The Franklin and Eleanor Roosevelt Institute Series on Diplomatic and Economic History

General Editors: Arthur M. Schlesinger, Jr., William vanden Heuvel, and Douglas Brinkley

FDR AND HIS CONTEMPORARIES
FOREIGN PERCEPTIONS OF AN AMERICAN PRESIDENT

Edited by Cornelis A. van Minnen and John F. Sears

NATO: THE FOUNDING OF THE ATLANTIC ALLIANCE AND THE INTEGRATION OF EUROPE

Edited by Francis H. Heller and John R. Gillingham

AMERICA UNBOUND
WORLD WAR II AND THE MAKING OF A SUPERPOWER

Edited by Warren F. Kimball

THE ORIGINS OF U.S. NUCLEAR STRATEGY, 1945-1953

Samuel R. Williamson, Jr. and Steven L. Rearden

AMERICAN DIPLOMATS IN THE NETHERLANDS, 1815-50

Cornelis A. van Minnen

EISENHOWER, KENNEDY, AND THE UNITED STATES OF EUROPE

Pascaline Winand

ALLIES AT WAR
THE SOVIET, AMERICAN, AND BRITISH EXPERIENCE, 1939-1945

Edited by David Reynolds, Warren F. Kimball, and A. O. Chubarian

THE ATLANTIC CHARTER

Edited by Douglas Brinkley and David R. Facey-Crowther

PEARL HARBOR REVISITED

Edited by Robert W. Love, Jr.

FDR AND THE HOLOCAUST

Edited by Verne W. Newton

THE UNITED STATES AND THE INTEGRATION OF EUROPE
LEGACIES OF THE POSTWAR ERA

Edited by Francis H. Heller and John R. Gillingham

ADENAUER AND KENNEDY
A STUDY IN GERMAN-AMERICAN RELATIONS

Frank A. Mayer

THEODORE ROOSEVELT AND THE BRITISH EMPIRE
A STUDY IN PRESIDENTIAL STATECRAFT

William N. Tilchin

TARIFFS, TRADE AND EURO-PEAN INTEGRATION, 1947-1957
FROM STUDY GROUP TO COMMON MARKET

Wendy Asbeek Brusse

SUMNER WELLES
FDR'S GLOBAL STRATEGIST

A Biography by Benjamin Welles

Sumner Welles:
FDR's Global Strategist

A Biography by
Benjamin Welles

St. Martin's Press
New York

Library of Congress Cataloging-in-Publication Data
Welles, Benjamin.
    Sumner Welles : FDR's global strategist : a biography / by
Benjamin Welles.
        p. cm.
    Includes bibliographical references and index.
    ISBN 0-312-17440-3
    1. Welles, Sumner, 1892- . 2. United States—Foreign
relations—1933-1945. 3. Diplomats—United States—Biography.
I. Title.
E748.W442W44 1997
327.73'092—dc21
    [B]   97-11579
                                              CIP
Design by Acme Art, Inc.
First edition: November 1997
10 9 8 7 6 5 4 3 2 1

CONTENTS

Ten pages of photos appear between pages 144 and 145

ACKNOWLEDGMENTS

Many have helped me down the years with time, recollections and advice but, among them, three especially merit my unstinted thanks. Dr. William M. Franklin, former director of the State Department's Historical Office, provided invaluable research into Sumner Welles's papers and early career, suggested preliminary chapters and generally exerted eagle-eyed vigilance over fact and form.

Dr. Arthur M. Schlesinger, Jr., my Harvard classmate and lifelong friend, sustained me through periodic discouragement with his compendious knowledge and unfailing support. Finally, my former editor in the *New York Times* Washington bureau, Robert H. "Bob" Phelps—who later, with Charles "Chip" Bohlen, co-authored *Witness to History* (N.Y., W.W. Norton & Co., 1973)— reviewed the entire mss. with professional skill and, together with his wife, Betty, bore in their home in Lincoln, Massachusetts, my presence (and cigar smoke) with Spartan forbearance. To all three, my gratitude. Without them this book might never have been written.

To the Bullitt family of Philadelphia goes my gratitude for their exceptional courtesy in providing me insights and materials essential to understanding the motives and machinations of their kinsman, William C. Bullitt, whose implacable jealousy of, and vendetta against, Welles helped end Welles's career—and his own as well. In addition, the FBI files helped me to trace the detailed maneuverings of Bullitt and of his accomplices—Cordell Hull, Arthur Krock, Senators Owen Brewster (R.-Me.) and Styles Bridges (R.-N.H.)—and other of Welles's political enemies who, collectively, forced FDR to accept his resignation—thus losing his services—in mid–World War II.

Others whose help I acknowledge include: Adolf A. Berle, Dr. Beatrice Bishop Berle, Brooke Astor, W. Averell Harriman, James L. Rowe, James Reston, Anna Louise Clarkson Bacon, Thomas G. Corcoran, Elliott Roosevelt, Franklin D. Roosevelt, Jr., William Fulbright, Anne Bullitt, Orville H. Bullitt, Dr. Orville Horowitz, Joseph P. Lash, Robert S. Murphy, Peter Grose, John Finney, Townshend Hoopes, H. Freeman Matthews, Benjamin V. Cohen, Loy Henderson, Norman Armour, Henry Norweb, James C. Dunn, Hugh Cumming, Paul Daniels, Dana G. Munro, Foy Kohler, Donald Heath, Walworth Barbour, William Phillips, Christopher Phillips and John and Anne Bryant.

In addition, Alice Roosevelt Longworth, Jonathan Daniels, Turner Catledge, Andrew Berding, Evan Wilson, Drew Pearson, Luvie Pearson, Robert S. Allen, Ugo Carusi, Ernest Cuneo, Douglas Macarthur II, Marion Oates Leiter Charles, Paul Nitze, Peter Krogh, Robert Woodward, Philip Bonsal, Carlton Savage, Bryce Wood, John Hickerson, Bradford Snell, Mrs. Orme Wilson, Theodore XanThaky, Margaret Cox, Robert Joyce, Frank Waldrop, Robert Alden, Frank Shulers, Cabot Coville, Cecilia May Vom Rath, Blanche Halla, Marion Christie, James Saylor, Julia Brambilla, Claude Erb and Paul Kramer.

My thanks, also, to William E. Jackson, William Braden, Rudolph Schoenfeld, Alger Hiss, Bradley Nash, Nevil Ford, Dr. Hugh Joseph, James J. Angleton, Eliahu Epstein-Elath, Campbell James, Ignatius Sargent, John H. Crimmins, Joseph H. Alsop, Susan Mary Alsop, Willard Beaulac, Diane Heinrichs, Frank and Joyce Graff, Walter Brown, Carroll Kilpatrick, Admiral R. H. Hillenkoeter, Mary Pyne Cutting, Courtney de Espil Adams, Robert Crasweller, Emilio Collado, Elizabeth Shannon, Elizabeth Anne Burton, Jane EngelHard, Thornton Wilson, Gail Hanson, James V. Reeks, Achiel and Mary Rawoens, Carol C. Franco, Jack Vietor and Susan McCarty.

Finally, no words can express my debt to Olive Cook and to Helen Louise Sanford (the "Delta Queen"), two ladies whose devotion to my wife and care of our home during her terminal illness enabled me to complete this book. For all who have helped me, my thanks. For my sins of omission or commission, I beg indulgence.

FOREWORD

This biography has grown erratically—like a child. For years, there was scant development; then, suddenly, it began shooting up and filling out as if driven by some inner force. Long before his death in 1961, my father had told me that his papers would eventually pass to me. I was to be his literary executor. Implied, though never stated, was his hope that, somehow, I would put them to use. In 1962, when they came into my possession, it seemed my filial duty to peruse them and decide whether to edit them for publication or try working them selectively into a biography.

The prospect, however, was daunting. I had no training in biography and was then about to return, permanently, to the United States with my family after seventeen years abroad as a foreign correspondent—the last six in Spain. I had contracted to write a book about Spain, a country I had come to love and, although ready to take a year or two off to write about a subject I knew first hand, I was not psychologically prepared to renounce competitive journalism for the lonely fastnesses of scholarly research into Welles's vast collection.

Welles's papers had been randomly stored in a Washington warehouse in thirteen steel filing cabinets crammed with 100,000 or more documents. The cabinets and files had been labeled by year or by broad subject matter (e.g. 1936 Correspondence, A-L, or M-Z) but the documents, themselves, had neither been indexed nor card-filed and merely to have read them attentively would have required a full year. I compromised.

They were moved to my Washington home and, early in 1963, an old friend, Thérèse E. Nadeau, took leave from the Ford Foundation to spend a year and a half indexing and card-filing every document in my basement. Next, Frank Graff, a young researcher who had written a doctoral dissertation on Welles for the University of Michigan, spent months with his wife, Joyce, reorganizing the collection and preparing an essential finder's-guide. Order was slowly emerging from chaos.

In 1966, after publication of my book on Spain, *Spain: The Gentle Anarchy* (New York: Praeger, 1965), I returned to active journalism and covered the State Department and national security affairs in Washington for the next six years. Eventually, Dr. William M. Franklin, retired as director of the State

Department's Office of History, examined the papers and conducted preliminary research in the State Department and National archives.

In 1972, after thirty-five years in journalism, I took early retirement, intending to edit the papers; but again problems, some beyond my control, delayed me. Serious family illness required my close attention for six years and, early in 1981, I accepted appointment as deputy spokesman in the Defense Department during the first Reagan administration. Little did I realize at the time that my three-year stint in government would furnish me with incomparable insights into the feuds and pitfalls of Federal service that Welles, himself, encountered in his decade of public duty (1933-1943) as FDR's Assistant and, later, Under Secretary of State.

In 1984, on returning to private life, I finally turned back full-time to the papers. Gradually, as I came to understand Welles's extraordinary contribution to his times and, especially, to the Franklin D. Roosevelt era, it was clear that only a full-scale biography could do justice to his dramatic, if tragic, life.

SOURCES

Published references to Welles's career are legion but while they provide facts—and, occasionally, valuable impressions by his contemporaries—they fail to provide the background essential to understanding those facts. By themselves, the facts are but scattered pieces of the mosaic.

Welles's papers (now open to researchers at the Franklin D. Roosevelt Library at Hyde Park, N.Y.) largely comprise copies of his official correspondence or of public State Department and National documents. His five books, while occasionally marred by minor inaccuracies as to dates, reflect his long experience in government and his policy views, but throw little light on his personal development as a man and public servant. The FBI files, obtained through the Freedom of Information Act, record without fully explaining the darker shadows of his life.

James Boswell, the greatest biographer in the English language, quotes Dr. Samuel Johnson as declaring that "Nobody can write the life of a man but those who have eat and drunk and lived in social intercourse with him."[1] This is largely true. Without having known Welles as a man and father; without having read his private letters to his family and friends; without knowing his origins, his upbringing, his adolescence, the forces that molded him as a youth and that later drove him as an adult; and, above all, without having known the men and, especially, the women, in his life, his story would be hard to tell.

The personal letters and recollections of R. H. Ives Gammell of Boston, Welles's closest friend during his adolescence and early manhood, have proved invaluable. The two remained close throughout their lives, despite occasional quarrels, and no one knew Welles's strengths and weaknesses better than Gammell. Albert Stagg of Fountain Hills, Arizona, my one-time tutor and friend for half a century, provided me unrivalled insights into Welles's activities and thinking during his turbulent years in the political wilderness (1927-1933) before FDR called him back to government.

Welles's voluminous correspondence with his Groton and Harvard classmate, Charles P. Curtis, Jr., of Boston, has also proved invaluable. Curtis served as an usher at Welles's marriage in 1915 and later became Godfather to his elder son, the author. A legal luminary, a member of the Harvard Corporation and a pillar of Boston society, Curtis coauthored with Ferris Greenslett *The Practical Cogitator* (Boston: Houghton, Mifflin, 1945, 1st edition), a work of rare erudition. Welles had long admired Curtis's brilliant, cultivated mind. Early in World War II, he called him to Washington as his special assistant and, throughout his life, confided to him intimate views about people and events as he did to no one else—excepting, possibly, Drew Pearson.

Unless otherwise indicated, all photos are from the author's private collection.

Sumner Welles: FDR's Global Strategist

For Cynthia, Serena and Mereda

BIRTH OF A SCANDAL

1940

ON A SWELTERING SEPTEMBER AFTERNOON IN 1940, Sumner Welles, Franklin D. Roosevelt's Under Secretary of State and lifelong friend, boarded the presidential train at Washington's Union Station. Tall, imposing and immaculately dressed, Welles was then at the peak of a brilliant career. A veteran diplomat and linguist, he had conceived and carried out for FDR, among other responsibilities, the Good Neighbor policy—arguably the high-water mark of U.S.–Latin American relations since the founding of the republic.

Age forty-eight—ten years younger than FDR—he, too, had attended Groton and Harvard. The Welles and Roosevelt families had long been close, and, as a twelve-year-old, Welles had served as a page at Franklin's wedding to Eleanor. Later FDR had sponsored his entry into the diplomatic service, had followed his career closely and, after taking office in 1932, had named Welles Assistant Secretary of State for Latin America. Ever since, FDR had come to rely on Welles's quick mind, tireless energy and compendious knowledge of foreign affairs. In 1940 many thought Welles the likely successor to Cordell Hull, FDR's elderly and chronically ill Secretary of State.

Few, however—and least of all Welles—would have suspected that the next thirty-six hours would start unraveling his career and generate a scandal that Roosevelt would struggle to suppress for the next three years.

Weeks earlier, Roosevelt's choice of the liberal Henry Wallace as his running mate for a third-term bid had affronted Hull and other Southern conservatives. His choice of Wallace and his decision to run for a third term had left the Democrats in disarray. As a political gesture, FDR asked the cabinet members to attend the funeral of the recently deceased House Speaker William Bankhead at his birthplace, Jasper, Alabama. "It was a very hot, uncomfortable journey," remembered Attorney General Robert H. Jackson. "It would not have been undertaken by the President, at that time, if it hadn't been for the campaign situation."[1]

The President's train pulled out of Washington's Union Station on Monday, September 16, at 5 P.M., carrying FDR and his cabinet members or their deputies. Hull had pleaded illness so Welles, representing him, was assigned a sleeping compartment in the car between the President's at the rear and the dining car. On one side was Navy Under Secretary James V. Forrestal; on the other, Labor Secretary Frances Perkins. Others aboard included Interior Secretary Harold Ickes, Supreme Court Justice Hugo Black, Federal Works Administrator John M. Carmody and Wallace. The train reached Jasper early Tuesday afternoon in ninety-degree heat.[2]

After changing into funeral attire, the President and cabinet members drove to the small First Methodist Church where 65,000 visitors, drawn by FDR's presence, gathered outside. Immediately after the service, the President and his party returned to the train which was soon clacking and swaying back to Washington. The next few hours would alter Welles's life.

Bone-weary, he began drinking in the dining car with colleagues. By 2 A.M. he was drunk. By then, all but Carmody and Wallace had gone to bed. Welles rambled on about his mission to Europe for FDR earlier that year and, according to Wallace, praised the Pope and Mussolini.[3] By 4 A.M., as the train neared Roanoke, Virginia, Wallace and Carmody retired, leaving Welles alone. After lurching and staggering to his compartment, he rang for coffee and the sleepy Pullman staff roused itself to serve him.

The first porter to appear, John Stone, a respected black veteran of the Pullman service, was allegedly offered money for immoral acts. Refusing politely but firmly, Stone returned to the dining car and recounted the incident to his colleagues. Other porters subsequently answered Welles's calls[4] and later reported "indirect" advances. The news soon reached the ears of W. F. Kush, the dining car manager; W. A. Brooks, a conductor; and D. J. Geohagen, a Pullman inspector. Luther Thomas, the Southern Railway's special assistant for security, alerted Dale Whiteside, chief of the President's Secret Service detail.

Whiteside ordered a porter to take Welles coffee and leave the compartment door open while he and Thomas waited in the corridor nearby. They were unable to hear the conversation, and, at this point, Welles suddenly emerged. Seeing Whiteside, he exclaimed: "What is Whiteside doing in this car?" He reentered his compartment, slammed the door and left the train without further incident on its arrival at the Union Station that afternoon. It was September 18, seven weeks before the 1940 election.

Thomas ordered the railway employees to say nothing, except to the proper authorities, and to put nothing in writing. Reports were to be solely oral. Possibly no one would believe that a senior government official in his right mind—least of all the patrician Under Secretary of State—would solicit Pullman porters on a train carrying the President, the cabinet, the Secret Service and railway officials. Welles, of course, had not been in his right mind. A railway flagman told the FBI later that the "tall, well-dressed, dignified man of about 45," whom he did not know, appeared "doped or highly intoxicated."[5]

Fate, however, had caught up with Welles at the wrong time and wrong place. Within weeks the story would reach the ears of his fanatic rival, William Christian Bullitt, FDR's ambassador to France, who, over the next three years, would spare neither time, nor trouble, nor expense to destroy Welles—and ironically, himself in the process.

Years of Youth

ONE

FAMILY AND GROTON

1892–1910

THE SUMNER WELLES WHO BROKE HIS HEALTH working for Franklin Roosevelt and then, through personal weakness, fell victim to political intriguers was born to a family molded for three centuries by New England's harsh climate and its Puritan values. From 1636, when Thomas, the first Welles to arrive in America, stepped ashore at Boston (later becoming third governor of Connecticut) until 1937, when FDR named Sumner Welles Under Secretary of State, the family had demanded achievement—and had reaped its rewards.

In 1892, the year of Sumner's birth, the United States was a contrast between opulence and violence. Jay Gould, the railroad magnate, died leaving $72 million (in today's terms, $1.5 billion) filched over a lifetime of speculation. New York's Metropolitan Opera opened with thirty-five parterre boxes, each costing $65,000 ($1.4 million today) and enriching the language with a new phrase: "the Golden Horseshoe." Months later the great house burned to the ground and was rebuilt more lavishly than before.

Industrial workers were organizing for better pay and conditions as management closed ranks against them. Andrew Carnegie, the Scots-born steelmaster, hired Pinkerton detectives to crush a strike at his Homestead mills in Pittsburgh. When the gunsmoke cleared, ten strikers lay dead and many more wounded. In New Orleans, "Gentleman Jim" Corbett, fighting with gloves for the first time under the new Marquess of Queensberry rules, battered John L.

Sullivan, the former bare-knuckle champion of the world, insensible in twenty-one bloody rounds.

Expansion was in the air: railways, shipping, banking, steel, even livestock. Prodded by Western cattle and sheep barons, the army was driving the last of the Plains Indians into reservations, and America's frontier stood at the Pacific.[1] Hungry eyes were already gazing out toward Hawaii, the Philippines and China, for American imperialism was on the march, although many preferred such euphemisms as "Manifest Destiny" or the "white man's burden." Meanwhile, a lachrymose new waltz, "After The Ball Is Over," was sweeping the nation.

The New York society into which Sumner Welles was born still clung to the rigid taboos and expensive monotony limned by his great-aunt, Edith Wharton, in *The House of Mirth*. His paternal grandmother, née Katherine Schermerhorn, was a sister of Caroline Schermerhorn Astor, the dumpy "Mystic Rose," who reigned supreme over Gotham society in her jewels and black wig. Her protégé, Ward McAllister, had coined the phrase "the 400" to equate true society with the capacity of Mrs. Astor's ballroom—although, in fact, it held 1,200.[2] McAllister also had designated Benjamin Welles, Sumner's father, a member of the Patriarchs, a clique of twenty-five men whom he had organized in 1872 to "create and lead" New York society.

Servants lubricated society, and without them it would have ground to a halt. Sumner's parents, for instance, were routinely attended by butlers, maids, coachmen and grooms while little Sumner and his sister, Emily, were pampered and cosseted from infancy by nurserymaids and governesses. Throughout his life, Sumner Welles would never conceive of a world without retainers as loyal to him as he to them.

In this privileged ambience, his childhood was apparently happy. His maternal grandfather, Frederick G. Swan of Oyster Bay, Long Island, came frequently to call. After one visit he wrote his brother, Edward:

> The last time I went to see Emily and Sumner, I told them to bring a great shawl—then I got a pillow for my head and I got down on the floor, putting the shawl over us three. All went well until I made a grunt like a bear. This was too much for Sumner for he jumped up and, speaking in my ear, informed me that he was "going home" and, before I could say anything, off Sumner and Emily ran, leaving me on the floor under a shawl. That was the end of "Children in the Wood" for me.[3]

From the day of his birth, Sumner's mother dominated his life. Poised and beautiful, she had an incalculable influence on his formative years. She became his champion and confidante, his ideal of feminine perfection and the woman against whom he would measure all others throughout his life. Devoted to music, to literature and art, Frances Swan Welles was also interested in politics and public affairs. She gave much of her time to charities and, in her later years, accepted appointments to state charitable boards from Governor Charles Evans Hughes of New York.[4] Many women would pass through Sumner Welles's life and he would marry three times, but his mother's memory remained sacrosanct to the end. From the day of her death, during his freshman year at Harvard, until his own death he wore black neckties in perpetual mourning.

At ten, Sumner was entered in Miss Kearny's Day School for Boys on Forty-second Street, between Fifth and Sixth Avenues. Mary Kearny was "quite a person," according to Charles Dickey, a fellow pupil. A strict disciplinarian, she loved and understood boys, and Sumner would speak of her always with affection and respect. His other classmates included such sprigs of New York's old Dutch-based Knickerbocker society as Schuyler Parsons, Winthrop Flagg, Winthrop Brooks of the Brooks Brothers clothing clan and Hall Roosevelt, who lived with his parents, the Elliott Roosevelts, and his sister, Eleanor,[5] on Thirty-seventh street, a block from the Welleses. The two families were close, and Eleanor, although eight years older, saw much of her younger brother's friend Sumner. It was then that their lifelong friendship began.

Many boys in that era roller-skated to and from school, but Sumner, self-conscious at ten, walked sedately the twelve blocks to school and back. At morning recess, the pupils often darted between the slow-moving carts and carriages plying Forty-second Street to play in Bryant Park behind the New York Public Library, but Sumner seldom joined them. "He was respected but always a little apart," Dickey remembered. "Never a fellow you could get close to."[6]

A year later his parents enrolled him in the Knickerbocker Greys, a fashionable cadet corps where small New Yorkers in gray caps and jackets and white duck pants drilled two afternoons a week in the Seventh Regiment Armory on Park Avenue. At parade rest, the cadet officers amused themselves by inserting the points of their swords into the floor cracks while Sumner and other privates stood mesmerized, watching the gleaming sabers sway back and forth but never breaking. Few were less cut out for close-order drill than Sumner Welles, but, whatever else the Greys taught him, he held himself like a guardsman throughout his life.

During the summers, the family moved out to Islip, on Long Island's southern shore, where the Atlantic breezes blew away the heat. Welles House, as it was called, was a large, wooden, Grant-era structure with rocking chairs on wide verandas, flower beds in front and kitchen gardens in the rear. When not attending their parents, Sumner and Emily rode bicycles and ponies, netted crabs in the warm, shallow coves or hung about the grooms in the stables or the gardeners in the greenhouses.

Children, in that age of formality, were essentially reared by servants who trotted them out for display whenever their parents' social schedule permitted. Like other moppets of their age, Sumner and Emily were taught to stand whenever grown-ups entered the room, to put up their cheeks to be kissed, to speak only when addressed, to be seen, not heard, and never to raise their voices. Decorum was the rule. Joseph Alsop, the journalist author, remembered his mother telling him how little Sumner came to play one day incongruously clad in white gloves.[7]

In September 1904, a month before his twelfth birthday, Sumner entered Groton School. The next six years there would mold his life. Set in rolling, wooded countryside thirty miles northeast of Boston, the school seemed to throw protective arms around an oval campus, dominated on one side by an exquisite little Gothic chapel and opening on the other onto playing fields and orchards. Bell-ringers and others willing to toil up the chapel's narrow stone steps to the spire could gaze for miles over unbroken country to Mounts Monadnock and Wachusett cresting the far horizon.

Groton was twenty years old when Sumner arrived and had already become known as a "temple of muscular Christianity." Christ and sports were its lodestars; education and deportment came next. Dominating the school and everyone in it was the headmaster and cofounder, the Reverend Endicott Peabody, known to all as the Rector. Peabody's father, an international banker, had educated his son at Cheltenham and Cambridge in England, where the youth had starred as an oar. Along the way he also had absorbed the principles of Christian education first developed by Dr. Thomas Arnold, headmaster of Rugby, and highly esteemed by American parents on the eastern seaboard.

Upon returning to Boston, Peabody had graduated from the Theological Seminary in Cambridge, Massachusetts, and later had served for six months as a "horseback" parson at Tombstone, in the lawless Arizona Territory. Local hoodlums, thinking to cow the eastern tenderfoot, had threatened to ride him out of town on a rail, but something about Peabody's steady gaze, his huge hands and massive frame had deterred them. Neither at Tombstone nor at Groton was Endicott Peabody to be trifled with.

In 1884, backed by J. P. Morgan and others, he had founded Groton School with two friends: the Reverend Sherrard Billings, his diminutive deputy, and William Amory Gardner, a frail but wealthy Boston classicist. In their first year they had one pupil,[8] but the school grew steadily and, by 1904, when Sumner arrived, the Rector, his wife, Fanny—a cousin and woman of rare beauty—and the small, hand-picked faculty had raised Groton to preeminence among schools where young American gentlemen could acquire a Christian education and the rudiments of broken-field running.

Compared with Sumner's luxurious New York home, Groton was Spartan. Like other boys, he slept in a narrow alcove, or cubicle, approximately five feet by ten, with a cot, a small window, a hard-backed chair, a chest of drawers and coathooks for suits. On weekday mornings a clanging "outside" bell awakened the school at 6:55; on Sundays all were allowed an extra half-hour in bed. After an obligatory cold shower came breakfast, twenty minutes of chapel and, except for midmorning calisthenics, classes until noon. After lunch came more study, organized sports, supper at six-thirty and more homework.

Twice weekly at 8 P.M., the thirty boys in the first, or youngest, form filed into the Peabodys' parlor, where Mrs. Peabody read aloud to them, glancing up at the first sign of squirming or whispering and restoring order with a quiet look. At nine came bedtime; the youngest boys then moved past the Rector and his smiling wife, each to have his hand shaken and to hear Peabody murmur "Goo' night, boy." Except for prefects and football stars, whose names he invariably remembered, everyone was "boy." None, however, would ever forget the probing gaze, the great hands or the sheer power of his personality.

From the day Sumner trudged up Groton's granite steps into its granite discipline, he was a misfit among the other boys. Gangling, fast-growing and ill-coordinated, he was a nonathlete in a school where sports had acquired the virtual status of religion. The stay of the nonathlete at Groton was "not so much hard . . . as inconsequential," wrote Frank Ashburn, the school's chronicler.[9]

In Peabody's view, hard knocks on the football field formed character. Football, he wrote Walter Camp, the celebrated coach, was of "profound importance for the moral, even more than for the physical, development of . . . boys. In these days of exceeding comfort, the boys need an opportunity to endure hardness and, it may be, suffering . . . Football has in it the element which goes to make a soldier."[10]

Isolated by his ineptitude at—and indifference to—sports, Sumner vented his hurt in sarcastic witticisms at the expense of classmates—thus isolating himself all the more. William Jay Schieffelin, a former classmate, remembered his bitter tongue. "In our first year, he taunted me about John Jay, an ancestor of whom I was proud," Schieffelin recalled. "He gloated that Jay had been burned in effigy after signing an unpopular treaty with Britain in 1794. We had a kid scrap and the master who pulled us apart whispered 'Good work, Sheffie.' Sumner turned many against him."[11] Ironically, Franklin D. Roosevelt also had been "very argumentative and sarcastic" at Groton and had "irritated the other boys considerably," wrote his son, Elliott.[12]

Sumner started off well scholastically, thanks to Miss Kearny's preparation, and although the youngest boy in his form, he led it the first semester. His mind, when stimulated, was quick, wide-ranging and retentive; when bored, his grades plummeted. "He was an extremist, at the top or bottom, seldom in between," remembered another former classmate, Louis Curtis.[13] Slowly, as he matured, his interests began to broaden. He acted in school dramatics, playing the role of a towering Spanish senorita in *The Dictator.* He also contributed to the *Groton Weekly.* The Russo-Japanese war had just ended, and American sympathies lay with the spunky Japanese who had humbled the Czar of All the Russias. "Japan [is] the only country we can come in contact with in the Far East," wrote Sumner at fourteen, little suspecting that ten years later he would be serving in Tokyo on his first diplomatic assignment.

Occasionally, like most adolescents, he engaged in horseplay. Dr. Hugh Joseph, another classmate, recalled riding astride Sumner's shoulders during midmorning recess when "riders" tried to wrench each other off rival "horses." Thanks to Sumner's height and Joseph's agility, they made a formidable pair, but Sumner remained basically a loner.[14] Curtis, who shared a study with him, remembered coming in from football practice late one wintry afternoon to find Sumner reading in a chair, trying to keep warm over the hot-air register in the floor. "I threw all the windows open. I was a real bum," Curtis remembered with a laugh. Curtis also remembered Sumner as "very sophisticated, talking about Japanese prints and things that boys of our age knew nothing about. He had more to offer than the rest of our form."[15]

Sumner began filling out as he approached seventeen during his fifth form year. Although still poorly coordinated and inept at ballgames, he now stood six feet three and was powerfully built. He won a place on Groton's second crew, gaining a measure of acceptance if not true popularity. Peabody appointed him to the Missionary Society, a school group dedicated to good works among the local poor, and made him an usher at Sunday chapel services where, as one contemporary remembered, he performed his duties with "cold courtesy."

Of the many acquaintances and few friends that Sumner made at Groton, his only real intimate was Ives R. H. Gammell, a small artistic boy from Providence, Rhode Island, who was a year younger and in the form behind his. They had met by chance when Sumner had been sent, for some trifling infraction of the rules, to eat with the younger boys and found himself seated beside a first former who used a French expression. French not being a normal mode of communication between Grotonians, then or now, Sumner had been intrigued and responded in French; soon a friendship had developed. Physically, the two were opposites—Sumner tall and sturdy; Gammell frail and delicate—but, intellectually, they were twins.

Friendships between boys in separate forms were frowned on, but Sumner and Ives discovered mutual interests in music, painting and the arts— sufficient in the sports-worshipping Groton of the day to brand them as outcasts. Of the 160 boys in the school, Gammell recalled, only 4 were interested in opera—Gammell himself; Welles; Grafton "Grubby" Minot; and Samuel L. M.

Barlow, who later became a career composer. Conformity was the rule, and one young mother, imploring Peabody not to expel her errant son because he was a "very unusual" boy, heard the stony response: "Groton, madam, is no place for the unusual boy."

Lonely misfits both, Sumner and Ives devised a secret code of their own: the aria *"Nous viverons à Paris, tous les deux,"* from Massenet's *Manon.* To live in Paris became their dream and they hummed the air conspiratorially whenever passing, confident that their secret was safe from less cultivated ears. Gammell had already decided on a career in painting. After Groton, he would attend the Boston Museum of Fine Arts School, then settle in Paris, rent an atelier and paint. Sumner agreed to join him. Family tradition would require his attending Harvard but, on graduating, he too would move to Paris, study architecture at the Beaux Arts and the two would share a studio.

During Sumner's final year, they became inseparable, roaming the country lanes and fields on Sundays and holidays, the younger boy struggling to keep up with his long-legged friend, planning and replanning as their dream took wing. They discussed everything: the Rector, the masters, schoolmates, courses, sports, colleges, politics, life—even sex. Both, nearing manhood, were alive to the primal urges yet both had been reared in homes and schools where sex, in theory, did not exist.

"Bull sessions," so called, were as common at Groton as at any boys' school, but Peabody's iron vigilance had largely spared Groton the blight of adolescent homosexuality. Sumner "recoiled from anything even suggestive of homosexuality," Gammell remembered. "He had an exaggerated horror of any kind of sex, or sex talk, verging on prudery. I remember his railing one day against student bull sessions, muttering gloomily, 'I understand in men's smokers it gets even worse.'"

Although normally perceptive in judging boys, Peabody made a strange miscalculation during Sumner's last year, calling him in before his graduation and suggesting a career in the Episcopal ministry. Sumner politely declined but, later, burst out angrily to Gammell about the Rector's "total misunderstanding" of him. From Peabody's perspective, however, it may not have been a total misunderstanding. He had watched the boy develop for six years, starting as an awkward misfit and gradually maturing, mentally and physically. His suggestion, although mistaken, was a mark of confidence not lightly conferred by a headmaster of Peabody's stature on a schoolboy of seventeen.

In June 1910 Groton's guest of honor, ex-President Theodore Roosevelt, handed Sumner his diploma. With two sons in the school, TR had become a frequent visitor and a hero to the boys—especially to Sumner, who idolized the former stripling who had fought his way through "grit" to the New York legislature, to ranching in the Dakota Badlands, to the Navy Department, the Rough Riders, San Juan Hill, the New York governorship and finally, the White House.

TR, however, was more than merely another example of muscular Christianity. He and Peabody believed, passionately, that Grotonians—and all born to privilege—owed their country public service. It was a belief that would leave its mark on Sumner, and for all who shared it, it was a golden era. Over an eleven-year span, Groton would graduate Franklin D. Roosevelt and Joseph C. Grew in 1900; Averell Harriman, 1909; Sumner Welles, 1910; and Dean Acheson, 1911.

In 1910, freed, finally, from Groton's iron discipline, Sumner lost no time testing his new wings. From the schools' summer camp at Lake Asquam, New Hampshire, where he was spending a fortnight counseling boys from the slums of New York and Boston, came a letter to Peabody apologizing for having smoked during the college entrance exams. "I am awfully sorry to have caused you so much trouble," he wrote contritely.[16] His camp duty over, he joined his mother at the rambling old Mt. Washington Hotel, at Bretton Woods, New Hampshire, while awaiting his examination results. Devoted though they were, mother and son soon clashed for both were cast in the same mold; both were iron-willed and Sumner was determined to enjoy himself.

"Mama, as usual, is having fits about what she amiably calls my 'second cut' acquaintances," he fumed in a letter to his sister Emily, recently married to Harry Pelham Robbins of New York. "There are two or three very pretty girls here. Naturally, I mean to have a good time and I have been dancing with them in the evenings and seeing them during the day." Concerned lest her eaglet fall into scheming hands, Mrs. Welles was monitoring his social gyrations with mounting irritation.

"Mama thinks I am having the most desperate flirtation with one of them and threatened, yesterday, to leave the hotel if I didn't 'behave myself,'" he groused. She expected him to "trail around" with a Miss X, a friend's daughter, whom he described, uncharitably, as the "most repulsive" girl he had ever seen. "I'm rather in hot water," he conceded, "as I plainly said 'No.'"[17]

Eventually his father joined them, and in Sumner's next letter to Emily came the first hint that their mother had been ill. "Mama, I think, is ever so much better," he wrote. "To me, she looks like a different person and, until Papa came back, she slept very well. I suppose," he added dourly, "his grumbling would keep a dormouse awake." He was enjoying himself despite his mother's vigilance. "It is too lovely up here," he went on. "The mountains are beautiful after Long Island and the woods, after the rain, are delightful . . . Must stop now. They are going on a drive and Papa's shouting. Do write me, dear, for it's lonely here, though don't let on."[18]

She never did let on but kept his secrets throughout the vicissitudes of his long, tempestuous life, his confidante and archdefender always. To his delight, word finally came that he had passed his examinations and would enter Harvard that fall.

TWO

HARVARD

1911–1912

"Very Contrary and Selfish"

HARVARD WAS IN A FERMENT WHEN WELLES ARRIVED. The year before, 1909, Charles William Eliot had finally handed over the presidency to Abbott Lawrence Lowell after a tenure of forty years. Eliot, a superb administrator, had transformed a small, moribund college into a world-class university, studding the faculty with giants, strengthening the research centers and professional schools and raising faculty salaries. Of his many reforms, the most controversial had been the "electives," which freed freshmen from traditional obligatory courses and allowed them to choose those that most interested them. Academic purists had criticized the electives but, by the time of Sumner's arrival, they had proved so popular that Harvard's enrollment had soared to 2,200. (In the 1990s, it exceeded 20,000, of whom more than 6,000 were undergraduates.)

Rapid growth also had brought social fragmentation, however, and on taking over, Lowell had found wealthy students living in luxurious private dormitories and eating in restaurants or clubs while the less wealthy roomed in the shabby Yard and fed in the vast, gloomy Memorial Hall. The poorest of all lived at home in Greater Boston and, as Samuel Eliot Morison observed, "commuted forlornly in trams and trolleys."[1] Determined to unify the student body, and financially backed by the philanthropist Edward Stephen Harkness,[2] Lowell had begun a massive building program, starting with three new freshman houses where first-year men would eat, sleep and, it was hoped, mix. For the next twenty-two years, wrote Morison, the sound of the "steel riveter, the carpenter and the mason, was never absent from Cambridge."[3]

The new freshman houses were still under construction when Sumner arrived so he settled with a Groton classmate, E. Kenneth Hadden, into one of the luxurious private dormitories on Mt. Auburn Street's "Gold Coast," which local entrepreneurs had fitted out with marble mantels, high ceilings, chandeliers and steam heat. Sumner and Hadden had little in common except for an interest in music, Gammell remembered. It was one of those "mutually protective alliances that unpopular Grotties made at Harvard pour se *donner une contenance.*" Like all freshmen, they ate in Memorial Hall, but even there class distinctions prevailed, and graduates of such private schools as Groton, St. Mark's and St. Paul's reserved their own tables.

Sumner's first weeks were apparently busy and happy. "He is working hard and having a fine time," his father wrote Edgar H. Wells, dean of freshmen, after a cautionary visit. He thought it would "flatter my boy and have a good effect" if Wells, or others in authority, called him in and saw him from time to time.[4] Sumner wrote a one-act play for his English class early in his freshman year that won him high praise. "The boy has been given an A for the [half]-course," Dean Wells wrote his father proudly.

Intent on finishing college as quickly as possible and joining Gammell in Paris, Sumner decided to graduate in three, instead of the customary four, years. He took on a heavy academic load: six courses, including English, French, Italian, History, Mathematics and, with an eye to a career in architecture, fine arts. He also took up singing lessons and gave a private recital, which Gammell thought a "*succes d'estime* . . . [he] entered very tall, erect . . . [with] a fine baritone and sang with gusto and fine delivery."[5] Walter Damrosch, the celebrated conductor, thought him sufficiently gifted to make singing a career. While nothing came of it, one of his singing teachers, on hearing Sumner broadcast over NBC thirty-four years later, wrote from retirement in California to congratulate him on his pitch and voice control.[6]

Meanwhile, across the Charles River in Boston, social diversions were soon vying for Sumner's attention. Ever since the 1880s, when eligible young Bostonians had began moving out West, Boston had become a "social leech on Harvard," wrote Morison. "The Boston mamas suddenly became aware that Harvard contained many appetizing young gentlemen from New York, Philadelphia and elsewhere."[7] Juniors and seniors were invited to debutante balls; sophomores to the Saturday Evening Sociables; freshmen to Messers. Papanti's and Foster's Friday Evenings. "Freshman fellowship, brisk enough in the opening days of college," wrote George Santayana, the Harvard philosopher, "soon blew away in a whiff of invitations to dances and weekend house parties."[8] For an eighteen year-old, newly freed from Groton's strict discipline, the pace was giddy.

Over Christmas Sumner returned to the family's new home at 110 East Fifty-fifth Street, where his mother, father, sister Emily and her husband, Harry, eagerly awaited him. Frances Swan Welles listened proudly as her tall freshman son described his professors, courses and classmates. Emily and Harry teased him affectionately; Bobby, his red setter, jumped on and off his lap; and Sumner's mustachioed father hovered amiably, as always, in the background. It was a glowing Yuletide: skating and sledding in Central Park, lunches and dinner-dances, theater and pretty girls to flirt with. Over New Year's, Sumner fell briefly ill with grippe but shook it off and returned to Harvard.

Suddenly fate dealt him two hammer-blows. On February 14, 1911, his favorite aunt, Helen (Mrs. George) Kingsland, his father's eldest sister, died unexpectedly. Eleven days later Sumner's mother followed her to the grave after a stroke at the Foord Sanatorium at Kerhonkson, near Kingston, in upstate New York, where she had been undergoing treatment for a nervous disorder.[9] The shock was devastating. Sumner was "almost prostrated by the two terrible losses within two weeks; not only a favorite aunt but the mother, whom he idolized, both taken," his father wrote Dean Wells.[10]

The family doctor recommended an early return to Harvard as the best therapy so Sumner struggled back, inconsolable, finding the noise and confusion of the university almost obscene. Fearing that his son might suffer a nervous breakdown, his father sought Dean Wells's help, suggesting that Sumner's faculty advisor, Julian Coolidge, a former Groton master and rising mathematics star, give the boy a "little more supervision." The dean was sympathetic.

"Sumner Welles, '14, has recently lost his aunt and mother and returns to college much stricken," he wrote Coolidge. "The boy has done remarkably well in English-D, for which he has been given an A, and received high praise for a play which he wrote."[11] Coolidge did his best, but only the atmosphere of Groton, the Peabodys and above all his friend Gammell seemed to offer haven in a sunless world. Sumner returned to Groton repeatedly seeking solace in Gammell's companionship. In May he wrote thanking Peabody for a letter of condolence, which he had delayed answering because of "sheer inability to respond, fittingly, to a letter that moved me as much as yours did."

It was three months exactly since he had been "left alone; it seemed nearer three years." Peabody, he knew, had been aware of the deep affection between mother and son, but, in addition, there had been a "perfect understanding and sympathy underlying our love. I have lost my all. I don't think I have ever loved anyone else in the world although . . . that may sound selfish to you. It seems so gray now; everything is so perfectly hopeless and worthless that I wonder how I can keep on living." At Peabody's suggestion, he had read and reread Tennyson's *In Memoriam,* a tribute to his friend Arthur Hallam, and had found it helpful. He also had written Mrs. Peabody that his mother's "perfect and unquestioning faith has borne me up and will still do so, I hope, all my life."[12] In fact, he would soon abandon the belief in Christ's divinity inculcated at Groton, although throughout his life he would continue believing in a "Supreme Being."

The summer eased his grief. Starting his sophomore year that fall, he thanked Peabody for a postcard on his nineteenth birthday—October 14, 1911[13] —and commiserated on the recent death of the Rector's mother. "I'm beginning to believe that there are things worth living for, after all," he wrote. "To have you say so, at a time when you have to bear the sorrow of losing your mother, gives me so much courage." He had seen Mrs. Peabody on a recent visit to school and had found her "splendidly sound view of the big things in life a tonic to a rather morbid person like myself." He was, in fact, dangerously morbid, unable to share his grief with anyone except the Peabodys and Gammell, and all three were thirty miles distant from Harvard.

College, meanwhile, remained a nightmare. He tried out for the Harvard *Crimson* but was rejected. "It was a critical dividing time in his life," remembered Gammell. "His mother's death, on top of his unpopularity with his fellows, seemed to snap his restraints. He threw off all controls."[14]

Sally Turner's was a brothel at 807 Shawmut Avenue in a tawdry district of Boston, known mainly for the furtive comings and goings of college undergraduates. Most who frequented it did so clandestinely after football games and usually when in their cups. Sumner now became a regular. Sex became a rite and harlots his escape. Years later, in bitter self-reproach, he would burst out to Gammell: "*You* would never have gone to a whorehouse right after your mother's death!"

Defiance of Boston's unwritten rules by an unpopular undergraduate isolated him further from his classmates, but, as always, he remained indifferent to criticism of his personal conduct. "The 'Kings' [college athletes] hated him and he hated them," Gammell remembered. His notoriety grew, and one debutante was heard whispering to another: "Sumner Welles likes black women." At a coming-out dance, an undergraduate usher asked him to leave because his peculiar style of dancing—leaning back with his pelvis forward— was causing comment. Sumner indignantly asked Gammell whether he should challenge the usher to fight, but Gammell thought not. "I do think you dance in a very peculiar manner," he observed mildly. Sumner was astonished. "Why didn't you ever tell me!?" he asked.

Virtually alone among his Groton classmates, he was elected to no club his sophomore year. The Harvard club system, although criticized by President

Lowell and others as elitist and snobbish, represented undergraduate success. Each autumn, approximately 10 percent of the sophomore class was elected to the catch-all Institute of 1770, which merged later with the Hasty Pudding Club, the nation's oldest amateur dramatic society. After further screening, virtually all elected to the institute were taken into one of Harvard's nine "final" clubs: Porcellian, AD, Fly, Owl and DU, among them.

The key to election was "conformity," wrote Morison. "Ambitious freshmen had to watch their step very carefully. No 'Harvard individualism' for them! They must say, do, wear the right thing, avoid the company of all ineligibles and, above all, eschew originality . . . Once having 'made' a club you could reassert your individuality; often, by then, you had none."[15] Stiff-necked, a nonathlete and womanizer, Sumner failed to be elected even to the grab-bag Institute–Hasty Pudding. "It broke young men when they didn't make Porcellian, or some such club," remembered a woman contemporary. "Sumner [was] totally indifferent."[16]

Too proud to bend the knee to his contemporaries, he sought acceptance among his elders and eventually, thanks in part to his family connections and recent bereavement, doors in Back Bay society that might otherwise have remained closed opened to him. Nancy Cabot [Mrs. Maurice M.] Osborne remembered the "shy, reedy, tall and lonely" youth who always seemed grateful for an invitation to her Cabot family's Sunday lunches. Self-conscious as he was, there was something about him that intrigued her for at times he could be surprisingly compassionate. At one dance, he went out of his way to be especially attentive to her house guest, an awkward, gauche girl. "It was strange," Nancy Osborne mused, "for he tended to dance only with the grand." His sophistication, compared with the young men of his time, also impressed her. "If one had a really good dress, Sumner would always notice it and remark on it in a quiet, appreciative way," she remembered. "Most men in Boston don't notice anything that isn't smashing, preferably fire-engine red. It always made me feel thankful that someone knew the difference."[17]

Eventually Sumner found haven in the home of his ultra-proper cousins, the Winthrop Sargents, and no better sponsors could have been found for a lonely undergraduate. Sargent's grandfather, Henry, had married into the Welles clan in 1807 and had later developed the nation's first great botanical collection at his summer estate, Wodenethe, near Fishkill on the Hudson. Sumner had been taken to Wodenethe as a child by his parents every spring or summer, and Winthrop Sargent had encouraged his early love of horticulture. Childless themselves, the Sargents opened their hearts and home at 207 Commonwealth Avenue to their young kinsman. In "Aunt Aimee" Sargent, Sumner found the mother missing in his life, and she the son missing in hers.

Born Aimee Rotch, of an old Salem family, she was "frail, but endowed with beauty, presence and an indomitable will," remembered her nieces, Aimee and Rosamund Lamb. "She knew nothing, intellectually, but she had a heart for those in trouble."[18] On arriving at Wodenethe as a young bride in 1874, appalled by the poverty of the local brickworkers, she had started cooking classes for their womenfolk in the kitchen of her palatial new home. Gradually her classes had developed into a domestic-science school from which eventually 10,000 local women graduated, raising living standards for miles around. On her death in 1918, schools throughout the Hudson valley closed for the day and flags flew at half staff in her memory.

Through the Sargents, Sumner began meeting eminent Bostonians: Brooks Adams, the historian-grandson of President John Quincy Adams; John La Farge, the muralist; and John Jay Chapman, the epistolaire, whom critic Edmund Wilson once described as the best writer on literature of his time. Bearded and dignified, Chapman had become a living legend. As a Harvard undergraduate, he had struck a fellow member of Porcellian in a fit of fury and, after brooding half the night, had thrust the offending hand into the fire, maiming himself for life. Sumner also met Langdon Warner, Sturgis Bigelow and Ernest Fenollosa, three of the leading exponents of Japanese art, a passion then sweeping Boston.

Born of Spanish ancestry in Salem, Fenollosa had graduated from Harvard first in his class before turning to drawing and painting at the Museum of Fine Arts. In 1878, as professor of philosophy at Tokyo University, he had revived an appreciation of Japanese culture, overshadowed in Japanese eyes by the apparent superiority of everything Western since Commodore Perry's visit in 1853-54. His students had dubbed him "Daijin Sensei," Teacher of Great Men.

Returning to Boston in 1890, he had been appointed curator of the Museum of Fine Arts, and Sumner, as a child, had been taken by his mother to hear him lecture at the home of Gammell's cousin, Mrs. Frederick Vanderbilt. The experience "bowled him over," Gammell remembered. "It opened his eyes." Langdon Warner, Fenollosa's disciple, also had studied art in the Orient before teaching at Harvard, where Sumner had attended his lectures.[19] Of the three Orientalists, however, it was Sturgis Bigelow whom Sumner came to know best. An "intellectual aristocrat," Bigelow later converted to Buddhism and died in Japan, but when Sumner met him he owned the greatest collection of Oriental art in Boston. "I remember his house on Beacon Hill as if I had been there yesterday," Sumner wrote a half century later. "I was enormously interested in him because of my own deep interest in Japanese philosophy and painting . . . I suppose that was the reason he was always especially kind to me."[20]

Kindness from his elders had eased, but not eliminated, Sumner's loneliness, and Aimee Sargent, with a woman's intuition, sensed it. "Sumner," she burst out, excitedly, one day, "I've met a girl with eyes like water dancing over rocks—brown and merry!" She arranged a small dinner and there Sumner met his future wife: Esther Slater, eldest daughter of the widowed Mrs. Horatio Nelson Slater and heiress to one of New England's great fortunes.

The Boston social season in the winter of 1912-13 was an "explosion of balls," Nancy Osborn remembered.[21] On December 6, 1,000 guests danced to the music of two bands at Mrs. Slater's coming out ball for Esther at the Somerset Hotel. Gobelin tapestries and Renaissance bas-reliefs had transformed the hotel ballroom into a replica of an old baronial hall. "For stateliness and artistic beauty," wrote the Boston Globe, "[it] has never been equalled at a private function in Boston." Boston expected nothing less of Mabel Hunt Slater.

A daughter of the painter William Morris Hunt and a niece of Richard Morris Hunt, the leading architect of his day, "Bay" Slater was an artist by birth and temperament. A pianist, violinist of concert quality, inventor[22] and ardent sailor (she was the first woman ever elected to both the New York and Marblehead yacht clubs), in 1891, at age twenty-six, she had startled staid Bar Harbor by marrying a sixty-six-year-old widower, Horatio Nelson Slater, heir to a textile fortune. Despite the forty-year difference in age, Bay and Slater had been happy. Four children were born to them: Esther, Nelson, Ray and Morris. In 1899, eight years after their marriage, Slater died and with the fortune left her Bay soon become celebrated for lavish entertaining.

Earlier that fall she had given an "autumn moon" ball at Pinebank, her country estate near Readville. Cornstalks had been arranged as decorations throughout the house and champagne "flowed like water," remembered Esther's younger sister, Ray. "Lots of Harvard students got drunk and started sliding down the banisters. Some even passed out on the beds—which made Mamma very cross!"[23] Among the sober undergraduate guests that night were Sumner Welles of Harvard and William C. Bullitt of Yale, whose paths would cross again twenty years later.

Many "proper" Bostonians thought Mabel Hunt Slater more Bohemian than Bostonian, but her ball for Esther at the Somerset Hotel was impeccably decorous. Watching her young guests whirl around the dance floor, Bay noted approvingly to her friend Aimee Sargent that young Sumner Welles of New York seemed to be paying marked attention to Esther, showing her the intricate new dance steps then the rage.

Frances Swan Welles had kept peace between her strong-willed son and his gentle father during her lifetime but, with her death, they soon began drifting apart. Lonely, his wife dead and his only daughter, Emily, newly married, the older man tried binding his son to him but Sumner resisted. The memory of his mother remained sacred; his love for her not to be shared. Letters to his father at the time reflect filial duty rather than love. "It's hard for me ever to express myself," he wrote awkwardly on returning to Harvard in 1912 for his third and final year. "Please don't think, when I seem to do things you mind, that it's because I don't care—for I do care for you far more than you realize, and can realize." He was grateful for all that his father had done to make his summer enjoyable: a car, improvements to the family estate at Islip, visits to friends. But the thanks were gestures and the affection strained.

Back at Harvard, he complained to his father about Lowell's controversial new policy of "majors and minors." Determined that his students know "a little of everything and something well," Lowell had decreed that of the sixteen courses required to graduate, six be concentrated in one academic field, six distributed among three others and the remaining four chosen at will. Sumner grumbled, with justification, that several of the obligatory courses—anthropology and Slavic languages, for instance—would be "useless to me." He had been hoping to concentrate on architecture and fine arts in preparation for his career and had asked Julian Coolidge to intercede, but to no avail.[24]

Meanwhile, music still entranced him, and he asked if his father would again promise him $100 at Christmas for an opera seat, which "I enjoyed more than anything else during the year." Soon after his twentieth birthday, and increasingly interested in public affairs, he wrote Corinne (Mrs. Douglas) Robinson, TR's sister and a family friend, condemning the "horrible attempt on your brother's life." The ex-president had narrowly escaped assassination in Milwaukee on October 14, 1912, while campaigning for reelection. His loss would be the "most tremendous disaster which could fall upon our country," wrote Sumner. TR was the "greatest force for good that the U.S. has ever known and to have that force taken at this time of great social crisis would mean ruin." He was praying that TR would soon recover and be reelected. "If not [re-elected] I hope, in four years, to cast my first vote for him."[25]

Sumner's first, and only, brush with the Harvard authorities came in his final weeks. Under his mother's will, he would receive a sizable sum (approximately $116,000 in today's terms) on his twenty-first birthday. Eager to ascertain the state of his finances before joining Gammell in Paris, he took a Friday night train to New York to see a family trustee, skipping an obligatory Saturday drawing class. Cutting classes at any time was hazardous, doubly so on the eve of the Easter recess. His absence was noted and, on April 29, 1913, he was placed on six months' probation.

"Benjamin [sic] behaved very frankly," Dean Byron S. Hurlburt wrote his father. He had wanted to see a man about his estate and it was "more convenient for the man to see him on that Saturday than . . . the next week, although not absolutely necessary." Welles père, more indignant at Harvard than at his errant offspring, sprang to Sumner's defense. It was the only censure that the boy had received in three years, he protested. Apart from this one lapse, Sumner's "exemplary conduct in scholarship and college life" should have carried weight with the Administrative (disciplinary) Board. Coming at a critical time in his studies, probation had "upset him. He thinks he has been punished with great severity."

Mr. Welles's reference to Sumner's "exemplary" scholarship is puzzling, for his son's mind, in fact, had been so focused on Paris that he was drifting— as his final grades showed. Apart from an A in oral French and a B in English, he received passing Cs in German, anthropology and Slavic languages; a C in one geology half course and a failing E in the other. Even in his major—fine arts—he received failing Ds in both half courses.[26]

His agitated parent alluded tactlessly to correspondence with President Lowell about funding a scholarship for "deserving descendants" of his grandfather, Benjamin Welles, Harvard 1800.[27] Whether or not impressed by the dangled scholarship, Dean Hurlburt replied soothingly that the boy would regain good standing in time to win his degree. With 2,000 or more students at Harvard, he pointed out, discipline had to be maintained, but the Administrative Board understood the situation. "Sumner is a fellow whom I like very much," concluded Hurlburt. "I do not think you need worry about him."[28]

Probation proved salutary. Alarmed lest his low grades cost him his degree and prevent his sailing for Paris that autumn, Sumner rejected his father's invitation to spend the summer at Islip, declined other holiday invitations and insisted on spending his time at the Harvard Architecture School. He had been "very contrary and selfish," he wrote contritely weeks later. "I wanted, immensely, to get my degree, now, and get a foundation for my work abroad." Before starting at the architecture school, he joined Gammell for a few days at Provincetown, Cape Cod, where they lived in a simple rooming house with neither plumbing nor running water and with every receptacle filled from a well. Sumner loved its extreme simplicity but suddenly fell ill. "He got a headache, probably a sunstroke," Gammell remembered.

Gammell offered to accompany him to Boston and let him use his apartment on Brimmer Street, but Sumner refused. "You certainly will not," he replied firmly. "There's nothing wrong with me." He returned to Boston alone and later Gammell discovered that he had been seriously ill. "He was very, very unselfish and quite heroic," Gammell recalled. Apparently Sumner's illness was prolonged, for he wrote his father that he had declined an invitation to join the Richard Sears family at their summer home at Islesboro, Maine, and that they had sent him "flowers and books," suggesting lengthy convalescence.

Despite his illness and the heat of midsummer Cambridge, he did well. His architectural instructor, Professor E. J. A. Duquesne,[29] singled out his "one completed" drawing as the best in rendering and conception, and his classmates congratulated him. It had especially pleased him, he wrote proudly, as he had "worked only for three weeks, really." Thirty years later a fellow student, Harden Pratt, would recall their summer studies at Robinson Hall. "We had a sort of gentleman's agreement," wrote Pratt. "I would take you to the Colonial Club (dreadful place but near the Arch. School) and, the following day, you would invite me to the Copley Plaza—certainly a most unfair exchange!"[30] The summer's hard work paid off and, on September 23, 1913, Harvard lifted his probation: "Your record for the degree being complete." He was granted a year's leave to study architecture in Paris and would officially graduate with the class of 1914.[31] The nightmare years were over.

He drove out to Groton to bid the Peabodys farewell but found them away and wrote them, later, from New York that he intended to remain in Europe at least three years. He had hoped to start preparing immediately for the Beaux Arts, but the doctors "unfortunately, have forbidden me to take up my studies until July [1914]." He vouchsafed no medical explanation. Meanwhile, he planned to visit Africa, India and China, start back via the Trans-Siberian railway around New Year's and commence his studies in Paris that June.[32] The thought of nine idle months traveling in Africa and Asia may well have caused the Rector's lips to purse in silent disapproval—with reason.

As Sumner's sailing day drew near, his father suddenly decided to accompany him and install his son safely in the French capital. Sumner was privately outraged. "Wouldn't you think this was the time I needed release?!" he fumed in a letter to Gammell, who was awaiting him in Paris. To his father, he was more diplomatic. His decision, Sumner wrote tactfully, had come as a "very welcome surprise. I hate to have you say that you look forward to nothing but loneliness. You know that so long as I am alive if there is a single thing that I can do to make you happier, I will do it." Fair words; but time would prove them hollow.

The boat-train pulled into the Gare St. Lazare and there stood Gammell awaiting them, wreathed in smiles and humming Lescaut's aria to *Manon*. After five long years, their schoolboy dream had come true. With the callousness of youth, they bundled Mr. Welles off to the Ritz alone in a taxi with the luggage and repaired to Maxim's to toast their future.

THREE

PARIS

1913–1914

"The Great Business at Hand
Was Pleasure"

PARIS, OCTOBER 1913. The "Belle Époque" is fading like a slow summer sunset; only nine months remain until World War I brings it to a close. Meanwhile, elegance still reigns. Society beauties and demi-mondaines drive gleaming little phaetons down the Champs-Elysées or through the Bois de Boulogne each afternoon, managing matched pairs with a flick of the reins as cavaliers trot alongside and liveried grooms follow discreetly at a distance.

Parisiennes in veiled hats and flowing skirts stroll the boulevards, window-shopping with top-hatted escorts, all gravitating toward the Place Vendôme, the center of elegance where can be found the jewelers: Mauboussan, Cartier and Boucheron; the perfumers: Lentheric, Houbigant, Roger et Gallet; the saddler: Hermès; purveyors of porcelain, crystal and china such as Baccarat, Christofle and Lalique; and the couturiers: Worth, Doucet and Charvet, "le roi de la mode masculine."[1]

With 3 million inhabitants, Paris is already one of the largest cities in the world. The underground Metro has been running since 1900 and traffic is doubling every two years. Bicycles and motorized buses clog the streets, and automobiles, hand-built by Panhard & Levassor, Renault, Peugeot, Mercedes and the Michelin brothers, are beginning to thrust into traffic, leaving horses rearing and coachmen cursing. With 27,000 cafés, wine shops and cabarets, Paris now boasts more drinking places than any city in the world.[2] Theaters, such as the Opéra Comique, l'Athenee and the Porte-Saint-Martin, offer matinees and evening performances. Four circuses are running to capacity, and the new "cinemas" are increasingly popular.

Children of all ages gather in the Tuileries Gardens each morning to watch the puppets of the Grand Guignol thwack each other lustily while respectable women skate and socialize at the rinks of the Palais de Glace or the Champs-Elysées in midafternoon. After 5 P.M. a racier crowd takes over, including the celebrated courtesans Emilienne d'Alençon, Liane de Pougy and Caroline "la Belle" Otero. Men of fashion spend their days at polo, pigeon-shooting or racing, followed by tea, a visit to their club, an hour of "dalliance," dinner and a ball. The comtesse de Chabrillon's Persian ball the year before is still the talk of the town. As recounted in Edward R. Tannenbaum's *1900: The Generation Before The Great War,* her ball plans stipulate that:

> Don Luis Ferdinand, Infante of Spain, will be naked. Nattie de Lucinge is marvellous in a sword dance, Emma d'Aremberg will come on an elephant, Boni de Castellane will wear a Turkish costume that belonged to his ancestor, Louis XV's ambassador to Constantinople. Henri de Mun will be stunning as a Persian archer, the Baronne de Brimont will make a delightful "houri," Comte Louis de Blacas in a turban is as handsome as a Bagdad youth and Suzanne de Montesquiou is a living miniature with her oval face outlined by veils.[3]

Those seeking nocturnal diversion flock to the "spectacles" at the Folies-Bergères, La Revue des Revues, l'Olympia or the Casino de Paris. The serious frequent museums such as the Louvre, the Grevin, the Carnavalet and the Oller; or public gardens, such as the Jardin de Plantes or the Jardin d'Acclimatation. Restaurants— Maxim's, La Tour d'Argent, Drouant, Ledoyen, Le Grand Vefour and Laperouse— are packed, and Fouquet's is the first to serve the new "cocktail." An Argentine dance, the tango, is sweeping the nation, and Americans are arriving in ever-growing numbers as the French press sniffs at their "money-spending lust." Into this world of gilded frivolity steps young Sumner Welles, just turned twenty-one, financially independent and eager to cast off parental control.

His father will install him in a luxurious garçonniere, or bachelor flat, at 2-bis Place du Pantheon, on the Left Bank, then sail forlornly home, while the young man engages a French couple, Jean Villain and wife, to cook and tend for him and horse-drawn vans start clattering up over cobblestones, bringing new fittings and furniture. Gammell, on his first visit, sees yellow silk brocade going up on the walls and smiles at his young friend's extravagance. Invited to move in, he declines, preferring to live in a garret on Montparnasse amid such budding artists as Chagall, Léger, Soutine and Modigliani.

In 1913 the Place du Pantheon on the Left Bank still swarmed with students. In the center stood the Pantheon itself: a domed marvel designed in 1755 by Soufflot, who had studied in Rome with Robert Adam. Secularized during the French Revolution, it now sheltered the remains of Rousseau, Voltaire and other French immortals. On seeing it for the first time in 1795, young Thomas Handasyd Perkins of Boston wrote his family that "it surpasses everything I have ever seen . . . Entirely of stone, not an inch of wood . . . Its height . . . is three hundred and eighty feet; and from its top all Paris is to be seen . . . one of the most enchanting scenes in nature."[4]

Nearby stood the multitiered College de Montaigu, the library of the Sorbonne, where Erasmus had studied in the fifteenth century. Students ascended and descended its worn stone stairs night and day, chattering, arguing, quarreling and flirting in a dozen languages. Sumner soon began exploring the quartier's bookstores, antiquaires, confectioners and cafés and walking his red setter, Bobby, his one link with home, in the Luxemburg Gardens each afternoon.

In Paris, wrote Cornelia Otis Skinner, "the great business at hand was pleasure, conducted by a people who knew the seriousness of that business."[5] Barred by his doctors from study and free for the first time in his life from parental or school discipline, Sumner threw himself into the pursuit of pleasure. Parisians had discovered the thrills of "slumming" on Montmartre. The Tabarin dance hall had opened in 1904, and night restaurants were multiplying rapidly. Each night, at the Moulin Rouge, "La Goulue," immortalized by Toulouse-Lautrec, performed her notorious "chahut," a frenzied dance whose high kicks and splits, wrote Tannenbaum, "freely displayed the performer's animal spirits and underclothes."[6] Night after night Sumner sallied up to the *boites* on Montparnasse with like-minded cronies.

One was Victor Chapman, a son of the Boston *homme-de-lettres* John Jay Chapman, as wild as his celebrated father was grave. Victor also had come to Paris ostensibly to study architecture. Another was the diminutive Carlo de Marroquetti, a self-styled Italian "baron" and fortune-hunter of ambiguous sex. A third was Sumner's Groton classmate, Charles P. Curtis, Jr., seeking occasional relief from the musty curriculum of l'Institut des Sciences Politiques, where his father had sent him. Gammell joined them now and then, more to please Sumner than for the revels, which he secretly detested.

The pace was frenzied and, one night, one of the group rolled a wine keg down the steep narrow streets, demolishing a café front and breaking a waiter's leg. On another, as dawn was breaking, they crammed themselves into a taxi that hurtled down the slopes. Chapman quarreled violently with Marroquetti, jumped out of the speeding vehicle and disappeared, reappearing the next day unscathed.[7] Thirty months later he would become the first American killed flying in the Lafayette Escadrille on the Western front.

Sumner by now had filled out, standing rigidly erect and broad-shouldered. His complexion was clear, his eyes hazel and his chestnut hair, plentiful at the time, was slightly wavy. Fastidiously groomed, he splashed 4711 eau-de-Cologne on his shirts and handkerchiefs, affected the pearl-gray spats then *en vogue,* wore a jeweled stickpin in his black cravats and carried a gold-headed Malacca cane. In another, such studied elegance might have smacked of the *flâneur,* or *boulevardier;* but there was a steely quality about Sumner that discouraged familiarity from men and intrigued women. Gammell remembered his friend's multiple love affairs, almost all with women nine or ten years older. Excess eventually took its toll, and he fainted one afternoon while walking Bobby in the Luxembourg Gardens, awakening to find himself sprawled on the gravel path, the gentle animal licking his face.

Whether it was a recurrence of the mysterious malady that had laid him low at Providence the summer before or the price of omniverous debauchery is unclear. In any event, women alone attracted him at the time, and he was repelled by the homosexuality then prevalent among the French upper classes. His homophobia, in fact, was to lead to a curious incident.

Sipping an aperitif in a café one morning, he was reading a message scrawled on the back of his calling card when a waiter approached with an invitation to join an older man at a nearby table. Glancing over, Sumner saw a total stranger and sensed the innuendo. He called for his bill, tore his card in half, dropped the pieces in an ashtray and walked out. Next morning, a gold cigarette case was delivered to his apartment. The stranger had discovered his name and address by retrieving the torn halves of his card. Weeks later, at a garden party in the south of France, the man turned up unexpectedly. Threading his way through the guests, he approached Sumner with a broad smile. "How wonderful that I've finally caught up with you," he began smoothly. Sumner, in a paroxysm of rage, struck him and stalked off.[8]

That Christmas of 1913, two roistering young Americans arrived in Paris to lure Sumner on safari. One was Nelson Slater, Esther's younger brother, just twenty and fresh out of the Massachusetts Institute of Technology. The other was Richard "Buck" Emmett, a rich but dense young Long Islander who had been briefly in Sumner's form at Groton before dropping back. The speed with which Sumner accepted the offer suggests that the safari had been planned long in advance. In fact, in his last letter to Peabody, Sumner had mentioned traveling to Africa and India before taking up his studies in Paris. Meanwhile, Mrs. Slater was just setting out with her daughters, Esther and Ray, on a world tour that would take them through the Orient, by the trans-Siberian railway to Moscow, and then on to Berlin and Paris before sailing home. Nelson intended to join his mother and sisters along the way—and to bring Sumner back into contact with them.

Sumner Welles and Nelson Slater were opposites in all but the pursuit of pleasure; in that they were twins. Short, stocky and spoiled since birth by his millionaire mother, Nelson had won a reputation in Boston for the love affairs with actresses and young married women carried on in his Newberry Street bachelor flat, a converted stable near his mother's Beacon Street mansion. Cars, airplanes and speedboats thrilled him, and nothing delighted him more than racing his lady loves in his open Peugeot to and from his mother's Readville estate, near Boston. Arrested repeatedly by local constables at his mother's request, he had turned the tables, bribing them to arrest her on her next outing in her chauffered limousine. Knowing her madcap son, she had burst out laughing.

Nelson's mechanical bent and fortune derived from his great-grandfather, Samuel Slater, a mechanical genius and founder of the American textile industry. Born in 1768 into a poor Derbyshire farm family, Slater had been apprenticed at fourteen to Richard Arkwright and Jedediah Strutt, cotton spinners at nearby Belper. Thirteen years earlier, Arkwright had built the world's first spinning mill, which allowed many threads to be spun at once, saving hand labor, improving quality and boosting demand. So valuable had the process become to Britain's economy that Parliament had made it a hanging offense for anyone with knowledge of it to emigrate. Determined nonetheless to seek his fortune in the newly independent colonies, young Slater had committed the mechanical details to memory, slipped past the London port authorities and sailed for America.[9]

After arriving in New York in September 1789, he had made his way to Providence, Rhode Island, where he entered into partnership with Moses Brown, a Quaker merchant, and his son-in-law, William Almy, whose efforts to replace hand-spinning by machinery had failed repeatedly. Working solely from memory, by 1790 Slater had built the first successful models of Arkwright's water-frame spinner and carding machine in the United States.[10] Joined by his brother, John, Slater later struck out on his own, building three mills along the main sources of power, the rivers flowing down from Massachusetts. After acquiring local water rights, he had built his fourth mill at Webster, Massachusetts, founding the town.

For the next twenty years he worked sixteen hours daily, often risking life and limb in winter by hanging by his hands from the mill wheels and kicking the ice free with his feet. By stimulating domestic manufacturing, the British blockade in the War of 1812 had made his fortune. By 1829, he owned or controlled cotton mills in four states and had branched out into woolen mills and iron manufacturing, becoming one of the wealthiest merchants in New England.

Reared in the piety of eighteenth-century Derbyshire, austere and God-fearing, Slater had founded schools where his millhands, many of them children, could acquire a rudimentary education on Sundays, the one day of the week when the mills fell silent. His schools, although secular, pioneered the nation's Sunday school system. When Slater died in 1835, President Andrew Jackson, who had been touring New England, paused by his deathbed at Webster to salute the "Father of American Industry."[11] Nelson had inherited part of his great-grandfather's fortune and a smattering of his mechanical bent but little of his interest in Sunday schools.

Early in 1914 Sumner, Nelson, and "Buck" Emmett boarded a scruffy little one-stack Italian freighter at Naples and, after traversing the Suez canal and the Red Sea, landed at Mombasa, on the Kenya coast. Karen Blixen, a young Danish writer later famous under the nom-de-plume Isak Dinesen, arrived at about the same time to marry Baron Bror von Blixen-Fineke and later left a vivid description of the port. "Mombasa has all the look of a picture of Paradise, painted by a small child," she wrote. "The deep sea-arm around the island forms an ideal harbor; the land is made out of whitish coral-cliff grown with broad green mango trees and fantastic bald gray Baobob trees. The sea . . . is as blue as a cornflower, and . . . the long breakers of the Indian ocean . . . give out a low thunder even in the calmest weather." Above the town rose a massive old fort which had repeatedly switched hands three centuries earlier as the Arabs and Portuguese had fought to control it. "The sun burns and scorches," she went on, "but the ancient mango trees have a dense dark-green foliage and give benignant shade, [creating] a circular pool of black coolness underneath them."[12]

Snapshots in Welles's albums, now eighty years old show, Mombasa as it was. Turkana tribesmen from the North mingle with towering Masai warriors, spears in hand, their half-naked women giggling shyly behind them. African runners stand in the shafts of canopied rickshaws; camels plod in single file down dirt streets and white British hunters pose in regulation pith helmets and khaki shorts. The most surprising photo of all, perhaps, shows the fastidious young Sumner Welles seated in the open fly of a tent, a towel around his neck, smiling wryly as a safari companion with comb and scissors crops his hair as close as that of any marine recruit at Parris Island. Another shows him in pith helmet and riding boots holding a baby rabbit in his lap.

The capital, Nairobi, eighteen hours from Mombasa by train, was like a "humdrum little South African 'dorp,' straggling listlessly in the sun and occupied," wrote Elspeth Huxley, who had grown up there, "most of the year by a handful of European officials and store-keepers, a mob of Indians packed into the insanitary and smelly bazaar and a drifting population of all breeds of natives." Two or three times a year, Nairobi would suddenly fill with "tattered settlers in broad-brimmed felt hats and revolver holsters. At such times, there was something of the eighteenth-century . . . about the place."[13]

British-ruled Kenya in 1914 was a sportsman's paradise, where wealthy young Americans could acquire virtually anything needed at minimum cost. After outfitting themselves and hiring white hunter guides, Sumner and his companions set out on native ponies, followed by a hundred African bearers who trudged over the plains or forded streams with guns, tents, ammunition, food and drink balanced on their heads. Rising at dawn, the three men hunted until the midday heat, ate sparingly, napped, then hunted again until dusk. By nightfall, their tents had been pitched, their canvas tubs filled with heated bathwater and dinner prepared.

Jaded by Paris, Sumner found the beauty of the veldt, the camaraderie of men his age and the danger of the chase exhilarating. "After two or three days in the wild," wrote Errol Trzebinski, biographer of Denys Finch-Hatton, Karen Blixen's lover, "the senses sharpen. Instincts, buried for aeons under the yoke of what is called civilization, reawaken. Complicity is the keynote of those who hunt in Africa. The closeness, possibly framed by danger and the very savagery of the act, binds . . . pursuants together."[14]

For the next three months Sumner, Nelson and Emmet crisscrossed Kenya and Tanganyika (now Tanzania), hunting lion, elephant, zebra, hartebeest, rhinoceros, hippopotamus and impala. Nelson shipped home, as a gift to Boston's Franklin Zoo, two lions along with a young African, Zaggi, to feed and water them on the long journey. After delivering his charges to the zoo, Zaggi turned up unexpectedly at Mrs. Slater's Readville estate, astonishing servants and neighbors. "He landed dressed in his jumble [sic] clothes, that is, he had on no garments except the fur with which nature had provided him," wrote a local newspaper in a flight of imagination. "Mrs. Slater rushed off, returning with trousers, a shirt and stiff collar into which Zaggi was stuffed." Now presentable by rural Massachusetts standards, Zaggi bicycled excitedly around the estate, causing further pandemonium until he was finally sent home to Africa. Nelson, not content with lions, also acquired a white baboon as a gift for his teenage sister Ray and, for reasons of his own, christened it "William Pig." For years Pig gamboled along the high mansard roofs of Mrs. Slater's manor, descending to eat and sleep but otherwise gazing forlornly over the New England countryside, so unlike his native African habitat.[15]

Spoiled and headstrong, the three young Nimrods inevitably quarreled at times. Big-game hunting, according to Trzebinski, "was a severe test of compatibility. Adverse conditions, fear, ignorance and fatigue can act as tripwires in relationships . . . For those who surmount and share the apprehension at the moment of death, the chafing from the day-long walk and the thorns, the harmony of this reward is rich indeed."[16] Their minor tiffs were soon forgotten, however, in the forbidden fruits of the Dark Continent. Young, lusty and reckless, they boasted in letters to friends at home of the sexual prowess of the native women available for a pittance in the stews and bagnios of the Kenya coast. Welles's later predilection for black sexual partners may have stemmed from this safari. Far from home and Groton, abetted and encouraged by young libertines his own age, he indulged in what Parisian friends might have called *nostalgie de la boue,* a craving to wallow.

Fit, bronzed and laden with trophies, the three left Kenya early in the spring of 1914. Emmett disappeared back into Long Island, Nelson settled temporarily in London, while Sumner returned to Paris and the revels that the faithful Jean Villain confided sadly to Gammell: "fatiguaient beaucoup monsieur." Still restless, however, Sumner soon joined Nelson in London, and they shared a houseboat on the Thames. Visiting Bostonians, including Charles Codman, regaled Back Bay friends with vivid accounts of the nymphs and naiads who flitted—or floated—around it. Sumner's constant companion, that summer, was Ethel Levey, an American musical comedy star once married to George M. Cohan and then appearing in the West End with the British stage idol Gerald du Maurier. Predictably, she was nine years older than Sumner.

London, in that sylvan summer of 1914, rivaled Paris in luxury; its tailors, hosiers, hatters, shoemakers, saddlers and gunsmiths were unsurpassed. Englishmen and their women were flocking nightly to Tango Suppers at the Hotel Savoy.[17] Americans, ex-President Theodore Roosevelt among them, filled the shops, hotels, restaurants and theaters. Chaliapin was singing *Prince Igor,* and Nijinsky and Karsavina were dancing *Le Sacre du Printemps* at Covent Garden. Basil Hallam was starring in a musical hit *The Passing Show* at the Palace Theater while Mrs. Patrick Campbell and Herbert Beerbohm were drawing capacity crowds in Shaw's *Pygmalion* at His Majesty's. The summer solstice was approaching and the sun, wrote Robert Pilpel, seemed to shine night and day.[18] World War I was only three months away.

Meanwhile, Mrs. Slater, Esther and Ray had just reached Berlin after a journey through the Orient and by trans-Siberian railway to Moscow where the American ambassador, Curtis Guild, an old Boston friend, had welcomed them, escorting them to a court ball, to the theater and to the Bolshoi, where Esther saw Russian aristocrats fling jewels onto the stage in tribute to a particularly brilliant performance. Independent at twenty, she had baffled an amorous young Russian noble by refusing, laughingly, to slip away with him from a court function and go on unchaperoned to his family's palace. "There'll be no one there but the servants," he had murmured. "Besides, my mother wants me to have anything I want."[19] Czarist autocracy had met its match in Bostonian obstinacy.

Once again in Berlin, Mabel Hunt Slater felt fully at home. As a child she had often visited Germany with her artist father, William Morris Hunt, learning the language and coming to love German art and, especially, music. Each summer for fifteen years since her husband's death she had taken her children to such German spas as Wilhelmshohe, near Cassel, where Kaiser Wilhelm II summered. At fifty, she was still strikingly handsome and her looks, wealth, vivacity and fluent German had won the approval of the "All Highest" and thus entrée into the old German nobility and the diplomatic corps. She dreamed that Esther would marry a diplomat and live in Germany, where she could visit her.

Sipping tea in the garden restaurant of the Bristol Hotel as the summer shadows lengthened over the lawn, she murmured to her daughters: "Girls, how peaceful and quiet it all is." Two waiters were whispering nearby, and one came over to confide that, that very morning, the archduke Franz Ferdinand, heir to the Austrian-Hungarian throne, had been assassinated in Sarajevo, an obscure town in faraway Bosnia.[20] The date was June 28, 1914.

Within days German headlines were shrilling for war as the tramp of soldiers grew louder. On August 3, Germany declared war on France and, the same day, von Kluck's army sliced through neutral Belgium and Luxembourg, driving deep into northern France and seeking to envelop Paris before the French could rally. The Slater ladies entrained hurriedly for the French capital, where Nelson awaited them. Meanwhile, hordes of panic-stricken Parisians fled south by every exit, some in horse-drawn vehicles packed with belongings, some trudging on foot. Mrs. Slater and Esther left Ray in Paris to follow with Nelson and made their way to Deauville on the Normandy coast, where they settled into the summer villa of an American banker friend, Herman Harjes.

Nelson and Ray eventually joined them, escaping from Paris on the last day automobiles were allowed to leave, then threading their way along refugee-clogged roads in Nelson's new Mercedes, piled with effects, including the white baboon.[21] Nelson donated the Mercedes to the mayor of Deauville for war use, then found passage on a cross-channel steamer that eventually landed them in England. London was packed with Americans all seeking passage home and, in Washington, President Woodrow Wilson had just proclaimed that the United States would remain "impartial, in thought as well as . . . action." Mabel defiantly donated $10,000 to equip a British regiment and sailed home with her daughters while Nelson returned to France to drive an ambulance on the Western Front.

Sumner, meanwhile, had started back on a separate steamer. On board, he discovered two American girls from Bernardsville, New Jersey, whom he had known since childhood: Mary Pyne, a sister of his Groton classmate Rivington Pyne, and her bosom companion Harriette Post, who would become his third wife thirty-seven years later. En route they teased him unmercifully about his precocious elegance and he conceded ruefully that he had been spending "much time" at Cartier's, the jeweler.[22] For better or worse, he had matured in the ten months since leaving Harvard. He had savored the delights of Paris, hunted across Africa and had tested the pleasures of a Thames houseboat. But the war had dashed his plan to study architecture at the Beaux Arts. He was still drifting.

Back in Boston, at convenient remove from his father in Islip, Long Island, he resumed the lifestyle appropriate to a Parisian *boulevardier* but egregiously out of place in the Puritan capital. When most men his age lived in a walk-up flat and few owned a car, he engaged a valet, a chauffeur for his new Renault and took a ground-floor apartment at the intersection of Commonwealth Avenue and Berkeley Street with twin entrances affording discreet entry and exit for lady visitors. Gammell, also back from Paris, called to inspect and, on seeing black satin pajamas on the bed, caught Sumner's eye and both burst out laughing. "Very few young men in Boston had so many affairs," Gammell remembered.

The after-theater parties also resumed: They were "good fun, with champagne, and regularly attended by actresses and a singular assortment of offbeat Bostonians, Harvard students, debutantes and racy young married couples," Gammell recalled. "The common denominator was a bowing acquaintance with the arts, music and drama."[23] In time, the aimlessness of his lifestyle began to pall. That autumn Sumner began contemplating marriage, pursuing Esther on one occasion to Pawtucket, Rhode Island, where she had gone to visit a girl friend. From a hotel in nearby Providence, Gammell received a cryptic note from his friend. He was there for "purposes of my own." Knowing Sumner's penchant for melodrama, Gammell shrugged it off but the thought crossed his mind that Sumner might finally be settling down.

Although they had been reared in the same milieu, Sumner Welles and Esther Slater were poles apart. His mind was quick, incisive and arrogant; hers, gentle and unsophisticated, formed largely by boarding school—Miss Porter's at Farmington, Connecticut—and travel abroad with her mother. Sumner had a sense of the ridiculous triggered by human frailty; Esther, a sense of humor, bubbling up from high spirits. A tomboy at heart, she had once shocked staid Boston by walking down Boylston Street in broad daylight with a girl friend, both dressed as men. Her delight during summers at Bar Harbor was racing her little A-boat around Frenchman's Bay, challenging one and all. "She was a very scrappy girl—fighting for every inch of wind," remembered a male competitor.[24]

Given an automobile by her mother as a coming-out present, she named it the "Red Devil" and drove it along the dusty lanes of Readville, accelerator to the floor, laughing with vexation as she tried passing everything in sight. Arrested repeatedly for exceeding the twenty-five mile-per-hour speed limit, she smilingly paid her fines—then raced off again, leaving horses snorting and rearing in her wake. Gentle and affectionate, she was adored by her mother, by her siblings and by the family servants; as unconventional as Sumner was stiff, she was as popular as he was unpopular. "She was always beautifully dressed and had a lovely smile," Nancy Cabot Osborne remembered, "but she probably never understood one-sixteenth of what Sumner said to her. She was not always tactful and in diplomacy it's very necessary. I can't think why they married."[25]

There were at least three reasons. Faced with the collapse of his architectural dreams, Sumner had begun weighing diplomacy—encouraged by Bay Slater, who pointed out that, with the outbreak of war, diplomacy would assume a new importance and he, with his education and languages, might rise fast. Aimee Sargent was urging him to marry, and Esther was clearly in love with him. Finally came Esther's fortune, no minor inducement for someone with his luxurious tastes. Prompted by Bay, Aimee and Esther, Sumner wrote Assistant Secretary of State William Phillips, a family connection, in late February 1915, asking about the diplomatic examinations.[26] Two of Mrs. Slater's influential friends lent their support. Governor David Walsh of Massachusetts wrote Wilson's Secretary of State, William Jennings Bryan, recommending Sumner as an "educated gentleman of independent means with four languages." Notwithstanding his "travels abroad," he was "American to the core."[27] Ambassador Guild wrote Bryan from Moscow citing the young couple's "real democracy." It had only been a few months, he noted, since "Miss Slater's personal charity of breakfasts for the unemployed was heralded in all the newspapers."[28]

Versed in the ways of Washington, Guild enlisted the support of four senators: James W. Wadsworth and James A. O'Gorman of New York, where Sumner paid taxes; and Henry Cabot Lodge and John W. Weeks of Massachusetts, where the Slaters paid far larger taxes. "I believe that [Sumner] is exceptionally well fitted," Lodge wrote Bryan.[29] Assistant Navy Secretary Franklin D. Roosevelt also lent a hand. "I have known [Sumner] since he was a small boy," FDR wrote Bryan. "He should give a very good account of himself in the [diplomatic] service."[30]

To press his case in person, Sumner took a train to Washington, calling first on Franklin D. Roosevelt who, in turn, sent him to Phillips. His wife, Caroline, was Sumner's distant cousin,[31] and the couple convinced their young kinsman that, with hard work and tutoring, he might be allowed to take the examinations that summer. That settled it; he returned to Boston determined to become a diplomat. Overjoyed, Mrs. Slater announced Esther's engagement and began channeling her formidable energies into wedding plans.

Esther, innocent and artless, was being swept by a dynamic mother into marriage with a man biologically her age but immeasurably more carnal and sophisticated. Within days she confessed to her closest friend, Miriam Sears, that she was totally unversed in what Bostonians of the day primly called the "facts of life." Sumner drove her out to Groton to introduce her to the Peabodys but found them away and wrote them later of his "great happiness." It seemed "almost miraculous contrasted with the unhappiness of my past few years," he concluded. "If I ever achieve anything in this world, and I mean to, it will be due very greatly to you and to my life at Groton."[32] At twenty-three, achievement was his major goal.

Yet shadows of the past still pursued him as his wedding day approached. Mrs. Slater received an anonymous telegram: "On no account let your daughter marry Sumner Welles. Charlie Curtis will explain." Curtis, mystified, conferred with Gammell, then wrote the prospective mother-in-law, "I've known Sumner Welles at school and at college and I've known nothing about him that wasn't worthy of an American gentleman."[33] Traced to a black-sheep Grotonian and unsuccessful rival for Esther's hand, the telegram was ignored; but more problems followed. Several of the contemporaries whom Sumner had invited to be wedding ushers declined. They were a "mixed bag," remembered Gammell, "Grotonian formmates and others chosen essentially for their ties to socially prominent Boston or New York families." Among them, Arnold Welles Hunnewell, a distant relative, saw Sumner passing in the Copley Plaza Hotel one day and remarked coolly to Curtis: "That's Sumner Welles, a sort of cousin of mine. I hardly know him, yet he's asked me to be an usher."[34] Eventually a quorum was formed; and each usher received as a wedding gift a black onyx tie-pin with his initials in tiny diamonds.

On April 14, 1915, the wedding unfolded in feudal style at Webster, seat of the family mills. That morning, at 8:30 A.M., a private train pulled out of Boston's South Station with the wedding party and thirty of Mabel Slater's friends, including Governor Walsh of Massachusetts and Isabella Stewart Gardner, doyenne of Fenway Court, the great private museum. WEBSTER MAKES GALA DAY OF ESTHER SLATER'S WEDDING: WHOLE TOWN HAS PART IN THE DEMOCRATIC CELEBRATION, shrilled a banner headline in the *Boston American.*[35] A thousand children from St. Joseph's parochial school lined the roads, waving American flags as the bride, resplendent in white, whirled by in a limousine with her sister and maid-of-honor, Ray.

Three thousand millhands, given the day off, cheered the bridal couple "displaying affection for [Esther] and her family," wrote the *Washington Post.*[36] George B. Dorr, a family friend, gave the bride away; Nelson served as Sumner's best man, and the Reverend Endicott Peabody helped officiate. On emerging from the church, the newlyweds were escorted to the railway station by fifty Civil War veterans of the "Slater Guard,"[37] and, as the train pulled away for Boston, mill employees and their families sat down to a wedding feast in a mammoth tent while a brass band pumped out Offenbach airs.

Meanwhile, in Boston, guests were arriving at Mrs. Slater's Beacon Street mansion, filing up the stairs into the Gothic drawing room decorated with palm fronds and greeting the animated mother, the shy bride and the stiff young groom. The new Mrs. Sumner Welles had been "exceptionally favored in the matter of wedding presents," reported the *Boston Transcript* with commendable delicacy.[38] At day's end the couple slipped away by train for New York, spending their wedding night at the St. Regis Hotel. Esther, in her innocence, had invited Gammell to join them on their honeymoon, but he had tactfully declined.

Their first week was spent at Islip, where Esther enchanted her new father-in-law and Sumner learned, to his delight, that he would be allowed to take the diplomatic examinations in June. Later they moved up to Bar Harbor, and friends picnicking with them on the Cranberry Islands noted that Esther seemed nervous and Sumner irritated by her awkward, if well-meant, efforts to help her hostess. It was a portent of much to come.[39]

On June 28, Sumner took the diplomatic examinations in Washington and wrote Peabody, soon after, that he had had the "good fortune of passing, first . . . with an average of 93." Not even his father could have been more surprised, he wrote exultantly. It was, in fact, a remarkable achievement; of all who took the examinations that year, only 44.4 percent even passed.[40] Sumner was being assigned to Tokyo, the "best post available," and was sure it would provide a "magnificent chance to show what ability I have. I am very proud and hope the period of inertia in my life is now over."[41]

Years of Promise

TWO

FOUR

JAPAN

1915–1917

"The Tall, Young, Friendly Man
with a Sharp Eye and an
Understanding Heart"

THE STATE DEPARTMENT ORDERED WELLES TO SAIL from San Francisco on August 25 with Ambassador George W. Guthrie, who was returning to his post after home leave. He and Esther crossed the country by train and joined the Guthries aboard *SS Mongolia,* pride of the Pacific Mail line. The war in the Pacific was spreading, and as they sailed out the Golden Gate the Chinese crew set off firecrackers to "placate the spirits." Sumner's career was off to a noisy start.[1]

Japan posed a formidable challenge to American diplomacy in 1915. The imperial government, then allied to Great Britain, had entered World War I for spoils virtually with the first shot. After seizing the great German naval base at Tsing-tao on China's Shantung peninsula and capturing 4,500 German and Austro-Hungarian troops, Japan had next overrun Germany's mid-Pacific possessions—the Caroline, Mariana and Marshall islands, thus overnight extending Japanese sway 2,000 miles closer to the United States. Emboldened by its rapid, bloodless conquests, Japan was already eyeing China, where the new republican government under Dr. Sun Yat-sen, its first leader, had overthrown the Manchu dynasty in 1912 and was facing immense problems.

Three months earlier Japan had handed China a secret ultimatum, the so-called Twenty-one demands, which would have reduced China to vassalage had China not leaked them to the American press, arousing world indignation. Even Wilson's pacifist Secretary of State Bryan had protested the flagrant violation of the U.S.-backed Open Door policy guaranteeing China's territorial integrity.[2] Japan had backed off, but its exclusionary policies in Manchuria left little doubt that China was its next victim. This and more Sumner would learn during the long Pacific voyage from his courtly, dignified new chief.

Born into a substantial Pittsburgh family, Guthrie had served as the city's reform mayor until named ambassador to Japan by Wilson in return for his support during the 1912 campaign. His mission had been difficult from the start. Soon after his arrival in 1913, Japanese mobs had demonstrated outside the American embassy to protest the new U.S. alien land bill, which virtually barred Asian settlement on the West Coast. Guthrie's tact and firmness had won the respect of the emperor and his officials, but relations between Washington and the Japanese foreign ministry, or *Gaimusho,* remained tense.

Nineteen days after departing San Francisco, the *Mongolia* docked at Yokohama. Japanese officials were waiting to greet the returning ambassador, and Sumner would long remember a talk on the train to Tokyo with Dr. (later Baron) Takuma Dan, a director of the powerful Mitsui industrial complex. Dan showed an impressive grasp of political and business conditions in the United States and in Western Europe, Welles wrote later, and exemplified the "liberal" group of Japanese who believed in constitutional government and in assimilating "the best that Western civilization had to offer."[3] In that autumn of 1915, he wrote, Japan was still led by men who had "turned its face to the West" and who believed that Japan could achieve preeminence in the Orient by developing a liberal, parliamentary system of government and cooperating with the Western powers.

Yet, he also noted, it would have been a "very casual" observer who failed to detect the "primeval military instinct" behind Japan's veneer of Westernization. In every part of Japan, the army or navy were the "dominating" factors in daily life.[4]

The American embassy in Tokyo, a Victorian-style frame mansion trimmed with Japanese-style gingerbread, was "quite large [and] built like a southern house with great big rooms and high ceilings," Esther noted in her diary.[5] The embassy staff comprised Post Wheeler, First Secretary and consul; Charles J. Arnell, a consul-interpreter; Sumner Welles, Third Secretary, seven Army and Navy attachés (an indication of Japan's growing military importance); four interpreters; a chaplain; and a handful of clerks.

Sumner's immediate superior, Wheeler, was a man of talent who dabbled in poetry and prose while his wife turned out best-sellers under the nom-de-plume Hallie Erminie Rives. Wheeler's prickly, suspicious nature had led to friction at his previous post, Rome, and he had been recalled to answer charges of trafficking in tax-free gasoline. Apparently he had cleared himself with Secretary of State Bryan, for subsequently he had been posted to Tokyo. The Wheelers took quickly to the new young Third Secretary and his dark, vivacious wife and taught them, along with much else, the intricacies of Japanese protocol. Japan, still emerging from feudalism, was avid for Western esteem, and the imperial government insisted on punctilious compliance with official etiquette.

"We dressed up in our very best and started off to call on the princes and the Imperial household," Esther wrote ten days after arriving. "S. got out and signed his name in the guest book. Most of the princes have very large foreign houses, connected to their palaces, in which they entertain; but I think they live in the latter." Archaic appurtenances brought out the Bostonian in her. "In some [palaces]," she sniffed, "the ink has dried up and the pens must have arrived with [Commodore Matthew Calbraith] Perry."[6] Their protocol duties completed, they began sightseeing, driving on weekends with friends to Kamakura, a seaside resort near Tokyo, and surfboarding the waves. After dark they inspected the Daibutsu, a thirteenth-century bronze Buddha, forty-two feet high and reputedly the largest in the world. "We went to gaze at it by moonlight. How impressive and mysterious, with such great poise and dignity," Esther marveled.

Back in Tokyo, she began lessons in flower arrangement and visited the famous Manyasuro teahouse with Sumner and a diplomatic colleague, Henry May. "Five or six geishas . . . squatted around me, gazing at my dress and jewelry," she wrote with amusement. "They weren't over twenty and most of them sixteen . . . decided to escort me . . . I have never had such a 'succes fou' with my own sex before." The medieval red-light district, Yoshiwara, a ritual for foreign visitors, depressed her. "The women all sit behind bars, which was the only thing about it that affected me," she wrote despondently. "They seemed more like caged animals. Most of the men [were] from the lowest classes. The women seemed to have very little mentality; they looked more like dolls. It is not a place to go twice as it's very depressing and rather ghastly . . . only once!"

After weeks in Frank Lloyd Wright's unfinished masterpiece, Tokyo's Imperial Hotel, they settled into a rented house at 44 Saksunada-cho. "How lovely to feel at home, really so again," she glowed. That night, with the limitless energy of youth, they took the overnight express to Kyoto, the ancient capital, and next day visited a local museum, admiring superb lacquer boxes and screens by the late seventeenth-century master Korin [Ogata].[7] It was the first of many visits to Kyoto: "more beautiful and picturesque each time I see it," wrote Esther. Swept up, like many Bostonians, in the craze for Japanese art and guided by the celebrated dealer Yamanaka, the young couple began collecting. A year later, Sumner would buy a pair of Korin screens from a Kyoto nobleman who, he wrote a friend, had "just lost his last cent."[8] In 1920 he would lend them for display in New York's Metropolitan Museum.[9]

At the end of 1915, Japan celebrated the coronation (more accurately, inauguration) of the young emperor, Yoshihito, with parades, state dinners and the courtesy visits of an American naval squadron. Sumner and Esther attended the ceremonies, he in prescribed white tie, white gloves and top hat, she in a court gown of richly embroidered peach satin and taffeta with elbow-length white kid gloves, a fan of black ostrich feathers and a diamond tiara atop her dark hair. The Wheelers thought them a striking couple; Sumner "tall and handsome and twenty-three."[10] Already a model of sartorial elegance, he now wore suits of China silk and Panama hats "as fine and light as a rose leaf," remembered his sister-in-law Ray Slater.[11] They drew their Japanese friends from many walks of life and in the home of Dr. Inazo Nitobe, whose wife was an American from Philadelphia, they met artists, writers, progressive thinkers from the universities and political leaders from the Diet and the House of Peers—all eager to know more of Western culture and Western political thinking.[12]

His work was "absorbing," Sumner wrote Endicott Peabody. "I hope the period of inertia in my life is past. So far as happiness is concerned, there is no comparison." He expected to remain two years in Tokyo. "After that, I should hope . . . to obtain a place in Washington."[13] Working for an ambassador whom he admired, with congenial colleagues and representing his country, he was taking quickly to diplomacy. He now began developing the powers of persuasion, concentration and precision that later would carry him far. Meanwhile, a challenging new assignment was about to start him up the diplomatic ladder.

The Japanese capture of Tsingtao had left them with 4,500 German and Austro-Hungarian prisoners—most of them middle-age reservists. The Japanese, however, were totally unprepared for the influx, and soon Berlin began charging Tokyo with mistreating its compatriots, and the neutral United States, representing German interests in Japan, soon was embroiled in the issue. Thirty years later, his recollections softened by time, Welles would write of the "decency and consideration" with which Japan had treated its prisoners.[14] U.S. diplomatic archives and eye-witness accounts, however, tell a different story.

The fall of Tsingtao "greatly increased the normal work of the Chancery," wrote Post Wheeler. "All of the German reserves in the Far East had been called to the defense of the fortress . . . The prisoners brought over to Japan, and parcelled out among the stockades built for them, numbered over three thousand." (The precise number was 4,592.)[15] "They were in the Embassy's care and must be looked after . . . We were deluged with telegrams, literally from all over the world, asking news of individual soldiers, dead, wounded or prisoners, each of which must be answered by code through Washington. In order to relieve suspense, a part of the staff had to work all day and a part of the night."

To ensure the health and good treatment of the prisoners, Americans had to supervise their camps and guard their rights and privileges. It was a task calling for "tact and good judgment and both," wrote Wheeler, "were provided by Sumner Welles. It was the beginning of a career which, for brilliance, has not been surpassed in our Service. He proved to be the most knowledgeable and efficient Secretary that I ever worked with."[16]

On Guthrie's orders, Wheeler had been trying for months to ease Japan's harsh treatment of its prisoners. Catholic Germans and Austro-Hungarians, for instance, were forbidden to speak to a priest except in the presence of a German-speaking Japanese officer. Wheeler repeatedly had pointed out that the sacrament of penance, performed only after confession, was a preliminary to the sacraments of the Holy Eucharist and Extreme Unction.[17] But his theological seed had fallen on stony ground. Catholic prisoners, many of high rank, continued to die without religious consolation even though Japanese Catholic priests were available. Soon U.S. diplomatic protests began verging on sharpness.

Guthrie now assigned Welles to handle daily negotiations about prisoners and civilian internees with the Gaimusho and to draft notes for his signature. German protests mounted and the Japanese press, in turn, began alleging mistreatment of Japanese civilians in Germany—with reason. In October 1915, Secretary of State Robert Lansing forwarded for transmittal to the Japanese an official German denial of the Japanese press reports. Nine days later, he forwarded a second denial, attaching a confidential report from the U.S. ambassador in Berlin, James W. Gerard, that cited threats to Japanese civilians in Germany. Gerard had had to request police escorts for the Japanese under his protection.[18] Welles drafted a note for Guthrie to Baron Ishii, the Japanese Foreign Minister, transmitting Germany's latest denial but omitting Gerard's ominous report. The kaiser's government continued protesting Japanese mis-treatment of its prisoners; Washington ordered a full-scale investigation, and Guthrie assigned the task to Welles, largely because of his fluent German.

Welles set out by train on February 29, 1916, with Joseph W. Ballantine, a Japanese-speaking colleague of twenty-seven. Over the next fortnight, they inspected ten prison camps scattered over 600 miles between Kurume, north of Tokyo, and Kyushu, Japan's southernmost island. Conditions in most camps ranged from tolerable to good, but in a few they were appalling. The Japanese had herded their prisoners indiscriminately into temples, into barracks formerly occupied by Japanese laborers or into ramshackle structures unsuited for Europeans, particularly in the cold Japanese winters. "The Europeans, accustomed neither to drafty structures nor to the use of a 'hibachi' in lieu of a stove, were extremely uncomfortable," wrote Charles Burdick and Ursula Moessner in *The German Prisoners-of-War in Japan: 1914-1920.* "Temples revealed a flimsily-constructed interior. Heating did not exist; windows and doors were covered with thin rice paper. Consequently, in wintertime—and the prisoners arrived in November—wind and cold readily penetrated the buildings."[19]

At the Fukuoka camp on Kyushu, 340 prisoners had been crowded into huts built originally for Japanese laborers; their low ceilings, small rooms and limited facilities made them "totally unsuited to the tall Europeans."[20] The worst was Kurume, also on Kyushu, where the Japanese held 1,314 prisoners. Overcrowding and poor housing had led to hostility between prisoners and guards, exacerbated by a brutal camp commander who permitted the guards to punish—even strike—prisoners for the least offense. "Once, quite unintentionally, a German officer dropped [cigarette] ashes in front of a wooden guardhouse," wrote Burdick and Moessner. "The Japanese guard dashed out . . . and deliberately struck the officer in the face. The striking of prisoners by guards occurred frequently . . . and created bitterness."[21]

Welles found that in many cases Japanese harshness stemmed from escape attempts. Several prisoners, in fact, had reached nearby villages or towns before being recaptured. Some had escaped by ship to China, and one—Paul Kempe—had managed to return to Germany, where his account of Japanese camp conditions had aroused national indignation. Tokyo, embarrassed, had ordered its camp commanders to redouble their vigilance. Welles discussed the problem with Alfred von Meyer-Waldeck, former governor of Tsingtao and the senior German prisoner in Japanese hands, but apparently little could be done.

The tour was grueling. In the better-run camps, where complaints were few, an inspection required at least three hours; in Kurume, the worst, it required seven. The camp commander and a squad of soldiers initially tried to prevent Welles from speaking with the prisoners, but the young diplomat drew himself up to his full height and referred the commander's attention to the imperial government's authorization. Eventually fifty prisoners were allowed to pour out grievances ranging from lice, inadequate latrines and lack of exercise to bad food and delayed mail. At Matsuyama, on Shikoku, an indignant German major handed Welles a twenty-six-page list of complaints, including impoliteness by the prison authorities and shoddy work by the local Japanese dentist.

Conditions varied. At some camps Welles found humane commanders. At Tokushima, on Shikoku, prisoners were allowed to conduct private business outside the camp grounds, to grow gardens, organize athletic societies and theater groups and even form an orchestra. At Narashino, near Tokyo, a sixty-man chorus, led by a former musical conductor from Stuttgart, delighted Welles with their professional rendition.[22]

He returned to Tokyo on March 15 and six days later submitted a 120-page report, including detailed plans of each camp plus copies, in English and German, of specific prisoner complaints. At the end he appended a four-page summary. The majority of camps were well run, although four were distinctly sub-standard, he indicated. All in all, however, the Japanese government seemed intent on treating its prisoners in accordance with prevailing Western standards. Although the tour had undoubtedly been arduous, not a word regarding personal discomfort appears in the report.

Wheeler thought the Welles report belonged on the "required reading-list of candidates for the [diplomatic] service as a model." Guthrie sent a copy to Washington, noting: "I desire to commend Mr. Welles's thorough and painstaking inquiry, which has resulted in this comprehensive and temperate report on present conditions."[23] Copies went to the Gaimusho and, later, to Berlin and Vienna. At year's end Welles made a four-day follow-up inspection and was gratified to find that the four camp commanders whom he had criticized had been replaced.[24] Apparently he had made an impression on the prisoners as well. One of them, interviewed a half century later in Germany, remembered the "tall, young, friendly man with a sharp eye and an understanding heart."[25]

Early in 1916 Esther realized that she was pregnant, but her joy was short-lived. From home came shattering news. Her youngest brother, Morris, age sixteen, the gentle idol of the family, had died of pneumonia at St. Paul's School in Concord, New Hampshire. Her grief poured into her diary: "Jan. 19, 1916; today has been one of the saddest of my life. Our darling Morris has been taken away. It must be that those whom the Gods love die young. I long to be with my darlings to shield Mama and help in every way I can . . . My Sumner has been my only staff. It is my first great sorrow. God knows best. I mustn't wonder at his ways . . . darling Morris, watch over us, keep us."[26]

Characteristically, her first thought had been for her mother alone in Boston with only Ray, her teenage younger daughter, to help her. Nelson was in France, still driving an ambulance on the Western Front and Esther was halfway around the world. In her grief, Mrs. Slater turned to Robert Payne, Morris's roommate at St. Paul's. Although only sixteen himself, young Payne handled the bereaved mother and the funeral arrangements with consummate sensitivity. By chance, his father was an executive of the Canadian Pacific company, stationed at Yokohama, and the young man persuaded Mrs. Slater and Ray to visit Japan, staying first with his parents at Yokohama, then moving on to Tokyo for the birth of Esther's baby.

They arrived in April bringing with them a young Boston-Irish nurse, Peggy Lynch, to help with the baby. The sight of her mother and sister sent Esther's spirits soaring. "My darling [Sumner] gave me a superb bouquet of orchids," she wrote glowingly in her diary on April 14, her first wedding anniversary. "How wonderfully happy I have been, except for the loss of darling Morris. I hope all the years of our lives will be as joyous." In expectation of the baby's arrival in midsummer, she and Sumner had rented a seaside house at Kamakura.

"Mama and I first lived at the Imperial Hotel [in Tokyo] before cherry blossom time," Ray recalled years after.

> Later we moved to Kamakura, where we enjoyed the services of a wonderful, whiskered French [hotel] manager who served langouste to Mama's liking . . . I spent time taking my skylarks out at dawn to let them fly from their tall wooden cages with an ivory pedestal in the center. We would visit old Japanese gentlemen [and] sit on silk cushions in rooms of typical Japanese matting on which there were numerous paper-enclosed cages. There, the adult nightingale would practice his chromatic scale teaching his young, each in a separate cage, to sing a few short notes, which was all they could accomplish.[27]

While Esther waited, Mrs. Slater and Ray toured the countryside, sleeping in village inns with balconies overhanging mountain streams and with meals brought to their rooms in lacquered dishes on lacquered trays. "At night, the 'ne-san' [maids] would place silk covers on the matted floor, stuffed with feathery silk from silkworm cocoons," Ray recalled. "As soon as the paper-and-wooden doors were slid shut a tiny opening could be observed with the eye of a crouching 'ne-san' peering through the door-crack."

Nelson eventually arrived from France, accompanied by young Robert Payne with whom he had joined forces in Montreal, an English valet aptly named Meek and a new automobile. Soon he was jolting Ray over the rutted Japanese roads in his new car, visiting Lake Hakone and other beauty spots and fording rivers. "We would be held back by boatmen who then pushed the car onto a raft," Ray remembered. "[They] poled it across, then forty-strong would push the car up the opposite incline."

Esther's baby—the author—made his appearance August 1, 1916, and was named Benjamin for his paternal grandfather. "Ben looks like his father," wrote Esther. "His hands are the miniature of Sumner's. We are delighted." World War I was entering its third year that day. The month before, in July, British casualties on the Western Front had totaled 59,675—slaughter unparalleled in the history of British arms—yet Field Marshal Earl Haig, the British commander-in-chief, was predicting "early" victory. Britain's press was reporting indiscriminate German aerial bombardment of England's east and southeast coasts while, in Russia, the czar's armies were meeting stiff German resistance on the Stoknod River front. In the neutral United States, two Yankee cavalrymen had just been killed in a border clash with Mexican raiders. Meanwhile, in Japan, the war seemed far away.

With Esther and her baby safe and well, Mrs. Slater, Nelson and Ray started home at the end of August. "How quickly the six months have fled," Esther wrote sadly as her loved ones sailed away. "I think they were very happy out here . . . It is just a year, today, that we left New York to start our life's work." For Sumner, it had been a banner year. He had won his first promotion three months earlier, and Guthrie had noted on his efficiency report: "Excellent, studious, anxious to work and attentive; always ready to respond." Esther seemed to be making friends, though, he added, "her health hampers her" and her brother's death had "distressed" her. As a couple, the young Welleses "seemed ready to do [their] share, are not pushers and appear to be acting discreetly."[28]

Woodrow Wilson's reelection that autumn on the slogan "He kept us out of war" dismayed Sumner and Esther, Republicans both. Early returns had indicated a landslide for the GOP candidate, former New York governor Charles Evans Hughes, a family friend. Esther's hopes had soared. "My heart sinks," she wrote when the embassy confirmed Wilson's narrow victory.[29] Rumors of a romance between the ex-Princeton educator and the widowed Edith Galt Bolling of Washington had reached Japan. "Four more years of the amorous professor!" Esther sniffed in her diary. "Of course, Ambassador and Mrs. Guthrie [are] delighted." Ironically, Hughes's defeat would redound, five years later, to Sumner's advantage. As Warren G. Harding's Secretary of State, (1921-25), Hughes would discern the younger man's ability, entrust him with high responsibility and become his lifelong friend.

In April 1917 two events shattered the even tenor of Sumner and Esther's lives. The United States entered the war and Ambassador Guthrie collapsed while golfing with an American reporter. On hearing the news, Post Wheeler sent Welles ahead and followed with the local hospital director. Guthrie was still conscious. "I've tried to do what was right," he murmured. His heart stopped en route to the hospital, and, despite restoratives, he died forty minutes later. "When I go," he had told Wheeler, "I hope to go out like a shooting star." Wheeler thought he had come close.[30] As a mark of respect, the imperial government returned Guthrie's body to San Francisco aboard its newest cruiser *Azuma*.

"America declared war on Germany last night," Esther wrote, in her diary on April 18. "The flag was flying at the embassy all day for the first time since Mr. Guthrie's death . . . Will the war be over quicker now that we have joined? . . . What is in store for us. I pray." For a young woman of twenty-four, reared in Puritan Boston, her next entry was surprising. "At six, Sumner and I went to the cathedral . . . I was confirmed by Bishop McKim."[31]

Sumner's tour was nearing its end; after two years in Japan he was due home leave and reassignment, but he offered to remain and help Wheeler until a new ambassador could arrive. The department gratefully accepted his offer.[32] Then disturbing news from home forced their immediate return—the great Slater mill complex at Webster was in peril.

On his death in 1899, Esther's father, Horatio Nelson Slater, had left approximately $4.6 million, one of the largest fortunes in New England and worth, in today's terms, more than $50 million. Half had been divided outright between Mabel, his surviving widow, and two grown children by his first marriage.[33] The remaining half, including the mills, had been left in trust for his and Mabel's children: Esther, Nelson, Morris and Ray. Before his death, Slater had named three trustees to help Mabel manage the mills, but the trustees, taking advantage of the young widow's inexperience, had offered to sell the mills to a bank at an artificially low price—provided it retain them for life as salaried managers. Mabel had blocked the sale in court; but for the next twenty years lawsuit and countersuit would follow, eroding her mental stability.

Meanwhile, war demand had sent profits soaring. By 1916 the value of the Slater trust had trebled, to nearly $15 million. Mrs. Slater had temporarily rid herself of the scheming trustees and had begun searching for a manager to run the mills for two years until Nelson, then twenty-three, reached twenty-five and could legally take over. Owing, however, to complex litigation, Esther's presence as a principal beneficiary was imperative. Thanks to Wheeler's sympathetic intercession, the department authorized their return.[34]

As sailing day drew near, the Tokyo club, a meeting place for leading Japanese and Americans, honored Sumner with a farewell dinner, attended by thirty of the city's most prominent Americans. The young diplomat's jingoistic address struck a popular chord. No other foreign colony in Japan, he declared, was so firmly bound by common interests and mutual responsibility. While due, in part, to the war, it was equally due to the "realization of our nationality . . . Our country, from San Francisco to New York, from Maine to Texas is awake, is as one and is prepared to win. [Our] cities are already becoming accustomed to the . . . presence of troops. Our men are already in France. Soon there will be more." The future, he proclaimed dramatically, was "at stake." The "northern barbarians, marshalled by the autocracy of Prussia, are once again marching with fire and sword upon civilization."

His analysis of U.S.-Japanese relations, more down-to-earth, hinted at Japanese complacency. "Some of our allies," he noted, dryly, "did not awaken to the full realization of what the war meant for months." During his own two years in Japan, the war had seemed "far away," although the "greatest struggle which ever convulsed the world" was taking place on the other side of the globe. In southern England, homes were vibrating to the sound of guns across the Channel in Belgium. "I have sometimes thought that it would not do us harm," he concluded, "if we, out here, could receive mental vibrations of the same kind; if, by war pictures, or war meetings, or war lectures the ghastly reality . . . could be brought home to us with vital force."[35]

On their last night the Wheelers gave them a farewell dinner. The next day, July 14, 1917, they boarded the SS *Empress of Russia* for home. "Great many came to see us off," wrote Esther. "Sorry to leave beautiful Japan and hope, some day, to return as First Secretary . . . We really love the country." Three days at sea, Sumner learned by cable of his second promotion in two years, an unusually rapid rise for a fledgling diplomat in that era.[36] Never again would he see Mount Fujiyama, stroll the museums and medieval streets of Kyoto or swim off Kamakura while bare-legged fishermen mended nets on the beach. He was leaving a Japan, he wrote many years later, "intensely proud of its recognition as a world power and determined that no word or act, by any Japanese official, should suggest that its standards of culture and civilization were in any way inferior to those in other parts of the world."[37]

Not for twenty years would he deal again with Japanese affairs—and then as Franklin Roosevelt's Under Secretary of State. By then Japan's claims to culture and civilization had been exposed by its brutal invasion of China and by the pitiless treatment it meted out to the prisoners—Americans, Europeans and Asians—who fell into its hands during World War II.

FIVE

ARGENTINA

1917–1919

Arrogance, Ambition and a
Marriage Doomed

THE UNITED STATES HAD BEEN AT WAR only four months when the Welles family docked in August, yet war fever was already sweeping the nation. Troops were drilling, new camps springing up and barracks being rushed to completion from Maine to California. George M. Cohan's stirring new march, "Over There," was the national rage, for America's eyes were increasingly "over there." General John J. "Black Jack" Pershing had just arrived in France to take command of the U.S. First Division, the first of forty-one that eventually would debark at Brest or Nantes before moving into the line. The war, however, was far from won.

German artillery and machine guns were still slaughtering British "Tommies" struggling through mud and barbed wire at an obscure Belgian hamlet, Passchendaele. German warplanes sporadically bombed Britain while, in Russia, a Communist-led revolution had just overthrown the czar, whose armies had suffered 7 million casualties. A year later he and his family would be executed by a Soviet firing squad in a cellar at Ekaterinburg, now Sverdlovsk. Meanwhile, Russia's new Communist boss, Vladimir Ilyich Lenin, would soon offer Imperial Germany vast territorial concessions for an armistice. Germany, while wounded, was still unbeaten.

In Washington, young Sumner Welles pondered his future. Two successive promotions at his first post, Japan, would normally have led to a good position in Washington or in Europe. The war, however, had closed many missions abroad, flooding the department with unemployed diplomats. Latin America seemed the best alternative—although few, at the time, would have chosen it. Washington's indifference to Latin America in 1917, Welles wrote in retrospect, struck him "even as a very young man." The United States and its allies, Britain and France, regarded Latin America as a collection of *petits pays chauds,* banana republics, where trade alone required negotiations and diplomatic assignments were reserved for the "unruly or incompetent."[1] Welles was clearly neither, and his choice of Latin America carefully thought out.

He had returned from Japan deeply disturbed by its growing militarism and convinced that the Japanese army and navy would continue expanding their sway across the Pacific, eventually threatening vital U.S. interests in the Western Hemisphere.[2] Therefore, U.S. friendship with Latin America was essential for strategic, political and commercial reasons. As U.S.-Latin American trade developed, foreign countries would see that the United States spoke "not as a single nation, but as a partner in an entire continent."[3] The seeds of the Good Neighbor policy, with its emphasis on collective security, were already germinating in his mind at age twenty-five. Flouting tradition and the advice of friendly superiors such as Assistant Secretary Phillips, who urged him to reconsider, he requested a post in Latin America and was assigned to Buenos Aires. It would prove a milestone in his career.

Argentina, rigidly neutral in World War I, was growing rich selling Britain and France the meat, hides, wool and grain needed to keep their armies fighting on the Western Front. Having imported few, if any, African slaves and having extirpated their own Indians during the 1800s, the ethnically proud Argentines of mainly Spanish-Italian stock[4] scorned their racially mixed sister republics and, above all, resented "Yanqui" intrusion into their sphere of influence.

The ruling classes wintered regularly in Paris, London, Madrid, Berlin and Rome, returning each spring with the latest in European fashions, furnishings and *objets d'art.* The capital, Buenos Aires, with a population of 1.6 million, gloried in its soubriquet: the "Paris of South America." No less than three opera houses played nightly to packed audiences.

Overseeing this dynamic scene was President Hipolito Irigoyen, a political mystic of Turkish origin, then approaching his seventies. Elected in 1916 in an upset victory that had broken the power of the landowners, Irigoyen had given the masses a "New Deal" and was immensely popular.

"On the rare occasions when he received me on official business," Welles wrote later, "I never failed to be impressed with a quality of innate force and inherent greatness that even his peculiar physical characteristics—a pineapple-shaped head, an evasive gaze and a Mongolian mask with straggling threads on either side of his mouth—could not dispel."[5] Even as president, Irigoyen refused to live in a government residence, preferring four rooms over a bootblack's shop "like a clandestine revolutionary," wrote an English observer. "In his home live his Austrian mistress and his illegitimate daughter. Neither have any influence over him."[6]

Irigoyen's adamant neutrality, although infuriating to the United States, Britain and France, was fully backed by the German-trained Argentine army, the powerful German business community, the university faculties and the masses. Deaf to Allied protests, to Woodrow Wilson's idealism, to liberal Argentine intellectuals and to the students, Irigoyen proclaimed that Argentina would never *ir a la zaga,* (trail in the wake) of the Yankee colossus. This seething cauldron had almost boiled over as Welles was arriving.

Imperial Germany, finding diplomatic protests over Argentine food shipments to the Allies ineffective, had ordered its minister in Buenos Aires, Count Karl von Luxburg, to block them by "any and all" means. When efforts to bribe Communist labor leaders to stage dock strikes failed, von Luxburg cabled Berlin proposing that Argentine ships be sunk *spurlos versenk* (without trace). Adding insult to injury, he also labeled the Argentine Foreign Minister, Honorio Pueyrredon, a "notorious Anglophile ass."[7] British intelligence intercepted his cables, passed them to Washington and, on September 9, Secretary of State Robert Lansing published them—without the normal diplomatic courtesy of forewarning Irigoyen.[8] The Argentine President was outraged.

Under normal circumstances, Argentina would have severed relations with Germany—but, by failing to inform Irigoyen in advance, Lansing had blundered. Berlin, adroitly recovered, recalled its maladroit minister, disavowed his insults, offered reparations and promised that no further Argentine lives would be lost at sea. (In fact, German U-boats continued torpedoeing Argentine ships throughout the war.) As Welles was arriving, pro-Allied *rupturistas* were demanding a break with Germany and denouncing Irigoyen for reaping profits while the Allies bled. Irigoyen characteristically was ignoring them.

Welles and his family docked in Buenos Aires on November 30. With the courtesy of an earlier age, his new chief, Ambassador Frederick J. Stimson, sent two embassy officers to greet them. Unlike his Republican cousin, Henry L. Stimson, Frederick Stimson was a politically active Democrat, a one-time professor of comparative legislation at Harvard and a former assistant attorney general of Massachusetts who wrote novels in his spare time. Slender, with shrewd, merry eyes and a Vandyke beard, he had an "unfailing, and somewhat puckish, sense of humor," wrote Hugh R. Wilson, a former subordinate. Mrs. Stimson, a Philadelphian, "read widely and discussed what she read with passionate interest . . . The couple lived simply and contributed from the spirit . . . not from the pocket. It did not take the Argentines long to appreciate their rarity."[9]

Three weeks after Welles's arrival, Stimson wrote Phillips in Washington that he was "delighted with his work" and was assigning him to commercial duties.[10] During the next two years, Welles would steep himself in Latin American trade and finance—becoming involved, in the process, with the clandestine trade war that Britain was waging to protect its rich Latin American markets from German—and American—competition. Although he had been briefed on the British campaign before leaving Washington, little would have led him to suspect that a genial fellow passenger on the ship taking them to Argentina—Sir Ernest Shackleton, the celebrated polar explorer—was a secret British agent. Shackleton had endeared himself to Sumner and Esther by teaching their eleven-month-old son to toddle the pitching decks during the tedious voyage and ostensibly was arriving to galvanize British propaganda. In fact, he was under secret War Cabinet orders to strangle trade competition—allied America's included.

He had sailed from New York, wrote his biographer, "with a crowd of American businessmen, all bent on pushing the trade of the U.S. in South America when British trade [was] strangled by war risks and restrictions." His mission involved not only study of the "policies and intrigues" of Argentine business firms under German control but, especially, of the "personal foibles" of leading Argentine officials.[11] Countering Shackleton's activities would dominate Welles's work over the next two years.

Meanwhile, the young diplomat's new commercial duties soon brought him into conflict with Consul General Henry W. Robertson, a crusty veteran whose insistence on his prerogatives provided Welles valuable training in bureaucratic warfare. The U.S. diplomatic and consular services were separately recruited and administered in 1917 and remained bitter rivals until the 1924 Rogers Act merged them into the Foreign Service. Consuls, at the time, routinely bypassed ambassadors and ministers, reporting directly to their own superiors in Washington, and they regarded their diplomatic counterparts as effete snobs. The diplomats, in turn, viewed consuls as glorified clerks concerned mainly with bills of lading or stranded seamen. Sumner Welles, the young and very self-confident commercial attaché, epitomized everything Robertson detested about diplomats.

After working for weeks in uneasy tandem, they clashed over the thorniest of many thorny issues on which they were forced to collaborate—the new U.S. "blacklist" of Argentine firms suspected of trading with the enemy. Blacklists, by their very nature, affected trade and often provoked the indignation of foreign governments, which felt their sovereignty was ignored.

The American blacklist, based largely on Britain's, had reached Buenos Aires at the same time as Welles—in fact, one of his first duties had been to draft a letter for Stimson ordering Robertson and his staff to comply.[12] When the American and British blacklists were found to differ markedly, fresh problems arose. How much credence was to be given anonymous or confidential tips? How should firms under German-Austrian control but not known to be trading with the enemy be treated? What was to be done with goods licensed in the United States for shipment to Argentina, then transshipped to other countries?

To establish the embassy's clear authority, Welles informed his consular colleague that henceforth interpretation of the Trading with the Enemy Act— previously Robertson's exclusive prerogative—would be submitted to the embassy (i.e., Welles himself) for approval. Robertson flared. This implied subordination to a novice. Fanatically anti-British, Robertson suspected, moreover—correctly, as it turned out—that Britain was using its blacklist to harass importers of U.S. goods.

At first, Stimson and Welles discounted Robertson's suspicions of British perfidy. After conferring with his British colleague, Sir Reginald Tower, and winning State Department approval, Stimson had Welles inform Robertson that the embassy in future also would consult its British and French allies before adding suspect firms to, or deleting them from, the American blacklist. Robertson was outraged. "I shall take this matter up, verbally, with Mr. Welles," he wrote the ambassador curtly. "I am, Sir, your obedient servant."[13]

Robertson smoldered for six months then, on September 18, 1918, he erupted in two angry dispatches to the Secretary of State. Since the start of hostilities, he charged, Britain had been waging "two separate and distinct wars." One was political, aimed at the Central Powers with troops and a blockade; the other was commercial, aimed at the rest of the world "including her allies and, particularly, the U.S." While pretending to destroy German commerce as a military necessity, Britain was attacking the trade of its friends through a blacklist: "a device selfish, short-sighted, internationally immoral and illegal."[14] In addition to its official blacklist, Britain was using a Suspect List, a Cloak List, a List of Undesirables and a White List—all, except for the blacklist, "absolutely secret from the trade, here and in the U.S." A British colleague had told him that such lists "kept people guessing" and were thus more effective. This, Consul General declared angrily, was "more or less, outrageous."[15]

Ironically, at war's end, Shackleton himself would confirm Robertson's charges. Britain's blacklist, he wrote his superiors in London, "not only damages British prestige but [has] failed entirely in its avowed object—to cripple and kill German trade. The Argentines . . . who have always been on friendly terms with England have entirely lost their sympathy on account of their utter disgust of our methods."[16]

Sumner and Esther had felt themselves essentially strangers in Japan; in Argentina they felt at home. Argentine society was entertaining frenziedly with its new war wealth and the young American couple—traveled, well educated, *simpatico,* and rapidly learning Spanish—were widely accepted. Formality "comes naturally to the Latin," a British ambassador wrote,[17] and Sumner was instinctively formal. He took up polo, the national sport, and soon weekend invitations to country *estancias,* to lunches, dinners, dances, the opera and the ballet were pouring in. Victoria Ocampo, the grande dame of Argentine letters, remembered a half century later the "tall, rather shy" young diplomat who came regularly with his wife to her Thursday afternoon receptions where, as one habitué recalled, "the dance continued until sundown, and conversation was subordinated to the dance."[18] Diplomacy, in World War I, took many forms.

Early in 1918, Esther realized she was pregnant again but, again her happiness was marred by news from home. An immigrant Russian anarchist, determined to attack American capitalism, had burst into her mother's Boston house, mortally wounding the butler before being disarmed. Mrs. Slater, terrified, had fled to New York. Worse followed. Sumner learned that his beloved "Aunt Aimee" Sargent, who had become a surrogate mother after his own mother's death, had just died. He was shattered; few people in his life had meant more. Aunt Aimee's devotion had supported him throughout his three unhappy college years. Upon coming into his mother's legacy at age twenty-one, his first act had been to buy her a diamond bracelet. Every day of his life thereafter, wherever he was, he had penned her a few affectionate lines. Her death exacerbated his inner loneliness. Characteristically, he sought to bury his grief in work—and casual love affairs.

He and Esther were already drifting apart. Despite two years as a diplomatic wife in Japan, she had remained essentially a capricious *jeune fille,* too fun-loving and immature for the ambitious young husband whom she often embarrassed by her pranks. Sensing her inadequacy yet uncertain how to surmount it, she let a new plaintiveness creep into her diary. She was tiring of charity teas, of fundraising for the American Patriotic Society, of ritual attendance on Mrs. Stimson, of Te Deums and military parades. "No ceremony in the world can be duller," she wrote after a crowded reception at the Casa Rosada, the presidential palace.

The initial thrill of Buenos Aires had passed and now nothing seemed right. The sets at the Teatro Colón, the city's leading opera house, were "not as good" as the New York Metropolitan's, and the orchestra "doesn't compare." The ballet at a performance of *Thaïs* was a "disgrace," and a noisy dinner party, arriving in an adjoining box at the opera at 11 P.M., an hour and a half late, kept up a "steady flow of conversation until the curtain fell."[19] Occasionally, to escape the summer heat, Esther and an embassy friend, Irene Robbins, took their children and nursemaids on the overnight boat to the beaches of Uruguay, but even there the beach regulations seemed "absurd, . . . One is not allowed to sit on the beach, even with wraps over a bathing suit. At noon, everyone must leave the water and come out and get dressed."

The Argentine women, she noted significantly, were "too much alike . . . the most self-conscious bunch I have ever met." Something was troubling her— probably jealousy. By then, Sumner's philandering had almost certainly reached her ears, for Argentine society was too porous to permit secrets, and love affairs, if discreetly handled, were widely winked at. The amatory exploits of a young American diplomat would have evoked amusement, not censure. Esther bottled up her hurt, allowing no hint of a rival to appear in her diary, but one day, driving in the countryside with a female friend, the two passed a cemetery and Esther murmured, as if to herself, "I wish I were there."[20]

The birth of her second son on September 19, raised her spirits. The delivery had been hard. "All is over, thank goodness. An enormous difficulty lifted off me," she wrote. "I had decided it would be a girl and Emily was the name." The new arrival, in fact, was christened Arnold, for a Revolutionary War descendant of the clan matriarch, Abigail Arnold, and Nelson, for Esther's brother, who had arrived from Boston to be with her for the birth and whose family news and high spirits delighted her. Sumner soon whisked his brother-in-law off to meet an Argentine beauty with whom he was dallying and whose nubile daughter, he suggested, might make Nelson a perfect wife. Nelson laughed the idea off, but the suggestion itself reflected the madcap relationship between the two since their safari days and the revels on the Thames.

A fortnight later Esther noted cryptically in her diary that "Sumner and his twin, Carlos A, went off to Cordoba for a spell." Why was not explained. Carlos A. was an Argentine *homme-du-monde,* polished, with European tastes, whom many thought resembled Welles physically. He moved to Paris after World War I, dissipating his wealthy Mexican wife's fortune until, as one contemporary remembered, he "slid down the path to end his days, patheti- cally."[21] It was a fate common to many rich Argentines at the time. Bored and jaded, they turned to drugs and homosexuality for stimulation. At one Buenos Aires dinner, a prominent Argentine bemoaning the loss of a handsome lover was consoled by one and all.

The stage is dark and the players have long departed but one Latin American who knew Welles at the time believed that his latent bisexuality first surfaced in the Argentine. "My suspicion, or conjecture, that he gave way to his innate tendencies first . . . in Argentina," this source wrote the author years later, "is because he found there a favorable environment. Respectable married men of high position, like himself, gave vent to deviation and he followed them . . .

I am convinced that . . . his preference for men was always there, only controlled by shame and a Puritan ethos. In Argentina, he found a different attitude and he let the reins slip."[22]

That Esther knew, or even suspected, is inconceivable; she would have left him instantly. In the Boston world in which she had been reared, sexual deviation was never discussed, let alone condoned. It was not the Argentine men whom she feared, but the women.

Germany's surrender, on November 11, 1918, abruptly ended Argentina's lucrative food sales to the Allies. Inflation sent prices soaring, political infighting—suspended during the war—resumed and labor violence escalated. Strikes at year's end closed the great port of Buenos Aires and Irigoyen, populist though he was, reacted savagely with troops. "In one week, 2,500 known killed were found in the streets of the capital [plus] 5,000 estimated wounded and 1,500 deported to . . . an antarctic penal colony, whence few return," wrote Stimson.[23] Sumner's and Esther's second Christmas in the Argentine, unlike their first, was somber.

Early in 1919, to escape the Argentine summer heat, they moved with children and servants to a *quinta,* or country house, at nearby Isidro on the Plate River. Violence was steadily escalating. "Trains . . . thrown over, a great many burned. Motormen killed. No taxis," Esther noted. "The stillness frightening." Newspapers had ceased publishing, and there were rumors of shooting in the city. Workers at the British-owned Alcorta Iron Works had, in fact, been killed, and sympathy strikes were spreading. Sumner took a suburban train to the embassy the next day as their chauffeur was "afraid to drive." Surprisingly, given his links to the wealthy classes, he sided with the strikers.

"The sympathy of any reasoning person must, unquestionably, be with the striking employees of the large department stores," he wrote in the embassy diary. "Their wages have, for years, been inadequate and, since the war, impossible for women employees to live on." Government claims that German funds or influence lay behind the strikes were "mischievous and misleading," nor had he been persuaded by claims of "leftist" instigation. The causes of labor unrest were "too deep-seated," he noted dryly, to be effaced by "police edicts or Patriotic Leagues."[24]

The war's end also had expanded Sumner's embassy duties. The United States, Britain and France, seeking war reparations, were competing for German assets in the Argentine—but national pride and lingering pro-German sentiment were complicating their task. Given "Argentine obstructionism," Welles warned Washington, it would be a "very serious error" to cooperate with the French or British in obtaining information about German assets. What facts could be obtained should be utilized "strictly for our own benefit."

If war prizes, such as the German Electric Company or the ships of the Hamburg South America line, could be acquired, control should be vested "only in American corporations." British influence should be "curtailed" and every effort directed toward the "enhancement of our own importance commercially, and consequently, politically."[25] Two years as commercial attaché in the Argentine had made Welles as ardent an economic jingoist as Consul General Robertson himself.

On September 9, 1919, Stimson returned from leave to find Welles on the verge of collapse. Although seriously ill, he had continued directing the embassy as chargé d'affaires, unwilling to leave his post in the ambassador's absence. The story was dramatic. Months earlier he had handled, or been bitten by, a dog found to be rabid and had undergone painful injections at the local Pasteur Institute to prevent hydrophobia. However, infection had set in—so serious that Stimson had vetoed Secretary Lansing's proposal that Welles, because of his "good work," be loaned to the embassy in Chile to help mediate a border dispute. Welles's health prevented his making the trip across the Andes, Stimson had replied before departing. He would leave him in charge of the embassy during his coming absence and send another officer to Santiago instead.[26]

The responsibility of directing the embassy at the young age of twenty-six had boosted Sumner's morale—and delighted Esther more for her husband's sake than for her own, as her Boston upbringing forbade the sin of pride. "I had expected that, to become the wife of the chargé d'affaires of the U.S. embassy, would cause me to feel very exalted," she wrote, "but so far I sail along feeling not in the least changed from what I did yesterday." Despite their youth, as the ranking American couple in Buenos Aires they were caught up in endless social obligations—fatiguing, especially, for Sumner. Esther, tireless and high-spirited, seemed oblivious to the strain on her convalescing young husband.

Esther's sense of humor bubbled up at a farewell dinner for the departing British envoy, Sir Reginald Tower. On the center table, an artificial garden had been arranged from which, she wrote, "several very lively ducks . . . quacked terribly" during Foreign Minister Honorio Pueyrredon's speech. Later a "ten-year-old nymph danced in a most scanty costume to the delight of the bald-headed gentlemen . . . the Papal Nuncio turned his back . . . but could hardly resist the temptation of peeking . . . his eyes rolled."[27]

By the fall of 1919, Sumner's two-year Argentine tour was drawing to a close. Phillips had hinted at a good post in the department's Latin American division, so the Welleses moved to the Plaza Hotel, preparing to sail home on October 31. On September 25, however, Esther's diary noted that Sumner had been

"suffering terribly" for several days. Their doctors recommended hot com-
presses changed every quarter hour, but when these brought no relief they
decided to operate. "I felt terribly anxious," wrote Esther. "Sumner came out of
the ether very quickly, before he was off the operating table."

Following an injection of morphine, he fell asleep. "He suffered
tremendously but he is mentally much better than he had been for several days."
Slowly, his strong constitution mended and, on October 3, she noted that "My
darling got up and came into the sitting room for lunch with me. Everybody was
delighted to see him up and about."

Their final weekend was spent with close friends, the Carlos Alberto
Tornquists, at their celebrated *estancia,* Miraflores, eighteen hours by train from
Buenos Aires. A "great, white stucco house, Renaissance-style, surrounded by
lawns and an artificial lake with a magnificent view of the 'pampa' and great
hills on the horizon," wrote Esther. Sumner went off with others to visit a
neighboring property, but she remained behind, alone, to inspect the milk house,
the piggery and other appurtenances and, as she put it, to "cool my thoughts."
Why, she did not explain.

Sumner returned by train to Buenos Aires the next day to wind up at the
embassy, but Esther stayed on for "four more divine days fishing, motoring,
walking, rowing and dancing." The overnight train trip back to Buenos Aires
brought out the tomboy in her. "Fun, apple-pie beds, rough-housing of all sorts,"
she wrote. "Carlos Alfredo [Tornquist] dropped me at the Plaza at the atrocious
hour of seven where I found Sumner peacefully sleeping."

On sailing day, the Stimsons and Argentine friends accompanied them
on the boat train and rode out with them in a launch for a final meal aboard the
familiar old SS *Vestris,* which had brought them down two years earlier. "I cried
very hard," Esther wrote, as the Argentine coast faded from sight. "We have
spent two wonderfully happy years." As the *Vestris* plowed its way north,
Stimson cabled the department extracts from *La Nacion,* the leading Buenos
Aires daily, citing Welles's "pleasing and sympathetic manner" and the "tact
and intelligence" that he had displayed. Thanks to his "judicious conduct," the
paper wrote, he had conquered Argentine society and was leaving behind a
throng of friends.

Stimson thought it highly unusual for a junior secretary of embassy to win
such marks of esteem, not only from Argentine friends but from the diplomatic
corps and the American colony as well. The Foreign Minister, he added, had
"repeatedly expressed satisfaction" with Welles's work as chargé d'affaires.[28]

Two years in the Argentine had honed Welles's diplomatic skills, providing him
a solid grounding in hemisphere trade and finance, flawless Spanish and an
insight into the Latin American mind that few contemporaries would ever

approach and none would surpass. Professionally, his star was rising; but, personally, he was in trouble. His self-assurance was verging on arrogance and a new ruthlessness was emerging that would soon brush aside anything, or anyone, in his way. He was emotionally parched—and his marriage to Esther was doomed.

SIX

DIRECTING LATIN AMERICAN AFFAIRS

1920–1922

"Overwhelmed with His Own Dignity"

WELLES HAD BEEN MORE SERIOUSLY ILL than he or anyone had suspected. His New York doctors found "intestinal disorder, protracted; wounds unhealed [and] a lowered tone evoked by residence abroad."[1] On the strength of this report the State Department added three months' sick leave to the two due him on change of station, so he and Esther sailed for Europe, leaving the children with relatives in New York. After a winter touring by car and collecting antiques in London, Paris and Madrid, they returned in May 1920 with a new gray-and-black "drop-nose" Renault cabriolet bought in Paris for $80,000 in today's terms.

Restored to health, Welles reported in June to LA, the department's division of Latin American affairs. Its chief, Dr. Leo Rowe, a leading economist recruited from the Treasury,[2] was leaving to become Secretary General of the Pan American Union and had already begun searching for a successor. The fortuitous arrival of young Welles, whose fluent Spanish and work in the Argentine had won him commendation, solved the problem. Nine days later Rowe named Welles the deputy chief of LA; when Rome left for the Pan

American Union on September 1, Welles became the department's acting chief.[3] At the time Sumner was six weeks short of twenty-eight.

Congratulations flowed in. Under Welles's direction, Rowe predicted, LA would move forward with "dispatch and efficiency."[4] Alvey A. Adee, the venerable Assistant Secretary whose eagle-eyed insistence on proper usage had cowed young diplomats for a half century, wrote Welles that his work in Buenos Aires had impressed him as "painstaking and thorough." His new position, he added, would afford ample scope for these "very necessary qualities."[5] Indeed it would. LA, while not in the forefront of world diplomacy, was nonetheless an arduous, demanding bureau involving eighteen countries in the Caribbean, and Central and South America.[6] Secretary Bainbridge Colby and Under Secretary Norman H. Davis concentrated primarily on postwar European and Asian affairs, leaving Welles to detect and devise solutions for problems in his own area.

The war's end had brought a new mood to Washington: less bellicose, more sensitive to foreign opinion and thus more in tune with Welles's own thinking. His two years in the Argentine had convinced him that the hatred of the United States common throughout much of Latin America stemmed largely from misunderstanding of the Monroe Doctrine.[7] To many Latin Americans it seemed a thinly disguised pretext for armed intervention in their affairs.

Proclaimed in 1823, eight years after Waterloo, by President James Monroe and his Secretary of State, John Quincy Adams, the Monroe Doctrine had grown out of a proposal by the British Foreign Secretary, George Canning, to prevent rival European powers—Bourbon France, Czarist Russia and Austro-Hungary—from seizing Spain's rebellious New World colonies. Canning had promptly recognized their independence and then, assuming that the fledgling United States would welcome the powerful support of the Royal Navy, had suggested a joint Anglo-American warning against foreign intrusion into the Western Hemisphere.

Monroe and Adams, however, had turned his proposal to their own advantage, unilaterally proclaiming U.S. opposition to all foreign intervention—Britain's included. The Monroe Doctrine was not addressed to the Latin American nations, wrote a legal authority, but to "overseas nations which threatened by force to introduce changes in the territorial or political conditions in America disturbing to the welfare of the U.S."[8] In solving one problem, however, the Monroe Doctrine had created another.

Barred from military intervention, the Europeans had turned to commercial penetration, accumulating large surpluses, especially in the Caribbean. Then, finding it impossible to collect their debts, Britain, France and Germany had begun bombarding laggard debtors from warships or landing troops. An Anglo-German attack on Venezuela in 1902 awakened Washington to its quandary. "If we intend to say 'Hands off!' to the powers of Europe," Theodore

Roosevelt had told his Secretary of State, Elihu Root, "then, sooner or later, we must keep order, ourselves."[9] TR's celebrated corollary to the Monroe Doctrine had been seen thereafter as White House sanction for keeping order, by force if necessary, in the strategic Central American–Caribbean arc where TR eventually planned to build an interocean canal.

In the decade prior to World War I, the United States, for example, had: established a protectorate over Panama; taken over the Dominican customs; twice reoccupied Cuba; landed marines in Nicaragua; and quarreled repeatedly with Mexico. In 1915, to forestall European bridgeheads near the new Panama Canal, the pacifist Woodrow Wilson had ordered the military occupation of Haiti and, in the following year, that of the adjoining Dominican Republic as well. The war's end had eliminated any threat to the canal but also had highlighted the contrast between Wilson's pious "self-rule for all" and continuing U.S. military occupation of small neighbors, such as Nicaragua, Haiti and the Dominican Republic. Not only prominent Americans but groups such as the American Federation of Labor and Latin American statesmen had begun pressing Wilson to withdraw U.S. forces and restore independence.

In mid-1920, as Welles was taking up his new duties, Wilson, Colby, Davis and Rowe had already begun deliberating how to extricate the United States from its occupation morasse. Thus Welles did not conceive the policy of withdrawal. However, he infused it with a new vigor, cutting bureaucratic red-tape and galvanizing the State Department and White House to act. Support soon arose from an unexpected quarter. Warren G. Harding, the Republican presidential candidate, seized on U.S. intervention in Latin America as a 1920 campaign issue.

Franklin D. Roosevelt, the flag-waving young Democratic vice-presidential contender, had recently boasted in a speech in Montana: "I wrote Haiti's constitution, myself, and, if I do say it, I think it is a pretty good constitution."[10] Haiti's constitution had, in fact, been drafted in the State Department and had crossed FDR's Navy Department desk en route to the U.S. occupation authorities in Port-au-Prince. Nonetheless, it was a political gaffe and Harding pounced. If elected, he proclaimed, he would not empower an Assistant Secretary of the Navy to draft a constitution for "helpless neighbors in the West Indies and jam it down their throats at the point of bayonets borne by U.S. Marines."[11]

Over the next two years, three of the eighteen countries under Welles's supervision—Cuba, Haiti and the Dominican Republic—would monopolize his attention. U.S. troops had already left Cuba by the time he took charge, but the 1901 Platt amendment[12] still required the United States to send forces back to Cuba in event of a foreign threat or domestic disorder. Cuba, in effect, remained a quasi-protectorate, while Haiti and the Dominican Republic were still being ruled by U.S. military proconsuls sent out by Washington. In all three republics demands for total, immediate independence were rising.

Wilson, Colby and Welles agreed with independence—in principle. The problem was timing. Premature withdrawal from the Dominican Republic or Haiti might spark violence, thereby postponing independence. Meanwhile, the the navy and the Marine Corps, finding occupation duty in the sunny Caribbean far more stimulating than routine shore duty, were covertly opposing withdrawal through friends in Congress. The lessons Welles would learn over the next two years would stand him in good stead when, thirteen years later, he became FDR's Assistant Secretary of State for Latin America. His successes and failures early in his career laid the groundwork for what later became the Roosevelt administration's signal success: the Good Neighbor policy.

CUBA

Cuba's case was unique. After freeing the island republic from Spanish rule in 1898, the United States had then handed it "conditional" independence, but the Platt Amendment, designed to prevent civil disorder, had boomeranged. Cuban politicians, whether defeated or facing defeat at the polls, had begun fomenting violence, hoping to provoke U.S. intervention and emerge with better terms. As a result, the United States had been forced to land troops to restore order in 1906 and 1912. In 1917, during World War I, it had had to threaten intervention. By war's end, weary of endemic violence, Washington had begun a tutelary process—creating a mixed Cuban-American Advisory Commission under General Enoch H. Crowder, an army administrator of genius who would later become the first U.S. Ambassador to Cuba. Under Crowder's guidance, the Cubans had reformed their civil service, had improved local government, had drafted electoral laws and had defined the powers of their presidents. As Welles was taking charge, Cuban elections were again approaching, but tension was rising—due largely to American tactlessness.

In 1919, Cuba's president, Mario Garcia Menocal, had invited Crowder back to update his electoral laws. A Cornell graduate, Menocal admired Crowder, as did most Cubans, but the State Department, pressing its advantage, had proposed that Menocal not only publicly pledge honest elections but also invite Crowder to "supervise" them. Catching wind of the U.S. demand, Menocal's Liberal opponents had denounced it as subservience, leaving Menocal angry and embarrassed and Welles facing his first crisis. Pressure to comply might provoke Menocal's resignation, leaving a dangerous power vacuum, yet his Conservative backers were turning increasingly to intimidation and fraud and, if unchecked, might drive the Liberals to boycott the election— or worse: to demand U.S. intervention. "What this nation must make every effort to avoid," Welles counseled his superiors on August 27, 1920, "is to be impelled to intervene, once more, in Cuba to preserve order."[13]

Welles proposed, and Colby agreed to, a face-saving compromise: the United States would "observe" but not "supervise" the coming poll. Nonetheless, as violence continued and Menocal refused to pledge an honest election, Welles recommended that Boaz Long, the American minister to Cuba, cut short his home leave and return immediately to his post, accompanied by Crowder as President Wilson's "Personal Representative." Wilson ordered Long back but held Crowder in reserve, and eventually Menocal issued the desired pledge. In return, Welles announced that the United States would remain strictly neutral in the coming poll but, as the Platt Amendment obliged the country to ensure a fair election, Washington would observe not only its conduct but its "spirit." His message was clear.

Meanwhile, in Havana, Boaz Long heard rumors that American-owned properties would go up in flames if civil war broke out and asked for election observers, including twenty Spanish-speaking marines, for "intelligence" duties. The State Department was "exceedingly reluctant" to have marines prowling around a Cuban election, Welles replied, but Long might broach the matter "confidentially" with Menocal. When Menocal posed no objection, Long, emboldened, next requested that U.S. warships deploy off Cuba's shores before election day. At this, President Wilson erupted. "We are authorized to intervene . . . only in case of revolution, not when we fancy that revolution is impending," he decreed. "To do that . . . would bring about the very thing that we want to avoid."[14]

The Cuban election of November 1920 ended in a deadlock, but the fraud and intimidation had been so glaring that Crowder persuaded Cuba's supreme court to annul the results and schedule fresh elections for March 1921. Cuba settled down to six months of tense waiting. While Wilson, Colby and Welles pondered their next move, a fresh crisis arose.

With the war's end low-priced European beet sugar had flooded back into world markets, collapsing Cuba's high-priced cane sugar sales. Facing bankruptcy, Menocal appealed to Washington for help, but Wilson, without consulting or even informing him, ordered Crowder back to Cuba aboard the USS *Minnesota*. Welles cabled Boaz Long, in strict confidence, that the presidential envoy would arrive New Year's day, 1921, but, within twenty-four hours, the story appeared on the front page of the *New York Times*. Offended again at being treated like a puppet, Menocal announced that, although he respected Crowder, he would not officially receive him until a face-saving exchange of notes had been published.[15] The indignant department directed Welles to draft a suitable rebuke for Under Secretary Davis's signature.

"It has not been customary, nor has it been thought necessary," Welles began icily, "for the President of the U.S. to obtain the prior consent of the President of Cuba to sending a special representative to confer regarding conditions seriously affecting the interests of both [countries]." Wilson expected Menocal to receive his envoy at the "earliest possible moment."[16] Menocal ordered Carlos Manuel de Cespedes, his minister in Washington, to protest, but Welles and Davis, tempering firmness with tact, assured the minister that Crowder's visit was intended to assist, not humiliate, Menocal. Two days later Menocal welcomed Crowder to the presidential palace. Wilson wrote that he had been "cheered" by Menocal's decision to "act like a gentleman."[17]

Before Crowder's departure, Welles had drafted his instructions, which Crowder would later describe as Washington's "New Conception." Henceforth, Welles wrote, the Platt Amendment would be used to "maintain, and not simply . . . restore stable government" in Cuba.[18] Whether preventive diplomacy or paternalistic meddling was irrelevant: Cuba was bankrupt and facing a political crisis. As Crowder continued firing off salvos of advice from the USS *Minnesota* in Havana harbor, Colby ordered Welles to join him and assess the situation at firsthand. Welles arrived in February to find a chaotic situation.

Many Liberals were demanding U.S. intervention, claiming that they had been "robbed" of victory at the polls, although some Liberals, disgusted by the feuding of their political leaders, José Miguel Gomez and Alfredo Zayas, were demanding that both step aside and yield the presidency to an acceptable "nonpartisan." Crowder, although initially dubious, had begun warming to the idea as Welles arrived, and after long discussions Welles agreed to recommend the idea to Washington. Neither Gomez nor Zayas seemed "desireable," he cabled. No matter which was elected, "nothing would be accomplished for four years." If the March runoffs ended again in deadlock, both men should be "induced" to withdraw in favor of a nonpartisan.[19]

Welles's preferred candidate was de Cespedes, the Cuban minister in Washington, whom he had come to know and respect. Twelve years later, as FDR's ambassador to Cuba in 1933, Welles would again support de Cespedes for the presidency; thus his reasoning in 1921 merits attention. De Cespedes's diplomatic career, he cabled, had "disassociated" him from politics. His other qualifications included his integrity, his prestige as the son of a hero in the struggle for independence,[20] his "thorough acquaintance with the desires" of the United States and his "amenability" to advice.[21] While no doubt compelling factors in the eyes of the twenty-eight-year-old chief of LA, de Cespedes's "amenability" to U.S. advice would surely have cost him the presidency had the Cubans learned of it. In any event, he was not needed.

Ignoring U.S. advice, Gomez's Liberals boycotted the March runoffs, handing the presidency by default to the moderate, pro-American Zayas. Predictably, Gomez appeared soon after in Washington, brandishing a seventy-four-page list of complaints about electoral fraud. By this time the Harding administration had taken office and the new Secretary of State, Charles Evans

Hughes, refused to intervene. Cuba's political crisis had been averted and Welles had won his first test.

Welles's rapid rise, his impatience with minds slower than his and the mass of work flowing over his desk inevitably led to friction. Older subordinates resented his self-assurance, and many contemporaries thought him overbearing. "He had an immense belief in his own ability to win people around to his own viewpoint, to get things done," remembered Dana G. Munro. Munro had joined the Latin American division at about the same time as Welles and, soon after, had been assigned to Santiago, Chile. After a long boat trip, he and his wife had rented a house, had begun their official rounds, had hired riding horses—had even laid in a stock of Chilean wine—when suddenly they were recalled to Washington. Welles was leaving for a few weeks in Paris on personal business—the wedding of his brother-in-law, Nelson Slater—and had recalled Munro to run the Latin American division in his absence. It was a mark of confidence with which Munro would gladly have dispensed. "When we got back, Sumner suggested we take some leave before starting work," Mrs. Munro recalled with a laugh years later. "I could have murdered him. We would so much rather have taken leave in Chile than in Washington."[22]

Welles's self-assurance even led to a newspaper report, possibly apocryphal. He had been summoned to Secretary Colby's office late one afternoon only to find that Colby had left for a social engagement. After waiting until 10 P.M., Welles went home. When Colby eventually returned, his secretary telephoned Welles's apartment to be told by his butler that Welles had retired for the night. Colby came on the line to hear the butler intone stonily: "Mr. Secretary, Mr. Welles told me—particularly if you called—to say that he had retired." Amused rather than irked by such sang-froid, Colby was overheard telling a dinner partner soon after that Welles "could become anything he wants. He is brilliant, tireless. When there is work to be done—the clock does not exist."[23]

Among the older men irked by Welles's self-esteem was Chandler P. Anderson, a prominent Washington lawyer and former State Department legal advisor then representing Nicaragua in a border dispute with Honduras. "I called on Mr. Wells [sic] and was ushered in without any considerable delay, for the first time in my experience with him," Anderson wrote in his diary. "It is the first time that he has not been so much overwhelmed with his own dignity that my suggestion of difference with him was not regarded as presumption."[24]

Not long before, in a stormy meeting with Anderson, Welles had threatened to "compel" Nicaragua to accept a boundary awarded by a mutually agreed arbiter, King Alfonso XIII of Spain. "I asked what he meant by 'compel,'" Anderson expostulated, "because it implied . . . interference with the rights of independent nations, which I could not believe he had in contemplation." In fact, this was precisely what Welles was contemplating. To ease tension in Central America, he warned Anderson, the State Department might use financial measures to "force" Nicaragua to accept the disputed boundary. At this, Anderson had flared.

Welles, he snapped, did not seem to realize that "[Woodrow] Wilson and all his works had been repudiated" by the American people in the 1920 election. If Welles was planning to resort to "Wilsonian autocracy," he had better do so before President-Elect Warren G. Harding took office on March 4, 1921. Unmoved, Welles had continued pressuring Nicaragua until Anderson went over his head, persuading Colby to disapprove any decision not acceptable to his Nicaraguan client. Despite their early clashes, Welles and Anderson became close friends, although the older man continued misspelling his name. "Talk with Sumner Wells [sic] at country club" Anderson noted in his diary on April 19. "Sumner Wells [sic] dined with me last night," he wrote on November 3. Anderson, in fact, was one of the few to whom Welles confided, early in 1922, that he was planning to leave diplomacy for the more lucrative field of banking. He had promised, however, to continue directing the Latin American division until the Washington arms conference, then in session, no longer monopolized Hughes's time.

As Welles's resignation drew near, Anderson noted that he seemed "exceedingly anxious to have the Honduran-Nicaraguan border dispute settled . . . as something to his credit before leaving." He would also, he told Anderson, urge Hughes to convene a Central American conference to create a Central American Court of Justice and settle other financial and political problems in the area.[25]

While many of Welles's colleagues resented him, others found him a loyal friend. Post and Hallie Wheeler returned from Japan in late 1921 and, while awaiting reassignment, spent a fortnight as houseguests in the Welleses' apartment. Still paranoid about plots to wreck his career, Wheeler poured out his woes and Welles, as an ex-officio member of the Personnel Board, brought them to Colby's attention. Thanks to Welles's intercession, Wheeler's career was saved. "Never was a friendship more loyally displayed," Wheeler wrote later.[26]

Another who developed a lifelong admiration for Welles was Anna Louise Clarkson, a young Virginian of brains and breeding who had recently been recruited into the State Department's clerical pool and was waiting assignment. She was spending a weekend with friends near New York when she received an urgent message to report to Welles on Monday morning. She arrived nervous. "I was wearing a navy blue suit with a white blouse and a friend had pinned a rose to my lapel," she remembered. "I'd bought a new hat, especially." Welles quickly put her at her ease by complimenting her on her neatness. "He talked and I listened," she remembered. "He said that he had been called in as acting chief of LA with a free hand to develop his thesis that the terms of the

Versailles Treaty made another world war inevitable and that every effort should be made to produce solidarity in the Western Hemisphere."

For the next twenty-three years Welles and Louise Clarkson worked together as a team, both in government and out, always addressing each other formally, as Mr. Welles and Miss Clarkson. In 1943, when Welles resigned, she loyally followed him into private life, eventually marrying Roger Bacon, an old beau. Only then did she and Welles agree to address each other by their first names.[27]

HAITI

Haiti was passing through a crisis of its own in 1920 as Welles was taking over the Latin American division. The American minister, Arthur Bailly-Blanchard, had just won a test of wills by blocking the salaries of Haitian president Philippe Sudre Dartiguenave and his entire cabinet. This unprecedented act, taken without the knowledge—let alone approval—of the State Department, characterized American occupation policy in the world's first black republic. Haiti had known little but turmoil since wresting its independence from France during the French revolution. As Robert and Nancy Gordon Heinl wrote in *Written in Blood: The Story of the Haitian People,* Haiti was a land of "beauty, romance, mystery, kindness, humor, selfishness, betrayal, cruelty, bloodshed, poverty and hunger."[28]

Early in the century, Haiti's chronic unrest had threatened the Monroe Doctrine. Determined to protect their nationals and collect overdue debts, France and Imperial Germany had begun landing troops, and both had begun eyeing Haiti's strategic harbors. "Germany, especially, was ready to go to great lengths to secure exclusive customs control and a coaling station at Mole St. Nicolas [controlling the strategic Windward Passage]," wrote Secretary of State Robert Lansing.[29] In 1915, culminating a bloodthirsty career, Haitian president Guillaume Sam had executed 167 political prisoners and had fled for safety to the French legation, where mobs had broken in, tearing him to pieces. French warships were already closing in when Woodrow Wilson had ordered Admiral William Caperton, to land marines and bluejackets and restore order.

From the start, the American occupation had been haphazard. Assuming the vague authority of senior officer present, Caperton had conferred with Haitian officials, had appointed Philippe Dartiguenave, the Senate leader, President and had then presented him with a stiff draft treaty granting the United States control over Haiti's finances, sanitation and public works and creating an American-officered gendarmerie to preserve order.[30] Thereafter, Washington had virtually forgotten Haiti. By the end of World War I, U.S. policy—such as it was—had devolved on a troika comprising the senior U.S. naval commander, a Treasury advisor and the minister, Bailly-Blanchard, a political appointee who reported sporadically, if at all, to the State Department.

On taking charge, Welles found Bailly-Blanchard and the Treasury advisor, John A. McIlhenny, justifying their freeze of Haitian salaries by claiming that the Haitians were resisting reforms and enacting decrees without their consent. Ordered by Colby to investigate, Welles informed the hapless American minister within twenty-four hours of the department's "surprise over action taken without previous reference for its decision." He was to cable, at once, by what authority he and McIlhenny had acted; to take "no further steps to commit" the United States or to prevent the State Department from "acting freely in its own best judgment." Finally, Bailly-Blanchard was to keep the department informed "daily."[31] The twenty-eight-year-old acting chief of the Latin American division was losing little time in establishing his own authority.

In Welles's view, the problem stemmed essentially from personality clashes. Bailly-Blanchard, like other Southern-born American officials, was indifferent to Haitian pride. To soothe local sensibilities, Welles secured McIlhenny's recall and then arranged for the visit of a high-ranking U.S. officer with the resounding title of Military Representative of the U.S. The choice fell fortunately on Rear Admiral Harry S. Knapp, a former military governor of the adjoining Dominican Republic, whose tact soon won Dartiguenave's cooperation and the crisis eased. Welles had hoped to use Knapp's presence in Haiti to launch overdue reforms, but these were set aside until the Harding administration took office in March.

On his first day in the White House, Harding found awaiting him a letter from Dartiguenave proposing sweeping changes in the U.S. occupation of Haiti. The hated "provost courts," in which U.S. military officers tried and sentenced Haitian offenders, should immediately be abolished, Dartiguenave proposed. Once the Haitian gendarmerie had been trained and equipped, the United States should restore independence and withdraw.[32] Given his campaign attacks on the Democrats for intervention in Latin America, Harding might well have been expected to agree—but, like presidents before and since, he found it easier to fly than to lower the Stars and Stripes. Haiti was bankrupt, lacked law enforcement, independent courts—even a civil service. Immediate withdrawal was out of the question.

To gain time, Harding directed Hughes to draft a conciliatory but noncommittal reply to Dartiguenave and prepare a "modification" of the occupation machinery to reflect the "high purpose" that the United States wished to pursue in Haiti.[33] Hughes assigned Welles the task; it proved excellent training. The first step would be to establish State Department control. Tact would be essential, for not only the Department but the navy, the army's Bureau of Insular Affairs and the Treasury were all involved, and all three would have to be persuaded to cooperate. Welles led off with a meeting in his office with General John A. LeJeune, the Marine Commandant; General Smedley Butler, U.S. Marine Corps, a former commander of the Haitian gendarmerie; Treasury's McIlhenny and Ferdinand L. Mayer, the State Department's Haitian desk officer.

The marine generals proved surprisingly conciliatory, agreeing that a reorganization of the occupation machinery was necessary but insisting on a continuation of the troika with disputes to be resolved by a vague entity: the U.S. "government." To Welles, this smacked ominously of a continuing scramble for the President's ear; therefore, he submitted to Hughes a counter-proposal tactfully leaving the trappings of power in military hands. The troika would continue as an "Advisory Council" to the Haitian government, but all occupation officials in Haiti would come under State Department (i.e., his own) control. As he awaited Hughes's decision, the navy overreached.

On June 13, Navy Secretary Edwin Denby ordered Marine Colonel John H. Russell, the U.S. troop commander in Haiti, to tighten press censorship, crack down on "agitation" and haul Haitian offenders into the provost courts. Denby's move played into Welles's hands. The navy, he warned Hughes, was ruling Haiti without considering "foreign policy implications," especially throughout Latin America. The time had come to decide "whether the Secretary of State or the Secretary of the Navy . . . determines policy." Haiti's stagnating economy could be resolved and a Wall Street loan raised within days, "if the banks knew whether the government was going to stay in Haiti, or get out."[34]

After extracting Welles's plan from his in-box, Hughes sent it to the White House with the recommendation that it be implemented quickly. "We cannot leave Haiti at the present time," he counseled, but it was the administration's "duty to perfect the occupation and benefit the Haitians."[35] Harding concurred and, on August 15, instructed Hughes to discuss with his colleague Denby the "exceedingly important" choice of a successor to Admiral Knapp, who was being transferred.[36] Asked for his own recommendation, Welles made an apparently incongruous choice: Major General Smedley Butler, known as the "Fighting Quaker." A notoriously tough, outspoken line officer, Butler had crushed an earlier Haitian uprising and seemed as unlikely to win Haitian cooperation as to take policy guidance from a State Department stripling. Welles, however, was rapidly learning the ways of Washington.

Aware that Denby favored Butler and that Denby's cooperation would be essential, Welles proposed Butler—certain that the White House would veto him. He proved right. Senator Medill McCormick of Illinois, the Senate's expert on the Caribbean, had just returned from an inspection trip and warned Harding that the Haitians detested Butler and preferred the more civilian-minded Colonel Russell.[37] As Welles had foreseen, Harding rejected Butler, promoted Russell to brigadier general and softened the martial overtones of the occupation by styling him High Commissioner.[38]

As with his earlier instructions to Crowder in Cuba, Welles's instructions to Russell in Haiti set U.S. policy. The history of the Haitian occupation, he wrote, was "not viewed with satisfaction by this government." Taking as his model War Secretary Root's 1900 instructions to William Howard Taft, first civil governor of the Philippines, Welles made clear that the U.S. intervention in Haiti had been undertaken "neither for the satisfaction of the U.S., for the accomplishment of its theoretical views, nor for any selfish purpose or ambition." Its goal remained the "happiness, welfare and tranquility of the Haitian people, plus their development toward self-government." Henceforth, U.S. policy in Haiti would have four aims: reorganization of the occupation machinery; stabilization of Haiti's finances; withdrawal of the marines once a Haitian gendarmerie had been trained; and, finally, economic and cultural development with emphasis on education. The measures Russell adopted should conform to the "customs, habits, even . . . the prejudices" of the Haitian people.

As a philosophy of military occupation, it seemed unassailable—yet many criticized Harding for choosing a marine general as high commissioner. Norman Thomas, the socialist editor of *The Nation* and the President's boyhood friend, wrote Harding that the choice of Russell would "nullify all your efforts toward mutual understanding." American help to the weak should not involve coercion; if U.S.-Haitian negotiations seemed desireable, they should be preceded by immediate independence. Thomas, however, was elaborating theory from an editorial chair while Harding, Hughes, Welles and the U.S. occupation officials in Haiti were grappling with poverty, illiteracy, superstition and graft. Five years later, when out of office in 1927, Welles would write his brother-in-law, Harry Robbins, extolling the occupation's benefits.

If one accepted its "legitimacy," he wrote, no sound criticism could be leveled against it. Where once the Haitian government's authority had extended only a few miles from the capital, Port-au-Prince, and isolated districts were ruled by *caciques* (local bosses), absolute peace now reigned. Robbery had been suppressed, revenues increased and surpluses channeled into roads, irrigation and schools. Reforms that Welles himself had promoted had prevented "rapacious" American individuals or corporations from seizing control of Haiti's wealth. The occupation had served as a "trustee," determined to hand Haiti back to the Haitians in a state that "several centuries of their own government could not have procured."[39] In his view, there was a difference between the well-intended Good Neighbor who expected instant democracy in an impoverished land where people were barely able to scratch a living from the soil and the practical Good Neighbor who brought public order, sanitation, roads, schools, hospitals, law courts and sound currency.

Welles, early in his career, was a benevolent imperialist in tune with his times. In eighteen months he had won White House approval for a major reorganization of Haiti's occupation; he had replaced military with State Department control; he had secured the appointment of the tactful Russell as High Commissioner; and had paved the way for U.S. loans and a revival of Haiti's economy. For a diplomat still under thirty, it was a creditable performance.

THE DOMINICAN REPUBLIC

The third of Welles's Caribbean time bombs, the Dominican Republic, was locked in a dialogue of the deaf, a *dialogue des sourds,* with Washington as Welles took over the Latin American division in 1920. Neither was listening to the other.

Like the Haitians, the Dominicans had expected that, with World War I ended, the Americans would wind up their occupation, restore independence and sail home. Like the Haitians, they were mistaken. President Wilson, then critically ill, was being shielded from all but the most pressing decisions, and the State Department, facing far graver issues in Europe and Asia, had shrugged off responsibility for the Dominican Republic onto the navy. The navy, untrained in colonial administration but loath to relinquish any perquisites, had in turn left Dominican affairs to its military governor, Rear Admiral Harry S. Knapp. Meanwhile, Dominican demands for independence were escalating.

As with other Caribbean republics, American involvement in the Dominican Republic had begun early in the century. In 1905, faced with continuing disorder and the complaints of European debtors unable to collect their debts, President Theodore Roosevelt had ordered the country's Customs, its main source of revenue, taken under U.S. control. Nevertheless, unrest had continued, and in 1916, after the outbreak of World War I, Woodrow Wilson had ordered the country occupied lest Imperial Germany establish a bridgehead close the Panama Canal.

Initially the U.S. occupation had won popular support. Knapp had restored order, stabilized the currency, improved sanitation, built elementary schools and transformed mule tracks into roads. But unlike Haiti, where the United States ruled through a puppet regime, the fiery Dominicans had refused to cooperate politically in any way. In his history of the Dominican Republic, *Naboth's Vineyard,* Welles described the "extraordinary anomaly of a Dominican government headed by an officer of the American Navy, with a cabinet composed of officers of the U.S. Navy or Marine Corps, none of whom had any knowledge, or experience, of Dominican affairs and the great majority of whom could not even speak the language of the country."[40]

In 1918, Knapp had been succeeded by Rear Admiral Thomas Snowden, a Southern martinet whose contempt for the racially mixed Dominicans had sparked anti-American sentiment. By 1920, as Welles was taking charge, atrocities committed by a handful of marines sent to stamp out "banditry" in the interior had brought Dominican indignation to fever heat.

Alarmed by criticism throughout Latin America, Wilson's Secretary of State, Bainbridge Colby, had won White House approval for an Advisory Commission of five prominent Dominicans empowered to discuss independence with Snowden. The admiral, however, resenting State Department intrusion into his military domain, had not only rejected the commission's mild opening suggestion for an easing of censorship but, to emphasize his authority, actually had tightened it, and the commission members, frustrated, had resigned. Meanwhile, a nationwide protest movement, the Union Nacionalista Dominicana (UND), had begun agitating for immediate independence, sending agents throughout Latin America to whip up anti-Yanqui sentiment.

Before handing over to Welles, Leo Rowe had persuaded Colby to overrule the admiral and appoint a new commission but, again, Snowden had balked. A new Commission, he protested, "would serve no useful purpose in view of . . . unrest and agitation."[41] Welles warned Colby of the danger of protracted hostility, suggesting that conciliation was essential. Colby, in full agreement, ordered him to draft a plan for Dominican self-rule on two conditions: The United States would retain control both of the Customs and of the American-officered Gendarmerie. To assuage hemisphere criticism and conciliate Dominican sentiment, Welles recommended that Washington make clear its policy by announcing its intention to "start the simple processes of . . . rapid withdrawal." Once this was clear, the Advisory Commission could amend the Dominican constitution, reform the electoral laws and prepare for national elections under U.S. supervision. Once a constitutional government was in place, U.S. troops could withdraw.

The White House approved, Colby sent Welles's plan to Navy Secretary Josephus Daniels for implementation and, on December 24, 1920, Snowden was ordered to announce the eventual withdrawal of U.S. forces—Wilson's "deathbed repentance," as one American observer described it.[42] Wilson, Colby and Welles had expected that the new U.S. policy would usher in an era of Dominican goodwill, but, to their chagrin, protests against U.S. supervision of Dominican elections swept the nation. Firebrands insisted that agitation alone would force the Americans out without protracted negotiations or demeaning concessions.[43] "Evacuation pure and simple" became the national cry. Welles's first evacuation plan died stillborn.

Evacuation pure and simple, however, was manifestly impossible. During four years of occupation, the U.S. military government had signed hundreds of contracts, awarded innumerable concessions and assumed financial obligations on behalf of the Dominican people. Before the marines could sail away, an elected Dominican government would have to assume these financial responsibilities and prove able to keep order. Meanwhile, only a month remained until the new Harding administration took office. The Dominicans, scenting better terms ahead, settled down to wait.

In the interim Welles revised his withdrawal plan, hedging it with safeguards as the navy still opposed withdrawal and he was uncertain as to which policies the incoming Secretary of State, Charles Evans Hughes, might choose to adopt.

Hughes's appointment as Secretary of State early in 1921 marked a turning point in Welles's career. His previous chiefs—Guthrie, Stimson, Colby and Norman Davis—had all won his respect and some his personal devotion. Hughes, the dignified, spade-bearded former governor of New York, Supreme Court justice and 1916 GOP presidential candidate, now became his idol.

"There was one thing [Hughes] would not tolerate," wrote Hugh R. Wilson, a former subordinate and later U.S. ambassador. "He would not talk to anyone who came to him who had not mastered the last word of his subject. It was admirable training . . . it was inspiring."[44] Hughes had "vision and great simplicity . . . , and was incapable of thinking a mean thought," wrote Caroline Phillips.[45] A jurist by training and temperament, unfamiliar with Latin American affairs, Hughes started out cautiously, continuing Wilson's policy of granting or withholding U.S. recognition of Latin American governments as a mark of approval or disapproval and insisting on strict observance of U.S. treaty rights and the right to "temporarily interpose" U.S. troops to protect American citizens and their property in an emergency.

Initially awed by his new chief's immense prestige and highly conscious at twenty-nine of the responsibilities of office, Welles went along with such policies. Gradually, however, over the next year, as he and Hughes began working in tandem, Welles was able to induce him first to question, then to abandon, long-standing policies described variously by historians as "protective" or "self-righteous" interventionism. Dexter Perkins among them cited Welles's influence in his biography of Hughes. No man, he wrote of Welles, had a "wider or more sympathetic knowledge of Latin America."[46] Hughes himself soon came to respect Welles's judgment. "I found him in charge of the Latin American division and I continued him as its chief," he wrote in his memoirs. "I recognized, at once, his exceptional ability, his poise and force of character."[47]

In due course, Welles presented Hughes his revised plan for Dominican independence. Among other safeguards, he had retained U.S. supervision of Dominican elections; continued American training of the Dominican gendarmerie; increased the control of the American Receiver General of Customs over

Dominican finances; and required ratification of all U.S. decrees and contracts by an incoming Dominican government. Finally he had included a "Platt Amendment" proviso authorizing the United States to send troops back in event of disorder. While such safeguards were all likely to affront Dominican pride, Welles's second plan, stiff as it was, was considerably more conciliatory than his first. His first had omitted a timetable for U.S. withdrawal; his second stipulated an eight-month period in which the Marines would phase out as an elected Dominican government phased in. Finally, as in Haiti, Welles recommended eliminating "controversial" personalities. Snowden should go.[48]

Hughes had found in Welles a subordinate attuned to his own views; both favored Dominican independence—with safeguards. Hughes had already warned that "controlling foreign peoples was a policy of mischief and disaster." America's true interest, he had proclaimed, lay in "prosperous, peaceful and law-abiding" neighbors. Accordingly, he dropped Welles's "Platt Amendment" proviso, scaled back the added fiscal power for the U.S. Receiver General, then sent the plan to the White House with his approval.[49] Harding gave it his imprimatur and, on June 14, Snowden's replacement, Rear Admiral Samuel S. Robison, was ordered to announce it.[50]

Again Washington's hopes ran high; again they were dashed. Welles's second plan fared no better than his first.[51] Three thousand Dominicans demonstrated angrily outside Governor Robison's residence, and the U.S. minister, William W. Russell, reported a "hot blast" of press protest against American supervision of Dominican elections, American training of the Dominican gendarmerie and, especially, Dominican ratification of U.S. contracts and decrees. No local politician dared approve such conditions nor could any who did be elected or survive politically.

Welles offered belated concessions but tension mounted as the Dominicans seethed. Weary and frustrated, Welles called for a showdown. If the United States presented the Dominican leaders with an "ultimatum," he wrote Hughes grimly, they would accept it. If they still boycotted elections under U.S. supervision, Washington should lay the blame "where it belonged" and proceed. The occupation might have to continue but, at least, a start could be made in "civilianizing" it.[52] As frustrated as Welles by Dominican intransigence, Hughes sent his recommendation to the White House, suggesting that it be "sweetened" with a $10 million loan.[53] Harding, bereft of alternatives, ordered Robison and Russell to resume talks with the Dominican leaders on February 21, 1922. The site chosen was the palace of the archbishop of Santo Domingo, but whether because of or despite its aura of sanctity, the Dominicans continued adamantly opposing U.S. supervision of their elections, sweetener or no sweetener.[54] The air had been cleared but not as Harding, Hughes or Welles would have wished. The deadlock hardened and on March 16, Harding ordered Admiral Robison to announce that the military occupation would continue for two more years: "approximately, until July 1, 1924."[55]

A new approach was clearly needed but, for Welles, the Dominican problem had become academic. The day before, professionally frustrated and his marriage in shambles, he had resigned.

SEVEN

THE DOMINICAN REPUBLIC, MATHILDE AND RESIGNATION

1922

An Attitude of "Ruthless Superiority"

ONLY A FEW INTIMATES had known of the personal and professional turmoil festering within Welles since his return from the Argentine. By 1922, two years later, his marriage was in trouble and morale in the Diplomatic Service had reached rock bottom.

For all his professed idealism, Woodrow Wilson had used the State Department as a political trough, shuffling off all but the most important diplomatic appointments onto his populist Secretary of State, William Jennings Bryan, whose chief concern was "jobs for deserving Democrats [distributed] equitably among the states," wrote a career diplomat, Dana G. Munro.[1] On taking charge of the Latin American division, Welles had found that most U.S. mission chiefs in the Western Hemisphere were political appointees. Nearly all, wrote Munro, were "incompetent" and some had "personal failings that . . . made their removal necessary."[2]

Nor was the Western Hemisphere the only area to suffer. The United States was being made "ridiculous" by its representatives abroad, Joseph C. Grew, the American minister in Paris, wrote a colleague. "Hardly one in twenty speaks a word of any foreign language and diplomatic posts are going to political hacks carried by career counsellors who have nothing to look forward to after ten or fifteen years at low pay but the scrap-heap." Without higher salaries and better allowances, he wrote another, "many men . . . will resign."[3] Under Secretary Phillips warned Congress: "We have lost, and are continuing to lose, some of the best men we have."[4]

Welles himself, despite commendations for his work in Japan and the Argentine, plus two years as acting chief of the Latin American division, was drawing an annual salary of $3,000 ($23,500 today) with no guarantee of promotion—let alone a legation or embassy of his own. "If I could feel any certainty that there was an assured future in the Diplomatic Service of this government," he wrote Hughes on leaving, "I should not have felt compelled to resign from a service to which I devoted a good many years and to give up a work which is of greater interest to me than any other."[5] If Hughes ever needed him, however, he would return.

Still more depressing than low salaries or uncertain promotion was the political climate. The American people had responded "magnificently" to Woodrow Wilson's call to arms in 1917, believing, Welles recalled, that his policy of international cooperation would ensure their future. By late 1919, however, their fervor had vanished. The battle over U.S. entry into the League of Nations had unleashed a wave of cynical isolationism, and, by the time of Harding's inauguration in 1921,Wilson's international cooperation had been replaced by a foreign policy of "no cooperation of any character" with other nations. "In the history of our foreign policy," wrote Welles, "this is probably the most ominous chapter."[6]

Compounding professional frustration, Welles's marriage had grown increasingly sterile since returning to Washington. He and Esther had settled into a large apartment on Sixteenth Street, near Scott Circle, where her fortune permitted the luxurious lifestyle to which he had grown accustomed and that he felt essential to his position. Their domestic staff comprised a governess for the children, a French chef; his wife, the laundress; a chauffeur for the new Renault; a maid for Esther; a valet for Sumner, and an English butler, James Reeks, who had been employed on a temporary basis. The young couple entertained lavishly and, to many, seemed happy and well matched, but Caroline Phillips, Sumner's cousin, noted shrewdly in her diary that Esther's "eccentric, unconventional streak irritates [Sumner] and sometimes drives him crazy."[7]

As his hours at the department lengthened and the summer heat suffocated Washington, Esther began visiting her ailing mother, in New York, leaving her young husband alone—a formula for trouble. A packet of love letters tossed casually into a file, some still unopened a half century later, show two sides of Welles's character as he was approaching twenty-nine. The random love affairs begun in the Argentine were continuing in Washington. Signed "Kina," the pseudonym of a flirtatious young Washingtonian married to an Englishman, the letters reveal the ruthlessness with which Welles's conquests—like their missives—were forgotten once the prize was won. He and Kina apparently had met at an embassy dinner in 1920, soon after his return, and their affair had blazed. She was about to sail for England with her husband and children, and, for the next seven weeks, she sent Welles impassioned notes virtually daily.

"My imagination carries me back to you faster than this train bears me away," she wrote en route to New York and the waiting steamer. "I shall think of you, always, as I saw you last night—straight like a pine tree with that glorious screen surrounding you." It was, almost certainly, one of the pair of Korin screens he had bought in Kyoto in 1916. Apparently the two were planning a tryst in England in April. "Till April, this April, last April, the Aprils of all the future and all the past," she wrote ecstatically, crossing the wintry Atlantic. "You will not fail, I know, and never, never shall I, for I love you with all my being, my heart, my soul . . . you have lighted a great fire in this cold room of my heart." Meeting mutual friends on board—Senator Medill McCormick of Illinois, Mabel Gerry, Mrs. Whitelaw Reid and a dashing Italian, Prince Caraciolo—only intensified her longing. "I wish I had torn down with my fingers the picture that hangs in your dining room above the fireplace," she wrote. "Torn it down to steal it away. I wonder if I can wait till Abril [sic]." To please him, she had used the Spanish spelling.

London was "incredible, depressing, hopeless . . . Barely anyone is living in the same way as when I left." She, her husband and children had settled temporarily into Claridge's hotel while house-hunting, and Prince Caraciolo had come to call with lilies. "Italians are the only men I have found who can be in love with a woman, worship and idealize her with a fire that leaves no ashes," she mused. Meanwhile, she would not leave London until April: "Nothing could make me . . . Nothing could prevent me, then."

Slowly hurt and fear crept in as her letters went unanswered. "Daily pain when the porter at Claridge's tells me there is no letter . . . nor the ring you spoke of. Oh, the agony of your silence. You have been very cruel not to have written me . . . twenty days since I saw you, with only your cable." Then a letter arrived and her heart leapt. "Your first letter—today!" Apparently, in self-defense, he had accused her of forgetting him. "Forget you! I have forgotten all, everyone, everything save you," she wrote. "My life, my heart, my soul, I myself, have I given you. A perfect understanding holds us. April, my heart stops at the very name."

"A perfect understanding" was an expression Welles would use with many women, but his affair with Kina was far from perfect and would end sadly. As a parting gift, he had given her a Chow puppy, Li, and from Knepp Castle in Kent where she was visiting friends, came her last letter, dated January 12, 1921. Little Li had died. "I am dreadfully grieved," she wrote. "He was such a beautiful little ball of life and he was a link." The puppy's death seemed a portent. "I think I must take the next boat to America. Can I wait till April? Can you? I ache for you, my eyes for the sight of you."[8]

From then on—silence. Two days earlier, Welles had met Mathilde Townsend Gerry, the only woman, apart from his mother and his "Aunt Aimee" Sargent, whom he would truly love and whom he would marry four years later.

Chancing at the time on a new book, *Psychological Types,* by the Swiss psychiatrist, Carl Gustav Jung, Ives Gammell was struck by Jung's analysis of the "extraverted intuitive." It fitted Welles like a glove.[9] The extraverted intuitive, wrote Jung, had a keen nose for "anything new or in the making" and would seize on new objects or situations with extraordinary enthusiasm only to abandon them "cold-bloodedly" once their range was known and no further development likely. The extraverted intuitive acted "irrationally"; his morality was governed by "neither feeling nor thinking," and his consideration for others was "weak." One passage especially intrigued Gammell: When the extraverted intuitive became entangled with a "highly unsuitable" woman, wrote Jung, he would claim exception from restraint, submitting his decisions to no rational judgment and relying entirely on his "nose." His attitude was one of "ruthless superiority." Gammell showed the passage to Welles, who studied it with fascination for two or three days, then tossed it aside.[10]

The "highly unsuitable" woman with whom Welles had suddenly become infatuated was Mathilde Townsend Gerry, then thirty-seven (thus eight years older than Welles), immensely wealthy and unhappily married to Senator Peter Goelet Gerry, a socially prominent Rhode Island Democrat. Still at the height of her fame as a Washington belle, she was tall and statuesque, with fair hair, a finely chiseled nose and large eyes that led Gammell to describe her maliciously once as "ox-eyed." An accomplished equestrienne in her youth, she still moved with the slow, easy grace of one born to constant adulation and to few responsibilities other than the dogs and horses on which, being childless, she lavished her affection.

Endowed with faultless taste in clothes, jewels and objets d'art, she was invariably surrounded by a swarm of social butterflies, a queen among her drones. Although shrewd about people and money, she was intellectually idle, her reading confined to headlines and gossip columns. Her interest in public affairs, such as it was, centered mainly on personalities. The countries she liked were those whose diplomats made amusing dinner partners. Dull diplomats meant dull countries.

An only child, spoiled since birth by her widowed, millionaire mother, Mary (Mrs. Richard) Townsend, Mathilde had been educated by a succession of governesses and tutors and by annual summer trips to the spas of Europe. Mrs. Townsend, like other rich Americans with daughters to marry off at the turn of the century, had dreamed of a brilliant match, preferably one with a title, and had thrilled at the sedulous attention paid Mathilde by "Jimmy," the Duke of Alba, premier grandee of Spain. Mathilde's laughing indifference to Alba and other titled suitors had vexed her imperious parent, but Mathilde had remained American to the core.

The fortune behind her stemmed from the post–Civil War boom. Her maternal grandfather, William L. Scott, of Richmond, Viriginia, orphaned at seven, had won appointment through family friends as a page in Congress, where his diligence and intelligence had caught the attention of Representative Charles M. Reed of Erie, Pennsylvania. Reed invited young Scott to join his coal-forwarding business in Erie on reaching eighteen, and Scott had shown a head for business. Striking out on his own at age twenty-two, he had amassed a fortune before he was thirty and, in 1886, had been elected to Congress. His wife, however, had refused to leave their comfortable lakeside home in Erie for the unfinished U.S. capital, so Scott had invited their elder daughter, Mary, to serve as his official hostess and bring her husband, Richard Townsend, a Philadelphia stock broker, and their only child, Mathilde, to Washington. At the time, Mathilde was seven.

On his death in 1891, Scott left a fortune estimated at $15 million ($350 million in today's terms), and Mary, captivated by Washington society, decided to stay. A decade later, she buttressed her social position by building a French Renaissance mansion at 2121 Massachusetts Avenue, then on the edge of Washington.[11] Designed by the fashionable New York architects Carrere and Hastings, and modeled on Versailles' Petit Trianon, her new home had become a showplace for entertaining. The main, or second, floor included a white-and-gold ballroom, a salon in silver, another in red and gold and a library in rich heavy green. Liveried footmen in powdered wigs held flambeaux as her guests ascended or descended the marble stairs, and invitations to "Minnie" Townsend's dinners and balls soon became the goal of society. In such a setting was Mathilde reared and her character formed.

In 1902, when Mathilde was eighteen, her father was killed in a riding accident. Although she postponed her debut into society for a year, suitors swarmed around her. None struck a spark until finally, on reaching twenty-six and wearied by her mother's importunings, she agreed to marry Peter Goelet Gerry of Newport. The wedding, attended by President Taft and his cabinet in her mother's marble palace, was the social event of 1910.

To Mrs. Townsend, Gerry seemed the ideal son-in-law. Handsome and comfortably off, he was descended from a Signer of the Declaration of Independence[12] and thus socially impeccable. Unfortunately, he was also dull and suffocated Mathilde with adulation. "We went to a dance and Mathilde 'killed' everyone in the room," he wrote his mother-in-law ecstatically, on his honeymoon. "A more beautiful woman doesn't exist in America."[13] Each letter brought fresh paeans of praise: "Toots [Mathilde's nickname] is becoming more beautiful every day." Years later Toots would confess to having been "spoiled by dog-like devotion."[14]

Gerry eventually entered Congress and, later, the Senate, but Mathilde's interest in politics soon flagged. To amuse herself, she began a series of mild flirtations with prominent men-about-town: Jerome Bonaparte, a nephew of the great emperor; Raoul d'Adhemar; Sylvanus Stokes; and Sam Pisa, a Latin American lady-killer. Gerry bore her *amitiés amoureuses* with patrician restraint, confident that they meant little, until at a Washington dinner on January 10, 1921, Mathilde met Sumner Welles. Three years later, on the anniversary of their meeting, she would write him "Tonight, at this very hour, I met you, and never have I loved anyone since, nor will I till I die."[15]

Discontented with his marriage and career and suddenly infatuated with Mathilde Gerry, Welles began weighing a divorce and resignation from the State Department early in 1921. Mathilde's wealth, however, posed a psychological problem. Resignation would end his government salary and divorce from Esther would leave him financially dependent on his moderate private income. Proud to a fault, he could not appear a pauper in Mathilde's eyes. A career in banking seemed the only solution. As a banker, he could augment his income, meet men of influence and, he hoped, return to government later at a policy level.

His contacts were excellent. As chief of the Latin American division, he had negotiated loans for several Latin American governments with New York banks, and former Under Secretary Norman H. Davis, now a Morgan partner, had hinted that Welles might represent the Morgan interests in Madrid or some other Spanish-speaking capital. Davis arranged an interview with J. P. Morgan, the founder's son, and in June 1921 Welles confided to Hughes that he was planning to resign.

In July, Esther sailed for a European vacation with her brother, Nelson Slater. "Delighted you saw Mr. Morgan," she wrote Sumner from Paris. "Anxious to know what you decided." Her next letter implied that Madrid had fallen through. "I am sorry we aren't going to Madrid. I think it would have been very interesting. Perhaps," she added philosophically, "it's better as it is."

Apparently, there remained a chance that he might work in New York for Morgan, and it brought out her New England practicality. "We must take an unfurnished apartment in New York and use your furniture," she wrote. "It is such an expense keeping it in storage."[16]

How much she suspected, or knew of, Mathilde's growing hold on her young husband is unclear, but her letters from Paris reflect foreboding. "I still hope we will go to Madrid next winter," she wrote wistfully, "I don't enjoy the thought of New York." Perhaps New York was too near Washington and Mathilde. At summer's end, before starting home, she sent Sumner a poignant note. "I certainly will be glad to get you away from Washington. It hasn't been as happy a place as it should have been for either of us."

Hughes promoted Welles that summer from "acting" chief to chief of the Latin American division—at twenty-nine, the youngest man ever to hold the position—and at Hughes's request Welles agreed to postpone his resignation until March 15, 1922. His decision to resign, however, remained firm, "You may have been amused to see in the New York papers of my promotion to the position that I have occupied for the past year," he wrote Norman Davis in August. "This compliment will not, however, cause me to modify my plans in any way."[17]

A faded chit found in Welles's papers after his death shows that the State Department was billing him at the time for personal telephone calls to a Mrs. Gerry in Atlantic City.

A week after Welles's resignation, ex-Secretary Bainbridge Colby wrote him from New York: "You have distinctly left your mark and a very fine reputation. To merely see you again would give me very great pleasure."[18] From Secretary Hughes came a letter extolling "ability of a very high order. I have always . . . prized your judgment."[19] Of all the tributes, however, one in particular touched Welles. The Washington correspondent of *La Prensa* of Buenos Aires cabled his paper that Welles had won the "esteem" of his Latin American colleagues by his "courtesy and ability to discharge his responsibilities, quickly and effectively."[20]

Freed from official responsibility for the first time in seven years, Welles and Esther rented a house that spring at Manchester, on the North Shore of Massachusetts, where she and the children could summer while he commuted to New York in search of a banking job—and, presumably, to meet Mathilde. His return to private life, however, was short-lived. Ten weeks later Hughes summoned him back. The Dominican logjam had suddenly eased and he was needed.

During his brief absence, Francisco J. Peynado, a leading member of the Dominican Advisory Council, had unexpectedly called on Hughes with three colleagues. Between them, they represented the country's main political parties, and, to end the deadlock, they proposed a new two-phase plan. Phase 1 would begin with the Advisory Council appointing an American-approved "provisional" government to administer the country and prepare for elections. Once an elected government was ready to maintain order and assume its fiscal and legal obligations, Phase 2 would follow. The U.S. military occupation would end and the marines would sail away.

Initially, Hughes turned it down. Dubious of Dominican good faith and weary of the protracted imbroglio, he decreed that the United States would not deal with a "provisional" regime but would hand over power only to an elected government. Welles's successor, Dana G. Munro, rescued the plan from the wastebasket. The more he pondered, the more it offered hope. Heretofore, Dominican refusal to hold elections under U.S. supervision had blocked agreement. By providing for a U.S.-approved "provisional" regime to conduct elections itself, thus saving Dominican face, Peynado's plan skirted the problem. What was needed was someone to steer it to completion. Why not Welles?[21]

Hughes deliberated and, on May 31, invited Welles back to confer with Peynado and his colleagues. By the end of June, Welles had reworked the broad Dominican outline into a detailed program that Hughes approved and sent to the White House. On July 1, President Harding named Welles U.S. Commissioner in the Dominican Republic with the rank of Envoy Extraordinary and Minister Plenipotentiary.[22] At twenty-nine, he had won the promotion and rank he had long craved. Officially, he would be "investigating and reporting," but, having written his own orders under Hughes's supervision, he would, in fact, be shepherding the Dominicans to independence. He accepted, he wrote long after, believing that the assignment would take "only a few months."[23] Had he known that it would take two grueling years, separate him from children, family and friends—and, above all, from Mathilde, straining their relationship to the breaking point—he might have declined.

In the interest of speed, Hughes asked the navy to rush the new U.S. Commissioner by torpedo boat from Puerto Rico to Santo Domingo, but Admiral Samuel Robison, the military governor, sent his official yacht, the USS *Nokomis,* and, on July 28, Welles was piped ashore with a U.S. navy band, an honor guard and a salute from Fort Ozama, the colonial Spanish fort high on a nearby hill.[24] The task facing him demanded extreme tact. Young as he was, as the president's envoy he outranked both Governor Robison, fifty-five, and the American minister, William W. Russell, sixty-three, and both men resented him. Moreover, six years of U.S. military rule had aroused fierce Dominican resistance—which often had been met by harsh U.S. countermeasures. Even as Welles was arriving, Robison had provoked national indignation by jailing a half-dozen young Dominicans for daring to criticize his new land law. Welles had them released but, for the next two years, he would find himself constantly battling on two fronts: Dominican resentment on the one hand, U.S. navy obduracy on the other.

He conferred with the Dominican leaders, approved the addition of Archbishop Adolfo Nouel of Santo Domingo to the Advisory Council, then set out to gauge grass-roots sentiment throughout the country. After visiting eight cities or large towns and meeting in each with twenty-five to fifty leading citizens, he found widespread suspicion of U.S. motives. "I felt it desireable to make quite plain," he cabled Hughes, "that orders issued by the Military government, during the life of the Provisional government, did not mean that the latter would not have all the necessary powers to carry out freely, without control from the former, the purposes for which it was installed."[25] In other words, he would ensure that the Dominicans took their first steps toward self-rule without undue U.S. interference.

His message slowly spread and, on returning to the capital, his hopes had begun rising. A handful of extreme nationalists still opposed the evacuation plan, but the bulk of the population was now well disposed. At this point, however, Admiral Robison laid down a series of demands clearly designed to hamstring the provisional government. While some were acceptable, Welles cabled Hughes, insistence on all might precipitate a Dominican walkout. Hughes agreed and, soon after, Assistant Navy Secretary Theodore Roosevelt, Jr., cabled Welles that Robison had been ordered to "cooperate."[26]

His authority now reinforced, Welles spent an uphill summer negotiating harmony between rival Dominican factions. "For the first time in the history of the Republic," he cabled, "all the leaders of the political parties are working in close cooperation." However, to prevent extremists or political independents from denouncing the evacuation plan for political advantage, he recommended certain "modifications which might appear trivial but which would be regarded as of great importance for sentimental reasons."[27] His feel for Latin American psychology, begun in the Argentine, was paying off.

The strain of incessant negotiation in a small Caribbean capital where the heat was oppressive, recreation nonexistent and Spanish-style formality mandatory was beginning to tell, however. "Sorry you were upset because I didn't write," Esther apologized in August from her North Shore eyrie. "Fearfully busy . . . people in the house all the time . . . wonderful week . . . the Spanish tennis players, Count Gomar and the Alonso brothers [here] from Madrid. I asked them down for the night and had a big dinner for them. Next week I am going to New York for the polo."[28] Without his brooding presence, Esther's spirits had lifted but, meanwhile, Welles felt cut off from home and friends.

His small staff consisted of his secretary, Louise Clarkson; a State Department translator-stenographer; a Scots valet, Ross McInnes, and Sigourney Thayer, an unlikely addition to a diplomatic mission. A son of Dr. William

Greenough Thayer, the ultra-respectable headmaster of St. Mark's School, Groton's rival, Thayer had won a reputation for bravery flying on the Western Front in World War I. After the armistice, however, his madcap antics in Paris had led to notoriety and even a brief jail term. Welles had met him on a transatlantic crossing and, amused by his eccentric brilliance, had invited him to Santo Domingo as an "outside courier," or jack-of-all-trades.

"There were very few women out in the field in those days," Louise Clarkson remembered. "I stayed in the office, took dictation and did much of the coding while Thayer took messages to and from the Foreign Ministry and performed a variety of chores." An avid horseman like Welles, Thayer accompanied him on early-morning rides, proved an excellent chef, a talented poet and, despite a pronounced harelip, an amusing raconteur who seemed to enchant the Dominican ladies. At summer's end, when Welles returned to the United States, he and Thayer parted, each going his separate way. But, dissimilar as they were, in that summer and autumn of 1922, with incessant work and limited diversion, Welles had found him an entertaining companion who knew the same people, spoke the same language and came from the same milieu from which Welles had temporarily cut himself off.

On September 18, seven weeks after Welles's arrival, the Dominican leaders formally approved the evacuation plan and authorized the Advisory Commission to name a provisional president and cabinet and start preparing for national elections. The last, however, had not been heard from Admiral Robison. Ordered to regroup his marines outside the three main cities before election day, he insisted that they be permitted to circulate freely inside the cities during liberty hours. The Dominicans insisted that they be confined to barracks election day, a request that Welles found reasonable but that Robison denounced as Dominican "dislike" of his forces and with which he refused to comply. Again Welles went over his head, cabling Hughes that the military governor supported "neither the [evacuation] plan, nor the military dispositions necessary to effect it." Robison was overruled and the final hurdle cleared.

On October 2 the Advisory Commission named Juan Vicini Burgos, a respected businessman, provisional president, and Robison, bowing to the inevitable, formally proclaimed the start of the evacuation plan. To avoid the impression that Robison was retreating under fire, Welles tactfully arranged that the inauguration of Vicini Burgos on October 21 uphold the dignity of both men. Robison was replaced soon after by Brigadier General Harry Lee of the U.S. Marine Corps, whom Welles and the Dominicans would find far more flexible.

Phase 1 of the two-phase evacuation plan had now been completed. The provisional government was in place, ready to administer the country, maintain order and negotiate with Washington the fiscal-legal obligations prerequisite to elections. Welles cabled the department that he was returning home. Hughes sent congratulations, and the provisional government cabled the White House urging that Welles return later and continue his mission until the elections had been completed and a constitutional president inaugurated.[29] On Welles's last night, Vicini Burgos and the cabinet tendered him a banquet followed by speeches "sprinkled with flowery terms to which the Spanish language lends itself," wrote William Ellis Pulliam, the U.S. Receiver General of Customs. At the end, Welles "rose to his full, commanding height, radiating dignity, and, without a prepared script, talked three times as long and beat them all at their own linguistic game. His Spanish was flawless."[30]

Weary and eager to get home, he set out by car next day crossing the mountainous border into Haiti and sailing from Port-au-Prince on October 27. Mathilde was in New York awaiting him. "Can't believe you are really due here tonight after all the delays of the past month," she wrote in a note left at his hotel. "If you can, dear, do come to me. If you can't, do call me up. I long so to tell you how I love you."

EIGHT

"PRESIDENTIAL TIMBER"

1923–1924

AFTER A QUICK REUNION WITH MATHILDE, Welles reported to Hughes in Washington, briefed State Department colleagues, then returned to New York to catch up with children, family and friends and resume his search for a banking job. With the Dominicans safely launched on the road to independence, his full-time presence there no longer seemed essential. Fate, however, again intervened. War was looming in Central America, and Hughes needed him.

Welles had urged Hughes repeatedly before resigning to convene a conference of the five Central American republics, help mediate their disputes and thus reduce the risk of war near the Panama Canal. In 1907 the United States and Mexico had cosponsored a similar conference in Washington with lasting results. The conferees had unanimously agreed not to recognize revolutionary new governments until legitimized by free elections, and, as the goal of most Central America revolutions had been U.S. recognition (i.e., Wall Street loans), the new policy had cut violence sharply. From 1911 to 1917 not a single Central American government had been overthrown.

By the end of World War I, however, a permanent ban on revolutions was clearly impossible in countries where neither free speech nor free elections existed and where opposition groups had no legitimate access to power. Many such groups were being armed and financed by hostile neighboring governments or by American fruit companies seeking political influence and lower taxes. Meanwhile, tension was rising.[1]

Hughes had initially opposed Welles's recommendation, noting that the United States was involved already in Cuba, Haiti and the Dominican Republic. He had no intention of embroiling it in Central America as well. But, with the danger of war rapidly rising, Welles's successor, Munro, won Hughes around by reporting that the five Central American envoys in Washington were now "entirely favorable" to a conference.[2] While Hughes was weighing his course, the Presidents of Honduras, Nicaragua and El Salvador—Diego Chamorro, Rafael Lopez and Jorge Melendez—seized the initiative and, in August, 1922, staged their own "summit" at Amapala, on the Honduran Pacific coast.

Increasingly eager to support peace around the Panama Canal, President Harding and Secretary Hughes sent the cruiser USS *Tacoma* to Amapala as "neutral" territory where the three presidents and their respective American ministers—John E. Ramer, Franklin E. Morales and Montgomery Schuyler— could confer in safety. The presidents agreed not only to keep peace among themselves but to invite their Guatemalan and Costa Rican colleagues to a follow-up five-power "summit" in December. Hughes, finally persuaded that Welles had been right, announced that the United States would participate and offered Washington as the conference site.

Given Welles's long advocacy, Hughes asked him to serve as his deputy, and Welles, flattered to share the spotlight with the Secretary of State, enthusiastically accepted. Under international protocol, Hughes, representing the host government, would automatically become conference chairman, and Welles, his deputy, would become vice chairman, directing proceedings in his absence. Welles's elation was short-lived, however, when he learned that Harding and Hughes both expected him to continue as U.S. Commissioner in the Dominican Republic until its formal independence—at least a year away. This posed major personal problems; not only did it mean a far longer commitment than he had contemplated originally, but it postponed his search for a banking position and separated him indefinitely from Mathilde.

Reminding Hughes that he had resigned from the Diplomatic Service and thus had no "tenure," Welles asked what personal security he could expect if he continued as commissioner. Hughes, he wrote later, assured him of "promotion satisfactory to me" if the Harding administration remained in office.[3] Satisfied that his government career was secure, Welles accepted and brought Esther to Washington for the conference opening.

Washington was in a "social frenzy" that winter, Caroline Phillips recorded in her diary. "Everyone entertaining Central Americans, dinners and dances every night, dinners beginning only at 8:30." As a nine-power arms parley was also in session, there was "no escape" for officials like her husband, the Under Secretary, who worked from 8 A.M. until 7 P.M., then faced a "hurried change into evening clothes and three hours of social duty before collapsing into bed at midnight." Better acquainted with the Old World than the New, she viewed Central Americans with patrician reserve. Some she thought "fairly intelligent" while others were "queer, childish people . . . opera bouffe types." One Central American delegate discussing women's suffrage with the courtly Hughes was heard to observe that women in his country "did not want independence but preferred to stay home and have children in chastity." This, Mrs. Phillips surmised, meant being "faithful to their husbands."[4]

On December 4, Hughes rapped the Central American conference to order and presided that evening at a gala reception in the ornate Pan American Union. Parrots cackled and fountains splashed in the tropical Aztec patio as the delegates, their wives and guests ascended the marble stairs to the colonnaded Hall of the Americas above where a marine band played and six marines in full-dress uniform held the Stars & Stripes and the flags of the five Central American republics. Heading the receiving line were Secretary and Mrs. Hughes, beside them Sumner and Esther Welles and then the five Central American delegates and their wives. A young Western congressman passing down the line was heard murmuring to a Central American lady: "Señora, I regret that I only know two words of your beautiful language: mañana, which means tomorrow, and pyjama, which means tonight."[5] The next day, the conference settled down to work.

Hughes and Welles had agreed in advance on three goals: a five-power Treaty of Amity to preserve peace around the Panama Canal, creation of joint U.S.–Central American tribunals to mediate disputes and, finally, disarmament. The Central Americans, however, had their own priority: five-power "Union," a dream dating from 1821 when Spain's colonies were struggling for independence. Union had failed repeatedly, however, and, to avoid interminable debate, Hughes and Welles had dropped it from the agenda as a condition of U.S. participation. Tempers flared nonetheless, for many Central Americans viewed union as their sole hope of greater influence in the hemisphere and beyond. One delegate even threatened to disrupt the conference unless "Union of the land of our forefathers" took priority.[6] Eventually he was dissuaded.

Hughes's heavy schedule permitted him to preside only at the opening ceremony, at six working sessions and at the close. At all others, Welles took his place, at thirty the model of the classic diplomat: attentive, tireless, never leaving his seat though sessions often dragged on till dawn. Occasionally he would extract a cigarette from a gold case, tap its end, light it with a match, then let the smoke filter slowly from his nostrils as he listened impassively to rolling floods of Spanish oratory. Conscious of his relative youth, he was studiously deferential to the older delegates, knowing their penchant for defying the Yankee colossus oratorically. He "skillfully steered the conference without arousing resentment," Munro wrote later.[7] By the close on February 7, 1923, Hughes and Welles had achieved two of their three goals: a five-power Treaty of Amity and mixed U.S.–Central American tribunals. Arms cuts, however, proved unattainable.

The conference, Hughes wrote in his memoirs, revealed the "special aptitude for negotiations with Latin Americans which Welles so brilliantly displayed [later] with Secretary Hull."[8] Welles himself was pleased with the outcome. Never before, he wrote a colleague, had the United States taken part in an international forum "in which it had less to gain for its own material ends." The overriding goal had been to help the Central American republics preserve their independence, and "by agreeing to participate in the joint tribunals, we placed ourselves on a par with those republics."[9] Equality, for Welles, was the key to dealing with Latin Americans and, ten years later, would become the cornerstone of his and FDR's Good Neighbor policy.

Publicly praised for his role at the conference, Welles was coming under private censure for his open liaison with Mathilde Gerry. Caroline Phillips, who saw much of her "young cousin"[10] that winter, confided her disapproval to her diary. Welles, she wrote, had a "grand air, and undeniable charm . . . was brilliantly clever, very ambitious but with a steely quality about him." He had behaved "outrageously" to Esther, a devoted wife and mother, whose "eccentric, unconventional streak" irritated him. He had begun paying attention to "that horrid vamp," Mrs. Peter Gerry, "a sort of Rubens beauty who amuses herself by breaking up happy homes."

It had become a public scandal. Esther had left him temporarily and Sumner had been "forced" to resign from the Diplomatic Service. Apparently the couple worked out their differences but Caroline Phillips still condemned Welles for "not behaving like a gentleman and for making his wife suffer. I can't approve of him," she concluded, "yet he does charm and interest me."[11]

Her assertion that Welles had been forced to resign is puzzling. As the Under Secretary's wife, she would have been privy to most departmental secrets; yet it is hard to reconcile with the fact that Hughes, a pillar of rectitude, not only recalled Welles six weeks after his resignation but persuaded Harding to appoint him U.S. Commissioner in the Dominican Republic with the rank of minister and, later, to make him deputy U.S. representative and vice-chairman of the Central American conference. Possibly Hughes so needed Welles that he was willing to close his mind to the younger man's character flaws. Eighteen years later Franklin D. Roosevelt would do the same—under far graver circumstances.

With the conference over, Welles reluctantly turned back to Dominican affairs. Predictably, in his four-month absence, they had deteriorated. The Advisory

Commission had pigeonholed the new electoral law, and its members, except for Archbishop Nouel, were all busily campaigning. Even the honest provisional President, Vicini Burgos, seemed to be faltering. His Interior Minister had resigned after quarreling with him, and his Finance and Health ministers had been dismissed for diverting public funds to political ends.[12] The timetable for independence was in jeopardy, and, at Hughes's urgent request, Welles agreed with heavy heart to return to Santo Domingo in late March. It was the worst possible time; his personal life was in turmoil. As a presidential appointee, he had momentarily patched up his uneasy relationship with Esther, essentially for the sake of form. But he remained desperately in love with Mathilde, who, despite repeated promises, was still procrastinating about starting her divorce.

Determined to force her hand before his departure, Welles met her at White Sulphur Springs, a West Virginia resort, in mid-February and threatened to remain married to Esther unless she acted soon. "I was so miserably unhappy at the White Sulphur," Mathilde wrote him later. "You left me there and I shall never forget my suffering when you told me, perhaps, you couldn't [divorce Esther]."

Whatever his motive—to pressure Mathilde, to quell gossip or both—Welles sailed back to the Dominican Republic in late March accompanied by Esther, her mother, and his son Ben, then seven. (Arnold, then five, had been left with relatives.) The gesture was pointless, for he and Esther had virtually reached the breaking point. A handwritten note dated March 22, two days before they sailed, states coldly: "I owe Esther Slater Welles the sum of $88,900 which I will refund her by installments, beginning with the present date, until the whole debt is cancelled."[13]

The year before he had borrowed $100,000 from Esther, ostensibly to join a New York banking syndicate but, instead, had bought Mathilde jewelry. It was a *geste* as senseless as it was indefensible, for Mathilde, whatever her faults, was not grasping. Money, however, seemed much on his mind at the time, his $3,000 salary having ended on his resignation from the diplomatic service on March 15, 1922, a year earlier. "As you know, I have accepted only a nominal salary of $10 a month [$80 in today's terms] since I was appointed," Welles wrote his State Department colleague, Francis White. "I feel, however, that expenses [for] entertaining should be borne by the government. Last year [they] averaged about $500 [$4,000 today] a month."

Early in April, the SS *Panama* dropped anchor in Port-au-Prince, Haiti's mountain-ringed capital, and the U.S. Commissioner, his family and staff disembarked. A Haitian band blared discordantly on the quai and a row of open limousines stood nearby, each equipped with "isinglass" (plastic) curtains that the chauffeurs could snap on when the tropical rains pelted down. The party set off in convoy for Santo Domingo, an overnight trip across the mountains, the cars slithering over muddy roads. Haitian men rode donkeys by the roadside, their women walked behind them balancing waterjars on their heads and half-naked children waved shyly from the underbrush.

They spent the night in a white government guesthouse high above the clouds, where Ben fell instantly asleep in a rusty iron cot with broken springs. The next morning, to his surprise, he awakened in a four-poster canopied bed. Dissatisfied with his son's cot, Welles had quietly changed places with him in the night—one of many small acts of tenderness which would bind father and son over the coming years.

Once back in the Dominican capital, Welles resumed his habitual breakneck pace. He convened the laggard Advisory Council and demanded that it complete the electoral law, appoint electoral boards and prepare for elections in October.[14] Speed was essential as Vicini Burgos's provisional presidency was due to expire in mid-August. Fearing delays and a dangerous power vacuum, Welles had its term extended until January 1, 1924, safely past the election date, then set off on a cross-country inspection of electoral boards, the key to an honest poll. Day after day, often far into the night, he conferred with local politicians in moldering provincial capitals, in rural towns with sun-baked plazas and wooden sidewalks and in jungle hamlets. Snapshots at the time show him towering over the slender Dominicans in a tailored tropical suit, cane in hand and a broad-brimmed Panama hat to shield him from the glare. Everywhere he went he spread his message: the U.S. occupation would end and the marines would sail home once the Dominicans had elected a president.

Meanwhile, Welles had now settled with his family in a seaside villa where, to his son's delight, marine sentries in "Smokey-bear" hats presented arms whenever the commissioner arrived or left. His schedule was unvarying. He left for his office early each morning, returning after 2 P.M. for a late lunch, then stretching out on a sofa in shirtsleeves for the ritual Dominican siesta. By late afternoon, when the government offices reopened, he would be off again until after dark. Esther and Ben spent their days on the beach watching the Caribbean breakers curl and foam, building sandcastles or chatting with a smiling native in a curious striped uniform raking seaweed whom they later learned was a "trusty" serving life at a local prison for a *crime passionelle*. By then he was their friend. Mrs. Slater eventually left for home. The days passed but Esther seemed increasingly sad and withdrawn until, one day, she too was gone, leaving Ben in his father's care. The child, inconsolable, asked repeatedly where his mother had gone, only to be gently put off by his father with a familiar nursery jingle: "She's gone to catch a rabbit skin to wrap her Baby Bunting in." At seven, Ben was too young to know that she had sailed for the Paris divorce courts, whose decrees at the time were legally recognized in the United States. French law, however, required that Sumner testify in person before Esther could be granted a divorce, so he cabled Hughes that there was little he could do until the October elections. All political parties had been duly registered and calm could be expected during the coming sixty days of voter registration. Meanwhile, he had urgent business in Paris. Returning to New York in late May, he left Ben with relatives and sailed for Europe, where Mathilde was awaiting him in Paris.

In time, the French courts summoned him to resume marital relations with his wife, but he refused, formally declaring: "I do not want to see my wife again. I refuse absolutely to take her back. I intend, henceforth, to live my life as it pleases me." On October 9, 1923, Esther was granted a preliminary decree on grounds of desertion.[15]

Sumner's father, Ives Gammell and other friends who loved Esther condemned him for deserting her; only his sister, Emily, who also loved Esther, stood by Sumner, refusing to censure her brother. Surprisingly, Mrs. Slater sent him a poignant note. She was thinking of him "with real affection and sympathy," she wrote sadly. "You two young people are bound to meet . . . and to love each other . . . even if it's years from now. It will be hard for you, both, but perhaps it's all for the best. God only knows. This is just a line from poor old Mim [her family nickname] to send you a heartful of love."[16]

Now legally free to live "as he pleased," Welles would find the price high. That August, while he had been divorcing Esther and dallying with Mathilde, the philandering, easygoing President Warren Gamaliel Harding had died suddenly. His successor, a dour Vermonter named Calvin Coolidge, would take a very bleak view of the marital misconduct of young government officials like Sumner Welles.

Hughes was glad to see him back, however. In his absence, the Dominican situation had soured again, threatening the U.S. evacuation plan. Political leaders were quarreling, gun-running was rampant and the elderly U.S. minister, William W. Russell, was proving ineffective. The elections, scheduled for October, would have to be postponed for at least six months—until March 1924—and Welles would have to return and remain until they had been duly carried out. The department booked him onto the first available ship, the SS *Huron,* a rusty little tub due to sail October 27.

As his departure drew near, Mathilde's letters reflected both frenzied infatuation and the congenital procrastination that were to infuriate him over the next three years. "I came up to try to end it all—and just can't yet," she wailed from her husband's home in Warwick, R.I. "I always have failed you and I always will, I fear." Four days later she wrote: "I can't let you leave me for long. I will join you any place, anywhere on earth, in late November or before, if I can. PS. [Gerry] says he will [agree to a divorce] if I insist upon killing him. Oh, Sumner, I long for you. I will look at the sailings on one of those good boats. No SS Huron for me if I can do better."

At their final meeting in New York before his sailing they quarreled bitterly when he hotly denied an ongoing affair with a woman in Santo Domingo, a charge for which Mathilde had some evidence. Nonetheless, she saw him off at the pier then poured out her grief.

> 4 A.M. You have just left me two hours ago and I can't sleep. I know you love me, no man could have proved his love more. Why, loving me, must you always have some woman to amuse you till you come back to me? I hated tonight . . . I adore you with all my heart, soul and body . . . I have made you suffer. What I have done was for pity for [Gerry] and from the best in me. It was hard and unfair to you. It's dark and now you are far out on the water on that awful little boat. If only I were Li [his Chow dog]. I envy his soft blue nose touching your hand tonight and I can't. I am torn to pieces, [Gerry] is ill and you gone, my darling. I love you. It's a madness, a worship, not love.

Dreading her empty house in Washington and her mother's hectoring, she stayed on alone in New York, writing him next day: "I am coming to Santo D. I simply must, soon, or I will be ill . . . Don't worry, my darling, it [her divorce] is going to be done soon . . . I am coming to you."[17] Again, she let him down.

Dominican problems, meanwhile, overshadowed his troubles with Mathilde. The situation was "electric," he cabled Hughes upon arriving. Election fever gripped the nation and passions were high. To prevent violence, he would have to ensure personally that each political party had equal representation at every level, from provincial governors down to rural sheriffs: *alcaldes pedáneos*. The Minister of the Interior had been accused of favoritism and, since his control of the police might affect the vote, he would have to be replaced. The Advisory Commission solved the problem by splitting the Interior Ministry in half, replacing one minister with two. "The humor of the situation," Welles cabled Hughes, "was heightened by the fact that the two appointees . . . had been close personal friends for many years and . . . were nicknamed . . . the Heavenly Twins. Extravagant as the solution appeared, in practice it worked well."[18]

On Thanksgiving day, Welles became a minor hero. While lunching as guest of honor of the American community at a beach club, he heard a young fisherman call for help from a dory capsized offshore. Stripping off his jacket and shoes, he swam out encumbered by white flannel trousers and dragged the youth to safety. In the struggle, Welles was bitten by a barracuda and strained his heart, suffering heart trouble the rest of his life. In appreciation, on December 3 the Ayuntamiento (City Council) of Santo Domingo awarded a gold medal to "Summer *[sic]* Welles, *por su accion heroica.*[19]

At thirty-one Welles, the ranking American in the country, tall, handsome and unencumbered by a wife, was socially much in demand. The leading Dominican families divided their time between town houses, seaside villas and country estates. On weekends he often joined the Oscar Michelena family at their estate, San Cristobal, west of the capital, riding horseback by day and playing poker with the men at night. At other times he swam with Francisco Peynado and his family off Boca Chica, a palm-fringed resort on the south coast. Humid little Santo Domingo had little diversion apart from dinners and Saturday night dances at the country club. "One always saw the same old faces," Louise Clarkson remembered.

At some point, Dominican tongues began wagging over Welles's marked attentions to a Mrs. Russell, the petite, Mexican-born wife of an American bank manager. "She was not pretty but she had sex appeal and was very flirtatious," a Dominican matron recalled a half century later. "Sumner often danced with her Saturday nights at the country club, or at private parties, and it caused a lot of talk because he was so tall and she so very small. She would close her eyes as she danced, as if she were asleep with her head on his chest."[20]

Clever, ambitious and much courted by Dominicans seeking favor with the U.S. occupation authorities, Mrs. Russell was providing Welles not only with political intelligence but, apparently, with romantic solace as well. It was these rumors that had reached Mathilde in faraway Washington.

Mathilde had promised to join him for Christmas but again her nerve failed. "In a few days it will be January 10 [the third anniversary of their meeting] . . . three long wretched years—fights and kisses to forget the fights," she wrote apologetically. Sumner had given her a ring during his divorce in Paris the previous summer, believing that she would soon start her own divorce, although Gerry had talked her out of it. "I have never taken my ring off my finger since last July in Paris," she wrote. "I never will. It will be there the day I am buried . . . Oh why didn't he [Gerry] let me do it all in Paris last year?"[21] Although angered by her failure to meet him for Christmas, Welles cabled her to join him for their anniversary.

"Insanely happy you cabled me to come," she wrote. "It will kill Peter [Gerry] if I go. If I stay—you will be lonely and forget me—or care for some other woman." Jealousy, fear and self-pity ran like a thread through her letters. "Are you coming back to me to take me away from it all or are you going back to her [Esther]? I can't come to you, alone, or I would." Rumors of his philandering and his denials irked her. "Will you ever be really frank and not lie, Sumner? It's just this that has parted us . . . my fear of being unhappy if married to you and making you wretched as I would hate you and leave you in a day if I found it so."

She struggled to justify her indecision. "I have tried, God knows, to do my duty and suffered all these months for pity because my heart was soft and . . . felt I would kill him if I left. Do you love me? Tell me, don't lie to me, dear. If only you had not, we might tonight be together." To retaliate for her reproaches and self-justification, he began returning her letters unopened. "Oh Sumner, how can you hurt anyone so!" she protested. "You are cruel and hard."

In May, despairing over Mathilde's irresolution and increasingly guilt-ridden over his own divorce, Welles wrote Esther suggesting that they resume married life before her decree became final, but she had crossed her Rubicon. "I have done nothing but think the situation over and I really believe it is better to let the divorce go through," she wrote back. "We have lived separate lives so much that it won't be the same. It seems hard now but I don't believe we could pull together again." The children, meanwhile, were in good health and Ben doing well in school, except for "conduct." He had begged to be allowed to rejoin his father in sunny Santo Domingo, but Esther did not want him removed again from school. Welles could have him throughout the summer, and she would keep Arnold, the younger child, with her. "Love from the boys," she ended, signing herself, coldly, ESW.[22]

Mathilde, meanwhile, had begun hearing criticism of her own role in breaking up Welles's marriage. A woman friend had told her that "everyone sides with [Esther] and thinks I am responsible. How can I come to Santo Domingo and have the world say I am rushing after you?" she wrote. "[Esther] tells everyone you are not really divorced." Mrs. Slater was boasting that Sumner had "finally gotten away from that blonde home-wrecker" and would soon return to his wife. "Pleasant, isn't it, for me!" Mathilde moaned. She passed him a political tip. Juan Riaño, the Spanish ambassador, had told her that Phillips would soon be named ambassador to Belgium and that Welles might succeed him as Under Secretary. "Do you want it, my darling?" she asked ingenuously.[23]

Nothing, in fact, would have pleased him more, nor was the idea far-fetched. Hughes had recently been overheard telling a dinner partner that Welles was the "outstanding man in the State Department: presidential timber."[24] Weeks earlier, on hearing that Welles might be sent to Central America on a six-month assignment, Mathilde reacted with frenzied extravagance, spending $400,000 ($3.2 million in today's terms) for a necklace of forty-two black pearls recently brought to the United States by Prince Felix Youssoupoff, Rasputin's assassin. "I shall be poor for years but they are so becoming," she prattled. "You will not like them. I adore them . . . huge with lights of pink, mauve and gray. I suppose I was crazy but I just get insane days."

Within days the New York Times commented editorially on the "desire, so common among savages and barbarians and the possessors of childish minds . . . to festoon themselves with shiny bits of metal and stone. This joy is innocent enough in itself," noted the *Times,* "but it is so—well, *primitive.*"[25]

The Dominican elections, set for March 15, 1924, were fast approaching, but every day brought Welles new problems. "It would be difficult to appreciate the inertia and sheer laziness of even the best politicians," he wrote his friend Francis White wearily. "Everything is left to the last minute." Compounding his problems, the State Department had rejected an increase in state revenues although the country faced bankruptcy. "If we are not able to increase [revenues] very substantially," Welles warned White, "we will have failed in our mission here and all the work which we are now doing will count for very little."[26]

In mid-January he set out on a final inspection of electoral boards in the twelve provincial capitals. "I have found by experience," he cabled Hughes, "that the establishment of a personal contact of this nature affords the only assurance that necessary measures will be carried out."[27] To ensure that a trained, disciplined police force was equipped and in place before the marines left, Welles persuaded the two leading candidates, General Horacio Vasquez and Francisco Peynado, to pledge publicly that, whichever man won, the American-trained constabulary (the Policia Nacional Dominicana, or PND) would remain nonpolitical. Appointments would be made "solely on merit."[28] In return, Welles announced that the United States would remain "neutral" in the coming poll.[29]

On election day the Dominicans overwhelmingly chose the grizzled old patriot Vasquez as their president and Peynado, his defeated rival, breaking a long tradition of electoral violence, accepted the outcome and offered congratulations. In Washington, Coolidge and Hughes breathed more easily. Hughes cabled Welles citing the "splendid work which you have performed, not only in bringing about . . . elections in Santo Domingo, but in having [them] conducted in such a thoroughly satisfactory manner and participated in by an unprecedented large proportion of the people."

The largest and most important step toward the program of evacuation had now been successfully accomplished, Hughes added, and the State Department "congratulates and commends you for the very important part that you have played in bringing about this result."[30] After two grueling years, Welles had crowned his mission with success.

NINE

CRISIS IN HONDURAS

1923

Three Whirlwind Weeks

WELLES'S DEFT HANDLING of the Central American conference and his success in the Dominican Republic won him star status. His choice of Latin America as his field had been wise; in no other area could a thirty-one-year-old diplomat, however able, have risen so fast. Latin America "must have the best of our thoughts . . . our energies . . . our men," Under Secretary Grew wrote at the time. "We must build up a selected corps of young men on whom we can depend in emergencies and whom we can advance to our most responsible positions . . . Of these, none are of greater importance . . . than . . . in Latin America."[1]

Mathilde, apparently, had been well informed, for Hughes was about to send his young troubleshooter to stave off another crisis. While Welles had been guiding the Dominicans to independence, Honduras had erupted in civil war. American lives and property were in danger, and the four other Central American republics were urging the United States to join them in another mediation effort at Amapala. Eager for fresh laurels, Welles wrote Francis White that the situation in Central America was "particularly interesting." It might be too late to use him, he wrote on February 24, but if the Secretary still wished to do so he would be happy to be informed. "I, personally, wish there were two of you," White wrote back, "as we need you for the work planned in Central America and, also, when you leave the Dominican Republic the wheels there stop turning."[2]

Welles's hopes were realized sooner than expected. On April 9, three weeks after the Dominican elections, Coolidge and Hughes ordered the destroyer USS *Richmond* from Guantanamo, Cuba, to pick him up and rush him to the scene. He boarded that evening, cabling the department for the latest information and suggesting that it direct Franklin P. Morales, the American minister in Honduras, to "cooperate."[3] Two years of tension with Russell in Santo Domingo had taught Welles the need for a clear chain of command.

Mountainous, wedge-shaped and approximately the size of Tennessee, Honduras had known little but domestic strife, foreign invasion or both since Columbus sighted it in 1502. Its predominantly Indian population of 1 million led a "simple life, anticipating the many feast days of the Roman Catholic church," wrote an American authority, dryly.[4] One of the poorest countries in the hemisphere, Honduras depended for survival on banana exports, although its largest plantations were owned almost exclusively by absentee U.S. corporations.

As Welles was racing to the scene, Honduras was approaching chaos. In presidential elections the previous autumn, none of the three candidates had won a majority. The faction-ridden Congress had failed to agree on a new chief executive and the incumbent, Rafael Lopez Gutierrez, had remained in office, ignoring cries of "dictatorship." The army had rebelled, taking control of the countryside, and was rapidly closing in on Tegucigalpa, the capital. Lopez Gutierrez had since died but his ultra-conservative cabinet, the Council of Ministers, was holding out in the beleaguered capital. Meanwhile Guatemala, Nicaragua, Costa Rica and El Salvador were urging Washington to mediate with them at Amapala.

Until Welles could arrive and report, however, Coolidge and Hughes were restricting themselves to banning arms shipments, ordering warships to patrol the Honduran coasts and landing marines and bluejackets to protect American lives. Welles had been authorized to mediate, single-handedly if necessary, but, when dealing with Latin American disputes, he invariably preferred consultation to unilateral U.S. action. Therefore he cabled Hughes from the destroyer, proposing that any U.S. peace proposal be submitted "jointly, with all other Central American governments, to avoid suspicion and further misunderstanding."[5]

Three days after leaving Santo Domingo, the USS *Richmond* dropped Welles at Puerto Cortez, on the Honduran Caribbean coast. The department had promised an airplane to fly him 130 miles across country to the capital but, finding neither an airplane nor even a message from the U.S. minister, and facing a trip alone through the revolution-infested countryside, Welles telegraphed the U.S. Legation to learn that the promised plane had been seized by the rebels. Striking out on his own, he boarded a banana train, which dropped him thirty miles inland at San Pedro de Sulla, where he encountered Fausto Davila, a prominent Honduran conservative whom the rebel generals had earmarked as their provisional President after victory.

Eager to ingratiate himself with Welles, Davila expressed interest in the "welfare and development" of the American fruit companies and offered thanks for the "material assistance" they were furnishing the rebels.[6] Welles took due note. Warning Davila that his hopes of becoming provisional President might be "premature," Welles boarded another train, which carried him twenty miles farther to Potrilleros. After some difficulty, he found an antiquated Ford and driver to take him on to Lake Yojoa. After crossing in a rented launch, he arrived at Pito Solo and, after more delay, found another car to take him thirty-five miles to Comayagua, where two of the four rebel generals—Vicente Tosta and Tiburcio Carias—were awaiting him.

They insisted that he proceed no further; their car had been fired on as they arrived. It was now past midnight and Welles had had not slept for thirty-six hours. After snatching three hours rest, he set off again at 4 A.M. with the two generals. On reaching their headquarters at San Juan de Flores, he learned their terms for a cease-fire and the formation of a "provisional" government. Eager to enter the besieged capital and arrange a cease-fire as quickly as possible, he set off on muleback, the only available transport. The sight of the elegant young diplomat astride a small Honduran mule, his long legs scraping the ground, with an escort of swarthy revolutionaries hung with pistols and bandoliers, might have delighted his debonair friends in Paris, Tokyo and Buenos Aires—to say nothing of the Reverend Endicott Peabody of Groton.

Weary and saddle-sore, Welles reached the radio station at Toncontin, on the capital's outskirts, at three the following morning. A message from Morales awaited him. Owing to lack of "sufficient guarantees" of his safety, the American minister could not leave the city and meet him until that afternoon.

Eventually Morales arrived with a naval aide and they drove Welles through sporadic rifle fire into the capital. His immediate task was to persuade the council to accept a cease-fire and the terms laid down by the insurgent generals: the appointment of a "provisional" president free to choose his cabinet, amendment of the constitution and the electoral laws and national elections for a constitutional President and Congress.

The council was "distinctly unfriendly," Welles cabled Hughes. After unsuccessfully challenging his credentials, it demanded that he transfer his mediation seventy miles north to Amapala, where delegates of the other Central American republics were expected. Meanwhile the cruiser USS *Milwaukee* had arrived in port as a "neutral" meeting ground. Welles suspected the council of stalling—hoping that the arrival of the Central American delegates would save it—but its chances of survival were rapidly deteriorating. The 800 troops still under its control were increasingly drunk and deserting in droves as the rebel columns closed in.

Racing to halt the fighting and start peace talks, Welles drove back the next day to Toncontin, where, after lengthy debate, he persuaded the rebel leaders to join him at Amapala and negotiate peace with Council delegates. At the last minute, however, General Gregorio Ferrera, another of the insurgent leaders, balked. His forces were ringing the capital and he saw no need to treat with a political corpse. Ferrara's opposition could not be disregarded lightly. A full-blooded Indian, he was a hero to the Honduran population, and a rebuff might inject dangerous racial overtones into an explosive situation. Telegraphing Ferrera to meet him on April 20, Welles succeeded after hours of discussion and appeals to patriotism—a favorite technique—in winning Ferrera's cooperation. Encouraged, he cabled Hughes:

> Ferrera impressed me favorably. He is a man of admitted personal integrity, has always maintained the most complete discipline over the forces under his command who, like him, are all Indians, and is, likewise, a man whose word can be depended on. I found him, with General Tosta, very solicitous for the welfare of his country and disposed to put the interests of the Republic above his personal ambitions. I can say this of no other Honduranian [sic] with whom I came in contact during the course of my mission.[7]

Seven days after arriving in Honduras, Welles welcomed Tosta and Carias and two council delegates aboard the USS *Milwaukee*. The talks quickly deadlocked, however. The Central American negotiators still had not arrived, notwithstanding U.S. appeals for speed, and the council, still stalling, now repudiated its earlier agreement to accept Tosta as provisional President. When Welles spent two days submitting alternative names, the council tried another bluff, protesting from its beleaguered capital that its two delegates were being "improperly imposed on" and prevented from communicating freely. If attempts at "coercion" continued and Welles remained "partial" to the rebel faction, the council would recall them. The council had misjudged its man.

Cold with anger, Welles showed the offending message to the council delegates, who immediately cabled Tegucigalpa their "astonishment." They had made no criticism of his impartiality, they protested. Seizing the moment, Welles warned the council that, unless its threat was withdrawn and a "satisfactory" apology received within twenty-four hours, he would withdraw as mediator. The council backed down, an apology arrived and Welles declared the incident closed.[8]

Having called the council's bluff, he stepped up pressure for an immediate cease-fire and agreement on Tosta as provisional President. There was no time to waste, he warned; the rebel armies were at the gates of the capital and each hour reduced the council's bargaining leverage. Again it yielded and agreed to negotiate a peace settlement once the Central American delegates had arrived. Welles's final demand was theater: His signature on the agreement would be construed by both parties as a "moral guarantee" that its terms would be faithfully carried out. He had won round one.

Confident that he had halted the fighting before the rebels could burst into the capital, he telegraphed Morales exultantly that a cease-fire had been agreed to and Tosta accepted as provisional President. His elation, however, was short-lived. Morales wired back that the rebels had brushed past the council's crumbling defenses that morning and had taken the city virtually without a shot. Flushed with victory, they were denouncing Welles's cease-fire, claiming that they had been tricked and, worse, were planning to reject their colleague, Tosta, as provisional President in favor of Fausto Davila, the tool of the American fruit companies. Welles's hopes plummeted.

Knowing that Ferrera would violently oppose Davila and that Davila could not form a government that the United States would recognize, Welles raced back to Tegucigalpa, arriving at midnight, and plunged back into negotiations. By dawn, after dangling U.S. recognition as his trump, he had persuaded the rebel generals to reverse themselves, accept Tosta as provisional President and negotiate constitutional reforms aboard the *Milwaukee*. The Central American delegates, finally arriving, would serve as guarantors. Back once again in Amapala, Welles was unanimously elected mediation chairman.

Within forty-eight hours the conferees had reached agreement and, on May 3, 1924, the five Central American delegations voted their thanks to President Coolidge for the use of the cruiser and a commendation to Welles for his "perfect tact, entire rectitude . . . impartiality and breadth of vision."[9] After a whirlwind twenty-one days, he had again accomplished his mission. The next day he sailed aboard the *Milwaukee* for Panama, en route back to Santo Domingo.

Despite initial friction, Welles and Morales had worked well together, and Morales would later pay his young colleague a handsome tribute. In his report to Hughes, Morales wrote that Welles had displayed:

> Tireless energy in the carrying out of his mission, together with great tact and firmness . . . Within the short space of seven days, he was able to bring about a preliminary agreement, just to all parties, and to . . . hold a mediation conference

with the delegates of both sides. In Amapala, he continued his efforts with such effect that on the very day . . . Tegucigalpa was captured by the Revolutionists, a Provisional President was unanimously elected and the preliminary peace pact signed by the delegates of all factions . . .

To the general surprise, Mr. Welles succeeded in obtaining the ratification of the preliminary pact by the victors in two days time [and] was then able to go on with the Central American Conference of Mediation and have the final agreement signed within a few days. I can speak of him and of the success of his mission only in terms of the highest praise.[10]

In his own report to Hughes, Welles charged the fruit companies with fomenting revolutions in Central America for their own politico-financial gain. The Honduran revolution, he reported, was "directly traceable . . . to the intervention of American interests." The rebel troops had been paid with funds advanced by the three American fruit companies—the United Fruit Company, the Cuyamel Fruit Company and the Standard Fruit & Steamship Company—which, in addition, had furnished the arms, ammunition, cannon, machine guns—even the airplane—used to bomb the capital. When properties owned by American companies "actively promoting revolution" were protected by sailors and warships of the U.S. government, Welles warned, U.S. "impartiality was discredited."

Tosta, meanwhile, needed immediate help; the financial situation in Honduras was "chaotic." Peace and government by "orderly methods" could be assured only by "quick, effective aid." Welles's plea fell on deaf ears. With the fighting over, the Coolidge administration lost interest. Three months later Honduras fell prey to another revolution. "The Pact of Amapala is already, practically, a dead letter in spite of Sumner Welles's fine work," Under Secretary Grew lamented in his diary.[11]

TEN

MARRIAGE AND DISMISSAL

1924–1925

"Let Him Be Dismissed at Once"

WHILE WELLES HAD BEEN STRUGGLING with the Honduras crisis, Hughes had named Grew Under Secretary of State and Mathilde was outraged. "How stupid of old Charles Evans [Hughes] to give Joe Grew . . . Philips' [sic] place and not you," she fumed in a letter awaiting Welles on his return to Santo Domingo. "In a way I'm glad that Charles Evans didn't want you—as I want you, Sumner, and I hope to God the State Department will never see you again and that it will be years before you go back there."[1] Within a year, her angry outburst would prove strangely prophetic.

Meanwhile, with Honduras calm and the Dominicans independent, Welles was eager to get back to Washington. Mathilde was veering between her infatuation with Welles and pity for her husband, and was reluctant to start divorce proceedings. Without Welles by her side to steel her resolve, she would continue procrastinating, leaving him indefinitely in limbo. Moreover, he had urgent family problems to discuss with Esther. Vasquez solved his dilemma. Weary after an arduous campaign and in need of change, the old cacique suggested a visit to Washington before his inauguration on July 13. Welles seized on the idea.

A Vasquez visit would be "highly beneficial," he cabled the department. The situation in Central America was "exceedingly precarious," and he had recommendations of the "utmost urgency" for Secretary Hughes. To wring the stoniest of bureaucratic hearts, he adduced "pressing personal" reasons for his return.[2] No precedent existed for a preinaugural visit, the department replied primly, but President Coolidge would tender Vasquez a White House lunch and Welles could return.

He docked in New York on May 24 to find a frigid letter from Esther. "I would rather not see you," she wrote. "We can settle all by letter."[3] She had sent his riding horses to a livery stable, his trunks to a warehouse and would forward his personal effects to Washington once he was settled. The children and their governess would join him for his allotted share of their vacation.

A bachelor for the first time in nine years, Welles took a small apartment at the Wardman Park Hotel where his sons, Ben, age eight, and Arnold, six, eventually arrived. They saw little of him during the hot summer days for he was away at the State Department, but when two bicycles arrived—a present from their mother—their spirits lifted. Soon they were pedaling over the hotel lawns and hot brick walks, awaiting with mounting excitement the day's end and their father's return. Each would then race to be the first to clamber onto his lap, fascinated by the fragrance of the 4711 eau-de-Cologne he habitually splashed on his handkerchiefs and shirts.

In the cool of the evening, they strolled in Rock Creek Park and, occasionally on Sundays, he took them to the circus where a statuesque, fair-haired lady in a summer dress and large hat joined them. Not knowing at first how to address her, they called her the "Circus Lady" until she became part of the family and they were told to call her simply Mathilde. It seemed a strange, foreign-sounding name, but when she joined them in teasing their father and roughhoused with them in a restrained, old-fashioned way, they accepted her as a friend.

Coolidge's lunch for President-elect Vasquez on June 24, 1924,[4] remained etched in Welles's memory as a disaster of protocol. The day was "hot to the sizzling point," wrote Ellis Pulliam, the U.S. Receiver General of Customs who had arrived with the Vasquez party.[5] Shortly before lunch Coolidge notified Hughes that he would wear a blue blazer and white flannel trousers, but the State Department somehow failed to notify the Dominicans, who had docked in New York that morning and who arrived at the White House after a hot train ride attired in the heavy, black wool cutaways *de rigueur* for presidential audiences in Latin America.

The luncheon comprised the "face cards" of Washington, wrote Pulliam: Secretary Hughes, Supreme Court justices, senators, chairmen of congressional committees, ranking military officers, Leo Rowe of the Pan American Union, J. Butler Wright, Assistant Secretary for Latin America, Pulliam and Welles. Coolidge and Vasquez, who spoke not a word of each other's language, sat side by side in stony silence, broken by an occasional banality that Wright translated.[6] Vasquez was "reserved, imposing and possessed," wrote Welles, of an "old-time courtesy modelled on the Spanish tradition" and highly susceptible to any slight. Coolidge, in "one of those petulant moods from which he frequently suffered," made no effort to converse with his guest of honor but replied in monosyllables whenever the Dominican president-elect addressed him.[7]

After lunch, Coolidge led the way to the south portico for coffee and cigars, engaging in desultory chitchat with his staff until, minutes later, he abruptly sent word to Vasquez that he was obliged to depart; presumably, wrote Welles, for his customary postprandial nap. Pulliam saw the President bearing down on him. Vasquez had said "nice things" about his work, Coolidge vouchsafed. Drawing close, he muttered, "How are they getting along down there?" "All right, Mr. President," replied Pulliam. "Are they paying the interest on their debts?" asked Coolidge. "Yes, indeed," answered Pulliam. "We see to that." Without another word, Coolidge turned on his heel and disappeared, trailed by his deferential staff.[8]

Despite Coolidge's boorishness, Welles and Pulliam were determined that Vasquez not return home empty-handed. To that end, they negotiated a trade pact during his visit that opened the American sugar market to Dominican cane and eased the tight U.S. grip on Dominican finances. Welles arranged also for a $25 million loan and wrote Russell in Santo Domingo that the Vasquez visit had been "highly gratifying."[9] Still more gratifying—and unexpected—was a summons to the White House. Unknown to Welles, Senator Medill McCormick, Republican from Illinois, had written Hughes of the "marvelous regeneration" he had found on a recent inspection of Santo Domingo and Haiti and felt duty-bound to bear witness to the "ability, diligence and tenacity" with which Welles had carried out his work.[10] Upon entering the Oval Office, Welles was agreeably surprised to hear the laconic Coolidge thank him for his "accomplishments."

Welles might have been well advised to have resigned, then and there, as U.S. Commissioner in the Dominican Republic. His task was completed; and Hughes had hinted at a legation in Central America. Problems, however, remained. "Since I had taken hold of the Dominican job and had been working on it so long," he wrote Norman Davis long after, "I felt that I would prefer to continue until the reconstruction program, and a complete program of financing, [had] been carried out."[11] Fate had other plans in store.

The 1924 Democratic convention opened on June 24 in sweltering heat in New York's Madison Square Garden. Mathilde, desperate to get away from her "lonely" house in Washington, begged Welles to accompany her, if only for a day. Gerry was in a "dreadful state, hopeless to talk to," she complained. Tense and nervous, she was also quarreling with Welles. "Don't be cross with me," she pleaded. "Please don't think I don't adore the children. I do . . . I admit the convention would amuse me more than the infants for one day only."[12]

Indifferent to the risk of being seen together in a political fishbowl, they watched their mutual friend, Franklin D. Roosevelt, stricken three years earlier by polio, struggle to the podium to nominate Governor Alfred E. "Al" Smith of New York: a gallant but futile gesture. Two weeks and 104 ballots later, the Democrats chose as their standard-bearer John W. Davis, a silver-haired West Virginia lawyer who was swept into oblivion that November. Buoyed by prosperity, the nation voted two-to-one for "Silent Cal" Coolidge, the idol of Middle America. Welles's presence at the convention with the wife of a leading Democratic senator, meanwhile, had not passed unnoticed in the White House.

After the convention ended, Mathilde summoned her courage and set out for the Paris divorce courts, ignoring her mother's pathological fear of scandal. Mother and daughter were constantly bickering. "I will have to sail and escape alone," Mathilde wrote Welles. "Just Ramona and you to help me in Paris." Ramona Lefevre, an animated young Panamanian friend, had agreed to accompany Mathilde until Welles could arrive. "I love you more each day, each hour, each second," Mathilde wrote him as her departure drew near.

Welles sailed in September to join her, taking his son Ben, who was ecstatic over a transatlantic trip alone with his father. Mathilde had left a note at Welles's Paris hotel: "Keep on loving me, please, until December." Not until then would her preliminary decree be granted and, meanwhile, discretion was essential. Their meetings, consequently, were held to a minimum, and much of the time in Paris, Welles and his son were alone together. It was then that the lifelong bond between them was forged.

They walked each morning in the Luxembourg Gardens where, as an architecture student ten years earlier, Welles had exercised his setter. They strolled the quais by the Seine, pausing at book stalls where Welles thumbed through Tauchnitz paperbacks and his son hung, stomach-first, on the balustrades envying children on barges passing below. They rode the miniature trains in the Jardins d'Acclimatation, sailed toy boats in the Tuilleries fountains and laughed together at the puppets of the Grands Guignols thwacking each other lustily. Occasionally, at day's end, Welles would halt at a *confiserie,* known to him of old, where the portly *patronne* slid caramels into a box, tied it deftly with a single motion, then solemnly handed it to the excited child as his father and she exchanged laughs.

For Ben, the day's highlight was lunch in the bustling Meurice Hotel dining room, where tail-coated waiters rolled up carts with hors d'oeuvres in revolving trays and he would ponder how many he could cram onto his plate. At meal's end he was allowed a choice from the pastry cart, a task requiring prolonged concentration. At a nearby table, a spare, elderly gentleman in gold-rimmed glasses followed his deliberations with evident amusement. One day Welles whispered that the onlooker was King Gustavus Adolphus of Sweden on his annual "incognito" visit to Paris. Ben, however, was dubious. Kings wore crowns and ermine-trimmed robes, carried scepters and were girt with swords; so his father must be teasing—or, hard as it was to believe, mistaken.

Mathilde started home in October, her divorce under way, while Welles and his child sailed, for discretion's sake, on a separate steamer a day later. Cables flew between the ships but Welles was morose, reading all day in a deck chair while Ben romped with children his own age. Each evening father and son would dine together. After tucking the child into his berth, Welles would console himself with shipboard acquaintances at the bar. Returning late one night and unable to sleep, he awoke Ben and regaled him with vivid descriptions of Africa, promising that one day they would safari together. Ben lay awake, visions of elephants, lions and zebras racing through his head. The next morning, he was ready to start buying safari gear, but Welles had already forgotten the conversation. Tipsy, he had been reliving one of the few happy moments of his life.

Mathilde docked in New York a day ahead of them. "I won't meet you as I really feel it's wiser," she apologized in a note to his hotel. Mrs. Townsend had arrived from Washington, still terrified of scandal, and both suspected that Esther might be at the pier to retrieve her son. "Mother and I are both scared to death of her," Mathilde confessed nervously. Gerry, meanwhile, had come down from Rhode Island and was imploring Mathilde to drop her divorce while time remained. "I have had two hard days," she wrote Welles. "I will be so thankful to see you tonight. Never again, pray God, will we be parted this way. Come up here as soon as you can. He [Gerry] has gone back to Rhode Island."

Had Welles known of a private talk between Hughes and Grew while he was in Paris, his hopes would have sunk. Alvey A. Adee, the venerable assistant Secretary of State, had just died, and Hughes was considering a successor. He had been hoping, he told Grew, to appoint a "former diplomatic officer" who was a specialist in Latin American affairs and, as such, would be of great help to him. Two reasons made it impossible. The officer in question—undoubtedly Welles—had recently been divorced under "unfortunate" circumstances and had, apparently, offended a cabinet wife by an act she considered discourteous. Hughes feared she might fight the appointment.[13]

The circumstances of Welles's divorce were widely known, but the identity of the aggrieved cabinet wife remains a mystery. Rumors circulating at the time suggest that Welles had angrily refuted aspersions cast at an official function against his friend Pulliam by the wife of Senator Charles Curtis, a powerful Kansas Republican. Curtis had been maneuvering to replace the honest, able Pulliam with a Kansas crony, and Welles had blocked it. Curtis was not actually in the cabinet (he became Vice-President in the succeeding Hoover administration) but, as a friend of Coolidge and a Senate leader with twenty-two years of seniority, he was a dangerous enemy—as Welles would soon discover.

Christmas 1924 marked a new low for Welles and Mathilde. He was ill again, back in the hands of his New York doctors, and Mathilde was imploring him from Washington to "do what the doctors say, *please.*" Her mother and she were still quarreling as the old lady vehemently opposed their being seen together. "If you come back Friday it will be hell again," wrote Mathilde. "She is so cross and horrid." Gerry, meanwhile, had abandoned hope that Mathilde would drop her divorce and had stormed out of his Washington house, preferring to be alone in New York over Christmas. "Our last wretched Christmas on earth," Mathilde wrote Welles. "I can't go back. I decided, yesterday, at his house. It's nearly over, thank God."

Welles had given her for Christmas a black Scottish terrier puppy, Felix. "All I have is Felix for company tonight," she wrote. "His soft black nose near me now. What a Christmas! Peter there alone, too, poor soul. You alone and wretched at the Ritz. I love you."[14]

Early in 1925, while preparing to leave office, Hughes warned Welles that Curtis was still maneuvering to replace Pulliam with his deputy, Thomas Kelly, a Kansas politician of unsavory reputation. Pulliam himself had heard the rumors in Santo Domingo the previous autumn and, after taking the first boat north, had secured interviews with President-elect Coolidge and Hughes. "We are all behind you," Hughes had told him, and Pulliam had returned to Santo Domingo reassured. Curtis, however, had continued his campaign.

At Hughes's suggestion, Welles prepared a memorandum emphasizing Pulliam's experience, his integrity and the support he enjoyed among leading Dominicans. By contrast, he noted, Kelly spoke no Spanish, had neither "experience nor demonstrated capacity" in Customs affairs and was "notoriously intemperate." Moreover, there was evidence that Kelly was offering influential Dominicans patronage plums for their support.

In their final interview, Hughes urged Coolidge to retain Pulliam but then left Welles's damning memorandum for the incoming Secretary of State, his successor, Frank B. Kellogg. Unfamiliar with the case, Kellogg sent it to the White House for Coolidge's routine attention—a blunder that would cost Welles dearly.

Capping four years of tempestuous courtship, Welles and Mathilde were married on June 27, 1925, at Mt. Vernon, then an obscure hamlet twenty miles from New York City, chosen for its very obscurity. Nevertheless, the news appeared the next day on the front page of the *New York Times*.[15] Welles had been planning to take Mathilde, after a brief honeymoon at Atlantic City, to the Dominican Republic where conditions again were deteriorating. Vice-President Velasquez, passing through Washington, had begged Welles to return and exert his influence on Vasquez to quell mounting disorder.[16] Grew, weighing a replacement for the ineffectual Russell, had warned Coolidge that the "constructive work accomplished by Sumner Welles will, more than likely, be wrecked unless a firm hand is on the throttle."[17]

Planning to sail on July 23, Welles drafted a five-point Dominican reconstruction plan, which Kellogg approved before leaving on a short trip, then wrote Dominican friends of his impending arrival. Meticulous, always, in matters of protocol, he drafted a friendly greeting from Coolidge to Vasquez, which Grew sent to the White House for routine approval along with a list of fifteen nominees for the Central American Tribunals of Inquiry, which Welles had helped create at the Central American conference two years earlier. Welles's name headed the list. Coolidge's reply on July 10 came like a thunderbolt.

"I think Mr. Welles better retire from the service," he scrawled over the greeting to Vasquez. Across the list of nominees he wrote: "All O.K. except Sumner Welles. If he is in the government service, let him be dismissed at once. C."[18]

Stunned, Grew kept Coolidge's fiat to himself until Kellogg returned three days later. On July 13 the Secretary called Welles in and broke the news. He could offer no explanation, he said; the President had given him none. Masking his humiliation, Welles dictated a short letter of resignation and a businesslike summary of pending matters for his successor then poured out his feelings in a private letter to his friend and colleague Francis White. "I am bitterly resentful of the treatment meted out to me," he wrote. "The Secretary told me that the whole thing was done quite over his head and without his knowledge—but, even so, when I remember the work I have done for the present Chief Executive during the past three years and the flattering commendation he has, personally, given me, the whole thing seems pretty raw—but so the world goes."[19] Six weeks later arrived a typewritten note from the summer White House at Swampscott, Massachusetts. Signed Calvin Coolidge, it thanked Welles for "very efficient and valuable" services.

Coolidge's curt dismissal of Welles remains a mystery. Dominican friends wrote Welles soon after that Kelly had been brandishing a letter from Curtis boasting that he [Curtis] had persuaded Coolidge to "refuse [Welles] any further appointment in the government service." Dana G. Munro, Welles's colleague, however, discounted the story. Munro had been on leave at the time and had learned of Welles's dismissal only on his return. Years later he wrote the author that it was "highly unlikely that Coolidge would have dismissed a distinguished public servant because Senator Curtis asked him to."

The real reason, Munro suspected, was Welles's highly publicized divorce and remarriage to Mathilde Gerry. "The public attitude toward divorce was somewhat different in 1925," he wrote. "The Coolidges were conservative people [and] there must have been a good deal of feeling in the Senate."[20] Munro's analysis is supported by an entry at the time in the diary of the former Republican Under Secretary of State, William R. Castle, who detested Welles. "I cannot but applaud the move," wrote Castle, "although, I think it should have come before, rather than after, he married the woman. Probably, the press printed lurid accounts of the wedding which the President saw."[21]

A brief epilogue followed. Months later Grew confided to Welles that he and Kellogg still hoped to bring him back to the department as Assistant Secretary for Latin America, and Welles's hopes soared. It was "exactly the type of work I am most interested in," he wrote Grew. Weeks passed, however, and Welles's inquiries invariably brought the same answer: Coolidge was proving "reluctant." Baffled and depressed, Welles turned to his former Under Secretary, Norman H. Davis. "No charges of any sort—so far as I know—have been made against me," he wrote. Grew himself had confirmed it. Would Davis intercede with his banking partner, Dwight D. Morrow, a close friend of Coolidge?[22] Davis did his best.

Morrow thought Welles "unusually well-qualified," he wrote back, but had made it a cardinal rule never to offer Coolidge advice. Perhaps former Secretary Hughes could help. At Davis's request, Hughes wrote Kellogg, citing Welles's dejection and suggesting that he "ought not to suffer for [his] opposition to Kelly."[23] Kellogg's answer, drafted but never sent, was found in his papers after his death. He still did not know what had motivated Coolidge, he wrote Hughes, and would try to find out. But Welles's marriage, he noted, had "come to Coolidge's attention and you know how particular he is about such things." Across the unsent draft a Kellogg aide had written: "Secretary talked to Mr. Hughes on the telephone, June 15, 1926, about the attached correspondence and he, Mr. Hughes, decided to do nothing about it."[24]

At thirty-four, Welles's contempt for convention had ended his spectacular career.

ELEVEN

IN THE POLITICAL WILDERNESS

1927–1928

Renewed Contact with FDR

TOO PROUD TO COMPLAIN, unable to explain, Welles booked passage to Europe for himself, Mathilde and the children. There, far from Washington, he could decide his future. Coolidge had expelled him from government but "I fully intend to return, if possible . . . some time in the future," he wrote Rowe.[1] Eight years, in fact, would pass before Franklin D. Roosevelt called him back to office. Meanwhile, he faced idleness.

He wrote Christian A. Herter, coeditor of a Boston weekly, *The Independent,* before sailing and proposed a series on Latin America, but Herter thought his readers likely to be "apathetic" unless it involved an attack on U.S. imperialism. Could Welles "strain his conscience and . . . ideas of good taste" by a rousing criticism of American schools and colleges for ignoring Latin American history?"[2] The issue was so important, Welles wrote back, that he would not have the "slightest reluctance" to strain his conscience or good taste to win public attention. He promised an outline in two weeks; but nothing came of it.[3]

The European trip set a pattern for summer vacations virtually every year until World War II. After a ritual week at the Paris Ritz, Welles and the family set out in chauffeured limousines for Munich, the Bavarian capital, where Welles's spirits slowly rose amid the German art and music he had loved since childhood. Each morning, Baedeker guide book in hand, he set off with his children to tour museums, churches and palaces, practicing his German wherever possible.

The summer's highlight for his sons came one afternoon when a burly Bavarian in lederhosen and Alpine hat with badger-hair brush appeared in their hotel sitting room. Unshouldering a felt bag, he dropped onto the sofa a dachshund puppy, which yapped and raced behind chairs as the boys pursued it. Frisky and fearless, it was named Schnitzel and became the family idol— notwithstanding its delight in gnawing books, Mathilde's handbags and Welles's bedroom slippers. At times, his patience exhausted and deaf to family protests, Welles administered a slap or two on Schnitzel's rump, but, like all dachshunds, the dog proved virtually immune to correction.

In September the family moved to Carlsbad, the fashionable Czechoslovak health spa, where Mathilde lay packed in medicinal mud each morning, emerging to sip the curative waters while Welles led his sons on brisk mountain walks, teaching them German jingles and raising his hat to a dignified fellow stroller: Dr. Thomas Masaryk, the "father" of Czechoslovakia.

His resignation, he wrote despondently to Frederick J. Stimson, his former chief in the Argentine, had left him with "no plans other than those dependent on my wife's health. . . . We manage to get in some bridge . . . I have a dachshund, six months old which, in figure, reminds me of [the portly French Field Marshal] Joffre."[4]

To kill time, at summer's end, after returning his sons to their mother, Welles set out for Egypt with Mathilde, where they rented a Nile houseboat and visited Luxor, Karnak, Thebes, Dendereh and the pyramids near Cairo. "For the last three months I have been getting over various ailments," he wrote Endicott Peabody. The Egyptian sun had done them both good, and they planned to return home via Paris in time for Christmas.[5] Mrs. Townsend was in Paris awaiting them and, overjoyed by her daughter's safe return from the imagined perils of the Middle East, impulsively presented her with a diamond and emerald bracelet—a harbinger of bad luck.

On the journey home, Welles suffered a heart attack in mid-Atlantic. On reaching New York, he was taken by stretcher to a hotel, where he convalesced over Christmas and New Year's. Mathilde, meanwhile, had failed to declare her bracelet to Customs and was fined $5,250 ($42,000 in today's terms). Thanks to the intervention of a family friend, Ogden Mills, Assistant Secretary of the Treasury, it was later halved on the specious plea that Mathile, distraught over her husband's illness, had confused "bought" with "brought" on her Customs declaration.

Except for their marriage, 1925 had been a miserable year for them both. Ill, idle and depressed, Welles was now entering on a savagely self-destructive period: drinking with shady cronies and frequenting "speakeasies," or drinking clubs, illegal in that age of prohibition. He also involved himself in a tasteless quarrel with his elderly father, precipitating a break that lasted until the older man's death in 1936, ten years later. Sumner, by chance, had learned through his ultra-respectable brother-in-law, Harry Pelham Robbins, that his father had begun a liaison in Paris some years earlier with a French actress, Lili Greuse. Lonely since the death of Sumner's mother fourteen years earlier, he had continued meeting Mme. Greuze on his annual summer visits to Paris and in New York, where she occasionally performed. Robbins had cited rumors of a financial settlement—and, possibly, a secret marriage.

"The poor old gentleman had every right to do as he chose, even if it did involve money which his family were waiting to inherit," Gammell observed long after. "The lady in question was an actress of some standing. . . . They reputedly lived in adjoining rooms at the St. Regis Hotel where they very correctly always entered by separate doors . . . Marriage was never contemplated. Had he made such a 'mésalliance,' he would no longer have been invited by New York's leading dowagers to the stuffy dinners that constituted his only activity in life and the rightful heirs would have been even worse off."[6]

Sumner reacted harshly nonetheless, engaging a Paris lawyer, Maître Adrien de Pachmann, and writing: "The interests of my sister and myself, my sister's child and my own two children . . . are . . . involved." Pachmann was to hire a discreet detective agency and ascertain the facts. By demanding a large down payment, Pachmann saved the day. Robbins hastily withdrew, leaving Sumner to drop the sordid investigation himself soon after. How much his father knew of it is unclear; but Sumner was ill-placed at the time to offer him moral advice.

They were poles apart, father and son. Sumner was steel beneath the surface charm, intolerant of the least criticism of his personal conduct. His father, by contrast, was benevolent and mild until outraged by any flouting of the rules of the society into which he had been born. On the "Three D's" that ruled his life—dining, dress and deportment—there could be no compromise. Sumner's desertion of the blameless Esther and his marriage to a divorcée eight years his senior had violated the principles expected of a gentleman. Loyal to Esther, his father, deaf to Sumner's furious protests, refused to meet Mathilde. The final break came August 20, 1926.

Sumner received a letter with no salutation. "I think it only fair to advise you," it began coldly, "that I have been compelled to make changes in the disposition of my estate." Sumner was being disinherited. Among the many "hard things" his son had forced him to endure was the "impossibility of complying with the wishes of my mother [née Katherine Schermerhorn] regarding the family estate at Islip. When you finally come to a realization of what you have done," wrote his father, "I shall feel sorry for you—deserting your father in his old age when he needs a son's help, depriving your children of the happy childhood to which they are entitled and which your father and mother labored to secure for you. Alas," he concluded, "this may come too late to secure the forgiveness of Your Father."[7]

Analyzing Welles's character at that time, Gammell remembered a "steadily decreasing sense of responsibility toward those bound to him by affection or family ties whenever these interfered with his increasingly powerful drives." Gammell and Welles often had berated each other as young men, and Gammell had made no secret of his disapproval of Welles's desertion of Esther and his marriage to Mathilde. Starting in 1924-25, he remembered, "I felt I was on dangerous ground. Sumner destroyed my letters without reading them, assuming they contained criticism of his conduct. With most of us, it is, precisely, interlocking obligations which keep us, more or less, on the tracks as we flounder through life. We don't want our behaviour to repercuss adversely on those who care."

The death of Sumner's mother during his freshman year at Harvard removed the greatest restraining influence on him, Gammell remembered, and, soon after, his conduct began changing radically. His callousness grew steadily into the "utter ruthlessness" of his latter years when it combined with a sadistic element that alienated his male friends. The combination, Gammell thought, should have evoked "pity and compassion, leading to forgiveness in friends who knew his superb qualities of heart and mind. Instead, it gave his compulsive lapses a strangely repelling character. He never, after these nineteen-twenties, faced them with shame, humility and regret, as most of us do."[8]

By mid-January of 1926, Welles had recovered sufficiently to return to Washington. The New York Guaranty Trust, on Norman Davis's recommendation, suggested that he represent them in Latin America, and his hopes soared—only to fall. Because of his recent heart attack, his doctors forbade full-time work for at least six months. "Nothing would have been more attractive to me," Welles wrote Davis dejectedly; the position might have led to "exceedingly successful" results.[9]

Barred from government by Coolidge and from banking by his doctors, he turned to writing. He had begun weighing a book on U.S. Caribbean policy during his illness and, meanwhile, Herter was still interested in a series on Latin America—although he warned that it was "terrifically difficult" to interest readers in the subject.[10] Welles decided to focus instead on the subject he knew best: the Dominican Republic. Admittedly of limited interest, if handled well it could provide him a platform for condemning past policies, proposing alternatives and keeping his name before the public. Secretary Kellogg granted him access to State Department files, and he wrote a colleague in Madrid for relevant Spanish documents.[11] The bulk of his research, however, would have to be done in Santo Domingo, so he notified Dominican friends of his impending arrival and sailed with Mathilde in March. The sight of the familiar Dominican shore was balm to his ego.

President Vasquez, delighted to welcome back his young American friend and meet his new wife, tendered them a formal reception; Vice-President Velasquez held a garden party. Coolidge's new minister, Evan Young, however, remained at arm's length, cabling the department rumors that Welles had arrived on a "secret mission" to oust Vasquez and replace him with Velasquez, who was allegedly more amenable to Wall Street loans. The department stiffly denied the rumors.[12]

Back among old friends and warmed by Dominican hospitality, Welles amassed documents and interviewed local dignitaries, particularly Vasquez, whose recollections ran back to the 1880s. Working with characteristic energy, he completed his research in three weeks and, before sailing home, bought a small beach property at Boca Chica, a palm-fringed resort near the capital, where he and Mathilde could escape Washington's dreary winters.[13] Their dream faded, however, when the Dominican dictator, Rafael Trujillo Molina, seized their property four years later without compensation.

Rumors pursued Welles even as he sailed away. His "research," it was whispered, had merely been cover for his plot to replace Vasquez with Velasquez. Welles's visit, Young cabled the department darkly, had been "highly unfortunate."[14]

Once home, Welles settled quickly into the discipline of writing, concentrating exclusively on his book for the next sixteen months, in Washington or Bar Harbor, Maine, where he and Mathilde summered. Each morning at nine-thirty, he would begin dictating to Louise Clarkson. "He had notes on his desk but there would be no interruptions until luncheon, at one o'clock," she remembered. "He was the only man I've ever known who knew what he wanted to say—and said it without changing a word."[15] His goal, he wrote Henry Kittredge Norton, a friend and fellow-specialist on Latin America, was not the "average, detailed" history of the Dominican Republic but, rather, to awaken American opinion to the "astonishingly, disproportionately large" role the little Caribbean nation had played in U.S. hemisphere policy. During Grant's administration, and on repeated subsequent occasions—"some heretofore confidential"—the United States had contemplated establishing a protectorate or annexing the Dominican Republic outright.[16]

Welles took his title, *Naboth's Vineyard,* from a dramatic Senate debate in 1870 when his collateral ancestor, Senator Charles Sumner of Massachusetts, chairman of the Foreign Relations Committee, had blocked President Grant from buying the Dominican Republic as a naval base. Citing the biblical legend of Naboth, the Jezreelite whom King Ahab had stoned to death for refusing to sell him his vineyard,[17] Senator Sumner had thundered: "All that is implied in good neighborhood—this we must give freely; but their independence is as precious to them as ours is to us and it is placed under the safeguard of natural laws which we cannot violate with impunity."[18] Faced by Charles Sumner's moral wrath, Grant had backed down.

By mid-1927, Welles had completed *Naboth's Vineyard* and was ready for another European vacation. None of the publishers whom Henry Norton had recommended proved receptive to a two-volume tome of limited interest until finally Payson & Clarke, a London house, accepted it, and Welles left the manuscript with them. The day before sailing, on running into Albert Stagg, a young Anglo-Ecuadorean whose family he knew and who was at loose ends in New York, Welles engaged him on the spot as a summer tutor for his sons and someone with whom he could converse in Spanish.

Mathilde and her mother spent their days in Paris at the dressmakers, returning exhausted and dining in dressing gowns in their hotel sitting room. Bored and restless, Welles found Stagg an ideal companion with whom to tour the night spots. Night after night, after putting the boys to bed, the two sallied forth in top hats, white ties and tails, de rigueur evening wear at the time.

Paris in 1927 was alive with sophisticated entertainment. Mistinguette was starring at the Foliès Bergeres; Fred Waring, his band and the Dolly sisters at Les Ambassadeurs. A visit by the American Negro Dance Company two years earlier had started the rage for black entertainers. Josephine Baker was appearing nightly at the Bal Tabarin and "Bricktop," another black American artiste, was packing the house at Chez Florence. Parisians were flocking to the Bal Negre in the rue Blomet, the Harlem of Paris, learning the Charleston, the shimmy and the beguine. Negro nightclubs, such as the Boule Blanche and the Cabane Cubaine, were springing up around Montmartre and Montparnasse. Limousines "disgorged elegant society neurotics avid to throw themselves into the arms of handsome, athletic Senegalese, Antillean, Guinean or Sudanese men," wrote one observer.[19]

For Welles, the nightly forays with Stagg were an intoxicating release, and, predictably, excess fed on excess. Emerging from an erotic "exhibition" in a gilded bordello early one morning, they saw emerging ahead of them a former New York police commissioner and one-time Groton master who knew them both. Fortunately, he failed to spot them, and for days they chuckled over the close call. Meanwhile, Mathilde and her mother seemed unaware of—or indifferent to—the nocturnal ramblings of Welles and his children's tutor.

The summer was over and, at thirty-five, Welles was still idle. For the next six years, he sought a variety of outlets for his energies. He joined the Council on Foreign Relations, the Academy of Political Science and the Foreign Policy Association. He followed hemisphere developments, subscribed to Latin American journals and kept up a running correspondence with Latin American diplomats and State Department friends. He built a country estate, entered Maryland politics and, most important, renewed contact with an old friend and rising Democratic politician, Franklin D. Roosevelt.

On returning from Europe, Welles had been dismayed by Coolidge's disastrous policy in Latin America. In the two years since Welles's resignation, Coolidge had embroiled the United States in an angry quarrel with Mexico and had landed 5,000 marines in Nicaragua. A young guerrilla chief, Augusto Cesar Sandino, was leading armed resistance, casualties were mounting on both sides and criticism of the United States was rising at home and abroad. The Hughes-Welles policy of close inter-American cooperation had been abandoned for the failed tactics of the past: armed intervention and moralizing. Welles began turning from the Republican orthodoxy of his youth to the Democratic Party as the sole hope of reversing Coolidge's ruinous course.

The Foreign Policy Association invited him to attack Coolidge's Latin American policy at a forum that autumn but, though tempted, he declined. Hughes had recently been named U.S. delegate to an inter-American conference opening shortly at Havana,[20] and Welles suspected that the United States would come under sharp attack there for its Nicaraguan intervention. To denounce the administration as Hughes was setting out would give the country's critics ammunition and jeopardize Hughes's chances of success. Instead, he laid out his policy ideas in a closely reasoned letter to Olivia (Mrs. Henry) James, an old friend and Foreign Policy Association official.

The American people were not "imperialistic" as many Latin Americans, and some North Americans, had charged, he wrote her. Once convinced of the importance of U.S.–Latin American ties, the American people would "force" their government to adopt consistent political, economic and intellectual policies. The United States admittedly had treaty responsibilities in certain "turbulent" republics where it could not tolerate conditions that might force it to intervene. But the bland assumption that the Monroe Doctrine had somehow made the Central American and Caribbean republics U.S. "protectorates" guaranteed their hostility. The United States was still treating Latin America as a closed market for its exports while barring Latin imports. Meanwhile, American scientists, artists and scholars knew little of what their Latin American counterparts were doing—and vice versa.

U.S. goals in Latin America could not be achieved by armed intervention or military occupation, Welles maintained, but rather by fostering economic prosperity, education and constitutional rule. It might take years but it was practicable, and the continuation of the United States as a great power, spiritually and materially, depended largely on its accomplishment.[21]

Early in 1928, concerned that Coolidge's policy would isolate the United States at Havana, Welles called on his old friend Franklin Roosevelt in New York. They had not seen each other for many years although their ties were close. In 1904 Welles, then twelve, had served as a page at Franklin's marriage to his cousin, Eleanor. In 1915, as Assistant Secretary of the Navy, FDR had sponsored Sumner's entry into the diplomatic service. "I had just passed my examinations . . . was living in Washington and saw a great deal of him," Welles remembered years later. "He was enthusiastic, enjoyed dinners at the Chevy Chase club and . . . a good time."[22] In 1920, when FDR ran as the Democratic vice-presidential candidate and Welles was directing Latin American affairs, their contacts resumed. Few knew better than Roosevelt the importance of peace in the Caribbean-Central American arc near the new Panama canal.

After FDR's polio attack in 1921, Welles asked to visit him, but Roosevelt was seeing only a handful of intimates at the time and declined. Two years later, during Welles's Dominican mission, he asked again and, this time, FDR agreed. Welles found a dramatic change. "It was exactly as if all trivialities in life had been burned [out] in him," he recalled. "A steel had entered his soul; he never made any reference to his tragedy. He was tremendously interested in Santo Domingo and reminded me that he had been there in 1918. We talked a lot about the country. He told me how absorbed he was by what was going on in the world . . . asking me to give him ideas. From then on, our contact was never broken."[23]

Arriving at Roosevelt's New York townhouse that wintry morning, Welles found him absorbed with his coming race for the New York governorship and with overall Democratic prospects for the 1928 presidential campaign. Welles's criticism of Coolidge's Latin American policy struck FDR as good campaign material, and he asked him to put his ideas on paper. Soon after he received a "Dear Franklin" letter highlighting three areas for attack: armed intervention in Nicaragua, high tariffs that excluded Latin imports, and the need for a "preventive policy . . . which suggests rather than commands."[24] Thanking Welles for an "interesting and constructively useful" set of ideas, FDR passed them to the Democratic standard-bearer, Governor Alfred E. "Al" Smith of New York, who, FDR wrote Welles later, had been "impressed."[25]

FDR next asked Welles to assess the Havana conference that had just opened. "Send me a line to Warm Springs, Ga.," he wrote.[26] Hughes had scored a personal success by blocking an anti-U.S. resolution, Welles wrote back, but the "palpitating" issue of armed intervention had merely been postponed, not resolved. The Latin Americans might hesitate to attack the United States, publicly, but the danger lay in "latent hostility," which would fester until the United States treated its neighbors along "strict lines of procedure": that is, consultation, not marines.[27] Welles's views were apparently hitting home, for FDR asked him next to confer with Judge Joseph Proskauer, a Smith advisor who had begun assembling planks for the Democratic platform.

That summer FDR incorporated Welles's ideas in an article that appeared under his own name in *Foreign Affairs* quarterly on the eve of the Democratic convention. Entitled "Our Foreign Policy: A Democratic View," the passage on Latin America was vintage Welles. If a sister nation fell on evil days and needed a temporary "helping hand" to end disorder and eliminate bad government, wrote FDR, the United States had "neither the right nor the duty to intervene, alone." By enlisting the cooperation of others, the United States would have "more order in the Hemisphere, and less dislike."[28] After publication, Welles congratulated Roosevelt with a twinge of parental pride, regretting only that he had not also called for an "intelligent downward" cut in U.S. tariffs. Roosevelt, in fact, had; but Smith, fearing protectionist outcries, had persuaded him to drop it. Increasingly caught up in the campaign, Welles offered to "contribute and work for [Smith's] election, speak at any time and in any place."[29] A Democratic victory, he wrote an Argentine friend, might "radically change U.S. policy in Latin America."[30]

The publication of *Naboth's Vineyard* that summer boosted Welles's stock as an authority on the Western Hemisphere. Former Secretary of State Hughes wrote congratulating him, complaining only that he had "underplayed" his own role. Arthur Bullard, former chief of the State Department's Russian division, wrote Sir Eric Drummond, Secretary General of the League of Nations, that Welles was "almost the only Gringo who could have carried it off with such a high degree of objectivity and authority."[31] Raymond Leslie Buell, reviewing Welles's book in the *New York Herald-Tribune,* thought its chief merit lay in its "frank criticism of the Latin American policy of the U.S. in which the author has been so intimately associated."

Some critics scored Welles's massive, two-volume tome for its use of privileged departmental records; others for minimizing sociological and economic factors.[32] The *New Republic* accused him of overlooking an axiom of foreign policy: that the United States should "never help collect the private debts of its nationals." Rounding indignantly on liberal "theorists," Welles wrote a colleague that unless the United States backed its businessmen, hemisphere trade would end up in the hands of Europeans or American "speculators and usurers, demanding exorbitant profits for their risks."[33] Some even accused Welles of being "anti-Negro," citing his vivid description of Toussaint L'Ouverture, the Haitian tyrant, who had led a bloodthirsty invasion of Santo Domingo in 1801:

Picture him as he rode through the narrow streets, followed by his numerous aides-de-camp, decked out with as much gold lace as they could muster, bearing themselves, like their leader, with simian self-importance.

All of the officers . . . were powdered and queued like their commanding general, and attempted to ape the expression of pompous determination depicted on the countenance of Toussaint, which, in his case, his noticeably prognathous jaw rendered easy. Behind him the common soldiers straggled, dressed in rags or in any incongruous garments they had been able to lay their hands on during the march, and brandishing a strangely assorted variety of weapons, ranging from the moreusual machete to the rare matchlock.[34]

Welles summarized his policy views in his final chapter. The United States, he charged, had "floundered too long between the sane and salutary, on one hand, and blustering intimidation on the other." If armed intervention was inescapable, at times, to preserve hemisphere peace, why should the United States incur "odium and suspicion" by itself? Why should the other American republics not share in the task of maintaining order when their own interests were involved?

If the United States hoped to live with peaceful, prosperous, law-abiding neighbors, it could not "stand aloof watching revolutions develop then hurrying, belatedly, to quell them by the rifles of American Marines." Preventive diplomacy meant cutting tariffs; fostering economic prosperity; offering financial, technical and educational aid; in short, promoting well-being. If the United States was to remain a great nation, its strength and support lay in the Western Hemisphere.[35]

Welles was a lonely prophet, crying into the wind in 1928, yet his book rode the crest of a wave. Thoughtful Americans, among them Franklin D. Roosevelt, were beginning to question failed Republican policies: armed intervention, high tariffs and moralizing. By praising Hughes's enlightened policy, Welles had avoided charges of narrow partisanship while providing the Democrats with campaign ammunition.

As the contest gathered speed, Roosevelt asked Welles to discuss speaking engagements with his wife, Eleanor, and with Senator Millard Tydings (D.-Md.) and also suggested that he try his hand at a "somewhat spectacular" campaign pamphlet to be entitled: "The Crime Against Our American Neighbors." The spectacular not being Welles's forte, he produced instead a twenty-four-page indictment of the GOP's Latin American policy that Eleanor Roosevelt thought the "best thing" on the subject she had ever read.[36] Her influence was growing and her support of her lifelong friend Sumner would later play an important role in his career.

One recommendation, especially, may have appealed to her and her husband. The cardinal need in American foreign policy, Welles had written, was "humanity . . . comprehension, willingness to make allowances for prejudices and weaknesses . . . the sincere wish to 'do unto others as you would wish to be done by.'"[37] Such sentiments might have seemed mawkish to some at the time, but not necessarily so to Franklin and Eleanor Roosevelt, both of whom had been reared, like Welles, in the Christian precepts embodied by the Reverend Endicott Peabody of Groton. The point, however, was moot.

Herbert Hoover crushed Al Smith at the polls that autumn though Roosevelt, breasting a Republican wave, slipped into the New York governorship by a razor-thin margin: 25,371 votes out of 4,234,822 cast. His victory alone alleviated Welles's gloom. "If anyone can hold the Democratic Party together," Welles wrote him prophetically, "that man is you."[38]

With Smith's defeat, Roosevelt had become, overnight, the leading contender for the 1932 Democratic nomination and, very likely, the presidency. Welles, while heartened, was cautious. His dismissal by Coolidge three years earlier had taught him a bitter lesson: Without a political base and allies of his own, his return to government would remain hostage to the whims of others. He and FDR were old friends—but Welles's hopes of office would depend on his help in electing Roosevelt.

Ever since his humiliating dismissal, Welles had contemplated moving from the (then) voteless District of Columbia, establishing a residence in nearby Maryland, entering local politics and, eventually, running for the Senate. On returning from Europe in late 1927, he and Mathilde had bought 250 acres overlooking the Potomac River at Oxon Hill, Maryland, a half hour's drive from Washington. Roosevelt's surprise victory in New York clinched his decision. He would build a political machine, work full time for FDR's election and await his own reward.

Construction of a house began in 1928. Virtually every day for the next year, Welles and Mathilde drove out each morning to supervise a small army of workmen digging foundations, laying brick, hammering beams, gouging a swimming pool out of the red earth behind plodding mule teams or hacking bridle paths through woods and meadows that ran down to the river. No expense was spared. Jules Henri de Sibour, a prominent Washington architect, was commissioned to design the manor house, and Ellen Payson Shipman, a leading New York landscape architect, to lay out the grounds.

Welles's early architectural training and passion for horticulture found full scope. In shirtsleeves, he hammered stakes to mark garden boundaries, paths or sites for hardy perennials as Mathilde swung in a hammock, chain-smoking and offering advice. By June 1929, at an estimated cost of $250,000 ($2.1 million in today's terms), Oxon Hill was ready for occupancy and the family and staff, ferried out from Washington in limousines and station wagons, moved in.

Oxon Hill was a showplace. One entered the estate through huge, antique wrought-iron gates bought in Charleston, South Carolina, then followed a gravel drive that wound a mile or more past meadows where horses and cattle grazed and past groves of trees through which the Potomac glimmered in the distance. Each spring white narcissus, gold jonquils and yellow daffodils carpeted the grounds as far as the eye could see. The Georgian colonial manor house, a two-story structure of red brick with white trim, crowned an eminence with a view across the river from Alexandria to Mt. Vernon on the Virginia side.

The entrance hall, of black-and-white marble, opened into a drawing room the width of the house decorated with Adam friezes, gray-green walls and parquet floors. Next came a pine-paneled library, hung in rose-red drapes, and then a dining room, seating forty, done in Chinese yellow with drapes of pale apricot and a blue Oriental rug. A ten-foot Coromandel screen dominated one end. Weather permitting, the family and guests gathered outside in wicker sofas and chairs on a broad brick terrace shaded from the sun by a huge striped awning. Flagstone steps led gently down to a swimming pool in a wide lawn beyond which, hidden by trees, lay the superintendent's cottage, a five-car garage, riding stables, kitchen gardens and chicken coops. Twelve servants attended the family inside the manor while eight "outside" hands drove up each morning in ancient Fords or Chevrolets to tend the grounds, feed the cows and chickens and hack honeysuckle from the bridle paths.

It was, in every sense, a seignorial estate, and Welles was in his element: the squire on his domain, inspecting his acres cane in hand, issuing orders, feeding the horses apples or carrots by hand as his dogs crisscrossed busily at his heels. Before breakfast each morning he rode his gray hunter for an hour and, on Sunday afternoons, listened with closed eyes to Beethoven, Brahms, Mozart or Wagner records in his ground-floor study, or "den."

His artist friend Ives Gammell had adorned the walls with pastel murals depicting the Greek legend of Daphnis and Chloe and on his desk stood autographed photographs of his idols, Charles Evans Hughes and FDR. Oxon Hill became Welles's passion and his escape from the pressures of office, especially during the frenzied years of World War II. Few were permitted to disturb him there, and the staff had standing orders to tell all who called, except close friends or government officials, that he and Mathilde were "out."

Diplomatic dinners at Oxon Hill were stately affairs, and visiting dignitaries and Maryland politicians vied for of an invitation. Contrary to rumor, Winston Churchill never saw it, but Foreign Secretary and, later, Prime Minister Anthony Eden dined there before, during and after World War II. While President, FDR himself drove out occasionally on summer afternoons to escape the capital's humidity. Secret Service agents would appear hours in advance and

Welles, tense and businesslike, would stride briskly from room to room, ensuring that all was in order.

The White House convoy eventually would arrive and the President, rolled onto the terrace in his wheelchair by a Secret Serviceman and handed a mint julep, would chat animatedly with Welles and others of his entourage, finally falling silent and refreshing his soul by gazing down on the lovely Potomac at dusk.

TWELVE

THE DAWES MISSION

1929

A Dream in Tatters

IN 1929, WITH OXON HILL COMPLETED, Welles sought a fresh outlet for his energies and soon found one in an economic rescue mission to the Dominican Republic. While visiting the country the previous autumn, he had listened with sinking heart as Vasquez poured out his woes: widespread corruption, the budget overspent by one-third, Customs revenues reserved for debt reduction and Wall Street loans forbidden without U.S. approval. Dismayed by the plight of the little country that he had helped to independence, Welles offered to help and warned Vasquez that "disaster" was imminent unless he sought expert advice.

Upon returning to New York, Welles turned to former Under Secretary Norman H. Davis, pointing out that Vasquez had no one to advise him. Graft was rampant, the executive departments "disorganized" and Dominican budgets "incomprehensible."[1] Welles and Davis agreed that the solution was an advisory mission of the type that Professor Edwin Kemmerer, a noted Princeton economist, had led to several countries facing bankruptcy. Kemmerer was in China and unavailable, and Davis himself was too busy.[2] Welles had an inspiration: Vice President Charles G. Dawes. A prominent Chicago banker, Dawes had served as the first director of the new Bureau of the Budget in 1921, and his reorganization of postwar Germany's shattered finances in 1924 had won him a Nobel Prize. He was about to resign as Vice President to become Hoover's ambassador to the court of St. James and would be free for a few weeks before assuming his new post.

Helped by Davis, Welles turned his powers of persuasion on Dawes and, after three long interviews and a private lunch, cabled Vasquez that the Vice-President had agreed to lead a team of administrators, bankers and businessmen to the Dominican Republic for three weeks. They would pay their own way and accept only living expenses. No economist in the world had "greater prestige," Welles cabled euphorically; Dawes's plan for stabilizing German finances had led to the "current rebirth" of Europe."[3]

Welles sailed with the Dawes mission from New York on March 28, 1929. The brisk, no-nonsense Vice President assured shipboard reporters that this was "no junket"; golf clubs and wives had been banned. Welles, however, having conceived the mission, characteristically assumed that such edicts did not affect him; predictably, Mathilde, her maid, his valet and Miss Clarkson all were on board. Once at sea, Dawes instructed his team to read *Naboth's Vineyard,* copies of which Welles had provided, and divided the group into task forces. Welles, because of his intimate knowledge of Dominican affairs and fluent Spanish, was assigned to government reorganization and named Dawes's official liaison with Vasquez.

Welles and Dawes clashed briefly at the outset over a matter of principle. Welles felt strongly that the Dominican tax structure, which weighed most heavily on the poor, should be reformed. Vasquez, he pointed out, was at the height of his popularity and in control of the legislature. If tax reform was ever to be carried out, now was the time. Dawes, however, argued that tax laws were political issues beyond his scope. His mandate was to reform government machinery, not involve himself in matters of sovereignty. He held to his views and Welles eventually gave way.

Once ashore, the Dawes mission plunged into a work schedule that left the easygoing Dominicans awe-struck. Day after day, on holidays, weekends and often far into the night, Dawes's experts interviewed local officials, pored over Dominican laws and regulations, analyzed fiscal and government records and drafted recommendations as the typewriters of their stenographers clacked relentlessly in the stone corridors of the headquarters. American reporters marveled. "Here were experts who, far from being carpet-baggers or junke-teers," wrote one, "had given up, for a moment, their own important personal affairs and come down to a little tropical country . . . to consider financial obligations which, two or three of them at least, might have discharged by simply reaching down into their own pockets."[4] Mathilde saw little of her husband for he drove himself and his colleagues without respite. One wrote Welles later that he would always treasure their association—although Welles had been "rather a hard task-master about office hours."[5]

The mission finished its work within the stipulated three weeks and, before sailing home, presented Vasquez with 200 pages of detailed recommendations.[6] The Dominican Congress voted Dawes its thanks and a gold medal, and Vasquez cabled Welles, then at sea, that the legislature had approved all major recommendations. No government had ever received "expert advice of this character for so small an amount," Welles wrote an Argentine friend on reaching Washington. The total cost to the Dominican taxpayers "had not exceeded $5,000."[7]

Ironically, the Dawes mission—conceived to save Vasquez's tottering regime—helped seal its doom. The new Budget Bureau, created at Dawes's suggestion and staffed with honest men, uncovered a trail of corruption leading to the sinister army chief, Rafael Trujillo. Knowing his record, Welles detested him. Starting as a constabulary lieutenant and Marine Corps spy during the U.S. occupation (1916-24), Trujillo had wormed his way up the promotion ladder by assiduously courting Vasquez.

In return, when the marines sailed away in 1925, Vasquez had named him colonel commandant of the Dominican Constabulary and, in 1927, when the Constabulary became the Dominican army, its chief of staff with the rank of brigadier general. Trujillo's rise from lieutenant to general in ten years had made him the power in the land. Welles had repeatedly warned Vasquez that to retain him would prove an "utter disaster," but the old cacique, ill and plagued by quarreling subordinates, had procrastinated.[8]

Scornful of rumored plots and supremely confident of his national popularity, he sailed in late 1929 for medical treatment at Johns Hopkins, near Baltimore. Welles drove out virtually daily from Washington to chat with him in Spanish and discuss his problems. Once restored to health, he told Welles, he would return home, run for another term and then, backed by a fresh mandate, begin rooting out Trujillo's corruption. Skeptical, Welles tactfully tried to persuade him to retire with honor, but the old warrior sailed back early in 1930 ready for battle.

"He is beginning to show that tendency to be domineering and querulous, which is characteristic of him when he is feeling well," the U.S. legation cabled Washington. A longtime American resident, Robert D. Crassweller, wrote later that Vasquez "threw himself into his old routine, dining on pork and champagne, holding political conferences at all hours and ordering his colleagues about as if nothing had happened. But the old fire and familiar command had faded and he was hardly equal to strong new challenges."[9]

The strongest of the new challenges was Trujillo's growing power. Sensing it, Welles warned Secretary of State Stimson through Francis White that U.S. treaty obligations—which Welles himself had drafted—might have to be "exercised" if conditions in the Dominican Republic were allowed to deteriorate. Still smarting, however, from the uproar caused by the marine landings in Nicaragua two years earlier, Stimson was in no mood for further entanglements. Time might solve the problem.

On February 23, 1930, while Stimson dozed, Trujillo lunged. Warned of Vasquez's coming corruption investigation, he staged a "rebellion" in the north, crushed it and ousted Vasquez in the process, replacing him with a puppet, Rafael Estrella Urena. "I have never in my life been more thoroughly discouraged," Welles wrote Pulliam. Had Stimson "even desultorily" heeded his warnings, had the U.S. legation "even negatively" supported him, he would not feel that "all the work accomplished since 1922 had. . . gone by the board."[10]

Emboldened by Stimson's hands-off policy, Trujillo shouldered aside Estrella Urena and offered himself to the cowed nation as its next president. Murders, beatings and intimidation increased, and when prominent Dominicans—Vasquez among them—began fleeing to Puerto Rico for their lives, Welles doubled his efforts to persuade Stimson to exert at least "moral pressure" on Trujillo for an honest poll. Frustrated, he wrote Dawes in London, urging that the American legation in Santo Domingo be ordered to "insist" that the coming elections be irreproachable. There might still be time to prevent "conditions which might force the U.S. to intervene."[11]

The United States, Welles wrote Pulliam, had accepted control of Dominican Customs revenues as a "trustee" for the Dominican people and was "morally obliged" to ensure that such funds were entrusted only to a "legitimate, constitutional and properly-elected government." The Dominican Republic was totally dependent on the United States for financing.[12] Determined to arouse American opinion, he persuaded Kent Cooper, general manager of the Associated Press, to send a special correspondent to cover the coming poll because local reporters had fallen "ominously" silent.

Stimson belatedly ordered the American legation to ask Trujillo "in the most friendly spirit" to conduct an honest election, but the fox was being asked to guard the hen-house. The time for preventive diplomacy had passed and, on May 16, Trujillo swept himself into power by more votes than there were voters. He would hold power at gun-point for thirty-one years until his assassination in 1961.

Trujillo's new regime, backed by "illiterates and crooks of the worst sort," as Welles put it, soon began rifling U.S. government premises, including those of the U.S. Receiver General of Customs, in its search for domestic opponents. Welles had been sending letters to Dominican friends via Pulliam's "Receptoria General" for safety's sake and now learned that his letters were being opened—a clear violation of diplomatic immunity.[13] Learning next that Trujillo had approached Washington for a loan, Welles persuaded Drew Pearson, a journalist friend, to visit the Dominican Republic and report. Pearson returned with a chilling series that ran in the *Baltimore Sun,* headlined: "Santo Domingo Under the Sway of Terrorists; All Federal Judges Removed; Eleven Persons Assassinated."[14] The loan was blocked.

Added to Trujillo's reign of terror, fate now dealt the Dominican Republic another crippling blow. On September 22, a hurricane devastated the country, including the vital Customs warehouses. "Destruction on all sides . . . havoc almost beyond belief . . . The house you once occupied completely demolished," Pulliam wrote Welles.[15] Welles rushed food, clothing and medical supplies to the Pulliams but the republic lay in ruins, its light and power system wrecked, crop prices at record lows, the treasury empty.

Six years had passed since Welles had set the Dominicans on the road to independence. Eighteen months had passed since the Dawes mission had drafted a blueprint for stability. The dream now lay in tatters, wrecked by Dominican ineptitude, by nature's own savagery and by Hoover's and Stimson's lethargy.

THIRTEEN

GROWING LINKS WITH FDR

1928–1932

First Clash with the Brain Trust

ROOSEVELT'S RECORD-BREAKING REELECTION as governor of New York in 1930 had made him the Democrat to watch, so Welles eagerly accepted an invitation to bring Mathilde to Albany for the night early in 1931. She declined at the last minute, owing to her mother's illness, but Welles went alone, using the occasion to discuss the coming presidential campaign with Roosevelt's closest confidant, Louis Howe. A year earlier Welles had begun a private journal that, although discursive (the index alone covers eight typewritten pages), provides a unique record of his contacts and conversations with FDR and his circle while awaiting his own return to government.

Howe, he wrote, was "over sixty . . . an extreme sufferer from asthma, living apparently on black coffee and cigarettes. He had hardly known . . . a night's sleep for months. As early as 1916, [he] had decided that Roosevelt would be the 1932 Democratic candidate and had concentrated, totally, thereafter on that goal. More than any other individual, Howe had been responsible for FDR's rally after his 1921 polio attack and for his determination to return to public life."[1] Howe and Welles were gauging each other that evening—apparently favorably, for two years later Howe would persuade FDR to ignore a whispering campaign launched by Welles's enemies to bar him from the New Deal.

FDR took Welles to his upstairs study after dinner where the two discussed domestic politics, the Maryland situation and world—especially Latin American—affairs until 2 A.M. The governor's ideas were "eminently sound," Welles noted, although he had not "kept himself thoroughly familiar" with developments overseas.[2] That night the Western hemisphere was much on their minds.

A week earlier Secretary of State Stimson, addressing the Council on Foreign Relations in New York, had denounced Woodrow Wilson's policy of refusing recognition to revolutionary Latin America governments until legitimized by free elections. The United States, declared Stimson, would no longer "propagate democratic institutions" in Latin America but, instead, would revert to the policy in existence from George Washington to William Howard Taft (1909-13). Henceforth it would recognize any government demonstrating control of its territory, respect for its debts and the "acquiescence" of its people."[3]

How was "acquiescence" to be proved without free elections? FDR and Welles, Wilsonians both, shared the late President's passionate conviction that the United States had a "moral duty" to promote democracy below the Rio Grande. The United States was "more than a friend of constitutional government," Wilson had proclaimed on taking office in 1913. "We are its champions."[4] Soon after he had told a visiting British statesman, former Prime Minister Arthur James Balfour, that he intended to "teach the South American republics to elect good men."[5] On his renomination in 1916, he had further declared that the United States would "refuse the hand of welcome to anyone obtaining power in a sister republic by treachery and violence."[6] With these sentiments, Welles and FDR profoundly agreed.

Stimson's new policy was an expedient for recognizing dictators, Welles warned FDR; only free elections could deter revolutions and promote hemisphere stability. In full agreement, Roosevelt suggested that a prominent Democrat issue a "reasoned and detailed" reply to Stimson and told Welles that former Under Secretary Norman H. Davis had already telephoned him to denounce Stimson's new course. Welles proposed that Davis be given the task and, when FDR concurred, wrote Davis a week later urging him to denounce Stimson's "cynical and negative" policy in an article for *Foreign Affairs* quarterly. He would be "only too happy," he added, to help in research or in preparing a draft.[7]

Davis chose a draft, so on April 6, Welles sent him a 12,000-word exposition of "my own faith as regards our dealings with Latin America." Davis thought it a more "thorough" analysis of Latin American policy than he had ever seen but warned that the editor, Hamilton Fish Armstrong, had stipulated 6,000 words.[8] Cut by half—and thus measurably improved—Welles's article appeared in the July, 1931, issue under Davis's name.

Since the start of Stimson's new policy, Welles pointed out, seven revolutions had erupted in Latin America—more than in any comparable period in history. Was it mere coincidence? Automatic recognition involved "greater intervention" in a country's affairs than withholding it as recognition enabled a dictatorship to secure Wall Street loans, "which may be all that it needs to maintain itself in power . . . through force, or corruption, and against the popular will."

The hostility, suspicion and fear of the United States found throughout Latin America sprang from three causes: the assertion of the U.S. "right" to intervene by force; the protectionist Smoot-Hawley tariff passed by the Republican-controlled Congress the year before; and, finally, the U.S. failure to consult Latin American republics about the "interpretation and enforcement" of the Monroe Doctrine.

The Monroe Doctrine barred foreign powers from intervening on the American continent to collect overdue debts but, Welles argued, "justice [demands] that reasonable grounds for such intervention be eliminated." The United States should prevent conditions such as these from arising in the first place. Failure to take "preventive, corrective" measures such as tariff cuts had led the United States to intervene repeatedly by force in Central America and the Caribbean without "permanent benefit" to the United States or to the peoples involved. American marines had been stationed in Nicaragua for twenty-one years "yet today Nicaragua is politically less stable and economically less advanced than almost any other country on the continent."

If the United States was forced, in an emergency, to resort to "single-handed" intervention in a Latin American republic, it should do so only after the "fullest and frankest" consultations with its Latin neighbors. The safety of the Panama Canal was vital to the United States but was also of intimate concern to the Latin American republics and depended on their goodwill. The United States should invite its sister republics to proclaim the Monroe Doctrine a "cardinal principle" of their own national policies, thus giving them a stake in continental defense and reducing fear of Yankee domination.

Misinterpretation of U.S. aims would no longer continue as a "festering sore," Welles concluded. The time had come for a new hemisphere policy and for "a leader convinced of its immediate necessity and immense importance to the future security of the American people." For Welles, that leader was Franklin D. Roosevelt.

The "Davis" article won wide approval. The Diplomatic Corps, the Latin American press and State Department correspondents praised its call for a new hemisphere policy, and Welles accepted Davis's name on his own ideas philosophically, realizing that they would thus receive a far wider audience.

Davis was soon mentioned as a future Democratic Secretary of State and told Welles it was a position he wanted. If appointed, he said, he would want Welles as his Under Secretary. Welles, although flattered, was skeptical. "If my obtaining that position depended upon his being appointed Secretary," he wrote warily in his journal, "my chances would probably be remote . . . [as] Franklin would feel under greater obligation to various other leaders of the party."[9] Events would prove him right.

Mathilde's mother, Mrs. Richard Townsend, died in March, 1931, while Welles was drafting the "Davis" article, and the full force of Mathilde's grief fell on Sumner. Deeply fond of the little tyrant, whom he invariably addressed with Victorian gallantry as "Dearest Mama," or "Dearest," Welles had joined Mathilde at her mother's bedside for months at day's end, soothing the old lady's fears and hearing out her grumbles. She, in turn, had come to rely increasingly on him to control her headstrong daughter. In her will she left Welles $50,000 and the rest of her vast fortune in trust for Mathilde.

With her death, the great mansion on Massachusetts Avenue became more sepulchral than ever, its tapestried salons and marbled halls silent except for the ticking of ormolu clocks or the low, canonical tones of the English butler, Frederick, responding to telephone inquiries. The French government, in need of an embassy residence, offered Mathilde $1 million for the house, a princely sum in that depression year ($9.2 million in today's terms), but she turned it down. Unwilling to face her first Christmas in forty-three years without her mother, Mathilde sailed with Welles for Paris early in December. After Christmas with friends, they would tour North Africa and be back by spring for the start of the 1932 campaign.

Welles notified FDR of his return and was invited to Albany on April 9, 1932. The governor's sweeping reelection two years earlier had convinced Welles that liberal new currents were stirring the electorate, making FDR's nomination and election virtually certain. Equally confident, Roosevelt asked him to open a Washington office and research and collate foreign policy material for his campaign. There was no one, FDR said, on whom he could depend "so thoroughly for accurate information."[10] The Washington office never materialized but, a month later, Welles wrote him: "I either have on hand, or have access to, all the material relating to foreign affairs which . . . might be of use to you, before or after the convention . . . I shall hold myself in readiness at any time for any call you may make upon me."[11]

Meanwhile, Welles's liberal instincts were being encouraged by his columnist friend Drew Pearson. A rising star at thirty-four, Pearson had coauthored a best-seller, *The Washington Merry-Go-Round,* the year before with his journalistic partner, Robert S. Allen. The public was fascinated with the private lives of government officials and the book had sold 100,000 copies, leading to a sequel and a syndicated column. Along with his readership, Pearson's political influence was growing.

He and Welles had met as young men-about-town in the early 1920s when Welles was divorcing Esther to marry Mathilde Gerry and Pearson was divorcing his first wife to marry Felicia Gyzicka, the daughter of Eleanor "Cissy" Patterson, the dynamic, red-haired publisher of the *Washington Times-Herald.* Although close friends, Welles and Pearson were totally dissimilar: Welles vice-regal, precise and formal; Pearson lean, foxy and ruthlessly inquisitive.

A Quaker by birth—Pearson and his brother, Leon, addressed each other as "thee" and "thou"—he had considered diplomacy before turning to journalism and, almost alone among Washington reporters, had followed Latin American affairs closely. Welles's encyclopedic knowledge and personal style had impressed him and, like Welles, he had come to believe that a new hemisphere policy was not only essential but that Roosevelt alone could bring it about.[12]

In Pearson's rambling Georgetown house, Welles now began meeting such prominent liberal Democrats as the two New Yorkers Senator Robert Wagner and Representative Fiorello LaGuardia; Senator Bronson Cutting of New Mexico; Lawrence Dennis, a black economist specializing in Latin America; and newsmen like Charles Ross of the *St. Louis Post-Dispatch,* who later would become Truman's press secretary, Henry Suydam of the *Brooklyn Eagle* and Pearson's partner, Robert S. "Bob" Allen. Instinctively reserved and accustomed to diplomatic protocol, Welles recoiled at first from the back-slapping and profanity natural to politicians and newsmen and, when Pearson twitted him about it, ruefully conceded that he lacked the "common touch." Gradually, however, he began to unbend, and many whom he first met at Pearson's house became his lasting friends.

Pearson had been a frequent visitor during the construction of Oxon Hill, driving out from Washington on fine evenings with lady friends to picnic with Welles and Mathilde. Eyes twinkling and mustache bristling, he regaled Mathilde with gossip and passed Welles political tips. One evening early in 1932 he and Welles retired to the library after dinner, and there, under Pearson's editorial eye, Welles drafted a seven-page foreign policy memorandum for the Democratic platform. Pearson would claim years later that Welles had blueprinted the Good Neighbor policy months before Roosevelt's nomination. "I was with him the night he drafted it," he told friends.[13]

Predictably, Welles focused on Latin America, where he felt Roosevelt could score an early success. An inter-American conference, due to open at Montevideo in eighteen months (December 1933), would provide an ideal forum for launching a new hemisphere policy. Welles led off by boldly asserting that the Democratic party recognized as a "cardinal principle" the need for a "new relationship" in the Americas based on four points: no armed intervention unless American lives were at stake; no recognition of revolutionary governments until legitimized by free elections; inter-American consultation in event of a crisis; and, finally, reciprocal trade agreements—a gesture to Senator Cordell Hull of Tennessee, a Democratic trade expert whom Roosevelt had recently named a foreign policy advisor.

Other world areas received more cursory treatment. Welles criticized Republican "indifference" to Europe and proposed that the United States participate in League of Nations peacekeeping and welfare activities and join the World Court, subject to its own veto. Echoing FDR's new militancy on repayment of war debts, he called on foreign debtors to honor their obligations but suggested, with a dash of realism, that these be scaled down by arms cuts, by elimination of trade barriers and by revising the crippling financial burdens imposed on Germany at Versailles.

Turning to Asia, he urged support of China's territorial integrity, opposed recognition of Japan's recent seizure of Manchuria and called, finally, for recognition of the Soviet Union—provided it abstain from "subversive propaganda" within the United States. His memorandum went to Roosevelt on May 5.

"I much like that draft," Roosevelt wrote him from Warm Springs a fortnight later. For platform purposes, however, it would have to be cut to three paragraphs—a task he mercifully agreed to do himself. Senator Hull would have "something to do" with the platform, so Welles should show him his draft and copies of his correspondence with FDR. "When I get back," Roosevelt concluded, "I want to have a talk with you."[14] When the Democratic platform finally emerged, Senator Hull had retained only four cryptic references to foreign affairs—and had brushed off Latin America in two pallid phrases: hemisphere "cooperation" to preserve the spirit of the Monroe Doctrine and "no interference" in the affairs of other states.[15] Hull was proud of his handiwork but Roosevelt and Welles were disappointed—an augury of much to come.

With the convention approaching, Welles plunged into the turbulent currents of Maryland politics, determined to rally the state for Roosevelt and win kudos for himself. His task was delicate. The state boss, Governor Albert C. Ritchie, wanted the nomination and regarded Roosevelt as his chief rival. Many Ritchie supporters secretly preferred FDR but were fearful of deserting their "favorite son" too soon, risking his wrath. Welles found a covert ally in Enos C. Ray, Ritchie's close aide and chairman of the Maryland Democratic Committee. Ray, ambitious for the governorship, had concluded that a Roosevelt victory would clear his way by elevating Ritchie to the cabinet.[16] To Welles's delight, Ray named him an alternate delegate to the Democratic convention in Chicago.

Before setting out early in June, Welles met in New York with an old friend, David Lawrence, publisher of the *United States Daily* (now *U.S. News & World Report*), who had an intriguing proposition. The ailing *Washington Post* might be up for sale for a relative song, he confided. Welles's interest rose. A major metropolitan daily read by Congress and the administration could be made influential and profitable.

The *Post* was losing $200,000 annually, Lawrence said. Its plant was obsolete and its only remaining assets comprised its real estate, its advertising and its name. Lawrence thought it could be acquired for $500,000 in cash. Initially skeptical, Welles wrote later in his journal: "the more I thought about it, the more sane it became."[17] More than sanity, however, was needed in that depression year, and neither Welles nor Mathilde were prepared to liquidate securities on a speculative venture. A year later Eugene Meyer bought the *Post* at a bankruptcy sale for $850, 000.

It is interesting to speculate what might have happened had Welles acquired a major interest in the *Washington Post* in 1932. Eleven years later, when his enemies combined in mid-World War II to drive him from office, the support of a powerful metropolitan daily might have saved his career.

On reaching Chicago, Welles dropped Mathilde at the Drake Hotel and went immediately to the headquarters of the Maryland delegation, where Ray confided that Ritchie's chances of nomination were far slimmer than the Maryland governor had led his delegates to believe. Roosevelt was still leading in delegates, but ex-Governor "Al" Smith of New York and other party bosses were trying desperately to forge a "stop Roosevelt" movement. Over the coming days, Welles would immerse himself in the convention and later leave a vivid 3,500-word account in his journal.

Roosevelt's floor manager, Louis Howe, was "not particularly optimistic" about FDR's chances, he told Welles. The New York governor had 690 delegates committed but needed eighty more (770) to clinch the nomination. These could come only from Tammany Hall, whose "sachems" detested FDR; from Ohio, whose governor, George White, wanted the vice presidential nomination for his support or from the Texas-California bloc of ninety controlled by House Speaker John N. "Cactus Jack" Garner, an ultra-conservative Texan who loathed the liberal Roosevelt.

Howe foresaw a bitter fight and, in fact, the battle seesawed for five days until Garner, pressured by William Randolph Hearst and by William G. McAdoo, Woodrow Wilson's son-in-law, finally released his delegates to FDR, ensuring his nomination.

There followed what Welles described as a "riot." Bands blared, crowds roared, the Roosevelt delegations paraded and Mathilde saw, from the galleries above, her tall, patrician husband in his shirtsleeves brandishing an FDR placard in the midst of the Maryland bloc. Next day, breaking all precedents, Roosevelt flew in from Albany with his family to accept the nomination. Welles wrote:

> It was late in the afternoon and the sun, which was sinking, shone in through the upper windows of the hall, [illuminating] the platform where he appeared without the aid of any artificial light. He came on the platform, leaning on Jim's [his eldest son's] arm, and stood for some time while the convention cheered. Not a boo was heard from the galleries. He made an admirable speech, which had a marked effect upon the delegates, as did his vigorous appearance, contrary to all the propaganda about his health which had been spread for so much time. I went to see him, immediately after the convention closed, and found him not in the least tired, and almost like a boy in his excitement over the enthusiasm of the reception he had had.

Eleanor Roosevelt invited Welles and Mathilde to hear the acceptance speech in her box the next day and also asked Welles to confer with the nominee the next morning. Welles and Mathilde, however, were leaving immediately for Oxon Hill and it was agreed that he would go instead to Albany or Hyde Park later to discuss a foreign policy speech Roosevelt was planning for the summer's end. Driving home through the stifling Midwest heat, for the first time since Coolidge had dismissed him seven years earlier, Welles felt confident of the nation's future and of his own. Roosevelt's vigor and dynamism, he wrote, had produced a "new current of optimism likely to sweep the nation."

FDR's nomination boosted Welles's political stock in Maryland, but Ritchie was brooding and Welles feared he might sit out the campaign, losing FDR the state. The time had come to assert his own authority. On August 12, with FDR's approval, he escorted to lunch at Albany two Maryland political allies: Enos Ray and Judge Joseph C. Mattingly, an Oxon Hill neighbor and Democratic leader of Prince George's County. Before accepting, Ray had cautiously checked with Ritchie and had learned that FDR had invited the Maryland governor up later. "It was evident," Welles recorded admiringly, "that all the contingencies were perfectly apparent to Franklin."

At lunch with them were FDR's confidential secretary, Marguerite "Missy" Lehand, and his new speechwriter, Judge Samuel I. Rosenman. Roosevelt talked with an "extraordinary charm . . . and quick-ranging mentality which," Welles wrote later, "I have only seen in one other individual . . . strangely enough, Theodore Roosevelt." He had impressed his Maryland guests with his ability to "captivate the individuals with him, no matter how unlike himself and dissimilar, in station or intelligence, they may be."

FDR took Welles aside for a half hour after lunch and confided that he had tried, by long-distance telephone, to retain in the platform two foreign policy planks that he and Welles both thought essential: an end to armed intervention in Latin America and repayment of war debts. He had failed and it was "water over the dam." What he now wanted were Welles's ideas on ending the Chaco war—a protracted Bolivian-Paraguayan conflict over an oil-rich border area. He went into it "in some detail," Welles wrote, because the conflict seemed to him a "local symptom of a broader danger threatening the entire hemisphere."

Roosevelt and Welles had often discussed how to halt Latin American conflicts before they spread, involving neighboring countries. The current Hoover-Stimson policy of dealing separately with each quarrel as it arose was "remedial, rather than preventive," they agreed, and resulted in frustration and delay. What was needed was to prevent—rather than repair—Latin American conflicts; for example, "inter-American machinery to act, automatically, before an emergency arose."

This meeting of minds eight months before FDR named Welles Assistant Secretary of State for Latin America was significant as prevention, rather than cure, became the hall-mark of their Good Neighbor policy. At the Buenos Aires conference of 1936, Welles would foil Argentine opposition and win unanimous agreement to "automatic" consultation if danger threatened the hemisphere. This principle, little noted at the time but strengthened at Lima in 1938 and at Havana in 1940, enabled the United States and its Latin American allies to cooperate, quickly and effectively, in defending the hemisphere after Pearl Harbor.

Welles spent the rest of the summer attending party picnics, clambakes and wienie roasts from Maryland's eastern shore to its traditionally Republican western counties, urging fractious Democrats to unite behind FDR. On September 12 Roosevelt called him to Hyde Park. He was leaving on a western swing and wanted, for his return, a "relatively brief" speech on foreign policy that he hoped to use at the end of the campaign. Europe's problems were "essentially economic," so Welles should concentrate on Latin America and, secondarily, on the Far East. To Welles's surprise, FDR asked how many career ambassadors and ministers he should retain and seemed "amazed" when Welles suggested only four. He thought him "undoubtedly right" and asked for a list of those to be kept.

Welles was asked to stay for lunch with thirty-five other guests and wrote later that the occasion was "typical of a usual Roosevelt day." Throughout the meal, Eleanor Roosevelt "was called to the telephone and Franklin and his wife and mother were all called out to sign autograph albums. The Roosevelt sons kept rushing in and out, either from riding or going to ride, and the noise and confusion was so terrific that it reminded me of only one thing and that was having lunch at Colonel Theodore Roosevelt's house at Oyster Bay, many years ago."

Notwithstanding FDR's request for a foreign policy speech on Latin America, Welles would soon feel the covert hostility of the small, jealous band of advisors known as the "Brain Trust." (Formed by FDR in Albany during his governorship and continued into his early presidency, this unofficial body of advisors originally comprised Columbia University professors Raymond Moley, Rexford G. Tugwell and Adolph A. Berle.) Weeks earlier, on meeting in Albany charter Brain Truster Adolph A. Berle, a Harvard prodigy and expert on corporate law,[18] Welles had thought him "one of the ablest men of the younger generation" that he had encountered. On September 28, Welles sent him a draft copy of his speech, requesting Berle's advice on reciprocal tariffs. The two would later become State Department colleagues and close friends, but Berle's reaction at the time was ominous.

"A purely practical question is whether anything ought to be said about Latin American matters in the campaign as it had developed to date," he wrote Welles. "Something will have to be said, sooner or later; the problem is whether a campaign which has thus far gone off, exclusively on domestic matters, should be widened in scope. Confidentially," he concluded, "there are those who believe that the Governor should follow the course of a Chinese Buddha and 'contemplate his navel' for a while."[19] Worse followed.

As the campaign drew to a close, on October 26, Roosevelt, largely at Welles's urging, visited Baltimore and delivered his celebrated attack on the Republican Four Horsemen of the Apocalypse: Destruction, Delay, Deceit and Despair. Later Welles called on him in his private railway car and there, for the first time, met Professor Raymond Moley, head of the Brain Trust. It was an inauspicious meeting; the two disliked each other on sight. Moley told Welles privately that Roosevelt had "just about decided" to make no speeches on foreign policy until after the election. For Welles it was a bitter blow. He had written the speech on Latin America specifically at FDR'S request, and upon reading it Senator Claude Swanson, Democrat of Virginia, the incoming chairman of the Foreign Relations committee, had asked Welles to tell Roosevelt that it was a "fine speech and one which you should, without fail, deliver."[20]

Now, hearing Moley decree that the speech should be pigeonholed until after the election, Welles could only swallow his chagrin. Moley and the Brain Trusters were clearly determined to keep foreign policy—and rivals for FDR's ear like Welles—out of the campaign. Welles had had his first clash with the Brain Trust—but not his last.

1. Sumner Welles's fourth form Groton portrait taken when he was 15 years old.

2. Esther Slater Welles, circa 1914, on her grand tour of Europe.

3. A sixth form theatrical at Groton. Sumner Welles played a Spanish señorita and is pictured, in costume with fan, in the second row, second from the right.

4. Opposite page: Esther Slater Welles's portrait by Ignazio Zuloaga in 1929.

5. In a garden on the Tigre near San Isidro. Welles is seated between Justo del Carril and Nenette Sanchez-Elia.

6. At the Japanese Embassy, Welles is pictured second from left and Mrs. Welles is first on the right.

7. At the U.S. Embassy in Buenos Aires, Welles is pictured at right in the first row.

8. Oxon Hill, Welles's Georgian house on the banks of the Potomac. It was designed by the prominent Washington, D.C. architect, J. H. de Sibour.

9. The drawing room at Oxon Hill. This magnificent room ran the entire width of the house. The walls were painted a grayish green with a delicate frieze in the Robert Adam tradition. The bulk of the furniture was collected during several trips to Europe.

10. In the Dominican Republic, from left to right, Dominican President Horacio Vasquez, U.S. Minister William W. Russell, Welles, Judge Richard Strong, Vice-President Federico Velasquez, Elias Brache and Dominican Advisory Council member Francisco J. Peynado.

11. Opposite page: Mrs. Mathilde Welles as photographed when Welles was Ambassador to Cuba.

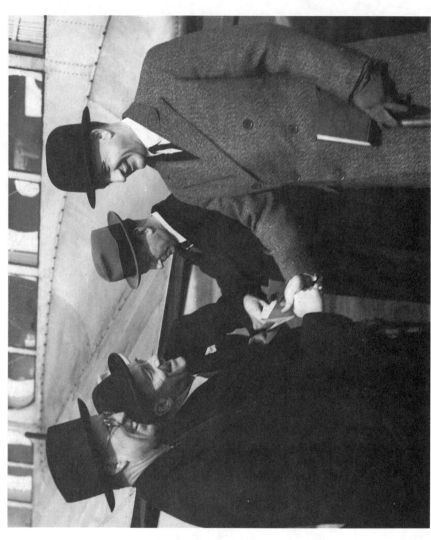

12. Welles, as FDR's personal envoy, arrives in England on March 10, 1940, escorted by French warplanes. Left to right: Mr. Joseph Kennedy, the American Ambassador, Sir Alexander Cadogan, Permanent Under Secretary of State at the British Foreign Office, an unidentified aide, and Welles.

Years of Achievement

THREE

ASSISTANT SECRETARY OF STATE FOR LATIN AMERICA

1933

Bright Prospects; Looming Clouds

ROOSEVELT'S ELECTORAL LANDSLIDE sent Welles's hopes soaring. His credentials for office seemed unrivaled. As a young man he had distinguished himself in diplomacy; he had written a well-received book on the Dominican Republic and was widely viewed as the Democrats' leading authority on the hemisphere. A lifelong friend of the President-elect and, particularly, of his wife, he had been advising FDR on foreign—and especially Latin American—policy since long before the election. His relations with Louis Howe, FDR's closest advisor, were good; those with Norman H. Davis, a likely Secretary of State, even better. He had helped carry Maryland for Roosevelt and, when appointments were made, his and Mathilde's contributions to the Democratic war chest would surely not pass unnoticed.

Yet for the next six months Welles's nerves remained taut. After twelve years in the political wilderness, the struggle for office among Democrats would be savage, even cut-throat, and the Brain Trust might stop at nothing to block him—or other rivals—for Roosevelt's favor.

FDR wrote him unexpectedly at Christmas: "Don't you want, once more, to try the impossible: a two-paragraph draft about inter-Americanism?" Already assembling themes for his March 19 inaugural address, FDR wanted Welles's ideas for a passage on foreign policy.[1] His allusion to the "impossible" was not entirely jocular; no one could compress Latin American policy into two paragraphs—least of all Welles, whose compendious knowledge often led him into prolixity. Nonetheless, Welles set to work over New Year's while recovering from influenza and promised to bring the draft to New York on January 10.[2]

Arriving a day early, he called on Norman Davis to inquire if he had had any further intimation about his prospects of becoming Secretary of State. Davis had not; in fact, his last talk with Roosevelt in Albany a few weeks earlier had left him distinctly uneasy. FDR had been evasive, intimating that he might be "his own" Secretary of State at the start, although he might name some "stop-gap individual" for the first year or two of his administration. He had asked Davis, meanwhile, to continue as a "roving" ambassador handling war debts, disarmament and European economic problems.

No "roving" envoy could conduct such negotiations, Davis had told him; only a Secretary of State could, by traveling periodically to Europe, provided he could leave some "reliable" individual to run the department. FDR had been noncommittal and there the matter stood.

Sensing his dejection, Welles told him that no one had the same contacts, experience or capacity to be Secretary of State. Davis then stated categorically that if he became Secretary, he wanted "nobody but [Welles]" as his Under Secretary. Before Welles left, Davis warned him of the protective ring of Brain Trusters around FDR. They were "theoreticians" with not the remotest understanding of foreign affairs, he said, and assumed that Roosevelt would be "entirely guided" by their ideas.[3]

Welles arrived the next morning at FDR's Sixty-fifth Street townhouse to find the President-elect, only fifty-one then, "tired and worn, his color . . . bad." For the first time in Welles's memory, his hands were "not quite steady."[4] All hopes of a private talk were dashed as Nathalie van Vleck, a New York society artist, was painting FDR's portrait and a Secret Service man had taken up his post by the open door. Welles handed Roosevelt the draft memorandum and asked how he planned to use it. If the inaugural address were sufficiently long, FDR said, he might incorporate it; if short, he might hold it for a special session of Congress. In any event, he was planning a major foreign policy speech at the "earliest" opportunity after the inauguration.

Suspecting that he was temporizing, Welles injudiciously pressed him. The situation in Latin America, he warned, was more "disquieting" than he had known it in fifteen years. Bolivia and Paraguay were warring over the Chaco; Colombia and Peru clashing over their Leticia border; and "unrest was rampant." Nothing would be more salutary than for Roosevelt to announce a new hemisphere policy before—not after—his inauguration. Latin America was waiting. Welles's plea fell on deaf ears. Roosevelt's "Dutch" was up, so Welles fell silent as the President-elect perused his draft memorandum—in three, not the requested two, paragraphs:

> The Monroe Doctrine, long suspect as a vehicle of U.S. imperialism, should be made common property. In his inaugural address, FDR should encourage every American republic to adopt principles of continental self-defense as a portion of its national policy;
>
> If friendship with Latin America [is] to become the keystone of FDR's foreign policy, a threat to hemisphere security should be followed, immediately, by inter-American consultation. U.S. lives, admittedly, [may] have to be protected at times, but this should never again lead to armed intervention in a sister republic;
>
> Reciprocal tariff cuts were essential if inter-American trade was to revive.[5]

Roosevelt read the memorandum very slowly and attentively—which, Welles wrote later, was very different from his usual habit of reading material of this character "very rapidly." After a pause he exclaimed, "I think it is admirable. I think it will hit them between the eyes." Welles specifically asked if he was in accord with the first, and most important, portion of the draft: namely, that dealing with the Monroe Doctrine. FDR answered without hesitation that he was fully in accord and felt that his policy should be so stated "without changing a word." Welles reminded him that, to his knowledge, the question had never before been approached in this manner. FDR would be doing something "new."

"How does this fit in with Wilson's Mobile speech?" Roosevelt asked. (Speaking at Mobile, Alabama, in 1913, Wilson had declared that the United States would "never again acquire a foot of territory by conquest.") The policy in his memorandum, Welles replied, was a "logical outcome" of that speech. FDR then reread certain portions with evident approval and said, "I think this is a very statesmanlike document and I am very grateful to you for giving me just what I wanted."[6]

Gratified, Welles took his leave, but his elation was short-lived. Descending the stairs, he encountered Marvin McIntyre, FDR's hard-bitten press secretary, who immediately challenged him. Weeks earlier Welles had offered Roosevelt the use of Mrs. Townsend's Washington mansion as a preinaugural retreat for himself, his large family and staff. Roosevelt had gratefully accepted, and Eleanor had written Mathilde about household arrangements. McIntyre now growled that FDR's use of the Townsend mansion would be "bad politics." FDR should go to "an ordinary hotel like anyone else."

Welles stiffened, unaccustomed to having his personal dealings with the Roosevelt family challenged by a staff subordinate. Roosevelt had approved the idea, he replied coldly, and he himself saw no "political drawback" in his using the home of a lifelong friend. McIntyre was "somewhat taken aback by the way in which I spoke to him," Welles later recorded, and asked that he not repeat their difference to the governor. Welles agreed; but when the inauguration rolled around, FDR, his family and staff settled into the Mayflower Hotel—proof of the power of the inner ring.

Roosevelt had disturbed Welles in their talk by alluding—erroneously, in Welles's view—to Wilson's refusal to recognize revolutionary Latin American governments. The outgoing Secretary of State, Stimson, had told him, said FDR, that Wilson had "never" made an official pronouncement opposing such recognition. After checking the record, Welles wrote FDR two weeks later that Stimson had been wrong and, in proof, cited Wilson's renomination speech of September 2, 1916: "So long as the power of recognition rests with me the government of the U.S. will refuse to extend the hand of welcome to anyone who obtains power in a sister republic by treachery and violence. I declared that to be the policy of this administration within three weeks after I assumed the Presidency. I here again vow it."

In Welles's view, no aspect of U.S. Hemisphere policy was more important than recognition—or non-recognition—of Latin American governments. Four years earlier, he and FDR had condemned Stimson for abandoning Wilson's policy and automatically recognizing any government that controlled its territory, paid its debts and claimed the "acquiescence" of its people. Welles, after long reflection, had now changed his mind and could no longer recommend resuming Wilson's policy without "modification."

If strictly applied, he wrote FDR, it would prevent official contacts with "existing dictatorships to our own detriment and . . . the prejudice of amicable inter-American relations." The Wilson Doctrine denied the right to "revolution which, in some instances, was the only manner in which the peoples of Latin America could change their governments." If carried to extremes, it would constitute "interference in the inherent rights of the Latin American peoples to determine their own destinies."

Instead, Welles recommended withholding recognition until the people themselves had expressed approval or disapproval through elections. Admittedly, there would be drawbacks: delays might occur before elections could be held, and often Latin American elections were "controlled." Nonetheless, the advantages would far outweigh the Stimson policy of automatically recognizing all dictatorships while, at the same time, avoiding the pitfalls of Wilson's refusal to recognize any.

Knowing FDR's penchant for ribaldry, Welles ended on a light note. The American minister in Bulgaria, he reported, had recently cabled the State Department: "The Queen of Bulgaria gave birth this morning to a daughter. I have just congratulated the Prime Minister." From Warm Springs came a joyous response: "I am very glad to have that clear picture of our policy relating to non-recognition from 1916 on. I love that classic cable from the American minister in Bulgaria!"[7]

As the inauguration approached, Welles's name began cropping up frequently in the newspapers, and his telephone rang constantly with requests for introductions to the Roosevelt entourage or for other favors. On January 27, Congressman Hamilton Fish, a right-wing Republican and Dutchess County neighbor of FDR's, asked him to support a Congressional resolution urging U.S. mediation in Cuba, where violence was rising. The Cuban president-dictator, Gerardo Machado, was repressing political opponents—many of them university students—with sickening brutality, and congressional indignation was mounting. Welles, however, was wary.

There were two things to avoid in Cuba, he warned: armed intervention (unless prolonged revolution and anarchy developed) or "humiliating" Cuba by forcing elections under U.S. supervision. The proper policy would be to negotiate an accord between Machado and the opposition, followed by free elections and a return to constitutional rule. Fish predicted that Welles himself might be sent as ambassador to Cuba, but Welles replied flatly—and, as it turned out, inaccurately—that it was "out of the question."[8] Knowing the awesome responsibility that the 1902 Platt Amendment imposed on the United States to keep order in the turbulent republic, his hope was to remain in Washington as Under Secretary to Secretary of State Norman H. Davis.

The winter dragged on, as rumors of appointments floated like thistledown on the wind. Welles waited, keeping in daily touch with Davis, who was also waiting. Davis told him that Senator Cordell Hull, an old friend and fellow Tennesseean, had sworn that Roosevelt had offered him "nothing specific." Hull was dissimulating. FDR, in fact, had already offered the elderly legislator the Secretaryship of State, and characteristically, Hull was taking a month to make up his mind. Accustomed to simple meals and early nights in their Carlton Hotel apartment, Hull and his wife thought the social demands of the great office "intimidating."[9]

Trusting Hull's word, Davis continued regarding himself as a possible Secretary of State. Meanwhile, Welles was growing increasingly despondent about Davis's prospects and his own. On February 17, to calm his fears, Davis passed him a tip from Louis Howe. Welles's chief rival, Moley, would not become Under Secretary. Apparently, Moley heard the news at about the same time. Later, upon hearing Davis extol Welles's qualifications in the White House one day, Moley rounded on Davis and snapped, "The trouble with Welles is that he's too ambitious. Why I, myself, am only going to be an assistant Secretary!"[10] What had happened?

Roosevelt, caught in a bitter struggle for the embassy in Rome between his former law partner, Grenville T. Emmett, and William Phillips, both old friends, had devised a truly Solomonic solution. He sent Emmett to Rome and made Phillips Under Secretary. Moley had been blocked—but so had Welles.

While bitterly disappointed by Hull's appointment as Secretary of State on February 21, Davis loyally continued stressing Welles's qualifications. Hull had expressed a "high opinion" of him, Davis told Welles, but had encountered "very strong" opposition to his being named Under Secretary. Welles's old friend "Daisy" (Mrs. Borden) Harriman, a Democratic national committee-woman, told him that she had heard rumors that the Senate Foreign Relations Committee might reject him if he were nominated for the Under Secretaryship. However, on checking with Hull, among others, she had found the rumors false.[11]

Francis White next confided that someone "close to FDR," whom he would not name, had asked the State Department to search its files for an "unfavorable" report on Welles. After investigating, the department had found "nothing not highly favorable." Someone was clearly mounting a whispering campaign—but who? Increasingly perturbed, Welles asked Davis to intercede with Howe, who replied enigmatically that there was no question about Welles's ability; the opposition would have "no effect, one way or another." But this could be taken in two ways. Had Welles already been blackballed? Or would the opposition itself be ignored?

Seizing hat and cane, Welles drove to Howe's office. No one, he declared, had recommended him to Roosevelt for any position with his "consent or prior knowledge." The President-elect had known him all his life and was aware of his qualifications. "I know that Franklin counts on you to help in the administration," Howe remarked soothingly. Still unsatisfied, Welles drove home his point. Certain charges had been made against him by persons close to the President-elect. If these concerned his ability, he had nothing to say. If they reflected on his integrity or character, he should be given a chance to refute them. Howe pondered at length.

"I want to be perfectly frank with you and tell you that charges of that character were made," he said finally. They were apparently based on the knowledge of certain people that a 1925 memorandum from Coolidge to Kellogg about Welles existed in the confidential files of the Secretary of State. As Coolidge was dead, Howe had turned to Chief Justice Hughes, who told him that no one had ever worked for him for whose ability or character he had a higher regard than for Welles. Howe had ordered the State Department files searched and, on finding only "highly flattering" material and the charges appearing "unjustified and unfounded," FDR and he had decided to ignore them.[12]

"It might as well be put down here with regard to the Coolidge memorandum," Welles wrote in his journal, "the only people who have access to the Secretary of State's confidential files are the Secretary, the Under Secretary and the confidential employees of the Secretary's office." Stimson, then about to leave office, would have no reason to refer to the matter; so the "presumption would seem to be very clear that [William R.] Castle is the only individual who could have had any interest, whatever, in taking the matter up and in making it the basis for the charges against me." Castle, the outgoing Republican Under Secretary, had been a jealous critic of Welles for years. As to who in Roosevelt's inner circle had dredged up the charges and brought them to FDR's attention, Welles concluded dryly: "I have no knowledge."[13]

Welles's interview with Howe cleared the air, and Davis heard soon after that Welles would be named ambassador either to the Argentine or to Cuba. Welles, however, wanted neither. In all his discussions with FDR, he reminded Davis, it had always been "inferred" that he would be wanted in Washington. If the President-elect had changed his mind, he would have to consider long and hard. Phillips compounded the confusion by telling Davis that, while Welles was to get "the best . . . to be had," Mathilde was unwilling to live abroad. Rising to her defense, Davis replied that she might not choose to go to the "end of the earth" but would loyally accompany her husband if he were offered a "first class post that interested him."[14]

Confusion escalated. Hull complained that Phillips seemed "out of touch" with European affairs and, when Davis reiterated Welles's qualifications for the position, seemed to "jump at the idea," asking Davis if Welles might agree to start as an Assistant Secretary and succeed as Under Secretary in six months if a suitable embassy overseas could be found for Phillips. Wary after the collapse of his own hopes, Davis replied that he would advise Welles to accept only on Hull's "utmost assurance" of promotion. Otherwise, he thought, the best thing for the administration and for Welles would be to send him as ambassador to Cuba. Hull had apparently decided to do so.

Roosevelt, like presidents before and since, distrusted the State Department's entrenched bureaucracy. Determined to be his own Secretary of State, he began naming friends to high departmental office with little or no consultation with Hull, whose experience in foreign affairs was limited and whom FDR had named Secretary of State, essentially, to be his chief liaison with the conservative congress. One appointment in particular disturbed Welles. Davis told him on March 9 that FDR was "insistent" on naming William C. Bullitt ambassador to France and had only been persuaded with the greatest difficulty that Bullitt's appointment to any position would be "disastrous."[15] Davis was wrong; FDR would soon name Bullitt his first ambassador to the Soviet Union.

Welles's antipathy to Bullitt as early as 1933 is significant, given their deadly feud ten years later. It stemmed essentially from Bullitt's slippery record in World War I and his later betrayal of Woodrow Wilson. Castle detested Welles but shared his misgivings about Bullitt. "When one considers that Woodrow Wilson loathed [Bullitt], that he has never been anything but a clever and quite unscrupulous intriguer, more or less of a communist," Castle wrote in his diary, Bullitt's appointment to Moscow was "almost impossible to understand."[16]

Hull himself barely knew Bullitt at the start of the administration but, after watching him maneuver for power at the 1933 London economic conference, soon came to loathe him second only to his pet detestation, Moley. Traveling by sea to an inter-American conference at Montevideo that autumn, Hull learned by cable that FDR was about to resume diplomatic relations with the Soviet Union. Turning to his young aide, Hugh S. Cumming, Hull muttered with the lisp that invariably connoted anger: "Well, I thuppose Roosevelt will thend that thon-of-a-bitch [Bullitt] to represent us."[17]

For the next seven years, Bullitt in Europe and Welles in Washington maintained cool but correct relations. In 1940, however, soon after the start of World War II, FDR sent Welles to explore the chances of peace in the European capitals—including Paris, Bullitt's personal fiefdom—and four months later, after the French surrender to the Nazis, shelved Bullitt as his ambassador to France. Jealous and vengeful, unjustly blaming Welles for his dismissal, Bullitt set out to destroy him and eventually he did so—while destroying himself in the process.

Meanwhile, the day of Roosevelt's inauguration, March 19, 1933, came and went, but Welles still waited. Rising violence in Cuba was spurring congressional demands for U.S. intervention, and Roosevelt, employing a favorite time-buying technique, sent Adolf Berle on a quick "fact-finding" trip to the island republic. Upon his return, Berle told Welles that he would recommend a "waiting" policy in Cuba—hoping that, somehow, the Cuban opposition would unite around an acceptable candidate before Machado's term expired. Welles disagreed: A waiting policy should be the last resort.

The correct policy would be "proper, behind-the-scenes" influence on Machado to resign. Cuba's constitution and electoral laws could then be amended, and when elections were held, the United States would not again be faced with demands for intervention on the grounds that the polling had been fraudulent. There should be "no question of intervention," Welles insisted. His own experience in Cuba, in 1920 and 1921 and in the Dominican Republic, from 1922 to 1924, had convinced him of the "futility" of intervention. Berle agreed that Machado should be "induced" to resign but thought such action would depend on the U.S. ambassador. No one, he insisted, was so well qualified as Welles.[18]

Welles's vigil was drawing to a close. In late March he was offered the ambassadorship to Argentina, which he declined. "Friendships [and] associations would make it the place, above all others, I would care to go," he wrote an Argentine friend. "The best three years of my life were spent there." But, in that era of steamship travel, he would not see his sons for two years, and, meanwhile, there would never be a more "propitious moment to radically reform and revise" U.S. policy toward Latin America.[19] Washington was still where he wanted to be.

At month's end his hopes soared again—only to plunge. A long-scheduled appointment with FDR was postponed for a week and Welles, his nerves at the breaking point, erupted in a rare fit of temper. The atmosphere in the White House, he wrote Davis bitterly, was like a "three-ring circus." FDR was appointing personal friends to office; Howe and James A. Farley, then chairman of the Democratic National Committee and later FDR's Postmaster General, were recommending politicians and Phillips was pushing "old, time-worn" career diplomats whose failure to receive important posts might "harm service morale." He himself was leaving Washington that night and would make "no effort to go to the White House until . . . sent for."[20]

On April 3, he finally was sent for. Roosevelt named him Assistant Secretary of State for Latin America, Senate confirmation followed and, on April 6, he took his oath. Forty years old, back in harness after eight frustrating years and serving a president whom he revered, Welles at last was in a position to reshape U.S. policy in Latin America along lines forming in his mind for fifteen years. Hull had hinted at promotion to the Under Secretaryship in six months, and, from every prospect, the outlook seemed bright. As always in Welles's stormy life, however, a cloud was looming on the horizon: Cuba.

FIFTEEN

AMBASSADOR TO CUBA

1933

"It Seemed a Miracle"

CUBA, ALTHOUGH RAPIDLY MOVING TOWARD REVOLUTION, was only one of Welles's new responsibilities. Bolivia and Paraguay were still clashing over the Chaco; Peru and Colombia over their Leticia border; and continuing unrest in Nicaragua was preventing the withdrawal of marines sent six years earlier to "preserve order." Latin America, however, ranked low among FDR's priorities in 1933. At home, banks were closed, credit frozen, trade stagnant, a quarter of the labor force unemployed and breadlines stretched across the nation. Domestic emergency measures monopolized his attention.

True, in his inaugural address he had pledged the United States to be a "Good Neighbor"; but he had been addressing the whole world, not solely Latin America. Welles and Leo Rowe persuaded him, nonetheless, to outline his hemisphere policy in an address to the Pan American Union on April 12. Welles drafted the speech and showed it to Rowe with the hope that the President would announce a new, constructive and concrete policy—not merely "good will and pious wishes."[1] His hopes were dashed.

Cautioned against committing himself too soon, FDR watered down Welles's bolder proposals.[2] Renunciation of U.S. intervention became "respect for the rights of others"; inter-American consultation, "fraternal cooperation." The boldest proposal—that FDR invite each Latin American republic to make the Monroe Doctrine "a portion of its national policy"—was emasculated. The Monroe Doctrine, FDR declared elliptically, was "purely defensive, menacing no one and intended, solely, for continental self-defense."[3]

Through this speech, Welles had been hoping to establish Latin America's—and his own—priority status at the start of the New Deal. Roosevelt's first foray into hemisphere affairs, therefore, disappointed him. Yet the President's courageous note of confidence struck a receptive chord below the Rio Grande. "All Latin Americans are in accord with President Roosevelt's Good Neighbor policy [as] enunciated," wrote the newspaper *Estrella de Panama,* "but this must be more than oratorical expression and must be . . . supported by facts."[4] Cuba would soon become the Good Neighbor policy's first test and the Platt Amendment its first major embarrassment.

Named for Senator Orville H. Platt (R.-Conn) who, as chairman of the Foreign Relations Committee had written it into the 1902 U.S.-Cuban treaty[5] at the end of the Spanish-American War, the Platt Amendment had hung, ever since, like a sword of Damocles over U.S.-Cuban relations. Still in force at the start of Roosevelt's administration, it committed the United States to protect Cuba from foreign threat and to preserve in the island a government "adequate for the protection of life, property and individual liberty." In short, the United States was legally bound to keep order in Cuba.[6]

Early in the New Deal, mounting Cuban opposition to Gerardo Machado—and especially reports that his police were throwing rebellious students to the sharks in Havana harbor—spurred congressional and public demands that the United States land troops to prevent civil war and protect American lives and investments worth at the time $2 billion. Norman Davis, lunching with FDR and Hull on the eve of the inauguration, had suggested Welles as the "one man" capable of solving the Cuban crisis. Roosevelt had thought it a "fine suggestion," and Hull had posed no objection.[7] On April 21, barely two weeks after naming Welles Assistant Secretary for Latin America, FDR suddenly changed his post to ambassador to Havana.

It was a post, Welles wrote a colleague, for which, he was not "keenly anxious."[8] FDR evidently considered it a temporary assignment for, on May 6, two days after Welles had sailed, he ordered Jefferson Caffery, then minister to Colombia, to be ready to relieve Welles "in about three months." Welles would return and resume his post as Assistant Secretary.[9] Widespread rumors that he was being sent temporarily to "oust" Machado, however, disturbed Welles. "If the Cuban government or . . . people [get] the idea that they would, later, have to deal with someone else," Welles warned FDR, "it would very probably jeopardize success."[10]

Asked if Welles would investigate reports of "murder, riots and sudden death," Hull told reporters that the new envoy would perform the "usual" functions of a diplomat, and Welles himself stressed at his Senate hearings that he was going as Roosevelt's "permanent" representative. He believed firmly in the Good Neighbor policy, would abide by its principles and hoped to negotiate a new trade treaty to benefit the Cuban people.[11] The *Baltimore Sun* thought he was approaching his task with a "healthy" regard for the fact that Cuba is "an independent country. It is not for us to meddle in its internal disputes."[12] Normally, Welles would have agreed; but conditions in Cuba were not normal, and the Platt amendment bound the United States to correct them.

In sending Welles, FDR was employing what both had long advocated: "preventive" diplomacy. An inter-American conference was due to open at Montevideo in December and the new Good Neighbor policy would come under critical scrutiny there. Intervention in Cuba, except to protect American lives, was therefore to be avoided at all costs. Welles's "preventive" task essentially would be two-fold: to end violence by bringing Machado and the opposition to the bargaining table, then to arrange for reform of Cuba's constitution and electoral laws and for free elections when Machado's term ended in May 1935. Concurrently, he was to negotiate a new trade pact granting Cuban sugar greater access to the U.S. market and alleviating its economic misery.

One important task remained before sailing. If Welles's mediation was to succeed, the various anti-Machado groups exiled in the United States would have to cooperate. Encouraged by FDR's election, all but one, the *Directorio Estudiantil Universitario* (DEU), representing Cuba's radical university students, agreed. Brutally suppressed by Machado, the DEU had turned to violence three years earlier and opposed mediation as certain to strengthen Machado's hand. Fanatically anti-American, the students were demanding a total change of regime ("no Machadismo without Machado") and immediate abrogation of the Platt Amendment which, they claimed, made Cuba a U.S. "puppet."

Welles set off for Cuba on May 4 with Roosevelt's authorization to communicate with him directly by cable or telephone.[13] The DEU's young leaders, meanwhile, were hiding from Machado's police in Cuba, in exile in the United States or roaming Latin America and Europe seeking funds and support. By its very obduracy, the DEU had isolated itself from the other opposition groups. In the coming months, it would prove itself Welles's most implacable foe.[14]

When Welles arrived, Cuba was under the rule of a "tyrannical dictatorship to which ninety-five percent of the people were fanatically opposed," he wrote later. "The authorities could only go abroad in armored cars, and usually at night, for fear of assassination. Bombings, terrorism and murder were daily occurrences."[15] Not only students but young Cuban professionals—lawyers, doctors, businessmen and university professors—were flocking to various underground movements of which ABC was the largest and most prestigious.[16]

Machado, then nine years in power, had been elected in 1924, when sugar prices were high and fortunes made overnight. At first, Cuban and American business interests had backed him as a guarantor of order; but, after winning a second term in 1928, he had illegally extended it by bribery and violence from four years to six. The 1929 Wall Street crash and the subsequent world depression had brought Cuba to the brink of collapse, eroding his popularity. Determined to crush rising discontent, he had unleashed a reign of terror.

"Utterly autocratic and reactionary . . . his life [was] in constant danger [and] his movements from the [presidential] palace in Havana to his country place in the outskirts . . . surreptitious," Welles recalled. "In the frequent conversations I had with him, in which we discussed the revolting details of the murders committed by his secret police, particularly those of young patriots hardly more than boys, he never gave the slightest indication that these acts of barbaric cruelty were anything but justified."[17]

On May 11, four days after arriving, Welles handed Machado his credentials and a letter from FDR describing Welles as an "old friend." Few envoys had ever arrived with broader powers: Welles had drafted his own. After citing Machado's transgressions and Cuba's slide toward anarchy, Welles emphasized that he was authorized only to offer "friendly advice," not to be construed as intervention. Machado said little but two days later, in a long, affable talk, he welcomed Welles's offer to mediate a political truce and hinted that he might resign before, or during, the next electoral period to ease tension. Gratified, Welles held out the prospect of a larger sugar allocation once calm had been restored; in turn, Machado offered a "practical monopoly" of the Cuban market for American exports. That night Welles outlined his coming strategy to Hull.

To divert Cuban opinion from politics, he intended to emphasize the benefits of the new trade pact, which would give the United States "practical control of a market we've been steadily losing for . . . ten years." At the same time he would urge reform of the constitution and electoral laws before the next presidential campaign. If, however, "hatred" of Machado persisted, it might be "highly desirable to replace him"—though not before the campaign. Machado controlled the army and the opposition was split, so ousting him prematurely might promote violence.[18]

Soon Machado began freeing political prisoners and easing censorship. Welles, in turn, urged American newsmen to check carefully before filing opposition versions of Machado's atrocities.

Eleven days after arriving, Welles wrote FDR that the situation was more "precarious and difficult" than he had foreseen. Nothing would be more prejudicial to U.S. policy in Latin America than U.S. intervention in Cuba by "force or by open diplomatic action," but Machado's acts of "hideous cruelty" had aroused a "detestation . . . unparalleled in Cuban history." Eventually it might be necessary to replace him—cautiously. His precipitous ouster might provoke chaos. In closing, Welles asked for "two lines, either approving, or disapproving," his program.[19] FDR never replied.

On May 29, an inspired editorial in the influential *Diario de la Marina* hinted that Machado was ready to negotiate with his adversaries.[20] However, the quarreling opposition factions were agreed only in demanding his immediate resignation. Welles, fearing a dangerous power vacuum, turned for help to Machado's most prestigious opponent, Dr. Cosme de la Torriente. A former president of the League of Nations General Assembly, Torriente's fame alone had spared him imprisonment or exile. Like Welles, he opposed violence and agreed to rally the opposition groups behind mediation.

With still neither approval nor disapproval of his program from FDR, on June 1 Welles proposed to Machado a cautious three-stage program for restoring constitutional rule. A new electoral law would be drafted with expert American advice, and political parties, after years in the underground, permitted to organize again. Once a new constitution had been promulgated, a "caretaker" Vice President would be elected. Only then would Machado step down, allowing the Vice President to supervise the coming elections. Initially, Machado seemed receptive, offering to resign as a "patriotic gesture" once the Vice President had been installed. Welles reported the news to Washington that night.[21] The next day Roosevelt wrote that he had been too busy with Congress to keep in more than "very sketchy" touch with Welles's activities but concluded cheerfully, "It seems to me, that things are going as well as you and I could possibly hope for."[22]

Asked if he and Welles were starting a "new" policy toward Machado, FDR told newsmen offhandedly that there was "really no story . . . I have been so darn busy with other things that I have not read a single dispatch from Welles. I saw him before he left and Phillips, since then, has given me a few high spots." Fortunately for Welles, FDR's comment had been off the record, but an erroneous United Press dispatch predicting that Caffery would soon replace him undercut his authority at a critical moment.

Cuban newspapers blazoned the report in headlines and opposition extremists, assuming that Welles would soon be gone, stepped up the violence. It could not have come at a "more unfortunate" time, Welles wrote Drew Pearson, bitterly. He had been working "around the clock to convince hot-headed" students and underground members to organize a new political party and work out Cuba's problem peacefully. The UP story had given the opposition the idea that "my own government was not backing me and that a new man would insist on [Machado's] immediate resignation." On the eve of his mediation, the setback had been "almost heart-breaking."[23] Worse followed.

The next day Washington dispatches reported that Roosevelt had virtually abandoned hope that the current Congress would approve a new U.S.-Cuba trade pact. Welles's trump had been snatched from his hand. Salvaging what little he could from the wreckage, he won permission to update the 1902 trade pact, but his bargaining leverage had been weakened and Cuba slid deeper into economic distress.[24]

A fortnight before the July 1 start of mediation, the outlook was grim. None of the opposition groups wanted to be first to sit down with the dictator so, to break the deadlock, Welles took a calculated risk: He confided his strategy to American reporters and urged them to back mediation with their opposition contacts—a "clever gesture," one reporter thought.[25] Eventually, persuaded by Torriente and the reporters, the leading underground faction, ABC, agreed to participate and the rest fell into line. On June 24, Welles was heartened by a letter from FDR stating "how proud I am of all that you have been accomplishing since you got down to Cuba. I have been so taken up with the European situation[26] that all I have been able to do is read your dispatches and dismiss them from my mind . . . You seemed to be getting the situation under control and to have the confidence of people who count."[27]

The Student Directorate, however, was still holding out. Warned by reporters that the students were planning a political assassination, Welles met privately with two of their leaders, and they dropped their plans. Violence diminished and on the eve of the July 1 deadline a truce of sorts had set in.

Welles and Mathilde, meanwhile, had settled into a large rented house in Miramar, Havana's fashionable suburb, and there his teenage sons joined him in late June for their school holiday. With the Victorian solicitude he invariably employed when trying to focus their scattered attention, he had written weeks before to warn them that he would have little time to spend with them, except on Sundays. "I think you will both have a pleasant time with the country clubs," he wrote. "You will, of course, need bathing suits and tennis rackets." That two teenagers might have thought this out for themselves had not occurred to him; in his eyes they were still children.

After the usual flurry of meticulous instructions, he had reluctantly consented to their taking a two-day boat trip from New York rather than the one-hour flight from Miami. "Please try to be business-like and see that the proper arrangements are carried out," he admonished.[28] Convinced that they would confuse the sailing date, misroute their luggage, or both, he instructed Mrs. Townsend's imperturbable English butler, Frederick Holmans, to meet them in New York on their arrival from their New England boarding school and shepherd them aboard ship. "You know how haphazard they both are," he wrote Frederick. "All arrangements about luggage, etc., must be made by you; otherwise, I am sure, some-thing will be mislaid."[29]

In that halcyon summer of 1933, Cuba seemed a tropical paradise, and his sons were soon swept up in swimming and tennis matches at the Jaimanitas Country Club or in offshore sailing races. In the evenings there were dinner parties in the homes of young Cuban friends or in open-air nightclubs, such as Sans Souci or the Chateau Madrid, where marimba bands played under the stars and the maraccas rattled till dawn.

Jai-alai was the national rage, and the *frontons* were packed, night and day, with cigar-chomping Cuban fans screaming excitedly as agile Basque players leapt up the concrete walls to snare the ball in *cestas* (curved wicker baskets strapped to their wrists), then snap it away with blinding speed. Odds rose and fell amid the din as local urchins tossed slit tennis balls stuffed with money or betting slips back and forth among the spectators. Fascinated by the game, Welles's elder son, Ben, began lessons with Millán, the Cuban champion, returning home his first day with an egg-size lump on the back of his head, the result of inattention. After that his concentration improved.

Havana's narrow colonial streets with their flower-filled balconies, horn-honking traffic and slow-moving pedestrians enchanted the Welles sons. Months later, back at Groton in wintry New England and still pining for sunny Cuba, Ben gave vent to his nostalgia in the school magazine:

> The city wakes to a new day. Like an ant-hill when disturbed, it gradually assumes a state of excitement. High above the streets, shutters are flung open, women greet one another noisily, and the general animation quickly spreads until the whole city is teeming with life . . . Vendors, pushing carts before them, cry out their wares. Newsboys shriek the names of the morning papers, their shrill voices pervading the innermost rooms of the houses and calling forth, from those still in bed, curses at being waked.
>
> The trolleys . . . clang by through the narrow streets, the harsh clash of their massive wheels on the tracks adding to the din. By now, the sun is high in the great cloudless vault of blue over Cuba. The beaches are crowded with those seeking relief from the heat before the noon-day meal. All who can get away, fare north to "La Playa," the people's bathing beach . . .
>
> Here and there, a few taxis cruise the streets; police in blue, with black stripes setting off their not-always perfect figures, stroll leisurely or lean lethargically against buildings, ready to bring down the full force of the law on

urchins who scribble "Abajo Machado" (Down with Machado) on the sidewalks. The afternoon wears on. The sun hangs over calm waters. The crowds flock to the Malecon—Havana's beautiful sea-drive. Here they sit, walk, talk, play and carry on the great part of their social intercourse.

Peddlers sell fish, badges, balloons. Women jabber, men lie on their backs. Children totter over the streets, their parents as unwatchful as the motorists that whiz by them at speed. The breezes swirl through the town, driving out the stench of the city and spreading the clean, cool salt smell everywhere.[30]

As foreseen, Welles found little time for his family, even on Sundays. Each morning at seven his English valet, Reeks, awakened him and, after a light breakfast and quick perusal of the Cuban papers, he would be off to the embassy, returning only after dark. Mathilde spoke no Spanish and found the days interminable until her Panamanian friend, Ramona Lefevre, arrived to interpret in the shops or accompany her on afternoon drives. Even the family meals were constrained for Welles suspected, rightly, that the Cuban servants were eavesdropping for Machado's police.

"The heat was intense and the mosquitoes added to our discomfort," Mathilde wrote despondently in her journal. "I meant to face it out with my husband, as much as I longed to go home. Nothing could have persuaded me to leave him. He was often at the point of exhaustion from work and no sleep, always ready to see anyone that wanted to talk with him, day or night. The Cubans," she added tartly, "can talk. They sleep late and go to bed at dawn."[31]

For Ben, seventeen and temporarily freed from Groton's Spartan discipline, Cuban hours—late to bed and later to rise—seemed ideal. His only problem was transportation. After dancing half the night at Sans Souci or the Chateau Madrid, he invariably had to beg a ride home from young Cuban friends. Eventually, he persuaded his father to rent for his use a white Ford roadster complete with "rumble seat."[32] Proud of his new mobility, Ben decided one evening on the spur of the moment to drive with two teenage American friends to Varadero, a beach resort eighty miles away. The night was clear and they expected to be home by midnight.

They reached Varadero around 10 P.M., found mutual friends, sipped Cuba libres, chatted on the moonlit beach, played records and the hours slipped by. It was past midnight when they started back, and Ben fell asleep at the wheel, fortunately traveling slowly along a dirt road. The Ford nosed gently into a ditch, expiring with a wheeze of steam. There the three sat until a passing milk cart hauled them out at dawn. More adventures followed.

Unknown to them, striking Cuban transport workers had scattered nails along the main highways to paralyze traffic and, within minutes, they experienced their first flat. Halting at a country store, they bought brooms, which they tied awkwardly onto the front bumper. Even so, four more flats followed in quick succession. The sun was high in the sky and Cuba's national radio was broadcasting their "abduction" when they crept, shamefaced, into their respective homes. Next day, a grim-visaged Welles put his sons onto a plane back to their mother in New York—he was too busy staving off revolution for adolescent shenanigans.

Welles's mediation, designed to bring Machado and the Cuban opposition leaders into a political "modus vivendi," opened as scheduled on July 1, at the U.S. embassy. The rival delegations refused, however, to meet face-to-face so he received Machado's three delegates at 10 A.M. and the seven representing the opposition, with Torriente at their head, an hour later. By day's end, he wrote Leo Rowe, his belief in "reasoned discussion" had been reaffirmed. "Luckily the appeal to patriotism meets with a vigorous response, and it is definitely on this that I base my hopes."[33]

Under Secretary Phillips cabled him a week later asking how long he thought he should stay. The talks had begun very favorably, he replied, but the "crisis point" would probably come in two to three weeks when the opposition would demand a firm date for Machado's resignation. His own immediate replacement, therefore, might lead to a "complete breakdown." If his mediation succeeded, he would stay until the constitution and electoral laws had been reformed. If it failed, a "new policy" would be required, and then it would be wise to replace him. In any event, he should be replaced by the end of September. He wanted two months to prepare for—and then star at—the Montevideo conference looming in December.[34]

A week later, cautiously optimistic, Welles wrote FDR thanking him for the June 24 letter, which had made him "very happy." After seventeen days, the mediation seemed distinctly encouraging. Machado and the important opposition groups were cooperating and he was "unable to attach much importance" to the students—a serious miscalculation, which he would later regret. Meanwhile, the timing of Machado's resignation remained crucial, yet the dictator was "changing his mind with the utmost frequency."

If he refused to resign after an impartial vice president had been sworn in, the opposition would boycott the coming elections and the United States would be left "facing the same problem." Admittedly, Machado would be relinquishing power a year before his term ended, but, since he had illegally extended it by two years, this would be his "only sacrifice." Before urging Machado to resign, however, Welles wanted Roosevelt's "specific authorization."[35] Machado lunged before Roosevelt could reply.

Persuaded against his will to negotiate with the opposition on "patriotic" grounds, Machado had seen his power eroding. The new electoral law, drafted by Professor Howard McBain of Columbia University, an American expert recruited by Welles, ended traditional voting fraud and sealed the dictator's fate. In a rambling, incoherent speech to the Cuban Congress a week later, Machado praised Welles as a "friend of Cuba" then set out to destroy him. His mediation, the dictator declared, was "personal, unauthorized and not at the instruction" of the American government. The gloves had finally come off. Welles cabled Washington to reaffirm his "full authorization" to mediate but, before it could act, a fresh crisis arose.[36]

On August 4, simmering labor troubles erupted in a general strike. Banks, shops, sugar mills, transport and public utilities across Cuba ground to a halt, and an ominous silence descended on the nation. Radio reports that the dictator had resigned—inspired, possibly, by Machado—sent delirious crowds milling into Havana's streets. Machado's gunmen, firing indiscriminately from speeding cars, killed or wounded large numbers, including many gathered around the American embassy for protection.

In an icy confrontation the next day, Welles virtually demanded that Machado replace his Secretary of State, the Sicilian-born Orestes Ferrara, with a new Secretary of State, agreeable to all, and take immediate leave of absence. The new Secretary would reorganize the cabinet to include members of the opposition. The Cuban Congress would reform the constitution and electoral laws and choose a caretaker Vice President to administer the country until the elections. Machado refused. Mediation was weakening his authority, he protested; U.S. intervention was preferable to being "thrown into the street." After Welles had left, he gloated to his henchmen: "I threw him out."[37]

The time had come, Welles cabled Washington, for "forceful and positive" action: immediate withdrawal of U.S. recognition of Machado. U.S. prestige in Cuba, and throughout Latin America, was being seriously prejudiced and a solution of Cuba's problem thwarted by the "unwillingness of one man to retire." So long as Machado remained in office, there was no hope of normal conditions. The day before, opposition members had warned Welles that a squad of Machado's gunmen had been assigned to assassinate him. By deliberately provoking U.S. intervention, Machado hoped to restore his image as a constitutional president quelling rebellion. "I shall, naturally, not change in the least my mode of existence nor take other than ordinary precautions," Welles added, "but I think the information will give you an indication of the state of affairs now existing here."[38]

Hull, absorbed with the coming Montevideo conference, was growing increasingly alarmed and, for the first time, reported adverse comments in the United States and Latin American press alleging that Welles was "coercing" rather than "persuading." At his next press conference, Hull added, he would stress that there was no "Welles" plan—only a Cuban plan. Welles should bear in mind that he was a mediator making a friendly effort to help the Cubans solve their problem. Although correct in theory, Hull was ignoring the fact that Machado had rejected "friendly" mediation by reverting to terror. With the dictator and the opposition locked in violent confrontation, there was no one to broker a solution except Welles.

Machado fought for time and, on August 9, ordered his ambassador in Washington, Oscar B. Cintas, to protest personally to Roosevelt that the American ambassador would not be "allowed to drive him from office." Welles was acting with his full authority, replied FDR; Machado would go down in history as a "great patriot" if he resigned.[39] Nonetheless, Machado clung to office for two more days as Welles, subsisting mainly on coffee and cigarettes, continued round-the-clock discussions with Cuba's political leaders in search of a constitutional solution. On August 12 the deadlock ended dramatically.

Shortly before dawn Welles was awakened to learn that the Cuban army officers would no longer tolerate Machado's indiscriminate slaughter. As he sped back to the embassy, crowds gathered nearby scattered in terror as six cars drove up, bristling with armed men. Out stepped Colonel Julio Sanguily, leader of the officers, to inform Welles that they had just handed Machado an ultimatum to leave the country immediately.

Guns booming from Morro Castle at noon signaled the tyrant's departure. Troops tried to seize him at the airport, but, at Welles's request, he was permitted to fly to Nassau, the wings of his plane riddled with bullets. Orestes Ferrara also escaped by plane with his wife, abandoning their luggage. On reaching Miami, she telephoned Welles for their missing bags. "You can look after your own luggage," snapped the exhausted envoy, his nerves at the breaking point.[40]

What Welles had most feared—a power vacuum—now stared him in the face. By overthrowing Machado, the rebel officers had torpedoed his plans for a constitutional handover and no one was now legally in charge. Before fleeing, Machado had hurriedly designated his War Secretary, General Alberto Herrera, as his successor, but Herrera was anathema to the officers, who insisted that he be replaced immediately. Welles plunged back into negotiations with the political and army leaders. With their unanimous approval, Herrera resigned that afternoon after designating a sixty-two-year-old diplomat, Carlos Manuel de Cespedes, as "provisional" President. Ironically, twelve years earlier as chief of the Latin American division, Welles had recommended de Cespedes for the same position under very different circumstances.

De Cespedes bore a proud name. The son of a hero executed by the Spanish in the struggle for independence, he had been born in New York, raised in Europe and, as a young man, had returned clandestinely to Cuba to join the insurrection. After independence, he had served in the Cuban Congress, in successive governments and, in 1914, had been named minister to Washington, where Welles had later come to know and respect him. He had also become Secretary of State and minister to France and Mexico. His name, his integrity and, above all, his immediate availability had led to his selection.

Critics would later charge that Welles had "hand-picked" de Cespedes. Spruille Braden, a future U.S. ambassador to Cuba, described the new President as a "boulevardier and gourmet who had lived and entertained lavishly in Paris and was more European than Cuban . . . He knew no more about Cuba and Cuban politics or was able to cope with the Cubans . . . than an average European did."[41] Ruby Hart Phillips, a veteran American journalist, thought de Cespedes "too gentle to rule; honorable and intellectual—but indecisive. He always carries his father's picture and consults it when puzzled."[42] Cuba, however, was facing a crisis, and acceptable candidates were few.

Learning that the political and army leaders had unanimously agreed on de Cespedes, Welles immediately conferred with him and announced that he had agreed to serve. The news brought crowds cheering into the streets. The solution, he cabled Washington that night, had been worked out "solely" by the Cubans and would be acceptable to the "enormous majority," The next few days would be difficult, but he was confident that the situation had been saved and that no "further action," (e.g., U.S. intervention) would be necessary.[43]

It seemed a miracle. Intervention had been averted and Machado replaced by a patriot, sworn to restore democracy. Bells pealed across Cuba and the press in both countries heaped encomiums on the weary envoy. Welles was the "most talked-of diplomat" in the American service, wrote the *New York Times*.[44] Roosevelt and Hull both cabled congratulations, and letters and telegrams poured in. "Talking this morning with Hull, he remembered how highly I recommended you and how thoroughly you have justified the opinion I had expressed," wrote Norman Davis.[45] From an Oxon Hill neighbor and friend, Judge Joseph C. Mattingly, came a letter particularly touching. "Your name, your wonderful achievement and, frequently, your picture, [are] on the front page of almost every paper and magazine in the country. We, who can claim you as a neighbor, feel especially proud."[46]

As calm returned, Drew Pearson wrote Welles suggesting that he return in triumph. "Some of your best friends are very much hoping that you will be getting back here while the getting is good," he noted shrewdly. "You have no idea how much kudos and acclaim you have acquired in the past two weeks. Your picture has been everywhere, your work has been approved by both liberals and conservatives. You are sitting prettier than almost any man I can think of right now." If he stayed on, he would be involved in "all the petty politics of the most difficult imbroglio in the world. Let [Jefferson] Caffery handle that," continued Pearson. "He is aching to come down and be ambassador, although he has been absolutely loyal to you and is one of your best friends. The [Montevideo] conference and much bigger things loom here."[47]

Welles agreed. He was constantly being appealed to for recommendations and advice "with which I should really have no connection," he wrote back. It was unwise both for U.S.-Cuban and for U.S.-hemisphere relations that the U.S. ambassador have "such control." He had cabled Roosevelt suggesting that Caffery replace him within two or three weeks, but FDR asked him to stay on another month, until September 15, to wind up the trade treaty and other pending measures owing to his "very close friendships . . . with [de Cespedes] and all the cabinet."[48] Welles would find, however, as he had in Honduras and the Dominican Republic, that governments in trouble were loath to drop the pilot.

SIXTEEN

END OF A CONTROVERSIAL MISSION

1933

"Before I Leave Cuba, What Little Personal Reputation I Have Will Be Gone."

AT FIRST, de Cespedes seemed to be settling in competently. His cabinet reflected a "thorough New Deal" for Cuba, Welles reported, choosing his words for maximum impact in the Oval Office. His ministers were men of ability and integrity, and the ABC was now represented after years in the underground. Its program, while "radical," aimed at honest administration and social reconstruction; nothing could be more "salutary."[1] Foreign countries had begun recognizing the new regime, and after de Cespedes agreed to honor Cuba's debts, Roosevelt, on Welles's recommendation, conferred U.S. recognition.[2]

Soon, however, the new President seemed incapable of imposing his authority. Machado's flight had opened the floodgates of revenge, and mobs began sacking the homes of Machadist officials—especially of their mistresses. A manhunt began for Machado's secret police, the dread Porristas, and, in three days, sixty were massacred. "Civilization stripped away in one stroke," wrote Ruby Hart Phillips. "The Army joins in . . . no discipline."[3] After Welles reported clashes between army officers and mutinous soldiers, two U.S. destroyers slipped into Havana and Santiago harbors lest violence turn against Americans. At this critical moment, Colonel Sanguily fell ill and the mutinous army became leaderless.

On August 24, eleven days after de Cespedes had taken office, Welles "abandoned hope" that the new government could last; general disintegration had set in. "So-called students and radicals of every shade" were raiding homes, lynching opponents and forcing terrified officials to resign. The Student Directorate, the "most pernicious" element in Cuba, was broadcasting inflammatory proclamations, and sugar workers were turning violent. Horacio Ferrer, de Cespedes's War Secretary, was already recommending that the United States assemble reinforcements at Guantanamo and Key West. "If conditions such as this continue," Welles cabled grimly, "a general state of chaos is inevitable."[4]

Belatedly attempting to ease tension and restore army discipline, de Cespedes promised the nation a purge of Machadist officials and early elections but, unwisely, appointed a retired army bureaucrat, Colonel Armando Montes, as the army's new chief. Years earlier Montes had slashed army pay, infuriating low-paid soldiers and noncoms, and his appointment fanned rumors of further cuts, playing into the hands of the Student Directorate and Communists, who called on "healthy" elements in the mutinous army to join them in overthrowing Welles's "puppet," de Cespedes.

As the mutiny spread, U.S. Consul General Frederick Dumont reported that officers at Camp Columbia, the big army base near Havana, no longer dared remain there overnight. Ruby Hart Phillips heard "astonishing" information: Mutinous troops, backed by students and Marxists, were planning a full-scale revolt against their officers. The students, she noted in her diary, "dislike Welles and will do anything to embarrass him. Their patriotic duty is to cast off the U.S. yoke."[5] Working feverishly to buttress de Cespedes's bankrupt regime, Welles had underestimated the pent-up resentment of ill-paid troops and workers and the appeal of visionary students promising instant reforms.

Confusion mounted and, on August 20, he cabled Hull requesting "several million" dollars in emergency aid and an immediate enlargement of Cuba's sugar quota. Congress was in recess, the New York banks reluctant to advance loans, and Cuba's distress and destitution could "hardly be exaggerated."[6] Unless the United States acted quickly on "repeatedly urged" financial and economic recommendations, chaotic conditions would arise "far more difficult to put down than to prevent."[7] Roosevelt was absorbed, however, with domestic problems and Hull was busy preparing for the upcoming Montevideo conference. De Cespedes had five days left in office.

On September 1 the Cuban president left to inspect hurricane damage along Cuba's north coast, taking with him the hated new army chief, Montes. Within hours the Student Directorate moved into the vacuum. On learning that mutinous sergeants had called an emergency meeting at Camp Columbia, student leaders raced to enlist their support. Soon what had begun as a grievance session turned into a coup d'etat. In a tumultuous meeting lasting till dawn, the sergeants, swept up by passionate student oratory, agreed to join in overthrowing de Cespedes. Years later Justo Carillo, a student militant, recalled the scene.

"When we set out for Camp Columbia, we didn't have the slightest idea that the sergeants would prove the solution," he wrote. "Power lay in the streets and the students were determined to seize it without knowing how, or when, but soon. Afterwards, they'd see."[8] Hastily cobbling together a five-man Junta, or "Pentarchy," the sergeants and students named Dr. Ramon Grau San Martin to head it. Grau was a popular anatomy professor who had fled to Miami during Machado's tyranny, returning a hero after the dictator's flight.[9] Meanwhile an obscure army stenographer, Sergeant Fulgencio Batista, signed the revolutionary decree as "Sergeant-Chief of the Revolutionary Armed Forces." Batista declined to join the Junta but agreed to serve as its liaison with the students; within weeks, he would emerge as Cuba's strongman.

The Junta installed itself in the presidential palace on September 5 and de Cespedes walked out, still draped in the ineffectual dignity with which he had entered it twenty three days earlier. His cabinet resigned soon after, and that afternoon Batista called on Welles to request immediate U.S. recognition of the Junta. Summoning every ounce of his self-control, Welles replied that any such notion was "premature." No political party, however liberal, he knew, would support a revolutionary Junta installed by rebellious noncoms and students and incapable of running the country. Party leaders had, in fact, already begun urging Welles to land troops and restore order while the American Chamber of Commerce was demanding protection for Americans and their properties. The armed overthrow of de Cespedes's legitimate government had ended FDR's plan to recall Welles in mid-September to his post as assistant secretary for Latin American affairs. Welles would now have to remain and help resolve the crisis.

Welles, for the first time, now recommended the use of "limited" force to suppress the mutiny and restore de Cespedes's legitimate government. Otherwise, he warned, Cuba would face mounting chaos and the risk of full-scale U.S. intervention.[10] Hull nonetheless rejected force as likely to lead to intervention. "If we go in," he telephoned Welles on September 6, "we'll never come out. It will be the same as thirty years ago." Fearful lest the United States be accused at Montevideo of "imposing" a solution, FDR and Hull consulted four key Latin American governments—Argentina, Brazil, Chile, and Mexico—that, FDR declared, would be given "complete and constant" information.

The United States had no desire to intervene and was seeking every means to avoid it.[11]

During the confusion, few noticed that Colonel Sanguily, the head of the army officers, had slipped quietly into the Hotel Nacional, an American-owned enclave where many Americans had moved for protection and over which flew a huge American flag. Sanguily's move to a hotel occupied by the American ambassador would soon have dramatic consequences.

With a grotesque sense of timing, FDR's elderly Secretary of the Navy, ex-Senator Claude Swanson, chose that moment to arrive in Havana harbor aboard the USS *Indianapolis,* his mission unclear. The city masses, alarmed by shrill DEU warnings of an imminent U.S. landing, gathered by the thousands along the waterfront as if daring the venerable Secretary to lead his marines and bluejackets ashore. Welles hurriedly dispatched a launch to the cruiser with a private message for Swanson; two hours later, the *Indianapolis* raised anchor and disappeared over the horizon.

Swanson's ill-timed visit, plus the arrival of warships off Cuba, however, soon led to U.S. press charges that the FDR administration was bungling and confused. Welles, the State and Navy departments were all acting with scant knowledge of, or interest in, what the others were doing, claimed the anti-New Deal *New York Herald-Tribune.* "Surrounded by Cuban officers," it wrote, Welles was issuing "ultimatums" to a de facto government and seemed to regard himself as a sort of "regent authorized to sit in his hotel and dictate to the revolutionaries how and by whom Cuba should be ruled." His usefulness had ended and the sooner he departed Havana the better.[12]

The next night, de Cespedes's War Secretary, Horacio Ferrer, called on Welles to confide a daring plot. Eighty army officers were planning, with de Cespedes's approval, to seize Cabana Fortress, certain that they could hold it. The nation would support them and the rebellion would collapse, Ferrer asserted. All, however, depended on U.S. support. Could they have it? After questioning Ferrer closely, Welles recommended "strictly limited" U.S. action to suppress the rebellion. The Cuban army, he noted, was in mutiny, and de Cespedes's government could not regain control unless the United States was willing to "lend assistance."

Full-scale intervention was to be avoided, but a Marine "police force" of 1,000 men was well within the limits of the Good Neighbor policy and as much a "friendly" act as a loan. In the one case "we would be lending the Cubans police and, in the other, money—neither of which they have." The only disadvantage would be the violent animosity of the extreme radical and Communist groups "which [exists], already."[13] Roosevelt overruled him.

"Any promise, implied or otherwise, relating to what the U.S. will do under any circumstances is impossible," the President decreed. "It would be regarded as a breach of neutrality, as favoring one faction of many, as attempting to set up a government which would be regarded by the whole world, and especially throughout Latin America, as a creation and creature of the U.S. government."[14] FDR left Welles a loophole. While observing "strict neutrality," he was not to "block, or in the least affect, any movement by any faction." In other words, if the Cubans could restore de Cespedes's lost authority themselves, well and good—but without American help.

Welles now verged on insubordination. Alarmed by the growing danger to Americans living throughout Cuba and, especially, to his embassy staff, he persisted. Backing de Cespedes through a "police" service was not favoring "one faction of many" but the legitimate Cuban government, he argued. Lending a small number of marines was "far wiser" than letting the situation slide into anarchy, eventually forcing intervention. His plea fell on deaf ears. FDR's decision ended any hope of restoring de Cespedes to power. Left with no alternative, Welles recommended recognition of Grau provided he won "popular" support and proved able to keep order. Privately he thought neither likely—and he was right.[15]

Meanwhile, the five Pentarchs, emboldened by FDR's hands-off policy, began churning out revolutionary decrees. Since each had separate—and often conflicting—agendas, the DEU perceived that collegial rule was a farce and, on September 10, dissolved the Pentarchy and named Grau president.[16] Despite a "pleasing" impression, Welles reported, the slight, bespectacled anatomy professor was "impracticable and vacillating, devoid of any knowledge of government and under complete student domination."[17]

Ruby Hart Phillips later described a typical cabinet meeting. Grau sat at the head of a long narrow table in the long narrow cabinet room surrounded, she wrote, by "youthful, shouting nation-savers. No one . . . pays the slightest attention to him, or has the courtesy to stop talking long enough for him to make himself heard."[18] Spruille Braden recalled the presidential palace in 1940 when Grau was again in power. Grau was "very much up in the clouds, with a lot of cock-eyed liberalism and nationalistic ideas . . . totally incompetent," he wrote. "The palace was just pandemonium. You'd be given an appointment at 4 A.M. [to] find great big Negro sugar workers, sweating and without shirts on 'tuteyando' [theeing and thouing] the president. Somebody would dash in and throw down a paper: 'Sign that,' and he'd sign that and he'd no more know what it was about than the man in the moon."[19]

Erratic as he was, Grau was shrewd enough to realize that his regime, without army support, would be powerless. His first priority, therefore, was to restore army discipline. Successive colonels had refused to be figureheads for mutinous sergeants, so Grau and the students solved the problem by promoting Batista overnight to colonel. Secretly they planned to replace him once he had served their purpose—but they underestimated their man. The semieducated son of a mestizo railway worker, Batista was a born leader. Suspecting their purpose, he began consolidating his power, in the process drawing Welles into one of the few seriocomic episodes of his mission.

As agreed with FDR, Welles had planned to return to Washington by mid-September and had moved with his family to the American-owned Hotel Nacional, Havana's best, where many Americans were living and where 200 deposed Cuban army officers, following Sanguily's lead, also had moved, turning the hotel into an armed camp. Foreseeing trouble, Welles warned the State Department that an agreement to remove the officers under safe-conduct would have to be negotiated before violence erupted. He had no intention of leaving the hotel himself as many Americans had moved in for protection and his presence might ensure their safety.

Batista, however, egged on by the students and Grau, considered the presence of armed officers in a hotel occupied by the American ambassador to be a time bomb. Violence came sooner than Welles had expected. Adolf Berle had recently joined him as an advisor on Cuban finances and, while they were conferring on the evening of September 11, word came that Batista's troops had begun surrounding the hotel. The terrified staff was disappearing. "Come on, Adolf," Welles said quietly. "We'd better go and see what's going on."

Batista's troops, commanded by a sergeant, were setting up machine guns in window embrasures on one side of the lobby as the officers, in various stages of undress, milled about defiantly on the other. Radiating authority, Welles identified himself to the sergeant in Spanish and asked for an explanation. His orders, replied the sergeant, were to search for weapons. At this point an officer interrupted to warn that a search would be resisted. Welles suggested discretion to the sergeant. The puzzled noncom asked what "discretion" meant; Welles suggested that he consult his superiors, as a search might lead to the death of American citizens. The sergeant departed, leaving his troops in place.

For the next half hour, Welles and Berle sat side by side in armchairs in the middle of the lobby, separating the adversaries. "Sumner was very cool," Berle remembered. "He talked about Emily Dickinson, of whose poetry he was very fond, and of Berkshire [Mass.] flower gardens, of which I am even fonder." Eventually the sergeant returned and redeployed his men outside. "Well, Adolf, we'd better get some sleep" was Welles's only comment. "We'll have to be up early in the morning." At 5 A.M., he arranged the safe evacuation of foreign diplomats living in the hotel and, months later, received in appreciation a silver salver engraved with their signatures.[20]

Welles's valet, Reeks, would never forget the rest of the day. As the hotel staff had disappeared, and he feared violence, Welles instructed him to transfer the family's effects to the nearby Presidente Hotel, then drove off to the embassy. Mathilde, meanwhile, sent Reeks out to forage for breakfast. After considerable difficulty, he managed to procure snacks at a corner cafe. Predictably, she found the coffee cold and the orange juice warm, but this was merely the start of his troubles. The hotel elevators had stopped running so, somehow, Reeks slid the trunks and suitcases down eight floors to the lobby, then set out on foot to find transport. Batista's men allowed him to proceed. In time he found a ramshackle truck with a driver and two helpers.

Mathilde had already driven off in the embassy limousine with her maid, her dogs and her Panamanian house guest, Ramona Lefevre, leaving Reeks to follow with the baggage, Ramona's teenage Indian maid, a half-dozen caged parakeets and a tame monkey, which bit Reeks in the confusion. No sooner had the caravan been loaded than the Cuban officers, seeing Reeks depart with Welles's effects, threatened to hold him hostage unless he agreed to intercede on their behalf with the ambassador. He agreed and they let him go.

Meanwhile, the two terrified baggage handlers had crowded into the truck's front seat with the driver, leaving Reeks to perch precariously in the open rear with the now-hysterical maid, the trunks, the suitcases, the hat boxes, the monkey and the parakeets. As the truck lurched away, Reeks tied one of Welles's white silk handkerchiefs to a Malacca cane, waving it as a signal of neutrality. Even so, bullets whistled overhead, barely missing him. Batista's troops presumably had been put off by so sterling an example of British phlegm in the midst of a Cuban revolution.[21] Cuba's economy, meanwhile, was grinding to a halt. "No one paying taxes," wrote Phillips, "merchants not importing . . . wholesalers refuse credit [and] demand cash. The lack of revenue will ultimately defeat Grau."[22] Notwithstanding the economic chaos, his Junta continued churning out revolutionary decrees: dissolution of political parties, tribunals to try suspected Machadists, elections for a constituent assembly, lower interest on loans, a new Department of Labor, an eight-hour workday, land reform, woman's suffrage, lower utility rates for students and a halt to the immigration of low-paid Jamaican and Haitian workers.[23]

With most of these reforms, Welles cabled, he was in sympathy and could have supported them, had they been carried out by a constitutional government with the consent of a majority of the Cuban people. Grau's regime, however, was adopting a virulently anti-U.S. tone, even falsifying Welles's position on key issues. The students, for instance, had cabled Latin American universities claiming that Welles had "urged" the officers in the Hotel Nacional to revolt as a pretext for landing U.S. troops. The continuing hostility of the students and their hold over Grau remained the prime barrier to a settlement.

Seizing the nettle, Welles met privately with thirty student leaders, among them four women, on September 15. "The first thing that surprised us was that he greeted every one of us by name," remembered Carillo. "He spoke to us in perfect Spanish." Welles began by reminding the students that FDR's New Deal also had begun with sweeping social reforms and was already adopting a "totally new" policy toward Latin America. The United States would welcome "any government capable of ruling the country" and would furnish aid if the Cuban people wanted it, Welles made clear. Meanwhile, all Cubans—students included—should put aside personal rivalries for the common good.

As the meeting broke up at 2 A.M., Welles made a final appeal to student idealism. Were he a Cuban himself he declared, he would consider it an "honor" to be a DEU member. The meeting had been "extremely cordial," he cabled Hull next day but, in fact, nothing had changed. The students had heard him out courteously but, as they scattered into the night, they knew in their hearts that he would continue opposing their leader, Grau.[24]

Batista soon learned of Welles's meeting with the students and called on him unexpectedly six days later. Sensing a message, Welles listened intently. The solution to Cuba's problem was U.S. recognition, Batista declared. Neither Grau nor the students should be "permitted to block it." He would be powerless, however, to bring about a solution so long as the party leaders continued subverting the army's loyalty to him. Until he was sure of the army, he would not move. His meaning was clear: Batista represented the only hope of ousting Grau's revolutionary Junta and replacing it with a moderate regime that the United States could recognize.

Choosing his words carefully, Welles assured him that the United States was neither "partial nor prejudiced" and would welcome any government meeting "accepted standards," no matter what individuals composed it. He would talk immediately to the various party leaders. That night he cabled Hull that he had been struck by Batista's "reasonableness, intelligence and apparent patriotism." The tall, imperturbable ambassador and the swart, stocky ex-sergeant had reached a meeting of minds.

The officers holed up in the Hotel Nacional, meanwhile, were growing desperate as food and water ran out. Sympathizers occasionally drove cars or trucks with emergency rations through the bored ring of surrounding soldiers, but the end was approaching. Batista had begun assembling gunboats in the harbor and massing artillery on the surrounding heights. At dawn on October 2, the thunder of guns announced the final assault. Soon the thick masonry walls of the Nacional were crumbling under Batista's shells.

The assault on the hotel broke the final resistance. Fighting desperately, the officers killed dozens of Batista's men before Welles and his Spanish colleague, the dean of the diplomatic corps, could persuade Batista to offer safe-conduct to those willing to surrender. Even so, fifteen officers were killed and seventeen wounded before the rest were carted off to prison. Hull telephoned Welles later that day to congratulate him on a "mighty fine piece of work."[25]

Welles and FDR, however, drew diametrically opposite conclusions from the battle. Welles saw it as consolidation of Batista's power; FDR, as proof of Grau's control. The President suggested, through Hull, that "perhaps the time had come for more latitude" in recognizing Grau. Public opinion might soon demand Grau's recognition, Hull cabled Welles.[26] Criticism of his opposition to Grau was growing in the United States and, in Latin America, was being ascribed to Grau's imagined threat to U.S. sugar interests.[27] Mexico, Peru and Uruguay already had recognized Grau, and other Latin states were waiting impatiently for the United States to act. Drew Pearson added a warning of his own.

"Forgive an old friend for writing you this way," he wrote Welles on October 12. "I have frequently thought that you have . . . one great quality which, sometimes, you carry to a fault. For instance, your loyalty to Jeffersonian democracy: the right of peoples to govern themselves. I sometimes think you would sacrifice your life for it." Grau's regime, admittedly, was not representative of the Cuban people, but "if I told you how public opinion has solidified, both among Latin American and official [U.S.] circles, for recognition," Pearson continued, "I fear you might get one of your stubborn streaks of loyalty and resign."

Caffery, acting Assistant Secretary, was supporting Welles, insisting that the man on the spot was the sole judge and refusing to go over his head. Except for Caffery, however, the President would have already recognized Grau. "I get the feeling," Pearson concluded, "that you have been working so hard and are so close to the situation that you have lost your perspective, somewhat."[28]

In a rare defense of his personal philosophy, Welles replied that "loyalty implies not only a taint of obstinacy but a tinge of principle." Grau had assumed power not by popular demand but after a mutiny of sergeants and soldiers exploited by "leftist students, a few self-seeking politicians of ill repute and a lunatic fringe." After six weeks in office, he had won no new support—except for "concession hunters linked to Tammany Hall and those urging recognition to feather their own nests." The opposition to Grau was overwhelming: every organized party, small merchants and farmers, Cuban and foreign business elements, the professional classes and a majority of the university professors and, probably, of the students themselves.

Grau's Junta had "utterly ruined" plans for government reorganization, and its power stemmed solely from the undisciplined army and Machado's legacy of terror, which still cowed the leaders of public opinion and the masses. U.S. recognition would clamp on Cuba a "military dictatorship fast becoming as bad as Machado's." So long as the Platt Amendment remained in force—"and I am only waiting for the time when [it] can be abolished"—the United States had a "moral responsibility" to the Cuban people and would earn their well-merited hostility if it recognized Grau.

Admittedly, recognition might reduce anti-U.S. propaganda and make it easier to deal with Grau's officials and with the coming Montevideo conference. But until Cuba had a popularly-supported government, withholding recognition was the "just and wise" policy. As to his own reputation, Welles concluded: "there is every likelihood that, before I leave Cuba, what little personal reputation I have will be gone."[29]

Welles's talk with Batista, nonetheless, soon began bearing fruit. Persuaded that the army chief represented their only hope of ousting Grau, the party leaders ceased suborning Batista's troops and, after meeting with him secretly, agreed that they would replace Grau soon with a respected moderate, Colonel Carlos Mendieta. A former chief of the anti-Machado exiles in the United States, Mendieta had participated in Welles's mediation, in de Cespedes's brief regime and was well thought of in Washington. Batista's secret pact with the political leaders, however, soon reached the ears of Grau and the students who, fearing that he might suddenly launch troops against them, decided on a showdown the night of November 3. Carillo left a vivid account of it.

Hauled before a revolutionary tribunal comprising fellow sergeants, the students, Grau and armed militants, Batista was ordered to explain his activities. Counting on Grau's support, the students were planning to arrest Batista, try him before a court-martial and execute him for treason. To their stupefaction, Grau let Batista talk his way out. "Instead of shooting him," fumed a DEU leader, "the idiot president expressed confidence in him!"[30] Aware that his future depended more on Batista than on the unruly students, Grau let him emerge stronger than before. Soon after, during another tumultuous all-night session, when Grau proved equally impervious to entreaties or insults, the embittered DEU voted to dissolve itself. Sixty days after thrusting the anatomy professor into the presidency, the students abandoned him.

A week later, when Batista crushed a halfhearted military revolt, Welles played his trump. Hull, about to leave for Montevideo, was urging Roosevelt to recognize Grau over Welles's objections. After Hull had sailed, Welles requested a personal interview with the President and, on November 19, flew to Warm Springs, where Roosevelt fully backed him. The United States would not recognize Grau's regime, FDR declared. Throughout Welles's mission, the United States had sought to be a "good neighbor" to Cuba, offering to modify the 1902 treaty (the Platt Amendment) and revise the U.S.-Cuban trade treaty.

No progress, however, could be made until Cuba had a government of "genuine stability," and only the Cubans could create it. Emphasizing his continuing confidence in Welles, FDR announced that he would resume as Assistant Secretary for Latin America after a brief wind-up visit to Havana.[31] The Warm Springs Declaration, a DEU leader wrote long after, was Welles's "great triumph."[32] Mathilde and their servants returned to Washington and Welles flew back to Cuba—to his astonishment, finding himself a hero. Cubans and Americans lined the streets, shouting *"Viva Welles"* and brandishing placards in Spanish and English.

Grau, meanwhile, continued maneuvering for time, promising Welles to hand over power to his democratic opponents on December 10 and then, as they arrived at the presidential palace, challenging them to oust him if they dared. Overnight he had persuaded Batista that to resign while Welles was still in Cuba would be personally humiliating. Yet the long, drawn-out drama was nearing its end. On December 13, Welles flew home.

"If any man can live in the satisfaction of having done his duty, Sumner Welles is that man," wrote the influential *Diario de la Marina.*[33] Letters flooded the embassy, one especially reflecting the consensus. "You have done your part with undisputable courage and ability," wrote a Cuban lawyer. "It is not your fault that the lack of comprehension and patriotism of many Cubans brought to naught your gallant efforts."[34] His efforts, however, had not been for naught. Welles had lost battles but had won the war.

A month later, as agreed, Batista replaced Grau with Mendieta.[35] U.S. recognition followed and, early in 1934, Congress abrogated the Platt Amendment at the urging of FDR and Welles—ending U.S. responsibility for Cuba's internal tranquility. Welles negotiated a new trade treaty granting Cuba a larger sugar quota, and relations under Mendieta steadily improved. Seven years later, when Japanese bombs rained down on Pearl Harbor, Cuba declared war within three days. Throughout World War II it proved a firm ally, providing the United States with bases from which to hunt down German U-boats prowling the Caribbean.

Welles's role in Cuba inevitably aroused controversy. Critics accused him of ignoring the pent-up aspirations of Cuba's masses and resisting reforms proposed by "radicals." By opposing Grau, they claimed, he had condemned Cuba to a series of corrupt right-wing regimes and mounting discontent—culminating, twenty-six years later, in Fidel Castro's Communist tyranny. His supporters, on the other hand, claimed that by holding firm against Grau's revolutionary radicalism in 1933, Welles had saved Cuba from civil war and almost certain U.S. intervention.

In retrospect, Welles had erred in pinning his hopes on de Cespedes—a venerable patriot more conspicuous for integrity than for competence. Cuba taught Welles that new forces were emerging alien to the world in which he had been reared. Previously he had resolved Latin American disputes by appealing to "reason and patriotism." Such appeals, however, passed over the heads of rebellious noncoms, radical students and Marxist ideologues. Welles also had erred in believing that U.S. military power could retrieve de Cespedes's lost authority. Perhaps, in the early 1920s, warships or marines might have sufficed; but by the 1930s, his brainchild, the Good Neighbor policy, had made armed intervention unthinkable.

In fairness, it should be noted that on the three occasions when Welles had been sent as a presidential trouble-shooter—to the Dominican Republic in 1922, to Honduras in 1924 and to Cuba in 1933—his early negotiating successes had later been vitiated by Washington's failure to provide emergency aid. Cuba was no more ready for Jeffersonian democracy on an empty stomach in 1933 than Honduras or the Dominican Republic had been a decade earlier. Preventive diplomacy required negotiating skill—but also economic follow-up.

Roosevelt may, in retrospect, have regretted not sending Caffery to replace Welles at the peak of Welles's success: when Machado fled on August 12, 1933. Caffery's Louisiana flexibility, in contrast to Welles's New England rigidity, might have eased the deadlock with Grau and, almost certainly, would have avoided Welles's friction with Hull. Returning from Montevideo by ship, Hull summoned Caffery from Havana to brief him at Key West. "I get on fine with that fellow Caffery," Hull told his young Virginia-born aide, Hugh Cumming, later, "much better than with that Yankee, Welles."[36]

The Cuban experience left its mark on Welles and, through Welles, on FDR's hemisphere policy. U.S. recognition had traditionally been viewed throughout Latin America as approval—in itself, a form of intervention. After Congressional repeal of the Platt Amendment in 1934, FDR and Welles adopted Mexico's Estrada Doctrine,[37] which, by automatically recognizing any government in power, avoided suspicion of intervention and made recognition what Welles thought it should be: "merely the official recognition of a fact."[38]

Had it not been for the Platt Amendment, Welles wrote Drew Pearson a decade later, "I would not have made any strong stand against recognizing [Grau's] government . . . It could, probably, have been able to carry on until its own inefficiency and unpopularity would have brought about its overthrow." So long, however, as the Amendment required the United States to keep order in Cuba, the administration would have been "derelict" had it recognized a "disastrously incompetent regime, not approved by the great majority of the Cuban people."[39]

The most damning criticism of Grau came, in fact, not from Welles but from Eduardo "Eddy" Chibas, a young Cuban founder of the Student Directorate. At the start, wrote Chibas, he and his fellow students had envisioned a "true revolution," but, under Grau's leadership, their dream had "fragmented between the army's irresponsible arrogance, administrative disorganization, demagoguery, plots, palace intrigues . . . personalism [and] vested interests."[40]

Welles's mission to Cuba had highlighted the danger of the Platt Amendment, leading Congress to repeal it, and had persuaded Roosevelt to concede, at Montevideo, a century-old hemisphere dream: U.S. renunciation of intervention in the affairs of its sister republics. By recognizing its limitations, the Good Neighbor policy now began moving toward success.

SEVENTEEN

BACK AT THE HELM: THE 1936 BUENOS AIRES CONFERENCE

1934–1936

"The Kind Of Man Who Asks No Favors."

DECEMBER 15, 1933: a typical Washington midwinter day. Rain spatters, winds gust and cold, bored police swing arms and stamp feet outside the old State Department near the White House. Precisely at 9:30 A.M., a chauffeured Rolls-Royce glides to a halt at the southeast corner and Welles, in a double-breasted overcoat, brown fedora and cane in hand, briskly ascends the granite steps. Behind him lumbers his portly chauffeur, Klenk, who hands Welles's briefcase to a waiting State Department usher.

Acknowledging murmured greetings, Welles rides an elevator to the second floor and walks rapidly, heels echoing on the marble, to his corner suite 202, adjoining Hull's. His veteran secretary, Louise Clarkson, and her three assistants rise smiling, happy to see him back after seven months in Cuba and again in charge of Latin American policy. Meanwhile, his in-box is overflowing with problems. Three demand his immediate attention: the festering Chaco war, tension with Mexico and Panama's grievances. Welles turns first to Panama.

PANAMA

The original 1903 U.S. treaty with Panama had, in effect, made Panama a U.S. colony—a fact that weighed on the conscience of successive American Presidents. Coolidge had offered concessions in 1926, but ones so trivial that Panama had rejected them. Welles himself writing as a jingoistic young diplomat in the *Atlantic Monthly,* two years earlier, had indignantly denied that the United States "controlled" Panama—an assertion that might well have brought a smile to the face of Theodore Roosevelt, who had not only wrenched Panama from Colombia at the turn of the century but had then bribed it to let him build a canal across it.

The passage of time had brought Welles greater maturity, and, by 1933, no one was more critical of the treaty than he. It had not only given the United States the right to "intervene by force" in Panama's affairs, he acknowledged, but also to seize any and all Panamanian lands or waters "which, at any time in our judgment, might be considered necessary for the security or maintenance of the canal." The Canal Zone, a strip ten miles wide running fifty miles from the Atlantic to the Pacific, split Panama in half. Even high Panamanian officials could not cross without U.S. consent. Zone commissaries imported duty-free goods, underselling Panamanian merchants and depriving them of the tourist trade. Moreover, the 1903 treaty had stipulated that the United States pay Panama $250,000 yearly in "gold," but the dollar had later been devalued and Panama had understandably protested being offered devalued dollars.[1]

Early in 1933, encouraged by Roosevelt's election and the start of the Good Neighbor policy, Panama's President, Harmodio Arias, suggested a fresh approach. Roosevelt invited Arias and his family to the White House as his first guests and, on October 21, the two chief executives issued a joint statement. Issues affecting the "defense and operation" of the canal would be left to further study but, meanwhile, the United States would try to alleviate Panama's grievances. Over the next six months, Welles reviewed Panama's complaints informally with Ambassador Ricardo Alfaro. In the fall of 1934, FDR authorized formal negotiations.

Welles and Alfaro would meet more than one hundred times over the next two years, the Panamanian envoy fighting doggedly for every concession. "I am beginning to think that the precept has been reversed," Welles observed at one point. "It is more blessed to receive, than to give." Alfaro had the last word. "We gave all we could in 1903!" he shot back. U.S. diplomats throughout Latin America were following the negotiations closely and, when George T. Summerlin, the ambassador to Mexico, wrote expressing amazement at Welles's willingness to consider Panama's "more frivolous" demands, Welles summed up his negotiating philosophy in his reply to Summerlin:

If I permit [the Panamanians] to discuss these concessions and to take up hours of my time with speeches on the subject, a good deal of steam is blown off and it does not do any harm whatever, except to my nervous system. If these concessions would impair, in any way, complete jurisdiction over the Canal Zone, they would naturally not be granted. If, on the other hand, they did not involve anything of detriment to us and would give us a palliative to use in Panama, I can see no reason why some adjustments should not be made.[2]

Welles's draft, for instance, dropped the 1903 right to "intervene by force," thus recognizing Panama's sovereignty outside the Canal Zone. When Panama agreed that the defense and operation of the canal were "joint" responsibilities, legitimizing the presence of U.S. troops in the country, Welles scaled down the U.S. right to seize "any lands." He increased Panama's annuity from $250,000 to $430,000, with no mention of gold, and barred tax-subsidized U.S. businesses in the Canal Zone from competing unfairly with Panama's heavily taxed merchants.[3]

The arduous Panamanian negotiations—sixteen exchanges of notes and three conventions—in addition to Welles's other duties brought on a heart attack early in 1935 (Welles was then 42), and Hull wrote expressing concern. "All of us here [are] hoping that you would soon be able to do what you really should have done months ago—get out somewhere and have a good period of solid rest," he counseled Welles. "Forget all phases of official affairs here. Those which you have been especially handling, such as the important provisions of the Panama negotiations, will be held in abeyance."[4] Under Secretary Phillips also urged Welles to "ease up," and on doctor's orders, he left for a three-week vacation with Mathilde in Florida.

On returning in March, Welles found the U.S. military adamantly opposing his concessions to Panama. In his absence, Secretary of War George H. Dern had warned FDR that the Army General Staff and the Panama Canal Administration both were insisting that the United States retain "all rights tantamount to sovereignty" enshrined in the 1903 treaty. Not only was Panama's port development to be restricted, the military were demanding the right to police the capital, Panama City, and the main Caribbean port, Colón, in an emergency and still more land for coast artillery batteries and a sealevel canal—or, alternatively, a third set of locks.

In November 1935, eighteen months after Welles had begun negotiating, acting War Secretary Harry B. Woodring and Navy Secretary Claude Swanson both warned FDR that the powerful Joint Army-Navy Board still opposed Welles's concessions. FDR passed him their letter, scribbling in the margin, "Will you see me about this?"[5] Together, he and Welles reviewed the text, article by article, in the Oval Office, weighing every possible loophole or grounds for objection. Finally satisfied, FDR thanked Welles for a "magnificent job" and authorized him to sign the new pact on March 2, 1936. Panama overwhelmingly ratified it soon after, and one American historian observed that, by voluntarily relinquishing the right of intervention, the United States had "restored Panama's full legal sovereignty."[6]

Roosevelt had ordered the U.S. military chiefs to support the treaty's ratification in Congress, but it was neither the first nor the last time that a presidential directive was ignored. Covertly pressured by the War and Navy departments, the Senate bottled up the Panama treaty for three years, releasing its stranglehold only in 1939 when World War II had engulfed Europe and was directly threatening the Americas.

MEXICO

Early in 1935, Mexican President Plutarco Calles secularized the country's educational system, banning Catholic schools and the teaching of religion—thus offending many American as well as Mexican Catholics. An ill-timed remark by the U.S. ambassador to Mexico, Josephus Daniels, praising Calles's goal of universal education fueled the controversy, and when Mexican officials began closing churches and harassing the native clergy, protests poured into the White House, spurred by the demagogic radio priest Father Charles Coughlin.[7] At Roosevelt's request, Welles met privately with leading U.S. prelates, warning them of the danger to the Good Neighbor policy of appearing to interfere in Mexico's internal affairs.[8] Eventually the stiff-necked Calles was succeeded by the more flexible Lazaro Cardenas, and the agitation died down.

Welles's talks with the American prelates and a coincidental visit by a Chilean education mission had convinced him, however, that more could—and should—be done to strengthen cultural ties with Latin America outside of government. The United States was moving rapidly toward a new "political and commercial" relationship with the continent, he wrote his Boston friend, Charles P. Curtis, Jr., a member of the prestigious Harvard Corporation. But government was "ineffective" in cultural fields whereas universities and foundations "[can] operate readily and without difficulty." Welles wondered whether their mutual alma mater, Harvard, might be induced to "break with tradition" and confer honorary degrees on two leading Latin American ambassadors: Oswaldo Aranha of Brazil and Felipe Espil of the Argentine. Such a gesture, he thought, would start an inter-American "cultural relationship."[9] Curtis tried, but to no avail. Harvard tradition proved stronger than the needs of hemisphere diplomacy.

Meanwhile, Welles's gadfly columnist friend, Drew Pearson, was constantly needling the President, Hull and other officials in a column syndicated by 600 papers and read by 50 million. Norman Davis wrote Welles protesting a particularly galling item, but Welles rose to the columnist's defense. Pearson, he explained, was bitter at being kept "at arm's length by FDR and Hull. You catch more flies with honey than vinegar but my views are not shared." Admittedly, White House anger at Pearson was a little embarrassing—although the columnist had not come to his office for months and they had met only socially in private homes.

Nonetheless, Welles intended to continue the same "close relationship" that had existed long before his return to the State Department. He had always found Pearson "absolutely loyal, on innumerable occasions exceedingly helpful and gifted with a very shrewd mentality."[10] Pearson, in fact, often tipped Welles off to developments he would not otherwise have known about—not only in the White House and in various government agencies but, occasionally, in the State Department itself.

THE CHACO WAR

In a June 1935 column Pearson paid Welles "large credit" for helping end the Chaco war.[11] Over the past two years, he wrote, Welles had been "quietly negotiating between the two belligerents, Bolivia and Paraguay, offering every conceivable proposal, sacrificing his vacations and working until late at night while remaining in the background to let Argentina take the credit." When the final story was told, Pearson wrote, it would feature the "prima donnas of peace" who had put their personal pride ahead of negotiating an early peace and considering the "dead they might have saved on the battlefield." This had been Welles's chief obstacle in terminating the war earlier.[12]

Bolivia and Paraguay had been fighting over their common Chaco border since 1932, exhausting their economies, decimating their populations and exposing the hollowness of existing peace machinery. Repeated efforts to end the war had failed. Stimson had proposed a ten-nation mediating group, only to run afoul of ingrained Argentine suspicion of U.S. motives. The League of Nations had proposed an arms embargo but without success, and the belligerents had continued fighting.

Long before his election, Roosevelt had developed a deep interest in Latin America, Welles recalled. Like Welles, he remembered the hatred of the United States prevalent throughout the hemisphere during World War I, a legacy of armed intervention and Big Stick diplomacy. Like Welles, he believed that the United States, in its own interest, should put relations with its Latin neighbors on a "new and completely different footing." In their talks in Albany and Hyde Park before the 1932 election, FDR and Welles had agreed on basic principles:

no further armed intervention, equality between all American republics and, most important, inter-American "consultation" if local disputes threatened neighboring republics or an outside threat imperiled the entire hemisphere.

By 1935, Japan's seizure of Manchuria, Italy's conquest of Ethiopia and Adolf Hitler's massive rearmament program had made the danger of war abundantly clear. Yet as Welles's deputy, Laurence Duggan, wrote:

> The American republics had never met to consider what they would do if an overseas power should attempt to gain a foothold in this Hemisphere. In general, Latin America had depended on the British navy to prevent aggression from any other European power. Fear of aggression from the U.S. had dwarfed dangers from other parts of the globe; the Latin American countries would have viewed with cynicism and hostility any U.S. proposals for joint action against Asiatic or European interference. The American republics entered the fateful years, when Japan was consolidating its hold on Manchuria and Hitler was building up an enormous army, without any plans for consultation or coordinated action.[13]

Ending the Chaco war now became, for Roosevelt and Welles, a golden opportunity to exert U.S. leadership in rallying the hemisphere before war erupted. Welles's role would bring him into close working relationship with Roosevelt and launch their later collaboration in a series of bold global moves that appealed especially to FDR's dramatic flair—but that also exacerbated Hull's innate caution and his jealousy. Welles's role as FDR'S global planner was now beginning.

Early in 1935, Argentina's astute but arrogant Foreign Minister, Carlos Saavedra Lamas, proposed a new approach to ending the Chaco war. A five-nation mediating group comprising Argentina, the United States, Brazil and the two belligerents would meet under his leadership in Buenos Aires on July 1. Bolivia and Paraguay, both too exhausted to decline, accepted, as did Brazil. Welles, though privately dubious that the haughty Saavedra Lamas could win significant cooperation, persuaded Roosevelt that, by joining the Buenos Aires talks, the United States could promote inter-American consultation; an essential first step toward hemisphere self-defense.[14]

Suspecting that proud, rich Argentina would oppose consultation as a U.S. ploy to assume hemisphere leadership, FDR and Welles decided to circumvent Argentina by adding friendly Latin republics and expanding the five-power Chaco talks into a "Special Conference on the Maintenance of Peace" embracing the entire hemisphere. To "exploit the favorable opportunity offered by an imminent end to the Chaco conflict and start discussing peace machinery," Welles directed Hugh Gibson, ambassador to Brazil and chief U.S. Chaco delegate, to propose to Saavedra Lamas that Mexico, Colombia and Cuba be added "lest these major republics be offended by being excluded."[15]

Saavedra Lamas predictably refused, and on June 18, 1935, Welles urged FDR to seize the initiative himself and start rallying hemisphere support for the special conference.

Roosevelt embraced the idea with "avidity," Welles wrote later. Warned that many might regard the conference as a U.S. maneuver to replace the ineffectual League of Nations, Roosevelt brushed it aside. In its handling of the Chaco problem, he observed, the League had shown itself "incompetent to deal with a purely inter-American problem." Maintenance of peace on the American continent was a matter in which "only an American nation could be vitally concerned."

Roosevelt indicated that he would send personal letters to his fellow Presidents, suggesting that the moment seemed opportune for a special conference and asking their reaction. This would be the first time that a U.S. President had acted in this manner, he told Welles.[16]

Hull, on learning of the project, protested that "the Latins are bound to ask us for the moon!" Nothing, he insisted, should be allowed to undercut the next inter-American conference at Lima in 1938, at which he planned a major role for himself.[17] FDR overruled him, directing Welles to draft a circular letter assuming an early end to the Chaco war and suggesting that the hemisphere Presidents seize the moment in an "eminently practical" way to meet and weigh their mutual resposibilities.[18]

The five-power Chaco talks opened on schedule in Buenos Aires. While awaiting the preliminary results, Welles locked FDR's circular draft letter in his safe and sailed with Mathilde in mid-August for his first European holiday in three years.

Returning in September, he found the Buenos Aires mediation dawdling along at a snail's pace. Increasingly impatient, FDR and Welles began stressing the importance of the proposed special conference to key Latin diplomats—but cautiously, lest they affront the prickly Saavedra Lamas by appearing to goad the lagging Chaco discussions or exploit the conference to boost Roosevelt's 1936 election chances. Hull still opposed the special conference, and many Latin diplomats, wedded to precedent, remained dubious. No previous U.S. President had ever proposed—let alone attended—such a meeting.

Early in 1936, the Chaco logjam unexpectedly eased and, on January 30, Welles persuaded FDR that no purpose would be served by further delaying the circular letter to his hemisphere colleagues. The Latin American Presidents responded favorably and, to ensure Saavedra Lamas's support, Roosevelt proposed that the conference open in Buenos Aires on December 1, thereby assuring himself a restful sea voyage after the autumn campaign. Welles began drafting an agenda.

"Lots of speculation . . . Why is FDR calling for an 'extraordinary' Pan American conference?" Castle wrote in his diary. "Little question . . . purpose [is] domestic political effect. Election approaching and no startling achievements in foreign policy to lay before the waiting public . . . I wonder whether this does not seem to Sumner Welles a golden opportunity to make a great name for himself. He very likely has an agenda pretty well under way for he's nobody's fool and knows his job, whatever one thinks of his personality."[19]

Castle was right. Welles's first two agenda items, in fact, embraced goals that FDR and he considered essential: first, "machinery" to operate, automatically, when armed conflict or an outside threat endangered hemisphere security; second, agreement—unprecedented at the time—that a threat to one republic threatened all. Unless these two goals could be achieved, Welles wrote later, "no regional security system could be developed nor could Hemisphere unity be guaranteed in time of danger."[20]

Warned that Saavedra Lamas intended to block the two U.S. goals, Roosevelt and Welles adopted a low-profile strategy. The wisest course, Welles wrote Ambassador Josephus Daniels in Mexico, would be to persuade "friendly and key governments" to take the initiative in sponsoring projects "in which we, ourselves, are interested."[21] Such a strategy, he wrote Ambassador Spruille Braden in Colombia, would avoid the impression of "some hidden, selfish" advantage to the United States. He, himself, would be more than willing for the United States to take "as much of a back seat as . . . necessary," providing the conference achieved what he hoped. He was not implying an "unduly retiring and shrinking" attitude but, rather, refraining from "pushing ourselves too much in the limelight," while taking a "dignified and cooperative position with full recognition of the importance of the U.S. on the continent." The President was "heartily in accord."[22]

Although busy preparing for Buenos Aires, Welles found time that summer for political fence-mending in Maryland, primarily for FDR, but not without thought to his own political ambitions. Diplomacy was temporarily shelved for the back-slapping bonhommie of rural politics as he crisscrossed the Free State, addressing rallies on the eastern shore, at La Plata, at Upper Marlboro and at other county seats, often in shirtsleeves.

Welles and Mathilde attended the Democratic convention in Philadelphia in June 1936, and reporters, seeing him marching with the Maryland delegation, suspected that he was working hard for the Under Secretaryship, vacant since Phillips's recent transfer as ambassador to Rome. One reporter regaled Castle later with an eyewitness account of Welles brandishing a placard and smiling broadly until, on seeing someone he knew, his face "froze."[23]

Hull, too, had arrived at Philadelphia, hoping to replace Vice President "Cactus Jack" Garner as FDR's running mate. At the President's insistence, however, the winning Roosevelt-Garner ticket was overwhelmingly renominated, and Hull left, feeling "personally repudiated and insulted." Adolf Berle wrote FDR in a letter addressed with the license of long friendship: "My dear Caesar . . . I was there; and I thought he was [badly treated]." Trouble was brewing in the State Department, Berle warned.

Hull thought Welles entitled to succeed Phillips as Under Secretary, but the elderly Secretary was sulking, unwilling to make recommendations to the White House "on any subject . . . If Hull were otherwise constituted," Berle added, "he would probably say so to you, but, as you know, Hull does not make representations, especially just now. It is possible Sumner would not care to remain, if passed over."

Not to make Welles Under Secretary would be "wholly unjust," Berle continued. "He has been doing [substantially] that work for the last three years; pulls his political weight, not only in Maryland, but also in the confidence which [Congressman Fiorello] LaGuardia and the majority of the Eastern liberals have in him. This may make considerable difference, both in Maryland and New York, and in the Congressional support in foreign affairs in the next Congress. Sumner," Berle concluded, "happens to be the kind of man who asks no favors."[24]

After the convention, Welles warned FDR that the Maryland situation was "troubling." The Democratic state boss, Governor Albert C. Ritchie, had died; other state leaders were feuding, and at least two would not "lift a finger" for FDR in the autumn election. A handsome Maryland majority for FDR was likely in November, but the current advantage should be consolidated. There was no better way to do so than by having a "small number of the real leaders . . . in the state have the privilege of meeting you, personally and informally."[25] A week later FDR drove out to Welles's Maryland home to meet the key state Democrats whom he had assembled.

Word of the visit spread rapidly. Soon after, Ambassador Daniels wrote Welles from Mexico asking about "the visit the President made to you at your home."[26] The Maryland situation was "singularly difficult," Welles wrote back. He had been working for two years to rally state Democrats behind FDR and managed to turn the Young Democratic Clubs, a "paper" organization in 1933, into an "efficient working unit, organized actively in every precinct in Baltimore and in twenty-one of the twenty-three Maryland counties." He himself had no "personal aspirations of any kind—so far as the State is concerned," he concluded disingenuously.[27]

Maryland went two-to-one for Roosevelt that autumn,[28] and Drew Pearson noted that Welles had become an "important state political figure." A year earlier Maryland had been considered hostile to FDR. The "pickup" in the Democratic vote had been due largely to the "intensive organization of Welles who had risen high in the inner councils of the President, not only through his foreign relations activities but, also, in domestic politics."[29]

FDR's landslide victory cleared the road to Buenos Aires, and he and Welles put the finishing touches on the agenda. "No conference, certainly no inter-American conference, had previously convened after more careful preparation," Welles recalled.[30] As a special mark of friendship, Roosevelt asked him to join the presidential party aboard the USS *Indianapolis* for the trip down, but Hull was brooding and Welles tactfully declined. He sailed instead with Hull's official delegation from New York on November 7, 1936, taking with him Mathilde, Louise Clarkson, two servants and, for once, no dogs.

Adolf Berle had been added to the delegation at Welles's request, and he had brought with him his wife, Dr. Beatrice Berle, an eminent pediatrician, and their seven-year-old daughter, Alice, whose precocious poise delighted Welles. Aware that her mother thought him overly solemn, Welles indulged his sense of the ridiculous by presenting Alice with a "horrible tin pan with rattles on it, instructing her," Dr. Berle wrote in her diary, "to 'shake it in Mummy's ears when Mummy makes Alice do arithmetic on Sunday.'" The ludicrous gift redeemed Welles in her eyes and, in turn, she told her daughter to "shake it in Sumner's ears when he looks too solemn . . . All this to his great amusement!"[31]

After eighteen days at sea and a stopover at Rio de Janeiro, the U.S. delegation disembarked in Buenos Aires on November 25. Memories flooded back as Argentine friends turned up at the pier to envelop Welles in warm, noisy *abrazos* and meet Mathilde. Roosevelt was at sea aboard the *Indianapolis* and not expected for several days, so Welles showed Mathilde the city and the house in the Calle Juncal where his younger son, Arnold, had been born eighteen years earlier. Winter in the Southern Hemisphere was turning to spring, he wrote Arnold. "The city is at its best, the Jacaranda trees in full flower . . . In all my experience, I have never known the local press so friendly. The President arrives next Monday and there is a tremendous expectation on the part of the public here."[32]

Welles and Mathilde spent their last free weekend at Miraflores, the celebrated *estancia* of his Argentine friends Angel and Nena Sanchez Elia, three hours by train from Buenos Aires. Mathilde marveled at the vastness of the pampas: "a superb sight but, at sunset, sad," she noted in her journal. "Miles and miles of flat land that seems to join the horizon." Little green parrots chattered each morning in the trees planted around the villa—the only trees in sight.[33] While her hostess took her driving, Welles and Sanchez Elia rode horseback over the great plains. Twenty years had passed since Welles had ridden the pampas of the Argentine, a country he had grown to love second only to his own.

The *Indianapolis* docked on November 30, and Roosevelt made his slow, painful way down the ramp to the pier where the Argentine President, Augustin P. Justo, and his cabinet waited to greet him. His arrival brought the city to fever pitch. Thousands burst through police lines, surrounding his car as it inched along the broad Avenida Alvear toward the American embassy.

"There wasn't a window, a terrace, a roof, a tree that wasn't filled with people through the entire route," remembered Spruille Braden.[34] Mathilde, an impassioned equestrienne since youth, had eyes only for the horses: "block after block of splendid-looking cavalry mounts," she wrote. "One block all blacks, another grays, another chestnuts and browns—lovely sight!"

Once in the embassy, FDR summoned Hull, Welles, Berle and U.S. Ambassador Alexander Weddell while he perused and edited the address Welles and Berle had drafted for him on the voyage down. "S. W. 'très emotioné,'" wrote Beatrice Berle. "This is the culmination and fruition of many years of work."[35] The next day, leaning on the arm of his eldest son, James, the President made his way onto the podium of the Argentine Congress.

"It is our duty to prevent any future war among ourselves by strengthening constitutional democratic government and preserving individual liberties," he declared. "We in the Americas stand shoulder to shoulder in our determination that others, who might seek to commit acts of aggression against us, will find a hemisphere wholly prepared to consult together for our mutual safety. Each one of us has learned the glories of independence. Let each one of us learn the glories of inter-dependence."[36] His address drew a standing ovation.

He had arrived "just when he was most needed," wrote *Noticias Graficas,* an Argentine journal often critical of the United States. "When we were being coaxed to believe that democracy [had] failed and we must choose between Fascism and Communism, this great man has communicated to us his optimistic faith in democracy."[37] Roosevelt, in fact, had arrived not a moment too soon. Days earlier a Fascist rabble-rouser dressed as Hitler had led a packed audience in a downtown theater in cries of "Death to the Jews! Death to the Protestants! Death to the Masons!" Even as Roosevelt was addressing the Argentine Congress, a heckler shouted "Down with Roosevelt! Down with the U.S.! Down with Imperialism!" Led away by police, he was later identified as a son of FDR's official host, President Justo.

FDR sailed home the next day, his message delivered, and the conference settled down to work. Hull had urged FDR before leaving Washington to flatter

Saavedra Lamas "with a steam shovel" and had worked behind the scenes to win his Argentine colleague the Nobel Peace Prize—to no avail. From the moment of Roosevelt's departure, wrote Braden, Saavedra Lamas proved "obstructionist all the way through and, particularly, anti-U.S."[38] Welles later would describe the Argentine Foreign Minister as a formidable opponent: "brilliant, dictatorial, steeped in foreign affairs and eloquent . . . one of the ablest Hemisphere statesmen of his time, and a dominating figure in any meeting in which he took part."[39]

The imperious Argentine dominated the conference at the start: demanding a stiffer resolution against U.S. intervention than that Hull had signed two years earlier at Montevideo and scuttling a Brazilian plan for a "continental defense pact." Dismissing a key U.S. proposal for a permanent Committee of Foreign Ministers to consult immediately in an emergency, Saavedra Lamas contemptuously termed it an "ambulatory" Pan American Union—a U.S. tool.

Out of touch with hemisphere affairs after years in Europe, Saavedra Lamas's disdain for the smaller republics—notably those of Central America— proved his undoing. Overplaying his hand as the conference began, he summoned the five Central American delegates to his residence and warned them to resist U.S. proposals as "traps," only to be told that his advice was neither wanted nor needed.

His efforts to revive fears of "Yanqui imperialism," also backfired. The threat of Axis aggression was now apparent; moreover, Saavedra Lamas had failed to sense the growing popularity of the U.S. Good Neighbor policy: abrogation of the Platt Amendment; the new treaty with Panama; recognition of Haiti's independence; a hands-off policy in Nicaragua; eight new reciprocal tariff agreements and, above all, U.S. renunciation of intervention at Montevideo. By patronizing the Central Americans, Saavedra Lamas blundered. Welles, who knew the countries' politics, history, and culture better than Saavedra Lamas, soon exploited it.

At the close of a grueling, all-night session, after days of haggling, Welles scored a personal victory. Louise Clarkson recalled the circumstances years later. He had escorted her to a plenary session that morning at her request and had gone on to a meeting of his subcommittee on inter-American consultation. "I did not see him later that day, at dinner, or almost until lunchtime the following day," she remembered. Henry Norweb, U.S. minister to Bolivia and a conference delegate, told her how Welles had "sat throughout the morning, afternoon and evening sessions, virtually until dawn without moving from his seat, while the demitasse cups and cigarette ashes mounted, talking his way to a solution that all could accept."[40]

Faced with overwhelming support for the U.S. position, and unable to block or further delay a vote, the Argentines grudgingly accepted the "principle" of hemisphere consultation in a crisis. It proved a major break-through. Three years later, when World War II erupted, agreement to "consult" provided the legal basis for the emergency meetings of foreign ministers at Panama in 1939, three weeks after Hitler's attack on Poland, and again in 1942 at Rio de Janeiro, five weeks after Pearl Harbor. Welles represented the United States at both meetings.

Thanks to the Central American and other small states—which Saavedra Lamas had patronized and Welles had cultivated—the United States also won its second major goal: agreement that a threat to one republic in the hemisphere represented a threat to all. These two agreements, Welles wrote later, provided the "underpinning . . . which preserved the unity of the Hemisphere at the outbreak of the second World War."[41]

The Buenos Aires conference was intrinsically "the most important inter-American gathering that [had] ever taken place,"[42] Welles wrote in retrospect. Roosevelt had impressed everyone with the "dangers . . . in the European situation and the imperative necessity for the American nations to pull together." By attending in person, he had won for the United States a "real friendship among the Latin American peoples which would have seemed incredible during the Hoover administration."[43]

In personal terms, however, the conference proved costly to Welles. Hull's fury over Saavedra Lamas's obstructionist tactics turned into a brooding hatred of Argentina that lasted throughout World War II. Welles vividly described his own efforts, as translator, to temper Hull's "aspersions on the views and conduct of Dr. Saavedra Lamas . . . to prevent an open brawl" at their climactic final meeting.[44] Indignant over the Argentine minister's sneering dismissal of his proposal for a Permanent Consultative Committee of Foreign Ministers, Hull offered to water it down further and merely authorize the ministers to "discuss how they might eventually cooperate." Even this Saavedra Lamas rejected, demanding another loophole: "if they so desire."[45]

Throughout the conference, Welles found himself caught between his own resentment at Saavedra Lamas's tactics—as bitter as Hull's—and his love of the Argentine people, their country and culture. Obdurate as Saavedra Lamas was, Welles reminded Hull, Argentine cooperation remained essential to hemisphere solidarity. Hull disagreed and vented his resentment on Welles. At Buenos Aires, Braden had his first experience of trying to remain in the good graces of both men. "Welles had Roosevelt's ear, much more than Hull, and Welles's opinions differed from Hull's," he wrote, "so I was trying to walk a tight-rope between them."[46]

Hull and Welles clashed violently Christmas day as the conference drew to a close. Hull was ill and considered Saavedra Lamas's closing speech "insulting" to the United States. He was "fit to be tied," Braden wrote later, on learning that the Argentine would not see him off at the pier. Hull announced that, before sailing, he would protest personally to President Justo that so long as Saavedra Lamas remained Foreign Minister, the United States would find it "impossible to get along with such a blankety-blank." Welles, seeing the success of the conference imperiled by an empty threat that Argentina and other Latin American governments would have denounced as interference in Argentina's internal affairs, "vehemently" opposed Hull's intention and, with Berle's help, dissuaded the irate old Secretary from carrying it out.[47]

But the flare-up at the end of an exhausting month strained Welles-Hull relations to the breaking point. Hull felt overshadowed. Welles had not only persuaded FDR to convene and attend a conference that Hull himself had strongly opposed, but, through his grasp of Latin American psychology, fluent Spanish and negotiating skill, had outmaneuvered the redoubtable Saavedra Lamas in his own capital. Hull seethed.

The U.S. delegation sailed for home the day after Christmas. Soon after embarking, Louise Clarkson noticed Hull glaring at Welles. "He looked at him with hatred in his eyes," she remembered. "I've never seen such loathing."[48]

EIGHTEEN

UNDER SECRETARY AND GLOBAL PLANNER

1937

"Sumner Moves with Lightning Speed"

WELLES'S PERFORMANCE AT BUENOS AIRES won him promotion—but only after a bitter struggle. The State Department had been in a state of "utter confusion" without an Under Secretary since Phillips's transfer to Rome, Castle noted in his diary. Welles "has done more for the foreign service in the few months that he has run the Department—for that is what he has done without any title—than Bill Phillips did in the years he was there."[1]

Roosevelt was moving cautiously, however, for Hull had a candidate of his own: Walton R. "Judge" Moore, a seventy-seven-year-old crony and former Virginia congressman whom he had named assistant Secretary for Congressional Relations. As inexperienced as Hull in foreign affairs, Moore viewed diplomatic problems from an "excessively legalistic and political viewpoint," wrote an observer, and his views were similar to the "more ardent isolationists" in Congress.[2]

Welles had never forgiven Moore for hastily and carelessly drafting an embargo on arms shipments to Spain in December 1936 while he and Hull were returning by ship from Buenos Aires and Moore was acting Secretary. Congress had enacted Moore's draft on January 8, 1937, five months after the outbreak of the Spanish Civil War; and on May 1, with Moore's help, had followed it up with the Neutrality Act, which tied Roosevelt's hands until World War II. Welles had recognized the act's potential danger, and his relations with Moore were glacial. The two waged a "bitter controversy" for months over the vacant Under Secretaryship, Hull wrote.[3]

On May 20, Roosevelt devised a face-saving compromise. He named Welles Under Secretary and revived the long-dormant position of Department Counselor for Moore. Both would draw equal pay and hold equal rank, but, in Hull's absence, Welles would run the department. "Mr. Welles has won his fight with the President and with the Secretary," Moore wrote bitterly to his friend and champion, Ambassador William C. Bullitt in Paris. Bullitt's father and Moore had been friends at law school, and, after the former's death, Moore had taken his place in the son's affections. "It is desired that I shall win the consolation prize," he wrote. "I heard someone say that if Welles is to be Under Secretary, the logical thing is to replace him as assistant Secretary by his spokesman, Drew Pearson. They are two persons whom I hold in utter contempt."[4]

Welles had won the contest, but, with Bullitt's help, Moore would even the score, four years later, on his deathbed.

Armed with new authority and FDR'S full approval, Welles began a sweeping reorganization of the State Department. Like presidents before and since, FDR had long chafed over the department's innate conservatism and had abandoned hope that Hull or Phillips, conservatives both, would prune deadwood or galvanize the bureaucracy. In Welles he had found an iron-willed veteran ready to act. Welles would be "ruthless with those he considered misfits," Castle predicted in his diary.[5] A year earlier, alluding to Welles's "great power . . . when he makes up his mind he wants something," Castle had noted that Welles "wants only men whom he can absolutely dominate."[6]

Meanwhile, others, too, predicted sweeping changes. The department had been "dozing through international disputes, taking its own sweet time," wrote Drew Pearson. "Now comes the revolution with the advent of Sumner Welles as Under Secretary."[7]

In 1937 the State Department was small: approximately 250 career officers, virtually all of whom knew each other personally. Hierarchy was strictly observed and access to the Secretary, the Under Secretary and the four assistant Secretaries restricted.[8]

Welles wrote Phillips in Rome that his goal was to abolish the semiautonomy of certain divisions, which had "frustrated efficiency and the determination of policy."[9] In his view, the chief culprit was the Eastern European division, which handled relations with the Soviet Union and whose head, Robert F. Kelley, was an anti-Soviet veteran closely linked to the Jesuit fathers at Georgetown University. So long as Kelley remained in charge, Welles suspected that U.S. ties with Moscow would continue to be strained. He quietly transferred Kelley overseas and merged the division into the European bureau covering all Europe. As division chief he named Jay Pierrepont Moffat, a fellow Grotonian, kinsman of J. P. Morgan and rising departmental star.

Two other semiautonomous divisions, Mexico and the Philippines, were similarly merged into bureaus covering Latin America and the Far East, respectively. Soon the department began functioning more rationally through four geographic divisions and an administrative division. To supervise sensitive areas—Europe, the Far East and international economic affairs, among others—Welles appointed Political Advisors, senior officers free from routine and able, at least in theory, to concentrate on long-range problems.[10] Latin American policy, however, he kept firmly in his own hands, directing it through his able young deputy, Laurence Duggan, and a staff of hand-picked subordinates.[11]

Welles's reforms predictably aroused intense opposition. Veterans accustomed to a leisurely pace found themselves transferred or retired; and one, long given to taking forty-eight hours to draft an aide-memoire, found a messenger standing at his desk with a memorandum from Welles outlining precisely what he wanted: "The messenger will wait and bring the note," Welles wrote pointedly.[12]

Some accused Welles of replacing Hull's men with his own. When, for instance, he offered James Clement Dunn, a Hull protégé, promotion as minister to Iran, Dunn's wife suggested that he first consult Hull. "Do you really want to go?" Hull asked, leaving no doubt as to his meaning. Dunn declined the promotion.[13] Junior officers, on the other hand, found Welles's imperturbable manner and fund of knowledge about foreign affairs awe-inspiring and sought out his memcons (memoranda of conversations) for their "elegant, precise English and total recall."[14] Among them, Jacob Beam, a future ambassador to the Soviet Union, thought Welles "terrifying."[15]

Not since the days of the legendary Charles Evans Hughes (1921-25), one young officer told a friend, had anyone had Welles's ability to "absorb a printed page and repeat it, letter-perfect."[16] His memory was "phenomenal," remembered Emilio "Pete" Collado, a Welles aide. "I'd report on a situation and within the first few words he'd zone in. I'd cut to the latest development but, if I ever slanted it a bit to favor one of my recommendations, he'd catch it right away and say 'That's not the way you put it to me last time.'"[17]

Working in Welles's office for three years, Collado never found him harsh or difficult—although there were days, he remembered, when Welles "smiled more than on others." Collado often had to wait until day's end to see his overworked chief, and, on one occasion, Welles motioned him to a chair where he normally placed long-winded diplomats. The nearby window was slightly ajar and the night air made Collado shiver. Welles smiled. "They don't usually stay there more than ten minutes," he observed, quietly.

Welles's close ties to FDR, his growing authority, and the publicity he was attracting exacerbated Hull's jealousy. Welles "wanted to be Secretary of State. He acted as Secretary," remembered Collado. "Hull was often at the Bethesda Naval Hospital, or elsewhere, and Welles would make prompt decisions. Hull couldn't bring himself to making decisions."[17] Pearson privately noted that Hull grew irked because "Sumner moves with lightning speed and Hull only wants to concentrate on one thing at a time . . . Sumner will come in with an idea, discuss it with Hull. Hull will nod his head and say 'Go ahead and look into it.' The first thing Hull knows, Sumner has done it. The Old Man reads the newspapers as no one else in the Department. If Sumner's move backfires, Hull is sore. If it goes across, he says nothing [but] is not averse to taking the credit."[18]

Welles was then forty-five, a career diplomat, a linguist, traveled, ambitious and determined to justify Roosevelt's confidence. Hull, by contrast, was sixty-six and frequently ill. Except for brief duty in Cuba during the turn-of-the-century occupation, Hull had never traveled abroad, spoke no foreign languages and, apart from trade and tariffs, on which he was an acknowledged expert, had little experience in foreign affairs. Roosevelt, determined to be his own Secretary of State, had chosen him essentially for his influence with Congress, where, after twelve terms in the House and two years in the Senate, his prestige was high.

A quarter century in Congress, however, had accustomed Hull to reaching decisions through protracted negotiation. His direction of the State Department was "collegial," and, when differences arose at staff meetings, he would wave his hands in the air and murmur reproachfully, "Gentlemen, I'm a busy man. Please go away and come back with an agreement."

Overworked and irked by Hull's congenital procrastination, Welles soon began skipping the Secretary's long-winded meetings, appearing only when Hull summoned him on his "squawkbox." Hull, sensing Welles's impatience, resented it. Their offices adjoined, and when the connecting door opened and Hull saw Welles reflected on the dial of a grandfather clock entering his office he instantly changed the subject, whomever he was talking to. With intimates, he would gesture with his thumb and refer to "that man" in the next office.

Welles's lights blazed late and many thought he was taking on too much, not delegating enough. Little escaped his attention—even press leaks, a source of constant irritation at the White House. Arthur Krock, the formidable *New York Times*'s bureau chief, scooped the capital early in 1938 by correctly predicting that FDR would name Joseph P. Kennedy ambassador to London. Furious, Roosevelt fumed to his new Under Secretary that Krock had sworn that the tip had come from the State Department. Leaks had become a "positive scandal," he complained. "If there is a leak in future, everyone down the line will be sent to Siam!"[19]

Aware of Krock's unrivaled contacts in the White House and his close friendship with Kennedy, Welles absolved the State Department—but the reproof rankled. "If there have been any leaks . . . from the Department, I wish to assume entire personal responsibility," he wrote FDR three days later.[20] Henceforth, only six individuals in the department, including Hull and himself, would know of impending appointments. Months later, after another leak, Welles pinpointed Senator Sherman Minton as the source.[21]

Roosevelt's irritation over leaks ran both ways, however. Once, when Welles sent him a report detailing Italian support for Franco's rebellion in Spain, he returned it with a handwritten buckslip: "Why not leak this to the press? FDR."[22]

Frustrated by congressional opposition to his domestic programs, by isolationism at home and totalitarian aggression abroad, FDR was undergoing a period of "malaise" in 1937, Welles recalled, and was "ostentatiously" leaving the conduct of foreign affairs to Hull.[23] Occasionally, at the end of a sweltering summer day, he would slip away to Welles's Maryland home, mulling over with his host and other intimates the darkening world scene and his limited options. Although aware of the threat to Europe posed by Hitler, Welles remembered, he was "far more preoccupied" by Japan, which had just invaded China.[24]

One evening at Oxon Hill, he confided a plan forming in his mind to halt Japan's invasion. Japanese merchant ships, he said, could be turned back by a U.S.-British naval blockade stretching from the Aleutians to Hawaii, the Philippines and Hong Kong. He had discussed details with his Chief of Naval Operations, Admiral William D. Leahy, and with other admirals. All agreed that Japan, still dependent on the United States and Britain for vital imports, was unready for war. Tokyo would halt if faced with sufficient "determination," FDR declared.[25]

Virtually alone among FDR's senior officials at the time, Welles agreed that Japanese aggression should be checked, sooner rather than later. Hull and his ranking Far Eastern advisor, Stanley K. Hornbeck, discounted Japan as a serious threat but Welles, having seen Japanese militarism firsthand as a young attaché in Tokyo twenty years earlier, "persistently used his influence to oppose any weakening of the Pacific fleet," remembered a colleague.[26] Halting Japanese aggression in 1937, however, depended on the certainty of British military cooperation and on American public support. Roosevelt had neither.

Weeks earlier, British Prime Minister Neville Chamberlain had sent him a secret memorandum, suggesting consultations on how to restrain the Japanese. The "greatest single contribution" the United States could make, noted Chamberlain, would be to amend its neutrality laws, distinguishing between "aggressors and victims." Roosevelt and Welles fully agreed; but Hull warned that the votes in Congress were not there and, instead, recommended "preachments," pleas to foreign governments to observe the standards of civilization Hull had outlined in an Eight Pillars of Peace speech at Buenos Aires the year before, and of which he was inordinately proud. Preachments and trade agreements, argued Hull, might "restrain the dictators and restore world sanity."

Accordingly, he instructed Welles to prepare a noncommittal reply to Chamberlain based on the Eight Pillars. In approving it, Roosevelt wrote Welles wearily that no one could refute its "completely pious principles. I can think of no other characteristics."[27] Pressed by reporters about U.S. policy toward Japan, FDR burst out angrily that everyone expected him to "pull a rabbit out of a hat. I haven't got a hat and I haven't got a rabbit in it!" he groused.[28]

No less frustrated, Welles wrote Groton's Endicott Peabody that the administration would somehow have to convince American opinion that it could "legitimately cooperate with like-minded nations." Neutrality was a mirage; no matter how successful the United States might be in keeping out of war, nothing could prevent the American people from suffering its consequences.[29]

Determined to awaken a somnolent nation, Roosevelt fired his first salvo on June 29, 1937, in a message to the University of Virginia Law School where his third son, Franklin, Jr., was about to graduate. Citing international "uncertainty, confusion and ill-will, the President predicted "disaster and human suffering beyond the mind of man" if such conditions continued. The solution was to divert revenues from armaments to higher living standards, ensuring economic and political peace. The United States and its Good Neighbors had successfully established "machinery for peace" at Buenos Aires the year before. It was a constructive beginning—and the rest of the world should emulate it.[30]

Speaking at the same forum a week later, Welles warned that the Spanish Civil War then raging was a "disease" infecting the world. Its roots lay in the intolerable moral and material burdens imposed by the victors on the vanquished after World War I. Permanent peace could not be based on "revenge," and foreign nations should begin political readjustments of the inequities resulting from that war. The United States bore no responsibility for them, he stressed, but they prevented international disarmament: "military and economic." Echoing FDR,

Welles also cited the Buenos Aires conference plus sixteen new reciprocal trade agreements as contributions to peace.

Sensitive to isolationist fears, Welles pledged that the administration would remain "wholly aloof" from foreign wars but then, more positively, proposed a four-point world rehabilitation program: arms limitation, abolition of trade barriers, free exchange of ideas and—with a nod to Hull's Eight Pillars—sanctity of the pledged word. The United States should play its part in grappling with the "disease" affecting mankind, he declared. American opinion would "overwhelmingly favor" such cooperation by its government.[31]

Though scarcely a clarion call, Welles's Charlottesville speech was hailed, abroad and at home, as evidence of a new mood in Washington. German newspapers praised his reference to the "iniquities" of Versailles,[32] and the British press approved his "frankness and friendly tone." The *Washington Post* agreed that the United States had an interest in preserving peace; and the *Houston Post* thought him "everlastingly right."[33] Constantine Brown, foreign affairs analyst for the *Washington Star,* praised his "somber frankness." Welles had been made the State Department's executive officer, he wrote, to instill "new life into that somnolent institution . . . The old policy of official optimism in the face of mounting danger [was] being abandoned."[34]

Isolationist newspapers were critical. "Can it be that [Welles] has talked too much with diplomats and not enough with the man in the street?" caviled the *Boston Post.* "He has yet to learn that the average American, who is eager for peace at any price, has a stubborn idea that the one way to achieve it is to keep out of Europe."[35] It was precisely to keep out of European—and Asian— disputes that Roosevelt and Welles were sounding the alarm. Even as Welles was speaking at Charlottesville, Japanese troops, staging an "incident" at the Marco Polo Bridge near Peking, had launched their invasion of China.

In mid-August 1937 Welles sailed with Mathilde for his customary three-week working holiday in Europe, the only time in the year when his weary mind and body could find rest. His two sons were in Paris awaiting him and, after conferring with French colleagues at the Quai d'Orsay, Welles took his family by train for a week in Lausanne, proceeding from there by easy stages to Geneva, Venice and, finally, Bellagio on Lake Como. It was the last European holiday Welles would ever have with both his sons, and, despite meticulous planning, as always it was highlighted by comic-opera contretemps.

Reeks, Welles's valet, was loading the family luggage onto the train at Geneva when he noticed, to his dismay, that it had begun moving. Racing with the last suitcase, he hurled it up through what he thought was an open window into the compartment he was sharing with Welles's younger son, Arnold, then scrambled aboard himself. Arnold, however, had closed the window, so the bag arrived with a shattering of glass. After a sleepless night with curtains drawn in a vain attempt to exclude the wind and soot of successive Alpine tunnels, Reeks and Arnold emerged at Venice looking, as Welles frostily observed, like two "minstrels in a black-face show."

The next morning, seeing Welles's elder son, Ben, stealing off in a gondola on a private tryst, they saluted him with a chorus of Bronx cheers that shattered the stillness of the Grand Canal. Welles, breakfasting on a balcony overhead, took in the scene with practiced eye and, summoning Reeks, observed that he was "too old to behave like a vulgar small boy, even if Arnold chooses to." Out of sight, Arnold and Reeks fell into each other's arms, tears of laughter coursing down their cheeks. Welles's retinue, in fact, led him a merry chase.

Days later, as the diminutive King Victor Emmanuel of Italy approached the hotel in a royal launch, bound for a lunch in his honor, Mathilde's anti-Fascist Spanish maid, Manuela, threatened to drop a flowerpot in the canal and drench the monarch as a protest against Italian aid to Franco's rebellion in Spain. Sternly reminding her of his official position, Welles warned in his gravest Castillian that there were limits to political disapproval.

In Bellagio, stretched out in a deck chair by the sunny lakeside each morning and absorbed in Tauchnitz paperback histories, biographies and novels in French, German or Spanish, Welles found the peace he craved. Afternoons were given over to excursions in a launch that cruised slowly past yellowing villas, half hidden by poplars and hydrangeas, finally dropping the family off for tea on the terrace of the ducal Villa d'Este Hotel as the sun dipped behind the Alps and church bells tolled over the darkening waters. Surrounded by his family, the reserve that intimidated Welles's subordinates—and often his colleagues—melted away. He could never quite rid himself of his Guards officer bearing or tolerate bores, but the affectionate raillery of his sons relaxed and amused him.

They twitted him about his sober holiday attire—his one concession being a wide-brimmed Panama hat and two-toned brown-and-white or black-and-white shoes. Such footwear, they observed in loud whispers, were known in England as "cad's" shoes. Mathilde, lazily tossing tidbits to the dogs, would protest, giggling, while Welles, involved in his book, would either look pained or pretend not to hear. Eventually, on completing his chapter, he would take on his irreverent progeny, expressing mock horror at their addiction to Benny Goodman jazz records, hot dogs, rumble-seat roadsters and the teenage girls touring Europe with their parents with whom they would slip away once dinner was over. Good natured as she was, Mathilde often seemed puzzled by these sallies.

Before starting home, Welles took his sons on a quick side trip to London for his annual visit to Davies, his tailor; Washington, Tremlett, his shirtmaker, and Thomas of St. James's Street, who had been making his shoes for a quarter century.

Between fittings, he managed a *tour d'horizon* with his British counterpart, Sir Alexander Cadogan, Permanent Under Secretary at the Foreign Office.

They reviewed world trouble spots—Spain, Ethiopia, China. Welles conceded widespread isolationism in the United States and thought one solution might be closer U.S.-British economic cooperation: early conclusion of the long-delayed Anglo-American reciprocal trade pact dear to Hull's heart. Time, he emphasized, was pressing but Cadogan, a small, waspish product of the old imperial school, thought otherwise. "Mr Welles," he noted dryly in his diary, "seemed rather insistent on the time factor."[36]

In sharp contrast to Britain's measured tread, Japanese troops, meanwhile, were pouring into north China, seizing Peking and Tientsin then racing south to ring Shanghai as Japanese warplanes bombed civilians, among them 3,000 Americans trapped in the city. Six months later, on December 12, 1937, Japanese planes also sank the U.S.S. *Panay,* a gunboat stationed on the Yangtze River, near Nanking, killing three crew members and wounding many despite the large American ensign at the stern and two American flags painted on the upper decks. It was a deliberate challenge.

Hull appealed to sixty nations to observe his Eight Pillars of Peace, and all—with one exception—agreed. To Hull's indignation, Portugal's hardheaded dictator, Antonio de Oliveira Salazar, dismissed the Pillars as "vague formulae."[37] Privately, Welles agreed. What was needed, he wrote later, was not a "reiteration of familiar principles, but a clear indication that the U.S. was willing to act."[38] It was not.

Welles was in Washington on October 5 when FDR launched his celebrated plea for a "quarantine" of aggressors on a visit to Chicago, the heartland of isolationism. "When an epidemic starts to spread," he declared, repeating the disease simile he and Welles had used at Charlottesville, "the community approves and joins in a quarantine."

Protests poured in from coast to coast. The reaction was "quick and violent," Hull wrote later. The speech had the effect of "setting back, for at least six months, our constant educational campaign . . . to create and strengthen public opinion toward international cooperation."[39] Samuel I. Rosenman, FDR's speechwriter, remembered that the quarantine address was condemned as "warmongering and saber-rattling . . . Telegrams of denunciation came in at once."[40]

Many would later claim credit for the term "quarantine," among them Interior Secretary Harold Ickes and Eugene Meyer, publisher of the *Washington Post.* Replying to a query from Rosenman in 1950, Welles recalled how the speech had evolved:

At that time, Roosevelt was more immediately concerned with the situation in the Pacific than . . . in Europe. He was talking with the Navy about drawing a . . . line in the Pacific to be maintained by the U.S., if the British would agree to cooperate, beyond which Japan would . . . not be permitted to trade or . . . expand [if] she persisted in the . . . military conquest of China upon which she . . . seemed bent. I remember very well . . . upon at least two, and I think three, occasions when I was with the President in his office in the White House . . . he had me walk over to the large map of the Pacific . . . on a stand in the rear of his office . . . that I might follow, point by point, the various lines that he had under consideration.

[He] used the word "quarantine" in connection with that line and the talks to which I refer took place in the earlier part and in the middle of the summer of 1937 . . . He did not discuss with me the so-called "quarantine" clause before the Chicago address was delivered . . . All that I can be certain of, however, is that it was a word that the President had used several times in talking with me long before the speech was drafted.[41]

The failure of the cabinet—and, especially, Hull—to back him left Roosevelt depressed and bitter. Welles approved the speech as "something you could get your teeth into." A trade embargo imposed on Japan in 1937 by the United States, Britain, France and other signatories to the 1921-22 Washington Naval Treaty and backed, if necessary, by force might have checked Tokyo, he wrote in retrospect. By rejecting FDR's call for collective action, the United States "lost its best chance to avoid war with Japan."[42]

FDR'S GLOBAL PLANNER

While the use—or even threat—of force in 1937 remained politically impossible, as the uproar over the quarantine speech had shown, Welles remained convinced that the United States should use its immense, if untested, influence to highlight the growing danger. It was now that his role as FDR's "global planner" began evolving further. After long deliberation, he submitted a two-phase plan to Roosevelt that fall. Phase one, "admittedly dramatic," was meant to capture the world's attention, he wrote later. Roosevelt would invite the Diplomatic Corps to the White House on Armistice Day—chosen to evoke the memory of 40 million dead in World War I—and appeal to the world to prevent another conflict, pledging U.S. cooperation in disarmament, tariff cuts and greater access to raw materials.

Phase two, however, was "wholly concrete," Welles wrote. If the world response was favorable, the President would invite nine small nations, representing Latin America and other regions, to join in an "executive committee" in Washington and prepare concrete proposals. (Five years later, in drafting the first United Nations charter in late 1942, FDR and Welles would retain both the executive committee and geographic regional concepts.)

His plan might have seemed "tenuous," Welles acknowledged in retrospect, but, at the time, it had four "immense" advantages: It involved no U.S. military commitments. U.S. leadership would have "heartened" the Europeans, Latin Americans and Asians, especially the Chinese. It would have warned aggressors not to count on American indifference, stiffening Italians who opposed Mussolini and Germans who detested Hitler. Finally, it posed no threat to the Soviet Union.[43]

Initially Hull showed little interest in Welles's plan, although he acknowledged in his memoirs later that Roosevelt "completely [embraced] it."[44] Seizing a pencil, the President began editing Welles's draft, promising to return it in a day or so. It came, therefore, as a double shock when FDR confided, soon after, that Hull's tepid acquiescence had turned overnight into violent opposition. As at Buenos Aires the year before, Welles had appealed to the dramatic in Roosevelt—and had alarmed the cautious in Hull.

Welles's plan, Hull argued, was illogical and impossible. FDR's meeting with the Diplomatic Corps would turn into a "peace congress," and it would be fatal to "lull the democracies into a feeling of tranquility."[45] Deaf to Welles's protest that his plan was designed to awaken—not lull—the democracies and that no peace congress was remotely contemplated, Hull remained unyielding. Roosevelt, loath to overrule his Secretary of State on the heels of the quarantine speech imbroglio, gave in.

"I have regretted few things so much," Welles wrote at the end of his life, "as that an opportunity, which Franklin Roosevelt was singularly qualified to grasp, should have so needlessly been thrown away."[46]

Norman Davis returned from Europe at the end of 1937, discouraged by yet another sterile disarmament conference, and learned, to his indignation, that Hull had vetoed the Welles plan which Davis had previously seen and had warmly endorsed. Warning FDR that "drift [is] no policy," he urged him to ignore Hull's objections and revive it. Early in 1938, prodded by the President and Davis, Hull grudgingly authorized Welles to proceed—then undercut him. Not only the British and French but Hitler and Mussolini, he decreed would have to approve it in advance. Welles was appalled.

To give the Axis dictators a virtual veto over a major U.S. policy initiative would be courting disaster. Downing Street was notorious for leaks, and premature disclosure would be fatal. Success depended on winning "public support so widespread and . . . enthusiastic that no government could refuse to cooperate."[47] Hull, however, remained adamant. Years later the Pulitzer Prize–

winning historian James MacGregor Burns would write that Welles's "key role" was part of the trouble.[48]

Roosevelt, though irritated by Hull's obduracy, decided to go ahead. At his direction, on the evening of January 11, 1938, Welles outlined the plan to the British ambassador, Sir Ronald Lindsay. A towering Scot, Lindsay was given to reading at a standing desk. Welles sat silently in the dimly lit embassy study as Lindsay stood perusing the proposal with evident approval. For two years he had been trying to enlist U.S. cooperation; here was the first concrete sign of a turning away from isolationism.

Later that evening Lindsay cabled London that FDR was planning to convene the Diplomatic Corps on January 22 and urge all governments to agree on certain "fundamentals of international cooperation": arms cuts, recognized laws of war and equal access to raw materials. If the response was favorable, the United States—"while maintaining its traditional freedom from political involvements"—would ask a small number of governments to help frame tentative proposals. Lindsay urged a quick, cordial acceptance of this "invaluable initiative [as] a rejection might destroy two years' progress."[49]

The dénoument is history. Foreign Secretary Anthony Eden was on holiday in France when Lindsay's cable arrived and, without consulting—or even informing—Eden, Prime Minister Neville Chamberlain tossed the FDR-Welles plan in the wastebasket, largely influenced by Sir Horace Wilson, his "very anti-Roosevelt" cabinet Secretary, by Cadogan and by his own prejudices. The plan would complicate his negotiations with Hitler and Mussolini for "appeasement" in Europe, he protested.[50] Cadogan sneered in his diary that Roosevelt had "wild ideas about formulating a world settlement . . . Must know Monday whether we agree . . . This is not the way to conduct such business."[51] On learning, two days later, from Lindsay that Roosevelt was "disappointed," Cadogan noted cynically: "We drafted a telegram to keep the President sweet."[52]

The moment, however, for the FDR-Welles diplomatic gambit had passed. Within a month, Eden resigned over Chamberlain's appeasement policy and, on March 12, Hitler, free from fear of possible Anglo-American cooperation, annexed Austria. From there, the road would lead inexorably to the dismemberment of Czechoslovakia that autumn, to the attack on Poland a year later and to World War II.

Chamberlain's rejection of the FDR-Welles plan in 1938 was one of the turning points on the road to war, Eden wrote in his memoirs. Welles had the "widest knowledge" of European problems among contemporary Americans and a "lucid mind, which I grew to respect."[53] Had the United States concerned itself with European affairs in "however moderate" a form, Eden told Drew

Middleton of the *New York Times* at the end of his life, it would have been a deterrent to the dictators and an encouragement to the free nations.[54]

Churchill, too, condemned Chamberlain—and, by implication, Hull—for having "cast away the last frail chance to save the world from tyranny, otherwise than by war." It left one breathless with amazement, he wrote, that Chamberlain should have "waved away the proffered hand stretched out across the Atlantic."[55]

NINETEEN

AT FDR'S RIGHT HAND

1938–1939

"The Department; the Dictator . . . Undisputed and Supreme"

ROOSEVELT AND WELLES HAD FAILED, but even failure seemed to strengthen FDR's confidence in his Under Secretary. Welles was "*the* Department; the dictator . . . undisputed and supreme," Castle heard while lunching in May with a State Department official and a *New York Times* reporter. By contrast, Hull was "not Secretary of State [but] stupid . . . fanatic on free trade, hopeless as head of the Department, morally noble, everywhere respected but [with] little, if any, idea of what was going on."[1] Columnists Joseph Alsop and Robert Kintner thought Welles one of the "most-discussed human enigmas" in Washington.

"This tall, powerfully-built, beautifully-tailored man with the glacial manner, and an expression which suggests that a morsel of bad fish has somehow or other lodged itself in his mustache," they wrote, was a shaper of America's course. He wielded a major influence in U.S. foreign policy, thought shrewdly, practically, forcefully and always to one end—maintaining a reasonably healthy international situation without involving the United States in dangerous commitments. Although privately a strong anti-Fascist, Welles wanted the United States to "ride on no crusades." The healthiest possible development, in his view, would be a restoration of the European balance of power. If that failed, he would take any other tack that seemed practical and sound. His point of view, they concluded, deserved the "compliment of imitation."[2]

Although normally deferential to the President, in the summer of 1938, Welles involved himself in a Maryland political dogfight that brought Roosevelt's wrath down on his head. The story illustrates Welles's political ambitions and, even more, his obstinacy when his personal word was concerned.

Smarting from his defeat in seeking to "pack" the Supreme Court the year before, FDR was determined to purge his political enemies in the 1938 congressional elections. High on his hit list was Senator Millard Tydings, a popular Maryland Democrat who had defied him. FDR gave orders to defeat Tydings by building up a little-known rival Democrat, David Lewis. Welles, deeply involved in state politics and planning a Senate run himself in 1940, protested vigorously.

The only state machine capable of building up Lewis, he argued, was controlled by the mayor of Baltimore, Howard Jackson, who was not only lukewarm toward the New Deal but had ambitions of his own for the governorship. Ignoring Welles, the White House agreed to back Jackson for the govenorship in return for his help in defeating Tydings. Welles was acutely embarrassed.

He had already begun cultivating political allies and had pledged his support for the governorship to Ghiselin Lansdale Sasscer, president of the state senate and a power in Prince George's County, where Welles lived. As governor, Sasscer would be powerfully placed to help Welles's 1940 Senate bid, and, having pledged his support, Welles was loath to withdraw it. He agreed to work for Tydings's defeat but insisted that Sasscer was a stronger gubernatorial candidate than Jackson, whose promise to build up Lewis he frankly questioned. If the White House would not support Sasscer for the governorship, Welles argued, it should at least help elect him state Attorney General.

"Welles doesn't know anything about politics, although he thinks he does," Ickes grumbled in his diary. "[He] is one of the most conceited men I have known."[3]

Weeks passed, and Welles found himself on a collision course. Finally the President told Ickes to phone Welles and tell him that he would "take care" of Sasscer later, if necessary. Meanwhile, his orders were to fall in line. "I did not think I was the person to convey this message," wrote Ickes. "He did not take it very well."

In fact, Welles told Ickes icily that he would personally telephone FDR to protest, but Ickes forestalled him by alerting Missy LeHand, FDR's confidential secretary. Soon after, Tommy "the Cork" Corcoran, a senior FDR political aide, told Ickes to phone Welles and say that FDR would not discuss the issue further. He had sent his orders and "expected them to be obeyed."[4] Welles fell into line and the storm passed.

It was the first, and only, time that Welles risked an open quarrel with FDR—admittedly over politics, not policy—and, for both, it proved an exercise in futility. Tydings won easy reelection that fall; Sasscer entered Congress a year later; and, by 1940, World War II had dashed Welles's hopes of a Senate seat. His place, FDR told him firmly, was in the State Department.

Welles and Mathilde sailed in August 1938 for their annual European holiday. Arnold, then a Yale junior, joined them in Lausanne. Europe seemed as peaceful that summer as the swans gliding over Lac Leman, but the newspapers were reporting mounting Nazi pressure on Czechoslovakia and Welles remained tense.

One evening, as he and Arnold were admiring the view from their hotel terrace, a cloud began forming in the cloudless sky, slowly taking the shape of Czechoslovakia. One end, roughly resembling the Sudentenland, began drifting away.[5] Little given to fantasy, Welles took it as an ill omen—and so it proved.

On returning to Paris, he conferred repeatedly with Ambassador Bullitt, with whom his relations were then correct, if not close. Bullitt invited the Under Secretary and his son to lunch with the French premier, Edouard Daladier, and Foreign Minister, Henri Bonnet—both of whom, like Bullitt, expected imminent war. After Welles had sailed for home, Bullitt wrote him that France would "unquestionably march" if Germany invaded Czechoslovakia. Hitler would "not dare take the risk," he predicted. An attack on Czechoslovakia would mean "immediate war with France . . . Great Britain would follow."[6] Bullitt proved as indifferent a prophet as the French leaders, whose views were molding his.

The Munich crisis broke when Welles was on the Atlantic. Upon arriving in Washington, on September 21, he found the capital confused but hopeful that war still could be averted. A week earlier Chamberlain had flown to Germany, umbrella in hand, to confer with Hitler, and FDR had cabled the gaunt old Briton: "Good man!" Ambassadors Bullitt in Paris and Kennedy in London were meanwhile urging yet another appeal to Hitler, and Welles and Berle drafted text after text. "Welles kept pushing the President, I kept advising him to go slow," Hull wrote later.[7] Negotiations collapsed, on September 24, and Europe began mobilizing. War seemed inevitable. The world seemed to "hang in the balance," wrote Hull.

In desperation, FDR tried a two-track approach: appealing personally to Mussolini and directing Welles to draft still another appeal to Hitler. On September 27, FDR cabled the Nazi dictator proposing an immediate conference of all nations "directly" interested in the Czechoslovak controversy (e.g. not the United States) at a neutral spot in Europe.[8] Hitler rejected it but invited Chamberlain, Daladier and Mussolini to join him the next day at Munich. The crisis eased and war was postponed for a time. But, as Hull noted, "Hitler got all he wanted without firing a single shot. Czechoslovakia now lay defenseless before him."[9]

Welles and Hull drew diametrically opposite conclusions from Munich, Hull's the more perceptive of the two. In a nationwide radio address on October 3, Welles praised the "superb" opportunity now afforded to establish a "new world system of law and order." Hull issued a coldly condemnatory statement. "Welles and I differed," he wrote later, "he being optimistic; I skeptical."[10] Drew Pearson, normally Hull's bitterest critic, noted that, while many State Department officials had "gone haywire" over the Munich pact, "one who hadn't was Cordell Hull." Hull had correctly predicted that Czechoslovakia would be sold short. (At Munich, Hitler had outmaneuvered the British and French to win virtual control over his intended next victim, Czechoslovakia.) Among those "a little off," wrote Pearson, was "sedate Sumner Welles."[11]

Welles later conceded that he had failed to foresee the "rapidity" with which the Munich crisis developed. Remembering the influence of the German General Staff in World War I, he had assumed that Hitler's generals would never "permit" him to risk war while Soviet Russia remained Germany's avowed enemy.[12] Welles had failed, however, to sense that Hitler, unlike Kaiser Wilhelm II in World War I, dominated his generals.

Munich marked a turning point in American foreign policy, Welles acknowledged, in an interview with Alsop and Kintner. He and other policy makers had "let matters slide long enough."[13] FDR conferred continually that autumn with Hull, Welles and Berle, often over breakfast in his bedroom. In his State of the Union message at the start of 1938, he had asked Congress for measures "short of war" to restrain the dictators. But, with the neutrality laws still tying his hands, there was little he could do except, as James MacGregor Burns aptly put it, the "old policy of protest and pinpricks—higher duties on German goods and jaw-boning."[14]

In frustration, FDR telephoned his envoys in Europe, suggesting an appeal to foreign governments to eliminate "offensive" weapons such tanks and airplanes and to rely, instead, on defensive arms. After discreet soundings, they tactfully persuaded him to drop the idea.[15] Nonetheless, slowly and fitfully, a new policy was taking shape: to prevent war, if possible. If impossible, at least to ensure victory for the democracies.[16]

Hitler occupied Czechoslovakia on March 15, 1939, and Welles, then Acting Secretary of State, condemned wanton lawlessness and the "extinguishment" of the liberties of a free people. Into his somewhat wooden statement Roosevelt inserted "temporary" before extinguishment. A fortnight later Chamberlain, conceding the failure of his appeasement policy, announced that Britain and France had jointly guaranteed the territorial integrity of Hitler's next victim: Poland.

Roosevelt and Welles had long viewed Italy as the weak link in the Axis chain and Mussolini as particularly susceptible to flattery. The fortuitous arrival of a new Italian ambassador to Washington, Ascanio dei Principi di Colonna, provided an opportunity to test the theory. Welles sat in on Colonna's first White House interview on April 5 and sent a memorandum of conversation later to key American ambassadors, among them Bullitt. War would be "ruinous" to Italy and to all other nations, Roosevelt told the Italian. The American people would insist on helping victims of aggression, and Congress was "speedily" preparing to lift the arms embargo.

Europe could not contain "two overlords," he continued. Hitler would throw Mussolini over whenever it suited him. By preventing war, Mussolini would win the world's gratitude and "just" concessions. Roosevelt was not thinking of a great conference, such as Vienna or Versailles, but rather of discussions among a limited number of states to consider all grievances. The United States would not take the initiative, lest Europe think it was "butting in," but, if Mussolini proposed such discussions himself, Roosevelt would back him.

Colonna asked if he could have it "in writing," but the President warily suggested that, instead, he report their conversation to Mussolini immediately. Concluding with a touch of his celebrated charm, FDR said he regretted never having met the Duce; he thought they "spoke the same language."[17] Apparently not. Two days later, on April 7, Mussolini invaded Albania.

Amid almost universal hopelessness and despair, wrote historians William L. Langer and S. Everettt Gleason, FDR stood out as the "moral leader" in the crusade against war.[18] On Pan American Day, April 14, he stressed the need for hemisphere solidarity and defense; and, the next day he appealed again to Hitler. The ill-fated gesture came to be known as the "Saturday surprise."

FDR proposed that Hitler publicly agree not to attack thirty-one specified nations in Europe and the Near East for at least ten years. In return, he would ask them not to attack Germany. This hapless proposition, which Welles helped draft,[19] met with predictable derision. Standing in the Reichstag, Hitler solemnly named each of FDR's thirty-one countries—including Portugal and Lebanon— as his Nazi deputies rocked with laughter.

Undeterred, FDR dusted off a fresh version of the Welles plan: an international conference on disarmament and trade, which the United States would attend, and parallel "political" negotiations, which it would not. When Hitler contemptuously rejected this too, Henry Wallace telephoned Roosevelt, criticizing his repeated appeals and insisting that the Axis "mad dogs" would heed only force.[20]

King George VI and Queen Elizabeth of England arrived on a state visit to the United States in June, and photographs of the royal couple democratically munching hot dogs with the Roosevelts at Hyde Park evoked a wave of pro-British goodwill. During the planning stage of the visit, Welles had told the British ambassador, Sir Ronald Lindsay, that he saw "no objection" to the inclusion of Foreign Secretary Lord Halifax in the royal party; in fact, he thought it an "excellent" idea. Lindsay was puzzled. Two days earlier, over a golf game, Secretary of War Stimson had warned him that the presence of Halifax would be a "fatal error"; and soon after, Roosevelt had added, "with a grimace," that the appearance of a British cabinet minister in the royal entourage would arouse speculation about an alliance. Welles was an "excellent official," Lindsay cabled London as the royal party was setting out, but he had often found his opinion on political issues "at fault."[21]

FDR's confident prediction to Colonna that Congress would "speedily" lift the arms embargo proved disastrously wrong. On July 18, meeting with Hull and congressional leaders in the Oval Office, FDR heard archisolationist Senator William E. Borah of Idaho flatly assert that there would be no repeal of the arms embargo—and no war. His sources, he claimed to Hull's fury, were better than the State Department's.[22] (They turned out to have been reporters.)

Meanwhile, tension in the Far East was rapidly rising. The Japanese humiliated the British during an incident at Tientsin, forcing them to back down, and the British and French both implored FDR to retaliate lest the Axis try similar tactics in Europe. The only available means to rein in Japan, however, lay in trade sanctions, and, on July 26, Roosevelt denounced the 1911 United States–Japanese commercial treaty, effective in six months. Virtually certain of retaliation sooner or later, he ordered Henry Morgenthau to start immediate planning for the use of ships and railways in event of war. Soon thereafter, Congress passed a $2 billion defense bill.

Despite Borah's assertion that there would be no war, Hitler was steadily escalating his demands on Poland—determined, from all indications, to prevent the Poles from backing down. Ominous reports of German troop movements toward Poland were now reaching the State Department.

Roosevelt had been planning a three-week vacation cruise along the New England coast, starting August 6. On August 2 he directed Welles and Louis Johnson, Assistant Secretary of War, to set up an advisory War Resources Board, and the next day, he reviewed with Welles measures essential if war erupted before his return. Welles drafted two standby messages: one to rally Latin American support, the other appealing against the bombing of open cities. FDR signed both on August 5 and departed the next day; Welles locked them in his safe.[23]

Reports that Hitler and Stalin were negotiating a nonaggression pact were mounting. Nine months earlier, in November 1938, the United States legation in Budapest had first reported secret German-Soviet talks.[24] In May 1939, when Stalin replaced his pro-Western Foreign Minister, Maxim Litvinov, with the hard-line Vyacheslav Molotov, fears of a Hitler-Stalin deal had escalated. On August 12, Welles telephoned the latest reports to FDR at sea. Roosevelt offered to return immediately, but Welles thought war not likely for at least a week or possibly ten days. Roosevelt decided to get what rest he could and return, as scheduled, on August 25. He told Welles and Berle, meanwhile, to draft a standby appeal to the king of Italy urging him to intercede with Hitler to avert war.

Welles had been planning his own European vacation for mid-August but, at the last minute, Admiral Stark sent him Rainbow One: the updated defense plan for the Western Hemisphere. If war erupted, the United States would defend the hemisphere as far south as a line from the "bulge" of Brazil on the Atlantic to Ecuador on the Pacific with the navy responsible for interdicting Axis communications with Latin America. Meanwhile, the U.S. Joint Chiefs also wanted his urgent help in acquiring bases around the Panama Canal and in the British Caribbean islands—a forerunner of the destroyers-for-bases deal Welles would help negotiate with Britain the following year.[25] He canceled his holiday.

The next day, with Roosevelt and Hull both away, he convened senior War, Navy, Justice and Treasury officials in his office, noting grimly that the situation was "now so bad I think we should prepare for the worst." The army set in motion a series of immediate-action measures,[26] and FDR ordered the Coast Guard to prevent Axis vessels from leaving American ports ahead of schedule." I have reason to believe," he warned, "that some . . . are carrying armaments which might conceivably be mounted after sailing."[27] Pierrepont Moffat noted in his diary, "We went over all the steps necessary should war break out: proclamations, supervision of neutrality, communications, prohibitions of loans and credit, cancellation of licenses, etc. Everything is reasonably well-organized. . . but, of course, if war should come there would be hundreds of new situations which have not been foreseen."[28]

Hitler's pact with Stalin was officially confirmed on Monday, August 21. Hoping to head it off, a week earlier Roosevelt had sent Stalin a personal letter via a diplomatic courier, Douglas MacArthur II, an officer in the Paris embassy and a nephew of the general. MacArthur arrived in Moscow by train, on August 15, and handed FDR's letter to Ambassador Laurence Steinhardt for immediate delivery to Foreign Commissar Molotov. That night, at a reception at the German embassy, MacArthur and his colleague, Charles "Chip" Bohlen, learned from a friendly, anti-Nazi German diplomat, Hans Heinrich "Johnny" von Herwarth,[29] that the pact had been initialed the night before.[30] In accepting FDR's letter to Stalin, Molotov had kept the initialing secret from the American ambassador.

On August 20, Bullitt telephoned from Paris that Hitler was expected to "break loose" in two or three days.[31] Welles cabled FDR at sea the next day, suggesting that the appeal to the king of Italy be sent simultaneously with the formal signing of the Hitler-Stalin pact.[32] FDR approved; and Welles cabled the appeal to Phillips in Rome for immediate delivery to the Italian monarch. On Friday, August 25, Welles met FDR at the Union Station. Six days later, at 4:30 A.M. on September 1, FDR appealed to Germany, Italy, Great Britain, France and Poland not to bomb civilians. The time for appeals had passed. That morning at dawn, Hitler's Wehrmacht began swarming over Poland while his Luftwaffe bombed Polish targets—including civilians. The war, which Roosevelt, Hull, Welles and others had fought so hard to avert, had finally arrived.

Awakened after midnight by Bullitt's calling from Paris to report Hitler's invasion of Poland, Roosevelt immediately telephoned Hull and Welles. Hull reached the State Department around 3 A.M.; Welles arrived from his Maryland home soon after, and other senior officials straggled in for an emergency meeting in Hull's office. Hours later Welles was in the White House, conferring at the President's bedside.

The immediate priority was to keep war far from the hemisphere, by avoiding the devastation World War I caused throughout Latin America: exports crippled, shipping disrupted, millions in distress. Three years earlier, at Buenos Aires, FDR and Welles had proposed machinery for collective hemisphere action in an emergency. Roosevelt moved swiftly to test it. On September 7, he proclaimed a "limited" national emergency, declared the United States officially neutral and convened an emergency meeting of Latin American Foreign Ministers in Panama on September 21.

Welles would represent the United States with three assigned goals: a maritime "neutrality zone" to bar naval hostilities from hemisphere waters,[33] security measures to combat Axis subversion, and an economic plan to help Latin American countries cut off from traditional European markets. Hull opposed the maritime zone (later nicknamed FDR's "chastity belt") as a violation of international law and likely to involve the United States in hostilities.[34] Unpersuaded, Roosevelt set Berle to studying legal precedents and the State Department geographer to drafting an area 300 miles wide encircling the hemisphere south of Canada. Seizing a ruler and pencil, he connected peripheral points by straight lines and handed the sketch to Welles for use at Panama.

Upon arriving in the Isthmus on September 20, Welles immediately conferred with his twenty Latin-American colleagues, then cabled Roosevelt that there was not the "slightest divergence" about the moral issues involved in the European war. For once, the countries refrained from bickering; even the Argentines were supporting U.S. efforts to keep the war at arm's length. In his opening address on September 25, Welles stressed that the conference was the first "direct result" of the 1936 Buenos Aires meeting in which every nation in the hemisphere had agreed to "consult" in an emergency.[35]

Notwithstanding the difficulties of shepherding twenty fiercely independent and disputatious delegations to a common goal, after ten days of intense negotiating Welles achieved unanimous agreement on FDR's maritime zone, on security measures to combat Axis subversion and on an inter-American Economic Board to be based in Washington.[36] Leo Rowe, observing the conference for the Pan American Union, wrote FDR later that Welles had placed "every-one under a deep debt of obligation." The Latins had looked to him for leadership; and he had achieved constructive results although, at times, these had seemed "in doubt."[37] Indeed they had.

At times, in fact, there had been moments of high and low comedy. At one critical juncture, when a unanimous vote was imperative, the Haitian delegate disappeared on a romantic tryst and Welles sent his aide, Paul Daniels, to retrieve the missing Lothario.[38] During the final public session, a *LIFE* photographer, moving stealthily to snap two unsuspecting Nazi journalists, tripped and landed in the lap of the regal Mathilde Welles, who "took it in good part," an American delegate remembered.[39]

Welles himself, exhausted by three weeks of nonstop negotiating in Panama's torrid heat, disappeared for a night of convivial drinking with Latin colleagues. This time Louise Clarkson sent the long-suffering Daniels to retrieve his own formidable chief. Clarkson saw Welles visibly affected by alcohol for the first time in their twenty-three-year collaboration. The Panamanian government tendered the delegates a ball on the last night, and Welles "passed me on the dance floor," she remembered. "I could see that his eyes were glazed."[40]

Welles had achieved FDR's three principal goals. Two of them, the Economic Board and security measures against Axis subversion, proved successful, but the futility of FDR's "neutrality zone" soon became apparent. The British protested it and three months later, when their cruisers drove the Nazi warship *Graf Spee* to its doom off Buenos Aires, the irrelevance of "proclamations," however high-minded, became clear.

Returning to Washington, Welles delivered a "dull but excellent" radio speech, Castle wrote in his diary. "He did not convince me about the neutral zone in the Atlantic and I had the idea that he did not, at all, convince himself. He made the best of a bad business and I greatly respected him for it."[41]

Years later, Welles would concede that FDR's maritime zone, officially the Declaration of Panama, marked the end of an era. It was, he wrote, the last "official expression" of a belief that the responsibility for avoiding war could be anything but global. Everyone at Panama had believed "perhaps blindly" that the war could be won without becoming universal.[42] Neutrality, as Welles himself had warned Endicott Peabody two years earlier, was a "mirage."

TWENTY

THE CREATION
OF ISRAEL

1937–1948

The Zionist Gentile

WITHIN HOURS OF THE BIRTH OF ISRAEL on May 15, 1948, its first president, Dr. Chaim Weizmann, telegraphed Welles: "I shall always remember your unfailing kindness, helpfulness and [the] unswerving support which you extended to our cause."[1] Weizmann was not flattering an old friend; Welles and he had traveled a long road together. Wary at first of Zionism, by mid–World War II Welles had concluded that there was no alternative to a Jewish homeland in Palestine. Thereafter, he became one of the few high-ranking Gentiles in the Roosevelt administration to support Weizmann's dream.

Critics have long accused FDR and his advisors of indifference to the plight of European Jewry, but the record tells a different story. For three years before Pearl Harbor, Roosevelt and, especially, Welles searched the world in vain for a refuge for Hitler's victims. The war blocked their search but, as Allied victory loomed increasingly certain, they threw their support increasingly behind Weizmann. The tale is one of missed opportunities, unforeseen events—and tragedy.

When Welles became Under Secretary of State in 1937, Hitler's persecution of Jews had become a matter of international alarm. Four years earlier, in 1933, the League of Nations had created a Refugee Commission headed by James G. McDonald, president of the New York–based Foreign Policy Association. But Hitler's persecution had continued and in 1935 McDonald resigned, blaming world indifference. As Welles was assuming his new global responsibilities, cables reporting Hitler's atrocities poured over his desk virtually daily, leaving their mark.

Welles's previous contacts with Jews had been virtually nonexistent. Born into an old New York Knickerbocker family whose social contacts with Jews were severely limited, he had been reared as a Protestant Episcopalian and educated in a New England boarding school where Christian precepts were drummed daily into the students and Jews had not yet been admitted.[2] His friends at Harvard and later in the Diplomatic Service had come from the same Eastern-seaboard milieu as himself. For Welles and his circle, Jews had fallen into two categories: artists, musicians, scientists and financiers—and the rest. By 1937, however, the grim daily cables and the responsibility of high office had begun to radically alter his outlook.

In March 1938, on reading a letter from Roosevelt's speechwriter, Samuel Rosenman, asking help for German Jewish friends, Welles told a subordinate that it was "shocking" that U.S. regulations made it impossible to grant visas to German Jews "solely because under present German law they have been convicted of 'Rassenschande' [racial shame]. We should . . . correct this injustice."[3] Hitler's annexation of Austria a week later exacerbated the Jewish refugee problem, and Roosevelt told the cabinet on March 18 that "something has to be done." Treasury Secretary Henry Morgenthau raised the issue with him over lunch three days later, and FDR told him to get in touch with Welles and bring him proposals the next morning before he left for Warm Springs. To Morgenthau's surprise, Welles had two proposals ready when they entered the Oval Office.

The first was minor: to add Austria's small immigration quota of about 1,300 yearly to the 25,000 admitted annually from "Greater Germany." The second, however, was important: an international conference to focus world attention on the plight of Jewish refugees. Latin American and other friendly states would be invited to form an international committee under League of Nations auspices to help "political" refugees emigrate from Germany and Austria. (Given anti-Semitism in Congress and certain sections of the country, FDR preferred the term "political" to racial or religious refugees.)[4] Roosevelt approved both recommendations, and invitations went out next day to thirty-three countries. Nazi Germany, having withdrawn from the League, was not invited; nor was Soviet Russia, which had made clear that it wanted nothing to do with Jewish refugees. Fascist Italy alone refused to attend.[5]

To emphasize the importance of the conference, Welles urged Roosevelt to appoint Hull, Welles himself and Assistant Secretary George Messersmith as U.S. delegates but FDR preferred a less official—that is, politically safer—team. Instead he named Myron C. Taylor, a former head of U.S. Steel, and two State Department technicians.[6] However, he approved Welles's suggestion for a Presidential Advisory Committee on Political Refugees with Morgenthau and Bernard Baruch as members, even though neither were leaders of recognized Jewish groups. When Morgenthau, in turn, proposed Rabbi Stephen Wise, president of the pro-Zionist American Jewish Congress, as a member, Welles, however, strongly objected.

Wise was the head of a "very bitter" faction of Jews, he warned FDR's secretary, Stephen Early. If Wise were appointed, Jews representing other factions would have to be included, giving the committee a politically risky "preponderance" of Jews. FDR, however, was fond of the contentious rabbi and overruled him. "Wise-yes," he minuted Early.[7] Welles and Wise would later cooperate closely in World War II and become friends, but, in 1938, Welles was aware that many American Jews opposed a Jewish homeland—in Palestine or elsewhere—convinced that their loyalty as Americans was solely to the United States.

Nonetheless, given the split in Jewish ranks, Welles also kept in close touch with Wise's rival, Rabbi Morris Lazaron of Baltimore, founder of the anti-Zionist American Council for Judaism.

The refugee conference opened in July 1938 at Evian, France, and proved a bitter disappointment. Despite torrents of rhetoric, not a single generous offer was made to help resettle Jewish refugees. Welles, however, achieved his main goal: permanent international machinery to help Jews escape Hitler. An Intergovernmental Committee on Political Refugees was set up in London with Myron Taylor as the U.S. delegate and George Rublee, a prominent New York attorney, as its director.[8]

The committee faced two immediate challenges: to persuade Hitler's regime to bring order into its chaotic expulsion of Jews and to find suitable areas for resettlement. Welles was the guiding spirit in both; Taylor and Rublee consulted him constantly. Hull played a passive role, possibly because his wife was Jewish, while other senior officials, if not anti-Semitic, remained largely preoccupied with their own problems.

Palestine would have been the logical resettlement area. For centuries the Holy Land had been the spiritual home of world Jewry. Theodor Herzl, the founder of Zionism, had convened the first World Zionist Congress in Basel, Switzerland, in 1897 to press for a Jewish homeland in Palestine, and during World War I the British government had pledged its support. On November 2, 1917, in recognition of the contribution of Dr. Chaim Weizmann, a brilliant

Jewish scientist, to Britain's wartime survival, Foreign Secretary Arthur James
Balfour had declared:

> His Majesty's Government view with favor the establishment in Palestine of a
> national home for the Jewish people and will use their best endeavors to facilitate
> the achievement of that objective, it being understood that nothing should be
> done that may prejudice the rights of existing non-Jewish [e.g., Arab]
> communities in Palestine or the rights and political status enjoyed by Jews in
> any other country.[9]

Britain's memory, however, proved short. After the war, the need for Arab
friendship to protect Middle East oil and imperial lifelines to India overrode its
pledge to the Jews. The dream of a Jewish homeland quickly faded. To placate
the Arabs, Britain accepted a League of Nations mandate to administer
Palestine, and in 1922 Trans-Jordan (now Jordan) was split off as a puppet
kingdom to reward the Hashemite dynasty for its support during the war. In
1936, following violent Arab-Jewish clashes, Britain cut Jewish immigration to
a minimum. By 1939, the eve of World War II, there were 500,000 Jews in
Palestine—half the Arab population.

Given Britain's stranglehold on Palestine, after the Evian conference
Roosevelt and Welles began searching for an alternative Jewish homeland. At
Welles's suggestion, FDR wrote his fellow Latin American presidents, but
their reactions were cool and financial and logistical problems complicated
the search. A Franco-Swiss Jewish group suggested Haiti, but Welles, knowing
the country, doubted that European Jews could thrive in a black republic whose
religion, history and culture were so alien to their own. The British offered
low-cost land in British Guiana, but again resettlement costs proved prohibi-
tive and few European Jews chose to live in the tropics. The Dominican
dictator, Rafael Trujillo, offered limited sanctuary, but, once again, shipping
shortages and high costs limited the number of Jewish families settling in the
Dominican Republic to 500.[10]

Disheartened by Latin America's reaction, FDR and Welles turned to
Africa. Dr. Isaiah Bowman, president of Johns Hopkins and a world-famous
geographer, had suggested the highlands of Italian-ruled Ethiopia, where
Italians settlers had begun arriving. On December 7, 1938, Welles drafted a letter
for Roosevelt urging Mussolini to allow European Jews to settle in Ethiopia.
Mussolini refused.[11] Bowman next suggested Portuguese Angola whose
possibilities "justify heroic efforts to overcome political obstacles," Welles
wrote FDR. Welles cabled Myron Taylor in London, urging him to persuade
Prime Minister Neville Chamberlain and Portugal's dictator-president, Antonio
de Oliveira Salazar, that Angola would be the "ideal supplemental homeland"

because of its temperate climate, its tranquil native population and its immense resources.[12] Again, political problems dashed their hopes.

Portugal was "extremely sensitive" about its colonies and almost certainly would refuse, the British warned. They proved right. The Portuguese minister in Washington discouraged the State Department even from broaching the matter officially to Lisbon, pointing out that Jewish colonies had already been tried in Angola and all had failed.[13] As a final resort, Welles suggested Mindanao, the second-largest of the Philippine islands. President Manuel Quezon and FDR's Advisory Committee both approved, but the outbreak of war in the Pacific strangled the project at birth.[14]

The Munich settlement in September 1938 had allayed fears of war for a time. To exploit Chamberlain's new contacts with Hitler, Welles drafted a message for FDR urging the British Prime Minister to persuade Hitler to increase the number of Jews allowed to emigrate and the amount of property they could take with them. Chamberlain suggested instead that the British and American ambassadors take up the matter in Berlin. With FDR's approval, Welles instructed U.S. ambassador Hugh Wilson to "act promptly." Early in November Wilson reported that Goering and Walther Funk, the Nazi minister for National Economy, would receive Rublee in Berlin.[15] Again fate intervened.

Herschl Grynszpan, a seventeen-year old Polish Jew whose family had been abandoned by the Nazis with no food, clothing or money in no-man's land between Germany and Poland, assassinated Ernst vom Rath, a junior diplomat at the German embassy in Paris. In reprisal, the Nazis unleashed *Kristallnacht*, an orgy of anti-Jewish terror during which 200 synagogues were burned, more than 800 Jewish-owned shops destroyed, and 7,500 looted, and thousands of Jewish homes ransacked.[16] In protest, FDR recalled Ambassador Wilson, but Welles, intent on saving as many Jews as possible, ordered Prentice Gilbert, the American chargé d'affaires in Berlin, to continue negotiations. Gilbert reported soon after that Goering was ready to send Hjalmar Schacht, president of the Reichsbank, to London to confer with Rublee and British financial experts.[17]

Goering's role was crucial for Hitler had just assigned him responsibility for *Judenrein,* ridding Germany of Jews, and he appeared willing to carry out the role without brutality, provided he could drive a hard bargain with the rich democracies. Acccording to Schacht, Goering planned to expel 150,000 able-bodied Jews from Germany in an "orderly" fashion over the next three years. Their expulsion would be financed by confiscating Jewish property and by a bond issue to which "international Jewry" would subscribe. Germany would thus obtain vital foreign exchange, offsetting the global Jewish boycott of German goods.

Welles's reaction was cool. After analyzing the Goering-Schacht plan with FDR's Advisory Committee and Treasury officials, he cabled Taylor and Rublee:

The plan is generally considered as asking the world to pay a ransom for the release of hostages in Germany and to barter human misery for increased exports . . . On the other hand, we . . . must proceed with care lest, by summary rejection, the plight of the Jews in Germany be made even more serious. It is . . . suggested that you merely emphazise the feeling of . . . all groups consulted that subscriptions to these bonds would not be forthcoming on the basis of Schacht's plan.[18]

Rublee adroitly followed Welles's instructions and was invited to confer with Goering in Berlin in January 1939. Goering appeared conciliatory. The Nazis, he said, would forgo bartering Jewish refugees for foreign currency and instead use confiscated Jewish property to buy goods and services in Germany or on German ships.[19] Once the 150,000 able-bodied Jews had been expelled, their dependents would be allowed to join them; meanwhile, private international refugee organizations would be allowed to work with Nazi agencies handling emigration.

American Jewish groups were initially skeptical but Welles and Rublee remained optimistic. The Goering-Schacht plan was "better than we had hoped for," Welles wrote Roosevelt in February.[20] The President appeared willing to test it, but again fate intervened. That March Hitler occupied Czechoslovakia, violating his Munich pledges six months earlier and destroying what faith remained in his word. Welles nonetheless urged FDR to continue the Berlin negotiations. "To give up what has already been accomplished with the German government would be an injustice to those whom the IGR was created to assist," he wrote.[21]

The time for negotiations, however, had passed. With war looming and Arab goodwill deemed vital to Middle East defense, the British announced that Jewish immigration into Palestine would be cut to 15,000 for each of the next five years and then would effectively end.[22] Britain's "infamous" 1939 White Paper, Welles wrote long after, "flagrantly dishonored the Balfour Declaration and the terms under which Britain had accepted the mandate."[23]

The United States itself, meanwhile, was far from blameless. Although 37 million foreign-born persons were living in the country, as Richard M. Ketchum pointed out in *The Borrowed Years: 1938-41,*[24] anti-immigrant sentiment was rampant. Xenophobia, recurrent in U.S. history, had soared after World War I as American servicemen streamed home seeking jobs. The 1921 Quota Act had cut European immigration to an annual 335,000; the 1924 Immigration Act further cut it in half. With the onset of the 1929 depression, patriotic groups—the American Legion and Daughters of the American Revolution, among them—lobbied Congress against admitting more foreigners. Sixty bills were introduced aimed at limiting or ending immigration during the 1930s, wrote Ketchum.

Congress insisted that no immigrant become a public charge, so after 1934, when Hitler limited the amount of money an emigrating Jew could take out to ten Reichsmarks ($4.00), Jews fleeing Germany found it increasingly difficult to enter the United States.[25] Welles told Eleanor Roosevelt that his desk was flooded with angry protests against admitting more Jews than the quotas allowed. Meanwhile the Roosevelt administration seemed paralyzed.

The plight of the German vessel *St. Louis* became a notorious example. After sailing from Germany in May 1939, bound for Cuba with 930 Jewish refugees, each of whom had paid $150 for Cuban landing rights and 734 of whom had U.S. immigration quota numbers, the Cuban government refused them entry unless President Federico Laredo Bru received a $350,000 bribe. As the sum was impossible to raise, the ship idled off Miami as the Jewish Joint Distribution Committee worked frantically to win landing rights for those with U.S. quota numbers. From Washington, wrote Ketchum, came "ominous silence."[26] Eventually Belgium, Holland, France and Britain accepted them, but three other vessels bearing Jewish refugees—the *Ordina,* the *Quanza* and the *Flanders*—suffered similar ordeals.[27]

With the outbreak of war in September 1939, Jews from Greater Germany living in Britain and France automatically became "enemy aliens." The United States tightened its visa regulations and, after Pearl Harbor, called on Latin American governments to do likewise.[28] Entry into the States now passed under the control of Assistant Secretary of State Breckinridge Long, a wealthy, ultra-conservative Southern Democrat close to Hull and closer still to Roosevelt with whom he had served in the Wilson administration in World War I. Whether anti-Semitic, as his critics claimed, or not, Long interpreted the immigration laws strictly, and his access to Hull and Roosevelt made his decisions virtually final.

Welles himself seldom dealt with visa matters, although those aware of special cases requiring sympathetic treatment found him their best hope. Eleanor Roosevelt, whose sympathy for the downtrodden led many to appeal to her personally, referred such appeals to her friend Sumner, knowing he would do what he could.[29] Long's fear of enemy agents posing as refugees, however, was not groundless. U.S. ambassador Laurence Steinhardt reported from Moscow in November 1940, eleven months before Pearl Harbor, that Soviet intelligence was forcing prospective emigrants to spy as the price of an exit visa. This was the first information reaching the department that placed "all persons emigrating from Soviet-controlled Europe under suspicion," Welles wrote FDR.[30]

Hitler's attack on the Soviet Union on June 22, 1941, exacerbated the plight of Europe's Jews. At first those captured by Nazi troops in east Poland or Soviet territory were shot by SS Einsatzkommandos, or murder squads, but when this technique proved too slow and cumbersome a more efficient system was required. In January 1942 Himmler's deputy, Reinhard Heydrich, summoned police and security chiefs to Wannsee, near Berlin, and issued Hitler's orders for the "Final Solution." Jews throughout Nazi-occupied Europe would henceforth be rounded up and shipped in freight cars to special death camps in Poland, far from the world's eyes.

For months few details leaked out, and those that did were discounted. The British and American governments and their civilian populations, Jews included, remained skeptical, recalling World War I atrocity stories.

American Jews suffered at the time from three "basic misconceptions," a Jewish commission on the Holocaust concluded forty years later: (1) Nazism was not essentially different from other forms of anti-Semitism and Jews would survive, as they always had; (2) there was no point trying to make a deal with Hitler's allies and satellites; and (3) the U.S. and British governments would give the rescue of Jews "serious priority."[31]

Jews in Europe, however, were already fleeing by any means available. In late 1941, 700 Romanian Jews chartered a decrepit Danube steamer, the *Struma,* in a desperate bid to reach Palestine. Its engines broke down off Istambul, but the Turkish authorities refused to allow the refugees ashore until Britain granted them permission to enter Palestine. Britain refused. Ten weeks later, on February 24, 1942, with the refugees packed together under hideous conditions, Turkey ordered the *Struma* back to the Black Sea. An explosion occurred a few miles from the Bosphorus and the vessel sank with all aboard.[32]

American opinion, both Gentile and Jewish, was outraged, and the British were condemned as harshly as the Turks. Defending its action in the House of Commons, the British government argued that it could not approve measures calculated to undermine the "existing policy regarding illegal immigration into Palestine in view of the wider issues involved"—that is, Arab goodwill.

Ironically, the *Struma* tragedy boosted Zionist prestige. Rabbi Wise wrote Eleanor Roosevelt in March that four other ships bearing Jewish refugees had encountered similar indifference or brutality. The only "realistic" solution, he wrote, was opening Palestine to Jewish immigration. She passed his letter to Welles.

> Dear Sumner: This memo seems perfectly shocking to me. We have taken British children (as war refugees) and I think the British government ought to pay some attention to us in return.
>
> They have set a very low quota in Palestine and the Arabs have agreed. After all, these are anti-Axis refugees and they certainly will help us rather than the Axis and, from what I read in the papers, we may be needing some help in that part of the world before long.[33]

The *Struma* episode was one of the "most shocking tragedies . . . in a tragic year," Welles replied. He would do everything he could to prevent a recurrence, but the British were "adamant" in their refusal to allow increased immigration into Palestine for fear of Arab unrest. Unimpressed, Eleanor wrote back next day: "Why not try to give asylum and guarantee that such refugees will continue to Africa and South America? This British policy is so cruel that, if it were generally known in this country, it would increase the dislike of Great Britain which is already too prevalent."

Welles wished that her suggestions could be carried out, he replied, but there were insurmountable problems. There were no ships available to transport refugees to Africa or South America, and a "well-founded" fear existed in the Latin American republics that enemy agents had been planted among refugees. Britain's east African colonies seemed a "logical" destination, but there were no facilities for refugees with "no means of livelihood . . . no funds . . . unable to speak the language [or] earn their own livelihood." The Intergovernmental Committee on Political Refugees had been created to deal with such tragedies, and he asked that the problem be referred to it.

Welles was fully aware that the war had left the committee virtually powerless. As Under Secretary of State, however, he was bound by war conditions and by British policy in Palestine. His private frustration erupted two days later. "If the British government did not wish this shipload of refugees to go to Palestine," he wrote a subordinate, Ray Atherton, "some arrangement should have been made, purely from humanitarian considerations, to have found some shelter for them during the war among the East African colonies."[34] Mrs. Roosevelt had sent his bureaucratic response to Wise and, after mulling it over, Wise wrote her April 1:

> If Palestine is to be ruled out, the situation of the unhappy refugees is, indeed, hopeless. Assuming that Mr Welles is right . . . that refuge cannot be found for these people in South America nor in Africa, is not the obvious answer that they should be admitted to the one country which they can call home, to which they could go, in the words of Mr. Churchill, "not on sufferance, but of right"?
>
> Palestine has been recognized as the Jewish Homeland, not only by Britain and fifty-two other nations of the world, but by unanimous resolution of the United States Congress [on June 30, 1922] . . .
>
> A word about the repercussions that Britain fears among the Arabs. . . the sacrifice of friends in the interest of appeasing the unfriendly has repeatedly been proven to be in vain.[35]

Chaim Weizmann arrived in Washington that spring of 1942 and, in two long interviews, impressed Welles deeply. The celebrated scientist, he wrote later, was "one of the greatest figures that Jewry has produced in modern times."[36] Weizmann had a solution to the Palestine problem: direct talks between himself and King Ibn Saud of Saudi Arabia. The Americans and British, he argued, should prepare the ground by letting the Saudi monarch know that they supported Zionism. He was certain that Ibn Saud would agree to a Jewish homeland in Palestine in return for political and financial "inducements."

His conviction stemmed from a meeting in September 1939, on the eve of World War II, with St. John Philby, a British Arabist close to Ibn Saud.[37] Philby had lived many years in Saudi Arabia, spoke fluent Arabic, had married a Saudi wife and had converted to Islam. Philby's formula was simple: Palestine west of the Jordan for the Jews in return for Anglo-American guarantees of postwar independence for all Arab nations plus 20 million pounds sterling to Ibn Saud for "resettling" Palestinian Arabs. If the Jews could raise the money, Philby had told Weizmann, he might be able to persuade the Arab monarch to accept the plan.

Weizmann had been impressed. Ibn Saud's prestige as the only independent monarch in the Arab world was unrivaled. In the 1920s he had won control of Saudi Arabia's vast oil reserves by crushing his Hashemite rivals virtually single-handed, and ever since had been courted by the Americans, to whom he had granted lucrative concessions, and by the British, eager for concessions of their own.

International Jewry could handle the "financial" part, Weizmann had told Philby, but only the British and American governments could guarantee the "political" part. Philby relayed this to Ibn Saud on January 8, 1940, and later told Weizmann that the king had intimated that he might consider the plan at an appropriate time—provided it was "firm." If it leaked, however, he would disavow Philby.[38]

Weizmann told Welles he had discussed Philby's proposal with Churchill before sailing for America. "I have a plan which, of course, can only be carried into effect when the war is over," Churchill had replied. "I would like to see Ibn Saud made lord of the Middle East—the boss of bosses—provided he settles with you. It will be up to you to get the best possible conditions. Of course, we shall help you. Keep this confidential but you might talk it over with Roosevelt when you get to America. There is nothing he and I cannot do if we set our minds on it."[39]

Sensing a ray of hope, Welles took Weizmann to see Roosevelt on July 7, 1942. The President had met Weizmann briefly two years earlier when the Zionist leader had pressed for Jewish settlement in Palestine and FDR, after querying its "absorptive" capacity and the cost of moving the Arabs out, had suggested that a "little baksheesh"—bribery—might help. In 1942, however, Roosevelt was not ready to commit himself. The United States had to be careful not to "upset" the British who, he reminded Weizmann, were facing formidable odds in the Middle East.[40] Characteristically, he steered the conversation away from Zionist aspirations to synthetic rubber: a subject on which the celebrated scientist was fully, albeit reluctantly, qualified to talk.[41]

The FDR-Weizmann interview produced little of substance, but it established a sympathetic bond between them and Weizmann was grateful to Welles for arranging it. Welles was "well-informed and well-disposed toward us," he wrote later. "The trouble began when it came to the experts in the State Department. The head of the Near Eastern division [Wallace Murray] was an avowed anti-Zionist and an outspoken pro-Arab . . . There was a definite cleavage between the White House and Welles, on the one hand, and the rest of the State Department, on the other."[42]

Four days before the FDR-Weizmann meeting, on July 3, Hitler and Mussolini had proclaimed their intent to "liberate the Near East from British domination." Lest the Axis ploy win Arab support, Hull cabled Ambassador John Winant in London that the United States itself was planning to promise postwar independence to Arab states backing the Allies. A century of American missionary, educational and philanthropic work in the Near East had "convinced" the Arabs, Hull asserted, that America's efforts had never been tarnished by "material motives or interests."

To capitalize on Arab goodwill and promote a United Nations victory, the U.S. Joint Chiefs would shortly send a military-economic mission to the Near East headed by Lieutenant Colonel Harold B. Hoskins, a reserve officer on "special" duty in the State Department. Hoskins spoke Arabic and had business experience in the Middle East. Winant was to inform the British that he had the "full support" of the State Department and the Joint Chiefs and seek British approval for his trip.[43]

Hoskins was something of a mystery. Soft-spoken, avuncular and slightly prissy,[44] he had been born forty-eight years earlier to missionary parents in Beirut and had moved to the United States as a teenager. After graduating from Princeton in 1917, he had served overseas with the marines during World War I and later had become a broker in Middle East textiles in New York, serving also as a trustee and board chairman of the American University of Beirut. Six months before Pearl Harbor, he had joined the State Department, which had loaned him to FDR's new intelligence arm, the Office of Strategic Services. The OSS, in turn, had sent him to develop "friendly" (i.e., intelligence) contacts in the Arab world.[45]

Suspecting United States intrusion into their traditional sphere of influence, the British protested that the Hoskins mission, on the heels of a U.S. pledge of postwar independence for the Arabs, would be misinterpreted by Arabs and Jews in Palestine and risk "dangerous" repercussions. Meanwhile, the U.S. Joint Chiefs, apparently in agreement with the British notwithstanding Hull's claim of "full support" for Hoskins, dragged their feet. Finally, in late

October, Welles wrote their chairman, Admiral Leahy, that the President "insisted" the Hoskins mission proceed and instructed Alexander Kirk, the U.S. minister in Cairo, to assist Hoskins whose mission had been delayed an "inordinate" period of time.[46]

In August 1942, shortly after taking Weizmann to see Roosevelt, Welles became caught up in the so-called Riegner reports: the first incontrovertible proof of Hitler's death camps to reach the West. Welles's role would lead later to bitter controversy.

Gerhard Riegner, a young lawyer of German-Jewish descent, represented the World Jewish Congress in Geneva and reported directly to its president, Rabbi Wise, in New York. In 1942 neutral Switzerland—adjoining Germany, free from air raids and comfortable by wartime standards—had become a favorite rest-and-recreation area for rich German businessmen with Nazi connections. Early in August, Riegner learned through Jewish friends that an anti-Nazi German industrialist had disclosed, at great personal peril, Hitler's plan to exterminate three or more million European Jews in special death camps.

Incredulous at first, Riegner hesitated to pass on such rumors; but they had come from unimpeachable sources. After further checking, he reported them to U.S. Legation officials in Berne, who also were initially skeptical. To conceal the source of Riegner's information from Swiss censorship, however, they finally agreed to forward his report in diplomatic code to Washington for relay to Rabbi Wise in New York.

Riegner's report reached the State Department on August 11, but Elbridge Durbrow, a middle-grade officer in the European division, thought it "not advisable" to transmit such "fantastic" allegations to Wise without confirmation. With Welles's concurrence, he relegated the report to the files.[47] Riegner, however, reported as well to the British branch of the World Jewish Congress and had sent a copy through British diplomatic channels to Sidney Silverman, a Member of Parliament and chairman of the World Jewish Congress's British section. At the end, he had added: "Inform and consult New York."

After a week's hesitation, on August 17 the British forwarded the report to New York over a low-priority Western Union circuit. By chance, that same day on the advice of his staff, Welles had cabled Bern that that Riegner's report would not be shown to Wise because of its "unsubstantiated" nature. The low-priority British message didn't reach the World Jewish Congress's New York office until Friday, August 28, the start of the Labor Day weekend. Rabbi Irving Miller was alone in the office at the time but, upon reading the message, immediately telephoned Wise at home. Wise, in turn, telephoned Welles for an urgent appointment.[48]

Perturbed by Wise's call, Welles consulted Ray Atherton, head of the European division. Atherton counseled caution: There was no confirmation. The State Department understood that Jews deported to Germany were put to work for the German war machine, as were Poles or Soviet prisoners. Welles passed this to Wise on Wednesday, September 9, and asked that he not publicize Riegner's information until it had been confirmed. Wise agreed.[49] Meanwhile, as Riegner and others continued forwarding information about death camps, Welles instructed Myron Taylor, FDR's representative at the Vatican, to consult the Holy See.

On September 25, Taylor urged the Pope to speak out publicly, but Vatican officials demurred, pointing out that the Pontiff also lacked proof. The next day, however, Washington cabled Taylor corroboration. Riegner's colleague Richard Lichtheim had just interviewed two recent escapees from Poland who told him that Jews in Warsaw were being taken from the ghetto and killed in special camps—one at Belzec. Jews from Germany, Belgium, Holland and Czechoslovakia, they warned, would soon meet the same fate.

No longer skeptical, the State Department passed Lichtheim's information to Wise who immediately took it up with Welles. Welles, in turn, cabled it triple-priority to Bern for relay to Taylor in Rome. Taylor was directed to seek confirmation from the Vatican plus any suggestions for action. Again the Vatican balked. His Holiness could not condemn the Nazis without also condemning the Bolsheviks, decreed Cardinal Maglione, the Pope's Secretary of State.[50]

Increasingly alarmed and frustrated, early in October Welles instructed Leland Harrison, the U.S. minister in Bern, to interview Riegner and Lichtheim and cable in code whatever information they feared entrusting to the mails. Welles's "persistent interest broke the logjam in Berne and Washington," Walter Laqueur and Richard Breitman wrote in *Breaking the Silence*. A fortnight later, on October 22, Riegner handed Harrison documents confirming Hitler's extermination policy; only at Harrison's personal insistence and with extreme reluctance did he agree to reveal, in a sealed envelope, the name of his source.[51] His documents reached Washington on November 23 and, the following day, Welles called Wise to his office and told him regretfully that he had to confirm the rabbi's worst fears. "For reasons you will understand, I cannot give the documents to the press," he told Wise, "but there is no reason why you should not. It might even help if you did."[52] Wise immediately called a press conference. The November 25 *New York Herald-Tribune* front-page headline read: WISE SAYS HITLER HAS ORDERED 4,000,000 JEWS SLAIN IN 1942.

Many, including the *New York Times*, remained dubious, but denunciations of Hitler poured into the White House. On December 17, Roosevelt and Churchill jointly declared that those responsible would be punished. Welles, meanwhile, had reached a more immediate conclusion. The Jewish refugee problem could be solved only by the creation of a Jewish state in Palestine, he told Britain's parliamentary Under Secretary, Richard Law.[53] After long misgivings, Welles had become a convinced Zionist.

Harrison was still forwarding Riegner's reports in coded cables marked "For the Under Secretary." His report #482 of January 26, 1943, included details of Nazi atrocities in Poland and Romania. On Welles's orders, the European division paraphrased the contents in a letter to Wise. Durbrow drafted the letter on February 6 and mailed it to Wise on February 9.[54] The next day, however, for reasons still unclear, he cabled Berne contradictory instructions.

> #354. In the future, reports submitted to you for transmission to private persons in the United States should not be accepted unless extraordinary circumstances make such action advisable . . . By sending such private messages which circumvent neutral countries' censorship we risk the possibility that neutral countries might . . . curtail or abolish our official secret means of communication.

Welles apparently signed Durbrow's cable hurriedly, along with scores of others crossing his desk daily, and it puzzled Harrison, who wrote asking for clarification. Welles's critics later charged that he had deliberately cut off reports of Nazi atrocities, but the charge was baseless. "Welles was . . . entirely sympathetic with efforts to rescue the Jews and did not understand the implications of the order," John Morton Blum wrote in *Roosevelt and Morgenthau.*[55] "Indeed, in April, 1943, obviously unaware of the restrictions he had inadvertently approved, he asked . . . Harrison for further reports from Riegner about the Jews."

By late 1942, Welles had concluded that the only hope of a Jewish homeland in Palestine lay in direct Jewish-Arab talks. To that end, he began regular meetings with Weizmann, Nahum Goldmann and other Zionist leaders. On December 12 he asked specifically if their program involved a "transfer" (expulsion) of Arabs from Palestine. Weizmann replied that there would be "ample room for Jews and Arabs to develop side by side." Welles pledged in return that the United States would make no "commitment" to the Arabs without consulting the Zionists and, "if possible," obtaining their consent. At the same time, he urged Weizmann to draft "specific proposals . . . One must have a program and go to Ibn Saud with it," Welles told him on January 26, 1943.[56]

Weizmann agreed—provided the United States and Britain officially supported a Jewish homeland in which there would be "room for everybody." Welles asked if he would repeat this to President Roosevelt, and Weizmann said he would.[57] His colleagues, however, were more skeptical about Ibn Saud's cooperation. After a State Department meeting on February 20, Goldmann noted that Welles had "praised Ibn Saud as the greatest Moslem since Mohammed . . . We . . . are always ready to speak with the Arabs," wrote Goldmann, "[but] as long as Ibn Saud knows the U.S. are not behind us, there is no use approaching him. The UN must pave the way."[58]

Goldmann was right; the huge, half-blind old Arab monarch fanatically opposed Zionism. In mid-April he received the American minister, Alexander Kirk, at his desert camp near Riyadh and told him that, as the "leading Arab and Moslem," Palestine was of more concern to him than to any other Arab. The Jews in Palestine were steadily encroaching on the Arabs, he claimed. He had warned Roosevelt of this before the war but had received only a noncommittal reply.[59] Because of his friendship for the United States and his sympathy for the Allied cause, however, he would remain silent.[60]

Nevertheless, two weeks later, in a letter to FDR headed "In the name of God, the Merciful and Compassionate," Ibn Saud protested that the Jews had "no right" to Palestine. A Jewish Palestine would "forever be a hotbed of troubles and disturbances," he insisted.[61] Undeterred and still convinced that direct Jewish-Arab talks alone could solve the Palestine problem, Welles wrote Roosevelt on May 10:

> I have found Dr. Weizmann the most constructive of all the Jewish leaders with regard to the Palestine question. He believes, as I think you do, that the solution to this problem should, if possible, be found by agreement between the Jews and Arabs, and it is his present hope that the way can be prepared for him to meet with King Ibn Saud and to try to work out the basis for an agreement which would obviate in the future the dangers and difficulties of the past twenty-five years.[62]

A week later Weizmann, about to return to England, asked Welles to arrange another interview with FDR. Welles agreed, but warned Weizmann that a Jewish advertising campaign urging anti-British violence in Palestine was "antagonizing" friends of Zionism. Weizmann assured him that the Zionists had had no part in it but pointed out that the British deadline for ending Jewish immigration into Palestine—1944—was "fast approaching." The Jews there were becoming desperate. If "reasonable" people like himself could not produce a solution, violence would follow.

The solution, he asserted, was to pave the way for Zionist talks with the Arabs. He himself would not be the first to make the approach—possibly "non-Jews" could prepare the ground—but the United States and Britain had to convince the Arabs that they were behind him. The issue should be tackled at once, not left until after the war.[63] "To bring Ibn Saud into the discussions does not mean we make Zionism dependent on the consent of Ibn Saud or [of] the

Arabs," Weizmann wrote Welles. "Zionism is based on our demands and the necessity of Palestine and our achievements and the justice of our cause."[64]

Welles escorted Weizmann to his third meeting with Roosevelt on June 11. As they walked the short distance from the old State Department to the White House, Weizmann said he would raise the Palestine issue. The current "drift" had to end. The Arabs should be told that the Jews had a right to Palestine. Welles observed that Ibn Saud had recently been writing "rather unpleasant" letters demanding an end to Jewish immigration; he thought them "childish." The President should be fully informed about Jewish aspirations, he said. The next three or four months would be a period of "crystallization . . . much would happen."

Roosevelt greeted them "very cordially," Weizmann wrote later, disclosing that he had persuaded Churchill of the need for an Arab-Jewish conference. "We will tell [the Arabs] what we both decided," said FDR, implying that he and Churchill both intended to be present. Weizmann recalled that the last Arab-Jewish conference, held in London in 1939, had "settled nothing." To avoid similar mistakes, the Arabs should be told, in advance, that the democracies had won important gains for them in two wars and thus had the right to determine what sort of a Palestine settlement they considered fair.

"Churchill and I agree on what kind of settlement we should have," Roosevelt declared. The Arabs had done "very badly" in the war. With vast countries at their disposal, they had done little to develop them. The Jews, or the United Nations, might help. Meanwhile, he still thought the Arabs "purchaseable." (Weizmann's notes cite the Arab term "baksheesh," or bribe.)

Weizmann warned that the situation in Palestine was increasingly dangerous. The Jews felt trapped and tension was rising. Fear of Arab violence, however, should not deter the democracies from doing "what was right" by the Jews. The Palestine issue should be settled at once, not after the war. At this point, Welles interjected that there was no use in waiting: The Palestine issue should be settled quickly. There would be no "demarcation" between the end of fighting and the beginning of peace, as after World War I.

FDR asked if Weizmann would personally attend an Arab-Jewish conference. When the Zionist leader said he would, Welles inquired whether the President wished to send someone to "prepare the ground" with Ibn Saud. Roosevelt thought it an "excellent" idea, provided Churchill was informed. Various names were raised, among them Philby and Hoskins. Welles thought Hoskins would "serve well" and, on this note, the hour-long meeting ended.[65]

Throughout the interview, Weizmann wrote later, "I was supported by Sumner Welles who had been somewhat cautious and reticent in our private conversations but, on this occasion, was outspoken in his desire to concretize my proposals. [He] expressed the belief that America would be prepared to help, financially, in the setting up of a Jewish National Home."[66]

Fearing leaks from the pro-Arab State Department, Roosevelt and Welles had kept no written record of the meeting, but Weizmann later sent a confidential report to the British Foreign Office. That summer—almost certainly with British connivance—it fell into the hands of Hoskins who was visiting Ibn Saud. On returning to Washington in September, Hoskins showed Weizmann's report to Wallace Murray, the pro-Arab director of the Near East division. Murray, in turn, passed it to Hull. "As far as I am aware," wrote Murray, "no other record exists of these important conversations regarding the future of Palestine which took place in the White House last June."[67]

In Roosevelt's presence, Weizmann had raised no objection to Hoskins as the U.S. emissary to Ibn Saud, but days later, three pro-Zionist U.S. officials—Justice Felix Frankfurter, David Niles and Benjamin Cohen—learned that Hoskins had begun circulating a memorandum about his coming mission on Capitol Hill and warned Wise to contact Welles quickly. On June 21, Wise and Goldmann told Welles that Hoskins was "one-sided, hostile and obsessed with the risk of an Arab revolt." He had not the "stature" to negotiate with Ibn Saud.

Welles sought to calm them. Hoskins was the son of missionaries and seemed to have a missionary's zeal, he observed: nothing was more dangerous than an "excess of zeal." His contacts with Congress would be stopped but no final decision as to who would visit Ibn Saud had been made. Whoever was sent would be "only a U.S. messenger" preparing the way for discussions. The Zionists remained skeptical. A Jewish-Arab understanding would depend on the "first approach," Weizmann warned. The Arabs were impressed by "prestige and high-standing. . . The gentleman mentioned during our discussion with the President [Hoskins] would be the least suitable to serve our . . . mission." If fear of Arabs remained its guiding motive, the mission would be doomed.[68]

Weizmann thanked Welles for arranging his interview with FDR, terming it a "concrete manifestation of your genuine desire to be helpful and to convey that desire to the President." Wise also thanked Welles, noting that Weizmann had found the interview "very satisfactory." Welles apparently had as well. It was the first time, he told the Zionists, that Roosevelt, apart from expressing sympathy for their cause, had "come down to business . . . At last, something constructive had been outlined and discussed."[69]

In choosing Hoskins, an American, rather than Weizmann's British friend Philby to approach Ibn Saud, Roosevelt and Welles were clearly exerting U.S. influence to win over the Arab monarch. Warned of growing British influence, Roosevelt had recently declared oil-rich Saudi Arabia "vital" to U.S. defense, flooding it with Lend-Lease arms and supplies. Hoskins, however, was an unlikely emissary to sell Ibn Saud on a Jewish Palestine; he, too, was fanatically anti-Zionist.

Although apparently a perfect choice as a presidential agent, Peter Grose noted in his *Israel in the Mind of America,* Hoskins entered "enthusiastically into the various anti-Zionist campaigns of the State Department . . . [Wallace Murray's] Near East division, initially skeptical of this unorthodox, independent agent, quickly recognized a kindred spirit."[70]

Hoskins had, in fact, warned Welles of the danger of Zionism soon after reaching Cairo in early 1943. A "very bloody" conflict between Jews and Arabs was looming, he reported. Unless quickly headed off, its repercussions might inflame the Moslem world "from Casablanca to Calcutta." The Jews in Palestine were arming and "goading" the Arabs to break their informal wartime truce. If fighting erupted, Arabs from eight bordering states would pour in and Jews throughout the Middle East might be massacred.[71]

His grim forecast had landed on Welles's desk while Weizmann was proposing direct talks with Ibn Saud. It almost certainly confirmed Welles's belief that only a face-to-face meeting, however difficult to arrange, could prevent a bloodbath.

Hoskins returned to Washington after a three-and-a-half month survey and, on May 7, 1943, Hull forwarded his conclusions to FDR. There was growing danger of Jewish-Arab hostilities in Palestine and a massacre of Jews in Arab lands, Hoskins warned. An Arab-Jewish conflict would exacerbate "dissension" among Jews in the United States and blur the distinction between Jews in Palestine and Jewish refugees in Europe. To win 60 million Arabs to the Allied cause, the United Nations should announce postponement of a final decision on Palestine until after the war—and then only after full consultation with both Arabs and Jews. In conclusion, he recommended admitting a half-million Jews into Palestine after victory, giving them parity with the Arabs in a "bi-national" state and, separately, creating a Jewish homeland in British-ruled Libya for a half-million more refugees.[72]

Whether influenced by Hoskins's warning of imminent bloodshed, by Ibn Saud's April outburst or by both, two weeks later FDR wrote his "Great and Good Friend," the Saudi monarch, suggesting that a "friendly understanding between Arabs and Jews would be highly desirable before the war's end." No decision altering the "basic situation" in Palestine would be reached, however, without full consultation between Arabs and Jews.[73] Reviewing the message before it was sent, Welles minuted Hull: "it would seem much more expedient for the President to be far less specific."[74]

The British officially learned of the Roosevelt-Welles plan for direct Weizmann–Ibn Saud talks when the Zionist leader returned to London in June and they immediately opposed it. Colonial Secretary Oliver Stanley tried to convince Weizmann that it would not work, but Weizmann persisted: "more and more at odds with the more militant Zionist leaders (David Ben Gurion among them) and . . . encouraged . . . to believe that Zionist aims could be reached by negotiation with Britain's help," wrote Nicholas Bethell in *The Palestine Triangle*.[75]

Weizmann's optimism puzzled the British. Their envoy to Saudi Arabia, Thomas Wikeley, had warned shortly before that Ibn Saud would "in no way act as the Americans expected." The king, he reported, was motivated by three factors: belief in Islam, Arabism and friendship for Britain. Of the three, religion was the strongest. "I am . . . convinced that [Ibn Saud] would not tolerate, let alone assist, a solution of the Palestine problem along Zionist lines," wrote Wikeley. "The proposal . . . that Weizmann should visit the King fills me with alarm. I am sure Ibn Saud would refuse to meet him."[76]

Wikeley was right. Ibn Saud received Roosevelt's emissary, Hoskins, in July 1943 and flatly rejected talks with Weizmann. It was his custom, he said in a verbal message to FDR that Hoskins summarized on August 20, to welcome "all, regardless of religion." The Jews, however, were on a "special footing . . . The noble President is well aware of the enmity that exists between us . . . We do not feel . . . safe from Jewish treachery and can neither hold discussions with them or trust their promises."

Weizmann had had the "outrageous impudence to single me out, among all the Arabs and Moslems, to address to me the base demand that I should turn traitor to my religion and my country." In 1940 Weizmann had sent him a "certain European"—Philby—with an offer of 20 million pounds for his help over Palestine. "Could there be baseness or impudence greater than this? Could there be a crime greater [than] making this request to me and . . . the noble President the guarantor of so dishonorable an act?"[77]

Hoskins later claimed that he had first learned of the 20 million pound offer and FDR's role as "guarantor" from Ibn Saud, but his claim strains credulity. Weizmann had discussed the offer with Welles a year earlier, and neither Roosevelt nor Welles would have sent Hoskins on a mission so critical to Middle East peace without briefing him fully.

Roosevelt's and Welles's hopes for direct Zionist-Arab talks had collapsed; whether the reason was Ibn Saud's obduracy, covert British resistance to American influence in the Middle East or Hoskins's own shadowy role will never be known. Hoskins told FDR that Ibn Saud had "broken" with Philby because of the alleged bribe but, when FDR ordered Hoskins to fly to London and confer with Weizmann, the Zionist leader brought Hoskins and Philby face-to-face. Challenging Hoskins's veracity, Philby produced a recent letter from Ibn Saud expressing warm friendship and inviting him to return to Saudi Arabia.[78]

The 20 million pound formula, wrote Grose, in some ways paralleled FDR's own thinking. David Niles, a White House aide, quoted FDR later as stating that he could "do anything with Ibn Saud with a few million dollars."[79]

Weizmann fought on, notwithstanding Ibn Saud's refusal to meet him, and pleaded with Welles in December 1943, to intercede again with Roosevelt.[80] Despite Hoskins's "adverse" report, he wrote Welles, a Jewish-Arab agreement on Palestine offered an "approach which should not be abandoned without further exploration." It would satisfy both the legitimate aspirations of Arabs and Jews and the "strategic and economic" interests of the United States and Britain. Philby and he remained convinced that Ibn Saud would accept—if it were offered "on behalf of Roosevelt and Churchill." By that time, however, Welles had resigned from the State Department and could do no more. The British, meanwhile, derided Weizmann's plea to Welles. "This correspondence does Dr. Weizmann no credit," wrote a Foreign Office official. "Anyone who thinks Ibn Saud will look at this hare-brained scheme, after what he has said about it, must be quite cracked."[81]

Cracked or not, Weizmann had offered perhaps the only hope of a Jewish homeland in Palestine without bloodshed. With Welles gone and U.S.-Soviet tension rising, State Department Arabists joined forces with U.S. military and oil interests to preserve British control of Palestine, the strategic key to the eastern Mediterranean. On November 19, three months after Welles's resignation, Wallace Murray laid down the law to Wise, Goldmann and Abba Hillel Silver, the American rabbi and Zionist leader. The future of Palestine was "not under discussion," he told them. The British had supreme responsibility in the Middle East, and the United States would be "most reluctant" to embarrass its ally while the war continued.

Citing earlier discussions with Welles, the Zionists protested that Britain alone could not be allowed to decide Palestine's future. They, too, should be consulted and not confronted with a decision that might later have to be "violently opposed." Murray was adamant. When the peace conference came, he observed coldly, a Jewish delegation would be present, as in Paris in 1919, and could then "submit" its demands.[82]

Except for Woodrow Wilson, Welles wrote in retrospect, no U.S. President had shown greater sympathy for Zionism than Franklin D. Roosevelt. The longer the war continued, the more his mind turned to Palestine as the only solution to the refugee problem. His motives, as always, were mixed: part geopolitical, part sentimental. He had never, for instance, forgotten that in April 1941, the most critical period of the war, the Jews in Palestine had proved the "one element in the Middle East unalterably loyal to the cause of democracy." "Hitler had occupied Greece, Rommel was at the gates of Egypt, a pro-Axis coup had erupted in Iraq and Britain's back was to the wall," Welles wrote in 1948. Had the Palestine Jews seized that moment to agitate, the course of history might have changed. "German air-borne forces . . . were poised in Greece and in Crete, ready to descend upon Iraq. With the German occupation of Iraq, the door would have been open for the Nazis to enter the Levant and Arabia . . . The United States was not yet a belligerent [and] the Japanese Navy could readily have joined the Germans and the Italians at the Suez Canal. The outcome of the war might . . . have been altogether different."[83]

Roosevelt envisioned a Jewish Palestine providing both refuge for hundreds of thousands of displaced European Jews and becoming an oasis of Western democracy in a feudal Arab wasteland; developing natural resources, attracting foreign capital, benefiting surrounding Arab states and, gradually, overcoming racial antagonisms.[84] In 1944 he formally endorsed a Jewish homeland in Palestine but, by then, the time for negotiation had passed. Returning from Yalta early in 1945, he sent a destroyer to bring Ibn Saud and his retinue of forty-eight (plus seven goats for sustenance) from Riyadh to the Great Bitter Lake, near Suez.

Convinced, as always, of the power of "reason and self-interest," the President tried negotiating a face-to-face solution with Ibn Saud along lines similar to Philby's: Palestine for the Jews, independence and economic aid for the Arabs and a guarantee against Jewish expansion into Arab lands. But his dream faded when the desert monarch told him flatly that Arabs and Jews could "never cooperate, neither in Palestine nor in any other country."[85] Roosevelt had underestimated the strength of Arab nationalism, Welles later conceded.[86] A half century of war would follow.

TWENTY-ONE

MISSION TO EUROPE

1940

A Forlorn Hope

HAD HITLER HAD HIS WAY IN 1939, there would have been no war. After his conquest of Poland, Britain and France would have faced facts and made peace. On October 6, he offered the Allies his "outstretched hand," suggesting that if problems still remained, it would seem "more sensible to resolve them before millions . . . are uselessly sent to death and billions of wealth destroyed."[1] Neville Chamberlain and Edouard Daladier, however, had been duped at Munich and spurned his offer, certain that what he really wanted was an armed truce.

Balked, Hitler ordered immediate planning for a full-scale attack on France through Belgium and Holland. His generals, although elated by their quick victory in Poland, still respected the hundred-division French army behind the Maginot defense line and insisted on more time for training. Winter brought operations on the Western Front to a halt and, in Washington, archisolationists like Senator William E. Borah sneered at the "phony" war.

Roosevelt sent Welles to Europe on a "fact-finding" mission that winter, and historians ever since have speculated about his motives. Some have seen it as a ploy to buy time for the Allies; others as a means of detaching Mussolini from

Hitler; others as a last-ditch effort to appease Hitler and forestall hostilities.[2] Roosevelt was a man of infinite complexity, however, and the Welles mission an example of multiple motivations. One may have been a letter from James W. Gerard, an old friend and U.S. ambassador to Germany during World War I. Three weeks before Hitler's attack on Poland, Gerard wrote FDR: "This country and the world expects [sic] you to make every effort for peace." Britain and France together had "one half of the land area of the world" and might help restore Germany's and Italy's lost colonies if FDR proposed it, secretly, as a contribution to peace. Gerard suggested that FDR send "three men in whom the country has confidence—one a Republican," to prepare the ground. "P. S. Don't think that I want the thankless job."[3]

Roosevelt asked Welles to draft a reply and, on August 10, Welles sent his draft to Hull, who then was vacationing at White Sulphur Springs, in West Virginia. Dismissing Gerard's proposal about restoring colonies as "exaggerated," Welles suggested nonetheless that if the European situation worsened, the President might consider sending "three representative" Americans to Europe to ascertain if grounds for a peaceful settlement still existed.

"It might, at least, have a deterrent effect, and might, remotely, prove to have some constructive value," he wrote. "I have not wanted to speak with the President until I have had an opportunity of getting your opinion."[4] Hitler's attack on Poland, on September 1 made the issue moot; three days later, the British and French declared war.

In a radio address to the nation soon after, FDR made clear that his primary goal was a major role for the United States when the fighting ended. This country, he declared, would concentrate its influence on a "final peace" to eliminate the continued use of force between nations.[5] In his message to Congress over New Year's, he lashed out at the Axis Powers, refused to compromise with the conqueror of Czechoslovakia and Poland and emphasized the importance of "human rights" to America's safety.[6]

Recalling that the State Department had failed during World War I to prepare adequate studies for Woodrow Wilson's peace goals, he directed Welles to form a small group of State Department experts and start postwar planning. To avoid isolationist and special-interest pressures, the work was to be conducted in "strict secrecy." Meanwhile, rumors of a German spring offensive were mounting and an American "peace movement" was coalescing. 1940 was an election year, and failure to act might subject FDR and the Democratic party to censure. The time seemed ripe for a U.S. initiative.

Traditionally, neutrals had sought to make their voices heard at peace conferences by concerting in advance, and this is what Roosevelt now proceeded to do. In August, a month before Hitler's attack, FDR had agreed to open diplomatic relations with the Vatican, at Welles and Hull's urging.[7] Over

Christmas that year he proposed sending a personal representative to Pius XII to discuss "parallel peace efforts." FDR surmised that the Pope, like himself, saw no early prospect of peace, but, when the time came, it would be important that "common ideals have united expression."[8] Pius agreed and, after consulting Christian and Jewish groups,[9] FDR named Myron C. Taylor, a former head of U.S. Steel, his personal representative.

Having established contact with Europe's most prestigious neutral (Italy then was still technically "nonbelligerent"), FDR directed Welles to prepare a conference of forty neutrals in Washington before the European war flared up. "We do not have to go to war," FDR told Congress, "but we can strive with other nations to encourage . . . peace."[10] The world, he added, expected the United States to "continue as a potent . . . active factor" in seeking to reestablish world peace.[11] Roosevelt was reflecting the national mood. Polls showed that millions of Americans opposed involvement in Europe's war but overwhelmingly favored active U.S. participation should Hitler make another peace offer.[12] The pressures on FDR to "do something" were increasing.

Into this bleak scene fell a ray of hope over Christmas. Roosevelt heard rumors that Hitler's deputy, Hermann Goering, and certain German generals opposed an attack on the West and favored more generous peace terms than Hitler had offered in October. FDR's source was James D. Mooney, chief of General Motors' overseas division and a veteran Roosevelt supporter with easy access to the White House. Thanks to GM's substantial investment in Europe, Mooney also claimed access to the Nazi leadership. (In 1938, in fact, Hitler had awarded him the order of the German Eagle, First Class.[13])

According to Mooney, Goering had hinted that Germany was ready to sign a pact of "eternal friendship" with France and Britain and, if agreement could be reached, might even cut its ties to Moscow and Tokyo. Eventually, Mooney asserted, Goering intended to "ease Hitler into an honorific position" and take over the Third Reich himself. Unaware that Mooney had been peddling the same rumors in London and Paris, and receiving a cold shoulder in each, Roosevelt was intrigued.

At the time he had no high-level contacts in the Axis capitals. Alexander Kirk, the able U.S. chargé d'affaires in Berlin, had been treated as a pariah since 1938 when FDR had recalled ambassador Hugh Wilson to protest anti-Jewish atrocities. In Rome, Ambassador William Phillips was feeling the brunt of Mussolini's anger at FDR's refusal to recognize his conquest of Ethiopia. Mooney's rumors seemed worth checking.

Early in January 1940, Myron Taylor called at the White House before leaving for his Vatican assignment and learned from FDR that he was contemplating sending an emissary on a "fact-finding" mission to Europe. He had not decided whether it would be Welles, Berle, or a "businessman" (presumably Mooney)[14] and had left the name blank in his handwritten press release. Soon after FDR apparently decided on Welles, for he broached it with him at about the same time.[15]

The idea to send Welles had come as an "impulse," he told Breckinridge Long. It could not do any harm and might do good. The Germans might launch an offensive at any time, and he foresaw the bombardment of English cities and ports "with horror." If Welles's trip could delay or possibly prevent an offensive, it would be worth a "great deal." A month, even a week, would help England and France obtain arms. Another reason for sending Welles was to get the "lowdown" on Hitler's and Mussolini's views. FDR already knew what the British and French were thinking so Welles's visits to their capitals would merely be "window-dressing."[16] Welles fell ill soon after, however, and, when his doctor ordered two weeks' convalescence, FDR agreed to wait.[17]

On January 24, with Welles ill, Mooney reappeared in the Oval Office, announcing his early return to Europe and requesting a diplomatic passport. Sidestepping the passport issue, the President genially stressed the "unofficial, confidential" nature of his trip. When Mooney asked for written instructions, FDR wrote noncommittally: "Dear Jim: I enjoyed our little chat this morning very much. Just a line to wish you good luck and I shall expect you to drop in to see me when you return."[18]

Armed with what he considered presidential carte blanche, Mooney turned up next day at the State Department to request diplomatic codes. With Hull and Welles away, he was received by a third-echelon officer, George Messersmith, who knew Europe well and had known Mooney for fifteen years. Messersmith had decided misgivings about the auto magnate's back-door forays into the White House. Until he could verify Mooney's "mandate," he merely emphasized the need for secrecy and warned Mooney against statements that might "commit" the President or the United States. Messersmith agreed to "consider" his request for diplomatic codes and noted later that "Mr. Mooney is not a person to be trusted with any such mission as that which he seems to be undertaking."[19]

Welles returned to the Department in late January, learned of Mooney's capers during his absence and asked the President for clarification. Roosevelt, embarrassed, acknowledged the risk of sending a businessman, untrained in diplomacy and linked financially to the Nazis, to roam Europe as his "peace" agent. He had given Mooney no official mission, he insisted; Mooney was returning to Europe solely in his private capacity and would not need State Department codes.[20]

With Mooney about to sail, however, FDR speeded up preparations for Welles's trip. In his previous talks with Mooney, FDR had not considered a visit to "nonbelligerent" Italy; but Welles stressed the importance of Italian neutrality to Anglo-French control of the eastern Mediterranean and won its inclusion.

On February 1, ten days before announcing Welles's mission, FDR called in Lord Lothian, the British ambassador, and explained its purpose. A "tremendous" German spring offensive would make peace far more difficult, he said. To satisfy himself and U.S. opinion, he was sending his Under Secretary to Berlin, Paris, London and Rome. He was not "hopeful" that Welles would find an acceptable basis for peace; if this proved the case, he would publicly condemn Hitler for fighting for "aggression, rather than security."[21]

Unpersuaded, the British opposed the Welles mission from the start. His trip would produce a "sensational" impression on the world, protested Chamberlain. Peace rumors were rampant, and Hitler was seeking a settlement that would guarantee his gains while leaving his armed forces intact. Welles's visit to Rome would make it appear that FDR was "negotiating peace" in concert with the Vatican. "What the President now proposes to do," Foreign Secretary Halifax cabled Lothian, "is precisely what Hitler hoped he would do."

To strangle the Welles mission at birth, Chamberlain played his trump—cabling Lothian to disclose to Roosevelt in the "strictest secrecy" that Britain and France were planning a joint military expedition to help Finland, which Soviet forces had invaded on November 29, 1939. Norwegian and Swedish cooperation would be necessary, Chamberlain added, and the Welles mission might "interfere with . . . success." If Norway and Sweden got the idea that "some sort of peace negotiations were under way," they would refuse. "Tell the President he is being entrusted with a secret we have told no one else," Chamberlain concluded.[22]

Roosevelt stood firm, agreeing only to notify the Norwegians and Swedes privately that Welles's trip was "solely for inquiry." He, himself, had no interest in a truce or unstable peace, and Welles would make clear in each capital that anything like a successful attack on Britain or France would inevitably bring the United States "nearer war." Faced with FDR's resolve, the British grudgingly yielded. "Half-baked idea of sending Sumner Welles over here with a flourish of trumpets to collect data on which Roosevelt is to provide basis of peace," Cadogan sneered in his diary.[23] Halifax suspected the influence of U.S. Ambassador Joseph P. Kennedy "whose opinions are well known to us" and of certain American businessmen with "dubious political connections" to Goering.

"Mr Mooney is on us again," minuted Sir Robert Vansittart, a towering, apoplectic Foreign Office official whose detestation of Germans had led him to write that "eighty percent of the race are the political and moral scum of the earth."[24] Vansittart's brother, Nicholas, was a European director of General Motors and had just seen Mooney in Rome. "This is what is in the wind," Sir Robert prattled.

FDR had been dissatisfied for some time with the reporting of his diplomats in Europe and was sending Welles to "check up" on them. Mooney would be checking up on Welles who was FDR's "open" representative and Mooney his "private and unofficial one." At some point, the credulous Briton continued, the two would meet and exchange impressions. Vansittart thought the proceeding "most unusual," and Halifax scrawled on his memorandum "They are a strange people and pursue strange methods!"[25]

Meanwhile, in Washington, the better-informed Lothian was urging that every courtesy be shown Welles, who had "very distinctive views regarding his own importance." Anthony Eden, then Dominions Secretary, wrote Halifax that Welles, "rather a stiff dog," had tendered him a banquet at his Maryland home the year before, and he would be happy to return the kindness.[26]

On February 9, Lothian cabled London that Roosevelt would announce the Welles mission "tomorrow morning . . . as Bullitt, his ambassador to France, [is] arriving in Washington tomorrow evening."[27] Anticipating Bullitt's violent reaction, Roosevelt had decided to forestall him. The next day two announcements in quick succession aroused world speculation. Hull told reporters that forty neutral nations were being invited to exchange views in Washington on disarmament and trade.[28] Two hours later Roosevelt announced the Welles mission, fueling further speculation.

Welles's trip would be solely for the purpose of advising him and Secretary Hull as to "present conditions" in Europe, FDR announced. Welles would make "no proposals or commitments," and statements made to him by government officials would be kept in strict confidence.[29] Reporters were puzzled. A month earlier FDR had ordered Welles to start postwar planning. Now he was sending him to three belligerent capitals and to Rome. Was he not receiving regular diplomatic reports from these capitals? What could Welles add? Roosevelt stonewalled. There was great value in having the "total situation surveyed by one mind," he replied blandly. The reporters persisted. Even if Welles made no commitments, would he not be reflecting the President's views on a possible peace? It was all in the prepared statement, Roosevelt replied. He had nothing to add.

With Welles about to hold the world's center stage, jealousies predictably flared. Hull learned of the mission at the last minute and violently opposed it, predicting that it would arouse false hopes and undermine the Anglo-French will to resist. Hull's resentment paled in comparison with that of Bullitt, who heard the news only on landing at the Washington airport from Paris that evening. "He was furious that Welles was about to make a swing around Europe for FDR—even going to Paris," Robert D. Murphy, his deputy, told the author years later. "Bullitt considered himself FDR's viceroy for Europe. He would have Europe and Sumner . . . everything else. This was the beginning of his insane jealousy of Welles and it was pursued implacably."[30]

Bullitt poured out his anger to all who would listen. "He did not relish the idea of Welles going over and, in effect, superceding the regularly accredited diplomatic representative," wrote his friend Harold Ickes.[31] The French, too, heard Bullitt's strictures. "[He] learned of the Welles mission yesterday, disembarking from his airplane, and wants me to inform [you] that, had he known previously, he would have opposed it," cabled the French ambassador, Count René de St. Quentin. "He attributes the principal responsibility to Welles, himself, who is anxious to step out in front [*"jouer les premiers roles"*] before the Secretaryship of State falls vacant, either after the elections, or before, should Mr. Hull become the Democratic presidential candidate."[32]

Welles sailed in a blaze of publicity for Naples on the Italian liner *Rex,* on February 17, carrying in his briefcase a numbered code for direct communication with the President.[33] and accompanied by Jay Pierrepont Moffat, chief of the Department's European division, a junior aide, Hartwell Johnson, and the usual large family entourage: Mathilde, her young cousin and traveling companion Thora Ronalds, their maids, Reeks and Welles's West Highland terrier, Toby. The presence aboard ship of Myron Taylor, en route to his Vatican post, aroused further speculation about United States–Vatican "peace moves" among the many reporters assigned to cover Welles. Welles confined himself, however, to bromides about the weather; and was wryly amused at the soubriquet "Sumner the Silent" that they fastened on him.

At Naples, Mussolini's officials had rolled out a huge red carpet, and a special train stood waiting to take Welles and his party to Rome. All seemed off to a good start—except that Toby calmly lifted his leg on a ceremonial urn during the welcoming ceremonies, embarrassing Reeks, who was holding his leash, and Welles, who looked stonily the other way.

In Rome, Welles found Mussolini's thirty-seven-year old son-in-law and Foreign Minister, Galeazzo Ciano, more intelligent and sympathetic than his playboy reputation had suggested. Ciano spoke colloquial English, was cordial and unaffected and made no secret of his contempt for France and Britain nor of his respect for German military power. He detested Hitler—and, even more, Joachim von Ribbentrop, his Foreign Minister—and told Welles that Hitler might have accepted peace after his conquest of Poland but now it was too late.

Ciano, alone of the Axis officials whom Welles would meet in the coming weeks, made clear without "subterfuge or hesitation" that he opposed the war, saw devastation for Europe if it spread and intended, by every means at his disposal, to prevent Italy's entry into the war. Sensing a covert ally, Welles emphasized the advantage to Italy in remaining neutral. Dangling the prospect of greater trade, Welles noted that the United States and Latin America together formed the "one great neutral influence" in the world. Italy should work with it to lay the groundwork for peace.

Ciano confided soon after to the famous red diary locked in his safe that Welles was a "gentleman" compared with high German officials who were "presumptuous barbarians." Welles "easily bore the weight of the mission which had thrust him into the world limelight . . . I did not hesitate to inform him [about] events concerning which he was not informed. He seemed pleased when I let him know my feelings and sympathies."[34]

Dissimilar as they were—Welles a towering, reserved Anglo-Saxon, Ciano a chubby, ebullient Latin—their common interest in halting the war seemed, at least to Welles, to have forged a bond. Nevertheless, he wrote FDR later that Ciano, although sympathetic, was also "wholly subservient" to his formidable father-in-law and "quailed" when confronted with the Duce's wrath.[35]

The next day, accompanied by Ciano and Ambassador Phillips, Welles had his first interview with Mussolini. The Duce, he wrote FDR, was "ponderous, moving with an elephantine motion, his face falling in rolls of flesh. He seemed to be laboring under some tremendous strain: physical, unquestionably, for he has procured a new and young Italian mistress only ten days ago, but . . . mental, as well. One could almost sense a leaden oppression." Mussolini had reason for oppression. Unknown to Welles, he was due to meet Hitler at the Brenner Pass in a few days and suspected that the Führer would demand his immediate entry into the war. Welles asked if a basis for peace still existed.

A "negotiated" peace was still possible, replied Mussolini—but not if the war spread. Citing Italy's territorial claims and its ties to Germany, he hinted at the terms Hitler might demand in return for peace. The Allies, he warned, were underestimating Hitler's military power. On arriving, Welles had presented Mussolini a handwritten letter from FDR, emphasizing his hopes that Italy would remain neutral and concluding cordially: "I still hope to meet you one day, soon!"

Mussolini expressed pleasure but demurred at the distance. When Welles suggested the Azores as a possible halfway point, Mussolini seemed to toy with the idea, promising to reply to FDR personally. He never did. Long after, Welles would write that a Roosevelt-Mussolini meeting "probably would have . . . spared the [Italian people] the tragedy which they have undergone."[36]

Ciano's private analysis of Welles's interview with Mussolini was somber. The meeting, he wrote in his diary, had been "icy." Welles had left the Duce's vast, dimly lit study "more depressed" than when he entered it.[37] On the other hand, Ambassador Phillips's wife, Caroline, presumably echoing her husband, thought that it had been a "great success." The ambassador had never seen the Italian dictator more amiable and friendly. Welles, she mused, was a "strange man: tall, handsome, distinguished-looking, essentially a gentleman, cold, reserved, stoical and very able."[38]

Welles had planned to visit Paris after Rome, but Bullitt persuaded Roosevelt that the French would be "upset" if he appeared there before Berlin so he set out next day by a special Italian train for Switzerland, leaving Mathilde in Rome and taking with him Moffat, Johnson and his valet.[39] Pausing in Zurich for two days, he drafted a report for FDR and left Reeks to await his return. As a British subject, Reeks would have been liable to internment in Germany. He would never forget Welles's last-minute request to him: "Forget for the moment that you are working for me and write down, exactly, what you think of Hitler." Before confronting the Nazi dictator, Welles wanted the gut reaction of an average, man-in-the-street Englishman.

Reporters tried to corner Welles in the lobby of his Zurich hotel on his last night, and a female writer for a New York tabloid donned a clinging black evening gown, hoping to extract secrets over dinner, but Welles remained Sumner-the-Silent. "We saw him next day standing in the window of his compartment as the train pulled out for Germany," remembered another reporter. "We waved but he made no response."[40] His mind was focused on the approaching critical phase of his mission.

Oppression set in as he crossed the frontier. Hitler had sent a special train to take him to Berlin but, remembering the World War I travels of Wilson's aide, Colonel E. M. House, and his covert contacts with the British, had ordered every blind in the train lowered. Welles whiled away the hours reading Nazi newspapers, appalled at the lies printed about the United States and Britain.[41] Hitler had decreed that Welles would "do the talking." Germany's October peace offer had been spurned, and Britain and France had repeatedly proclaimed their intention to "dismember and annihilate" the Third Reich. Hitler would handle specific questions about Poland, Austria and the Bohemia-Moravia protectorate himself, but on the subject of peace, Germany would have "nothing to say."[42]

Welles's opening interview with Foreign Minister Joachim von Ribbentrop, on March 1, was one of the "most unpleasant" in his life, he wrote later. [43] Accompanied by Alexander Kirk, whom Ribbentrop previously had refused to receive, Welles entered the foreign ministry past storm troopers in "stained uniforms . . . their faces . . . subnormal in their startling brutality." Ribbentrop lectured Welles for two hours, his arms extended along the sides of his chair and his eyes closed like a Delphic oracle. His mind was "completely closed. The man is saturated with hate for England," Welles wrote FDR. "He is clearly without background in international affairs, and was guilty of a hundred inaccuracies in his presentation of German policy during recent years. I have rarely seen a man I disliked more."[44]

The following morning at eleven Hitler received Welles pleasantly but with great formality. He was taller than expected and had none of the "ludicrous" features often shown in his photographs. He seemed in excellent physical condition, his color good and his eyes, while tired, clear. He was dignified, spoke with clarity and precision, and Welles, who understood German, followed every word though the interpreter, Dr. Paul Schmidt, interpreted at times inaccurately. Hitler's voice was low, and well modulated. Only once during their hour-and-a-half conversation did it take on the raucous stridency heard in his speeches. Only then, wrote Welles, did his features lose their composure.[45]

Welles had opened with a short statement. He had brought no proposals; his mission was solely to learn the "purpose" of the German government so that Roosevelt might judge for himself whether a just, durable peace was still possible. Hitler then launched into a ninety-minute diatribe. He had sought peace with Britain unsuccessfully, he claimed. So long as Britain and France intended to "destroy" the Reich, there was no hope of real peace. Germany would assert its economic supremacy in Central and Eastern Europe, and no state "to the East" (i.e. , Soviet Russia) would be "permitted to constitute a threat." The German people would fight to preserve the unity Hitler had won for them; German victory was inevitable. On this grim note, the interview ended.

Welles and Kirk left, escorted by uniformed Nazi guards marching in measured tread past bowing servitors in blue satin livery and powdered hair. "It was . . . tragically plain," Welles reflected as he drove away, "that all decisions had already been made. The best that could be hoped for was delay." At a reception for Welles at Kirk's residence that night, Mooney appeared, uninvited, hoping to tell Hitler when they next met that he had "conferred" with Welles. To his chagrin, Welles remained icily distant.[46]

Welles's next interview, with Hermann Goering, Hitler's deputy, was memorable. Despite the freezing March weather, Goering sent an open limousine to drive Welles an hour across the north German plain to his residence, Karinhall, an ornate palace built around a former hunting lodge. Throughout the drive, snow whirled past flapping canvas curtains into Welles's face.

Goering's girth was monstrous, his thighs and arms "tremendous," Welles wrote FDR. His hands were shaped like the "digging paws of a badger." On his right hand he wore an enormous ring set with six huge diamonds and, on his left, an emerald an inch square. His face gave the impression of having been "heavily rouged, but, since at the end of our three-hour conversation the color had vanished," Welles added, "the effect was probably due to some form of physical maladjustment."[47]

Goering was more frank and cordial than the other Nazi leaders, but his account of German history over the past seven years parroted Hitler's. Germany's armed strength vis-à-vis the Allies was far greater than in 1914, he boasted. The Luftwaffe (German air force) was "supreme." The war would be short, Germany victorious and, even if the war lasted five or ten years, Germany would grow steadily stronger and emerge triumphant.

Listening in a low, easy chair by the fire as the snow gusted outside, Welles reflected that Goering had at least traveled outside Germany and had some concept of foreign psychology. He alone in Hitler's entourage might grasp the impact of a German war on the American people. War would inevitably affect America's "vital" interests, Welles warned, but Goering brushed it aside. Britain and France were determined to crush Germany, he insisted; war was inevitable. If the United States could prevent it, it would be "the greatest thing which human beings could desire." The United States, however, should feel no cause for alarm, concluded Goering. Germany had no ambitions that could "affect the Western Hemisphere."[48] Better informed about Axis penetration into Latin America than anyone except Roosevelt, Welles knew that statement for the lie it was.

His interviews with other Nazi officials were equally sinister. Rudolf Hess, a deputy Führer, seemed "of the lowest order of intelligence . . . forehead . . . low and narrow . . . deep-set eyes very close together," he reported.[49] Baron Ernst Von Weizsaecher, Welles's opposite number at the Foreign Ministry, drew their chairs to the center of his office to foil microphones in the walls. Hjalmar Schacht, Hitler's fiscal wizard, whispered to Welles at Kirk's house that he would be "dead within a week" if what he was about to relate was repeated. He then confided a plot by unidentified German generals to oust Hitler and pleaded with Welles to be allowed to visit the United States, presumably to further the plot. German atrocities in Poland, he confided, were "beyond imagination."[50] On his last night, walking across the snow covered Paris er-platz to the Adlon hotel where he was staying, Welles paused to chat in German with four old country women encumbered with heavy bags and satchels who had stopped to rest. Dressed in the long, heavy skirts and tight corsets of an earlier era, they had the "decent, kindly faces" he remembered from his childhood visits to Germany. What struck him most was that one had already lost three sons, and the others one each, in the Polish campaign, six months earlier.[51]

Welles left Germany the next day, profoundly depressed. What influence Mussolini had ever had on Hitler was gone. The key to war or peace now lay solely in Berlin.

After two days in Switzerland drafting an interim report to the President, Welles set out for Paris. His train passed through Milan, where Joseph P. Kennedy, returning to his London embassy from home leave, boarded. Learning of Welles's presence, Kennedy joined him and for the next few hours, as their train sped toward Paris, the two exchanged impressions. Kennedy was a compulsive note-taker, and his records provide the only private account of Welles's activities and views on this final stage of his mission.

In 1950, ten years later, James M. Landis, the wartime director of civilian defense, helped edit Kennedy's papers and sent Welles a draft chapter covering the period. Welles studied it "very carefully," he wrote Landis. No stenographer had been present, so direct quotations ascribed to him could not be wholly accurate, but he had "no criticism of any of the essential facts."[52]

Kennedy cited rumors that Hitler would send Ribbentrop to Rome to neutralize Welles's influence on Mussolini and reap propaganda benefits by offering Pope Pius a Nazi "peace plan." The chance of a negotiated peace was still one in a thousand, Welles conceded. Even if his mission failed, however, it might still prove useful in "consolidating" official American opinion about the war. "In the State Department," he confessed, "we are too much at sea."[53]

Welles found Paris in a mood of sullen apathy.[54] Bullitt had refused to return to his embassy post while his archrival was on the scene, so Welles called on French officials escorted by Bullitt's deputy, Robert Murphy.[55] The French cabinet, defeatist to a man, still insisted on the protocol of *l'ancien regime,* and guests in business suits at a stag dinner given for Welles at the Quai d'Orsay were served by footmen in knee breeches.[56] The French press, starved for news, filled its columns with "personal tidbits . . . about Sumner's English valet, Reeks, laying out his clothes or drawing his bath at the Ritz hotel," noted Moffat.[57]

One incident especially revealed how deeply Nazi ideology had permeated the French masses. After Welles had paid a courtesy call on the ex-Premier, Leon Blum, more than 3,000 letters flooded the American embassy protesting in "violent, insulting terms" that a representative of the President of the United States had dared call on a Jew.[58]

Entering the final round of his mission, Welles flew to England, on March 11, in a French government plane, escorted by fighters. Kennedy and Cadogan met him at the airport, and soon after, Welles told Kennedy that Hitler's military strength was being "seriously underestimated." In all three capitals—Rome, Berlin and Paris—he had heard the same demand for security. "Security is the thing everyone wants," he said. What was lacking was confidence, and there was only one solution: a "mechanical" peace based on phased disarmament with automatic sanctions to enforce compliance. How it was to be done, he did not know: possibly through a "strong bloc of neutrals or an international air police."[59]

Roosevelt had directed Welles to make no "proposals or commitments," but the evidence suggests that they had a secret agenda. The President "wants nothing more than to make a dramatic move for peace," Welles confided to Kennedy. "If he sees anything in my report which will encourage him in such a move, he will jump at it; Hull, notwithstanding."[60] Welles, however, had found Hitler set on war, Mussolini vacillating and the French blind to any solution except military victory. If grounds for a "dramatic" peace move were to be found for FDR, they would have be found in London.

Welles pressed his "security through disarmament" formula in his first talk with Foreign Secretary Lord Halifax. The Germans were convinced, he said, that Britain and France meant to destroy and dismember the Reich. Mussolini hoped to keep Italy out of the war but had warned that this would become increasingly difficult if hostilities began. Lasting peace depended, therefore, on reestablishing "general security." Only then could political issues such as Poland, Czechoslovakia and Germany's economic demands be addressed. Immediate disarmament was not necessary; the belligerents could remain mobilized, and Britain's blockade continue, while Europe's political problems were being negotiated. Everyone realized that general security was the objective so the important point was that "hostilities not begin."

That night, meeting Chamberlain and Halifax at 10 Downing Street, Welles handed the Prime Minister a letter from FDR introducing him as "my boyhood friend." His credentials established, Welles reverted to his theme: disarmament as the only way of restoring confidence before war laid Europe in ruins. Chamberlain was courteous but cool. It was impossible to deal with Hitler's regime, he declared. There could be no real peace without confidence and, without confidence, no disarmament.

Halifax interjected that neither could there be a peace that allowed Hitler to remain in power and "save face" with the German people. The Germans would have to learn the penalty of aggression. Faced with the same intransigence he had found in Rome, Berlin and Paris, Welles persisted. It was not beyond the "wit of man" to find a solution, he argued. The problems, admittedly, were difficult—but not more than war's destruction. If war was to be avoided, someone would have to start. Citing the adage of the chicken and the egg, Welles asked which came first: disarmament or confidence? Halifax reported later to King George VI and the cabinet that "Mr Welles . . . inclined to . . . the first. The Prime Minister argued vigorously for the second."[61] The interview ended after an hour in deadlock.

In need of fresh air, Welles walked with Kennedy through the gathering dusk to the Dorchester Hotel, where he was staying. Chamberlain seemed tired, he said, and Kennedy agreed. Kennedy would write later that the "old men" running the British government were "so near the grave that they ran the war as if there were no generations to follow. There seems no real fire anywhere, no genius, no sense of the shambles that are to come."[62] That night the cabinet tendered Welles an official dinner, and on seeing him next morning, Kennedy asked how it had gone. "Pathetic" was Welles's reply. "We seemed to be dining in 1892."

Vansittart exploded on reading the minutes of Welles's talk with Chamberlain. Welles, he fumed, was a man of "no practical experience . . . exceedingly dangerous." The Prime Minister had been "entirely right" in putting confidence before disarmament and Welles was "hopelessly wrong" in putting it the other way, seeking refuge in "rubbish about the hen and the egg." Welles's suggestion that the United States might "associate" itself in some system of international inspection of disarmament was worthless—unless the Americans were prepared to "go to war with anybody (i.e., the Germans) who would be found . . . infringing any disarmament clauses within a short while."

Vansittart suspected that Welles was planning to put his "ensuing nonsense" to Roosevelt with the "consolation" that FDR would inform Britain before taking action. The only consolation, he growled, would be if the President consulted Britain before taking any particular action. "That, of course, he will not do because he is electioneering." Welles's proposal was playing "ostrich," and the situation was far too serious for ostriches. While dining with Welles that night, Halifax should point out the fatal flaw in his reasoning. "We are going to have trouble from this gentleman," Vansittart warned darkly.[63]

Of the many British officials with whom Welles conferred, Churchill, then First Lord of the Admiralty, alone impressed him. Welles arrived at his office at day's end, weary after three weeks of travel and innumerable interviews, and expecting to find concentration difficult. To the contrary, he wrote Roosevelt, Churchill held him spellbound:

> He was sitting in front of the fire, smoking a 24-inch [*sic*] cigar and drinking a
> whisky-and-soda. It was obvious that he had consumed a good many whiskies
> before I arrived. [He] commenced an address which lasted exactly one hour and
> fifty minutes . . . a cascade of oratory, brilliant and always effective, interlarded
> with considerable wit.

For twenty years, Churchill claimed, British governments had failed to pursue a realistic policy toward Germany. After World War I, the "victors forgot, the vanquished plotted on."[64] The Germans had not changed; nor would they. Germany's objectives—military conquest and world supremacy—endangered the United States as much as the British empire. The only solution was the outright and complete defeat of Hitler, the destruction of National Socialism and postwar arrangements to control Germany "for at least . . . a hundred years."[65]

Sensing that his meeting with Welles had ended in a stalemate, Chamberlain invited him back on his last night in England. He would not deal with Hitler's regime, the Prime Minister repeated, but, if the Nazis were replaced by the German army or "some other group that publicly avowed that it had nothing to do with. . . Hitler," a disarmament program might be worked out, together with political problems such as Poland and Czechoslovakia. Unknown to Welles, Chamberlain had confided his secret war aims to his private secretary, Sir Arthur Rucker. His goal was not to fight "Germany," he told Rucker, but to oust Hitler and make peace with the German General Staff. Soviet communism was a greater danger than Nazi Germany, a plague that did not stop at national boundaries. Given the Soviet advance into Poland and its threat to East Europe, it was vital not to destroy the possibility of "uniting with a new German government against the common danger."[66]

Sensing a subtle shift in Chamberlain's earlier intransigence, Welles asked if he would still refuse to deal with Hitler, provided he withdrew his troops and reconstituted Poland, made Bohemia and Moravia separate political units, held a plebiscite in Austria and agreed to disarmament under a "central authority" comprising the nations of Europe.

Chamberlain reflected, then replied that he would not deal personally with Hitler, but he was not speaking for the cabinet. If Welles's ideas could be worked out with Hitler, it would be a "miracle, and we are perfectly willing to see a miracle happen." The chance was one in a 1,000, or one in 10,000, said Welles, but "there seems to me a chance and, therefore, I must explore every possible angle."

Welles left England the next morning, March 14, in a blinding snowstorm. Seeing him off, Kennedy thought he had been encouraged by Chamberlain's "definite drawback" from his initial obduracy. To have persuaded Chamberlain and Halifax to argue a different position, wrote Kennedy, had been a "step forward." Nothing, however, had fundamentally changed.

After Welles departed, Halifax cabled Lothian his impression that Welles would propose to Roosevelt an "outline for peace" that would afford the Allies security without requiring the elimination of Hitler's regime. The general outline of his plan—"if such it can be called"—ran as follows:

1. Germany would withdraw its troops from Poland and Bohemia within areas to be negotiated;
2. Hitler's assurances and signature being "valueless," plans should be prepared for the rapid, progressive disarmament of all belligerents and the destruction of offensive ground and air weapons and the factories which produced them. Simultaneously, an international air force should be created;
3. The belligerent armies would remain mobilized and the British blockade continue up to an agreed cut-off date;
4. The United States would "associate" itself with international inspection of disarmament and with European economic reconstruction.[67]

When pressed for details of his disarmament ideas, however, Welles had replied "disconcertingly" that this was essentially a European problem in which the United States had "no part to play."[68] By implying that this country would limit itself to helping supervise disarmament and participating in economic reconstruction, Welles seemed to believe that disarmament could precede security—without a guarantee of U.S. military support.[69] He had appeared disappointed on receiving the impression, from all his interlocutors, that his ideas on disarmament were "impractical."[70] His formula for peace had fallen on deaf ears.

Welles returned to Rome on March 16. While he had been meeting with other leaders, Hitler had sent Ribbentrop to hold Mussolini in line and had assured the Duce that Welles's visit to Berlin had contributed "nothing new." His real purpose had been to "paralyze" German plans for an offensive, but Germany's war plans were based on military considerations and would not be affected "in any way."[71] Ciano told Welles that Ribbentrop had intimated an all-out German offensive in the near future and had made clear that Hitler was not considering any peace short of a military victory. After that, he would decide peace terms by "diktat." Ciano confided, too, that Mussolini would meet Hitler at the Brenner Pass in two days and offered a confidential report if Welles postponed his departure, which was scheduled for March 18. Welles agreed.

In a meeting with Pope Pius XII in the interim, Welles assured the Pontiff that no one in the Allied capitals expressed the desire to "destroy" Germany, as Hitler claimed, but he saw little hope of a durable peace until certain categories of offensive weapons had been abolished. The Pontiff, having just seen Ribbentrop, agreed. Roosevelt's immediate task was to try to keep Italy neutral, he said. When the time came for a peace move, cooperation between the United States, the Vatican and Italy would be important.[72]

Mussolini received Welles again soon after and confirmed his coming meeting with Hitler. If he was to persuade Hitler to postpone his offensive, he began, would have to offer some hope that Germany's demands would be met. Would Welles authorize him to reveal to Hitler his ideas of a possible negotiated solution to Europe's problems? A "just" peace (e. g. , settlement of German and Italian claims) would be vital.

Aware of the danger of negotiating peace terms with the Axis, Welles telephoned Roosevelt that night, recommending that Mussolini's proposal be rejected. Roosevelt concurred. The Italians were apparently tapping the line, for Ciano noted in his diary soon thereafter that Welles and FDR had discussed a "vague peace initiative." From the tone of their conversation, it appeared that FDR did not wish to "commit himself" beyond a certain point and certainly not before assessing the results of Welles's trip.[73]

On Welles's last day, Ciano invited him to lunch at the fashionable Rome Country Club and provided a warped, truncated version of the Brenner Pass meeting. Captured Axis documents have since revealed that Mussolini pleaded for time to prepare but agreed to enter the war after Hitler lectured him about military planning. Britain's "negative" attitude toward the Welles mission, said Hitler, proved that the Allies were determined to "crush" the Reich.[74] Ciano said nothing of this to Welles but hinted that Hitler might be receptive to a negotiated peace in the not-too distant future. Roosevelt could then seize the initiative and use Italy as a "point of support." Bidding Welles farewell, he reiterated his admiration for FDR and pledged again that Italy would stay out of the war so long as he remained Foreign Minister.[75] Within ninety days, his word would prove worthless.

Sumner-the-Silent still kept reporters at arm's length, and, predictably, they fell to speculating. On the eve of his departure, the veteran *New York Times* Rome correspondent, Herbert L. Matthews, duped by Vatican underlings, reported that Welles and Ribbentrop had, separately, discussed with the Pope an eleven-point "peace" proposal of Hitler's. The grossly inaccurate story drew world attention. Hull demanded an immediate denial, and Welles, furious over Matthews's gullibility, promptly issued it. Roosevelt himself underscored his fear of congressional and isolationist reaction by repeating the denial at a White House press conference, on March 29, the day after Welles's return.

The prospect of a stable, lasting peace appeared "scant," the President told reporters, although Welles's "contacts and conversations had clarified" the situation and, in certain instances, would help achieve "more friendly" relations. Exactly with whom, FDR left vague. Some thought he meant Italy; the German chargé d'affaires cabled Berlin that he was referring to the Reich. In any event, FDR insisted, discretion was imperative, as Welles might have to return for further information from the "same sources."[76]

Welles's report left little doubt that luring Mussolini from Hitler's embrace had been a prime goal of his mission. Italy would move, however, "as Mussolini, alone, decides," he warned the President. The Duce, a man of "genius," remained "at heart and instinct, a peasant who admired force and power." If Germany obtained some rapid victories, such as the occupation of Holland and Belgium, "I fear very much that Mussolini would . . . force Italy in on the German side." Ciano, the Pope and Cardinal Luigi Maglione, Papal Secretary of State, had all urged that Roosevelt use his influence on Mussolini to keep Italy out of the war.

The President could not exert his influence effectively, however, unless relations between the United States and Italy became "closer and more friendly." A confidential, friendly contact between FDR and Mussolini would do much to prevent Italy's entry of into the war and might prove of "exceptional value" should a negotiated peace in Europe prove practicable.[77] Welles, unquestionably, saw himself in the role.

Virtually overnight, Welles had become an international celebrity. Offers for his story poured in from newspaper syndicates and magazines—one for $50,000, a sizable sum in 1940—but he declined them all and made copies of his report only for the President, for Hull and for himself. Hull praised his "superb" report in his memoirs. "No one could have gleaned more information," he wrote, "although nothing he learned gave us any basis for action."[78]

Robert Sherwood observed that Welles had come back with "discouraging reports about everything but the temper of the British," but had also brought back "much useful information on the personalities he had met and Roosevelt knew how to use such information. It was always of tremendous importance to him to be able to size up the characters of the leaders of both enemy, and friendly, states."[79]

Welles apparently discussed his impressions privately with Drew Pearson later. The columnist's notes indicate that Welles, like others in the State Department, had set out believing that the Allies could not win and that the outcome would be a "stalemate." His visit to Berlin had changed that impression. The Nazi leaders had discussed their military strength in the frankest detail. Although Welles thought the French army good, German mobility and airpower were "tremendous." Hitler was stronger than at any time since his seizure of power in 1933. There was no unrest in Germany and, given his string of victories, the German people regarded him as a savior.

If an upset or government "turnover" occurred in Germany, Italy would be the key to peace. Mussolini admired German military genius, believed Hitler was winning and probably would join him if he launched a blitzkrieg in Europe. Welles therefore had put "everything he had" into establishing friendship with Mussolini and had recommended to Roosevelt continuing efforts to improve U.S.-Italian ties.[80]

Years later Welles would acknowledge that his mission had been a "forlorn hope."[81] Neither Congress nor American public opinion had authorized Roosevelt to exercise "real influence" in Europe. No treaty obliged the United States in 1940 to join in sanctions against Hitler, and Congress, through its neutrality laws, had barred even nations attacked by Hitler from obtaining arms in this country. The "maximum" that could be hoped for was to keep Italy out of the war.

Welles's somber report left Roosevelt two alternatives: He could accept Hitler's domination of Europe or confront Congress and the isolationists, speed aid to the Allies and accelerate national rearmament. Hitler's lightning attack on Norway and Denmark two weeks later made his choice inescapable.

TWENTY-TWO

HULL'S PROBLEM WITH WELLES

1940–1941

"He Thinks So Fast, Moves So Rapidly, He Gets Way Out in Front"

THE BRITISH HAD SECRETLY BEGUN MINING NORWEGIAN WATERS on April 9, hoping to sink or capture German ships carrying high-grade Swedish ore down the coast to Nazi war plants. Ill-prepared and overconfident, they failed to foresee Hitler's reaction. Within twenty-four hours, German forces occupied Denmark and, after crossing waters wider and rougher than the English Channel, landed in Norway. The British and French rushed in scattered units, but lack of air and naval support forced their early evacuation. "The British stupidly brought the whole thing on," Breckinridge Long wrote in his diary. "The British navy must have been asleep."[1]

Meanwhile, reports of an imminent German offensive on the Western Front were mounting. Bullitt telephoned Roosevelt from Paris virtually daily, indifferent to the risk of interception. When the Germans later published extracts of his conversations, Long thought them "more truth than fiction." Hull observed that files in German hands about Bullitt might prove "still more disconcerting."

Bullitt, he said, was drinking and his conduct, diplomatic and otherwise, had been "unorthodox."

For a time Bullitt's erratic behavior eased Hull's chronic suspicion of Welles, of whom he was "very fond" and whose ability he appreciated, he told Long during Welles's mission to Europe a month earlier.[2] Hull's problem with Welles, wrote Long, was that Welles "thinks so fast and moves so rapidly that he gets way out in front and leaves no trace of positions taken or commitments made." Occasionally, the department was left in the dark as to his meaning and actions, and men who owed key positions to him acted as if they were part of "his" organization, as distinct from Hull's.[3]

Roosevelt's mercurial sense of humor often played over Welles's desk like a ray of sun breaking through clouds. "Here is a real job for you, and you alone," he wrote Welles tongue-in-cheek in April. "How in the blankety-blank do I answer Lady Oxford?" Margot, Countess of Oxford and Asquith, a celebrated but waspish political personality, was the widow of former Prime Minister Herbert Asquith and the mother of the beautiful Princess Elizabeth Bibesco whom FDR and Welles had both known when she was married to a Romanian diplomat in Washington in the 1920s. Lady Oxford had written FDR praising Welles's recent visit to London and suggesting that he appoint Welles ambassador to the Court of St. James in place of the unpopular Joseph P. Kennedy.

"It's because she evidently loves you (just as much as she does me!) that I wish you would try your hand," wrote FDR. "I knew Elizabeth Bibesco, of course, but I only saw Mommer [*sic*] once in New York when she came and spent an hour while I was recuperating from infantile paralysis." To answer her, Welles wrote back, would be a "very puzzling" task. He, too, knew Princess Bibesco well but, like FDR, he had met Lady Oxford only once. "Perhaps unlike you," he added uncharitably, "I found her one of the greatest pests I have encountered." Welles thought her letter "amazingly impertinent" and was sending the President a draft reply that ignored her criticism of Kennedy. "As you know," he warned FDR," she will carry your reply around with her and show it to everyone . . . in London."[4]

A year later, on receiving a rambling "Dearest Franklin" letter from Princess Bibesco in Romania asking for Washington gossip, FDR again turned to Welles. "How, oh, how does one reply to this?" the President wrote. "You are, Thank God, not a career diplomat, but you may have imbibed enough savoir faire from the P. P. (Profession of Perfection) to prepare a brilliant or a Rabelaisian answer. You probably knew Elizabeth Bibesco about the time of the Civil War as I did! FDR"[5]

Although enlivened periodically by FDR's sallies, Welles's growing workload was draining his reserves. On May 8, 1940, he and Berle left the old

State Department building around midnight and walked a block to the Metropolitan Club. Welles was "furious with desire to sleep, but totally unable to do so," Berle recorded. "We drank four scotches in a row in quick succession." For once, Welles let down his habitual reserve. The third-term issue was on everyone's mind, and he and Berle both agreed that FDR probably would wait until the last minute, then support Hull as his successor.

Welles thought that Norman Davis would become Secretary of State and that "there would be nothing for him." The London embassy would undoubtedly be offered him, but it would be "boring to a degree" and he did not think he could afford it. Kennedy and Bullitt were not speaking; Kennedy admired him but Bullitt "hated" him. Berle ascribed Welles's pessimism later to "great fatigue."[6]

Whatever slender hopes FDR and Welles had retained of detaching Mussolini from Hitler collapsed, on June 10, with Italy's attack on France. Roosevelt's bitterness erupted in a speech that night at the University of Virginia. "The hand that held the dagger has struck it into the back of its neighbor," he declared. Welles had spent the afternoon urging him to omit the dagger simile lest it end any hope of Mussolini's cooperation when peace came. Roosevelt had reluctantly agreed to do so— only to reinsert it in midspeech.[7]

That same day, with the Germans closing in on Paris, the French government fled first to Tours then to Bordeaux, where it expired a week later. Anticipating its flight, Bullitt had cabled on June 6, requesting twelve submachine guns and predicting that, once the government had fled, its place would be taken by a "communist mob." Three days later, on June 9, reminding FDR that "no American ambassador in history ever left Paris," he proposed that Anthony J. D. Biddle, a debonair fellow Philadelphian, be named FDR's "special representative" to the French government. Biddle's role as ambassador to Poland had ended eight months earlier with the German occupation, and he had turned up in Paris at loose ends.

On checking the records, Welles found that a similar procedure had been followed in 1914 when the French government had fled Paris but Myron T. Herrick, the U.S. ambassador, had remained at his post. Welles drafted a cable to Bullitt recommending the same procedure; FDR approved it and Bullitt was informed that final orders would not be cabled until the "contingency foreseen [e.g., the government's flight] has actually arisen."[8] Roosevelt's response makes clear that he previously had authorized Bullitt to remain in Paris but had now changed his mind. "Preferable to alter . . . plans we had previously agreed on," he cabled. "You may inform French government that you are leaving Paris with the other chiefs of mission at my express request."

Bullitt ignored FDR's express request. "It may be that I, as the only representative of the Diplomatic Corps remaining in Paris, will be obliged, in the interest of public safety, to take control of the city pending the arrival of the German army," he replied. Increasingly impatient, FDR reiterated his orders: "Strongly recommend that if all foreign chiefs of mission follow the French government to its temporary capital, you should do likewise." Bullitt, however, had tied himself to the mast; glory beckoned. "I have never run away from anything," he replied defiantly. Two days later, on June 12, the Germans entered the city to find Bullitt in the embassy but no "communist mob."[9]

Bullitt's refusal to accompany the French government, as ordered, was based on the "Quixotic theory that an ambassador did not run away from his post," wrote his political counselor, H. Freeman "Doc" Matthews. At that critical moment, the American embassy had three main tasks: (1) to save the French fleet; (2) to keep alive, in North Africa, if necessary, a free, independent French government backed by its empire, its air force and half a million troops outside metropolitan France; and (3) to keep the remaining French gold out of German hands. "On the first we failed, largely," wrote Mattews. "On the second we failed, completely. On the third we were successful."

Deaf to the pleas of his staff that the French government would need his advice and encouragement, Bullitt was "helpless to do anything after June 10," Matthews wrote. Whether any man could have persuaded the French authorities in Bordeaux to keep up the fight and give their fleet to the British, or send it overseas, Matthews did not know. There was "one man, however, who, with his enjoyment of their confidence and his dynamic personality, might at one or two critical moments have tipped the scales. That man was . . . Bullitt." The last person in the world likely to stiffen the morale of the crumbling French government, Matthews concluded, was the "nice, genial, playboy [Biddle]. . selected for the job."[10]

Long afterward, Hull wrote, that had Bullitt continued representing the United States during the fall of France," it is possible that the [French] government would have taken the fleet, gone to North Africa and continued the fight from there." No less an authority than Charles de Gaulle wrote that Bullitt's "refusal to remain with the French government in its final days left the impression that the United States no longer had much use for France."[11]

Bullitt's eyes were on bigger game. Nine months earlier, during the German conquest of Poland, he had written FDR: "Put me in the cabinet . . . My work here has nearly ended."[12] In February 1940, as Welles was setting out on his European mission, Bullitt had dined in the White House with FDR and his confidential assistant, Missy Lehand, with whom Bullitt had once been romantically linked. During dinner Roosevelt had suffered a slight heart attack[13] but had quickly recovered, and Bullitt had returned to Paris, confident that soon he would be Secretary of the Navy.

Brimming with optimism, he reported that Welles's "eulogies" of Mussolini had undermined French morale, and, to whet FDR's prurient appetite, passed him gossip about Premier Paul Reynaud's mistress, Hélène, comtesse de Portes, who "completely dominates" him. Not only had she "dictated" the latest cabinet changes, but Bullitt's aide, Carmel Offie, was "close to her . . . She summons him for intimate conversations to her 'love nest' almost daily . . . Offie is the power behind the throne."[14]

Bullitt's extraordinary involvement in French domestic politics led later to charges that he had misled the French government about American support. True or not, on June 16 Reynaud—abandoned by Bullitt and importuned by his hysterical mistress and by defeatist ministers—threw up his hands in Bordeaux and resigned. Four days later his successor, the aged Marshal Philippe Pétain, sued Hitler for an armistice. With Bullitt at Reynaud's side, Hull wrote," we should have had a reasonable chance to induce the French cabinet to continue the fight with the fleet and colonies."[15]

Following the French surrender, Roosevelt reshuffled his cabinet, bringing in two prominent Republicans: Henry L. Stimson and Frank Knox, respectively Secretaries of War and Navy. Bullitt's dream of a cabinet post had collapsed. Making his way belatedly through the German lines with his aide Offie, he paused at Vichy, where Pétain had installed his collaborationist regime. At nearby La Bourboule, he was handed a "Dear Bill" cable from FDR, ordering him to remain at his post in France. Tearing up the message, he ordered the operator to say that he—Bullitt—had never seen it and started home. At Lisbon, he telephoned Roosevelt and, when asked "What are you doing in Lisbon?" claimed he had never received FDR's order.[16]

Arriving at La Guardia airport on Saturday, July 20, Bullitt held an impromptu press conference before reporting to the President of Secretary of State, which violated diplomatic procedure, and proposed U.S. recognition of the Vichy government. On Sunday night, he dined with FDR at the White House and on Monday accompanied him on the presidential train to Hyder Park, where again he lauded Vichy to reporters.

The next day, however, Roosevelt seemed studiedly noncommittal when asked at a press conference if Bullitt might soon return to France. The ambassador, replied the President, had "earned a vacation."[18] Roosevelt was dissembling. He would not forgive Bullitt's loose tongue, but, meanwhile, he wanted no open quarrel with his combative friend before the autumn election, when he himself was secretly planning an unprecedented third-term bid. Even Harold Ickes, Bullitt's close friend, acknowledged that Bullitt had been "out of order in making an announcement of foreign policy which should, properly, have come, either from the State Department or from the President . . . But then," added Ickes," Bill has always been an 'insurrecto' so far as the State Department is concerned. The two hate each other very cordially."[19]

FDR's third-term campaign brought winging home a gaggle of ambassadors, all determined to repair their nerves—and political fences—at the Democratic convention in mid-July. When FDR commented very critically on this "collective fatigue,"[20] Welles warned that Kennedy, still in London, was convinced of a Nazi victory, threatening to resign and, unless carefully handled, might join the GOP candidate, Wendell Willkie, and preach isolationism. As if to confirm his disgruntlement, Kennedy telephoned Welles on July 12, violently protesting the impending visit of FDR's new spymaster, Colonel William J. "Wild Bill" Donovan, who, he insisted, would be unable to gather any information except through the U.S. military and naval attachés and whose visit would result in "confusion and misunderstanding."[21] Before Kennedy flew home in October, Roosevelt had Welles draft a cable warning him how to behave on his arrival:

> A great deal of unnecessary confusion and undesirable complications have been caused in the last few months by statements which have been made to the press by some of our chiefs of mission who have been coming back to this country. I am, consequently, asking you, specifically, not to make any statements to the press on your way over, nor when you arrive in New York, until you and I have had a chance to agree upon what should be said. Please come straight through to Washington on your arrival since I will want to talk with you as soon as you get here.[22]

Discontent was rife throughout the administration. Wallace found Hull in a "black mood," complaining that the President had treated him "abominably" by dealing directly with Bullitt over his head. He would round out six more months, then resign. "He feels he has been kicked around about all he can stand," Wallace recorded.[23] Ickes lunched with Drew Pearson and wrote that the "disorganized" State Department was the President's direct fault. Hull had told him on taking office that he would have "nothing to do with personnel . . . Welles is ambitious," growled Ickes, "and Berle . . . even more so. Both are arrogant."[24]

Had Welles known of a private talk between FDR and Attorney General Robert H. Jackson on the eve of the Democratic convention, he would have been deeply depressed. Lunching alone with Jackson in the Oval office, FDR confided his decision to run again, then proposed and eliminated a dozen possible running mates. The man he really wanted, if he would accept, wrote Jackson, was Hull. FDR and Jackson agreed that Hull, then sixty-nine, was "along in years and not too strong a campaigner," but Roosevelt thought that Hull looked like a "statesman: his picture was very effective."

If Hull accepted, said FDR, he would ask Jackson to take over the State Department. Dismissing the latter's protest that he had no preparation, FDR cited the "extremely competent" men in the department, among them Welles. He knew that

Jackson and Welles were friends. Welles would be a tower of strength to him, but, for "political" reasons, he did not think it advisable to make Welles Secretary of State. What these reasons were, FDR did not volunteer—nor, apparently, did Jackson ask.[25]

On the eve of the convention, Long heard that Hull might not seek the nomination for fear of "severe attacks" on his wife, the former Frances Witz, who was Jewish. Long urged him to run with FDR if the vice presidency were offered him at the convention by acclamation, but the old Tennessee mountaineer grumbled that his field was foreign affairs. As Vice President, he would be "in a pocket with no function." He was sailing shortly for the Havana conference and would tell Roosevelt so before leaving. After a two-and-a-half-hour talk with FDR in the Oval Office, Hull sailed away, abandoning the vice presidency to Henry Wallace by default.[26]

A week later the Roosevelt-Wallace ticket swept to easy victory at Chicago, thanks largely to Mayor Ed "Boss" Kelly, an experienced politico who left little to chance. What opposition arose was quickly stifled by thunderous cries of "WE WANT ROOSEVELT" from a Kelly henchman hidden in the basement with a microphone and bullhorn and later immortalized in political annals as the "Voice from the Sewer."

Welles spent six days at Chicago, finding the marching bands, flag-waving delegates and general pandemonium a welcome relief from the drear discipline of foreign affairs. As always at a convention, the patrician diplomat became a shirt-sleeved powerbroker, almost—but never fully—one of "the boys." Reporter John O'Donnell, recalling the scene years later, wrote that the "distinguished, frigid and aristocratic Sumner Welles leaped for the banner of the Free State of Maryland, captured the emblem and gaily pranced down the convention aisles with more gusto than he had shown since the morning, forty years ago, when he was page boy at the marriage which united the cousins, Franklin and Eleanor Roosevelt, in the bonds of matrimony."[27]

With Hull at the Havana conference, Welles's workload doubled. He was not only running the department but defending its interests in cabinet meetings. Attorney General Jackson left a vivid account of a typical FDR cabinet session. The President, he wrote:

> Would be wheeled in, take his place at head of the table, *Washington Star* on his lap, [John] Berryman cartoon always very popular . . . quips about some member of cabinet in a cartoon. He'd then call on Hull [whose] reply was almost invariably: "Well, there isn't much in our Department that you haven't already read in the newspapers."
>
> Hull was a very silent member of the cabinet . . . If Welles were representing the State Department, as frequently he was, he usually gave a quick

and very intelligent resume of the week's developments and trends. He was a much more informative person, and a much more informed person to all appearances although it was never possible to tell how much Hull might know because he was so reserved.[28]

Welles and Morgenthau clashed violently at a cabinet meeting on July 25. The Treasury Secretary, backed by Stimson, Knox and Ickes, insisted that the United States would inevitably be drawn into the war sooner or later and wanted a total, not partial, embargo on oil and scrap metal exports to Japan. Oil was the enemy's Achilles' heel, and to cripple the Japanese and German war machines, they urged not only a total embargo on exports to Japan but destruction of oil installations in the Dutch East Indies and intensified British bombing of petroleum targets in Europe. Britain's oil needs, they asserted, could be met from Western Hemisphere—Venezuelan and Colombian—production.[29]

Suspecting that Welles would oppose a total embargo as dangerously provocative, before the meeting Morgenthau had gone behind Welles's back and had persuaded FDR to approve it. Welles objected "very strenuously" on learning of Morgenthau's maneuver, Ickes wrote later, and Roosevelt himself was "impatient" at discovering that a measure of such importance had been presented to him without clearing other interested departments. Stimson described a "frantic" meeting with FDR "throwing his hands in the air" and telling Welles and Morgenthau to "go into a corner and settle it."[30]

Welles, however, stood firm, knowing that Marshall and Stark were behind him. In sharp disagreement with their civilian superiors, the two military chiefs had warned Stimson and Knox that a total embargo might provoke Japan into a sudden attack on the Dutch East Indies and, possibly, on British Malaysia. It was a moment of "supreme danger," Welles wrote in retrospect.

Hitler had just subjugated France, the fate of England hung in the balance and to have risked goading an "already berserk" Japanese army into an attack in 1940 might have been the spark setting off the powder keg—possibly involving the United States in a war for which it was not ready.[31] On Welles's "most earnest" appeal, Roosevelt reversed himself, authorizing only a partial embargo on oil and scrap. Welles had won against formidable odds.

Later Morgenthau complained to his staff about the "beautiful Chamberlain talk" Welles had given in cabinet. "Everything was going to be lovely, Japan was going to come over and kiss our big toe."[32] Ickes growled that he would have thought more of Welles "had he put a little feeling into a discussion—especially when he had strong feelings." Even in a fight, grumbled the cabinet's self-styled curmudgeon, Welles remained "glacierly top-lofty."[33] Yet vital time had been won, and sixteen months later, when the Japanese attacked Pearl Harbor, U.S. naval power in the Pacific had increased dramatically.

Each day brought new problems. In May, as Hitler's armies overran France and Britain stood in imminent danger of invasion, the British urgently requested forty-eight overage U.S. destroyers and as many torpedo boats as the U.S. Navy could spare. Noting the threat of German parachute attacks, London also had asked for half a million rifles and ammunition. The rifles and ammunition were rushed to them and negotiations for the destroyers began. In June, to ease congressional fears, Churchill had pledged publicly, at FDR's suggestion, that if British waters became untenable, the British fleet would not be surrendered or scuttled but would sail to Canada or to other empire ports.

On August 8, Welles sent Roosevelt a letter and two memoranda from Lord Lothian, the British ambassador, formally offering to lease eight bases in British territories—Newfoundland, Bermuda, the Bahamas, Jamaica, St. Lucia, Trinidad, and British Guiana—to the United States for ninety-nine years in return for ninety-six destroyers (twice the number originally requested), torpedo boats, fifty long-range naval patrol bombers (PBYs), a few Vought-Sikorski dive bombers and ammunition.[34] FDR cut the destroyers to fifty, eliminated most of the aircraft and approved the rest. Hull returned from the Havana conference at this point and left, almost immediately, on vacation. Four days later, on August 12, Welles drafted the agreements and cleared them with Knox, Morgenthau and Stimson, and Attorney General Jackson certified their legality. FDR announced the agreement, stressing that the British bases would "greatly strengthen Hemisphere defense."

Before the agreements actually had been signed, however, Hull returned and Welles left for his own vacation. Therefore, Welles did not handle the final, closing exchange. With Hull in charge, wrote Jackson, a "serious blunder" ensued. The requisite notification to Congress failed to specify the matériel promised Britain over and above the fifty destroyers, and Churchill was indignant. "What about the torpedo boats and ammunition?" he cabled angrily. "We consider this was promised us and we want it!"

At the next cabinet meeting, Stimson suggested a "forthright explanation," but for obvious reasons neither Hull nor FDR were "much in favor," wrote Jackson. It was decided to handle the oversight "quietly."[35]

In addition to his other duties, Welles began exhaustive negotiations in the summer of 1940 to improve U.S. -Soviet relations. He had returned from his European mission in March disturbed not only by Hitler's military power but equally by Stalin's cynical policies. The Soviet dictator's pact with Hitler in August 1939, his attack on Finland that November, his seizure of east Poland and absorption of the Baltic states had outraged American opinion, leading to a "moral embargo." U.S. -Soviet trade had been cut to a trickle, and Washington and Moscow were barely speaking.[36]

Welles suspected that the Stalin-Hitler alliance was based solely on expediency and likely to be short-lived. Diplomacy might still pry Stalin from the Axis, cutting Soviet aid, particularly in oil, and reducing Germany's war potential.

With the approval of FDR and Hull, he began exploratory talks with the rough-tongued Soviet ambassador, Konstantin Oumansky, whom Hull had once labeled a "walking insult."[37] Oumansky fully lived up to his billing. Convinced, like most Soviet envoys, that invective produced results, he led off with a catalogue of complaints that taxed Welles's patience to the breaking point.

While rejecting Oumansky's demand for U.S. recognition of Soviet sovereignty over the Baltic states, Welles agreed to speed the export of American supplies for which the Soviets had already paid. Over their twenty-seven subsequent meetings, Welles kept control of his temper, and, gradually, as Oumansky sensed the futility of abuse, a thaw set in. The lessons Welles learned in breaking bottlenecks and accelerating aid shipments proved valuable following the German attack on the Soviet Union on June 22, 1941.

It was Welles, in fact, who warned Oumansky of the coming attack in March 1941, four months before it occurred. "[He] turned very white," Welles wrote later. "He was silent for a moment and then merely said: 'I fully realize the gravity of the message you have given me. My government will be grateful for your confidence and I will inform it, immediately, of our conversation.'"[38]

The story is dramatic. Reports of Soviet-German tension had begun reaching the State Department in late 1940. Early in 1941, they were confirmed by the U.S. commercial attaché in Berlin, Sam E. Woods, who had obtained a copy of Hitler's war plan under spy-thriller circumstances. A German general staff officer, appalled at the prospect of a two-front war, had passed it through intermediaries to an anti-Nazi Catholic economics professor who knew Woods socially. Arranging to sit beside him in a darkened Berlin theater, the professor had slipped Woods the plan. The document, rushed to Washington, was authenticated by ex-Chancellor Heinrich Bruening, then in the United States in exile. According to Breckinridge Long, it was "probably the most important document to have arrived in the Department since the war's start."[39]

Years later Ladislas Farago, a writer of popular spy-fiction, would claim that Welles had shown Oumansky an intercepted cable from the Japanese embassy in Berlin to Tokyo predicting the attack.[40] Had a seasoned diplomat like Welles committed so monumental a security breach, it would have revealed to Moscow—then Hitler's ally—that the United States had broken Japan's purple (diplomatic) code, the prime source of U.S. intelligence. The charge, in fact, was false and was refuted in 1981 by Ruth B. Harris, a recognized authority, in an article in the *Pacific Historical Review*.[41] Hull himself wrote in his memoirs that he had authorized Welles to pass Oumansky the "contents of the [Woods] report."[42]

Welles had long been fearful that U.S. codes were insecure and had warned Roosevelt on April 21, 1941: "I have held the view for a long time, as I know you have, that our codes have been broken." He had discussed the situation that morning with Marshall and Stark, and all three believed that an urgent review was imperative.[43] They had reason for concern. A year earlier, in June 1940, Tyler Kent, a young code clerk (and Hull protégé) at the American embassy in London had been arrested. A search of his rooms had revealed a complete history of U.S. diplomatic correspondence since 1938.

"Appalling," wrote Long. "Hundreds of . . . dispatches—cables, messages. Some months, every single message going in and out from the London embassy was copied. It means, not only that our codes are cracked a dozen ways, but that our every diplomatic maneuver was exposed to Germany and Russia. [Kent's] girl friend was a Russian."[44] Worse had followed.

Donald R. Heath, an attaché in the U. S embassy in Berlin, wrote Welles in the autumn of 1940 that Hjalmar Schacht, the Nazi financier who had passed Welles secrets during his trip to Berlin, had confided that every coded U.S. telegram was known, sooner or later, to the German government "no matter whether . . . sent from Berlin, Switzerland or Portugal."[45] So concerned was Welles about code security that Joseph Grew, the American ambassador in Tokyo, complained of being kept "out of touch." Welles, in reply, cited his "extreme reluctance" to entrust sensitive material to cables or radio. Soon after, the Japanese Prime Minister, Prince Fumimaro Konoye, warned Grew privately that the United States had only one "unbreakable" code, and Grew conceded that Welles's "excessive caution" had been justified.[46]

On October 26, 1940, an ominous report from Sir Samuel Hoare, British ambassador in Madrid, predicted Hitler's armistice terms for France. From an "absolutely sure" source, cabled Hoare, Hitler would demand from Vichy:

1. The French fleet "at the service of the Axis";
2. Alsace-Lorraine;
3. An international corridor across France from Switzerland to the sea;
4. Naval and air bases in northern France for the duration of hostilities;
5. A tripartite German-Italian-French mandate over all French colonies.

France would also be forced to cede the Department of the Alpes Maritimes, Tunisia and half of Algeria to Italy; French Morocco to Spain; and Indo-China to Japan. Pétain, he reported, had rejected Hitler's terms, but his cabinet was "equally divided."

The danger was stark. Axis control of the French fleet, with its 238 ships, including 11 battleships and 103 submarines, might tip the naval balance in the Atlantic, Long wrote after an emergency Sunday meeting with Hull, Welles and other senior officials on June 16, the day before the French surrender. "If Germany seizes the French fleet, the fate of England would be sealed and the U. S would face the victorious Axis and Japan unarmed, unready and alone."[47]

Roosevelt, a lifelong naval strategist, moved swiftly when Churchill warned that Vichy might soon transfer its two greatest battleships, *Jean Bart* and *Richelieu,* to the Mediterranean for reconditioning or repair. The American chargé d'affaires in Vichy, he replied, had been ordered to inform Pétain that it was of "vital interest" to the United States that the two warships not pass to Axis control. "For your personal information only," FDR added," I am letting the [Vichy] French government know that this government would be prepared to buy these two ships with the assurance that they would not be used during the present war."[48]

Pétain was still resisting Hitler's demands, but appeasers in his cabinet, notably the sinister Pierre Laval, might soon wear him down; it was imperative, therefore, to strengthen U.S. influence at Vichy. FDR had Welles draft a letter to General "Black Jack" Pershing, commander-in-chief of the American Expeditionary Force in World War I and a former colleague of Pétain's, offering him appointment as ambassador to France in place of Bullitt.

"It is in the interest of . . . our country that the French government at Vichy should not enter into any agreement with Germany which would directly or indirectly facilitate the attempt of the Axis powers to defeat Great Britain," FDR wrote Pershing on November 13. "Your personal prestige . . . and close relationship with Marshall Pétain would undoubtedly make it easier for the views of this government to be expressed to him through you in a friendly way but without reserve."[49]

Pershing, an octogenarian then convalescing at Walter Reed Hospital, declined, so FDR asked Welles to bring him other suggestions the next morning. "As I was driving into town," Welles recalled," the name of Admiral William D. Leahy suddenly occurred to me."[50] Leahy previously had served as FDR's naval aide and Chief of Naval Operations and, at the time, was governor of Puerto Rico. Welles arrived at the White House to find Roosevelt in bed, his blue navy cloak around his shoulders, eating his usual hearty breakfast of grapefruit, coffee, cereal and eggs. "Have you any ideas?" he asked. When Welles suggested Leahy, FDR's face "lit up, as it always did when a new idea appealed to him," Welles wrote later. At FDR's direction, he drafted a cable to Leahy:

> There is . . . the possibility that France may actually engage in the war against
> Great Britain and, in particular, that the French fleet may be utilized under the

control of Germany. We need in France at this time an ambassador who can gain the confidence of Marshall Pétain . . . the one powerful element in the French government who is standing firm against selling out to Germany . . . The position which you have held in our own Navy would undoubtedly give you great influence with the higher officers of the French Navy who are now openly hostile to Great Britain."[51]

Seizing the telephone, FDR also called Leahy in Puerto Rico. When the admiral-governor accepted the assignment, Bullitt's days in government were numbered.

TWENTY-THREE

IN THE NATIONAL SPOTLIGHT

1940–1942

"A Field-Marshal in the War of Brains"

ON NOVEMBER 7, the eve of the 1940 election, Bullitt submitted a pro-forma resignation as ambassador to France. "I am ready for any work you want," he wrote FDR confidently. Two days later he received a disarming reply: "(1) Resignation not accepted; (2) We will talk about that and the future later; (3) Hope to see you very soon. FDR."[1]

Unknown to Bullitt, however, his refusal to follow Roosevelt's orders and remain with the French government after its flight from Paris in June, his precipitate rush home for a cabinet post and his public demand for recognition of Vichy had eroded Roosevelt's confidence. Bullitt "talked too much . . . was too quick on the trigger," the President told Ickes.[2] When Ickes repeated the comment, Bullitt conceded that he had been "unfortunately hasty and careless."[3]

Soon after, on learning to his fury that the State Department had requested Vichy's "agrément" for Leahy and that he had, in effect, been shelved, Bullitt turned his brilliant malevolence on Welles, the imagined architect of his downfall. In Walton R. "Judge" Moore, a critically ill friend in the State Department, he found the perfect instrument for revenge.

Reporters, meanwhile, had begun hearing rumors of Welles's alleged proposals to porters on the presidential train in September. Felix Belair, a *Time* magazine correspondent, learned about it within twenty-four hours. Belair knew several of the Pullman employees, including S. C. "Mitch" Mitchell, the porter on the presidential press car. "Mitch was quickly transferred to the White House, obviously to keep him quiet," Belair remembered. "He was a very fine person and rose to be a senior White House usher."[4]

Robert S. Allen, Drew Pearson's columnist partner, heard the story from friends on the *Phildelphia Record* who, in turn, had heard it from Bullitt. Allen did not believe it. Marquis Childs, the syndicated columnist, traveled on Truman's campaign train in 1948, five years later, and fell into conversation with a dignified porter in his forties who had been involved. "He didn't want to discuss it," Childs remembered. "The Southern Railway president sent an emissary with orders to recount the facts. His job was at stake and he complied, but he was sorry he had done so."[5]

The rumors soon reached the Senate. With the election approaching, two anti-FDR isolationists, Burton K. Wheeler, Democrat of Montana, and Hendrik Shipstead, a Farm-Laborite from Minnesota, asked for a private interview with Cissy Patterson, publisher of the anti–New Deal *Washington Times-Herald*. Scenting trouble, she asked her managing editor, Frank Waldrop, to sit in. After hemming and hawing, the senators drove to the point. Would she print the train story if they supplied affidavits? Incredulous, she refused.[6]

Welles himself heard the rumors and turned to his friend, Adolf Berle, the State Department's liaison with the FBI. "I asked him if there was any truth to the story and he said no," Berle remembered years later. "I said I'd have the FBI run a check to see who was spreading it. Looking back, I think I gave him poor advice."[7]

By late November, the story had reached the ears of "Judge" Moore, the State Department Counsellor, who had never forgiven Welles for wresting the Under Secretaryship from him in a bitter struggle three years earlier. Moore, too, was incredulous, but the story had come to him from an old friend and fellow Virginian: Ernest E. Norris, president of the Southern Railway. Norris warned Moore that the danger of scandal was so explosive that Hull, or the President, should be told. Moore agreed; but he was terminally ill and the more he pondered, the more thankless his duty appeared. "Moore was not a forthright man," remembered Ernest Cuneo, a prominent Washington lawyer. "He was a Southern courthouse lawyer, someone gamblers call a 'larry-player,' his cards always close to his chest."[8] After long soul-searching, Moore devised a solution.

On November 25, at his suggestion, Norris and Luther Thomas brought the incriminating affidavits to Bullitt's apartment at the Anchorage Building, and Bullitt and his henchman, Carmel Offie, took copious notes. Two months later, after relating the story to Hull, Moore died, still pursuing Welles from the grave. A quarter century later, after Bullitt's death in 1967, his daughter, Anne, found hidden under the floorboards of his home in Ashfield, Massachussetts, a metal box containing an envelope with the original affidavits. On the envelope Moore had written instructions that the contents be turned over after his death to Bullitt "for his use."[9]

On January 3, 1941, with Roosevelt safely reelected, his military assistant, General Edwin M. "Pa" Watson, summoned FBI director J. Edgar Hoover, Dale Whiteside of the Secret Service and Rudolph Forster, a veteran White House functionary, to his office. Whiteside related details of the train incident and Forster observed—inaccurately—that Welles had been "barred" from the White House during Theodore Roosevelt's administration, 1901 to 1909. (Welles, at the time, had been a student at Groton.) Watson directed Hoover to conduct a discreet investigation for the President, and Hoover assigned the task to Edwin A. Tamm, the FBI liaison with the State Department.[10] Three weeks later Tamm's report was on FDR's desk.

Welles apparently had made the alleged advances and had been involved in a similar incident two weeks later, while traveling by Pennsylvania railroad to a speaking engagement in Cleveland.[11] A Filipino attendant had been approached. On both occasions Welles had been drunk; but the story was spreading and Senator Wheeler had already heard it from a reporter who had heard it, in turn, from Bullitt. Bullitt had told him that he did not dare take it directly to the President for fear of "getting his legs cut off." He was, however, urging Moore to do so and was also taking steps to see that Colonel Edmund W. Starling, the veteran Secret Service chief, was informed. According to Hoover and Tamm, Wheeler had been "indignant" over Bullitt's behavior and had urged the reporter to warn Welles.

In fact, they reported, another reporter had. Welles had heard him out impassively, had thanked him and had intimated that he might ask the Secret Service to investigate. Instead, he had gone to his friend, Attorney General Jackson, acknowledging that he had been drinking heavily on the train. He remembered suffering a heart attack, taking barbiturates and ringing for coffee, which eased the angina pain. Beyond that, Welles told Jackson, he remembered nothing. Roosevelt asked for Hoover's recommendations.

There seemed no doubt, said Hoover, that Welles had made improper advances. However, the only porter to whom a "specific" proposal had been made—namely Stone—had died two weeks before the FBI investigation began. There was no affidavit, therefore, from anyone "directly" propositioned, although other porters had mentioned "indirect" approaches. Welles had been drunk, Hoover concluded: more a "mental" condition than anything else. Roosevelt agreed: Welles, he thought, had behaved without really knowing "what he was doing." The President, however, faced a dilemma. While no specific "act" had occurred, under Virginia law an indecent proposal made even while drunk was punishable by fines, imprisonment or both, and the alleged proposals had been made in Virginia. FDR reflected.

Welles's resignation or sudden transfer would arouse world speculation, and there was little time to train a successor. Hull was seventy, mentally fatigued and often ill. Welles was forty-eight, a prodigious worker who sensed FDR's wishes intuitively and executed them promptly. At the time—a year before Pearl Harbor—the nation was still torn between interventionists and isolationists. Hitler was master of Europe. Britain's back was to the wall, and a Nazi invasion was possible at any moment. France's surrender, moreover, had left the fate of the French fleet in the scales, and its seizure by the Axis might alter the naval balance in the Atlantic, directly threatening the Western Hemisphere.

Then came the personal factor. The Roosevelt and Welles families had long been close. Eleanor Roosevelt had known Sumner since childhood. He had been a page at their wedding, and FDR himself had helped launch Welles's diplomatic career, following it closely and coming to know Welles's strengths and his weaknesses better than most. No prude himself, FDR viewed sexual frailty on a par with financial or political frailty—especially when alcohol was involved. "I have heard it said by many close friends of the President," Spruille Braden recalled years later, "that Roosevelt would forgive anything if the man were able to prove that he was drunk at the time. He had kindness in his heart for a man who had sinned under the influence of alcohol. He felt he wasn't responsible and shouldn't be held responsible for that—a curious quirk."[12]

Hoover's report throws light on FDR's mental process. If the President did not wish to "tell Welles himself," Hoover suggested, he might have someone travel with him in future to prevent a recurrence. It should, however, be someone mature: not a "young man who might lend credence to the stories circulating." Roosevelt thought this the proper solution. He needed Welles and would keep him. Watson was ordered to have a friend of Welles's (presumably Berle) assign him a bodyguard for future travels, and Hoover told to impose silence on all concerned. The only three copies of the FBI report were to be locked in Watson's safe. His decision made, Roosevelt turned to his other problems.

How much Welles himself knew of what had happened in his alcoholic mist remains a mystery. Almost certainly he "blacked out," remembering nothing later. His ability to snap back after a night of hard drinking was phenomenal. The following morning he would be his brisk, authoritative self, off to the State Department as if nothing had occurred, and no one had seen him in his cups. No hint of remorse or chagrin ever escaped his lips at such times. Moreover, commandingly tall and forbiddingly formal, he was not one to be lightly rebuked by friends, family or even Mathilde, whose complaints about his drinking he dismissed as "slush."

As Hoover's report implies, the President himself was loath to raise an embarrassing personal issue with his Under Secretary; and the two officials whom Welles consulted—Berle and Jackson—were friends anxious to shield the administration from scandal. In short, no one, went to the mat with Welles.

Later some claimed that Welles had been ensnared. In 1944 Charles Marsh, a wealthy Texas newspaper owner, told Vice President Wallace that Hoover had "framed" Welles with the connivance of Carmody.[13] Elliott Roosevelt told the author in 1975 that the President always believed that Bullitt had "set Welles up for public disgrace. Father hated Bullitt and wouldn't see him," said Elliott.[14] In his book *A Rendezvous with Destiny,* Elliott wrote that FDR "believed Welles's version—that it was the porter, bribed on Bullitt's behalf, who had made the overtures."[15]

Meanwhile, the public, unaware of the train incident, saw Welles emerging as an "associate" Secretary of State, a man to whom the President turned increasingly for fresh ideas and quick action. Not only metropolitan dailies but small rural newspapers were noting his spectacular rise. It was Welles who had been involved in the destroyers-for-bases deal, wrote the *Greensboro* (N.C.) *News;* Welles whom FDR had consulted on the Canadian defense agreement; Welles who had been named U.S. representative on the Inter-American committee to administer the hemisphere's European colonies. By contrast, Hull had been "left out" of major international developments in recent weeks. "The shadow and influence of Under Secretary Welles are projected into the future," wrote the News.[16]

Francis Biddle, the new Attorney General,[17] noted in his diary that Hull "tired easily" and Welles then would "run things." Cabinet officers, who normally dealt only with their peers, did not "disturb" Hull but telephoned Welles directly. Foreign diplomats made a perfunctory call on Hull then spent two hours with Welles, who usually spoke their language. In every way, wrote Biddle, Welles was "Hull's opposite: under fifty, robust, a tireless worker, intelligent rather than imaginative, instinctively liberal in a Department where this quality was not often apparent."[18]

Eleanor Roosevelt, when frustrated by bureaucratic red tape, turned to her childhood friend Sumner. "You are one of the grandest people in government," she wrote him jointly with her secretary, Malvina C. Thompson, early in 1941. "You can be reached on the telephone without delay, you give an answer when you are reached and our many questions are settled quickly! With appreciation and, on my part, affection, Eleanor."[19]

Assistant Secretary Breckenridge Long, comparing his two chiefs, Hull and Welles, wrote that Welles was "daring, thorough, quick-witted, clear-headed if, occasionally, a little on the too-daring side in trying to do whatever the President wanted, even when not thoroughly considered." Hull, by contrast, was "wary, slow to conclusion, less clear in preliminary thought and critical of any proposal for which he assumed responsibility—even the President's.[20]

Welles was the department's "operating chief," wrote Bernard Gladieux of the Budget Bureau. Hull had "no interest in, and took little part in, running the State Department."[21] Even Hull's protégé, James C. Dunn, conceded that the President "very obviously" sought Welles's advice in preference to Hull's.[22] "I don't see the President very often," Hull told former Postmaster General James A. Farley. "Most of the details are handled through Welles."[23]

Inevitably, the department began splitting into rival cliques. The more Hull pondered, or challenged, the President's wishes, the more FDR turned to Welles to carry them out promptly. "Judge" Moore's death, in February 1941, added to Hull's isolation. A friend and congressional colleague for many years, Moore had made no secret of his detestation of Welles, affording Hull a confidant to whom he could pour out his own bitterness. Lonely, brooding and infuriated by a Drew Pearson column of December 20, 1940, alleging that Hull had urged a $100 million loan to the Spanish dictator Francisco Franco and that Welles had blocked it by going over his head to FDR, the Secretary called Welles in and "castigated him as he had never been spoken to in his life," Welles told Pearson reproachfully.

The story was "completely untrue," and Welles wanted Pearson to publish the "true facts" in his column. Neither the department nor any high official had approved or recommended a $100 million credit to the Spanish government. There had not been the "slightest divergency" about it between Hull and himself, and he had "never communicated with the President . . . with regard to any aspect of this government's policy toward Spain."[24]

Four days later, Pearson wrote him:

> Dear Sumner: I deeply regret the repercussions. Certain gentlemen in the State Department seem to be anxious to use anything they possibly can against you. It would probably be best if you were not to talk to me regarding anything about foreign policy in the future. You and I know you have never revealed any of these things, such as the story regarding the Spanish credit, but, unfortunately, our friendship has been misconstrued.[25]

To placate Hull, Welles called a press conference and repeated his denial. It would have been humanly impossible, he declared, for two people to agree over eight years more "consistently and thoroughly" than Hull and himself. There had never been the slightest "important" difference of opinion between them. Moreover, it would also have been impossible for a man in Welles's position, knowing Hull's "extraordinary moral courage, consistency and almost unique intellectual integrity," to have anything except "deep devotion" for him.[26]

The effort failed. Pearson's Spanish loan story had exacerbated Hull's suspicion of Welles's loyalty, and Welles would pay dearly for it later.

In 1941, Welles was entering his eighth year in office, his fourth as Under Secretary, and the strain on him was mounting. Each morning, after little or no sleep, he returned to the State Department for another ten-hour day of conferences, cables and crises, driving himself unsparingly and depleting his diminishing reserves. With the onset of war, the State Department had burgeoned to 5,700 career employees deployed between Washington and 20 embassies, 33 legations, 49 consulates-general, 172 consulates, 13 vice-consulates and 24 consular agencies overseas.[27]

Breckenridge Long, who supervised twenty-three of the department's forty-two divisions, wrote that Welles was carrying a "very large responsibility: practically all conversations with ambassadors and ministers, secret liaison with the Army and Navy, contacts with the White House."[28] American diplomats streaming home from Europe through Lisbon heard that Welles was the man to see in Washington to "get anything done."[29]

Mathilde's journal that summer noted "trying, nerve-wracking days . . . Many nights my husband was called to the telephone by the President or State Department and would dress hurriedly and dash into town, sometimes well after 2 A.M."[30] Alone all day at Oxon Hill, a half-hour's drive from the capital, she whiled away the hours in telephone gossip, writing letters, ordering meals, inviting an occasional woman friend to lunch or strolling the grounds with her dogs, cane in hand.

Except for the occasional tidbits Welles tossed her at dinner, she was uninterested in public affairs and unable to provide him mental stimulus. Moreover, deaf to her doctor's insistence on a bland diet and addicted to rich food, she was frequently ill and, by day's end, would be fretfully scanning the evening headlines while awaiting the sound of his car wheels over the gravel drive. Night after night Welles returned bone-weary to endure her complaints in silence.

Alcohol was served sparingly at Oxon Hill on her orders, and, for months, Welles would drink nothing stronger than home-brewed beer. Then, as cumulative fatigue mounted, the cycle resumed. First he would ask for a spritzer (white wine and soda water), days later for a Scotch and soda and then Reeks would sense trouble ahead. Alcohol became Welles's release: whether a drink or two at the Metropolitan Club on his way home or drinking at Latin American stag dinners all night with convivial companions, usually to excess. An eighteen-page letter in Mathilde's handwriting, headed 2 A.M., undated but almost certainly written that summer, was found in Welles's papers after his death.

A few months ago you gave me your promise and suggested it, yourself, that you would accept no more stag dinners. As all your promises, this is just another failure. It is already past 1:30 A.M. Why do you have to go to stag dinners and Mr. Hull doesn't?

I see you exactly ten minutes each day, at breakfast or passing upstairs to your bath. Your work, your job, your Latin American friends all come before me. I cannot forgive this utter selfishness to one who has never failed you. I am proud of your efforts to "be someone," but this, alone, cannot fill a woman's heart or life. Your word means nothing: when you leave me at night, I know you will be drinking.

I feel so alone, so horribly alone, Sumner. I cannot face any more and would rather be away where I might have to make my own life but, at least, feel peaceful and have my health. You are killing my love for you. I know you cannot stop drinking, and I pity you, but it's no use ranting and scolding. After sixteen years, I know you are weak and have not the courage to stop.

You owe it to me to say frankly, like a man, that you cannot stop and let me go my own very lonely way, alone. I love you, Sumner, but I just can't face life this way. Try to understand.

Then came a frantic postscript. Since writing what he called her "slush," he had come in, drunk.

Oh Sumner, for you in your position, it will get you yet, my dear. I can't help you. It's you I care for, not the Under Secretary of State. God help us, both, but there is no God. Just you and me and this unhappy life and struggle.

Neither could have known that Bullitt, meanwhile, had laid the Southern Railway dossier about Welles on the President's desk on April 23, unaware that FDR had already seen it. It was "Judge" Moore's "dying wish," said Bullitt, that Welles be dismissed as a potential victim of blackmail. If the train story leaked, public confidence in the administration would be shaken. FDR read the first page and glanced at others. "I have had a full report on it," he said. "There is truth in the allegations." He thought, however, no newspaper would publish such scandalous material.

Bullitt cited information from a personal friend, Martin Clement, president of the Pennsylvania Railroad, alleging that Welles had been involved in a similar incident the same month while traveling by train to Cleveland. Roosevelt confirmed it but added that Welles would never again be able to repeat the performance. As a public official, he would be accompanied on future trips by a bodyguard. Bullitt's temper now rose.

It was not a matter of future actions but of "past crimes," he insisted. He had discussed the matter with Hull who thought Welles "worse than a murderer." Roosevelt agreed that solicitation was a prosecutable offense but did not think anyone would initiate prosecution. At this, Bullitt let fly, announcing defiantly that he would accept no position in the State Department or in the foreign service so long as Welles remained in office.

Roosevelt rang for General Watson. "Pa, I don't feel well," he said. "Please cancel all appointments for the rest of the day." He was wheeled to his quarters and Bullitt left, dictating a memorandum of the conversation soon after to Offie.[31]

Days later Bullitt told Robert D. Murphy, his former deputy in Paris, that he would "force" Roosevelt's hand by taking the story to Senator Styles H. Bridges, a rabidly anti-FDR New Hampshire Republican. Murphy begged him to desist but he turned a deaf ear. "He was never again given anything of substance to do," Murphy remembered. When Hull asked Roosevelt later for a diplomatic post for Bullitt, the President leaned back, cocked his cigarette holder and contemplated the ceiling. "That's right, Cordell," he finally replied. "What about Liberia? I hear that's available."[32]

Rather than diminishing Welles in Roosevelt's eyes, Bullitt's vendetta seemed to enhance his stature, stiffening the President's native obstinacy. Inured to throat-cutting after a quarter century in politics, FDR remained too much the Grotonian to condone personal viciousness within his entourage. Welles's drunken behavior had been unpardonable; but it was FDR's problem, not Bullitt's. Bullitt's threats, moreover, brought out the steel in FDR. With the war news steadily worsening, Welles seemed all the more irreplaceable.

Britain's gallant but Quixotic effort to stem the German invasion of Greece that spring was failing. German paratroopers were driving British forces from Crete, threatening Britain's control of the eastern Mediterranean. As German bombing of the United Kingdom intensified, Welles wondered whether Britain itself could hold out three more months. Hitler's U-boats were sinking three times as many ships as Britain could build in a year; twice as many as Britain and the United States combined.[33] If the arms trickling from American factories were not to end on the ocean floor, the U.S. Navy would have to escort Allied convoys as far east as Iceland. Roosevelt rushed fleet units from the Pacific to the Atlantic, sent U.S. Marines to replace Britain's 13, 000 troops in Iceland, and told Welles and Harry Hopkins to "work out the details."[34]

Hemisphere defense would be the key to rallying the nation and winning congressional support. Roosevelt had Robert Sherwood and Samuel Rosenman draft an "unlimited" emergency proclamation, replacing the "limited" emergency of 1939. Hull thought it too bold and sent Welles and Berle to tone it down, but, fortunately, wrote Rosenman, they were not so cautious as Hull and won him around.[35] FDR was putting the finishing touches on his proclamation when Hitler, defying him, sent his mightiest battleship, the *Bismark,* and the cruiser *Prinz Eugen* to prowl the Atlantic, leaving FDR to ponder how to react should the deadly pair turn up in the Caribbean near the Panama Canal.

His fears mounted on May 24 when the *Bismark* sank its only British rival, HMS *Hood,* with one salvo—threatening not only Allied convoys but control of the Atlantic itself. Suddenly the wheel of fate spun back. Roosevelt had begun broadcasting his proclamation in the White House when word came that a U.S.-built Catalina, a long-range naval patrol aircraft furnished to the Royal Air Force under Lend-Lease and carrying an American observer, had sighted the *Bismarck* limping home to repair battle damage. Hours later the Royal Navy cornered and sank it off Brest. It had been, as the Duke of Wellington reportedly observed after Waterloo, a "damn'd near-run thing."

Hitler's attack on Soviet Russia on June 21 dramatized the need to rush aid and help Stalin hold out. "I have been doing my utmost to expedite . . . assistance," Welles wrote FDR on July 19, enclosing a draft of orders to Stimson, Knox, Major General James H. Burns, coordinator of Defense Aid Reports, and William S. Knudsen, director of the Office of Production Management. "I have reached the conclusion that the only way in which satisfactory results can be obtained is for these letters to be sent by yourself."[36]

Scribbling "OK" on the orders, FDR told Welles to issue them himself as acting Secretary of State. It was of the "utmost importance," Welles wrote Stimson, Knox, Burns and Knudsen, to "cooperate in every way so that prompt and effective assistance may reach the USSR before winter [makes] ocean and land transportation difficult."[37] Aiding Communist Russia, however, aroused fierce resistance in conservative, especially Catholic, circles. In August two ranking prelates, the Most Reverend Edward Mooney, Archbishop of Detroit, and Right Reverend Monsignor Michael J. Ready, General Secretary of the Administrative Board of the National Catholic Welfare Conference, agreed to back assistance but warned Welles that Roosevelt should make clear that backing Soviet Russia "in no way implied support of communism."[38]

Meanwhile, tension was mounting in the Pacific as well as the Atlantic. In late July, exploiting the French surrender in June, Japan occupied all Indochina, threatening the Philippines and the raw materials vital to the Allies: oil from Dutch East Indies, tin and rubber from Malaysia, the meat and grain from Australia needed to feed Britain. A month earlier Harold Ickes, the testy Interior Secretary (and National Petroleum Coordinator) had threatened to halt all oil shipments to Japan, encroaching on one of the most sensitive issues in American foreign policy.

At FDR's direction, Welles drafted an unusually peremptory order reining Ickes in. "Lest there be any confusion whatever," the President ordered, "please do not issue any directions, as Petroleum Coordinator, forbidding any export from or to the U.S. This can be qualified only if you obtain my approval or that of the Secretary of State." Oil exports to Japan were so much a part of foreign policy that the policy "must not be affected in any shape, manner or form by anyone except the Secretary of State or the President."[39] Ickes, unrepentant, nonetheless continued raising the issue in heated cabinet quarrels with Welles.

Like others in the months before Pearl Harbor, Welles believed that Roosevelt was moving too cautiously: first leading, then following, public opinion as it wrestled with the risks of aiding Britain and the Soviet Union—or even of rearming itself. Welles repeatedly urged him to speak out, insisting that the American people would unite only if the dangers were frankly outlined and the nation's goals made clear. Roosevelt agreed in principle; but, still haunted by the uproar following his 1937 "quarantine" speech, he hesitated to find himself again out ahead of his troops. Characteristically, he solved the problem by tacitly permitting Welles to launch trial balloons outlining the world of the future.

On July 22, 1941, speaking at the Norwegian Legation in the presence of FDR's friend, the exiled Princess Martha, Welles made the first public reference to postwar aims voiced by a high administration official since the war's start. The world would know no peace, he declared, until Hitler had been "finally, and utterly, destroyed." Millions were asking if the future meant merely a return to "ruined homes, the graves of slaughtered wives and children, poverty, want, the same gray and empty years" that had followed World War I. It was not "premature" to start thinking about the postwar.

Only an "association of nations" could rebuild a shattered world and, whatever its mechanism, two basic principles would remain: disarmament of aggressors under strict international supervision and the "natural" right of victors and vanquished alike to share in the world's resources.[40] Translated into twenty-five languages, Welles's speech was repeatedly broadcast into occupied Europe.

The New York Times called it the "most significant" declaration on peace aims since the outbreak of war; the Cincinnati Enquirer thought it "likely to correspond to the ideas of most Americans."[41] The St. Louis Post Dispatch cited Welles as the first American—or Briton—who had begun thinking about victory "at the peace table, as well as on the battlefield."[42]

Progressive Republicans, weary of the GOP'S sterile isolationism, applauded Welles, and John Foster Dulles, a future Republican Secretary of State then heading a Federal Council of Churches Commission on Future Peace, wrote that he was "strongly in agreement. Nothing is more sure to fail than a national policy dedicated to the status quo." In offering Welles his "warm approbation," Dulles was reflecting the views of the "entire commission."[43]

There were, of course, critics. The *Denver Post* thought it "ridiculous" to believe that all peoples could expect equal access to the world's resources. The *Troy* (N.Y.) *Record* condemned Welles as a "dreamer of Utopia."[44] The isolationist *New York Daily News* suspected him of trying to revive the discredited League of Nations and lashed out at the "same old clichés . . . what the hell is going on, anyway?"[45] In Washington, its sister paper, the *Times-Herald,* provided the answer. When Welles made an official speech, it wrote, he was saying "what the President wants said."[46]

Welles's ground-breaking discussion of postwar aims predictably focused national attention on him. He was a "professional" in manner, outlook and appearance with the "dignity to be viceroy of India" and the influence to make his ideas "count with the President, whom he [sees] virtually daily," wrote James Reston in the *New York Times.* In his youth Welles had been considered "quite a blade" by Latin Americans, who remembered his engaging in a little "serenading" after duty hours in Santo Domingo. Now forty-nine, he possessed the six qualities listed by British historian Harold Nicolson as requisite to the finished diplomat: precision, calm, loyalty, patience, modesty and truthfulness.

Welles's mind was already ranging ahead to Hitler's ultimate destruction, continued Reston, and to a new era in which U.S. policy would rest on three legs: intimate ties with Latin America, friendship with all nations and the "freest possible" world trade to prevent future wars. Peace, for Welles, was not just a momentary abstention from war. It was positive, not negative, and Reston thought it hard-headed and pragmatic, a professional diplomat's philosophy, aimed not merely at winning the war but, more important, at the peace to follow.[47]

Time magazine featured Welles on its front cover a week later, describing him as a "Field-Marshal in the war of brains" against the Axis. He was tough-minded, with an intellectual defense in depth, a mental resilience that could absorb pressures and withstand shocks. Some New Dealers had dismissed him as an "appeasement-minded gentleman" who played high politics with the ruling castes. This idea stemmed, in part, from his appearance. He had never learned to unbend. To newsmen and the "great unwashed public," he seemed too impressive to be real: glacially dignified, ramrod stiff, as "reserved as a box at the opera."

His role in Cuba had been criticized, but it had eliminated the reactionary Platt Amendment, proving the good faith of the Good Neighbor program and leading to a "progressive success" in Cuba that almost no American fully appreciated. He had urged recognition of Franco during the Spanish civil war and this, too, had been criticized; but it had swung the anti-Marxist, Catholic republics of Latin America solidly behind U.S. leadership. Like Roosevelt, Welles had favored a peaceful settlement at Munich; and though some had called it appeasement, once convinced of Hitler's treachery, Welles had stood shoulder to shoulder with Roosevelt and Hull in every move thereafter, and all had been aimed against Nazism.

Welles, *Time* concluded, was "precise, imperturbable, accurate, honest, sophisticated, thorough, cultured, traveled and financially independent." He would like, above all, to be senator from Maryland. He had been through the mill—the only surprises left for him were those of "destiny."[48]

TWENTY-FOUR

DE GAULLE AND THE FREE FRENCH

1940–1944

On June 18, 1940, with France on the verge of collapse, an obscure French general became world famous with a single broadcast. "France is not alone," Charles de Gaulle proclaimed over the BBC from London. "Continue the fight. Get in touch with me!" Weeks later Pétain's collaborationist regime at Vichy broke relations with Britain following a bloody Anglo-French naval clash off Oran. Churchill promptly recognized de Gaulle as the symbol of French resistance and promised him what arms and funds Britain could spare. Slowly at first, then with gathering speed, French men and women inside and outside France began rallying to de Gaulle's banner.

For strategic reasons, Roosevelt had continued recognizing Pétain's puppet regime after the French surrender. Pétain alone could keep the French fleet—238 ships, including 11 battleships and 103 submarines—out of Axis hands and prevent the Germans and Italians from establishing bases in French North Africa, bases that would jeopardize future Allied landings.

American public opinion, however, unaware of these strategic considerations, clamored for a break with Vichy and immediate recognition of de Gaulle's fighting Free French. Encouraged by Gaullist propaganda and by British intelligence, which viewed de Gaulle as the key to rallying French colonies to the Allied cause, American liberals accused the State Department of "contemptible appeasement" and unleashed what Welles later called a "torrent of vituperation, unequalled in American history."[1]

Welles understood and supported FDR's recognition of Vichy, but Hull took criticism of the State Department as a personal affront. Bitter over Roosevelt's decision to run for a third term and the resulting collapse of his own presidential hopes, Hull suspected the White House of deliberately deflecting criticism of its Vichy policy onto him to shield FDR.[2] Roosevelt eventually named Welles his trouble-shooter with de Gaulle and his Free French, a role for which Welles's intimate knowledge of French affairs and fluent French well fitted him. But, over the years ahead, de Gaulle's arrogance, the ceaseless quarreling of his followers and Britain's all-out support of de Gaulle for its own postwar goals often drove Welles to the brink of distraction.

In March 1941 Congressional approval of Lend-Lease raised hopes in London that the United States might help arm—and even recognize—de Gaulle's fledgling movement. At Churchill's suggestion, de Gaulle sent René Pleven, an early adherent, to Washington in July to request Lend-Lease and recognition and to organize a Free French Committee to rally U.S. public support. To smooth Pleven's path, de Gaulle had previously offered the United States bases in Free French Africa for ferrying arms and aircraft to the British in the Middle East. Pan American Airways teams had already set out to survey routes.

Pleven, a lawyer and economist, knew America well.[3] "Very busy week," he cabled de Gaulle after seeing Morgenthau, Hopkins, Knox, British ambassador Lord Halifax and Welles. American opinion about the Free French was "improving," but so long as the United States continued recognizing Vichy, the State Department would oppose even "moral support" for de Gaulle.[4]

Throughout the summer of 1941, Pleven tried unsuccessfully to recruit various eminent French exiles to head de Gaulle's U.S. committee. Among them were Alexis Léger, former director-general of the Quai Dorsays[5]; Jean Monnet of the French purchasing mission[6]; and Jacques Maritain, a philosophy professor then teaching at Columbia University. All, however, refused, as de Gaulle was still an unknown quantity and rumored to be inflexibly authoritarian.

Eventually Pleven fell back on a fractious Socialist labor leader, Adrien Tixier, whose prewar links with the International Labor Office in Geneva might, he hoped, offset rumors of ultra-right-wing tendencies in de Gaulle's entourage.[7] Other committee members included Raoul Roussy de Sales, a half-American correspondent of the French news agency Havas; Étienne Boegner, a son of the Reverend Marc Boegner, head of the Protestant churches in France; Jacques de Sieyès, general manager of the perfumer Patou; and Raoul Aglion, a junior French diplomat.

Japan occupied French Indo-China in July 1941, and Welles, as acting Secretary of State, publicly condemned Vichy for yielding its colony without a fight.

Henceforth, he announced, U.S. policy toward French overseas territories would be determined by the "manifest effectiveness" with which they defended themselves.[8] His statement represented an important "turning point" in U.S. policy toward Vichy and, by implication, toward French colonies "which fight," Pleven cabled de Gaulle.[9] Soon after, for whatever reasons, four other French African colonies—Chad, the Cameroons, Gabon and the French Congo—cast off allegiance to Vichy and hoisted de Gaulle's symbol, the Cross of Lorraine.[10]

Washington, nonetheless, remained skeptical about de Gaulle's military ability and his appeal to Frenchmen overseas. A year earlier, in late 1940, de Gaulle had tried seizing Dakar, Vichy's great naval base on the west African coast. Word of the expedition, however, had leaked and his Free French–British landing force had been humiliatingly repulsed. Welles made no secret of U.S. reservations in an interview with Pleven October 1, 1941. The United States, he said, hoped to see the integrity of France and of the French empire restored— not for sentimental reasons but because it was essential that France again play an important world role.

There was an identity of "goals" between the United States and the Free French, said Welles, but differences over "methods." The United States had just learned from the British, for instance, that de Gaulle had formed a French National Committee in London. The United States would not, however, appoint a liaison officer to it or furnish it Lend-Lease, as Pleven had requested. The U.S. Lend-Lease law specified "governments," and this would imply recognition.[11] Welles was always "très froid," Pleven cabled de Gaulle. "He and his school think that they know more about France than the British or ourselves." The United States was apparently fearful of compromising its influence in Vichy and in French North Africa by openly supporting de Gaulle. There was, however, no doubt that the "bulk of U.S. sympathy remains in our favor."[12]

In September 1941, Pétain yielded to German pressure and dismissed France's ranking soldier, General Maxime Weygand, as delegate-general in North Africa—a serious setback for Roosevelt who, knowing Weygand's anti-German sentiments, had been hoping to win him over secretly to the Allied side. Fearful lest the Germans exploit his ouster by demanding bases in French North Africa, FDR authorized the British to furnish the Free French Lend-Lease arms from their own stocks. The defense of "any territory under Free French control," he proclaimed on Armistice Day of 1941, was "vital" to U.S. defense. This was not, however, to be construed as "recognition."[13]

Later that month two Free French officials—Roussy de Sales and Étienne Boegner—arrived from New York to see Welles and found him "very pessimistic." Pétain had just met publicly with Hitler's deputy, Hermann Goering, and Welles feared increasing German-Vichy collaboration. Resistance in metropolitan France and in French North Africa had virtually ceased, he told them. The United States was planning no "sudden move," but a break with Vichy was inevitable.[14]

This had important implications for the Free French, claimed the Gaullists. Vichy's collaboration with Hitler would make 40 million Frenchmen appear "odious" in world eyes; the United States could prevent it by supporting de Gaulle and his resistance program. Welles, they reported, agreed "energetically" and told them that the State Department probably would give the Free French movement growing support if it could "personify" the French Resistance. However, alluding to reports of third-degree interrogation methods being used on suspected French opponents by de Gaulle's security service, he had warned that the Free French should emphasize their "democratic" views. From London came a characteristically Olympian response: "De Gaulle sees the situation the same way as Sumner Welles."[15] By chance, his cable reached New York the day before Pearl Harbor.

In the confusion following the Japanese attack, de Gaulle staged a coup-de-main that virtually severed his relations with Washington. On Christmas Eve he ordered Free French warships (without notifying "the foreigners"[16]) to seize St. Pierre and Miquelon, two small French islands under Vichy control off the Canadian coast. The American and Canadian governments were outraged, fearing that Pétain might grant Hitler bases in North Africa in retaliation, and Hull angrily denounced the "so-called" Free French. The State Department was inundated with protests over his gratuitous slight,[17] and Roosevelt, thinking his statement ill-advised, refused to back him. Whereupon, wrote Welles, Hull's anger turned to "white heat."[18]

Churchill by then had arrived in Washington to plan Allied landings in North Africa (Operation TORCH) with FDR. While embarrassed by his French protégé's duplicity, he nonetheless defended him in a heated quarrel with Hull who departed, days later, for a two-month vacation in Florida—so angry, wrote Welles, that he refused for some time even to speak to the President by telephone.[19] De Gaulle's power play on the heels of Pearl Harbor cost him "all hopes of early diplomatic recognition by Roosevelt and sealed his complete exclusion from the higher political and military councils of the war, all the way to the Potsdam conference in the summer of 1945," wrote his biographer, Don Cook.[20]

In reprisal, FDR barred the Free French from signing the Declaration of United Nations with forty other nations in the White House on New Year's day, 1942. Hoping to avert an Allied quarrel, British ambassador Lord Halifax urged Welles to intercede with FDR to allow Gaullist "observers" at least to attend the ceremony, but Welles, equally angry, replied that the President had not asked his advice. If he did, he added coldly, he would recommend against it.[21]

The United States had been "moving heaven and earth" to stay on close terms with Vichy and keep the French fleet and North Africa out of German hands, he reminded Halifax. The appearance of Gaullist officials at the White House so soon after St. Pierre-Miquelon would convince Vichy that the United States was playing "both sides against the middle" and allow the Germans to reduce American influence still further. Britain had recognized de Gaulle but the United States had not. It was in the "highest degree expedient" for strategic reasons for the U.S. to continue recognizing Vichy—provided it did not become completely subservient to Germany. If it did, the United States would consider recognizing de Gaulle. Welles's personal assessment of the general, early in the war, emerged in his memorandum of conversation:

> I was unable to see that the Free French movement, at the present moment, had anything very much to commend it, from the practical standpoint. Unfortunately, there were no outstanding men with qualities of leadership and of initiative directing the Free French movement and providing that kind of inspiration to free men, both in France and in other parts of the world, to join in a movement against their German oppressors . . . If some man like [former Prime Minister Edouard] Herriot could get out of France and lead the movement, the situation would, undoubtedly, be very different, but I could not see that either General de Gaulle or his associates provided any rallying point for French patriotism.[22]

Welles was wrong, as history proves; but, like Roosevelt and Hull, at the time he was incensed by de Gaulle's devious power play, worried lest Vichy grant Hitler bases in North Africa and irked by Hull's pointless quarrel with FDR and Churchill. Early in 1942 the U.S. Pacific fleet lay crippled at Pearl Harbor, the Axis was winning on all fronts and de Gaulle seemed a minor irritant.

On February 19, as acting Secretary, Welles granted Tixier his first interview. Turning aside the Gaullist's opening demand for official recognition, he suggested instead that Tixier fly to London and persuade de Gaulle to "democratize" (i.e., expand) the French National Committee, which, in U.S. eyes, seemed exclusively Gaullist. Three weeks later, in view of the increasing use of Free French bases in Africa as ferry routes, Welles announced the appointment of a U.S. consul general to de Gaulle's African headquarters of Brazzaville.

Vichy, predictably, protested, and Welles's pent-up contempt for Pétain's puppet regime and its Nazi overlords erupted in an open letter to Gaston Henry-Haye, the Vichy ambassador in Washington. Only the "total destruction of the present criminal regime" in Germany, the defeat of its armies and those of the dictatorships aligned with Hitler could restore French independence Welles wrote:

That is well-known to all of the people of France, including even that handful of Frenchmen who have sordidly and abjectly attempted to prostitute their country to that regime in Germany which is bent upon the permanent enslavement of France. A part of France's overseas territories remains under the effective jurisdiction of [Vichy]; others are under the effective control of French authorities who do not recognize Vichy, but who are fighting actively [with] the forces of freedom . . . The United States will continue to maintain, or enter into, relations with those French citizens who are in actual control [of] French territories in Africa or the Pacific."[23]

In other words, Washington would recognize de Gaulle's authority over French colonies that rallied to him. The break with Vichy was approaching but hopes that de Gaulle might now prove grateful—thus more tractable—soon faded. A fortnight later Pétain reappointed the archcollaborator Pierre Laval, Vichy's Prime Minister, and, in reprisal, Roosevelt recalled Ambassador Leahy, naming him his personal chief of staff. De Gaulle saw the tide turning inexorably in his favor; not only did he become more obdurate, but, to pressure the Anglo-Americans, he began playing his "Russian card."[24]

Enraged on learning in May that the British had invaded Madagascar, a Vichy-controlled island off east Africa, without consulting him, de Gaulle staged a public row with Churchill, conferred ostentatiously with Soviet Foreign Minister Vyacheslav Molotov, who was passing through London en route to Washington, and embarrassed the Allies by openly backing Soviet demands for a second front.[25] His anger mounted still further when he learned that Roosevelt had told Molotov in the White House that France would need no army after the war; only the United States, Britain and Soviet Russia would have armies.[26]

Meanwhile, the more Vichy truckled to Hitler, the higher rose de Gaulle's star. In late May, when his Free French forces held out heroically against German panzers at Bir-Hakeim in North Africa, winning world acclaim, John G. Winant, Roosevelt's ambassador to London, met with de Gaulle and wrote FDR urging him to clear the air by inviting the imperious Frenchman to Washington.[27] Roosevelt, however, had not forgiven the French for their abject surrender in 1940 nor de Gaulle for his role at St. Pierre-Miquelon.

De Gaulle's claim that destiny had designated him alone to represent France stiffened Roosevelt's refusal to recognize his Free French—or any resistance movement—as the future French government. After victory the French themselves would choose their leaders, he decreed. The Allies would not foist de Gaulle on them during the war.[28]

The British, however, had other ideas. After victory, de Gaulle would be their instrument for dominating postwar Europe. As head of a French government presumably grateful for Britain's wartime support, de Gaulle would help keep Germany permanently disarmed and Britain would resume its historic role as Europe's kingmaker.

On May 11, soon after de Gaulle's flare-up over Madagascar, Halifax complained to Welles that he found himself at "cross purposes" with Hull about the Free French. Could Welles explain U.S. policy?[29] Emphasizing that he was speaking for neither the President nor Hull but solely for himself, Welles suggested that the United States and Britain coordinate their policies as U.S. relations with Vichy might soon be "drastically" modified. French resistance to Germany should be "focussed," said Welles, and there was no way to do it but by expanding de Gaulle's French National Committee to reflect "all political tendencies of liberal, democratic" French thought.

De Gaulle could remain a committee member—but not its head. His Free French movement was "breaking to pieces" in England, the United States and every other part of the world. By enlarging the French National Committee, Welles suggested, de Gaulle could be "controlled" to a greater degree.[30]

While Halifax was passing Welles's proposal to London, Tixier reappeared with a catalogue of complaints, causing Welles to warn him wearily that Gaullist feuding was having a "disastrous" effect on American opinion. The Free French seemed to be spending "ninety five percent of their time on petty quarrels." Days later Welles learned to his indignation that the British had scuttled his proposal to "control" de Gaulle by leaking it to the *New York Times*.[31] On Halifax's next visit, the normally cordial Under Secretary was frigid.

"It would seem almost incredible," he rebuked Halifax, "that highly confidential views, intended solely for the secret information of the British government, should have appeared 'in extenso' in recent despatches in the American press from London. It became necessary to question the wisdom of [discussing] matters of this character, informally and confidentially, with the British government."[32]

Almost certainly, Welles had advanced his hope of "controlling" de Gaulle by injecting liberal French elements into his hand-picked French National Committee with Roosevelt's concurrence; but London had torpedoed it and, meanwhile the date for the Anglo-American TORCH landing in North Africa was fast approaching. Discussing the operation with Churchill in June, Roosevelt ruled out Free French participation lest it stiffen Vichy's resistance. Nonetheless, once Allied troops were safely ashore, Vichy's usefulness to the United States would end and de Gaulle would loom ever larger on the scene.

Meanwhile, Laval's collaboration with Hitler was driving the French increasingly to de Gaulle. In July, at Churchill's urging, FDR agreed to provide Lend-Lease arms and supplies directly to de Gaulle's Free French as a "symbol of resistance" to the Axis. De Gaulle would be allowed a military mission in Washington, and Admiral Harold R. Stark, the former CNO whom Roosevelt had sent to London, would serve as his U.S. liaison for military—but not political—matters.

"It was de Gaulle's constant insistence on political recognition that excited so much suspicion against him," wrote Hull. "His own dictatorial attitude, coupled with his adventures in the political field, inevitably inspired the thought that he was trying to develop a political standing that would make him the next ruler of France."[33]

De Gaulle meanwhile had concluded that Tixier had not the requisite stature to represent him effectively in Washington. The Free French were still quarreling among themselves and the United States still recognized Vichy's ambassador, Gaston Henri-Haye, as the official representative of France. What was needed was a Resistance hero to convince Roosevelt that the French underground— from Catholics to Communists—accepted de Gaulle as their leader. In June 1942 he sent Emmanuel d'Astier de la Vigerie, who had just escaped from the Germans, to Washington for this purpose. His visit was to be "top secret," de Gaulle cabled Tixier. Roosevelt, Hull and Welles were too busy to see d'Astier— although apparently Harry Hopkins did—and Tixier, highly indignant, decided to bring the French hero's presence forcibly to America's attention.

Ignoring de Gaulle's order for secrecy, he arranged an interview with *LIFE* magazine, complete with photographs of d'Astier conferring melodramatically with Free French confrères, his back to the camera and his face in shadow. D'Astier's public prediction that Mistinguett, the cabaret star, and Georges Carpentier, the world-famous boxer, might be among the "collaborators" tried and shot after victory did little, however, to enhance de Gaulle's "democratic" image.[34] Welles told Richard Law, Eden's parliamentary undersecretary, soon after that the time was coming when de Gaulle would have to be "shelved." It might shock French opinion but, if de Gaulle arrived in North Africa with the Allied forces and established a provisional government, the Allies could "never remove him."[35]

On the heels of d'Astier's visit, de Gaulle sent another Resistance figure, Andre Philip, to seek Roosevelt's support. Philip, a former Socialist cabinet minister, also had escaped from occupied France, and de Gaulle had added him to his French National Committee. On reaching Washington in late October, Philip handed Welles a personal letter for Roosevelt from de Gaulle setting forth his policy.

He had not set out as a "political leader," de Gaulle wrote FDR; circumstances had made him a "moral entity" uniquely qualified to represent France. Evidently aware of U.S. suspicions, he claimed that "no one in France has accused us of aspiring to dictatorship," subconsciously slipping into the royal "we" and weakening his case. The Free French were not demanding recognition as the government of France, de Gaulle went on, but did insist on being consulted when French interests, such as the use of French troops or the administration of liberated territories, arose.[36]

Roosevelt never answered his letter. It had come two years too late, Ray Atherton, chief of the State Department's European division, minuted Welles. "If this letter had been written on the outset of the Free French movement, it would have been a great asset in our relations with them," wrote Atherton. "Unhappily, de Gaulle seems to have no conception of the reasons for our relations with Vichy. This blindness is more tragic in view of our ever-increasing collaboration with him. I fear [he] will attempt to force himself and his Committee on the French people by [Allied] arms."[37]

Precisely this fear haunted FDR and Welles at the time, and it was being powerfully reinforced by Alexis Léger whose democratic views and long experience at the Quai Dorsay were respected by both Roosevelt and Welles.[38] Welles, in fact, had included Leger in a small private dinner given for the President at Oxon Hill months earlier. Leger had refused repeated invitations to join de Gaulle and had just turned down a personal plea from Churchill to fly to London and become de Gaulle's chief advisor. A memorandum Welles sent FDR on August 13, 1942, explained Léger's mistrust of de Gaulle.

Léger, he reported, had just seen a French scientist and old friend named Istel who had arrived from London with yet another invitation to join de Gaulle's French National Committee. Before leaving England, Istel had talked at length with the general, apparently falling under his spell, and his report of the conversation had profoundly alarmed Léger. According to Istel, de Gaulle intended to press for recognition of the Free French as a "provisional government" with full diplomatic relations with the United Nations and "complete" authority over all French in or outside France. He intended also to seek an invitation from Roosevelt to visit Washington, thus enhancing his own influence in France, but he would oppose any shift in the supreme direction of the war from London to Washington.

De Gaulle had told Istel that the British favored a provisional government under his direction for six months after the armistice, to be followed by national elections. His postwar policy toward Britain would include "suitable" recognition of its role in France's liberation—but no more. His policy toward the United States would be "on a par . . . with the republics of Latin America." In general, he had said, his foreign policy would be based on the "closest" military and political ties with Soviet Russia. Only in this way could France prevent a "preponderance" of U.S.-British influence in the world.

Legér thought de Gaulle "totally opposed to any type of international cooperation or world organization," Welles stressed in conclusion.[39] For Roosevelt and Welles, both determined to create a United Nations Organization before the war's end, this alone was sufficient to damn de Gaulle.

While visiting Beirut in August 1942, de Gaulle heard rumors of impending Allied landings in French North Africa, and his phobia about Anglo-Saxon designs on the French empire soared. "I am convinced that the U.S. has decided to land troops in French North Africa," he cabled his aides Pleven and Maurice Dejean, in London. "The British . . . are ready to exploit any American success around Casablanca by penetrating, militarily, into French West Africa [i.e., Dakar]."[40] Two days later Dejean replied that he had talked with former U.S. ambassador William C. Bullitt, then in London on special assignment for Navy Secretary Frank Knox, and had gained the impression that "the so-called naval questions on which [Bullitt] is occupied appear to be in connection with the coming operation."[41]

Bullitt's indiscretion was notorious. Soon after, therefore, General Marshall warned Roosevelt in the presence of Averell Harriman that the U.S. Army had proof (presumably from wiretaps) that Bullitt had been leaking details of the approaching landings to curry favor with de Gaulle. "What are we to do with Billy?!" exploded FDR. "Perhaps we ought to send him to Alaska where he can leak to the Eskimos."[42]

Bullitt continued pressing FDR for a variety of war-related jobs for two more years. Finally recognizing failure, he joined the Free French forces in 1944 and served out the rest of the war under de Gaulle's command.

FDR had barred the Free French from the TORCH landings November 8, 1942, lest their presence stiffen Vichy resistance. However, if de Gaulle was to be excluded, he would have to be mollified. Therefore, on October 25, FDR had Welles notify Andre Philip that the President would see him and Tixier on November 6. For the Gaullists it was a milestone—their first interview with FDR—but, for reasons best known to themselves, they arrived four hours late and the meeting was cancelled.[43] Two days later American and British troops began disembarking in Morocco and Algeria, and within twenty-four hours, Dwight D. Eisenhower had concluded his celebrated "deal" with Admiral Jean François Darlan, the Vichy vice-premier, who had arrived in Algiers the night before to visit an ailing son and had found himself a prisoner.

The Eisenhower-Darlan pact ended Vichy resistance, ensuring Allied success, but Eisenhower's appointment of the turncoat Vichyite as senior French civil administrator in North Africa was widely condemned. De Gaulle ordered Philip and Tixier to protest vehemently to Welles, who heard them out in silence. Roosevelt, too, had been politically embarrassed, although he defended the deal on military grounds. At best, however, it was cynical expediency and, ironically, enhanced de Gaulle's prestige. Suspecting as much, FDR had Welles reschedule the meeting with Philip and Tixier for November 20. Welles later described it as a disaster.

Roosevelt, he wrote, received the Gaullists in a friendly manner then stated disarmingly that it would be "useful" for him and de Gaulle to talk. He would welcome the general to Washington whenever he wished to come. As to the Eisenhower-Darlan pact, U.S. military operations in North Africa had "subordinated" all other considerations, said FDR. Nothing could be allowed to interfere with victory, which alone could hasten the liberation of France.

Darlan's appointment had been based solely on military considerations, continued FDR, and he would remove him at once if, at any moment, he had reason to believe Darlan was not satisfactory. This applied equally to all other French officials in North Africa. Until France had been freed, decisions as to which Frenchmen would administer liberated territories were "solely, for the [U.S.] to determine."

At this, Welles wrote, Philip and Tixier immediately and categorically protested. The French National Committee would never "permit" any French town, village or farmhouse to be administered by "foreign powers." Administration of the liberated areas would have to be in Free French hands "not later than two or three weeks from now, which," they told Roosevelt, "will give you time to occupy Tunisia." At no time in the fifty-minute interview did either Gaullist express the "slightest gratitude or recognition" of the liberation of French North Africa by American forces. Facing deadlock, Welles suggested that the President might wish to end the meeting, noting that, if de Gaulle came to Washington later, FDR and he could then discuss "high policy." Roosevelt gratefully agreed.

The Gaullists left a "deplorable" impression on FDR; he found them filled with "personal ambition, totally incomprehensible [and] characterized by stupidity and rudeness," wrote Roussy de Sales.[44] In fact, the interview was to have a dramatic aftermath. Days later Roosevelt told Welles that he would not invite de Gaulle to Washington but would see him early in January 1943 if he asked to come. The day after Christmas 1942, de Gaulle was driving to the London airport bound for Washington when Churchill sent word that Darlan had been assassinated in Algiers the night before. FDR cancelled the visit.

With the Allied forces starting their slow, fitful drive east and Montgomery's Eighth Army, closing in from Libya, herding Rommel's Afrika Korps into Tunisia, Hitler occupied all French territory. The Americans, seeking a rival to de Gaulle, meanwhile had smuggled a lackluster four-star French general, Henri Giraud, by submarine from France to Algiers, where Eisenhower promptly named him commander-in-chief of all French forces—further infuriating de Gaulle. Months earlier Giraud had escaped from a German prison camp and, after making his way to Vichy, had pledged Pétain his "perfect loyalty," a declaration that, wrote Don Cook, somewhat embarrassed the Allies.[45]

However, with the Axis forces in North Africa relentlessly being herded into Tunisia to face mass surrender and the invasions of Sicily and Italy still to be planned, Roosevelt and Churchill agreed to meet in Casablanca from January 14 to 26, 1943, with Giraud—there was no thought at first of also inviting de Gaulle.[46] Affronted by his exclusion, de Gaulle publicly blasted Washington and, on January 2, two weeks before the parley, cabled Giraud suggesting that they meet in Algiers to "enlarge a provisional Central Authority."[47] De Gaulle's maneuver, Welles told Tixier indignantly, had introduced "unnecessary and diversionary political" questions into what was "primarily a military situation."[48]

Roosevelt and Churchill, however, faced awesome problems —among them arming, equipping, training and, it was hoped, unifying 300,000 French troops in North Africa for the coming liberation of Europe. It was Churchill who persuaded Roosevelt that a conference without de Gaulle would be meaningless. De Gaulle and his equally vainglorious, if less politically astute, rival Giraud would somehow have to be reconciled, if only for military reasons.

De Gaulle sulked at first, threatening to boycott the meeting, but, under intense pressure from Churchill and Eden, he finally flew from London to Casablanca in the closing days of the conference and, at FDR's request, posed stiffly for the famous "shotgun wedding" handshake with Giraud. Even so, FDR continued cold-shouldering him, naming Giraud "trustee" for French interests in North Africa, agreeing to equip and place all French forces under his command and authorizing him a military—but not a diplomatic—mission in Washington. De Gaulle bided his time. Three months later, in May 1943, when the Axis forces in North Africa surrendered en masse, he flew to Algiers and established his own headquarters alongside Giraud's on French soil.[49] De Gaulle was closing in.

In addition to roiling U.S.-British relations, the Giraud–de Gaulle feud reflected little-known but bitter Anglo-American rivalry for postwar influence in French Africa, notably around Dakar. The great French naval base on Africa's westernmost tip dominated the Atlantic narrows, and Roosevelt and Welles had long viewed it as a potential jumping-off point for an Axis invasion of Latin America. In fact, in May 1941, six months before Pearl Harbor, Welles had urged FDR to expand the Monroe Doctrine unilaterally to cover Dakar and all French, British, Belgian, Spanish and Portuguese colonies north of the equator. FDR initially had agreed, but Hull had talked him out of it.[50] Neither the President nor Welles, however, had lost sight of the danger of Dakar in unfriendly hands.

In March 1943, with Giraud–de Gaulle tension still straining Anglo-American ties, Welles alerted Roosevelt that the British were "rapidly expanding" their influence around Dakar. Roosevelt himself had recently stated that Dakar should "never again constitute a threat" to the Western Hemisphere but should remain in the hands of people "friendly to us," Welles reminded him. Unless prompt, effective measures were taken, "we shall, inevitably, lose the position which should belong to us at Dakar." Given recent aviation developments, Dakar's significance to the United States and to other American republics could "scarcely be exaggerated."

The next day, on Welles's recommendation, FDR named Admiral William A. Glassford of the U.S. Navy his personal representative at Dakar with the rank of minister.[51]

Meanwhile, in uneasy alliance in Algiers, de Gaulle and Giraud had formed a French Committee of National Liberation (FCNL) to direct the French overseas war effort and, after victory, hand over power to a provisional French government. Each was a "co-chairman" of the new committee, but their mutual mistrust involved more than a clash of personalities; it involved postwar power. Giraud planned to keep the FCNL under his military control and dominate it largely through three Vichyite governors in French Africa, each personally loyal to him—General Auguste Nogues in Morocco, Marcel Peyrouton in Algeria and Pierre Boisson in French West Africa. As a sop to de Gaulle, he offered to include some Gaullist governors of the Free French colonies of Equatorial Africa, Madagascar, Syria and New Caledonia, but essentially the FCNL was to be military and right-wing and to concern itself solely with French territories already liberated. Giraud's eyes were on the present, de Gaulle's on the future.

De Gaulle's main strength derived from the Resistance inside France— particularly the Communists, who had recognized his leadership on April 1— so he insisted that metropolitan France be given equal representation with the colonies on the FCNL. The specter of Communist influence on the committee, however, was anathema to Giraud and even more to the Americans, so the power struggle intensified with de Gaulle skillfully undermining his rival by accusing him, with considerable justification, of surrounding himself with Vichyites.

Eden arrived in Washington in March 1943 to discuss postwar issues— notably the tense de Gaulle–Giraud rivalry—and, in sparring with Roosevelt, Hull and Welles in the White House, "yielded not an iota," Breckinridge Long noted in his diary: "de Gaulle is their baby." The British opposed Giraud because he was not "pliable" to their plans and opposed U.S. policy because "we are looking to [Giraud] to play ball behind our military lines."[52] When Eden protested that FDR was being "very hard" on the French, the President retorted that the French would need help after the war and, in return, certain French territories could be earmarked as United Nations bases—a favorite FDR theme.

Welles reminded him that the United States was on record for the restoration of "all" French possessions. FDR thought this applied only to North Africa, but Welles insisted that there was no such modification. Roosevelt brushed it aside. In the "ironing out" of things after the war, he observed airily, this could be rectified.[53]

At the end of June, Giraud paid his first official visit to Washington, which now boasted rival French delegations, his and de Gaulle's, each with large military and civilian staffs. Confusion reigned. Earlier that month FDR had recognized the Algiers FCNL as "administering those French overseas territories which acknowledge its authority," although this did not constitute "recognition of a government of France or of the French empire by . . . the U.S." he insisted.

In mid-August, on the eve of the first Quebec conference, Ickes learned from Drew Pearson that Hull, hearing rumors that the United Nations was about to recognize the FCNL, had telephoned Leahy for confirmation to be told that Leahy was in Canada, fishing with FDR. Hull had asked if anyone in the White House could confirm the rumors and had learned from Leahy's secretary that a cable to that effect, signed by Leahy, had just gone to Eisenhower. "One of the most astonishing things I have ever heard," Ickes gloated in his diary. "The Secretary of State did not know the latest diplomatic move in North Africa!"[54]

As weary and frustrated by French bickering as Welles, Hull complained to Giraud's chief delegate, Henri Hoppenot (another Vichyite) about "incessant" French criticism of U.S. policy and about de Gaulle's "personal, tyrannical power" over the French empire.[55] Assistant War Secretary John McCloy told Hoppenot that de Gaulle was "violent, impulsive, talks too much of French sovereignty [and] claims that France will win, alone." The Gaullists, McCloy insisted, were demeaning Giraud; he himself had opposed Giraud's visit to Washington because it highlighted his image as a U.S. "puppet."[56]

Giraud's political ineptitude, in fact, was embarrassing the administration, which tried to mute his visit. Hull offered him no official dinner; he was given no role in the Bastille Day—July 14—celebrations in New York, and American reporters were encouraged to ask him military rather than political questions. Welles was away in Maine on holiday at the time, and his absence sparked rumors that he had left town deliberately to avoid being drawn further into the French morasse.

Soon after his return, Tixier reappeared with a drumbeat of familiar complaints, protesting, among other things, that the United States was not sufficiently backing a Gaullist candidate for a minor post in French Guiana. Welles's patience snapped. The situation, he retorted undiplomatically, reminded him of an "old-fashioned French farce . . . It was pitiful to see men like de Gaulle maneuvering in war time for personal political advantage. De Gaulle and Giraud should come to an urgent meeting of minds—the French were fighting each other."[57]

Except for agreement on a four-power declaration creating a United Nations Organization, wrote Sherwood, the principal political accomplishment at the

QUADRANT conference held at Quebec on August 11 to 24, 1943, was Roosevelt's "agreement to disagree with Churchill about the French. They formally recognized the FCNL, militarily though not politically, with de Gaulle and Giraud each co-presidents but, for FDR, it was a face-saving compromise. By then de Gaulle already dominated it."[58]

In October, while en route to the Moscow meeting of foreign ministers, Hull stopped off in Algiers to see de Gaulle, and their relations improved. A month later the United States formally severed ties with Vichy, for by then de Gaulle had formed his own French Committee of National Defense (FCND), shouldering Giraud aside and emerging as the unchallenged leader of the French. Even then FDR's hostility persisted. Returning from Tehran in December 1943, he told Wallace, Biddle and others that de Gaulle's influence was "decreasing." Reports from the French underground indicated that de Gaulle would "hardly last after France was freed," he told them. French leaders thought him purely a "temporary arrangement."[59]

Years later, in analyzing Roosevelt's antipathy to de Gaulle, Welles wrote that FDR thought France's recovery would be impossible if it continued spending the greater part of its revenues on armaments and a standing army. Since Germany was to be disarmed and placed under international control, there was no reason for France to continue as a military power. Welles strongly disagreed:

> I believed that only harm would result if he persisted in his views. I argued with him, pointing out that, if Germany was to be disarmed and divided into a number of states, Great Britain, alone, could not balance, in Western Europe, the weight of the Soviet Union in Eastern Europe. The loss of France as a strong, well-armed power would create a vacuum which the Soviet Union would fill. I doubt that my arguments had much effect.
>
> Two years later, however, the President, himself, [urged] the Soviet Union to let France participate in the military control of Germany. He also dropped all ideas of French disarmament, probably as a result of representations by Churchill. It may be that the vigor with which he expressed these beliefs was due to his feeling that, if postwar France came under the domination of chauvinistic leaders [like] de Gaulle, she would prove a major stumbling block to any healthy reorganization of the world.[60]

Welles acknowledged that he himself had underestimated de Gaulle in 1941. Three years later, in his best-seller, *The Time for Decision,* he wrote that:

> The ability of the Free French Committee in London, even with the support given it by the British government, to maintain a nucleus of patriotic resistance and gradually to increase its scope and its authority seemed for more than a year

to be very doubtful. But the committee succeeded and later proved to be of outstanding value in the war effort of the United Nations.[61]

Not until the second Quebec conference, held in September, 1944, eight months before the war's end, did Roosevelt finally bow to reality and recognize de Gaulle's FCND as the de facto civil and military authority of France, paving the way for its recognition as the Provisional French Government on October 23 following the liberation of Paris. The wheel had come full turn. In four years, starting from scratch, de Gaulle had outmaneuvered the most powerful statesman in the world.

TWENTY-FIVE

THE ATLANTIC CHARTER CONFERENCE

1941

"A Goodly Company at Sea"

MEANWHILE, ROOSEVELT AND WELLES were collaborating ever more closely in trying to shape the postwar world. Early in August 1941, Roosevelt confided that he would meet Churchill shortly off the Newfoundland coast. Very few knew of the meeting; nothing was to be announced until it was over.[1] Their encounter, he told Welles, would offer hope to the "enslaved" peoples of the world. The English-speaking democracies stood for freedom and justice and should bind themselves to establishing a new world order based on these principles.[2]

Roosevelt had three goals in meeting Churchill, Welles wrote later. Britain was losing the war and needed stiffening. Britain would have to foreswear the secret territorial deals that had so embittered the United States after World War I, fostering isolationism. Finally, the American people had to be convinced that, by aiding Britain, they were not merely defending the British empire and the status quo but ensuring America's own safety and a better world to come.

Roosevelt and Churchill barely knew each other at the time. Their meeting stemmed from a 4,000-word letter Churchill had sent FDR after the 1940 election, nine months earlier, warning that Britain's dollar reserves were fast disappearing. If Britain was to continue fighting Hitler, immediate massive aid was imperative. Roosevelt had been cruising the Caribbean when the letter arrived and had had time to weigh its importance.

He had immediately sent Harry Hopkins to confer with Churchill, and the passage of Lend-Lease in March 1941 had prepared the way.[3] Britain's military reverses in North Africa and Hitler's attack on the Soviet Union on June 22, however, had postponed the meeting date until August. Meanwhile, Hull's two-month illness had brought Welles into closer contact with Roosevelt's thinking, making him the logical choice to accompany FDR to Newfoundland.

Hull returned to the State Department on August 5 and, the next day, handed Welles travel orders melodramatic in their opacity: "It is desired that you proceed to an unnamed destination in New England to perform a special mission, the nature of which has been made known to you, orally."[4] Two days later Welles and Averell Harriman, a fellow Grotonian and "expediter" of Lend-Lease to Britain, boarded a navy PBY in Boston and landed at Argentia on the Newfoundland coast. That night Welles dined with the President aboard his flagship, the USS *Augusta,* and briefed him on world developments.

As always when at sea, Roosevelt was in high spirits, delighted at having outwitted the press by setting out ostensibly for a leisurely coastal cruise on the presidential yacht, *Potomac,* then transferring secretly to the *Augusta,* which had brought him the rest of the way, escorted by the USS *Tuscaloosa* and a screen of destroyers. The press, meanwhile, was still shadowing the presidential yacht as it slowly traversed the Cape Cod canal, an FDR "double" complete with the President's celebrated cigarette holder fishing ostentatiously on the fan-tail.[5]

In addition to Welles and Harriman, FDR had included Harry Hopkins; General George C. Marshall, army chief of staff; General Henry H. "Hap" Arnold, head of the Army Air Corps; Admiral Harold R. "Betty" Stark, Chief of Naval Operations; and Admiral Ernest "Ernie" King, Commander-in-Chief of the Atlantic Fleet; and two of his four sons: Major Elliott of the Air Corps and Ensign Franklin D., Jr., then on destroyer duty.

Next morning Ensign Roosevelt received an order to report in dress blues to the "Commander-in-Chief" on USS *Augusta.* Fearing a reprimand for some infraction from the formidable Admiral King, he duly reported and was shown to an empty wardroom. Puzzled, he heard a familiar chuckle. The President, in his wheelchair, had hidden himself behind the door to surprise his son. They embraced, discussed family matters and, on turning to the coming meeting, FDR Jr. asked his father why he had brought Welles instead of Hull. "One, I trust him," replied the President succinctly. "Two, he doesn't argue with me. Three, he gets things done."[5]

On Saturday, August 9, Britain's newest battle cruiser, the HMS *Prince of Wales,* threaded its way slowly past twenty-two American warships, halting near the *Augusta.* As the great anchors splashed down in the icy water of Argentia bay, the sun broke through the mist as if in welcome. On the bridge stood Churchill, cigar in hand, flanked by Harry Hopkins, who had crossed the Atlantic with him after a flying visit to Stalin.

Others included Welles's opposite number, Sir Alexander Cadogan, permanent Under Secretary at the Foreign Office, and British military chiefs. Roosevelt lunched with Churchill and Hopkins aboard the *Augusta* while their staffs turned in the wardroom to a U.S. Navy cold plate, which the high-born Cadogan, fifth son of an earl, dismissed in his diary as "very unsatisfactory."[7]

Following this inauspicious start, Welles led Cadogan to his quarters aboard the *Tuscaloosa,* sat at a desk piled with papers and "went, drily, over agenda items like a judge," Cadogan wrote later.[8] Welles asked Cadogan pointedly if Britain had any "secret commitments" that might affect the United States after the war and seemed reassured when the latter replied categorically that there were none.

Welles and Cadogan, each a product of his country's elite, were warily taking the other's measure. Welles's disgust over Britain's appeasement policies in the 1930s and his suspicion of all British bureaucrats had led to a reserve so marked that Cadogan had described him, during Welles's mission to Europe the year before, as "clamlike."[9] Welles, in turn, wrote later that while Cadogan was "competent, high-minded and honorable not, by the widest stretch of the imagination, could he be regarded as possessing vision or a capacity for initiative," qualities on which Welles prided himself.[10]

In his opening talk with Cadogan, Welles was fully aware that Churchill's main purpose in crossing the Atlantic was to engage the United States in a joint warning to Japan: if it continued its aggression, war would be inevitable. Weeks earlier Japan had occupied French Indochina, threatening Britain's lifelines to the Far East, the Dutch East Indies and the U.S.-administered Philippines. In retaliation, FDR had frozen Japan's assets on July 26 and had further tightened the embargo on oil and scrap metal exports. Cable intercepts indicated that Thailand might soon become Japan's next victim, but FDR still worried that the United States might be drawn into war before it was militarily ready.

Noting the President's freeze, Welles told Cadogan that America's "extreme" patience with Japan had ended. He himself had warned Kaname Wakasugi, the Japanese minister in Washington, that war was inevitable if Japan continued its course. Nonetheless, he thought an immediate showdown should be avoided—if only to gain time for rearmament. The War and Navy departments had warned that war in the Pacific would tie up the U.S. fleet, straining military and production resources needed for the Atlantic. Churchill would probably agree, said Cadogan, although he had already concluded that only a stiff U.S. warning would have any effect. The Japanese, he thought, were "ready to take on the whole world."[11]

Over dinner that night, FDR, Churchill, Welles, Hopkins and Cadogan weighed the pros and cons of a joint warning. Roosevelt thought it likely to provoke, rather than restrain, the Japanese and certain to arouse American isolationists but agreed to consider a warning if Churchill would draft it. Churchill said he would. They turned next to the Joint Declaration, or Atlantic Charter, whose parentage remains obscure.

Testifying before Congress after the war, Welles recalled that the President had told him weeks before that he was considering "some kind of public statement of objectives" to keep alive the principles of international law, moral and human decency in a darkening world.[12] He had made no mention of a "joint statement," although he had been considering one and had been awaiting an opportunity.

"When we arrived [at Argentia]," Welles recalled, "we found that Churchill had some specific suggestions. The Charter contains some of FDR's original ideas and Churchill's original ideas."[13] There had been "no prior exchange," he said. Churchill had suggested the joint statement on the evening of his arrival.[14] Churchill himself ascribed paternity to Roosevelt. "President Roosevelt told me, at one of our first conversations," he wrote, "that he thought it would be well if we could draw up a Joint Declaration laying down certain broad principles which should guide our policies along the same road."[15]

Robert Sherwood had a third version. While crossing the Atlantic, Churchill and Hopkins, he wrote, had discussed the "phraseolgy of the Atlantic Charter which the Prime Minister was to present to the President. Churchill hoped that from the meeting some momentuous agreement might be reached . . . The agreement that Churchill hoped for was definitely not the Atlantic Charter: it was the establishment of a common policy of resistance to further Japanese aggression."[16]

Whatever the facts, on returning to the *Prince of Wales* after dinner, Churchill outlined both the warning to Japan and the Joint Declaration to Cadogan and, before retiring to bed, assigned him the overnight drafting.

The next morning—Sunday, August 10—Roosevelt, Churchill and their staffs assembled for religious services on the *Prince of Wales*'s quarterdeck. Roosevelt was in his wheelchair, bare-headed; Churchill seated beside him, his cigar for once absent. Behind them, amid generals, admirals and air marshals, stood Welles, Harriman, Hopkins and the two Roosevelt sons, hymnals in hand, lustily singing "Onward Christian Soldiers," "O God Our Help in Ages Past," and other hymns,[17] which undoubtedly evoked for FDR and his four fellow Grotonians[18] memories of Endicott Peabody and school days long past.

The service completed, Roosevelt rolled himself in his wheelchair along the huge deck, inspecting guns and equipment with professional interest as Churchill took Welles aside and made an impassioned plea for the joint warning to Japan. If Tokyo took advantage of Britain's "solitary" struggle in Europe and the Middle East to seize its Far Eastern possessions, he warned, Britain's very survival might be at stake.[19] Welles escorted FDR back to the USS *Augusta* and, at the gangplank, Cadogan handed him Churchill's draft of the Joint Declaration.

FDR and Welles perused it, word for word, in the President's quarters. After a preamble, Churchill had drafted five clauses pledging political freedom, personal security and economic justice for victors and vanquished alike after Hitler's defeat. The first three "glowed with Churchill's genius," Welles wrote later, but the last two seemed "too vague or too sweeping." Roosevelt insisted that Congress would have to be assured that no secret commitments had been made; only "parallel principles, voluntarily adopted." He indicated the changes he wanted and Welles returned to the *Tuscaloosa*, spending the afternoon editing the prose of a master.

Churchill's preamble implied an alliance, so he changed "their" policy to policies of "their respective governments." Churchill's first three clauses— no aggrandizement, no forced territorial changes and self-rule for all—seemed essential in their import and admirable in their clarity, he wrote later, but the fourth, or economic, clause promising "fair and equitable" distribution of the world's resources seemed meaningless; "the same pious hope which had characterized countless economic conferences, changing nothing." By contrast, Hull's reciprocal trade program had begun moving the United States away from high tariffs, expanding trade and easing tensions.

Unless Britain agreed to scrap imperial preferences (e.g., the 1932 Ottawa Agreements) that bound members of the British empire to trade exclusively among themselves, virtually barring U.S. goods, hopes of a new and better world order would be stillborn.[20] Accordingly, Welles redrafted Churchill's economic clause—binding Britain, the United States and future signatories to eliminate "any" discrimination and to open markets and natural resources to "all peoples (victors and vanquished alike) on equal terms," after the war.

Churchill's final, or disarmament, clause also seemed vague so Welles strengthened it—carefully retaining his proposal for a postwar "international organization," a goal for which Welles had fought for a quarter century and whose time, he felt, had come.[21] That night he dined as Cadogan's guest aboard the *Prince of Wales,* staying on after the other Americans had left. Lord Halifax, Britain's Foreign Secretary, had written Cadogan before the meeting: "Try to get along with Welles who has been playing the game very well, lately, and is all out to help." Cadogan was beginning to agree. Welles, he wrote in his diary, "improves upon acquaintance. It is a pity that he swallowed a ram-rod in his youth."[22]

Early on Monday, August 11, Welles handed FDR his revisions of Churchill's draft. Seizing a pencil, the President strengthened the disarmament clause, stipulating that not only nations which threatened aggression but those which "may threaten" would be disarmed. To Welles's disappointment, however, he dropped Churchill's proposed "international organization," arguing that no such body would be needed until the United States and Britain had disarmed countries whose quarrels had repeatedly involved the major powers in war and whose armaments had bankrupted their peoples. France was, almost certainly, on his mind.

Anglo-American "policing" of the postwar world was uppermost in FDR's thinking at Argentia, wrote Welles, Cooperation with Soviet Russia, then desperately staving off Hitler's invasion, did not occur to him. Finally satisfied, he told Welles to join him at eleven that morning for a meeting with Churchill, Cadogan and Hopkins.[23] The meeting proved stormy.

Churchill objected strenuously when Roosevelt suggested issuing the Joint Declaration with a statement making clear that he and Churchill had discussed Lend-Lease but "no future commitments," thus avoiding any hint of a treaty requiring Senate confirmation. The Germans would seize on any such statement, and it would discourage the British people, the neutrals and "all under the Nazi yoke," Churchill protested. Roosevelt argued that the disclaimer was essential to quell isolationist fears of secret agreements but gave way when Churchill urged him to emphasize the positive, not the negative.

Churchill now turned to Welles's revisions. On reaching the economic clause and Welles's "without any discrimination" and "all peoples on equal terms," he asked balefully whether this was not aimed at the Ottawa Agreements. Of course it was, Welles acknowledged: For nine years, the United States had been trying to eliminate artificial barriers to world trade. "I could not help mentioning," Churchill wrote later, "the British experience in adhering to free trade for eighty years in the face of ever-mounting American tariffs. Mr Welles seemed to be a little taken aback."[24]

He had opposed the Ottawa Agreements when they were adopted in 1932, and still opposed them, Churchill asserted, but he could not abandon them without consulting the Dominions—and this would take a week. If Welles's "without any discrimination" were replaced by "with due respect for their existing obligations" (e. g. , the Ottawa Agreements), he might persuade the cabinet to approve the Joint Declaration immediately. Hopkins, seeing the declaration's world impact threatened by delay, suggested that Welles and Cadogan draft new "phraseology" but Welles's obstinacy now surfaced. It was not a question of phraseology but of vital principle, he insisted. If the British and American governments could not agree to restore free, liberal trade after the war, "we might as well throw in the sponge."

Persuaded by Hopkins's preference for speed over principle, Roosevelt told Welles to iron out the differences with Churchill and Cadogan before the next meeting at 3 P.M. In the interim, Hopkins won FDR over. At five minutes before three, Welles received a handwritten note: "Dear Sumner: Time being of the essence, I think I can stand on my own former formulas—to wit: access to raw materials. This omits, entirely, discrimination in trade. The other subject which is the only one in conflict: For *me*, that is consistent. Yrs. FDR"[25] Welles had been overruled and imperial preferences saved. "Welles was right on principle and Hopkins was wrong," Sherwood wrote later. "Hopkins did not like the hedging phrase any better than Welles but he was less aware of its consequences and he so persuaded the President."[26]

Alone with FDR at day's end, Welles confessed that he had been "surprised and somewhat discouraged" by the President's morning suggestion that that nothing could be more "futile" than a body like the Assembly of the League of Nations. If the President foresaw a postwar transition period during which Great Britain and the United States "policed" the world, it would be enormously desirable to have a "safety valve" such as an assembly in which that the smaller powers could air complaints and make recommendations to the policing powers. To exclude Nazi-occupied countries such as Belgium, the Netherlands or Norway or the Latin American republics would be impossible.

Roosevelt agreed: he had intended only to make clear that, during the postwar transition when the United States and Britain would be disarming aggressors and policing the world, no organization like the Council or Assembly of the League of Nations could exercise the same "powers and prerogatives" as they had during the League's existence. A solution might be found through the "ostensible" joining of the smaller powers to Great Britain and the United States. But it would only be ostensible, as none of the smaller nations would have the "practical means of taking any effective, or considerable, part in policing."[27]

Churchill and Hopkins had been as dismayed as Welles by FDR's refusal to consider an "international" organization and begged him to retain it. FDR argued that any reference to such an organization would arouse congressional misgivings; indeed, even as they were meeting, the House of Representatives in Washington extended the draft by a mere one-vote margin—an example of congressional truculence not lost on Churchill. Roosevelt knew in his heart that civilization could not survive without some form of international organization, Welles wrote, but in August 1941 his mind was on the immediate, not the ultimate. "First things first," he told his Under Secretary.

Eventually, persuaded by Churchill, Welles and Hopkins, Roosevelt accepted an oblique formula that Churchill himself drafted. Disarmament of aggressors would be essential, it read, pending the establishment of a "wider and permanent system of general security." Out of this mouse of circumlocution emerged the United Nations.

The joint warning to Japan, meanwhile, remained unsettled. Six months earlier, Roosevelt had sent Welles a MAGIC (a U.S. term for Japanese codes) decrypt of Foreign Minister Matsuoka's instructions to Nomura in Washington, noting that they reflected "a mind deeply disturbed and unable to think quietly, or logically."[28] His freeze of Japan's assets had shocked Tokyo, leading to new proposals, he reminded Churchill. He had no illusions about Japanese negotiating tactics but thought them worth pursuing, if only to gain an extra month for rearmament.

He would keep the "economic screws on tight," but a public warning might cost the Japanese loss of face, which would be dangerously provocative in their current frame of mind. He preferred "parallel" warnings to a "joint" warning. On returning to Washington, he would summon Nomura and, in the privacy of the Oval Office, hand him a note incorporating Churchill's "hard language": in other words, specifying U.S. countermeasures leading to war if Japan continued its aggression.[29]

Suspecting FDR of temporizing, Churchill asked to see the text but was told it had not yet been drafted. In fact, it never was. Hull protested that a stiff warning might derail his talks with the Japanese with whom he had been negotiating for months. Hull's heart, wrote Sherwood, was "set on peace above everything."[30] On Tuesday, August 12, Roosevelt and Churchill approved the final Welles-Cadogan draft of the Joint Declaration, and the Atlantic Charter was officially born. Now comprising eight (not five) clauses, it read:

FIRST, their countries seek no aggrandizement, territorial or other;

SECOND, they desire to see no territorial changes that do not accord with the freely expressed wishes of the people concerned;

THIRD, they respect the right of all peoples to choose the form of government under which they live; and they wish to see sovereign rights and self-government restored to those who have been forcibly deprived of them;

FOURTH, they will endeavor, with due respect for their existing obligations, to further the enjoyment by all States, great or small, victor or vanquished, of access, on equal terms, to the trade and to the raw materials of the world which are needed for their economic prosperity;

FIFTH, they desire to bring about the fullest collaboration between all nations in the economic field with the object of securing, for all, improved labor standards, economic advancement and social security;

SIXTH, after the final destruction of the Nazi tyranny, they hope to see established a peace which will afford to all nations the means of dwelling in safety within their own boundaries, and which will afford assurance that all the men in all the lands may live out their lives in freedom from fear and want;

SEVENTH, such a peace should enable all men to traverse the high seas and oceans without hindrance;

EIGHTH, they believe that all of the nations of the world, for realistic as well as spiritual reasons, must come to the abandonment of the use of force. Since no future peace can be maintained if land, sea or air armaments continue to be employed by nations which threaten, or may threaten, aggression outside of their frontiers, they believe, pending the establishment of a wider and permanent system of general security, that the disarmament of such nations is essential. They will likewise aid and encourage all other practicable measures which will lighten for peace-loving peoples the crushing burden of armaments.

by Franklin D. Roosevelt

Winston Churchill

During their four days at sea, Roosevelt and Churchill had come to know each other and appreciate each other's problems. Welles and Cadogan, too, had begun to thaw. "I have hobnobbed with [Welles] a lot and have tried to get through his reserve," wrote the tart little Englishman. "I believe him to be sound at heart and Edward [Lord] Halifax assures me this is so."[31]

Welles played no part in the military talks, and, in fact, the only decision of military importance at Argentia was FDR's order to the U.S. Navy to escort convoys as far east as Iceland, freeing Britain's hard-pressed destroyers for other duties. Elliott Roosevelt wrote later that the afternoon military sessions were "something of a breakdown from the ideal unity" of the morning political talks. The British fought for additional Lend-Lease for the United Kingdom while Marshall, King and Arnold argued that more should go to the Soviet Union, "which was fighting the Germans."[32]

The Atlantic Charter meeting, in personal terms, marked the peak of Welles's career. "Sumner Welles was the man who worked hardest on the Charter and who contributed most," Elliott Roosevelt remembered. "It was his baby from the time it was first considered back in Washington. He'd flown from Washington with a working draft of the final agreement in his briefcase; and all the world knows how important a statement it was, and is."[33]

Roosevelt and Churchill had not achieved all that they would have wished, Welles wrote later, but their meeting marked the end of U.S. isolationism, assuring peoples beyond the Western Hemisphere that the United States was "finally turning from a negative to a positive foreign policy . . .

enlightened international cooperation."[34] Within six weeks the Soviet Union and thirty-nine other nations had endorsed the charter. On New Year's day, 1942, it became the only formal link binding these united nations together through World War II.

The Atlantic Charter was announced simultaneously in Washington and London on August 14, 1941. FDR ordered Welles to withhold the names of those attending for two more days. "He wants the press release to stand out like a 'sore thumb' with nothing to detract from it, or cause any other discussion," Admiral Stark wrote Welles. "Then, when it has had time to be thoroughly digested, just of itself, go ahead and give out the names of the rest of the party."[35] By then Churchill was racing home aboard the *Prince of Wales,* dodging Hitler's U-boats.

The Atlantic Charter was an "interim, partial" statement of war aims, not the complete structure to be created after victory, he cabled the cabinet. Quick approval was essential, however, as Roosevelt thought it might "affect the whole movement of U.S. opinion." Churchill thought it astonishing that the neutral United States had signed such a document with belligerent Britain. The reference to final destruction of Nazi tyranny implied "war-like U.S. action," and the final clause left no doubt that the United States would "join us in policing the world" after victory.[36]

As to the joint warning to Japan, he had tried but failed. "Our hope had been to induce the President to give a strong warning to Japan," he cabled London, but, apart from economic pressures and calling in Nomura, the President seemed to think that this was the "most that he could do . . . He may have been under the influence of Mr. Sumner Welles who seemed to be of the opinion that the time for warnings was past."[37]

Once home, Churchill broadcast this message to his people: "We came back across the ocean waves, uplifted in spirit, fortified in resolve. Some American destroyers, which were carrying mail to the U.S. Marines in Iceland, happened to be going the same way, too, so we made a goodly company at sea together."[38] Aboard one of them was Ensign Franklin D. Roosevelt, Jr.

American reaction to the Atlantic Charter was favorable; world reaction was muted. The Axis Powers paid it scant attention, while the British had been hoping for something more concrete than high-flown principles. Wary of isolationist outcries, Roosevelt himself seemed initially to tiptoe away from his and Churchill's brainchild, telling newsmen who asked to see the charter that it "did not exist." Like the British constitution, the whole world understood and appreciated it. He and Churchill had dictated parts; Welles and Cadogan had handwritten other parts. On examining the only copy in his files, the President had found both signatures in his own handwriting. The important thing, said

FDR, was that Britain had been losing the war when the charter was drafted and it had given the British hope.[39]

The Atlantic Charter became "incalculably more powerful as an instrument of human freedom" than Churchill and his colleagues had imagined, Sherwood wrote later. The subject peoples of India, Burma, Malaya and Indonesia began asking if it also extended to the Pacific and Asia, and the doughty old champion of empire had to reassure a restive House of Commons that the charter, when written, had been aimed at "Europe's enslaved millions, quite separate," he said, from the "progressive evolution toward self-government" found in the regions and peoples owing allegiance to the Crown.[40]

FDR told Wallace later that it had been "his idea all along" that the charter applied to the Pacific as well as to the Atlantic. Churchill had been responsible for calling it the Atlantic Charter. Churchill also thought it applied to the wider area until he got "mixed up in the Indian trouble [India's demand for independence] and took the slant that it would not apply to the East."[41]

Consciously or not, Roosevelt, Churchill, Welles, Hopkins and Cadogan had lit a small candle of hope on warships off the Newfoundland coast in August 1941. Ten years later, fanned by postwar discontent and delays in providing the better world promised at Argentia, their candle would blaze up into global anticolonialism, ending centuries of white rule over Africa and Asia.

After the clean air and high purpose of Argentia, Washington seemed a purgatory to Welles: the same back-biting and jealousy. Hull, bitter at having been excluded, blamed Welles for failing to scuttle the Ottawa Agreements, baffling Moffat, who had heard Hull predict before the meeting that "all that could be expected from the British at Argentia was a general statement of policy." The only explanation was fatigue, wrote Moffat, "everyone, from highest to lowest, is so tired that the quality of work and thinking is not up to its usual standard."[42]

The White House was in an equally sullen mood. Breckinridge Long asked for an urgent appointment with FDR at Welles's suggestion, and found "Pa" Watson truculently protective of the President's time and energy, blaming Welles for "constantly" asking for appointments. Hull was threatening again to resign, said Watson. He was the "best thing" in the cabinet and the administration's greatest asset. Welles was trying to take over his functions by continually conferring with FDR who "felt the same way."[43] Weary in mind and body, Welles entrained with Mathilde at the end of August for a vacation in Maine, eager to flee the capital's poisonous atmosphere for the fresh winds of Mt. Desert island.

"Too glorious!" Mathilde wrote a friend in Washington. "Open fires all day but hot in the sun. I've had five perfect swims with water at 54! Sumner refuses to go in, too icy. We walk miles and go [sailing] on water in P. M. [He] feels so well. How I hate to leave this place."[44]

In a large, rented house facing Blue Hill Bay and surrounded by Douglas firs, Welles began weighing how to exploit the impact of the Atlantic Charter before world, and especially American, interest faded: how to transform broad principles into concrete policies before the war ended. The peace conferences of Vienna (1815) and Paris (1919) had shown that victorious allies inevitably quarreled over spoils. The only "spoils" the United States was seeking was a just peace, based on practical common sense, but it would not be achieved if the country postponed action until the victors were quarreling again around the peace table.[45] The time had come to start serious planning for the postwar period.

Roosevelt, however, while paying lip service to postwar planning, was still hesitant. Unlike Welles, he did not believe that the failure of the United States to join the League of Nations in 1919-20 had led to its later collapse. He had repeatedly advocated joining the League during his 1920 vice-presidential campaign but then had grown bitter over Britain's cynical use of it for its own purposes in the 1930s. Moreover, having just renewed contact with Churchill after a quarter century, he suspected rightly that the Briton's goal was to bring the United States into the war. Wary of entanglements, he had rejected Churchill's "international organization" proposal at Argentia, reluctantly accepting a pallid euphemism under pressure.

Not until Pearl Harbor did Roosevelt believe that an organization of nontotalitarian states was feasible or that the United States should help create one, Welles remembered. By then, however, three developments had begun reshaping his thinking. The 1936 Buenos Aires conference had impressed him as an example of "regional cooperation." The violent policies of Hitler, Mussolini and Stalin in 1939-40 had "revolted" him. Finally, the Atlantic Charter conference had opened fresh vistas of international collaboration. After Pearl Harbor, Welles recalled, Roosevelt become "engrossed for the first time in the possibility of an effective international organization."[46]

Meanwhile, Bullitt had called on Ickes during Welles's Maine vacation, distressed at learning from FDR that there was to be no place for him in the defense buildup. He was "terribly hurt," wrote Ickes. "He told about his interview with a laugh, but it wasn't a merry laugh." FDR had been "stringing" him since his resignation as ambassador to France, Bullitt claimed, insisting that he intended to name him to some important post, then one first-class job after another would appear above the horizon and someone else would get it. Edward R. Stettinius, Jr. , for example, had just been named administrator of Lend-Lease—a position Bullitt wanted.

Suspecting a run-around and determined to force the issue, Bullitt had gone to Roosevelt, who had confirmed that he still intended to use him but had no available position commensurate with his abilities. Bullitt had blamed Harry Hopkins for his exclusion: Four people, he asserted, had related incidents to prove it. FDR had flared. "You may say to these people that the President of the United States says this is a damned lie."

Bullitt and Ickes agreed that Hopkins was, in effect, "assistant President." FDR seemed to like people near him who were "pale, sick and gaunt," Bullitt observed. Louis Howe had been one; Hopkins was another. Each was "cadaverous and bent and thin."[47]

Two months after the Atlantic Charter meeting, Welles resumed his campaign for postwar planning. Addressing the National Foreign Trade Convention in New York on October 7, he cited the prohibitively high, Republican-sponsored Smoot-Hawley tariff of 1930 and the further tariff increase of 1932 as "colossal blunders" that had brought poverty and despair to virtually every corner of the earth. America's export trade, faced by reciprocal discrimination and trade barriers, had been "immediately and disastrously" affected.

Warning against a return to "misguided" high-tariff policies, Welles reminded the nation's leading traders that the new Atlantic Charter aimed at promoting economic prosperity for "all nations, great, small, victors and vanquished, alike." There could be no greater misfortune than postponing planning until the war's end—a policy of "wait and see."[48]

A month later, on Armistice Day, he pursued his theme of preparation at the tomb of Woodrow Wilson in the Washington cathedral. Twenty-three years earlier to the day, he recalled, Wilson had notified Congress of the end of World War I. Now the United States was in far greater peril than in 1917. Japan was menacing every nation in the Far East and Hitler had reduced half of Europe to serfdom. Would the most powerful nation on earth again stand aloof, not lifting a finger while the "raucous voice of a criminal paranoiac, speaking from the cellar of a Munich beer hall," proclaimed the destruction of United States security and the annihilation of religious, political and economic liberty throughout the earth?

The American people would defend their freedom until Hitler's defeat—but what then? The high objectives proclaimed by Roosevelt and Churchill three months earlier at Argentia—liberty, security, freedom from want and fear—had to be "realized." The American people could decide the world they wanted to live in. Was it conceivable that they would again spurn that opportunity?

"War may be forced upon us at any moment," warned Welles—twenty-six days before the Japanese attacked Pearl Harbor.[49]

TWENTY-SIX

DEFENDING THE HEMISPHERE: THE RIO CONFERENCE

1942

"If Ever I Achieve Anything Worth Doing"

ON SUNDAY, DECEMBER 7, 1941, Welles arrived at the State Department shortly before 10 A.M. After a staff meeting, he and Berle turned to a presidential message to Congress, which they had begun drafting for FDR the day before. Around 2 P.M., they were leaving for a quick lunch at the nearby Mayflower Hotel when the President called Welles to report the Japanese attack on Pearl Harbor.[1]

Hull, too, had come in that morning. The Japanese embassy had asked for an urgent appointment at precisely 1:45 P.M. to allow Ambassador Kichisaburo Nomura and his "peace envoy" colleague, Saburo Kurusu, to deliver a 1,500-word cable from Tokyo. Seeking to ease U.S.-Japanese tension, Hull had met with them sixty times over the preceding ten months, usually at night in his Carlton Hotel apartment.

The Japanese arrived late. By then Hull had learned from the President of the attack, which had occurred at 1:20 P.M. Washington time. Knox had telephoned FDR with the news at 1:47 P.M. As the Japanese arrived, Hull had also learned of the contents of the cable from decrypts and deliberately kept them waiting fifteen minutes. He received them standing at his desk, obliging them to stand as well. Glancing contemptuously at their message, he said that never in fifty years of public life had he seen a document more crowded with "infamous falsehoods and distortions."

Twelve icy minutes later, the Japanese trailed forlornly out past reporters as Welles and Berle entered Hull's office and heard him telephone FDR with news of his scathing condemnation and the Japanese reaction. "That's grand, Cordell" was Roosevelt's only comment.[2] The White House announced the attack at 2:25 P.M.

Hull crossed Executive Avenue to the White House, leaving Welles to alert U.S. missions and friendly governments around the world; Berle to arrange for the confinement of Japanese diplomats and their isolation (along with the Germans and Italians) from all communications; and Long to order U.S. frontiers closed to enemy aliens. The President conferred throughout the afternoon and evening with Hull, Stimson, Knox, Marshall, Stark and senior military commanders, making the Oval Office a national war room.

The cabinet arrived at 8:30 P.M., forming a ring around FDR as he sat solemnly at his desk, noting that it was the most important cabinet meeting since Lincoln summoned his cabinet at the start of the Civil War. He read his war message to Congress aloud. Hull thought it inadequate but FDR stuck to his guns, determined, Hopkins remembered, to make it an understatement. "Nothing too explosive."[3] At 9:30 congressional leaders arrived and agreed that the President would deliver his message at the Capitol the next day at noon. Shortly before 11 P.M. Hull left for home, exhausted, and Welles replaced him, remaining an hour. When he left, FDR cleared everyone out and announced that he was going to bed.[4]

His immediate priority was to reinforce the Pacific fleet, protect the vital Panama Canal and rally the hemisphere. Thanks largely to the Good Neighbor policy, Latin American support for the United States was immediate. Within three days, nine countries had declared war on the Axis—Panama, the Dominican Republic, Cuba, Haiti, and the five Central American states: Guatemala, Nicaragua, El Salvador, Honduras and Costa Rica—two weeks later Mexico, Colombia and Venezuela broke relations. Meanwhile, the "Big Three"—Argentina, Brazil and Chile—were awaiting U.S. leadership. On December 10, Roosevelt convened an emergency meeting of hemisphere Foreign Ministers to gather at Rio de Janeiro on January 15. Welles would represent the United States.

Rio had been selected deliberately. Brazil had traditionally been the strongest supporter of the U.S. in the hemisphere and, with Rio as the conference site, Welles's close friend, Foreign Minister Oswaldo Aranha, would automatically become chairman. Welles and Aranha began planning for a unanimous break with the Axis. Early in January, however, the Argentine Foreign Minister, Enrique Ruiz-Guiñazu, announced that hemisphere solidarity implied "neither military alliances nor automatic arrangements."[5] It was clear that Argentina, and probably Chile, would resist. The year before Welles had heard Ruiz-Guiñazu praise Mussolini and Spain's dictator, Francisco Franco, in Washington and wrote later that he was "one of the stupidest men ever to hold office in Argentina's proud history."[6]

To round up hemisphere support, Welles began holding out hope of faster arms deliveries. Following the passage of Lend-Lease the year before, Roosevelt had allocated $400 million for arms to Latin America over the next three years: $100 million of it in 1942. General Marshall protested, however, that "shortages make it practically impossible to find anything for immediate, or even reasonably prompt, delivery." Welles took it to Roosevelt. The United States had signed seven Lend-Lease arms agreements with Latin American republics, and others were pending, he pointed out. Failure to honor these commitments would have an "exceedingly unfortunate" effect at Rio.

The outlook for a diplomatic victory at Rio was grim. In the early-morning Japanese air attack on Pearl Harbor, Sunday, December 7, 1941, the U.S. had lost nineteen naval vessels (including eight battleships) sunk or seriously damaged. In addition, 188 military aircraft were destroyed; 2,280 U.S. military personnel were killed and 1,109 wounded. Sixty-eight U.S. civilians were also killed or wounded. The attack had exposed the entire Pacific coast from Canada to Chile to Japanese attack. The bulk of the U.S. fleet was pinned down in the Atlantic escorting convoys to Britain and to the Soviet Union, highlighting the navy's dread of a two-ocean war and a one-ocean navy. Marshall and Stark were opposing further Latin American declarations of war lest the United States be forced to disperse its limited resources protecting weak republics from the Rio Grande to Tierra del Fuego. Except for obsolete aircraft and coast artillery, the Panama Canal was virtually defenseless. Peru and Ecuador were still fighting over their jungle border, and, meanwhile, growing numbers of Latin Americans were beginning to believe that an Axis victory was inevitable.[8]

Nonetheless, there was reason for hope. The Good Neighbor policy and Hull's reciprocal trade program had won the United States unprecedented friendship, and, eighteen Latin republics, apart from Argentina and Chile, had indicated their approval for a break.

Reviewing strategy in the White House on January 7, Welles's last night in Washington before the conference, FDR and he agreed that the chief U.S. goal should be a unanimous break with the Axis Powers. U.S. military and economic aid would be offered Latin American republics willing to resist Axis pressure. Argentina and Chile, however, would almost certainly oppose a break. Argentina's democratic president, Roberto Ortiz, had resigned recently because of illness, and his successor, Vice President Ramon Castillo, was a confirmed isolationist and narrow reactionary.

Backed by a German-trained army, by ultra-nationalists and rich landowners, Castillo had declared a state of siege and was ruling by decree, muzzling the press and stifling criticism of his Axis leanings. In Chile, elections were imminent and the provisional government probably would not risk a Japanese attack on its undefended, 3,000-mile coast.

In bidding Roosevelt farewell, Welles made a final plea: Whatever the difficulties, every effort should be made to preserve hemisphere unity. Roosevelt gave his "whole-hearted approval," Welles wrote later. "He wished me good luck with a smile and characteristic wave of the hand."[9] Roosevelt's approval in advance of Welles's policy at Rio later saved the hemisphere from a catastrophic split—and Welles's career as well.

Mathilde was ill, unable to make the arduous journey, so he penned her a farewell note that night. "Never forget how much I love you. No one on earth means so much to me as you and, if ever I achieve anything worth doing, it will be because of your help, and your love, and your confidence." Achievement, as always, was uppermost in his mind as he approached a major challenge.

After an "appalling" three-day flight from Miami through tropical storms and over jungle, Welles's seaplane taxied into Rio harbor. "Bedlam broke loose," he wrote Mathilde. "The crowd surged in, cheering, all police lines vanished. I found myself being grabbed one way by Aranha, another by [War Minister Gaspar] Dutra, pushed this way and that, losing hats, papers, etc."[10]

Weighing strategy in advance, Welles took a calculated risk, bringing American reporters covering the conference into his confidence. Many were veteran foreign affairs analysts and some, like Drew Pearson, personal friends. Each morning he predicted on background what he thought might happen; at day's end, what had actually happened. He spoke with the "utmost frankness," Eric Sevareid remembered. Argentina could not be permitted to jeopardize U.S. security but hemisphere unity remained paramount.[11]

"The U.S. press [can] do as much to further our foreign policy as our official diplomacy," Welles wrote later. "By reporting the facts, accurately and objectively, the press can make it possible for the American public to know, not only what that policy is but—quite as important—the reasons for it. Throughout the conference, I reported every development whether confidential or not."[12]

On the eve of the conference, Welles was studying official papers in his Copacabana Hotel suite when his aide, Emilio "Pete" Collado, walked in without knocking, thinking him out. Collado's arms were filled with documents, but he had forgotten the ocean wind; on opening the door, it blew the papers around the room and slammed the door shut behind him with a deafening bang. He tripped, fell flat and looked up to see Welles observing him with amusement. "Are you having trouble, Pete?" he asked mildly. Collado was ecstatic. Never before had his awesome chief addressed him by his nickname.[13]

The conference opened on January 15 at the aptly named Tiradentes (Tooth-puller) Palace. In his address Welles urged the hemisphere republics to sever ties immediately and unanimously with the Axis. The "shibboleth of classic neutrality" no longer applied. Despite Pearl Harbor, the United States would fight and in the coming year—1942—would build 45,000 warplanes, 45,000 tanks and 600 merchant ships.[14] Economic warfare was equally important, and the United States would provide financial and technical aid to Latin American republics that suppressed Axis economic activity.[15]

Hours after his address, Welles fell mysteriously ill and his delegation feared a heart attack. Ambassador Jefferson Caffery prepared to sit in for him, but Welles insisted that nothing be reported to Hull lest he be replaced. The next day, Collado remembered, he appeared "as if nothing had happened."[16]

During the conference, Mexico, Colombia and Venezuela urged their sister republics to follow their example and break with the Axis. Predictably, Argentina objected and Berle cabled Welles: "Feeling in Department, from Secretary Hull down, is [that] a breach in unanimity . . . preferable to a compromise formula. The Argentines must accept the situation or go their own way."[17] Welles, at that juncture, agreed. Aranha was still optimistic about Argentine cooperation, although Welles personally suspected only a "fifty-fifty" chance of getting it. "Every effort should be made to preserve unanimity," he cabled Hull, "[but] if the Argentine government is unwilling to join in a continental declaration for a severance of relations with the Axis powers, Argentina should be allowed to proceed alone."[18] A week later, faced with the danger of a hemisphere split, Welles would reverse course.

The key to success lay in keeping Brazil in line. "The issue did not turn around the attitude of Argentina, but of Brazil," Duggan wrote later. "The situation facing Welles was never adequately disclosed."[19] Long isolated among its Spanish-speaking neighbors, Portuguese-speaking Brazil had traditionally sought friendship with the United States to counter its major rival, Argentina.

Brazil would break with the Axis, Aranha assured Welles, but he privately confided that the three Axis ambassadors had threatened a "state of war" if Brazil cut diplomatic ties with their countries. Given the large German, Italian and Japanese communities in southern Brazil near the Argentine border, the Brazilian President, Getulio Vargas, was taking the threat seriously.

Nazi Germany had been pouring money, organizers and propaganda into German communities, especially in southern Brazil, for years, Sevareid reported from Rio. Berlin regarded Brazil as its "greatest overseas plum." Nazi pilots had plotted every potential air and naval base on the country's long, unprotected coast, and many Brazilian army officers were of German descent. General Pedro Aurelio Goes Monteiro, the army Chief of Staff, held Hitler's Grand Cross of the German Eagle and reminded Sevareid that 2 million Germans and Italians and 300,000 Japanese had settled in southern Brazil. If Hitler seized Dakar, across the Atlantic narrows in West Africa, he warned, this "fifth column would rise."[20]

Determined to hold Brazil in line, Welles sent FDR a triple-priority cable on January 18, urging immediate arms deliveries. Brazil had received virtually no U.S. arms for eighteen months, and its High Command was not "enthusiastic" about risking war with the Axis. The situation was critical; the Nazis could exploit it.

"Marshall says it is not safe to give Brazil arms which they may use against us," he cabled, "but [an Axis-inspired] revolution in Brazil might have fatal repercussions . . . If we felt it necessary to move by force into Northeast Brazil, the effort might be far greater than we care to envisage. Vargas believes he can depend on you. I'd like to be specifically authorized to tell him you'll give orders if he'll give me a list of military requirements."[21]

Welles was also working to win over Chile. Its Foreign Minister, Juan Bautista Rossetti, assured him in a four-hour talk that he was expecting momentarily instructions to vote for a diplomatic rupture. As an added inducement, Welles recommended priority Lend-Lease arms for Chile as well. "Please do not sign the agreement in Washington at this time but, rather, let me use it in my discussions here," he cabled.[22]

Hoping to use Chile to pressure Argentina, he wired Norman Armour, the U.S. ambassador in Buenos Aires: "Aranha and I have agreed to wait until we are sure that we have Chile positively with us. If and when that time comes, I shall telegraph you, urgently, to seek an immediate interview with Castillo."[23]

Ruiz-Guiñazu had argued initially that Japan's attack on Pearl Harbor was not an attack on a "hemisphere" country, despite the Stars-and-Stripes flying over the Hawaiian islands. When Welles, Aranha and their Latin allies laid this tortured logic to rest, Welles reported that the Argentine Foreign Minister was "wavering, vacillating and increasingly unhappy about his country's isolation."

The pressure was mounting and the next day, January 21, Aranha told Welles triumphantly that the Argentine had finally consented to a break with the Axis. This was a "welcome surprise," Welles wrote laconically.[24]

He spent the afternoon with his fellow delegates drafting a resolution. Ruiz-Guiñazu "haggled over this and that word," Welles wrote, but eventually agreed to a resolution stating that the twenty-one hemisphere nations "cannot continue" relations since Japan had attacked, and Germany and Italy had declared war on, a continental American nation.

At day's end, reporters saw Welles smiling broadly as he descended the foreign ministry steps. Briefing them later, he predicted that a unanimous resolution to break with the Axis would be adopted by all twenty-one delegations—including Argentina's—the next day. Their euphoric dispatches sent Washington's hopes soaring.

The next day, in fact, proved one of the worst in Welles's career. Aranha called early to report that, overnight, Argentine President Castillo had reversed his Foreign Minister, refusing to break with the Axis and leaving the conference in chaos. A compromise was imperative. Brazil's military chiefs would not risk war with the Axis unless Argentina was equally committed. If the Axis attacked Brazil, Argentina might seize the occasion to invade Brazil's southern provinces. Stunned, Welles asked for an immediate meeting with President Vargas, who received him at his mountaintop hideout. Confirming Aranha's grim warning, Vargas begged Welles not to force Brazil into an open quarrel with Argentina, splitting the hemisphere.

After reporting to Washington, Welles returned to the foreign ministry, finding his fellow delegates as indignant as he over Castillo's overnight switch yet determined to preserve hemisphere unity. If Argentina and Chile were drummed out, they warned, each could become a hotbed of Axis subversion. Attempts to draft an acceptable compromise resumed, with the Argentines and Chileans rejecting formula after formula. Finally, importuned by their weary colleagues after hours of fruitless discussion, they agreed to "recommend" breaking with the Axis to their respective legislatures. Welles now faced a dilemma.

While neither as "peremptory or clear-cut" as the earlier version, he wrote later, the compromise involved no essential difference. For the first time, Argentina and Chile had gone on record in "recommending" that the hemisphere nations, themselves included, break with the Axis. Eventually every legislature, including the U.S. Congress, would have to ratify resolutions adopted at Rio. Brazil would not break relations unless Argentina and Chile agreed to, and, without Brazil, the conference would collapse.

Delay would give Argentina further excuse for backtracking, and the war situation was critical. Singapore had just fallen to the Japanese, General (later Field

Marshall) Erwin Rommel's Afrika Korps was advancing on Egypt and the U.S. Joint Chiefs feared that Germany might at any time invade the bulge of Brazil.[25] The conference was waiting and his decision would spell success or failure.

Recalling Roosevelt's parting instructions to "preserve unity," Welles seized the nettle and accepted the compromise. That night—Friday, January 23—the twenty-one hemisphere republics, including Argentina and Chile, voted unanimously to "recommend" breaking with the Axis. After the vote, Welles cabled Hull that the "concrete" effect was "exactly the same" as that in the text previously agreed on two days earlier.[26] Unity had been preserved—at a price.

Meanwhile, in Washington, Hull had begun hearing late-night radio reports of an Argentine "victory." The United States, they said, had accepted a nonbinding "milk-and-water" resolution; the "lowest common denominator;" United States prestige was at "low ebb." Summoning Berle and Duggan to his hotel apartment, he seized the telephone at 2 A.M.—midnight in Rio. Welles was climbing into bed, exhausted after forty-eight hours' nonstop negotiating, when his telephone rang. The half-hour conversation was "violent," Berle remembered years later. Quivering with fury, Hull accused Welles of having "gotten us into a fine mess . . . I never gave you 'carty blanchy' [sic] to act for us!" he roared. Welles was to inform the conference next day that he had not been authorized to accept the compromise, to switch his vote and oppose it. Argentina, Hull's pet detestation since the 1936 Buenos Aires conference, was to be treated as an "outlaw."

Weary, angry and better aware of the situation, Welles stood his ground. "I tried to remind Secretary Hull that I had received specific authorization from President Roosevelt to take precisely [the] action that I had taken," he wrote later. Hull refused to listen. Welles, he snapped, was being "ingenuous—not a single government would carry out its commitments." Facing the most critical moment of his career, Welles demanded to speak personally to the President, who, fortunately, was in the White House.

After a three-way conversation, Roosevelt made his decision. "I'm sorry, Cordell, but in this case I am going to take the judgment of the man on the spot," he said. "Sumner, I approve what you have done. I authorize you to follow the lines you have recommended."[27] As in the case of Cuba nine years earlier, he had taken Welles's advice over Hull's; and Hull would never forgive either of them.

Meanwhile, Caffery, too, was backing Welles: "General feeling here," he cabled Hull, "far better . . . to secure . . . adhesion of Argentina and Chile to this formula [e.g., to *recommend* a break] than . . . to a more ideal formula [e.g., to *insist on* a break] without them."[28] Elated by FDR's support, Welles and Caffery "really tied one on that night," Reeks remembered. The next morning he awakened Welles at the usual 7 A.M., and Miss Clarkson arrived with urgent cables for approval. Welles struggled to his desk in a dressing gown, scrawled his signature, threw down the pen, glared at them both and returned to bed without a word.[29]

Later that day he wrote thanking FDR for his support. "You will understand my feeling of amazement and complete confusion as a result of my conversation with the Secretary of State last night," he wrote.

> It has been manifestly impossible for me in the . . . constant turmoil and continuous [meetings] . . . to request prior authorization for . . . every word . . . I took it for granted that, so long as the desired objectives were attained and . . . the policy you and the Secretary of State had approved was carried out, I was entitled to have sufficient confidence from the Secretary . . . to agree upon texts.

Meaniwhile, the Brazilian press was hailing a "triumph." Brazil, Mexico and other republics thought the compromise "stronger and more satisfactory" than the original. Had the United States forced Argentina and Chile out of the American line-up, it would have been criticized from one end of the continent to the other for breaking a united front and forcing its own views on Argentina and Chile to "save American skins." Nothing would have pleased the Axis more. "We have achieved . . . a result which is the safest for the interests of our own country," he concluded. "May I say, again, how deeply grateful I am for your [support] last night."[30]

The United States won other important goals at Rio. An inter-American Defense Board was set up in Washington and an Emergency Committee for Political Defense (to combat enemy subversion) in Montevideo. Sixteen trade pacts were signed, a half-million tons of Axis shipping added to the inter-American shipping pool and agreements reached on orderly distribution of hemisphere surpluses. The festering Peruvian-Ecuadorean border war was ended with Welles's help. His appearance on the closing day, January 28, brought "thunderous cheers," wrote the *Chicago Daily News*. "Many thought he had saved the conference."[31]

Boarding his plane for home the next day, he was handed a cable— extraordinary in the circumstances: "Heartiest congratulations on the fine and outstanding part you played all the way through the meeting at Rio. Your leadership was powerfully effective throughout the proceedings. [signed] Hull."[32]

American press reaction was strikingly favorable. The *New York Journal of Commerce* thought Argentina had won a "diplomatic victory,"[33] but the *Washington Post* called the conference an "overwhelming success" for the United States.[34] The *Philadelphia Inquirer* hailed Welles's "personal achieve-ment,"[35] and Marquis Childs, in the *St. Louis Post-Dispatch,* thought Rio a "diplomatic miracle."[36] *Time* praised Welles's decision as "statesmanlike and shrewd . . . From being practically isolated from its twenty sister American republics nine years ago," it wrote, "the U.S. has become one of the most popular nations in the hemisphere. Argentina has isolated herself."[37] Even Hull's favorite eulogist, Arthur Krock of the *New York Times,* wrote that Welles had returned "with his country's praises."[38]

As at Buenos Aires six years earlier, however, the price had been high. Adolf Berle and Laurence Duggan, two of Welles's closest associates, sided with Hull. Duggan thought the compromise a "disaster," while Berle noted that "our moral leadership has been lost. There is a breach between the Secretary and Sumner which will never be healed."[39] Since his "blow-up" with Welles over Rio, Berle continued, Hull had been nervously and spiritually "torn to pieces," confined to bed by his doctor.

> The Rio incident raises the question as to who is the real Secretary of State. In cabling [sic] the President in defense of his course, Sumner intimated that there had been a major decision of policy which he had agreed on with the President, without reporting to Secretary Hull. At least, Hull had no recollection of it . . . I propose . . . tackling Sumner . . . and trying to bring some kind of a working relationship between the two men. A breach in wartime would be fatal . . .
>
> It will be difficult. Sumner is . . . preserving a direct line of power through the White House, irrespective of the Secretary; the Secretary will be satisfied with nothing less than cutting that off . . . [Hull] is slow in making up his mind . . . but his judgment is far better than Sumner's. Sumner, on the other hand, will move like a shot in all directions. It is essential that the values of both be preserved.[40]

Nine months later, on the eve of operation TORCH, the Anglo-American landings in North Africa on November 8, 1942, Welles sent Caffery a dramatic, triple-priority cable: "On receipt of a flash message which will be sent to you very shortly and which will consist solely of two words 'Deliver message,' please deliver, personally the following from the President to Vargas." The message, drafted by Welles, read:

> For the defense of all the Americas and, particularly Brazil, it is imperative that action be taken to prevent an occupation by the Axis of French Africa. It would be difficult for me to express the full appreciation of this government of the invaluable assistance which Brazil has given and is giving in our joint war effort. Warmest regards. FDR.[41]

FDR's tribute to Brazil's "invaluable" assistance was not hyperbole. Without Brazil, Welles wrote later, U.S. intelligence in the hemisphere would have been crippled. Axis sabotage and coups d'etat would have been more likely, and the hemisphere would have been split, arousing widespread anti-U.S. feeling. A neutral Brazil, moreover, would have barred the United States from using its ports in the war on Hitler's U-boats in the south Atlantic or from building the airfields on its north eastern "bulge" through which ferried the U.S. warplanes that turned the tide at El Alamein, supported the landings in North Africa and, eventually, carried the war to Japan.[42] Two years later, in a remarkable volte face, Hull wrote:

> At the blackest moment of the war, during the meeting of foreign ministers at Rio de Janeiro, our sister republics raised their banners alongside ours. They opened their ports to our ships. They welcomed and quartered our troops on their soil. They devoted their mines, their forests and their fields to the intensive production of strategic war materials. They rounded up Axis spies and saboteurs and they shut off trade of benefit to the Axis. They cooperated in the defense of the Panama canal and in the suppression of the submarine menace.
>
> When Rommel was hammering at the gates of Egypt, it was planes and light-tank ammunition ferried [through] northeastern Brazil that helped turn the tide. The value to our cause of the use of these Brazilian airports and of the cooperation of the Brazilian army and navy, cannot be overstated.[43]

By then Hull presumably had forgotten branding Welles "ingenuous" and predicting that "not a single Latin government would carry out its commitments."

By preserving hemisphere unity at Rio, Roosevelt and Welles had enrolled Brazil as an ally and, nine months later with Brazil's "invaluable" assistance, FDR landed the forces in North Africa that ended any threat to the hemisphere. It was a further step in Welles's and the President's joint vision of a safe postwar world.

TWENTY-SEVEN

PLANNING FOR PEACE

1942–1943

Drafting the United Nations Charter

ROOSEVELT SHARED HIS DREAM OF A POSTWAR WORLD with Churchill and Stalin, but it was Welles, his global planner, whom he assigned to put it on paper. At his direction, Welles began drafting the original United Nations charter in late 1942. In the process he became caught up in one of the bitterest, if least-known, battles of wartime Washington, pitting him against Hull, Hopkins, Marshall and others who believed in winning the war rather than in planning for its ultimate goal: peace.

Hull opposed postwar planning as premature and also resented Welles's growing influence with Roosevelt. In time the feud between the wily old Tennessee politician and the patrician diplomat from the eastern establishment shook the capital.

Roosevelt's approval for postwar planning came late. Disillusioned by the failure of the League of Nations, he repeatedly told Welles that if "any good" came out of World War II, it would not be another ineffectual body like the League but the opportunity for the United States and Britain to disarm aggressors and keep postwar peace on their own terms.(Early in the war, Soviet Russia played little part in his thinking.)

Pearl Harbor changed his mind. After the Japanese attack, FDR realized that Anglo-Saxon "policing" would not suffice. Britain would emerge from the war destitute, and revolutionary new forces were rising that even the United States with its vast resources could not control alone. Only "collective" security could guarantee postwar peace.[1]

Welles's own belief in planning stemmed from his experience in World War I. As a young diplomat, he had seen President Wilson's failure to prepare for the 1919 Paris peace conference leave U.S. objectives "unclear," contributing to the collapse of the conference, to the failure of the League and, eventually, to American isolationism.[2] Had Wilson used his unrivaled influence to create an international organization and negotiate peace settlements during the war when the Allies needed American help, Welles wrote in retrospect, the United States would have had "far greater leverage" in achieving its goals.[3] He had never forgotten the lesson and, throughout World War II, pressed FDR unsuccessfully to start planning for peace. When FDR eventually did, the hour had passed.

Early in 1940, just weeks after Hitler's attack on Poland, Welles proposed a Washington conference of forty neutrals to plan wartime economic collaboration and postwar disarmament. Roosevelt approved but travel conditions made it impossible so, at Welles's request, Hull named him head of a small departmental committee to start postwar planning called the Advisory Committee on the Problems of Foreign Relations. Its deliberations, he wrote later, were "desultory." Returning in March from a fact-finding mission to Europe for FDR, Welles warned him that, if war spread across the globe, U.S. leadership alone could create an international security system and prevent future wars. His recommendations fell on deaf ears.

Cordell Hull, Harry Hopkins, congressional leaders and military advisors all warned FDR that discussion of postwar problems would revive fears of a new League of Nations, alarm the isolationists and further split the nation. Hitler's blitzkrieg in May made the issue moot. Faced by the collapse of France, the likely invasion of Britain, Axis control of the Atlantic and enemy subversion throughout Latin America, Roosevelt shelved postwar planning for the next fifteen months.

The German attack on Soviet Russia on June 22, 1941, however, highlighted the need for U.S.-Soviet coordination. Roosevelt sent Hopkins to ascertain Stalin's needs and agreed to meet Churchill off the Newfoundland coast in mid-August. Hopkins reported from Moscow that Stalin was confident his forces could withstand the Nazis, but that his supply problem would become serious by the following spring and he would need American help. Meanwhile he would "welcome" American troops on any part of the Russian front under their own command. Hitler's chief weakness, Stalin told Hopkins, was the vast number of "oppressed" peoples who hated him. Only the United States could give them the moral strength to resist. Roosevelt's world influence was "enormous."[4]

Facing a common foe, Stalin and Churchill began negotiating a military alliance. London reported that Stalin was asking only for military aid and a pledge of no separate peace with Hitler, but Roosevelt's suspicions mounted when Foreign Commissar Vyacheslav Molotov hinted that the Soviet Union also would demand guarantees of its pre-invasion borders (e.g. recognition of its 1939 annexation of the Baltic republics of Latvia, Lithuania and Esthonia). In meeting Churchill off Newfoundland, one of FDR's chief aims was to forestall the secret territorial deals that had embittered American opinion after World War I, fostering isolationism, Welles wrote later.

Before setting out, the President had Welles seek assurances from British ambassador Lord Halifax that the coming Anglo-Soviet military pact contained no "secret" clauses. Halifax gave the assurances and the pact was signed in Moscow on July 12, 1941. The next day Roosevelt cabled Churchill, suggesting a public statement that no political or economic commitments had been made. He would back it up in "very strong terms." It was too early for commitments, insisted FDR. The United States and Britain intended eventually to "disarm troublemakers" and "revive" small states, possibly through plebiscites, one of his favorite panaceas.

Following Roosevelt's meeting with Churchill at Argentia in mid-August, Welles pleaded with him repeatedly to speak out about the need to plan for peace and how the country could help avert future wars. FDR, however, insisted that his primary obligation was to concentrate American opinion on rearmament. If he spoke out about postwar problems, controversies would arise, jeopardizing national unity and diverting the nation's attention from victory. He would exert American leadership to build the world promised in the Atlantic Charter when "the time was ripe."[5]

Meanwhile, Stalin had not been told in advance of the Roosevelt-Churchill meeting at Argentia. Suspecting Anglo-American designs to dominate the postwar world, he delayed endorsing the charter's principles for several weeks and, when he did, it was with an ominous warning that the charter's practical application would necessarily "adapt" itself to the circumstances, needs and historic peculiarities of "particular countries."[6]

Alarmed by this cool reaction, Roosevelt and Churchill sent Averell Harriman and Lord Beaverbrook, then British Minister of Aircraft Production, to reassure Stalin that massive Allied aid was on its way. On October 30, FDR cabled that he was allocating the Soviets $1 billion in Lend-Lease. Stalin expressed perfunctory thanks then reverted immediately to "peace aims," proposing to

Beaverbrook that the Soviet-British military pact be expanded into a twenty-year political alliance covering not only the war but the "postwar" as well.

By early December 1941, winter weather and stiffening Soviet resistance had slowed the Nazi drive on Moscow. When Marshal Semyon Konstantinovitch Timoshenko recaptured Rostov, the first important point to be retaken, Stalin stepped up pressure on the British to agree in advance to a list of postwar territorial demands, including recognition of the 1939 Soviet annexation of the Baltic states. Unless these were included as "secret" protocols, he hinted, the Soviets might not sign the twenty-year treaty.

Alarmed, British Foreign Secretary Anthony Eden prepared to fly to Moscow on December 7 to discuss Stalin's demands. Meanwhile, FDR, concerned lest the British give in, told Hull on December 5 to send Eden a strong private message, pointing out that the United States, Britain and the Soviet Union had all bound themselves to be guided in postwar settlements by the Atlantic Charter and that, therefore, no specific terms, should be agreed before the peace conference. Above all, there should be no "secret commitments." The message reached Eden the day before Pearl Harbor and went "much further than a mere note of warning," Welles wrote later. It created a "precedent on which a policy was soon erected," a policy disastrous in Welles's view.

Eleven days later, on December 17, with Hitler's forces twelve miles from Moscow, Welles telephoned Roosevelt the text of an extraordinary cable from Stalin to the Chinese leader, Chiang Kai-shek, virtually begging him not to insist that the Soviet Union declare war immediately on Japan. Shown by the Chinese to their American supporters, it read:

> Soviet Russia today has the principal burden of war against Germany . . . Under the circumstances, the Soviet Union today ought not to divert its strength to the Far East when it is beginning to attack German armies. By dispersing our strength, the difficulties of the German armies will be lessened. I beg you, therefore, not to insist that Soviet Russia at once declare war against Japan. Soviet Russia must [eventually] fight Japan . . . but it takes time to prepare. I again implore you not to take the lead in demanding that Soviet Russia at once declare war against Japan."

With Stalin critically dependent on U.S. aid to halt the Nazi drive, politically at his weakest and "imploring" Chiang not to force him into a two-front war, Welles believed that FDR should have seized the moment to begin negotiating postwar settlements with Moscow. Never again would the American President have such leverage.

In the wake of Pearl Harbor, Churchill flew to Washington to concert strategy with FDR and agreed strongly that Stalin's territorial demands were a violation of the Atlantic Charter. The transfer of the Baltic peoples against their will would be "contrary to all the principles for which we are fighting this war and would dishonor our cause," Churchill cabled Eden on January 8, 1942. "There can be no question of settling frontiers until the peace conference . . . President Roosevelt holds this view as strongly as I do."[8]

Thus, wrote Welles, barely a month after the United States entered the war, the U.S. and British governments agreed to make no commitments on postwar territorial and political settlements until the war's end.[9] It was a decision fraught with danger, and with which he profoundly disagreed.

Five weeks after Pearl Harbor, in mid-January 1942, Roosevelt convened a conference of hemisphere Foreign Ministers at Rio de Janeiro and sent Welles to win an immediate, unanimous break in relations with the Axis Powers. After intense maneuvering, Welles won the unanimous agreement of the delegates to "recommend" a break to their respective legislatures, a play on words that FDR approved but that infuriated Hull, who refused to see or brief Welles on world developments when he returned to Washington in early February after a three-week absence. Days later Hull left for a two-month "convalescence" in Florida.

Welles was initially too busy, as acting Secretary, to add postwar planning to his workload, but virtually all the Latin American leaders at Rio had urged that the United States start planning for the postwar world promised in the Atlantic Charter. On hearing this, Roosevelt was impressed. The Good Neighbor policy had proved successful at Rio, and both he and Welles viewed the inter-American system as a potential building block for the postwar world.

Stalin's territorial demands, meanwhile, still weighed on Welles's mind: If rejected or ignored, they could fester, creating strains between the Allies. Welles had negotiated with Soviet ambassador Konstantin Oumansky two years earlier, easing U.S.-Soviet tension. The more he thought, the more convinced he became that Stalin's territorial demands and other postwar problems should be tackled immediately under the auspices of the twenty-six united nations who had pledged themselves on January 1 and 2, 1942, to wage war on Japan and the Axis. Given Hull's stranglehold on planning, his fortuitous absence in Florida gave Welles an unprecedented opportunity.

At his urgent plea, FDR approved a "new approach" and authorized him to form a special committee and start drafting "preparatory" peace plans. He would not be drawn into details about frontiers and similar problems, the President made clear, since compromises would be inevitable. "What I expect you to do," he told Welles, "is to prepare . . . the necessary number of baskets and the necessary number of alternative solutions for each problem. When the time comes, all I have to do is reach into a basket and fish out solutions that are sound and from which I can make my own choice."[10]

Welles held his first meeting on February 12.[11] His co-planners included hand-picked subordinates—Dean Acheson, Adolf Berle, Herbert Feis and Leo Pasvolsky, among them—plus a half-dozen experts drawn from private life: Isaiah Bowman, president of Johns Hopkins University and a world-famed geographer[12]; Norman H. Davis, chairman of the American Red Cross; Hamilton Fish Armstrong, editor of *Foreign Affairs* quarterly; Myron C. Taylor, FDR's representative at the Vatican; Anne O'Hare McCormick, the *New York Times* foreign affairs columnist; and Benjamin V. Cohen, general counsel of the National Power Policy Committee.

Senators Tom Connally (D-Texas), chairman of the Foreign Relations Committee and the ranking Republican, Warren Austin of Vermont, were invited to participate and, as the work expanded, Welles turned to the Council on Foreign Relations in New York for special studies. It was an example, virtually unique to the American system of government, of combining officials and private experts to find solutions to unprecedented problems.

Welles and his staff analyzed the 1919 peace conference and the failure of the League of Nations, then concluded that the "wisest" policy would be to negotiate "as detailed agreements as possible" with Soviet Russia before the war's end. If U.S. views on frontiers, transfers of populations, armistice and occupation terms were left to the peace conference, there was no guarantee that Stalin would accept them. Nothing bound him but the lofty principles of the Atlantic Charter. The time to negotiate, Welles believed, had arrived. America's growing industrial-military strength, Stalin's critical need for Lend-Lease and Roosevelt's world prestige would give the United States "immense leverage." He wrote:

> We could assume that our views coincided largely with those of the British Commonwealth, of . . . the Western Hemisphere and the lesser powers of Western Europe. But, in the light of our past experience with the Soviet Union, what possible assurance could we have that, at the peace conference, Moscow would accept even a small percentage of our recommendations?
>
> Would it not be wise, as soon as our own views were formed . . . to set up, officially, an international group . . . to plan for future peace? When the peace conference was held, it could be presented with postwar settlements and policies already agreed upon, in principle.[13]

Two months later Welles and his planners had drafted a United Nations "Authority."[14] A champion of small countries, Welles believed that the views of the European states occupied by Hitler, and of the Latin Americans, would be invaluable. Roosevelt, however, had repeatedly dismissed small countries as able to contribute little to disarming aggressors. Only after the Big Four—United

States, Britain, the Soviet Union and China—had completed postwar "policing" would a UN organization be useful, he felt.

Accordingly, Welles blended Roosevelt's ideas with his own, combining the Big Four and representatives of small countries into a UN "Executive Committee." On April 4, 1942, with the approval of the State Department's official Advisory Committee on Post-War Foreign Policy,[15] he recommended that:

> A United Nations Authority . . . be created, composed of representatives of all the United Nations; an Executive Committee, thereof, should be composed of representatives of the four major powers [United States, Great Britain, Russia and China] with the addition of approximately five representatives from the regions of eastern Europe, the western democracies of Europe, the [Latin] American republics, the Far East and, possibly, the Mohammedan peoples.[16]

The Executive Committee, he pointed out, would provide a "mechanism for negotiating postwar agreements" and could later be expanded into a United Nations Organization.[17]

To Welles's lifelong regret, his proposal was "summarily turned down at the highest level," presumably in a telephone call from Roosevelt, as no written record has been found.[18] The intrinsic idea appealed to the President, Welles wrote, but the early months of 1942 were the "darkest" period of the war and Roosevelt was preoccupied by military problems. Japan dominated the Pacific. Axis forces were driving the British from Libya, Greece and Crete, threatening their hold on the Middle East. The United States Joint Chiefs were warning that Stalin might exploit negotiations to demand guarantees not only of his preinvasion borders (the Baltic states) but also control of the Dardanelles, a dominant position in Iran and concessions in the Far East.[19]

Hull, characteristically, preferred postponing difficult decisions and, early in 1942, Roosevelt was especially solicitous of the Secretary of State, given their recent clash over Rio. Finally, Welles wrote, the President feared that negotiations might leak, arousing powerful ethnic voting blocs. FDR saw no danger in delay, confident, as always, that his negotiating skills would win Stalin over at the peace table.[20]

Walter Lippmann, the foreign affairs analyst, called on Welles soon after to inquire whether the United States intended seeking agreement with its allies on postwar issues while the fighting continued. After World War I, he recalled, the Allies had failed to agree on political and territorial problems before the armistice—a factor contributing to "unsound and unwise" decisions.[21] This time the United States had only the Atlantic Charter to fall back on, and its terms were even vaguer than Wilson's Fourteen Points. What of the future of Germany, of Poland, of the Baltic states? The President and the Secretary of State were officially committed to a policy of no agreements on territorial adjustments or political settlements until the war's end, Welles told him.

"I was, naturally, not able to say that I was strongly opposed to the position taken . . . by the administration in which I served," he wrote long after. "There was little I could do . . . the decision was based almost entirely on military factors."[22]

Meanwhile, the British, fearful of an open break with Stalin and the risk of a separate Soviet-German peace, were prepared to concede his territorial demands. Failure to recognize the Soviet Union's preinvasion frontiers might lead to a "complete reversal" of Stalin's attitude toward the war, Sir Stafford Cripps, the British ambassador in Moscow, warned London. Stalin had become increasingly suspicious of delay and regarded acceptance of his claims as the "acid test" of Allied good faith and whether the Atlantic Charter was to be used against him.[23]

Halifax emerged from the Oval Office on February 17, confident that the President might be persuaded to accept, if not full Soviet sovereignty over the Baltic republics, at least Soviet control of their foreign and defense policies. "We did not want to recognize any Soviet position in the Baltic states," Eden wrote later, "but, if Hitler were overthrown, Russian forces would end the war much deeper in Europe than they began it in 1941. It, therefore, seemed prudent to tie the Soviet government to agreements as early as possible."[24]

Roosevelt was playing for time while Stalin was turning up the pressure. Even after cabling FDR his "sincere gratitude" for a second $1 billion Lend-Lease credit on February 22, 1942,[25] Stalin ominously omitted any mention of Anglo-American aid, hinted that the Soviet armies might eventually halt at the preinvasion frontiers and, in a special Order of the Day to the Red Army, alone of the three Allies, made no demand for Hitler's elimination.[26] His warning was clear.

Indignant on learning of Cripps's alarmist views, Roosevelt scribbled Welles in longhand: "Churchill to tell Cripps most unwise to advocate now any approval of pre-1939 Russian frontiers. In addition, contrary to Atlantic Charter . . . feel sure Cripps will not want to make me call attention to that fact. The matter had best be handled between Stalin and me, a bit later on."[27] The next day Welles told Halifax that the President had decided to discuss Stalin's demands with him directly—which alarmed the British. "When Halifax saw the President and Harry Hopkins on March 9th," wrote Eden,

> he found it impossible to dissuade Mr Roosevelt from direct negotiations.
>
> The President proposed to tell Stalin that, while everyone recognized Russia's need for security, it was too dangerous to put anything on paper, now. But there was no need to worry about the Baltic states since their future clearly depended on Russian military progress and, if Russia reoccupied them, neither

the United States nor Britain could, or would, turn her out. I did not like . . . this statement because I was sure it would fail to satisfy Stalin and because it seemed to me to give us the worst of all worlds. We would be ungraciously conniving at the inevitable, without getting any return for it.[28]

Welles was in the Oval office on March 12 when FDR told Soviet ambassador Maxim Litvinov that "under no conditions would he subscribe to any secret treaty, nor to any public treaty, with regard to definitive frontiers, until the war had been won."[29] To soften the blow, possibly at Halifax's urging, he promised that the United States would support Russia's legitimate postwar security.[30] But the President was determined to stiffen British resistance, and he instructed Welles to throw up fresh roadblocks. Welles told Halifax on April 1 that the impending Anglo-Soviet treaty should, at least, allow Baltic citizens unwilling to live under Soviet rule to emigrate with their property. Moscow, as expected, turned this proposal down, and FDR played his trump.

In a friendly, personal message to Stalin dated April 11, he suggested a meeting that summer near Fairbanks, Alaska, to consider a "very important military proposal involving the utilization of our armed forces in a manner to relieve your critical Western front."[31] What Roosevelt had in mind were the coming TORCH landings in North Africa that autumn; but Stalin, lured by hopes of an Allied landing in Europe, sent Molotov to London, where, on May 26, the Foreign Commissar signed the twenty-year Anglo-Soviet treaty—stripped of its territorial demands.[32] Molotov flew on to Washington, where FDR outlined his view of the postwar world over cocktails in the White House.

Churchill had ideas about a revived League of Nations, he confided, but this was impractical: too many nations would be involved. After victory, the Big Four would have to act as the world's "policemen," preventing clandestine rearmament. All other countries, France included, would be disarmed. If any nation menaced the peace, it could be blockaded and, if still recalcitrant, bombed. Gratified by the prospect of the Soviet colossus bestriding east Europe and the Middle East, Molotov nonetheless observed that compulsory disarmament might be a "bitter blow" to Poland and Turkey. How would France react?

France, FDR replied airily, might be admitted to the "great power club" in, perhaps, ten to twenty years. Meanwhile, he thought the Anglo-Soviet treaty "all to the good" and was glad that the frontier problems had been dropped—postwar Soviet borders might better be discussed later. Molotov observed blandly that while he and his government had very definite convictions in the "opposite direction," they were deferring to Britain's preference and what they understood to be the President's attitude.[33]

Roosevelt had momentarily sidetracked Stalin's territorial demands, but it was Stalin who emerged with a propaganda victory. On June 11 the joint U.S.-

Soviet communiqué announced "full agreement with regard to the urgent tasks [*sic*] of creating a Second Front in Europe in 1942."[34] The pledge would come back later to haunt Roosevelt and Churchill.

Molotov was still in Washington when Welles forecast the postwar world in a speech at Arlington Cemetery on Memorial Day. Coming from a Roosevelt intimate, it won wide attention—a fact that infuriated Hull. Welles cited the 90,000 Americans killed in World War I[35] and charged the United States with "unenlightened selfishness" in refusing to join the League of Nations and "share responsibility for peace . . . We are now reaping the bitter fruit of our own folly and lack of vision," he declared. Victory was certain but only the United States could help restore a shattered world.

After victory, he predicted, an international "police power" would disarm aggressors and keep order until the permanent system of general security forecast in the Atlantic Charter had been established. The United Nations would form the nucleus of a world organization, responsible for global relief, reconstruction and determining a just, durable peace. World War II was a "people's war" and would not truly be won until the rights of all peoples had been secured.

Those responsible for the war should be punished; but no people should be made to atone for crimes for which they were not responsible—and no nation forced to look forward to "endless years of want and starvation," as had the German people after World War I. Victory should bring the liberation of all peoples; discrimination because of race, creed or color should be abolished and the right to freedom in the Atlantic Charter extended to the whole world. "The age of imperialism is ended," Welles declared.[36]

After brooding for three weeks, Hull summoned Welles to his office and excoriated him for announcing "new policy" without his sanction. Welles stiffly denied it, offering to make no further speeches, but Hull insisted that he continue his "splendid" speeches provided they were first cleared with him. Welles agreed but, before ending their icy confrontation, told Hull that Roosevelt himself planned no speeches on postwar issues but had authorized others to launch "trial balloons."[37] Later he told Pierpont Moffat that Roosevelt had commissioned him to "keep the issue before the public and educate it, instead of confronting it with a 'fait accompli' as after World War I.[38]

The Hull-Welles feud over postwar planning intensified, further dividing the State Department into rival cliques. Hull told Breckinridge Long that he no longer trusted Welles, who was "laying plans for himself" and making speeches with an "illusory consent 'weasled' out of the White House."[39] Things were going badly, Berle noted in his diary:

> The Secretary and Sumner are further apart than ever—in this case I am afraid
> it is so definitely Sumner's fault as not to be arguable. Briefly, he committed the

fatal mistake of speaking as though he were the Secretary of State, when there is an alive and very active Secretary of State in the immediate vicinity. The Secretary, thereupon, went to work to clear the decks; and Sumner, on his part, has been retaliating by getting control of all the Departmental machinery he can. This bodes no good for anybody.[40]

Hull had refused to take charge of postwar planning upon his return from Florida in late April, and by July the department's Advisory Committee, which he nominally headed, had ceased functioning, its work devolving on Welles and his planners.[41] Allied successes at El Alamein and Midway, stiffer Soviet resistance at Stalingrad and the impending TORCH landings in North Africa, meanwhile, suggested, if not the beginning of victory, at least the end of defeat.

Roosevelt's interest in postwar problems now renewed and he summoned Welles and his team to the White House virtually weekly, studying every detail of their draft international organization, more and more convinced, Welles recalled, that no lasting peace was possible unless an "effective international organization were founded, if possible, before the conclusion of the war."[42] Finally satisfied with their outline, on October 23 he formally authorized Welles to start drafting the United Nations Charter.[43]

Early in 1943, after repeated requests, Roosevelt gave Welles an "uninterrupted" two hours in the White House to review his draft. It was late afternoon, the day's appointments had ended, and the President had signed the basketsful of urgent papers flowing endlessly over his desk, Welles remembered. "For once, he was not in a digressive mood. He read very carefully the memoranda and charts that I placed before him."[44] Fleshed out and more detailed than the blueprint Welles had submitted—and which FDR had rejected—in April, they nonetheless retained important similarities.

FDR's Big Four "policemen" remained the core of an Executive Council, expanded from nine to eleven members. The Big Four would have permanent status and an (undefined) veto; the seven members representing geographic regions would rotate periodically. In general, FDR approved his draft, Welles wrote later, including the concept of "regions" derived from the inter-American system. He questioned, however, whether regional organizations could function efficiently in the Near East or Asia, given their lack of experience in self-government.

Hull, on the other hand, vehemently opposed Welles's regional concept, claiming that he was merely echoing FDR and Churchill, both of whom "thought the world should be organized after the war on a regional basis." FDR, he wrote, favored "the creation of regional organizations . . . but the Big Four . . . would handle all security questions . . . policing the world. All other [countries], including France, were to be disarmed." Hull acknowledged a "basic cleavage" between himself and Roosevelt over postwar organization.[45]

Meanwhile, rising tension with Moscow and an anti-Soviet mood sweeping Congress and the nation early in 1943 confirmed Welles's belief that a United Nations Organization was imperative before the war's end. The situation was "very bad," he told Vice President Wallace in February; the "most important thing" was better understanding with Moscow.[46]

Roscoe Drummond of the *Christian Science Monitor* interviewed Welles then listed the main obstacles: the lack of a formal U.S.-Soviet agreement; the "stranglehold" over U.S. foreign policy exercised by thirty senators (at the time one-third of the Senate)[47] and, finally, Stalin's lack of confidence in the American ambassador to Moscow, Admiral William H. Standley, and in his own ambassador to Washington, Maxim Litvinov.[48] Litvinov's presence in Washington had indicated Stalin's willingness to cooperate with the West; his replacement that spring by the hard-line Andrei Gromyko boded ill.

On March 8, 1943, Standley exacerbated U.S.-Soviet tension by publicly accusing the Kremlin of concealing U.S. aid from the Soviet people and implying that the Soviet Union alone was fighting the war. Welles sought to minimize the damage, but Standley's intemperate outburst led to his recall. The British embassy in Washington reported "rival cliques" in the State Department: the experts, delighted by Standley's "tough talk," and the group "led by Welles, which [believes] that gentler treatment and certain concessions would break down USSR reserve and suspicion, indispensable for a common, successful prosecution both of war and peace."[49]

Tacitly encouraged by Roosevelt, Welles's "educational campaign" in Congress was gathering momentum. After conferring with Welles in mid-March, Senator Joseph H. Ball (R-Minn.) introduced a sense-of-the-Senate resolution[50] calling on the administration to create a United Nations Organization to prosecute the war, establish provisional governments in freed territories, supervise global rehabilitation, set up a World Court and mobilize a world police to enforce UN decisions.[51]

Hull accused Welles of "stirring up" the Senate and worked with Senators Connally and the influential Michigan Republican, Arthur H. Vandenberg, to substitute a weaker resolution,[52] but Welles was committing neither the State Department nor himself to "specifics," noted a British embassy observer. He was "throwing his weight behind Congressional forces fighting a return to postwar isolationism."[53] That autumn the House of Representatives overwhelmingly adopted a parallel resolution introduced by a freshman Democratic congressman from Arkansas, J. William Fulbright.

Irked by his young colleague's temerity in introducing such sweeping legislation, Sol Bloom, Democrat of New York, the irascible committee chairman, growled that the State Department should be consulted, but, when Fulbright produced Welles's written approval, Bloom fell silent.[54] The Fulbright resolution reflected growing national support for a United Nations Organization but, in Welles's view, the hour was dangerously late. The Allies might win the war but, without a UN agency for resolving disputes, could they win the peace?

The British, meanwhile, also had begun contemplating the future. Eden arrived in mid-March to canvass U.S. thinking, and Roosevelt ordered Welles's UN draft rushed to the White House for a meeting on March 27 between himself, Eden, Halifax, Hopkins, Hull, Welles, and William Strang, Assistant Under Secretary British Foreign Office. The President asked Welles to explain the details while Hull apparently sat silent.[55] Days before Churchill had broadcast a proposal for "independent" regional councils, which FDR and Welles both "emphatically opposed," Hopkins wrote later. Roosevelt wanted a global organization with "advisory" powers to which all UN members would belong. Under that would be regional councils with similar advisory powers. The "real decisions," however, would be made by the Big Four.[56] Welles later confirmed Hopkins's account. Roosevelt told Eden "rather more strongly than I had hoped," he wrote, that the Big Four should assert for a long time the "right to make all basic decisions affecting world order."[57]

Roosevelt took Welles with him on a state visit to Mexico in April and, as their train rolled through Mexico's low brown hills to Monterrey, where Mexican President Manuel Avila Camacho awaited them, they reviewed the problems of building a world organization based on regions. The great question mark on FDR's mind, wrote Welles, was whether Stalin would join the United Nations or stay out. "It may well be that all our plans will amount to no more than paper," the President observed forebodingly.[58] In a speech at Monterrey, FDR pursued what one observer described as the "Welles line: Pan-Americanism as a model for the postwar world, a new doctrine toward which both FDR and Welles are conspicuously moving."[59]

At the end of June, before leaving for a vacation in Maine, Welles handed Roosevelt the final draft of the UN Charter. Two major problems remained, both involving the veto. How much scope should the Big Four be allowed for military sanctions against aggressors? And how should small nations be protected?

"We could not admit the right of any power, great or small, to veto action against itself, if it pursued aggression," Welles recalled later.[60] By insisting on unanimity, the League of Nations had allowed aggressors to veto sanctions and thus escape punishment. The inter-American system had a fatal flaw: no provision for force. Welles, therefore, proposed a strict limit on the veto. Military sanctions would take effect with the approval of nine (of the eleven) members of the Security Council, including three of the Big Four. Roosevelt doubted that Stalin would join a world organization empowered to use force against him, and he proved right.

At meetings at Dumbarton Oaks in late 1944 and again at Yalta in early 1945 Stalin insisted on a veto over the use of force—and even on UN discussion of aggression. At FDR's urging, he dropped his demand for a veto on discussion—but not on the use of force. Welles recalled that the veto in his original draft charter was "far more limited" than that which the Big Four eventually granted each other.[61]

By mid-1943 the Allied invasion of Sicily, successful landings in Italy and the surrender of the Badoglio government there[62] had made defeat of the Axis Powers virtually certain. FDR and Churchill met in Quebec for the QUAD-RANT conference from August 17 to 24 to plan future operations and, while Stalin declined to join them, pleading military commitments, he suggested a Big Four foreign ministers conference in Moscow in October to announce the "early establishment of a United Nations Organization." Roosevelt approved and agreed, as well, to meet Stalin and Churchill in late November at Tehran, where he hoped to persuade Stalin to join and support the United Nations. On the eve of the FDR-Churchill meeting at Quebec, however, a political crisis arose: Hull demanded Welles's resignation. After ten years, his festering jealousy of his deputy had boiled over.

Nevertheless, on September 19, FDR summoned Welles to Hyde Park and asked him to represent the United States at Moscow: No one knew FDR's hopes for the UN better than he. Welles declined but, at Roosevelt's insistence, agreed to reconsider, and the two discussed the projected UN organization in detail. The key to postwar peace, said FDR, depended on whether Stalin agreed immediately to join the United Nations or remained outside. In the latter event, there would be no guarantee of postwar peace. His immediate agreement was "essential."

Welles eventually turned down Roosevelt's mission to Moscow and Hull went in his place. The day before FDR left for Tehran, he called Welles back to the White House. Welles wrote:

> The President was unusually serious. He felt deeply the import of the conferences ahead and spoke, far more than was customary, of the future after the war. At times, his face had that luminous aspect and his eyes that remote look, which struck so deeply into the hearts of those who loved him, as his life drew to a close.
>
> During the two hours I was with him, the greatest part of the conversation was devoted to international organization; how to achieve agree-

ment with Stalin on its nature and how to establish it. He had on his bed a copy of the draft which I had given him in June. He had been studying it again the night before and on the backs of some pages had jotted down notes and suggestions. "We won't get any strong international organization unless the Soviet Union and the U.S. work together to build it up as the years go by," he said. That, to him, was the key.[63]

Roosevelt used Welles's draft at Tehran to explain to Stalin how the United Nations would function. There would be three main bodies: an Assembly of (then forty) member nations to make recommendations; an Executive Committee (the Big Four, plus six regional representatives) to handle nonmilitary matters; and, finally, the Four Policemen to serve as an "enforcing" agency in event of war or other emergencies. To illustrate, he drew three circles: the Executive Committee in the center; on the right, the "4 Policemen"; and, on the left, the forty United Nations under which he wrote "ILO [International Labor Organization]-Health-Agriculture-Food."[64]

Stalin first wanted no international organization of any kind, Welles wrote. He preferred a continuing U.S.-Soviet-British military alliance to control Germany and Japan and objected also to the inclusion of China as a great power. Stalin, like Churchill, preferred "regional" councils in Europe and the Far East to a global body almost certain to be dominated by the United States. Roosevelt, however, overcame his objections and "saved the UN," Welles wrote later.[65]

Sherwood thought that the Tehran conference marked the "supreme peak" in Roosevelt's career.[66] Returning, buoyed by his success, FDR wrote Welles early in 1944: "I want to tell you all about Cairo and Tehran. I think that, as a roving ambassador for the first time, I did not 'pull any boners.'"[67]

In the general euphoria, however, little significance had been paid to Stalin's refusal to discuss the Baltic states, which, he said, had "already voted" to join the Soviet Union, or to his evasiveness about Poland's future borders and government. Churchill asked what future territorial interests the Soviet Union might have and Stalin replied that there was no need to speak of them then. "When the time comes," he added ominously, "we will speak."

FDR, Churchill and Stalin met again at Yalta in early 1945, fourteen months later. By then Stalin's armies had swept across the Baltic republics, Poland, Romania and most of Hungary and Czechoslovakia. The Soviet Union had become the most powerful entity in Europe and Asia, and the first successful U.S. atom bomb was still six months away. As Welles had foreseen, U.S. influence in the Kremlin had shriveled.

In 1950, five years after FDR's death, Welles wrote that his refusal, early in 1942, to create a United Nations panel and begin negotiating postwar settlements when

Stalin critically needed U.S. help had been "largely responsible for dividing the post-war world into two warring camps . . . The immense influence we had, immediately after Pearl Harbor, was not exercised," he wrote. "When we did attempt to negotiate political settlements, our influence was no longer decisive."[68]

When penning his criticism of the President he had revered, Welles was gravely ill and depressed by the outbreak of war in Korea and the threat of a nuclear conflict. Planning could have avoided—or mitigated—the Cold War, he maintained until his death. After Pearl Harbor, he wrote, the United States had two alternatives: to negotiate postwar issues with the Soviets during the war or to refuse resolutely to discuss them until the war's end. "By sticking to neither one nor the other," he wrote, "we fell between two stools." At Tehran and Yalta, Roosevelt and Churchill began "drifting" into a series of "haphazard" political and territorial concessions to ensure Stalin's cooperation.

In 1942-43, United States influence was at its peak, Welles recalled. Stalin had been so shaken by Hitler's 1941 invasion that he had "begged" the British and Americans to send divisions to fight on Soviet soil under their own command. Lend-Lease arms had saved Moscow; the United States was "supreme" in the field of production; and Stalin himself acknowledged at Tehran that the war would have been "lost" without American production.

The United States and Britain feared that Stalin might seek peace with Hitler if his politico-territorial demands were rejected, but both "misread" him. Stalin was equally fearful that his Western allies might seek a separate peace. Stalin's territorial claims were not "unreasonable," Welles argued. They had been presented to Eden in December 1941, when Hitler's armies were twelve miles from Moscow. Stalin had not been "bargaining." His demands represented his nation's minimal postwar security needs.

Annexation of the Baltic states would have been "unacceptable," Welles wrote, but the problem might have been solved "if we had broached the matter in the early days of the war and given Stalin assurance of security against a future attack by a rearmed Germany—an obsession governing all his . . . dealing with his major allies." Except for Poland, there were no "serious" disputes between the Kremlin and the Allies, Welles noted.

Stalin had, admittedly, broken his pledge to FDR at Yalta to allow free elections in Poland and other east European states freed from Nazi rule, but he had warned FDR that Poland was a matter of "life and death" for the Soviet Union. Poland had been the traditional invasion route for Napoleon and Hitler.[69]

Had FDR exerted U.S. influence in 1942-43 to negotiate agreements that insured the Soviet people "legitimate" security and appeared wise and just to the Western Allies, it probably would have been "conclusive," Welles claimed. After the battle of Stalingrad (November 1942 to February 1943), however, when an entire German army surrendered to Soviet forces and which is generally considered a turning point in the European war, the great Soviet offensives began and the time for negotiation had passed. Soviet military influence was greater by war's end than at any time since 1917, and it should have been foreseen that, without "prior [written] commitments," Stalin would align himself with his marshals and generals and that the appetite of a victorious Soviet army might become "inordinate" if no effort was made to check it in time.[70]

Had Roosevelt lived, Stalin would have lived up to his commitments, Welles believed. After years of dealing with FDR, the Soviet leader had come to trust him. "Stalin never broke his word to me," Churchill told the *New York Times* columnist C. L. Sulzberger in 1956. "We agreed on the Balkans. I said he could have Rumania and Bulgaria; he said we could have Greece (of course, only in our sphere you know). He signed a slip of paper. And he never broke his word. We saved Greece that way. When we went in, in 1944, Stalin didn't interfere."[71]

FDR was not blind to the Kremlin's fanaticism or ulterior motives, Welles wrote, but Stalin was not immortal and, in time, the enemies of the United States in his regime would be eliminated from leadership.[72] Stalin was not unyielding; he had compromised with FDR at Yalta over UN voting rights and the veto and, until the Potsdam conference in mid-July 1945, had observed his military commitments, entering the war against Japan ninety days after the German surrender, as promised.

Potsdam marked the turning point. With Roosevelt dead and American forces in Europe rapidly demobilizing, with no written commitments to bind him and with the new, suspect team of President Harry S. Truman and James F. Byrnes[73] in control of the atom bomb, Stalin reverted to primal instinct and power, allying himself with his military chiefs and Politburo hard-liners. The Cold War, which Welles had foreseen and had fought to avert, would dominate U.S. policy for the next forty years.

TWENTY-EIGHT

RESIGNATION

1943

"Finishing . . . His Brilliant but Stormy Career"

WHILE WELLES HAD BEEN DRAFTING A UN CHARTER, supervising relations with Latin America, dealing with the Free French, searching for a postwar homeland for the Jews and, in effect, running the day-to-day State Department, Hull and Bullitt had been forging an unholy alliance.

At loose ends since the fall of France and the end of his ambassadorship, Bullitt had found temporary refuge in 1941 as a special assistant to Hull. But, given little to do, bored and restless, he had stormed out of the State Department late in the year after quarreling with Berle and accusing him of rifling his desk. To be spared his importunings, Roosevelt had sent Bullitt on a two-month fact-finding trip to the Middle East. Before setting out, Bullitt had entrusted his friend, Interior Secretary Ickes, with a briefcase, confiding that it contained memoranda of conversations with FDR concerning Welles's "sex life."[1]

Returning in March 1942, Bullitt first called on Vice President Wallace, adverting to rumors about Welles.[2] By chance, Felix Belair of the *New York Times* had interviewed Wallace the day before, knowing that he had been on the presidential train after Speaker Bankhead's funeral in 1940. Belair had raised the same rumors. Welles was "perfectly grand" on some matters, he noted, but "not quite understandable" on others. Unwilling to be drawn out, Wallace merely had confirmed that Welles had drunk a "great deal of liquor" on the train that night.[3]

Meanwhile Bullitt, embittered by Roosevelt's refusal to use him in the war effort, pursued his vendetta, spreading the rumors to all who would listen. Wallace dined with him in May in the Georgetown home of his henchman, Carmel Offie, and heard Attorney General Francis Biddle relate how Welles had "hit the ceiling" when Biddle had proposed naming Bullitt to a government committee. "It is obvious that Welles is fully familiar with the story Bullitt has told about him in various places," Wallace noted in his diary.[4]

Too busy, or weary, to care, Welles relegated Bullitt's whispering campaign to the back of his mind, but the rumors spread, fanned not only by Bullitt and Offie, but by Theodore Roosevelt's viperish daughter, Alice Roosevelt Longworth, a onetime Bullitt flame who detested "Cousin Franklin" and his entire New Deal. Drew Pearson told Ickes in March that FBI director J. Edgar Hoover was allegedly homosexual. He had heard similar stories about Welles— but did not believe them. Pearson had known Welles for years and, as a younger man, Welles had "circulated very freely and intimately" among women.[5]

Dining with Bullitt a month later, Wallace heard him tell two guests, Navy Secretary Frank Knox and Loy Henderson, a senior State Department official, that the department had, in effect, four chiefs: Hull, Welles, Berle and Acheson. Some, Bullitt said darkly, were "criminals."[6] Castle heard Supreme Court Justice James C. McReynolds condemn "immorality" in the Roosevelt administration and cite stories about Welles. Castle noted that many were being spread by Bullitt, who would "do anything to secure the hide of Welles."[7]

Early in September, Welles and Mathilde left Washington for a brief vacation in Maine. On September 11, with Welles away, Hull called Breckin-ridge Long to his office. He was disturbed by a personal scandal, a "nasty rumor" in circulation, Long wrote in his diary. "It is not new to [Hull] but it now has, apparently, gained considerable currency. I shall not repeat it. I heard of it some months ago and dismissed it as malicious, impossible and incredible.[Hull] takes it very seriously, has made some inquiries...and is very much inclined to believe [it]. He has no documentary proof but has apparently had reports from sources he considers trustworthy, accurate and informed."

Uncertain whether to report the rumor to FDR or let it take its natural course, Hull asked Long's advice. "I had little to offer," wrote Long, "except that the person in question [undoubtedly Welles] be confronted with the charge and given an opportunity to disprove it. That was . . . an honest way to deal with an able man and a nasty situation."[8] That, however, was not Hull's way.

Six weeks later, on October 24, Hull summoned J. Edgar Hoover to his hotel apartment. Employing a favorite ploy when probing for information, Hull said that his wife had been hearing stories from the wives of several senators about Welles's "improper" actions. These had given him great concern. He understood that Hoover had made an investigation for the President the year before and asked to see his report. Hoover confirmed the investigation but warily told Hull that he had turned over the report to Marvin McIntyre, a veteran FDR aide, in the White House and suggested that Hull ask McIntyre for it.

Hull discussed the Welles rumors "at some length," Hoover recorded, and indicated that he would contact McIntyre or possibly even the President himself. The situation might lead to embarrassing publicity unless steps were taken promptly.[9]

As 1942 drew to a close, Bullitt confided that Hull was very "bitter" and Mrs. Hull very "outspoken" about Welles's "physical idiosyncracy." He had asked Hull why he had not gone directly to the President to demand Welles's resignation, but Hull, Bullitt told Ickes, had given him no answer.[10] Meanwhile, a copy of the FBI report on Welles found its way to the desk of Attorney General Biddle, who asked his deputy, James Rowe, Jr., how to handle it. Rowe, a former FDR aide, suggested that he take it to the President; Biddle seemed reluctant and Rowe suspected the "old Grotonian net." Eventually Biddle mustered his courage and took the report to FDR, returning shaken. FDR had "frosted" him, he told Rowe, had been very cross and had ordered him to "leave it alone."[11]

Bullitt ought to "burn in hell" for the stories he was circulating about Welles, Roosevelt told Wallace soon after,[12] but not even the President could still Bullitt's tongue. With the 1944 election in view, Senate isolationists—Owen Brewster (R-Me.), Styles Bridges (R-N.H.) and Burton K. Wheeler (D-Mont.) among them— were hungry for political ammunition. Wheeler, especially, was a "deadly enemy of FDR," Rowe remembered. "He got his information on Welles from Bullitt." Roosevelt needed Welles and fought for time—but the noose was tightening.

By 1943, Hull was moving in for the kill. Fearful of FDR's wrath and of being excluded from the inner circle, he temporized at first, but his wife, who thought Welles a threat to her elderly husband, and Bullitt were constantly by his side, egging him on. A Tennessee mountaineer to the core, Hull was slow to act but ruthless when aroused.

Early in January, he summoned Breckinridge Long and Green Hackworth, the department's legal advisor, to his office. The 1940 train story was spreading, he said, and asked their advice. When Hackworth suggested that Welles could still be prosecuted under Virginia law, Hull sent a State Department security agent to interview Bullitt's chief sources: Dale Whiteside of the Secret Service and Luther Thomas, vice president of the Southern Railway. Whiteside refused to talk but Thomas furnished full details.

Armed with Thomas's details, Hull warned Roosevelt that a scandal was about to explode and asked permission to read the FBI affidavits. Roosevelt, then about to leave for the Casablanca conference with Churchill scheduled for January 14 to 26, "looked miserably at the ceiling," Hull told Bullitt later. He refused to send the affidavits to the State Department but said Hull could read them in the White House on his return. Ever since, Hull confided, FDR had "excluded" him, dealing solely with Welles, Hopkins and Henry Wallace.[13] Bullitt again urged him to threaten to resign unless Roosevelt dismissed Welles "within forty-eight hours," even offering to accompany him to the White House, but Hull temporized, fearful of a showdown with a furious President.

Hull continued to brood. On January 27, the day after FDR's return, Hull told Bullitt that he had "categorically" demanded Welles's resignation though conceding that he had not dared threaten to resign himself.[14] A month later Roosevelt's military aide, "Pa" Watson, provided Hull the FBI affidavits in the White House. They proved voluminous and Hull read only the summaries. Meanwhile, he told Bullitt, Mrs. Hull was "constantly" hearing rumors about Welles from the wives of senators, congressmen and Supreme Court justices.[15] Resentment over Welles's alleged misconduct was so widespread in the House and Senate that he might not have to "act." The story might explode in Congress any day, forcing Welles to resign.[16]

Welles and Hull were now barely speaking. At the end of March, Hull gave a farewell dinner for the British Foreign Secretary, Anthony Eden, who was returning home after talks on postwar issues with the President, Welles and other officials. "I had been in the State Department saying goodbye," Eden wrote in his memoirs. "As I took leave of Sumner Welles, I checked myself, adding, 'but, of course, I shall see you at the dinner tonight.' Mr Welles flushed but replied firmly, 'I have not been asked.'"[17]

Over Easter, Hull and Bullitt discussed their vendetta in Hull's apartment. When Bullitt noted that the President had taken Welles, not Hull, on his state visit to Mexico, Hull said that he had told the President before his departure that he would not have "tolerated his own brother in the American government fifteen minutes had he committed such crimes." FDR, he added, had angrily denounced Bullitt's "whispering campaign." At this point, Mrs. Hull rejoined her husband and Bullitt and, overhearing their conversation, remarked: "Mr. Bullitt, won't you shoot that man for me?"[18]

At the end of April, Hull and Bullitt recruited a key accomplice: Senator Owen Brewster, an isolationist Maine Republican and inveterate Roosevelt-hater. At Hull and Bullitt's suggestion, Brewster asked J. Edgar Hoover for the Welles file, but the wary FBI director put him off. Reporting Brewster's request later to his superior, Attorney General Biddle, Hoover observed that the Welles case was "puzzling." There was no pattern of homosexual behavior; the only explanation seemed to be lack of self-control as the incidents had occurred only when Welles was "so drunk he could not remember them."[19]

Scenting political paydirt, Brewster returned to Hoover's office in May, intimating that he might ask the Senate investigating committee headed by Missouri Democrat Harry S Truman to open an investigation. He had asked Hull why he had not gone directly to FDR about the Welles case. Hull had replied that he had—but that FDR "wouldn't act."[20] Roosevelt provided the reason, soon after, telling Biddle that Welles was the "only man in the State Department who really knew what was going on." He had to depend on him.[21]

Still determined to force FDR's hand, Hull warned him early in June that "everyone" in the Senate knew that Welles was subject to blackmail. Unless the President acted quickly, it would be impossible to get major international pacts ratified. FDR again had sat back, "looked miserably at the ceiling" and had said nothing.[22] At month's end, warned by his doctors that he could no longer keep up the pace, Welles left with Mathilde for a vacation in Maine—abandoning the field to his enemies.

With Welles away, Bullitt called on FDR at the White House on July 27 and brought up his charges. A violent quarrel ensued. Paling with anger, FDR shouted that Bullitt was being "un-Christian" and accused him of leaking to that "bitch friend of yours," Cissy Patterson, publisher of the isolationist *Washington Times-Herald,* with whom Bullitt had been romantically involved. He needed Welles, FDR declared; Welles was younger and more intelligent than "that old fool, Hull." Bullitt was also growing angry. It was his duty as a friend and supporter, he snapped, to point out that Welles could be blackmailed. Keeping him in office was a bad example to the Foreign Service. FDR rang the bell, had himself wheeled to his quarters and Bullitt left, dictating a memorandum about their second "furious row" to Carmel Offie immediately after.[23]

Bullitt had come to see him demanding Welles's dismissal, FDR told Berle later. He had replied that he was going to "play Saint Peter." Two men came before him at the Pearly Gates. Welles confessed and was admitted. Bullitt also confessed but FDR told him: "Bill, you've tried to destroy a fellow being." With a gesture of his thumb, he had added: "Get out of here and never come back . . . I don't suppose he'll ever forgive me," FDR concluded with a laugh.[24]

The noose, meanwhile, was tightening. On July 29, Welles left the serene beauty of Mt. Desert Island to return to the Washington snakepit. "He hated so to leave this heavenly air and adorable place," Mathilde wrote a friend. "I feel lost, three days with Sumner gone."[25] Neither she nor Welles could have known that, during Welles's absence, Hull, Bullitt and Arthur Krock, of the *New York Times,* a venomous Roosevelt critic, had put the finishing touches on Welles's destruction. The first rumble of the approaching storm came on August 4, with a front-page story in the *Times.*

The State Department's efficiency was being impaired at a critical period in the war by "conflicting" personalities and lack of cohesive policy, wrote John

H. Crider, a staff reporter. The rivalry between Hull and Welles was "common knowledge." Foreign diplomats were "confused," and the Budget Bureau had begun preparing a reorganization of the State Department for the President's approval. Soon thereafter *The Nation,* a liberal weekly, noted that "identical" stories had appeared simultaneously in the *Chicago Tribune* and the *Washington Times-Herald* but "nowhere else." All three papers, *The Nation* added, were "champions of Hull in his long-standing feud with his second-in-command."[26]

Krock was on holiday at Hot Springs, Virginia, when Crider's story appeared, but he hurried back and, two days later, blamed Roosevelt in a long, analytical column for the alleged mess in the State Department. Roosevelt had given Welles "too much freedom" and had not backed Hull, Krock charged. As a three-time Pulitzer Prize winner, Krock was widely read and his analysis swept the capital.

Hull professed outrage over the Crider story in a meeting with the *Times*'s publisher, Arthur Hays Sulzberger, soon after, but those aware of Hull's close ties to Krock remained skeptical. Turner Catledge, a future *New York Times* managing editor, learned from James F. Byrnes, director of War Mobilization, that Hull had telephoned him "jubilantly" the morning the story appeared.[27]

In 1948, five years later, Crider heard that Welles was critically ill and wrote him a long, personal letter, insisting that Krock had played no part in his article. Crider had been wrapping up Washington political gossip on a dull news day, he wrote, and had been aghast to find his speculative story on the front page next morning. Crider also confirmed this version to the author in 1949; but Felix Belair, a *Times* Washington editor, challenged his account. "Krock told him to strengthen the lead [paragraphs]," Belair remembered.[28]

Roosevelt had been fishing in Canada when the Crider story broke. Returning to Washington three days later, he immediately lunched with Hull and called him back to the White House the next day, August 10. Although Stalin had just agreed to a meeting of Big Four foreign ministers in Moscow in October, Welles, not Stalin, was uppermost on their minds. Hull saw his chance—and struck. Roosevelt could accept either Welles's resignation or his, he decreed. One or the other would have to go.

Hull had carefully prepared the ground with Byrnes, Senators Connally and Brewster and others during Welles's vacation and had Roosevelt cornered. The President was leaving the next day for Hyde Park where Churchill was waiting to confer with him before QUADRANT, the first Quebec conference. Hull, too, was scheduled to attend; his resignation at that moment would have been a political bombshell.

At noon on August 11, FDR called Welles to the Oval Office and broke the news. Welles offered his immediate resignation, but Roosevelt refused it. He had a special mission for him, he said. He wanted him to represent the United States at the coming Moscow conference. Welles was to think it over and give

Roosevelt his answer when he returned in a few days from Hyde Park before going on to Quebec.

Alone the next night at Oxon Hill, Welles wrote Mathilde in Bar Harbor an eight-page *cri-de-coeur* describing his talk with the President. He asked her to burn it, but she did not, and it was found in his papers after his death:

> Darling: I realized very soon after I came back that Mr Hull's attitude to me was very much the same as after Rio de Janeiro but I paid very little attention to it. The President was, of course, away until three days ago.
>
> Then there appeared the article in the New York Times by Crider, a man I have never seen and who has never been at the State Department. Many of Mr Hull's friends told him that I had been responsible for the story. The atmosphere has been worse than I have ever known it, and I have proof that the Republican National Committee has been mixed in.
>
> Yesterday, the President asked me to see him. He said that he had never been angrier in his life at the situation in the State Department, which has now reached an impossible climax. Shortly before I returned from my vacation, Mr Hull had said to him that he had been trying for a year and a half to make it clear that he wished me replaced. The President said that under present circumstances, with the position [Hull] held in the country, and abroad, he could not let him go. I said I had always recognized that.
>
> The President then said there are two main problems: first, for two years or more you have been making admirable speeches, which he couldn't make and wasn't prepared to make, and have been taking the lead in post-war policy, which he should, but couldn't do. This he resents bitterly, and particularly so since Rio de Janeiro.
>
> Second, while I don't think he does it, deliberately, Mr Hull complains about you to every Senator and newspaperman he talks to. The result is the kind of story that has now again been published and repercussions among the conservatives on the Hill. The President spoke also of the poison Bullitt had spread and how he would never permit him to return to Washington.
>
> I said that if Mr Hull had ever indicated to me that he wanted me to resign I would have done so in 24 hours. My devotion and affection for the President was the issue. I would never embarrass him, particularly in wartime. I would resign at once. After ten years my health had broken—which is literally true in many ways. That was that.
>
> The President immediately said I won't allow you to do that and I shall never forget his next words: I have known you since you were a little boy before you went to Groton. I have seen you develop into what you now are. I need you for the country. After all, whom have I got? Harry Hopkins is a sick man. I thought he would die when he joined me last week. We are just moving into the

first critical stages of peace talks. You know more about that than anyone, and you can be of more value than anyone.

He then read me a cable from Stalin saying that the [Tehran] meeting was to take place a little later and asking him to send his personal representative to a preliminary meeting with Molotov and Eden. The President said: I have no one to send but you; no one to do the rounding-up work with the Latin Americans and other governments and, eventually, to see the whole thing through—which really means seeing the war we won isn't lost.

I said that I was very deeply moved and touched but didn't see how this remedied the situation. If I did what he wanted, I would still necessarily be in contact with Mr Hull all the time. The mere fact that I remained Under Secretary even for a few months, going back and forth all the time, would give me just the kind of publicity and Presidential authority which Mr Hull so greatly resented. I wished to resign: that was the best and wisest course.

The President said he wouldn't for a moment agree. I then said I would think it over and let him have my final decision Monday, August 16, when he comes back for a day before going to [Quebec]. I have not yet spoken to Mr Hull. You can imagine the nervous strain in this hideous weather. Last night, I couldn't get to sleep even with [sleeping] pills, and couldn't even keep my mind on a book.

Thank God Almighty for those happy peaceful days at Bar Harbor with you. I have never realized until now how much I love you and how much I need you. I am looking forward to hearing your voice tonight.[29]

Hull later described to Bullitt his final meeting with Welles. A day or two after seeing Roosevelt, Welles had come to his office. The President, he said, had told him that Hull had wanted him replaced for a year and a half. Why hadn't Hull told him so himself? "Stop right there!" Hull had thundered.

I didn't speak to you because you're an intimate friend of the President, much closer to him than I. I based my request on your personal habits.

For more than two years, I concealed it from my wife. It was brought to her attention by wives of prominent members of Congress. You knew it was known to them, to the Soviet government, the Free French, the British and South American countries. You should have come to me. Your continuation in office would be, for the President and State Department, the greatest national scandal since the existence of the United States.

Welles had risen, shaken his hand without a word and walked out. That was the last time Welles ever saw him.[30]

His career in ruins, Welles suffered a heart attack that weekend. On Monday, August 16, FDR returned from Hyde Park, conferred with Byrnes, Knox and the Democratic party boss, Postmaster General Frank Walker, then lunched again with Hull. Welles had been scheduled to see FDR next, but the White House appointment list shows his name scratched out and "sick" penciled in by General Watson.[31] That afternoon Welles dictated a formal letter of resignation from Oxon Hill and a personal note to FDR.

He had been "laid up for two days in bed with a bad heart attack or I would have come in to see you, as you said I might," he wrote. "Whatever you think the best course in this situation I will, of course, loyally follow. But I want you to know that, so long as I live, I shall never forget the friendship and kindness you showed me in our last talk."[32]

FDR left for Quebec the next day and Hull followed a day later, leaving Welles acting Secretary of State. That night, August 19, he wrote Mathilde again:

> You will never know what you have been to me these past ten days. Your letters, your encouragement, your voice in the evening and the fact, above everything else, that you love me have got me through the bitterest days of my life. I have learned a great deal that I will tell you when I see you—about plans and arrangements that were so carefully worked out when I was happily away with you last month.
>
> But it is almost all finished now, thank God, and I want to get through with my head up, and not as if there were room for public doubt as to my abilities. The one thing I look forward to is to get up to you, away from this inferno, and stay there until October. I can reply to the President's public offer to me [the Moscow conference] as well from Bar Harbor as from Washington. You and I are in complete agreement. From now on my life will be with you. That is the essential thing—what does the rest of it count in comparison?[33]

On Sunday, August 22, his last day in office, Welles asked Berle to meet him at the State Department late in the afternoon. Welles was exhausted, clearing out his desk and dictating letters of farewell, Berle remembered. Welles said that he had submitted his resignation and that the President had accepted it.(FDR, in fact, had not.) Welles said he would never forget the President's remarks about his service to the nation. He was leaving next day for Bar Harbor and asked Berle to assume charge of the department. Hull, in Quebec, had agreed.

Berle tried to persuade him to stay until Hull returned, pointing out that his resignation could not fail to get out if he left, but Welles thought it best to get away. There would be a week of unpleasant and difficult comment then "complete obscurity." Berle urged him also to attend the Moscow conference.

It was the biggest challenge ahead, he said. An unresolved relationship with the Soviet Union could mean a head-on collision later; there was little time left. "It is five minutes of midnight," Welles replied. "If the situation runs much longer, it will be insoluble."

But he could go to Moscow only with the State Department's full confidence and support. In view of Hull's attitude, he obviously would not have it. "I said farewell," wrote Berle, "and left him in a dusty, sunlit office in an empty building finishing, as he believed, his brilliant but stormy career."[34]

Welles asked Pearson to dine alone with him at Oxon Hill that last night and asked his advice. Pearson urged him to accept FDR's Moscow offer, but two days later he wrote that Welles should "stand pat," remaining loyal to the President but accepting no further diplomatic missions. Hull would undercut him in the Senate and "sour" any agreement he brought back from Moscow.[35] The next morning Welles entrained for Bar Harbor, arriving at day's end "looking awful," his valet, Reeks, remembered. Mathilde upbraided him for his appearance but he was too weary to argue. "Reeks, please lay out my clothes and draw a hot bath," he said quietly. "Let me know when it's ready." In the weeks ahead, Reeks often saw him sitting on the porch overlooking Frenchman's Bay, plunged in thought, "terribly depressed."[36]

Within twenty-four hours, Pearson's brother, Leon, a radio journalist, reported Welles's resignation and, "almost immediately," wrote Berle, "the left-wing press began to make Sumner a hero, the only friend of Russia, the sole bulwark against a Fascist State Department."[37] A week later, in a radio broadcast, Drew Pearson himself accused Hull of secretly hoping to see Russia "bled white" by the Germans. Hull denounced this "diabolical falsehood," and Roosevelt publicly branded Pearson a "chronic liar."[38] Never before had reporters heard the President assail one of their tribe so bitterly.

Drew Pearson's broadcast was the "final straw," Hull told Bullitt. Until then he had been willing to accede to FDR's desire to ease Welles out gracefully by sending him to Moscow or making him a roving presidential envoy in Latin America. Eleanor Roosevelt and other of Welles's friends had urged FDR not to accept his resignation, and, in fact, the President had pigeonholed it. Then, said Hull, that "dirty polecat" Drew Pearson, had made a violent attack on him, calling him an enemy of the Russians and Welles their only friend. After that he had gone to FDR, demanding that he accept Welles's resignation immediately.[39]

In the silver silence of the Maine coast Welles's spirits slowly began lifting, boosted by press eulogies and letters and telegrams of support. Welles had the "firmest grasp of anyone in the State Department on the problems of the future," wrote the *New York Herald-Tribune*. Eliminating him meant eliminating one of the "younger, abler and more forward-looking" minds in the department in favor of an "elderly chief, living largely in a rather remote past," whose policies had seldom been notable and whose administrative control of his department had been "lamentable."[40] By what right or reason, asked the *St.Louis Post-Dispatch,* was the nation's "greatest public servant in the field of foreign affairs" being asked to give up the post he had held with "honor"?[41]

Time magazine noted widespread press support for Welles and severe condemnation of Hull and Roosevelt.[42] The liberal *Nation* praised Welles as the department's most "far-sighted internationalist" and its leading advocate of friendly relations with the Soviet Union.[43] William L. Shirer described Welles in the *Washington Post* as the "only liberal and, by far, the most able" of the department's ranking officials.[44] The isolationist *Washington Times-Herald,* seizing on Welles's dismissal to attack Roosevelt, called Welles a diplomat of "extraordinary talent."[45] Messages of support poured in.

"Sumner busy answering hundreds of wonderful letters and wires," Mathilde wrote a friend. "I worried about him, at first, but he is too superb. Old 'Moss Back' [Hull] and his viper wife can't hurt him. Someday we'll tell you the dirty underhand way they and Krock did it while we were here in July for our holiday. A real man would have gone to Sumner and had it out. Not [Hull]. His insane jealousy and hers is disgusting and small."[46] A week later she wrote again.

"The old viper [Frances Hull] wrote me a 'devotedly, with love' letter after Sumner had [resigned.] Can you beat this for hypocrisy? Sumner's fan mail still arrives. Over 700 wonderful letters to date. He is really superb, calm and loyal. I can't be [loyal to the Hulls] and will say what I damn please, as usual."[47]

Meanwhile in Washington, Hull, irked by press eulogies of his former subordinate, sent a security agent to roam the Metropolitan Club as a "temporary guest" and pry details of Welles's drinking habits from the staff.[48] He called in James Reston, the rising star of the *New York Times,* and offered to leak him the Southern Railway affidavits about Welles, but Reston walked out, disgusted.[49] Hull was also telephoning James F. Byrnes, FDR's new chief of staff, virtually daily, worried that the President had the "wrong impression" about his demand for Welles's resignation and begging Byrnes to "clarify" it. Hull thought Welles should issue a statement correcting Pearson's "lies" about his attitude toward Russia.

Byrnes wrote FDR soon after that Hull was not "unqualifiedly" opposed to Welles going to the Moscow conference and that he himself thought Welles should attend. "He is qualified and I'd give him this recognition," he wrote. The chances were that, afterward, Welles would leave the government voluntarily. "I am confident I can get Hull to help, instead of hurt," Byrnes concluded.[50]

On August 30, Pearson wrote Welles that Byrnes "feels very much that you should go [to Moscow]." Byrnes had been with FDR on his fishing expedition and had taken no part in the controversy. "The only time your name was mentioned by the President during his Great Lakes trip," wrote Pearson, "was when [he] received a telegram from you regarding the Vatican and the message you proposed sending the Pope. After reading [it] the President remarked that you had one of the finest minds he knew and could always be trusted to handle any international situation which arose."[51]

Hoping to retain Welles's services, FDR summoned him to Hyde Park on September 19 and again asked him to represent the United States at Moscow—but first he wanted Welles to write Hull, making clear that he had not instigated Pearson's attacks. He asked Welles "point-blank" if he had dined with Pearson the night before news of his resignation was broadcast. Welles confirmed that he had but pointed out that Pearson had learned of it already from Leo T. Crowley, a senior administrator close to Hull. Two days later, on September 21, Welles wrote FDR, "regretfully and reluctantly," declining the Moscow mission and asking that his resignation be announced:

> I would value, tremendously, the opportunity of continuing to serve you and there is no negotiation I can think of which . . . would be of greater significance . . . But the insight you gave me . . . concerning Secretary Hull's feelings toward me makes me feel that this decision is the right one. It required many unhappy hours for me to reach it.

In announcing his resignation, he hoped that the President would "let it be known" that he had asked Welles to represent the United States at Moscow but that Mrs. Welles's "health" made it impossible.[52] The same day he wrote Hull as requested. The President had told him, he began icily, that Hull thought him responsible for Pearson's attacks. After ten years, Hull should have known that he did not "stoop" to such tactics. He had instigated attacks neither by Pearson nor by any other reporter, and had not the slightest responsibility for reports of Hull's views about the Soviet Union. During his ten years in office, he had talked with many newsmen and "not one can, truthfully, say that I have ever referred to you, except with the utmost loyalty."[53]

Welles's resignation, although a professional and, still more, a personal loss to Roosevelt, solved several of his problems. The President's indifference to—or inability to control—interagency feuding had led to severe criticism. "In every theater of war," wrote Byrnes, "the Army and Navy were confronted with chaos because of . . . conflicting policies."[54] For months Byrnes, Crowley, Wayne Coy of the Budget Bureau, and other senior administrators had been urging FDR to knock heads and merge quarreling agencies under a strong chief. Roosevelt had asked Averell Harriman at Quebec to succeed Welles as Under Secretary but Harriman had opted for the Moscow embassy.[55] The situation was critical and, after nineteen months of war, only Lend-Lease under Edward R. Stettinius seemed to be functioning smoothly.

"If you have not definitely decided the appointment of the Under Secretary," Byrnes wrote FDR on September 21, two days after Welles's resignation, "move Stettinius to that post." Lend-Lease and four quarreling agencies could then be merged into a new Foreign Economic Administration (FEA) under Crowley, who was on good terms with Hull and Congress. To avoid further delay and friction with Hull, Roosevelt settled on Stettinius,[56] announced Welles's resignation on September 25 and added "with deep and sincere regret" to the White House press release. Five days later Senator Brewster told Wallace of his happiness that Hull had "finally gotten rid of Welles." He had worked "very closely" with Hull on the problem, he boasted.[57]

Welles's friends, meanwhile, had not forgotten him. In October Morris L. Ernst, a leading New York lawyer close to FDR, organized a small dinner at New York's Waldorf-Astoria to show their "affection and esteem." Among the guests were Arthur H. Sulzberger, publisher of the *New York Times,* and Anne O'Hare McCormick, its foreign affairs columnist; John Gunther, the author; Raymond Gram Swing, the broadcaster; Myron C. Taylor, FDR's representative to the Vatican; and Helen Reid, wife of the publisher of the *New York Herald-Tribune.* That evening Mrs Reid asked Welles to write a foreign affairs column for the *Tribune* syndicate, and he gratefully accepted. Roosevelt wrote him, regretting that he could not attend the dinner and referring to his resignation. At the top he wrote "Private" in longhand.

> I think you were perfectly right in your decision, though I did honestly think it would be best for you, and for the country, if you could go to this Moscow conference. However, the final decision has removed the whole matter from the papers and the columnists . . . Incidentally, the Secretary very suddenly decided that he wished, most urgently, to go himself—and he has gone.
>
> In view of the fact that he made this decision known to one or two of his friends before I got your letter, I could not very well say that I had asked you to undertake the Moscow trip because it would have been said that the Secretary, on realizing this, had insisted on going in your place. That would have only added fuel to the fire—which I am confident is now out . . .
>
> I do hope . . . you will come in to see me. There are many things I want to talk over with you. I wish much that I could come to that dinner for you. Thank the Lord you have not retired to innocuous desuetude. Good luck![58]

It was a strange letter: more of relief that embarrassing publicity was "out" than of regret over losing a valued public servant and lifelong friend. Roosevelt the politician, not the man, had wielded the pen.

Far from retiring to "innocuous desuetude" Welles challenged the administration the next day to clarify its peace aims. In a nationally broadcast speech to the Foreign Policy Association in New York, his first in ten years as a private citizen, he urged the "immediate" establishment of a UN Executive Council. A fortnight later he began a weekly column for the *Herald-Tribune* syndicate and was at work on a new book, *The Time for Decision,* in Palm Beach early in November when Hull returned in triumph from Moscow.

Stalin had approved the Four Power declaration that Welles had drafted shortly before his resignation. After three weeks in Moscow, wrote Edgar Ansell Mowrer of the *Philadelphia Inquirer,* Hull had signed an "inspired plan—almost identical with that outlined by [Welles] at New York while the conference was going on."[59]

Pearson reported that Welles had shown the draft declaration to Hull in April or May, but Hull "would have none of it," although Roosevelt and Churchill both approved it later at Quebec.[60] Ickes, who detested Hull, noted in his diary that Welles was the "author of the much-vaunted Hull plan which Hull had been credited with putting over at Moscow. When Hull, as a result of Welles's resignation, found himself in such a jam that he had to go to Moscow, personally," Ickes continued, "he was probably delighted to have something tangible to take along in the way of a plan. It was extremely fortunate for all concerned that he did have such a plan and that it was acceptable to Russia, Great Britain and China."[61]

At year's end, Bullitt called on the Hulls to offer season's greetings. After a brief exchange of pleasantries, Mrs. Hull withdrew, leaving her husband and Bullitt to savor their triumph. The passage of time had done little to assuage Hull's "vindictiveness," Bullitt wrote later; he spoke of Welles with the same "intensity" as before, Their victory, however, was not totally unalloyed. Hull confided that Roosevelt was so angry with Bullitt after their "violent altercation" that he would not have him in the government. Hull, nonetheless, had not given up hope of finding Bullitt an official position and would speak again to the President.

Two days later Hull conceded failure. He had recommended Bullitt as either chief U.S. liaison officer with the Free French in North Africa or as a presidential envoy in the Middle East. To each FDR's reply had been a resounding "No!"[62]

Bullitt had destroyed Welles, with Hull's connivance, but he also had destroyed himself. Never again would he serve in the U.S. government. To be rid of him, FDR hinted that he might back him if he ran for mayor of Philadelphia, and Bullitt swallowed the bait. The arch-intriguer had met his match. Behind his back, FDR sent word to the Pennsylvania bosses: "Cut his throat."[63]

Years of Decline

TWENTY-NINE

FOUR

READY TO DEPART

1943–1961

"The Fire of Life Had Sunk"

WELLES LIVED ANOTHER EIGHTEEN YEARS, years initially marked by success as an author, syndicated columnist, radio broadcaster and lecturer. His views were widely sought and his prestige was intact, for few knew the story behind his resignation. Head high, he threw himself into his new labors with the demonic passion for work that had led to repeated heart attacks through the years. With the Allied victory in sight, he was determined to awaken Congress and the nation to the need for U.S.-Soviet agreement on postwar issues before the war ended and the Allies quarreled again.

In the early years, after leaving government, he displayed the same incisive thinking that had clarified foreign policy problems for three decades and the same devotion to FDR's policies that made him a beacon for those pondering America's course after Roosevelt's death. But his resignation from office had relegated him to the sidelines, and, with mounting frustration, he watched the Cold War unfold and his hopes for an effective United Nations collapse. Gradually he lost touch with the shapers of policy.

Unable, or unwilling, to discipline himself, he began drinking to keep up a crushing writing and lecture schedule; the carnal passions in his nature blazed up again, fueled by alcohol. After Mathilde's death in 1949, his remaining years were marked by loneliness, illness and suicidal dissipation.

In 1944, the year after his resignation, the success of his book, *The Time for Decision,* revived his morale. An international best-seller, it was praised by reviewers and, to his delight, brought out in paperback for U.S. troops overseas. "Of capital importance," wrote Anne O'Hare McCormick of the *New York Times* in a front-page review in the Sunday book section. "Required reading for every American, and a spur to the thinking of other peoples." Welles was one of the "best-informed men of our time" on the interrelations of governments.

In three sections, his book dealt with errors of the past, problems of the present and demands of the future—for most of which he offered solutions. The work of a policy maker rather than a diplomat, it was essentially an argument, first for the immediate establishment of a United Nations Executive Council to serve as a supreme authority until a permanent international organization was practicable, and, second, for a world order that ensured U.S. security.

His recommendations included: freedom of information; the division of Germany into three states[1]; eradication of the German general staff (the "root of evil"); economic union in southeastern Europe; and settlement of the Palestine problem through a union of Jews and Arabs in an autonomous Palestine within a Palestinian-Syrian-Lebanese-Jordanian federation.

"Unless the U.S. succeeds in establishing . . . an international organization in the immediate future," Welles wrote a year before Allied victory, "we will drift into the armistice period to find ourselves once more in the position President Wilson found himself in Paris in January, 1919. But this time our government will possess neither the prestige nor the influence Wilson then had."[2] History would prove him right. Welles's judgment could be challenged on "this or that" point, wrote McCormick, but he had developed his arguments with "logic and passion" and his competence to pass judgment was beyond dispute.

Welles had performed an "immense service" in putting his experience at the disposal of his country, wrote William Allen Neilson in the *New York Herald-Tribune.* His criticism of past events was "frank, temperate and without malice." His blueprint for the postwar had been thought out with immense care and a frank facing of its difficulties. The most important lesson of his book was the need to plan and establish the main lines of postwar settlement while the war was still on. "Unless we are prepared to apply ourselves to such plans," Neilson concluded, "there is no escaping a repetition of the present catastrophe."[3]

Like others dismayed by Roosevelt's death on the eve of victory, Welles viewed Harry Truman with extreme reserve. The new President's earlier links to Missouri's Pendergast machine, his inexperience in foreign affairs and his appointment of the equally inexperienced James F. Byrnes as Secretary of State left Welles profoundly depressed. FDR's flair, experience, knowledge and capacity for "daring initiative as well as prudence" had been replaced, he wrote, by "sincerity, devoted patriotism and the best of intentions but, unfortuntely, by neither knowledge, experience or strength."[4]

In *Where Are We Heading?*, a cantankerous jeremiad published in late 1946, Welles criticized the failure of Truman and the Allies to agree on a common policy toward Germany—let alone a peace treaty—fourteen months after the German surrender. By contrast, he noted, seven months after World War I the Allies had signed a German peace treaty. Truman should either have agreed with the Allies on a common policy toward Germany before its surrender or the UN should have supervised the occupation.

The United States had been at the "peak" of its military-political strength on the eve of the Potsdam conference in July 1945, he wrote. Yet to placate Stalin and ignoring Churchill's warnings, Truman and Byrnes had failed to ensure access to Berlin and had withdrawn U.S. forces from Czechoslovakia. Vacillating between concessions to the Soviet Union and "strong-arm" tactics, they had adopted a policy of "drift and hope for the best," not controlling but being controlled by events.[5] Stalin had dominated the Potsdam conference. "We were outplayed in every move," wrote Welles.[6] Unless the United States and the Soviet Union reached early agreement, he foresaw a "fatal drift" toward a world of two blocs.[7]

Following Hull's resignation in 1944, Welles's own name had frequently cropped up as a possible Democratic Secretary of State. "I believe Roosevelt would have preferred [Welles] to all others," wrote Robert Sherwood, "but his appointment would have been a direct affront to Hull and provocative of intense resentment on Capitol Hill."[8] In May 1947, Welles's friend Charles P. Curtis, Jr., heard fresh rumors and brought them to his attention. There was not the slightest truth to them, Welles wrote back. So long as Hull lived (he died in 1955), no offer would be made him. "I am now 54," Welles wrote, "and will never again accept any position in the government where my own views and convictions as to policy would have to be subordinated to those of some other individual in the State Department."[9]

Meeting in Palm Beach that spring, Welles and Churchill revived memories of their collaboration at the 1941 Atlantic Charter conference. Churchill was the "last survivor of the great generation," Welles wrote Curtis. The contrast between Churchill, on one hand, and Truman, Byrnes and British Prime Minister Clement Atlee, on the other, added to his depression. He differed profoundly with Churchill's belief that the British empire could survive but agreed entirely with his analysis of what could be done to "save something of that for which we . . . fought." In a dramatic speech at Fulton,

Missouri, on March 5, 1946, Churchill won world attention by proposing what should be done.

Choosing Truman's home state for maximum impact in the White House, he called on the West to unite in self-defense against the new danger to mankind: Soviet Russia. An "iron curtain" was descending across Europe from Stettin on the Baltic to Trieste on the Adriatic, he warned. Many assailed the ex-Prime Minister for saber-rattling, but Welles approved the speech, which had shocked U.S. opinion into realizing that Truman's "complacent drift could only end in a new war." Few learned by experience, he wrote Curtis; history was repeating itself.[11]

Four months later he wrote Curtis that he had never felt more thoroughly "disheartened and gloomy . . . Sitting on the side-lines as I do, I can see one opportunity after another in the field of foreign policy going by." Soon it would be too late for further opportunities. If the Republicans had the sense to nominate a Liberal in 1948, it would "probably be good for the country and, in the long run, for my own [Democratic] party."

In September 1946 he wrote his elder son, Ben, then in Peiping covering the Chinese civil war for the *New York Times,* that the United States had not had "so incompetent" an administration since James Buchanan (1857-61). "I hate to write in so pessimistic a vein," he added, "but have reluctantly been forced to the unhappy conclusion that world is very rapidly drifting toward the edge of the precipice."[12]

Many at the time might have agreed. Early in 1947 the collapse of the Truman-Marshall mediation effort in China led to fear that Mao Tse-tung's Communists might soon overthrow Chiang Kai-shek's American-backed but corrupt Nationalist regime, creating a Sino-Soviet bloc of 1.2 billion "hostiles." Political recrimination swept the nation. Republicans charged the Truman administration with "losing" China, fueling hysteria about Communist subversion and, later, to the persecution of anyone suspected of Communist sympathies by the Republican junior senator from Wisconsin, Joseph R. McCarthy.

Meanwhile, the growing threat of Communist coups in Western Europe in the autumn of 1947 reinforced Welles's conviction that only force—or the threat of force—could forestall them. In his next column, he wrote Curtis, he would "go out on a limb" and urge Congress to declare that the armed overthrow of a freely elected Western European government by Communist organizations would be tantamount to an "attack upon the U.S." Such a declaration would make armed insurrections impossible. Had Congress authorized Roosevelt, in 1939-40, to declare that Axis aggression against the democracies would be regarded as aggression against the United States, "Hitler's blitzkrieg and the result that we now confront" would have been prevented.

What shocked him most was the persistent conviction of many Americans that the United States could avoid having to use force in certain contingencies. Two Midwest senators, Arthur Vandenberg (R.-Mich.) and Robert LaFollette (Progressive.-Wis.), and Raymond Brandt, a columnist for the *St. Louis Post-Dispatch,* had recently dined with him and had expressed "horror" at his suggestion that force might be necessary to protect Europe. In the Midwest, it was fatal even to speak of another "shooting" war, they had warned. The American public seemed willing to "spend dollars" on the Marshall Plan and emergency relief, Welles wrote Curtis indignantly but would not even consider a "display of force" so that the dollars could be spent successfully.[13]

Early in 1948, Welles learned that Hull's memoirs would soon appear and asked Pearson to send him an advance copy as he would "probably have to make a statement refuting Hull's references to me."[14] His fears were confirmed when his Cuban friend, Cosme de la Torriente, wrote that excerpts in Havana newspapers showed Hull claiming credit for Welles's 1933 mediation between Cuban dictator Gerardo Machado and the opposition. Welles had been "wholly in disagreement with FDR" in demanding intervention, Hull claimed. After perusing Pearson's advance copy, Welles wrote angrily that it was full of "untrue and malicious" references to himself.

Hull had not had the "foggiest idea" of what was going on in Cuba. Throughout his mission, Welles had consistently counseled *against intervention.* "It was President Roosevelt whom I consulted and from whom I took orders," he wrote. "At the end, the President [told] me that he had been 100% in agreement on every step I had taken and on every recommendation I had made."

Among other "fabrications," Hull had charged that Welles had been responsible for the President's sending him to Europe in 1940. "I never thought of that possibility until the President suggested it on his own and told me I was the only person he could send," Welles asserted. Hull had further claimed that Welles's 1942 speeches had been made "against the wishes" of the President.

In fact, Welles wrote, he had discussed the speeches in advance with the President who had told him that he "heartily endorsed every word [and] was thankful that someone was speaking for the administration with regard to the objectives for which we were fighting." Hull had alleged that Roosevelt had wanted to send him to the Moscow conference in October 1943 and that Welles had been "only a possible substitute." To the contrary, Welles retorted, Roosevelt had insisted for six weeks that he go and had continued insisting until Hull announced publicly that he himself was going.

Welles's loathing for Hull poured out. The "psychopathic vanity, the pettiness, venom and inarticulate incapacity which operated behind the saintly mask and the assumed modesty that so long misled the general public," he wrote Pearson, would be apparent to any "thinking" reader. But how many were thinking readers? Pearson urged him to counterattack, issue a statement to newspapers carrying Hull's memoirs and challenge Hull in his column, but Welles refused. Hull's misrepresentations were "infuriating," he replied, but he doubted that anything would be gained by a public dispute.[15]

Galled by Hull's memoirs, Welles was drinking heavily and Mathilde threatened to leave him. Apparently it shook him, for a handwritten note, dated March 11, 1948, and found in her papers after her death, reads: "I state that the next time I take any alcoholic beverage of any kind I will leave whatever house my wife and I may be occupying and agree to a legal separation, should my wife desire one. [signed] Sumner Welles."[16] Like previous pledges, it was soon forgotten.

With the 1948 campaign gathering speed, Welles became tangentially involved in Republican attacks on Truman and the Democrats for lax security and indifference to communism. The year before, bowing to political pressure, Truman had signed a Loyalty Order requiring the investigation of all Executive Branch employees. On August 3, 1948, Whittaker Chambers, an admitted former Communist courier, identified the State Department's Alger Hiss as part of a prewar Washington Communist ring. Hiss had worked for Welles in drafting the UN Charter, had been a member of FDR's staff at Yalta, and Welles had formed an impression of him that made it "almost impossible for me to believe that there was a shred of foundation for the present charges," he wrote Curtis, who had written supporting Hiss.

"I wish I could have the confidence you have in the Hiss case," he added. Walter Lippmann, the foreign affairs analyst, had dined with him two nights earlier and had passed on a warning from Bert Andrews, the *New York Herald-Tribune*'s White House correspondent, not to support Hiss in his syndicated column. According to Andrews, Hiss had repeatedly lied and his outlook "seemed black."[17]

On December 8, scenting political pay-dirt, the Republican-controlled House Un-American Affairs Committee (HUAC) opened hearings on the so-called pumpkin papers: government documents hidden in pumpkins on Whittaker Chambers's Maryland farm. Called to testify, Welles identified them as having been filched from the Department in 1937 and 1938 while he was Under Secretary. He thought them so confidential that they should be withheld from publication. Asked whether publication after a decade or more would still jeopardize national security, Welles suspected a trap to smear the Roosevelt administration and coolly referred the committee to the State Department's security staff.

His indignation flared, however, when HUAC members sought to link his former assistant, Laurence Duggan, with espionage. After years of close collaboration, Welles respected Duggan's judgment, had come to regard him as a personal friend and had been saddened when the younger man had left the State Department at war's end for a senior position with the Carnegie Foundation in New York. Rejecting HUAC's insinuations with contempt, Welles asserted that Duggan was one of the "most brilliant, devoted and patriotic public servants I have ever known."

A fortnight later, on Monday, December 20, under circumstances that are still a mystery, Duggan plunged to his death from his sixteenth-floor office on New York's Forty-fifth street. When his body was found around 7 P.M. he was wearing one overshoe. The other was later found in his office, along with his hat, coat, Christmas cards, letters referring to future engagements and an airplane ticket to Washington for the next day. Within hours the acting HUAC chairman, Representative Karl E. Mundt (R.-S.D.), called a subcommittee meeting comprising himself and Representative Richard M. Nixon (R-Cal.) and hinted to reporters that Duggan had been linked to communism.[18]

Outraged, Welles telegraphed New York Mayor William O'Dwyer suggesting foul play and demanding an immediate investigation while the *New York Times* condemned Mundt editorially the next morning for leveling charges against a man "whose body was hardly cold." Welles, Adolf A. Berle, Francis B. Sayre and other of Duggan's former State Department associates "vouch for his loyalty and . . . honesty," noted the *Times*.[19] The world in which Welles had been reared was collapsing, its standards replaced by cutthroat insinuations, character assassination and smears.

Lecturing in universities and colleges across the nation, Welles was increasingly concerned that revisionist historians were sullying Roosevelt's record in the minds of young Americans. Robert Sherwood's new book, *Roosevelt and Hopkins*,[20] was "magnificent," he wrote Curtis, but it made no effort to show up as "malignant and psychopathic the outpourings of the Roosevelt-haters" who were trying to persuade the American people that Roosevelt had deliberately forced them into war or that his conduct of foreign policy and military affairs had been "ignorant, inefficient and prejudicial." Cass Canfield, whose firm Harper's had published *The Time for Decision*, and Hamilton Fish Armstrong, the editor of *Foreign Affairs Quarterly*, had both suggested that Welles write a new book to prevent misconceptions about FDR from "jelling" in the public mind. He had begun writing and was planning to call it *Ten Decisions That Shaped History*.[21]

Meanwhile, his lecture schedule, though "back-breaking," was reward-ing. "Every time I get out into other parts of the country, I come back feeling— mentally, at least—25 years younger, tremendously invigorated and gladder than ever to be an American," Welles wrote. In Pittsburgh he had addressed a luncheon of 150 "survivors of the dinosaurs and pterodactyls of the Andrew W. Mellon age,"[22] then another group of 300 and, after a cocktail party and dinner, an audience of 2,000 at the University of Pittsburgh. His reception at Kent State University in Ohio the next morning had been the "best of all." More than 3,000 "intensely interested" young Americans had packed the auditorium. He had been scheduled to speak for forty minutes but had spoken for an hour and a half, and no one had moved. The younger generation was "starving for some sign of hope," fearful of becoming what was so desperately on its mind: a "lost" generation.

After Kent State, he had driven to Cleveland, had taken part in a television interview, had made a dinner speech, had later addressed an audience of 2,000 at the Council on World Affairs and, afterward, had driven forty-five miles through dense fog to Akron to catch his train back to Washington. "I wish I could do that sort of stunt more often," he wrote Curtis early in December 1948, although it was "physically crucifying."[23]

Welles, in fact, was on the verge of collapse. Traveling, lecturing, broadcasting, writing books and two columns a week, he was dependent on sodium amytal for three or four hours' sleep a night and on alcohol to keep going. Physically exhausted, he was also emotionally depressed by Truman's reelection that fall, by his continuing "drift" in Western Europe and by anti-American riots, led by a Cuban firebrand named Fidel Castro, which recently had disrupted a hemisphere conference at Bogota. The Good Neighbor policy and hemisphere unity, for which Welles had worked a quarter century, were being abandoned.

Five years out of office, Welles was losing touch with important news sources. His columns were didactic or platitudinous, and his contract to broadcast for the Waltham Watch Company was about to expire, not to be renewed. Worse, his veteran English valet-factotum, James Reeks, had retired the year before after a heart attack, and his loss, after two decades of devoted service, was to have a disastrous effect on Welles's remaining years. Reeks's place was taken by a psychopathic bisexual, Gustave van Hamme, whose hard drinking and turbulent influence hastened Welles's rush to self-destruction.

Christmas 1948 marked a new low in Welles's life. Depressed by the sinister death of his friend and colleague Duggan and fearful that Mathilde might divorce him, he attempted suicide. A guest who had dined at Oxon Hill two nights earlier remembered that he seemed "terribly distraught . . . He hardly spoke."[24] A handwritten note, dated Christmas 1948 and found in Mathilde's papers after her death, suggests that her husband had come to the end of his road:

> Darling: No man on earth has had a more loyal and devoted wife than you. I
> thank you from the bottom of my heart for all that you have done for me. If it
> had not been for you during these past five years I would never have wanted to

work to try to keep my head up. All I can say is that, these past five years, I have worked like a dog to . . . pay my way and have you realize you hadn't married a heel.

When you think of me, try always to remember two things. You are the one person in life that I have really loved—and that, during the past five years since I left the government, I have never missed one day of work. Darling, darling—bless you always—you have been a benediction to me. One last favor I ask of you. I want to have my body cremated, and the ashes buried [near] your dear mother's mausoleum. I want no tombstone nor other memorial. [signed] Sumner.

At the same time, he wrote his elder son, Ben, who was working in London and whose wife, Cynthia, was expecting their first child, that he could not visit them as planned. "This is a sad letter to send you just as I hoped to be with you both but I just cannot stand existence any more," he wrote. "I don't know . . . what there is ahead but I do know that it couldn't be any worse than the present."

On Saturday, Christmas night, a dozen family friends gathered at Oxon Hill for the traditional Yuletide dinner. Welles was unusually morose. "It was evident something preoccupied him a great deal," one friend remembered. The guests left shortly before midnight, Mathilde retired upstairs, but Welles bade the staff good night and remained in the ground floor library. At 2 A.M., Sunday morning, the night watchman making his rounds saw the library lights still blazing and the door to the terrace open. He thought little of it; Welles often stepped out for a breath of air before retiring.

Twenty-four hours later, on Monday, December 27, the *New York Times* carried a front-page headline: "Welles, Stricken, Lies in Field for Hours in Icy Weather." Local neighbors, the Brooke Kerby family, returning from church at 8 A.M. Sunday morning, had seen a man lying in a field a mile or so from the Oxon Hill estate. Kerby, a carpenter who had helped build the house, had immediately recognized Welles and had called the police who had taken the numbed and all but unconscious man to Washington's Casualty Hospital. Welles's clothes had been frozen to his body and covered with mud, suggesting that he had fallen in a stream a hundred yards from where he was found.

His personal physician, Dr. George R. Huffman, confirmed severe exposure, fingers and toes frozen, but would not know for two or three days whether amputations would be necessary. The night had been cold, fifteen degrees, with snow on the ground. Welles had not worn a hat but Huffman thought his fur-collared coat had saved his life. On recovering consciousness, Welles complained of severe chest pains but remembered little. "I suddenly felt a pain in my heart and started to take a shortcut to my house," he recalled weeks later. "Somehow, in the semi-darkness, I took a wrong turn and found myself in the creek. I can't recall what followed."[25] Messages of sympathy flooded in and the *New York Times* wrote editorially the next day:

> We hope that Sumner Welles . . . will soon be sufficiently recovered to learn the esteem in which he is held and the general sympathy which goes out to him. Mr Welles's . . . natural reserve has often been mistaken for coldness. But his record shows . . . not only a keen intellect, but a warmth and unselfish enthusiasm for good causes . . . We need him.[26]

Fortunately, Welles had fallen into the hands of Dr. J. Ross Veal of Casualty Hospital, a brilliant young vascular surgeon, who saved his life. Welles lost both big toes, the small finger of his left hand, and suffered loss of balance and circulatory problems until his death. Except for Veal, Welles wrote Curtis weeks later, it would have been in the "highest degree improbable that I could have pulled through, or, at best, without major amputations."[27]

A month later he returned to Oxon Hill to start a slow, painful convalescence. Setback followed setback. Mathilde, too, fell ill, fearing a malignancy though a specialist restored her confidence. She had refused to obey any doctor's orders for the past twelve years, Welles wrote his sister, Emily Robbins. "You can imagine the effect on my own nervous system which has been shot to pieces." He still had day and night nurses and his surgeon had to "overhaul" him each morning.

"I have got to take an absolute rest during the next few months [and] give up all regular work," he continued. "This means, of course, abandonment of my column which, after five years of steady grind, is not a pleasing prospect."[28] Looking back, he had suddenly realized that he had "literally, not had a real rest for more than sixteen years."[29]

Two weeks later he wrote Eugene Meyer, publisher of the *Washington Post,* that "with deep disappointment . . . I must give up my column [and] take a complete rest . . . I greatly appreciate the interest the Washington Post has taken in my column from the time it was first started."[30]

Seeing Welles in July for the first time since his accident, Pearson noted that he had "lost thirty-five pounds and had aged ten years." He had wanted to travel since war's end but Mathilde had always refused. Now they were finally leaving for a rest cure in Europe. "Inevitably, a man . . . pays when he marries a rich wife," noted Pearson. "Sumner has had great advantages [but] has paid in the end, rather heavily."[31] Concerned with her health, Mathilde drew up a new will before sailing, leaving Welles $200,000 outright and the income of her fortune for life. She also left generous bequests to friends, family and old retainers and her portrait by John Singer Sargent to the National Gallery. Her will proved an ill omen.

Welles and Mathilde sailed on July 7, 1949, on the old SS *De Grasse* with the customary servants, dogs and mountain of luggage. After a few days at the Paris Ritz, they moved to Ouchy-Lausanne, on Lac Leman, where they planned to spend several weeks restoring their shattered health and allowing Welles to complete his new book, now retitled *Seven Decisions That Shaped History.* "I feel OK now," Mathilde wrote a friend from Lausanne on August 2. "Felt like hell for several days . . . exhaustion after trip and worry if Sumner could make it. [He is] much better and so happy in this place, busy as a bird dog with his book and daily massage and so contented here. It's divine as a rest cure. Ouchy is his heaven."[32] It was her last letter.

On August 5, three days later, contrite at having overlooked his elder son's birthday days earlier, Welles wrote him, "You were in my thoughts all morning of [the] 1st and it was my intention to send you a telegram . . . Then there was a serious 'crise' (Mathilde's health had suddenly worsened) and the whole thing went out of my mind . . . Forgive me, but I know you understand." Mathilde was a little better and there was a chance that she would recover before too long, but "I am on my last inch of staying power. I cannot eat or sleep and, needless to say, the only work I can do is some research now and then." Before sailing home on October 4, he planned to ask Mathilde's young niece, Thora "Bunny" Ronalds,[33] to stay with her in Paris for two weeks. "I would stay on here to try to get some rest," he wrote. "I could then finish my [book] and have some reserve strength. I only know I cannot last much longer."

Three days later, on August 8, Mathilde died suddenly of peritonitis. In despair, Welles telephoned his son Ben, who flew from London to join him, and together they entered her room. On seeing her at peace, all lines of pain gone and her face beautiful in repose, Welles exploded in a cry of anguish. Drew Pearson cabled from Washington: "Mathilde was one of our dearest, most thoughtful and loyal friends. Cable and I will come, immediately." Ben was obliged to return to his London post the next day, and, for the following two nights, Gustave, the valet, slept on Welles's balcony lest he take his life. Thora Ronalds arrived soon after, and she and Welles brought Mathilde's body home.

A month later, seeing Welles again, Pearson thought him "in terrible shape—his wife dead, his big toes gone, some of his fingers off. He has no interest in life, won't see his friends, can't eat or sleep at night. I'm afraid he wants to die." Had Welles remained in the State Department in 1943, the "peace of the world would not be so garbled. Sumner has plenty of faults, and is a difficult man, at times, to get along with but he has a perspective far beyond anyone else I have known in the State Department."[34]

Alone in the vast silence of Oxon Hill, lost without Mathilde, Welles turned to solitary drinking and reading, often until dawn. Many of his friends and former colleagues had died: James Forrestal, Ellis Pulliam, Rabbi Stephen Wise, Sol Bloom, Jan Masaryk and Bert Hulen, the *New York Times* State Department correspondent. Another, Admiral William D. Leahy, was seriously ill. It was now, during these long months of loneliness, that the malign influence of Gustave, his new valet, began taking hold.

Small and highly strung, Gustave van Hamme had been born in Belgium thirty-nine years earlier and had been brought to the United States as a child by his Belgian father, a hard-drinking carpenter. During World War II he had served in the Pacific as a soldier-servant to an army general. Afterward he had worked briefly as a valet for Governor Thomas Dewey of New York and, later, as a steward aboard Marjorie Merriwether Post Davies's yacht, *Sea Cloud*. After Reeks's retirement in 1947, he had been recommended to Welles and, at first, had seemed competent. The staff, however, soon noticed that he was both bisexual and an alcoholic.

"He was all right, except when he was drunk," one remembered. "Then he became noisy and impossible. The other servants didn't like him but he gave money away freely when drinking and they'd cluster around and take it. One of the maids was romancing the chauffeur and Gustave was jealous. He didn't want her but he didn't want anyone else to have her. He'd chase her around the kitchen with a knife in his drunken rages."[35]

In Welles, the little valet had found a father figure, a celebrity and security. Welles became the sun around which his life revolved, and Welles, ill, semicrippled and grateful, became increasingly dependent on him. Gustave's drinking and dissolute lifestyle, however, would have far-reaching consequences.

Early in 1950, while convalescing in Palm Beach, Welles was astonished to hear on the radio that his recently divorced younger son, Arnold, was about to remarry. Arnold had intended to tell his father but had been scooped by the Broadway columnist Walter Winchell. Swallowing his chagrin, Welles invited the newlyweds to spend part of their honeymoon with him in his Palm Beach house, where another guest was his lifelong friend, Harriette Post of Bernardsville, New Jersey.

Around midnight on their first night, Arnold and his bride, the former Mariana Ledbetter of Savannah, Georgia, were awakened by sounds of a drunken brawl. Jealous of the gentle Harriette, Gustave had flown into a rage and was screaming insults at her as Welles stood by, ineffectually trying to calm him. The next morning Arnold and his bride departed, a portent of worse to come.

Later that year, Carmel Offie, Bullitt's henchman, was arrested by the Washington vice squad for soliciting in Franklin Square. Seven years earlier Offie had helped Bullitt hound Welles from office on charges of homosexuality and, at the time of his arrest, was working for his friend Frank Wisner, chief of the CIA's ultra-clandestine arm, the Office of Policy Coordination (OPC). On reading the police report, CIA director Admiral Roscoe Hillenkoeter immediately dismissed Offie. Asked years later if he had been forced to let Offie go, Hillenkoeter replied with a laugh, "I wasn't forced to let him go. I had to force him to go!"[36]

Offie would later claim that Welles had "set him up" for arrest, but the CIA's veteran counterespionage chief, James J. Angleton, had read the FBI report and told this author categorically that Welles had "no involvement whatever."[37] Notwithstanding, in 1956, six years later, Offie and Bullitt avenged themselves by planting a vicious attack on Welles in *Confidential,* a scandal magazine.

In 1951, two years after Mathilde's death, Welles and Harriette became engaged. To mark the occasion, Welles invited his sister Emily, her husband, Harry Robbins, and his oldest friend, Ives Gammell, to Oxon Hill for the weekend and gave a small dinner in Harriette's honor. After dinner Welles took his guests to his study to display a set of murals depicting the Greek legend of Daphnis and Chloe, which Gammell had spent two years painting when Oxon Hill was built twenty years earlier.

Gammell retired after dinner but was awakened around midnight by shouting. Gustave, jealous of Harriette, had erupted in a drunken rage, hurling the contents of an inkwell around the study, ruining Gammell's murals. Gammell left early the next morning but Welles seemed curiously indifferent, offering no apology but stressing the valet's "utter devotion" to him and how he had spent two nights on his hotel balcony in Switzerland after Mathilde's death, protecting him.[38] Gammell never saw Welles again.

Harriette Post had known Welles since childhood. Vivacious, warm-hearted and impeccably turned out, she realized that no one would replace Mathilde in Welles's heart and accepted it gracefully. Her first marriage, to Welles's distant cousin, Thornton Wilson of New York, had failed and she had later married an Austro-Hungarian landowner and ardent Nazi, Emmerich von Jeszensky, on whose estate near Salzburg she spent the war years. Back in New York, briefly ostracized for her Nazi marriage, she had divorced von Jeszensky. In time her charm and good looks had won back her many friends, among them Welles. Both were lonely, both moved in the same circles and Welles was not only celebrated but, by Harriette's standards, rich.

They married on January 8, 1952, in a private ceremony in New York and settled into her Bernardsville home. A crumbling Scottish baronial mansion designed by her architect-grandfather George Post, it urgently needed repairs, and Welles began footing the bills.

Oxon Hill, however, remained a problem. Welles and Mathilde had found the site together, had built and furnished the great manor house, had laid out the grounds, the gardens, the swimming pool, the stables and bridle paths. It had been his home for a quarter century, and there his two sons had grown up. Everything about it reminded him of Mathilde, but the expense of staffing and maintaining the huge estate was more than he could afford and with heavy heart he put it on the market.

"Sumner [is selling] Oxon Hill, which makes me feel a little old," wrote Pearson, who had gone there first twenty-five years earlier, before the foundations were laid, to find Welles chopping trees. Oxon Hill had been one of the most "palatial" mansions in Maryland; Welles had entertained presidents and potentates, had dominated the State Department and was now "almost a forgotten man."[39]

Heartsick over the coming sale and increasingly ill, in June 1952 Welles wrote his older son, then stationed in Paris, "I've been suffering the tortures of the damned. You have no idea what angina pectoris is and I hope you never will." To ease the pain, his doctors had had him on narcotics for two months. "Thank God, that is over. I am better now, but life seems to have been intolerable lately. I can only hope that, in my case, it will soon be over." Oxon Hill was in the hands of the auctioneers, and he was returning for the last time the next day. "Harriette has been wonderful," he wrote. "I couldn't have lived this last two months without her. But, I know the time is drawing close when I shall have to say goodbye."[40]

Gustave's drunken tantrums eventually became so intolerable that Harriette, deaf to Welles's remonstrances, barred him from her Bernardsville home. Welles arranged alternate accommodations for his valet in Washington and visited him there periodically. The dissipation escalated. On the night of Monday, May 4, 1953, according to FBI records, Welles arrived in Washington by train, checked into the Mayflower Hotel for four nights, cashed a check for $100 and left immediately in the cab that had brought him.

Shortly after midnight the FBI agent-in-charge received a telephone call from one Gustave van Hamme, who described himself as Welles's "personal secretary" and demanded that an agent be sent immediately to the Mayflower as a Robert Chambers was detaining him in the lobby and preventing van Hamme from going to his room. Chambers, whom he described as forty to forty-two, about five foot six inches tall, with light brown hair, was "blackmailing" Welles. Told to call the D.C. police since the FBI had no jurisdiction, Gustave said that was out of the question because of "publicity." At 1:30 A.M. he called again to know if FBI agents were on their way. Ten minutes later he called a third time, upbraiding the FBI for not sending agents as demanded and reporting that Welles was "missing." The hotel night manager reported later that Welles had returned at 2 A.M. "intoxicated."[41]

Welles's obtuse belief that such public carousing would pass unnoticed or was solely his own business was rudely shattered three years later when a scandal magazine, *Confidential,* published his photograph on its front cover in

March 1956 and under it, in large letters: WE ACCUSE. Inside, an anonymous article revived details of the 1940 Bankhead train incident and claimed that Welles's retirement in 1943 and his winter accident in 1948 were both results of "grave, moral turpitude." It further accused him of homosexual "cruising" during a meeting of the Cleveland Council on World Affairs in September 1947.[42]

Presumably, few of Welles's friends or acquaintances would have read a magazine of this stripe. On the death of its publisher, Robert Harrison, in 1978, the *New York Times* observed that he had created the "girlie-book format" in the 1940s and had been involved, ten years later, in a court trial on charges of publishing "obscene and criminally libellous" material. The case had been dropped on his agreement to cease publishing such material.[43]

Nonetheless, for Welles and his family, the attack was harrowing. Ben was then working in London but his younger son, Arnold, was living in Savannah and caught in the eye of the storm. He urged his father to sue for libel. A fortnight later Welles wrote Ben that he had been in a mental collapse for ten days. He had learned of the "nightmare" from Charles Curtis and had immediately contacted an old (unidentified) friend who had worked with him in government and was then a partner in a leading New York law firm. His friend had suggested an investigation of certain "salient points" before taking action. It was "no coincidence," wrote Welles, that a libel of this kind had been published "sixteen years after the alleged occurrences were supposed to have taken place, thirteen years after I had left public office and at the start of a bitter political campaign."

The article had been handed in—not prepared by a staff writer; Offie had been in touch with Harrison, the publisher, and Bullitt was in Washington, working closely with Senator Styles Bridges (R.-N.H.) and the Republican campaign committee. Welles now brought up an "intensely humiliating" subject that he had never raised before.

In October (actually, it had been September) 1940, he continued, President Roosevelt had insisted that the entire cabinet go with him in his private train to Bankhead's Alabama funeral. On the way back, unable to sleep despite two barbiturates, Welles had dressed, gone back to the club car, had gotten extremely drunk and apparently had discussed "indecent" subjects with the "Negro waiters." Months later the President told him that the affidavits showed he had said "nothing that any other man who was drunk might not have said." It was on this that the "Bullitt concoction" had hinged. The FBI investigation had given him "entire clearance . . . I need only add," he concluded, "if it were not so, the President would not have given me increasing authority during the next three years or offered me the mission to Moscow or a White House assistantship after I left the government."

He enclosed a separate letter to Arnold, which Ben was to give his brother at his discretion. In it Welles states that he had never heard of the magazine nor had he read the article. Curtis had brought it to his attention. He had engaged a New York law firm and would be guided by their advice. What he called "this monstrous fabrication" fell, roughly, into two parts. The train incident he had already discussed with Ben; on Welles's death, the full documentation, including letters from the President, would pass to Ben in toto. (They were never found. Presumably Welles or someone acting on his behalf had destroyed them.)

As to the "winter accident," he concluded, "no one, except myself—but you, yourself—can judge for the malignant falsehood it is." Mathilde had been threatening a divorce. "It was that, and that alone, that drove me out that night into the snow and all that followed."[44]

Weeks later he wrote Ben from Bar Harbor that he had suffered nervous prostration in April, a month after the *Confidential* attack. In May, heart and digestive problems had confined him to the Bernardsville house. The change of climate in Maine had done him good, although he still could not walk without severe pain. Meanwhile, he had spent thousands of dollars on private detectives who had convinced his lawyers that there had indeed been a criminal conspiracy. The weak link was lack of proof that Bullitt had instigated Offie to plant the attack "however much people knew the relationship between jackal [and] hyena." A Democratic Senate friend had told him that Senator Bridges had been "in on it" and that politics had been "very much involved."

His lawyers, however, were adamant against a libel suit, which might become a campaign issue to smear Roosevelt's memory. Reputable newspapers would have to print it and millions of decent people who would otherwise not know of the slander might learn of it. "I won't get clean of the mud spattered on me by jumping into a cesspool," Welles wrote. Eisenhower's reelection that fall ended the mud-slinging and the *Confidential* attack was soon forgotten.

Ben had begun flying back from his post in Madrid each summer in the late 1950s to spend a vacation week with his father in Maine. Arnold summered nearby and the two brothers invariably discussed Welles's drinking and Gustave's malignant influence. The solution, they agreed, was for Reeks to return. Welles trusted him, and the Englishman's good humor and competence might loosen Gustave's hold as Welles struggled with increasing infirmity. In 1959, two years before Welles's death, Ben urged his father to ask Reeks back. Without a moment's hesitation—almost thankfully, in fact—Welles seized the telephone and called Reeks at his retirement home in Florida. Within days Reeks had returned, and the sight of him, after a twelve-year separation, brought a rare smile of joy to Welles's face. Reeks resumed his duties as if he had never been away.

Harriette had barred Gustave from Bernardsville but, under Mathilde's will, the Bar Harbor house belonged to Welles for life. Gustave reappeared there each summer, giving rein to his drunken antics. Within days of his return, Reeks saw the inebriated little valet chase the stately English cook, Mrs. Fitzgerald, and her portly Irish kitchen maid, Mary Dunne, around the kitchen with a meat cleaver. The two women spent part of the night hiding in the woods, Reeks remembered.[45]

Despite increasing illness, Welles maintained his accustomed lifestyle: a butler, valet, a household staff of half-a-dozen and a chauffeured limousine for afternoon drives or occasional dinners with friends on Mt. Desert Island. Each Thursday he attended the weekly lunch meeting of the Pot and Kettle Club, a coterie of summer residents who gathered to socialize and hear visiting dignitaries lecture on current affairs. To deflate pomposity, club rules required members and guests to don white aprons and billowing chef's hats. Welles invariably complied although highly self-conscious about his incongruous appearance.

Sensing his approaching end, in the summer of 1960 Welles invited his six small grandchildren[46] and their nannies to tea in his Bar Harbor house. As the children prattled happily, consuming cake and ice cream around the round oak dining table, he watched them intently, fixing their features in his mind for the last time. He never saw them again. Ben himself saw ominous signs that summer. Driving his father slowly over a dirt road to a campsite, he was surprised to hear him ask almost apologetically to drive more slowly. "If I squeak," he murmured, "pay no attention." It was an incongruous turn of phrase, never heard before, and Ben sensed that he was terminally ill.

A year later, in September 1961, Ben flew again from Europe to spend a week with his father in Maine. Harriette had returned to Bernardsville to await Welles's arrival so father and son were alone, enjoying each other's company, chatting about world affairs in Spanish, which pleased Welles, and lunching or dining with mutual friends. Welles was on his best behavior, drinking in moderation.

On Ben's last day, he went to bid his father farewell and, to his surprise, found him still in bed at noon. Welles was cheerful but obviously ill, his stomach bloated. He was looking forward to visiting Ben and his family in Madrid the following spring, he said. Ben left and Gustave tried to help Welles dress, but he sent instead for Reeks. "I shall never see Honfleur [his summer home] again," he told Reeks quietly. The next day he insisted on being driven to Bernardsville in a straight run of thirteen hours, arriving semiconscious. Suspecting the worst, Welles had long refused intrusive examination by his doctors.

For five days he struggled for life. Ben, alerted by Harriette, flew back from Europe, and with the help of Arnold, Reeks, Gustave and a male nurse periodically moved Welles's massive frame from his bed to an armchair, where he sat uncomplaining, his jaw sagging, unable to speak except with his eyes. The house was hushed; even his dogs sensed death. On September 24, 1961, the suffering ended and Sumner Welles died, age sixty-nine, of pancreatic cancer, the toll of years of drinking.

He had been a "diplomat of the old school in the best sense," the *New York Times* observed the next day. "Few Americans were better known or more highly regarded in the chanceries of the world . . . There is no fear that he will be forgotten . . . He has made his mark on the history of the twentieth century."[47]

In the lovely words of Walter Savage Landor, Welles had "warmed both hands before the fire of life." It had sunk and he was ready to depart.

A LIFE OF LIGHT AND SHADOWS

SUMNER WELLES made four major contributions to the Roosevelt era. He conceived and carried out the Good Neighbor policy, arguably the all-time high-water mark in U.S.–Latin American relations. With Roosevelt, Churchill and Alexander Cadogan, he wrote the Atlantic Charter, the cornerstone of the United Nations. In mid–World War II, at FDR'S direction, he drafted the original UN Charter. And during and after the war, he threw his support behind a national homeland for the Jews: Israel. The Good Neighbor policy and the Atlantic Charter are largely memories. The United Nations and Israel endure.

Roosevelt and his world planner, Welles, shared a historic dream: a world without war. Both had lived through World War I and, afterward, had seen the Allies quarrel, the League of Nations collapse, American isolationism and high American tariffs begin—all contributing to global depression, unemployment, starvation, the rise of the dictators and World War II. It should never happen again, they agreed; the cycle must be broken. The inter-American system became their model. Their joint success in forging a new hemisphere unity at Buenos Aires in 1936 pointed to a postwar world built around self-policing regions under a supreme authority: the United Nations.

    After victory, the United Nations would disarm aggressors and establish the world forecast in the Atlantic Charter: freedom of speech and religion, freedom from want and fear, the right of all peoples to choose their government, no territorial changes without the consent of those involved and equal access to trade and raw materials for all nations—victors and vanquished alike.

The conundrum was Stalin. Would he join the United Nations and work for peace—or would he play a lone hand? His preference, expressed at Tehran in 1943, for a continuing postwar U.S.-Soviet-British military alliance was impractical. Alliances dissolved once the danger was past, and small nations would never accept indefinite Big Three dictation. For FDR and Welles, the only hope of postwar peace lay in the United Nations.

Strong personalities both, FDR and Welles each believed in his negotiating skill. Their difference lay in timing. FDR, the politician, played cards close to his chest, choosing his moment to deal. Early in the war, absorbed with military problems, he wanted no UN organization with a chorus of small nations proffering advice. After victory would come time for a UN organization. Then, as leader of the world's greatest power, he would lay out the broad future, winning Stalin's cooperation by sheer force of personality and bargaining skill.

Welles, the diplomat, believed instead in negotiating at the outset, in pinning Stalin down with written agreements before unforeseen events arose and rival U.S. and Soviet positions hardened. FDR's refusal to "clarify" U.S. peace aims until late in the war—at the Tehran conference in 1943 and the Yalta conference in 1945—dismayed Welles. "The time for [clarification] was when our partnership in the war was young," Welles wrote in retrospect.[1]

To his dying day, Welles believed that the Cold War could have been avoided, or mitigated, had FDR created a United Nations "executive council" early in 1942 and begun negotiating postwar issues of frontiers, armistice terms, population transfers, and the like when Stalin vitally needed U.S. arms and the United States had "immense leverage." But FDR refused, preoccupied with military affairs and counseled by Hull, Hopkins and his military advisors to postpone postwar issues until the fighting ended.

Belatedly, he came around to Welles's view that a UN organization was imperative before—not after—victory. In late 1942 FDR authorized him to start drafting the United Nations charter. By then, however, the moment for negotiation had passed. Stalin's armies were already defeating the Germans and U.S. influence in the Kremlin had withered. FDR's death on the eve of victory left the fledgling United Nations leaderless, and for the next forty years, it moldered.

Welles revered Roosevelt but differed with him on many issues. He disagreed profoundly, for example, with FDR's conviction that defeated France was no longer a great power. Welles and Churchill both insisted that Germany's collapse made the revival of France imperative as a bulwark against Soviet domination of Western Europe; and eventually they won the President over. Welles also deplored FDR's indifference to the views of small nations, notably the occupied countries of Europe and those of Latin America—countries, Welles believed—that had suggestions worth hearing. He also questioned FDR's predilection for "panaceas" such as plebiscites and free ports to solve postwar problems.

FDR's refusal to dictate memoranda of important conversations, leaving no written record of agreements, created major problems for Welles and his colleagues. This refusal stemmed, Welles wrote, from the President's ingrained suspicion that American diplomats and permanent State Department officials were reactionaries opposed to his policies, and it almost certainly accounted for his refusal to take departmental Asian experts to the 1943 Cairo and the 1945 Yalta conferences, even though the futures of Japan, China, Manchuria and Korea were all on the agenda.[2]

By inference, Welles blamed FDR for failing to exert leadership early in World War II to find refuge for Jews fleeing Hitler. In 1938, Hitler's atrocities had led Roosevelt to approve Welles's proposal for an Inter-Governmental Committee on Refugees. Yet the "government of the U.S., itself, permitted the committee to become a nullity," Welles charged.[3] Had the "leadership of the U.S. been truly effective," the committee could have drawn up a resettlement program and, by negotiation with individual governments early in the war, could have prepared for the transfer of refugees to their new homes as soon as hostilities in Europe ended. "This could have saved the lives of many hundreds of thousands," he wrote in 1946. "The concentration camps for displaced persons would not still be filled fifteen months after Germany's defeat."[4]

In his books, Welles acknowledged his own errors. Before World War II, he had assumed that the German General Staff would never "permit" Hitler to wage a two-front war while the Soviet Union remained Germany's enemy. He misread the 1938 Munich settlement, believing that it had ended the threat of war. He failed to foresee the 1939 Hitler-Stalin pact and the "rapidity" with which the war began. Even after Hitler's lightning conquest of Poland, he still believed that the European democracies could withstand rearmed Germany.[5] His mission to Europe for Roosevelt early in 1940 and his interviews with Hitler and Mussolini ended that illusion.

A student of history, Welles often gave undue weight to the lessons of World War I. Like FDR, he believed that a revival of German militarism could be averted only by splitting Germany into three states. He erred in predicting that a defeated Germany would "thirst for revenge" again in 1945, that Nazi doctrines had "corrupted" all German youth and that the German General Staff ("the real master of the German race") was plotting a comeback. A new German "communism . . . directed by the cold and ruthless brains of the German General Staff, would find in many parts of the world a situation made to order for . . . Pan-Germanism," he wrote on the eve of victory.[6]

The rise of Asian nationalism, sparked by Japan's early victories over its foes at Pearl Harbor and later, led Welles to exaggerate Japanese resentment following its defeat. The Japanese were "biding their time," he wrote in 1946. Hatred of the American victors was "rising," he believed, and, once freed from occupation, the Japanese would "scrap" MacArthur's constitution.[7] Fear of a Communist China also led him to overstate the stature of Chiang Kai-shek, the Chinese Nationalist leader, whose "vision and statesmanship," Welles predicted, would mark him as one of the "greatest figures in . . . the New Asia."[8] In 1949, three years after Welles had penned his eulogy, Chiang and the remnants of his corrupt regime fled to Taiwan, leaving Mao Tse-tung and his Communist armies masters of China.

Welles believed that the inchoate United Nations and its newborn agencies—United Nations Educational, Scientific, and Cultural Organization (UNESCO) and the Trusteeship Council—should have supervised the occupation of Germany and Japan, the reconstruction of war-shattered Europe and the future of Palestine, but he overestimated their capacity. Believing passionately that small nations as well as the Big Four of the United States, the Soviet Union, Britain and China should help guide the future, he let his wish become father to the thought. Had the United States and the Soviet Union been bound at war's end by prior agreements—as Welles had urged—the United Nations might have functioned as he and FDR had intended. But, without written commitments between the world's two greatest powers, the United Nations fell victim to Stalin's veto.

Welles relied excessively on logic. The Soviet Union's postwar course would largely depend, he wrote, on whether the United States could "persuade" the Soviet people and their government that their "permanent and truest interest [lay] in cooperating with us in the creation and maintenance of a democratic and effective world organization."[9] Stalin surely would see that Soviet Russia's "prosperity and security" lay in joining an international organization capable of maintaining world peace.[10]

Neither Roosevelt nor Welles was blind to Stalin's rapacity or duplicity; they had dealt with him for years. The Soviet Union could become the greatest "force for peace" or, equally, the greatest "menace" that the world had ever seen, Welles predicted in 1944.[11] He and Roosevelt, however, believed that Stalin, once secure in victory, would shelve world revolution, concentrate on rebuilding his war-shattered country and turn to the United States for the aid and credits it was then ready to offer. Their assumption was logical, but Stalin was less motivated by logic than by power. After FDR's death and the shift of U.S. authority—and the new atom bomb—into the untested hands of Truman and Byrnes, he moved ruthlessly to consolidate and expand Soviet power. The Cold War was on.

Welles's vision of the future, nonetheless, proved prescient in many respects. The Good Neighbor policy, which he and FDR had carried out for nine years, assured the United States the support of Latin America and the protection of the vital Panama Canal at a time of national peril after Pearl Harbor. The revival of France helped defend postwar Europe from Soviet aggression. The creation of Israel provided the United States a permanent democratic bastion in the turbulent Middle East, and, as Welles correctly predicted, the practical safety valve against renewed German or Japanese militarism lay in the "realm of economics."[12] He also lived to see the end of colonialism. The right of self-determination, he declared in 1946, was not "limited . . . by the Atlantic Charter to the white race."[13]

For Welles, the best long-term foreign policy for the United States was "enlightened selfishness": the independence and integrity of the Western Hemisphere, defense of the Panama Canal, the continued existence of the British Commonwealth as distinct from the British empire, aid to France in resuming its traditional role as a great power and continuing efforts to reach understanding with Soviet Russia.[14] Without U.S.-Soviet agreement, he warned in 1946, a "fatal drift toward a two-world order" was inevitable.[15] Tragically, he proved right.

As the Cold War intensified, Welles supported continuing U.S. military strength and "containment" of Soviet Russia, yet he never abandoned hope that mutual hostility would end sooner rather than later. Stalin was not immortal, he wrote, and Soviet "isolationism" gradually would diminish. Time was on the side of peace, and, if war could be avoided, the "Iron Curtain will rust away."[16] Again he was right, a half century before his time.

"Wherever he has gone, he has made friends among those who had the right to be our friends," the *New York Times* wrote as Welles lay critically ill in 1948. "In the Far East, in Latin America, in Europe, he has promoted a Good Neighbor policy of his own . . . He has realized that we were living in a changed world to which we must adapt ourselves. He has worked hard . . . for democracy and peace. He has been a servant of the people, in appointive office and out . . . He has worn himself out in the useful labors to which he chose to assign himself."[17]

There lay the tragedy. Welles indeed had worn himself out. The world saw only the towering, imposing statesman-diplomat: few saw the secret drinker, physically and emotionally exhausted by ten years of crushing responsibility. Weary and in his cups, he let the bisexual urges latent in his nature burst their bonds, leading to tawdry advances to railway porters and others. This, however, was not the Welles endowed, as Roosevelt told Byrnes, with one of the "finest minds he had ever known"; nor the Welles with a "Jacksonian sense of duty," as Eric Sevareid, the radio-television commentator, wrote; nor the Welles with the "dignity to be viceroy of India," in the words of the *New York Times*'s James Reston.

This was the other Welles: stiff-necked, proud, deaf to warnings, indifferent to the risk of disgrace. Roosevelt tried for three years to suppress the 1940 train scandal but failed and, in midwar, when he most needed Welles to help create and guide the fledgling United Nations and negotiate postwar settlements, was forced to accept his resignation. A quatrain from the *Rubaiyat of Omar Khayyam* bears on Welles's fate:

> So when that Angel of the darker drink,
> At last shall find you by the river-brink,
> And, offering his cup, invite your soul
> Forth to your lips to quaff—
> You shall not shrink.[18]

It was not the Angel of Death but the Angel of Self-Destruction who had found Welles by the river brink. Casually, almost indifferently, he had tossed his enemies—Hull, Bullitt and others—the means to destroy him, and they had. His life had truly been one of light and shadows.

NOTES

PROLOGUE

1. Columbia Oral History Collection, Columbia University, New York, Attorney General Robert H. Jackson, p. 850.
2. *The Secret Diary of Harold L. Ickes* (New York: Simon & Schuster, 1953), pp. 326 ff.
3. Henry A. Wallace, *The Price of Vision: The Diary of Henry A. Wallace: 1942-46,* ed. John Morton Blum (Boston: Houghton Mifflin, 1973), p. 68.
4. Among them, Henry Calloway, James Hewitt, S. C. Mitchell of the press car and S. D. Lucas of the President's car, FBI records, obtained under the Freedom of Information Act (FOIA).
5. Memorandum for the Director, January 26, 1941, FBI records, obtained under the FOIA.

CHAPTER 1

1. The frontier was officially "closed" in 1894.
2. Richard Schermerhorn, *Schermerhorn Genealogy & Family Chronicles* (New York: Tobias A. Wright, 1914), pp. 161-169.
3. Frederick G. Swan to Edward H. Swan, February 7, 1895; Sumner Welles Papers, Franklin D. Roosevelt Library, Hyde Park, N.Y. (hereafter cited as SWP).
4. Sumner Welles (hereafter cited as SW) interview with Bela Kornitzer, September 3, 1947, SWP.
5. Later Mrs. Franklin Delano Roosevelt.
6. Interview, Charles Dickey, Northeast Harbor, Maine, 1977.
7. Interview, Joseph Alsop, Washington, DC, 1977.
8. George Rublee, later a prominent attorney who would work closely with Roosevelt and Welles on international refugee problems before and during World War II.
9. Frank D. Ashburn, *Peabody of Groton* (New York: Coward, McCann, 1944), p. 193.
10. Ibid.
11. Interview, William Jay Schieffelin, 1976, Mt. Desert, Maine.
12. Elliott Roosevelt, *FDR: His Personal Letters, Early Years* (New York: Duell, Sloan & Pearce, 1947-50), vol. 1, p. 34.
13. Interview, Louis Curtis, Boston, 1977.
14. Interview, Dr. Hugh Joseph, Baltimore, MD, 1977.
15. Interview, Louis Curtis, Boston, 1977.
16. SW to Peabody, undated, from the Groton Missionary Society's camp, Peabody Papers, Houghton Library, Harvard University, Cambridge, Massachusetts.

17. SW to Emily Welles Robbins, 1910, from Bretton Woods, New Hampshire, Benjamin Welles Papers (hereafter cited as BWP).
18. Ibid.

CHAPTER 2

1. Samuel Eliot Morison, *Three Centuries of Harvard* (Cambridge, MA: Harvard University Press, 1936), pp. 441-442.
2. Yale had rejected Harkness's offer of a similar program so he had turned to Harvard.
3. Morison, *Three Centuries of Harvard*, p. 449.
4. Harvard University records, 1910-13.
5. R.H. Ives Gammell, letter to author, November 24, 1977 (hereafter cited as Gammell letter).
6. Laura Kelsey Allen to SW, December 18, 1944, SWP.
7. Morison, *Three Centuries of Harvard*, p. 420.
8. Santayana quoted in Ibid., 421.
9. Five years earlier Dr. Andrew Green Foord, a pioneer in the use of therapy and psychiatry for the nervously ill, had opened a clinic there. Correspondence, Katherine T. Terwilliger, former Town Historian, Wawarsing, near Ellenville, New York.
10. Harvard alumni records, 1911.
11. Edgar H. Wells to Coolidge, March 4, 1911, Harvard Alumni records.
12. SW to Peabody, Peabody Papers, Houghton Library, Harvard University, Cambridge, Massachusetts.
13. Peabody invariably sent every graduate a birthday card.
14. Gammell letter.
15. Morison, *Three Centuries of Harvard, p. 422.*
16. Interview, Ernesta Drinker Bullitt Barlow, Gloucester, Massachusetts, 1978.
17. Interview, Nancy Cabot Osborne, Boston, 1977.
18. Interview, Rosamund and Aimee Lamb, Boston, Massachusetts, 1965.
19. As Under Secretary of State in World War II, Welles collaborated with Warner to spare Kyoto and Nara, two of Japan's most celebrated beauty spots, from U.S. bombing.
20. SW to Charles P. Curtis, Jr., June 14, 1949, SWP.
21. Notes read by Mrs. M. M. Osborn, (née Nancy Cabot), to the fiftieth anniversary of her Sewing Circle, Boston, Massachusetts 1962.
22. Among her inventions was a waterproof poncho for use in the trenches in World War I and postcards of children with huge eyes whose pupils swiveled around in plastic containers.
23. Interview, Ray Slater Murphy Blakeman, New York, 1973.
24. SW to Benjamin Welles, September 25, 1912; SWP. Harvard records show that he did, in fact, study architecture under George Henry Chase and took lessons in painting, drawing and the technique and historical development of medieval architecture under Herbert Langford Warren, Nelson Robinson, Jr., Professor of Architecture; Harvard Archives, Pusey Library.
25. SW to Mrs. Douglas Robinson, October 28, 1912, Robinson papers, Houghton Library, Harvard University.
26. Harvard Alumni records, class of 1914.

27. On his death in 1936, Sumner's father bequeathed Harvard $10,000 for the proposed scholarship. Owing to Harvard's ultra-conservative fiduciary policies, however, forty years later (in 1976), the book value had increased only to $18,000, or, $450 per annum.
28. Hurlburt to Benjamin Welles, 1913, Harvard Alumni records.
29. Author of a plan to improve Harvard Square in the Georgian tradition.
30. Harden de V. Pratt, Westerly, Rhode Island, to SW, February 16, 1942, SWP.
31. Harvard Alumni records, Class of 1914.
32. SW to Endicott Peabody, undated (probably autumn 1913), Peabody Papers.

CHAPTER 3

1. Edward R. Tannenbaum, *1900: The Generation Before the Great War* (Garden City, NY: Anchor Press-Doubleday, 1976), p. 250.
2. Michael Marrus, "Social Drinking In The Belle Epoque," *Journal of Social History* 7, no. 2, (1974), p. 130.
3. Tannenbaum, *1900,* pp. 45-46.
4. Thomas C. Cary, *Memoirs of Thomas Handasyd Perkins; Containing Extracts from His Diaries and Letters* (Boston: Little, Brown & Co., 1856), pp. 90-91.
5. Cornelia Otis Skinner, *Elegant Wits And Grand Horizontals* (Boston: Houghton Mifflin, 1962), p. 9.
6. Tannenbaum, *1900,* p. 74.
7. Gammell letter.
8. Ibid.
9. John Steele Gordon, "Technology Transfer," *American Heritage* (February 1990).
10. They are now on exhibit at the Smithsonian Institution in Washington, D.C.
11. George S. White, *Memoir of Samuel Slater,* printed at 46 Carpenter St., Philadelphia, 1836; Frederick L. Lewton, curator of textiles, U.S. National Museum, Samuel Slater and The Oldest Cotton Machinery in America, from the Smithsonian report for 1926, (New York: S. Slater & Sons, Inc., 1936). M. D. C. Crawford, *The Samuel Slater Story* (Pawtucket, Rhode Island: Old Slater Mill Assn., 1948); E. H. Cameron, *Samuel Slater: Father Of American Manufacturers,* The Bond, Wheelwright Co., Freeport, Maine, 1960.
12. Isak Dinesen, *Out of Africa* (London: Putnam, 1937), p. 319 ff.
13. Quoted in Errol Trzebinski, *Silence Will Speak* (Chicago: University of Chicago Press, 1977), p. 77.
14. Ibid, p. 157.
15. Recollections of Ray Slater Murphy Blakeman (hereafter cited as Recollections of RSMB).
16. Trzebinski, *Silence,* p. 77.
17. Carlos Fuentes, *The Buried Mirror: Reflections on Spain and the New World* (New York: Houghton Mifflin, 1992), p. 290.
18. Robert Pilpel, *To The Honor Of The Fleet* (New York: Athenaeum, 1979).
19. Post Wheeler and Hallie Erminie Rives Wheeler, *Dome Of Many Colored Glass* (New York: Doubleday, 1955), p. 352.
20. Recollections of RSMB.
21. Ibid.
22. Recollections of Mary Pyne Filley Cutting, Bernardsville, New Jersey, 1976.

23. Gammell letter.
24. Interview, Charles Dickey, Northeast Harbor, Maine, 1975.
25. Interview, Mrs. M. M. (Nancy Cabot) Osborne, Boston, Massachusetts, 1965.
26. SW to Phillips, February 25, 1915, Department of State jacket on Sumner Welles (hereafter cited as State jacket).
27. Walsh to Bryan, March 17, 1915; State jacket.
28. Guild to Bryan, March 26, 1915; State jacket.
29. Lodge to Bryan, March 26, 1915; State jacket.
30. FDR to Bryan, March 20, 1915; State jacket.
31. Born Caroline Astor Drayton, she and Sumner were both descended from Abraham Schermerhorn.
32. SW to Peabody, undated, Peabody Papers, Houghton Library, Harvard University, Cambridge, Massachusetts.
33. Gammell letter.
34. Ibid.
35. *Boston American,* April 14, 1915, p. 1.
36. *Washington Post,* April 14, 1915.
37. Grand Army of the Republic Royal Lyon post 61.
38. *Boston Transcript,* April 14, 1915.
39. Recollections of Aimee and Rosamund Lamb, Boston, Massachusetts, 1965.
40. Warren Frederick Ilchman, *Professional Diplomacy In The U.S.: 1779-1939* (Chicago: University of Chicago Press, 1961), p. 133.
41. SW to Peabody, undated, 1915, Peabody Papers.

CHAPTER 4

1. *San Francisco Examiner,* August 26, 1915.
2. For the Twenty-one demands and U.S. reaction see Foreign Relations of the United States Department of State publication (FRUS), 1915 (Washington, D.C.: U.S. Government Printing Office, 1924), pp. 79ff.
3. Sumner Welles, *The Time for Decision* (New York: Harper Brothers, 1944), pp. 272-273.
4. Ibid, p. 275.
5. Esther Slater Welles (hereafter cited as ESW), diary, 1915-17, BWP.
6. Ibid.
7. Ogata, born 1655, died 1716. Celebrated for his lacquer work, he revolutionized the Tosa school by his modern art conceptions.
8. SW to Agnes (Mrs. Eugene) Meyer, September 29, 1949, SWP.
9. Bulletin, Metropolitan Museum, 1920, vol. 15, p. 43. They are now in the possession of his granddaughters: Serena Welles Moss and Merida Welles Holman.
10. Post Wheeler and Hallie Erminie Rives, *Dome Of Many Colored Glass* (New York: Doubleday, 1955), chapters 39 and 40.
11. Recollections of RSMB to the author, 1979.
12. Welles, *Time for Decision,* p. 273.
13. SW to Peabody, undated, probably 1915 or 1916, Peabody Papers, Houghton Library, Harvard University, Cambridge, Massachusetts.
14. Welles, *Time for Decision,* p. 275.

15. Charles Burdick and Ursula Moessner, *The German Prisoners-of-War in Japan: 1914-1920* (Lanham, Maryland: University Press of America, 1984), p. 67.
16. Wheeler and Rives, *Dome,* pp. 554-555.
17. Ibid, pp. 555-556.
18. Tokyo post files, correspondence, 1915; class 703, part VIII, letters of October 15, 18, 19; same file, instructions # 195, 201, 208.
19. Burdick and Moessner, *German Prisoners-of-War,* p. 9.
20. Ibid, p. 10.
21. Ibid, p. 11.
22. Ibid, p. 64.
23. Ambassador's dispatch #493, April 11, 1916, and Welles's report are in Department of State (hereafter DS) records 763.72114/1491.
24. Guthrie's dispatch #697 and Welles's second report are in DS records 763.72114/2414.
25. Burdick and Moessner, *German Prisoners-of-War,* p. 61.
26. ESW diary, January 19, 1916.
27. Recollections of RSMB.
28. DS, personnel jacket: Sumner Welles, February 1916.
29. California provided Wilson's margin of 277 electoral votes to Hughes's 254; of 9.1 million popular votes to Hughes's 8.5 million.
30. Wheeler and Rives, *Dome,* p. 578.
31. Sumner had already been confirmed at Groton.
32. DS records, 123 W 451; telegram from Tokyo to DS, April 9, 1917; Department's reply, April 18.
33. Samuel Slater and Caroline Slater Washburn.
34. DS Records 123 W 451; Wheeler's telegram to Secretary Lansing, June 20, 1917, and Lansing's reply.
35. *Japan Advertiser,* July 12, 1917, pp. 1 and 10.
36. DS records, 123 W 451, telegram of July 16, 1917, from embassy Tokyo to DS; Department's reply and vice versa.
37. Welles, *Time for Decision,* p. 273.

CHAPTER 5

1. Sumner Welles, *Where Are We Heading?* (New York: Harper & Brothers, 1946), p. 182.
2. Japan's "New Order" during World War II called, in fact, for the "relegation of the Western Hemisphere to a subordinate position," after victory. Sumner Welles, *The Time for Decision* (New York: Harper & Brothers, 1944), p. 276.
3. Ibid., p. 183.
4. Almost 3 million immigrants had arrived from Europe in the preceding quarter century; Carlos Fuentes, *The Buried Mirror: Reflections on Spain and the New World* (New York: Houghton Mifflin, 1992), pp. 288-289.
5. Welles, *Where Are We Heading?*, p. 189.
6. Roland Huntford, *Shackleton* (New York: Athenaeum, 1986), p. 659.
7. Frederick Jesup Stimson, *My United States* (New York: Charles Scribner's Sons, 1931), p. 399.
8. *FRUS,* 1917, Supplement 1, (Washington, DC: U.S. Government Printing Office, 1931), pp. 322-323.

9. Hugh R. Wilson, *The Education of a Diplomat* (New York: Longmans, Green & Co., 1938), p. 119.

10. Stimson to Phillips, December 10, 1917.

11. Hugh Robert Mill, *The Life Of Sir Ernest Shackleton* (London: William Heinemann, Ltd., 1923), pp. 252-253.

12. Buenos Aires embassy records, correspondence, 1917, part VI, class 711.3.

13. *FRUS,* 1918, Supplement 1, vol. 2, pp.1013ff; SW-Robertson correspondence, February 25-26, 1918, same file.

14. Robertson to Secretary of State, dispatch #831, Buenos Aires embassy records, Correspondence, 1918, Part VII, Class 711.3.

15. Dispatch #833, same file.

16. Huntford, *Shackleton,* p. 659.

17. Sir David Kelly, *The Ruling Few* (London: Hollis & Carter, 1952), p. 135.

18. Guillermo Uriburu Roca, Buenos Aires, to author, 1978.

19. ESW diary, BWP.

20. Interview, Martha Lyon Slater, New York, 1977.

21. Private interview, Buenos Aires, Argentina, 1978.

22. Private correspondence, 1977, BWP.

23. Stimson, *My United States,* p. 417.

24. Argentine office diary, 1919: entries for February 17, April 14 and 22, May 6, August 7 and 13; Welles pouched copies, weekly, to the department.

25. Argentine office diary, February 6, 1919.

26. Warren Delano Robbins, a cousin of FDR: DS records, 123 W 451/16a.

27. ESW diary, September, 1919.

28. Stimson to Secretary of State, Dispatch #988, November 12, 1919; DS records 123 W 451/24.

CHAPTER 6

1. SW to Secretary of State, December 10, 1919, DS records, 123 W 451/83.

2. An authority also on municipal administration, Rowe had been professor of political science and international law at the University of Pennsylvania.

3. Bainbridge Colby to SW, June 3, 1920, DS records, 123 W 451/24b.

4. Rowe to SW, June 10, 1920, SWP.

5. Adee to SW, September 1, 1920, SWP.

6. Mexico, because of its size and special relationship to the United States, remained a separate subdivision until 1937 when Welles, then Under Secretary, merged it into Latin America.

7. Sumner Welles, *Seven Decisions That Shaped History* (New York: Harper Brothers & Co., 1950), pp. 97-98.

8. Chandler P. Anderson, "The Monroe Doctrine," *in American Journal of International Law,* Vol. 30, no. 3, June 16, 1936, pp. 477-479.

9. Quoted in Dana G Munro, *Intervention and Dollar Diplomacy in the Caribbean: 1900-1921* (Princeton, NJ: Princeton University Press, 1964), p. 77.

10. Quoted in Frank Freidel, *Franklin D. Roosevelt, The Ordeal* (Boston: Little, Brown & Co., 1954), p. 81.

11. Robert K. Murray, *The Harding Era* (Minneapolis: University of Minnesota Press, 1969), pp. 332-333.

12. Attached as a rider to the 1901 Army Appropriations Act by Senator Orville H. Platt (R-Conn.)

13. *FRUS*, 1920, vol. 2, pp. 17-18.

14. Ibid.

15. Boaz Long to Secretary of State, rush, teleg. #2, January 3, 1921, FRUS, 1921, vol. 1, pp. 670-671.

16. Davis to Long, teleg. #3, January 4, 1921, Ibid., pp. 671-672.

17. Wilson to Davis, January 7, 1921, DS records, 837.00/2118.

18. Crowder to SW, April 29, 1921, DS records 837.00/2208.

19. Welles report on his trip to Havana, March 1, 1921, DS records, files of Division of Latin American affairs, box 7.

20. De Cespedes's father had been shot by the Spaniards.

21. Welles report.

22. Interview, Dr. and Mrs. Dana G. Munro, Princeton, New Jersey, 1976.

23. Hallie Erminie Rives Wheeler to SW, May 11, 1932, SWP.

24. Chandler P. Anderson diaries, December 10, 1920, Library of Congress.

25. Ibid., January 22, 1922.

26. Post Wheeler and Hallie Erminie Rives, *Dome of Many Colored Glass* (New York: Doubleday, 1955), p. 637.

27. Interview, Anna Louise Clarkson (Mrs. Roger) Bacon, Hancock Point, Maine, 1968.

28. Robert and Nancy Gordon Heinl, *Written In Blood: The Story Of The Haitian People* (Boston: Houghton Mifflin Co., 1978), p. 1.

29. Quoted in Arthur C. Millspaugh, "Haiti Under American Control: 1950-1930," Boston World Peace Foundation, 1931, p. 32.

30. The treaty was originally set to run until 1926, but was later extended to 1936. In fact, U.S. forces began withdrawing in 1933 when FDR took office. Munro, *Intervention,* p. 358.

31. *FRUS,* 1920, vol. 2, pp. 771-772.

32. Ibid., pp. 191-199.

33. Harding to Hughes, March 28, 1921, DS records 711.38/1701.

34. SW to Under Secretary Davis, June 15, 1921, DS records, FW 711.38/180.

35. DS records, 711.38/165.

36. Harding to Hughes, August 15, 1921, DS records 711.38/148.

37. Kenneth J. Grieb, *The Latin American Policy of Warren G. Harding* (Fort Worth, TX: Christian University Press, 1976), p. 91.

38. Two years later, as U.S. Commissioner in the Dominican Republic, Welles would form a close friendship with General and Mrs. Russell and with their daughter, Brooke, who later married Welles's distant cousin, Vincent Astor.

39. SW to Harry Pelham Robbins, March 31, 1927, SWP.

40. Sumner Welles, *Naboth's Vineyard, Vol. 2* (London: Payson & Clarke, Ltd., 1928), pp. 797-798.

41. *FRUS,* 1920, vol. 2, pp. 110-115.

42. Horace G. Knowles, a former American minister to the Dominican Republic.

43. Welles, *Naboth's Vineyard, Vol. 2,* p. 832.

44. Hugh R. Wilson, *Diplomat Between Wars* (London: Longmans, Green & Co., 1961), pp. 162-163.

45. Caroline A. D. Phillips, Diaries, December 1922, p. 280, Schlesinger Library, Radcliffe College, Cambridge, Massachusetts.

46. Dexter Perkins, *Charles Evans Hughes and American Democratic Statesmanship* (Boston: Little, Brown & Co., 1956), pp. 129-130.

47. David J. Danelski and Joseph S. Tulchin, eds., *The Autobiographical Notes of Charles Evans Hughes* (Cambridge, MA: Harvard University Press, 1973), p. 269.

48. Welles, *Naboth's Vineyard, Vol. 2,* p. 839.

49. Hughes's comments on Welles's second evacuation plan were apparently made orally, as no paper on the subject has been found. See Munro, *Intervention,* p. 46.

50. Welles, *Naboth's Vineyard, Vol. 2,* pp. 840-841.

51. Ibid., p. 845.

52. SW to Hughes, October 11, 1921, DS records 839.00/2452.

53. *FRUS,* 1922, vol. 2, pp. 5-19; Hughes to Harding, February 2, 1922, DS records 839/2461-2.

54. Welles, *Naboth's Vineyard, Vol. 2,* p. 853.

55. Ibid.

CHAPTER 7

1. Dana G. Munro, *Intervention and Dollar Diplomacy in the Caribbean: 1900-1921* (Princeton, NJ: Princeton University Press, 1964), p. 274.

2. Ibid.

3. Grew to Hugh Gibson, January 18, 1920; Grew to Butler Wright, February 18, 1920; Grew diaries, Houghton Library, Harvard University, Cambridge, Massachusetts.

4. Phillips to Congress, February 18, 1918; Warren Frederick Ichman, *Professional Diplomacy in the U.S.: 1779-1939* (Chicago: University of Chicago Press, 1961), p. 142.

5. SW to Hughes, March 15, 1922, SWP.

6. Sumner Welles, *Time for Decision* (New York: Harper & Brothers, 1944), pp. 393 ff.

7. Caroline A. D. Phillips Diaries, 1922, Schlesinger Library, Radcliffe College, Cambridge, Massachusetts.

8. SWP, personal file.

9. Carl Gustav Jung, *Psychological Types* (New York: Harcourt, Brace Co., 1925), p. 368.

10. Interview, R. H. Ives Gammell, Boston, 1975; cited hereafter as RHIG.

11. It is now the Cosmos Club.

12. Elbridge Gerry of Massachusetts (1744-1814). As governor from 1810 to 1812, his manipulation of electoral districts led to the pejorative term gerrymandering. Later he served as U.S. Vice President under Madison.

13. P. G. Gerry to Mrs. Richard Townsend, August 12, 1910, SWP.

14. Mathilde Townsend Gerry (hereafter cited as MTG) to SW, October 14, 1923, SWP.

15. MTG to SW, January 10, 1924, SWP.

16. ESW to SW, 1921, SWP.

17. SW to Davis, August 29, 1921, Davis papers, Library of Congress, box 63.

18. Colby to SW, March 21, 1922, SWP.

19. Hughes to SW, March 13, 1922, DS records, 123 W 451/34.

20. *La Prensa* (Buenos Aires), March 17, 1922.

21. Munro to Hughes, April 11 and May 5, 1922, DS records 839.00/2678-79-80.

22. *FRUS,* 1922, vol. II, pp. 53, 64-68.

23. SW to Davis, April 29, 1926, SWP.

24. Hughes to acting Secretary of the Navy, July 23, 1922, DS records 839.00/2541.

25. SW to Hughes, August 8, 1922, DS records 839.00/2571.

26. Hughes-Welles correspondence, FRUS, 1922, vol. 2, pp. 39-42, 43, 45.

27. *FRUS,* 1922, vol. 2, pp. 49-52.

28. ESW to SW, August 8, 1922, SWP.

29. Hughes to SW, October 20, 1922, DS records 839.00/2631; *FRUS,* 1922, vol. 2, p.77.

30. W. E. Pulliam diary, courtesy of Pulliam family.

CHAPTER 8

1. Dana G. Munro, *The U.S. and the Caribbean Republics: 1921-33* (Princeton, NJ: Princeton University Press, 1974), p. 116.

2. Munro to Hughes, April 21, 1922, DS records 813.00 Tacoma/8.

3. SW to Davis, April 29,1926, SWP.

4. Caroline A. D. Phillips Diaries, Schlesinger Library, Radcliffe College, Cambridge, Massachusetts, December, 1922.

5. Frances Parkinson Keyes, *Capital Kaleidoscope: The Story of a Washington Hostess* (New York: Harper & Bros., 1937, pp. 99-103.

6. Proceedings, in English and Spanish, may be found in *Conference on Central American Affairs,* (Washington, DC: U.S. Government Printing Office, December 4, 1922– February 7,1923), pp. 32-36.

7. Munro, *U.S. and Caribbean,* p. 124.

8. David J. Danelski and Joseph S. Tulchin, eds., *The Autobiographical Notes of Charles Evans Hughes* (Cambridge, MA: Harvard University Press, 1973), p. 269.

9. SW to Herbert Jordan Stabler, undated, 1926, SWP.

10. Both Caroline Phillips and Sumner Welles were descended from Abraham Schermerhorn.

11. Caroline A. D. Phillips Diaries, 1922-23.

12. Munro, *U.S. and Caribbean,* p. 60.

13. The note is in the SWP, 1923. Welles finally repaid the debt in full in 1942 after Esther had personally appealed to Henry L. Stimson, an old family friend and FDR's Secretary of War.

14. *FRUS,* 1923, vol. 1, p. 839.

15. New York *Herald-Tribune,* October 14, 1923.

16. Letter, Mrs. H. N. Slater to Welles, BWP.

17. MTG to Welles, October 28, 1923, BWP.

18. Sumner Welles, *Naboth's Vineyard* (London: Payson & Clarke, Ltd., 1928), vol. 2, pp. 886-887.

19. Now in the possession of his eldest grandson, Benjamin Sumner Moss, of Coral Gables, Florida.

20. Private interview, Santo Domingo, 1973.

21. MTG to SW, January 6 and February 2, 1924, SWP; the ring was still on her finger when she died in 1949.

22. ESW to SW, May 29, 1924, BWP.

23. MTG to Welles, May 1924.

24. Interview, James V. Reeks, Englewood, Florida, 1975.

25. The *New York Times,* "Topics of the Times," January 26, 1924.
26. SW to White, January, 1924, SWP.
27. SW to Hughes, January 17, 1924, SWP.
28. *FRUS,* 1924, vol. 1, p. 618.
29. Ibid., pp. 618-619.
30. Hughes to SW, March 22, 1924, DS records 839.00/2812.

CHAPTER 9

1. Joseph C. Grew Diaries, March 16, 1924, Houghton Library, Harvard University.
2. SW to White, February 19, 1924, White to SW, March 7,1924, SWP.
3. *FRUS,* 1924, vol. 2, pp. 300-302; SW to Hughes, April 9, 1924, DS records 815.00/3082.
4. Rollin S. Attwood, "Honduras" *World Book Encyclopedia,* vol. 8, (Chicago: Field Enterprises Educational Corp., 1951).
5. *FRUS,* 1924, vol. 2, p. 304.
6. Ibid., p. 305.
7. SW to Hughes, June 2, 1924, DS records, 815.00/3185.
8. SW to Hughes, tel. #12, April 27, 1924, DS records, 815.00/3130.
9. Text of agreement and Welles's report on the signing are in FRUS, 1924, vol. 2, pp. 316-320.
10. Morales to Hughes, May 7, 1924, DS records, 123 W 451/65.
11. Grew Diaries, August 3, 1924.

CHAPTER 10

1. MTG to SW, March 11, 1924, SWP.
2. *FRUS,* 1924, vol. 1, pp. 625-628.
3. ESW letters to SW filed chronologically in BWP.
4. *New York Times,* p. 23, col. 5.
5. William Ellis Pulliam, unpublished memoirs, in his family's possession.
6. *New York Times,* June 24, 1924, p.23; Pulliam memoirs.
7. Sumner Welles, *The Time For Decision* (New York: Harper & Brothers, 1944), p. 188.
8. William Ellis Pulliam, unpublished memoirs, in his family's possession.
9. SW to Russell, June 27, 1924, SWP.
10. McCormick to Hughes, May 31, 1924, signed copy in SWP.
11. SW to Norman H. Davis, April 29, 1926, SWP.
12. MTG to SW, 1924, undated, SWP.
13. Joseph C. Grew Diaries, September 16, 1924, Houghton Library, Harvard University.
14. MTG to Welles, December, 1924, SWP.
15. *New York Times,* June 28, 1925.
16. SW to Kellogg, May 26, 1925, DS records, 839.51/2626.
17. Grew diaries, April 4, 1925.
18. The correspondence is in the Calvin Coolidge papers, series 1, file 20, Library of Congress, and in DS records, 123 W 451/75b, Confidential.
19. SW to White, undated, filed under 1925, White Papers, Evergreen House, John Hopkins University, Baltimore, Maryland.
20. Munro to author, July 4, 1977, BWP.

21. Castle Diaries, July 14, 1925, Houghton Library, Harvard University.

22. SW to Davis, April 29, 1926, SWP.

23. SW correspondence with Hughes in SWP; Hughes to Kellogg, June 5, 1926; Frank B. Kellogg Papers, Personal and Confidential, Minnesota Historical Society, St. Paul, Minnesota.

24. Kellogg to Hughes, June 7, 1926; Kellogg Papers.

CHAPTER 11

1.   SW to Rowe, July 22, 1925, SWP.

2.   Herter to SW, July 22, 1925, SWP.

3.   SW to Herter, July 23, 1925, SWP.

4.   SW to Stimson, September 9, 1925, Stimson Papers, Houghton Library, Harvard University.

5.   SW to Peabody, November 19, 1925, Peabody Papers, Houghton Library, Harvard University.

6.   Gammell letter, 1973.

7.   Benjamin Welles to his son, Sumner, August 20, 1926, SWP.

8.   Gammell letter.

9.   SW to Davis, March 12, 1926, SWP.

10. SW to Herter, January 12, 1926; Herter to SW, January 16, 1926, SWP.

11. SW to John Martin, February 8, 1926, SWP.

12. Young to Secretary of State, teleg. #19, March 17, 1926, DS records 123 W 451/84; Kellogg to Young, teleg. #25, March 20, 1926, DS records, same file.

13. SW to Francisco J. Peynado, May 1926, SWP.

14. Young to Orme Wilson, Jr., March 23, 1926, DS records, 123 W 451/87.

15. Interview, Anna Louise Clarkson Bacon, Prettymarsh, Maine, 1963.

16. SW to Norton, August 7, 1926, SWP.

17. 1 Kings 21, 2 Kings 9.21-37.

18. Quoted in Sumner Welles, *Naboth's Vineyard* (London: Payson & Clarke, Ltd., 1928), vol. 1, p. 393.

19. Brassai, *The Secret Paris* (New York, Pantheon, 1976).

20. The Sixth inter-American conference, Havana, January 16–February 20, 1928.

21. SW to Mrs. Henry James, FPA, November 5, 1927, SWP.

22. Aluizio Napoleao, Second Secretary Brazilian embassy, interview with SW, June 13, 1947, at Oxon Hill, Maryland, SWP.

23. Ibid.

24. SW to FDR, January 20, 1928, SWP.

25. FDR to SW, February 24, 1928, SWP.

26. FDR to SW, March 8, 1928, SWP.

27. SW to FDR, March 15, 1928, SWP.

28. *Foreign Affairs Quarterly* (summer, 1928).

29. SW to FDR, June 18, 1928, SWP.

30. SW to Carlos Alfredo Tornquist, Buenos Aires, September 9, 1928, SWP.

31. Mrs. Arthur Bullard to SW, April 10, 1935, with copy of letter from Bullard to Drummond, SWP.

32. See reviews by Melvin M. Knight in *The Nation,* November 14, 1928. Professor Knight had just published *The Americans in Santo Domingo* in Harry Elmer Barnes's iconoclastic series, *Studies in American Imperialism;* see also J. Fred Rippy and Charles E. Chapman in *The Hispanic American Historical Review* 10, no. 1 (February 1930), pp. 81-88. C. C. Tansill's definitive study, *The U.S. and Santo Domingo: 1798-1873* (1938), cites *Naboth's Vineyard* only twice.

33. SW to Herbert Jordan Stabler, January 4, 1929, SWP.

34. Sumner Welles, *Naboth's Vineyard,* introduction, p. 22.

35. Ibid., vol. 2, pp. 929-937.

36. Eleanor Roosevelt to SW, October 23 and 29, 1928, SWP.

37. Memorandum enclosed with letter from SW to Eleanor Roosevelt, October 15, 1928, SWP.

38. SW to FDR, November 10, 1928, SWP.

CHAPTER 12

1. SW to Norman H. Davis, February 14, 1929, SWP.

2. SW to American Consul, Shanghai, for Kemmerer, undated copy, Kemmerer to SW, February 15, 1929, SWP.

3. SW to Dawes, February 20, 1929; SW to Vasquez, February 28 and March 1, 1929; Vasquez to SW, March 1 and 2, 1929, SWP.

4. Arthur Ruhl, New York *Herald Tribune,* May 5, 1929.

5. Theodore W. Robinson to SW, May 15, 1929, SWP.

6. *Report of the Dominican Economic Mission,* (Chicago: Lakeside Press, 1929), SWP.

7. SW to Felipe Espil, May 2, 1929, SWP.

8. SW to Pulliam, March 19, 1929, SWP.

9. Robert D. Crasweller, *Trujillo: The Life and Times of a Caribbean Dictator* (New York: Macmillan, 1966), p. 63.

10. SW to Pulliam, March 19, 1929, SWP.

11. SW to Dawes, March 18, 1930, SWP.

12. SW to Pulliam, April 23, 1930, SWP.

13. SW to Pulliam, May 28, 1930, SWP.

14. SW personal journal covering 1929-32, pp. 120 ff, SWP.

15. Pulliam to SW, September 22, 1930, SWP.

CHAPTER 13

1. SW Journal, pp. 127, 193-94.

2. Ibid. p. 130.

3. Address to the Council on Foreign Relations, New York, February 6, 1931; reprinted in *Foreign Affairs Quarterly,* 9, no. 3, special supplement.

4. Wilson message to Congress, December 1913.

5. *Life and Letters of Walter H. Page* (Garden City, NY: Doubleday, Page & Co., 1922), vol. 2, p. 204, cited in Dana G. Munro, *Intervention and Dollar Diplomacy in the Caribbean: 1900-1921* (Princeton, NJ: Princeton University Press, 1964), p. 217.

6. SW to FDR, January 23, 1933, FDRL/PPF/2961.

7. SW to Davis, February 2, 1931, SWP.

8. Davis to SW, April 8, 1931, SWP.
9. SW Journal, May 13, 1931, p. 144.
10. Ibid., p. 174.
11. SW to FDR, May 5, 1932, SWP.
12. SW Journal, p. 120.
13. Interview, Drew Pearson, Washington, D.C., 1965.
14. FDR to SW, from Warm Springs, Georgia, May 19, 1932, SWP.
15. The platform is in Arthur M. Schlesinger, Jr.'s *History of U.S. Political Parties* (New York: Chelsea House, 1973), pp. 1967-1970.
16. SW Journal, p. 206.
17. Ibid., pp. 182-186.
18. Berle's book, *The Modern Corporation and Private Property* (New York: Macmillan), coauthored with G. C. Means in 1933, became a classic.
19. Berle to SW, September 30, 1932, SWP.
20. SW to FDR, October 6, 1932, SWP.

CHAPTER 14

1. FDR to SW, December 27, 1932, SWP.
2. SW to FDR, January 3, 1933, SWP.
3. SW Journal, p. 298 ff.
4. Ibid., p. 290ff.
5. The memorandum was published by Charles G. Griffin in the *Hispanic American Historic Review* 34 (1954), pp. 190-192; and republished by Edgar Nixon in *Franklin D. Roosevelt and Foreign Affairs* (Cambridge, Massachusetts: Belknap Press, 1969), pp. 18-19.
6. SW Journal, pp. 290ff.
7. SW to FDR, January 23, 1933; FDR to SW, February 1, 1933, SWP.
8. SW Journal, pp. 316-17.
9. Frank Freidel, *FDR: Launching The New Deal* (Boston: Little, Brown & Co., 1973), p. 144.
10. SW Journal, p. 364.
11. Ibid., p. 353.
12. Ibid., p. 362.
13. Ibid.
14. Ibid. p. 375.
15. Ibid. p. 376.
16. Castle Diaries, March 28, 1933, Houghton Library, Harvard University.
17. Interview, Hugh S. Cumming, Washington, D.C., 1976.
18. SW Journal, p. 377ff.
19. SW to Angel Sanchez Elia, May 10, 1933, SWP.
20. SW to Davis, March 30, 1933, SWP.

CHAPTER 15

1. SW to Rowe, April 7, 1933, SWP.

2. Rowe to Merrill for White House, March 21, 1933; Phillips to Louis Howe, March 30, 1933; DS records, 811.415, Pan American Day/68 and 73.
3. The address may be found in Samuel I. Rosenman, ed., *The Public Papers and Addresses of Franklin D. Roosevelt* (New York: Random House, 1938), vol. 2, pp. 129-133.
4. *New York Times,* April 14, 1933, p. 5.
5. It was also incorporated into Cuba's first constitution.
6. Council on Foreign Relations, *Survey of Foreign Affairs: 1929* (New Haven, CT: Yale University Press, 1929), pp. 16-19.
7. Davis to SW, March 18, 1933, SWP.
8. SW to Franklin Mott Gunther, April 21, 1933, SWP.
9. Phillips to Caffery, May 6, 1933, FRUS, 1933, vol. 5, p. 286.
10. SW Memo to files following meeting with FDR, April 24, 1933, SWP.
11. *New York Times,* April 24, 1933.
12. *Baltimore Sun,* April 13, 1933.
13. SW memorandum of conversation with FDR, April 24, 1933, SWP.
14. For an account of the DEU's origins, policy and demise see Justo Carillo, *Cuba 1933: Students, Yankees and Soldiers* (Miami: Institute of Inter-American Studies, University of Miami, 1985).
15. Sumner Welles to the Young Democratic Clubs of America, March 29, 1934, Willard Hotel, Washington, D.C., broadcast nationally by NBC.
16. The name derived from the hierarchy of cells in the underground organization. The three founders, Carlos Saladrigas, Ramon Hermida and Joaquin Martinez Saenz, were known respectively as A-1, B-1 and C-1. Each was responsible for recruiting ten members designated A-2, B-2 or C-2 and upward, numerically. Each in turn was responsible for recruiting ten more members. For security reasons, each cell member knew only his leader, and the leader only the members of his cell. The overall organization was known as ABC. Luis E. Aguilar, *Cuba, 1933: Prologue and Revolution* (Ithaca, NY: Cornell University Press, 1972); Alicia de Espinosa, Coral Gables, Florida, letter to author, July 27, 1991.
17. Sumner Welles, *The Time For Decision* (New York: Harper & Row, 1944), pp. 195-196.
18. SW to Hull, May 13, 1933, *FRUS,* pp. 287ff.
19. SW to FDR, May 18, 1933, SWP.
20. *Diario de la Marina,* May 29, 1933, *FRUS,* p. 296.
21. SW to Phillips, June 2, 1933, *FRUS,* pp. 299-300.
22. FDR to SW, June 8, 1933, SWP.
23. SW to Pearson, June 7, 1933, SWP.
24. *FRUS,* p. 307.
25. Ruby Hart Phillips, *Cuban Sideshow,* (Havana: Cuban Press, 1935), p. 16.
26. The London Economic Conference sought to check the world depression through currency stabilization. FDR's decision to take the United States off the gold standard hastened its collapse.
27. FDR to SW, June 24, 1933, Franklin D. Roosevelt Library, 470.
28. SW to author, June 9, 1933, BWP.
29. SW to Frederick Holmans, June 9, 1933, SWP.
30. *The Grotonian* (December 1933), pp. 36-39.
31. Mathilde Townsend Welles diary, p. 52, SWP.
32. The round back of the car opened up into a seat in which the occupants were fully exposed to dust, rain and wind.

33. SW to Rowe, July 1, 1933, SWP.
34. SW to Phillips, July 8, 1933, *FRUS,* p. 319.
35. SW to FDR, July 17, 1933, *FRUS,* p. 323.
36. *FRUS,* pp. 330-332.
37. *El Pais* (Havana), August 13, 1933.
38. SW to Hull, August 9, 1933, *FRUS,* pp. 345-346.
39. Hull to SW, August 9, 1933, *FRUS,* pp. 347-348.
40. Drew Pearson column, August 17, 1933.
41. Spruille Braden transcript, pp. 2916-2917, Columbia Oral History Project, Columbia University, New York.
42. Phillips, *Cuban Sideshow,* p. 44.
43. *FRUS,* p. 359.
44. New York Times Sunday magazine, Aug. 20, 1933, p. 3.
45. Davis to SW, August 15, 1933, SWP.
46. Mattingly to SW, August 15, 1933, SWP.
47. Pearson to SW, August 16, 1933, SWP.
48. FDR-SW correspondence can be found in *FRUS,* pp. 367-369.

CHAPTER 16

1. SW to Hull, August 14, *FRUS,* 1933, Vol. 5, p. 364.
2. Ibid., pp. 373-376.
3. Ruby Hart Phillips, *Cuban Sideshow* (Havana: Cuban Press, 1935), pp. 38-40.
4. *FRUS,* 1933, Vol. 5, p. 372.
5. Phillips, *Cuban Sideshow,* p. 53.
6. *FRUS,* 1933, Vol. 5, pp. 377-378.
7. SW to Hull, August 30, *FRUS,* 1933, Vol. pp. 377-378.
8. Justo Carillo, *Cuba 1933: Students, Yankees and Soldiers* (Miami: Institute of Inter-American Studies, University of Miami, 1985), pp. 117-118.
9. Others included José Miguel Irrisari, a DEU ideologue; Guillermo Portela, a professor of penal law; Sergio Carbo, a radical journalist, and Porfirio Franca, a conservative businessman, chosen as window-dressing.
10. Carillo, *Cuba,* p. 281.
11. Hull, *Memoirs,* p. 316.
12. *New York Herald-Tribune,* editorials, September 10 and 12, 1933.
13. SW to Hull, September 8, *FRUS,* 1933, Vol. 5, SWP.
14. *FRUS,* 1933, Vol. 5, pp. 386-387.
15. SW to Hull, September 10, 1933, pp. 416-417.
16. Carillo, *Cuba,* p. 218.
17. SW to Hull, September 10, 1933, SWP.
18. Phillips, *Cuban Sideshow,* p. 7.
19. Braden, p. 2918.
20. Interview, Adolf A. Berle, New York, January 13, 1975.
21. Recollections, James V. Reeks.
22. Phillips, *Cuban Sideshow,* p. 83.
23. Luis E. Aguilar, *Cuba 1933: Prologue to Revolution* (Ithaca, NY: Cornell University Press, 1972), p. 174.

24. Carillo, *Cuba,* p. 273.
25. Hull to SW, October 2, *FRUS,* 1933, Vol. 5, p. 464.
26. Hull to SW, October 5, 1933, SWP.
27. Laurence Duggan, *The Americas: The Search for Hemisphere Security* (New York: Henry Holt Co., 1949), p. 62.
28. Pearson to SW, October 12, 1933, SWP.
29. SW to Pearson, October 17, 1933, SWP.
30. Carillo, *Cuba,* p. 318.
31. SD press release, November 24, 1933.
32. Carillo, *Cuba,* p. 338.
33. *Diario de la Marina,* (Havana), December 13, 1933.
34. José Augustin Martinez to SW, December 13, 1933, SWP.
35. January 17, 1934; FRUS, 1934, vol. 5, pp. 95-97, 349; Manuel Marquez Sterling, *Proceso Historico de la Enmienda Platt* (Havana, 1941), pp. 402-404.
36. Interview, Hugh S. Cumming, Washington, D.C., 1976.
37. Named for Mexico's then minister of foreign affairs, Engaro Estrada.
38. Sumner Welles, *The Time For Decision* (New York: Harper & Brothers, 1944), pp. 198-199.
39. SW to Pearson, December 31, 1943, SWP.
40. Carillo, *Cuba,* p. 378.

CHAPTER 17

1. Sumner Welles, *The Time for Decision* (New York: Harper & Brothers, 1944), p. 201.
2. Langley Lester, "Negotiating New Treaties With Panama: 1936," *The Hispanic American Historic Review* (May 1968), p. 232.
3. *FRUS,* 1935, vol. 5, p. 855.
4. Hull to SW, January 18, 1935, SWP.
5. FDR to SW, November 15, 1935, SWP.
6. Edward O. Guerrant, *Roosevelt's Good Neighbor Policy* (Albuquerque: University of New Mexico Press, 1950), p. 14.
7. David E. Cronon, *Josephus Daniels in Mexico* (Madison: University of Wisconsin Press, 1960), pp. 89-103.
8. See SW memoranda of conversations with FDR, May 3 and 16, June 25 and July 12, 1935, SWP; SW to FDR, November 11 and December 21, 1935; also *FRUS,* 1935, vol. 4, pp. 782-806.
9. SW to Curtis, March 21, 1935, SWP.
10. SW to Davis, April 8, 1935, SWP.
11. Although hostilities ceased that year, the final Chaco treaty was not signed until July 21, 1938, and even then it did not include agreement on the definitive Bolivian-Paraguayan border.
12. Drew Pearson "Washington Merry-Go Round" column, June 30, 1935.
13. Lawrence Duggan, *The Americas: The Search for Hemisphere Security* (New York: Holt, 1949), pp. 70-72.
14. See Leslie B. Rout, *Politics of the Chaco Peace Conference* (Austin: University of Texas Press, 1970).

15. *FRUS,* 1935, vol. 4, pp. 77 ff; The final Chaco treaty was not signed until July 21, 1938, and even then did not include agreement on the definitive Bolivian-Paraguayan boundary.

16. SW memo of conversation with FDR, June 18, 1935, SWP.

17. Sumner Welles, *Seven Decisions That Shaped History* (New York: Harper & Row, 1950), p. 104.

18. The text is in *FRUS,* 1936, vol. 5, pp. 3-5.

19. Castle Diaries, February 18, 1936, Houghton Library, Harvard University, Cambridge, Massachusetts.

20. Welles, *Time for Decision,* p. 206.

21. SW to Daniels, September 8, 1936, SWP.

22. SW to Braden, August 5, 1936, SWP.

23. Castle Diaries, July 23, 1936.

24. Berle to FDR, June 30, 1936, FDRL/State/Berle.

25. SW to FDR, June 19, 1936, FDRL/PPF/2961.

26. Daniels to SW, August 20, 1936, SWP.

27. SW to Daniels, August 26, 1936, SWP.

28. FDR won 62.4 percent of the Maryland vote; Alf Landon, his GOP rival, 37 percent; Congressional Quarterly, Inc., *Guide to U.S. Elections,* 1975.

29. Drew Pearson column, November 7, 1936.

30. Sumner Welles, *The Accomplishments of the Inter-American Conference for the Maintenance of Peace* (Washington, D.C.: U.S. Government Printing Office, Department of State, Conference Series #26, 1937), p. 4.

31. Dr. Beatrice Bishop Berle diary, in family's possession.

32. SW to Arnold Nelson Welles, November 26, 1936, SWP.

33. MTW Journal, December 1936, SWP.

34. Spruille Braden transcript, p. 1639, Columbia Oral History Project, Columbia University, New York.

35. Beatrice Bishop Berle and Travis Beal Jacobs, *Navigating the Rapids* (New York: Harcourt, Brace, Jovanovich, 1973), p. 119.

36. Samuel I. Rosenman, ed., *The Public Papers and Addresses of Franklin D. Roosevelt* (New York: Random House, 1936).

37. *Noticias Graficas,* December 3, 1936; quoted in Samuel Guy Inman, *Inter-American Conferences, 1826-1954: History and Problems.* (Washington, D.C., 1965).

38. Braden transcript, p. 1640.

39. Welles, *Time for Decision,* p. 207.

40. Anna Louise Clarkson to author, January 22, 1968, BWP.

41. Welles, *Time for Decision,* p. 208.

42. Ibid., p. 206.

43. Welles, *Seven Decisions,* pp. 103-104.

44. Ibid., pp. 104-105.

45. Two years later, at Lima, Hull won approval for the Permanent Consultative Committee.

46. Braden transcript, p. 2182.

47. Ibid.

48. Anna Louise Clarkson to author, July 29, 1974, BWP.

CHAPTER 18

1. Castle Diaries, March 21, 1937, Houghton Library, Harvard University, Cambridge, Massachusetts.
2. Richard Traina, *American Diplomacy and the Spanish Civil War* (Bloomington: Indiana University Press, 1968), p. 23.
3. Cordell Hull, *The Memoirs of Cordell Hull* (New York: Macmilan, 1948), pp. 509-510.
4. Orville H. Bullitt, ed., *For the President: Personnal and Secret* (Boston: Houghton Mifflin, 1972).
5. Castle Diaries, May 22, 1937.
6. Castle Diaries, April 30, 1936.
7. Drew Pearson column, July 6, 1937.
8. SW recollections to author.
9. SW to Phillips, June 4, 1937, SWP.
10. He named James C. Dunn for Europe, Stanley K. Hornbeck for the Far East and Herbert Feis for International Economic affairs. In 1941 Laurence Duggan became political advisor for Latin America and, a year later, Wallace Murray for the Near Eastern division.
11. Among them were Philip W. Bonsal, Ellis Briggs, Paul C. Daniels, Gerald S. Drew, Robert F. Woodward, Walter N. Walmsley and Emilio P. Collado.
12. Drew Pearson column, November 9, 1937.
13. Interview, James C. Dunn, New York, 1976.
14. Charles C. Griffin to author, January 6, 1975, BWP.
15. Interview, Jacob Beam, Washington, D.C., June 1, 1974.
16. Drew Pearson column, November 9, 1937.
17. Interview, Emilio Collado, New York, 1976.
18. Handwritten notes, Drew Pearson personal papers, Lyndon B. Johnson Library, Austin, Texas, container G-236, undated.
19. FDR to SW, January 7, 1938, SWP.
20. SW to FDR, January 10, 1938, SWP.
21. SW to FDR, February 26, 1938, SWP.
22. FDR to SW, November 15, 1938, SWP.
23. Sumner Welles, *The Time for Decision,* (New York: Harper & Brothers, 1944), p. 8.
24. Ibid.
25. Ibid.
26. Interview, Alger Hiss, New York City, June 1975.
27. FDR to SW, DS records, 740.00/184, May 28, 1937.
28. Quoted in Dorothy Borg, *The U.S. and the Far Eastern Crisis of 1933-38* (Cambridge, MA: Harvard University Press, 1964), p. 374.
29. SW to Peabody, July 9, 1937, Peabody papers, Houghton Library, Harvard University, Cambridge, Massachusetts.
30. Text in Samuel I. Rosenman, ed., *The Public Papers and Addresses of Franklin D. Roosevelt* (New York: Macmillan, 1941), pp. 284-285.
31. University of Virginia, Institute of Public Affairs Proceedings, 11th session, 1937, vol. 1.
32. Editorial, *Boston Post,* July 9, 1937.
33. See July 9 editions of the *London Daily Mail,* the *Washington Post* and the *Houston Post.*
34. *Washington Star,* July 18, 1937.
35. *Boston Post,* July 9, 1937.

36. PRO, FO 371/20673, A-6974/4/5, September 24, 1937.
37. Hull, *Memoirs,* p. 536.
38. Sumner Welles, *Seven Decisions that Shaped History* (New York: Harper & Brothers, 1950), pp. 10-11.
39. Hull *Memoirs,* p. 545.
40. Samuel I. Rosenman, *Working with Roosevelt* (New York: Harper & Bros., 1952), p. 166.
41. Quoted in ibid., pp. 164-165.
42. Welles, *Seven Decisions,* p. 13.
43. Ibid., p. 16ff.
44. Hull, *Memoirs,* p. 546.
45. Ibid., p. 547.
46. Welles, *Seven Decisions,* p. 34.
47. Ibid., pp. 25-26.
48. James MacGregor Burns, *Roosevelt: The Lion and the Fox,* (New York: Harcourt Brace & Co., 1965), p. 353.
49. Winston S. Churchill, *The Gathering Storm* (Boston: Houghton Mifflin, 1948), p. 255.
50. Welles, *Seven Decisions,* p. 27.
51. David Dilks, ed., *Diaries of Sir Alexander Cadogan* (London: Cassell, 1971), summary covering January 1938.
52. Ibid., entries for January 13, 1938, and January 15, 1938.
53. Memoirs of Anthony Eden, Earl of Avon: *The Reckoning* (Boston: Houghton Mifflin, 1956), p. 48.
54. Drew Middleton, *New York Times,* August 31, 1969.
55. Churchill, *Gathering Storm,* p. 254.

CHAPTER 19

1. Castle Diaries, May 27, 1938, Haughton Library, Harvard University, Cambridge, Massachusetts.
2. Joseph Alsop and Robert Kintner, *Washington Evening Star,* May 18, 1938.
3. Quoted in Harold L. Ickes, *Secret Diaries* (New York: Simon and Schuster, 1953-54), July 9, 1938 entry, Library of Congress.
4. Ibid.
5. Arnold N. Welles to author.
6. Bullitt to SW, August 31, 1938, SWP.
7. Cordell Hull, *The Memoirs of Cordell Hull* (New York: Macmillan, 1948), p. 591.
8. Welles's draft shows signs of FDR's penciled editing, SWP.
9. Hull, *Memoirs,* p. 595.
10. Ibid., p. 596.
11. Drew Pearson column, October 20, 1938.
12. Sumner Welles, *Seven Decisions That Shaped History* (New York: Harper and Brothers, 1950), pp. 13-14.
13. Joseph Alsop and Robert Kintner, *American White Paper: The Story of American Diplomacy and the Second World War* (New York: Simon & Schuster, 1940), p. 6.
14. James MacGregor Burns, *Roosevelt: The Lion and the Fox* (New York: Harcout Brace and Co., 1965), p. 390.
15. Alsop and Kintner, p. 15.

16. Ibid., p. 15.

17. SW to Bullitt, April 5, 1939, SWP.

18. William Langer and Everett Gleason, *The Challenge to Isolationism, 1937-1940* (New York: Harper, 1952), p. 90.

19. The typewritten copy in Welles's files shows editing in his handwriting, SWP.

20. H. Wallace to FDR, FDRL/PSF/Agriculture. April 14,1939

21. PRO/FO/371/24405-8.

22. Hull, *Memoirs,* p.650.

23. Alsop and Kintner, pp. 50-58.

24. Hull, *Memoirs,* pp. 657-658.

25. Langer and Gleason, p. 134.

26. Stetson Conn and Byron Fairchild, *The U.S. Army in World War II, The Western Hemisphere, The Framework of Hemisphere Defense,* Office of the Chief of Military History, Dept. of the Army, Chapter 1, p. 20.

27. FDR to State and Treasury departments, August 18, 1939, copy SWP.

28. Moffat diaries, August 17, 1939.

29. Hans Heinrich Herwarth von Bittenfeld, an English-speaking junior diplomat, detested Hitler and furnished Bohlen, then in the U.S. embassy in Moscow, with valuable information. cf: Charles Bohlen and Robert H. Phelps, *Witness to History* (New York: W. W. Norton & Co., 1973).

30. Douglas MacArthur II, interview, Washington D.C., March 3, 1993.

31. SW to FDR at sea, August 21, 1939, SWP.

32. Ibid., August 22, 1939, SWP.

33. Argentina had proposed a similar zone during World War I, with mixed results.

34. Cordell Hull, *The Memoirs of Cordell Hull* (New York: Macmillan, 1948), p. 650.

35. SW address to meeting of Hemisphere Foreign Ministers, September 25, 1939; *The World of the Four Freedoms,* (New York: Columbia University Press, 1943), p. 1.

36. The Inter-American Financial and Economic Advisory Board was established in late 1939 and Welles was elected its first chairman.

37. Rowe to FDR, October 12, 1939, FDRL/PPF/2961.

38. Paul Daniels, interview, Washington, D.C., 1976.

39. Sheldon Thomas to author, July 15, 1978, BWP.

40. Anna Louise Clarkson Bacon, interview, Hancock Point, Maine, July 9, 1974.

41. Castle Diaries, November 14, 1939, Houghton Library, Harvard University, Cambridge, Massachusetts.

42. Sumner Welles, *The Time for Decision* (New York: Harper and Brothers, 1944), p. 212.

CHAPTER 20

1. Sumner Welles Papers.

2. The first Jewish student entered Groton in the early 1930s, twenty years after Welles graduated.

3. SW to George Messersmith, March 12, 1938, SWP.

4. Undated memorandum in SWP. On April 6, 1938, Welles wrote FDR, referring to the Welles-Morgenthau memorandum that the President had approved before leaving for Warm Springs. The approved version of the memorandum is with letter from Welles to

Morgenthau, March 23, 1938, Morgenthau diary, box 116, FDRL. See also Morgenthau diary entry for March 22, 1938.

5.   Invitations and related correspondence are in FRUS, 1938, vol. 1, p. 740ff.

6.   Henry L. Feingold, *The Politics of Rescue* (New Brunswick, NJ: Rutgers University Press, 1970), p. 28.

7.   Memo, Early to FDR with reply, April 11, 1938, FDRL/OF/3186.

8.   Rublee was also the first graduate of Groton, founded in 1884 and from which FDR graduated in 1900 and Welles in 1910.

9.   Quoted in Sumner Welles, *We Need Not Fail* (Boston: Houghton Mifflin, Co., 1948), p. 6.

10.   *FRUS,* 1938, vol. 1, pp. 785-786, 791, 835-842; Ibid., vol. 2, pp. 89-90; Feingold, *Politics of Rescue,* pp. 48-9, 99-102, 111-113.

11.   FDR's letter and Mussolini's reply are in *FRUS,* 1938, vol. 1, pp. 858-60 as modified by pp. 880-886 and *FRUS,* 1939, vol. 2, pp. 63-64.

12.   Ibid., 1939, vol. 2, pp. 65-69.

13.   Ibid., pp. 101-02.

14.   Feingold, *Politics of Rescue,* pp. 97-99.

15.   *FRUS,* 1938, vol. 1, pp. 791-815.

16.   Richard M. Ketchum, *The Borrowed Years: 1938-41: America on the Way to War* (New York: Random House, 1989), p. 121.

17.   *FRUS,* vol. 1, pp. 864-865.

18.   Ibid., pp. 873-877.

19.   In his book *We Need Not Fail,*, Welles cites Eliahu Ben-Horin's *The Middle East* on Nazi-Zionist deals to exchange refugees for foreign currency.

20.   Moffat Diary, February 13, 1939.

21.   *FRUS,* 1939, vol. 1, p. 99.

22.   After the five-year period from 1939 to 1944, Jewish immigration would be subject to Arab consent--effectively terminating it.

23.   Welles, *We Need Not Fail,* p. 14.

24.   Ketchum, *The Borrowed Years.*

25.   Ibid., p. 113ff.

26.   Ibid., p. 115ff.

27.   Feingold, *The Politics of Reason,* p. 65ff.

28.   Circular telegram to other American republics, February 14 1942, DS records: 862. 20200/46.

29.   SW-Eleanor Roosevelt correspondence file, SWP.

30.   FDRL, PSF/Welles, November 22, 1940.

31.   Report of the American Jewish Commission on the Holocaust, *New York Times,* March 21, 1984, p. 1.

32.   Feingold, *The Politics of Reason,* pp. 308-309.

33.   Both the Zionist memorandum and Eleanor Roosevelt letter are in SWP.

34.   SW to Atherton, DS records, 819. 857/111 and 112A.

35.   Wise to Eleanor Roosevelt, April 1, 1942, copy in SWP.

36.   Welles, We Need Not Fail, p. 5.

37.   Philby was the father, by an English wife, of H. A. R. "Kim" Philby, the Soviet double agent who penetrated British intelligence in World War II.

38.   H. St. John H. B. Philby, *Arabian Jubilee* (New York: John Day Co., 1953), pp. 206-207.

39.   Ibid.

40. Weizmann speech to American Emergency Committee for Zionist Affairs, December 12, 1942, Central Zionist Archives, Rehovot, Israel, Z-5, 1415.

41. Barnet Litvinoff, ed., *The Letters and Papers of Chaim Weizmann* (New Brunswick, NJ: Transaction Books, 1979), Series A, vol. 20, pp. 329-330.

42. Chaim Weizmann, *Trial and Error: Autobiography of Chaim Weizmann* (New York: Harper & Brothers, 1949), p. 425.

43. *FRUS,* 1942, vol. 4, pp. 24ff.

44. The author served briefly under him in the Office of Strategic Services during the war.

45. Peter Grose, *Israel in the Mind of America* (New York: Knopf, 1983), p. 125.

46. *FRUS,* 1942, vol. 4, pp. 32-35.

47. Walter Laqueur and Richard Breitman, *Breaking the Silence* (New York: Simon & Schuster, 1986), p. 150.

48. Grose, *Israel,* p. 125.

49. Laqueur and Breitman, *Breaking the Silence,* pp. 152-153.

50. Ibid., pp. 155-156.

51. In 1986, Laqueur and Breitman identified Riegner's source as Dr. Eduard Schulte, an executive of Giesche, a mining firm closely tied to the Nazi war effort.

52. Stephen Wise, *Challenging Years* (New York: G. P. Putnam's Sons, 1949), pp. 275-276; copies of corroborating documents in SWP.

53. Evan Wilson, *Decision on Palestine* (Stanford, CA: Stanford University, Hoover Institution Press, 1979), p. 28.

54. Feingold errs in asserting, on p. 180, that this report was suppressed. See SW to Wise, February 9, 1943, DS records 840. 48 Refugees/2256A.

55. John Morton Blum, *Roosevelt & Morgenthau* (Boston: Houghton Mifflin Co., 1970), p. 521.

56. Central Zionist Archives, Z-5, 1377.

57. Ibid.

58. Goldmann Memo, February 20, 1943, Central Zionist Archives, Z5/1220.

59. Ibn Saud to FDR, November 29, 1938, *FRUS,* 1938, vol. 2, pp. 994ff; FDR to Ibn Saud, January 9, 1939; *FRUS,* 1939, vol. 4, pp 64ff.

60. Kirk to Hull and Welles, April 17, 1943, *FRUS,* 1943, vol. 4, p. 768.

61. Ibn Saud to FDR, April 30, 1943, *FRUS,* 1943, vol. 4, pp. 773-775.

62. SW to FDR, May 10, 1943, SWP.

63. Nahum Goldmann notes of meeting, copy in SWP.

64. Weizmann archives, Rehovot, Israel, Central Zionist Archives, Z-5/1220.

65. Weizmann, memo of conversation, June 12, 1943, Central Zionist Archives, Z-5, 1377.

66. Weizmann, *Trial and Error,* p. 435.

67. *FRUS,* 1943, vol. 4, p. 792-794.

68. Weizmann to SW, June 25, 1943, Central Zionist Archives, Z5/1444.

69. Minutes of conversation, June 21, 1943, Central Zionist Archives, Z5/666.

70. Grose, *Israel,* p. 141.

71. Hoskins to Welles, January 23, 1943, *FRUS,* 1943, vol. 4, p. 747.

72. FDRL/PSF/Confidential/SD, May 7, 1943.

73. FDR to Ibn Saud, May 26, 1943, FDRL/PSF/Confidential File/SD.

74. SW to Hull, May 15, 1943, SWP.

75. Nicholas Bethel, *The Palestine Triangle,* (New York: G. P. Putnam, 1979), pp. 148ff.

76. Ibid.

77. Ibid.

78. Henry A. Wallace interview with Louis Bean, April 3, 1944, Wallace Papers, Columbia Oral History Collection.
79. Grose, *Israel,* p. 150.
80. Weizmann to SW, December 12, 1943, Central Zionist Archives, Z4/15113; copy in SWP.
81. PRO/FO/371/40319, quoted in Bethel, *Palestine Triangle,* p. 149.
82. Central Zionist Archives, Z5/666.
83. Welles, *We Need Not Fail,* p. 21.
84. Ibid., pp. 28-30.
85. *FRUS,* 1945, vol. 8, p. 2.
86. Welles, *We Need Not Fail,* pp. 28-30.

CHAPTER 21

1. Documents on German Foreign Policy, Series D, vol. 8, p. 229, National Archives, microfilm.
2. See Stanley C. Hilton, "The Welles Mission to Europe, February-March, 1940: Illusion or Realism?" *Journal of American History,* 58, (June 1971); also Arnold A. Offner, "Appeasement Revisited: The U.S., Great Britain and Germany, 1933-40," *Journal of American History* 64 (September 1977).
3. James W. Gerard to FDR, August 7, 1939, FDRL/PPF/977.
4. SW to Hull, August 10, 1939, SWP.
5. Harley A. Notter, *Postwar Foreign Policy Preparation, 1939-1945* (Washington, D.C.: U.S. Government Printing Office, 1950), pp. 18-22.
6. Samuel I. Rosenman, Public Papers, 1940 volume, pp. 4, 9.
7. SW to FDR, August 1, 1 939, SWP.
8. *FRUS,* 1939, vol. 2, pp. 869-874; ibid., 1940, vol. 1, pp. 123-129.
9. The Federal Council of Churches and the Jewish Theological Seminary, among others.
10. Notter, *Postwar Foreign Policy,* pp. 23-26.
11. Rosenman, p. 3.
12. George H. Gallup, *The Gallup Poll, 1935-71* (New York: Random House, 1971), vol. 1, pp. 200-201.
13. SW to FDR, June 8, 1940, SWP.
14. Joseph P. Kennedy and James M. Landis, unpublished Kennedy Memoirs, p. 538, James M. Landis papers, Library of Congress, box 51 (hereafter cited as Kennedy Memoirs).
15. FDRL/PSF, box 62.
16. Fred L. Israel, ed., *The War Diary of Breckinridge Long* (Lincoln: University of Nebraska Press, 1966) p. 64.
17. Sumner Welles, *The Time for Decision* (New York: Harper and Brothers, 1944), p. 73.
18. Louis P. Lochner, *Always the Unexpected* (New York: Macmillan, 1956), pp. 268-270.
19. Messersmith memorandum, January 25, 1940, DS records, 740. 00119, European war, 1939/104.
20. Messersmith memorandum, February 13, 1940, same DS records, 740. 00119, European war, 1939/104. An enclosure to a report of March 11, 1940, by Hans Thomsen, German chargé d'affaires in Washington, confirms the connection between Mooney and the Welles mission; cf. German Foreign Office document 2422/511869-72 on microfilm in National Archives. See also William L. Shirer, *The Rise and Fall of the Third Reich*

(New York: Simon & Schuster, 1960), p. 906. For Mooney's reputation as an appeaser, see Harold L. Ickes, *Secret Diaries,* Library of Congress, vol. 3, p. 395.

21. PRO/FO/800, Halifax private papers, February 1, 1940.
22. PRO/FO/800, February 7, 1940.
23. David Dilks, ed., *Diaries of Sir Alexander Cadogan* (London: Cassell, 1971), February 2, 1940.
24. Norman Rose, *Vansittart: Study of a Diplomat* (London: Heinemann, 1978), p. 242.
25. PRO/FO/371/24418/5958, February 16, 1940.
26. PRO/FO/800, Eden to Halifax, undated, Halifax papers.
27. Lothian to Halifax, February 8, 1940.
28. DS bulletin, February 10, 1940.
29. FRUS, 1940, vol. 1, p. 4.
30. Interview, Robert C. Murphy, New York, 1974.
31. Ickes, *Secret Diaries,* February 17, 1940.
32. Quai d'Orsay archives, très secret, #235-37, February 10, 1940. The file containing St. Quentin's dispatch was seized, along with others, by the Germans during their occupation of Paris. It was recovered by the U.S. Army after Germany's surrender, sent to Welles in 1946 for his perusal and found among his papers after his death in 1961. It has since been returned to the French government.
33. Despite searches in the FDRL and in Welles's personal files, it has not been found.
34. Ciano helped bring about Mussolini's fall in 1943. Arrested by the Germans, he was later executed by the Fascist republic in North Italy. His widow, Edda, Mussolini's daughter, smuggled the diary into Switzerland. Welles wrote the introduction when it was published in the United States in 1946: Hugh Gibson, ed., *The Ciano Diaries 1939-43* (Garden City, NY: Doubleday, 1946).
35. Welles, *Time for Decision,* pp. 78 ff.
36. Ibid., p. 86.
37. Gibson, ed., *Ciano Diaries,* p. 212.
38. Caroline A. Phillips Diaries, February 27, 1940, Schlesinger Library, Radcliffe College, Cambridge, Massachusetts.
39. Moffat diary (Cambridge, MA: Harvard University Press, 1956), February 15, 1940.
40. Interview, J. M. Dow, New York, 1979.
41. Welles, *Time for Decision,* pp. 90-91.
42. Documents on German Foreign Policy, Series D, vol. 1, p. 41, National Archives, microfilm.
43. Welles, *Time for Decision,* p. 90.
44. *FRUS,* 1940, vol. 1, pp. 57-58.
45. Welles, *Time for Decision,* p. 102.
46. Louis Lochner, *Always the Unexpected,* pp. 268-270; also Documents on German Foreign Policy, Series D, vol. 8, pp. 865-6.
47. Welles, *Time for Decision,* pp. 112-113.
48. Ibid., pp. 116-118.
49. Ibid., p. 110.
50. *FRUS,* 1940, vol. 1, pp. 57-58.
51. TFD, pp. 109-110.
52. SW to James M. Landis, November 28, 1950, SWP.
53. Kennedy Memoirs, p. 542.
54. Welles, *Time for Decision,* p. 121.

55. Admiral Roscoe H. Hillenkoeter, interview, New York, 1976.
56. Moffat diaries, p. 19.
57. Ibid., p. 24.
58. Welles, *Time for Decision,* p. 129.
59. Kennedy Memoirs, pp. 556, 559.
60. Ibid., p. 556.
61. PR/FO/371/24406, March 11, 1940.
62. Kennedy Memoirs, p. 572.
63. PRO/FO/24406, Vansittart to Secretary of State, March 13, 1940.
64. SW, *Time for Decision,* p. 133.
65. Ibid.
66. Sir John Colville, *The Fringes of Power* (New York: Norton, 1985), p. 40; cited in Anthony Cave Brown, *"C": The Secret Life of Sir Stewart Graham Menzies: Spymaster to Winston Churchill* (New York: Macmillan, 1987), pp. 212-213.
67. PRO/FO/371/24406, Halifax to Lothian, March 11, 1940.
68. *FRUS,* 1940, vol. 1, pp. 75-78.
69. PRO/FO/371/24407, Foreign Office to Lothian, March 17, 1940.
70. PRO/FO/371/24407, Foreign Office to Lothian, March 27, 1940.
71. Documents on German Foreign Policy, Series D, vol. 8, p. 864, footnote.
72. Kennedy to Hull, #639, March 14, 1940, SWP.
73. Gibson, ed., *Ciano Diaries,* p. 222.
74. Documents on German Foreign Policy, Series D, vol. 8, p. 864, footnote.
75. *FRUS,* 1940, vol. 1, p. 113.
76. Ibid., 1940, vol. 1, p. 20.
77. Ibid., pp. 113ff.
78. Cordell Hull, *The Memoirs of Cordell Hull* (New York: Macmillan, 1948), p. 740.
79. Robert E. Sherwood, *The White House Papers of Harry L. Hopkins* (London: Eyre & Spottiswoode, 1948), p. 139.
80. Drew Pearson, notes of conversations April 22 and June 25, 1940, Pearson Papers, Lyndon B. Johnson Library, University of Texas, Austin, Texas.
81. Welles, *Time for Decision,* p.77.

CHAPTER 22

1. Fred L. Israel, ed., *The War Diary of Breckinridge Long,* (Lincoln: University of Nebraska Press, 1966), p. 76.
2. Ibid.
3. Ibid, p. 67.
4. Franklin D. Roosevelt Library/PSF/State, April 13, 1940.
5. FDR to SW, April 15, 1941, SWP.
6. Adolph A. Berle and Travis B. Jacobs, *Navigating the Rapids: 1917-1971* (New York: Harcourt, Brace, Jovanovic, 1971), entry for May 8, 1940.
7. Cordell Hull, *The Memoirs of Cordell Hull* (New York: Macmillan, 1948), p. 784; Henry H. Adams, *Harry Hopkins: A Biography* (New York: Putnam, 1977), p. 169.
8. SW to FDR, May 25, 1940; SW to Bullitt, May 25, 1940, SWP.
9. Orville H. Bullitt, ed., *For the President: Personal and Secret* (Boston: Haughton Mifflin, 1972), pp. 455 ff.

10. H. Freeman Matthews, *Memories of a Passing Era* (Washington, DC: privately printed, 1974), pp. 179-180. Courtesy of the Matthews family.
11. Charles de Gaulle, *War Memoirs* (London: Collins, 1955), vol. 1, p. 67.
12. Bullitt to FDR, Sept. 8, 1939, Bullitt, ed., *For the President,* p. 369.
13. As diagnosed by Vice Admiral Ross T. McIntire, the White House doctor; Carmel Offie memo to John Bullitt, Orville H. Bullitt, private papers. Philadelphia. Courtesy Bullitt family.
14. Bullitt, ed., *For the President,* chapters 22 and 23.
15. Hull, *Memoirs,* p. 791.
16. Douglas MacArthur II, interview, Washington, D. C., January 19, 1989.
17. Hugh Cumming, interview, Washington, D.C., 1976.
18. Will Brownell and Richard N. Billings, *So Close to Greatness: A Biography of William C. Bullitt* (New York: Macmillan, 1987), pp. 266-267.
19. Harold L. Ickes, *Secret Diaries,* Library of Congress, entry for August 3, 1940, p. 277.
20. Israel, ed., *War Diary of Breckinridge Long,* p. 141.
21. SW to FDR, July 12, 1940, SWP.
22. SW to FDR, October 15, 1940; FDR to Kennedy, October 17, 1940, SWP.
23. Henry A. Wallace, *The Price of Vision; The Diary of Henry A. Wallace, 1942-1946,* ed., John Morton Blum (Boston: Houghton Mifflin, 1973), p. 1182.
24. Ickes, *Secret Diaries,* June 29, 1940.
25. Robert H. Jackson Papers, Columbia Oral History Collection, p. 850.
26. Israel, ed., *War Diary of Beckenridge Long,* pp. 118-122.
27. John O'Donnell, *Washington Times-Herald,* August 31, 1943.
28. Jackson Papers, COHC, p. 802.
29. John Morton Blum, *Roosevelt & Morgenthau* (Boston: Houghton Mifflin, 1970) p. 396.
30. Ibid., p. 396.
31. Sumner Welles, *Seven Decisions That Shaped History* (New York: Harper and Brothers, 1950), pp. 80-81.
32. Blum, *Roosevelt and Morgenthau,* 393-394.
33. Ickes, *Secret Diaries,* July 27, 1940.
34. SW's correspondence with FDR, Stimson, Knox and Stark plus relevant British documents are in SWP.
35. Jackson Papers, COHC, p. 904; Blum, *Roosevelt and Morgenthau,* pp. 334-335.
36. Sumner Welles, *The Time for Decision* (New York: Harper and Brothers, 1944), p. 169.
37. Hull, *Memoirs,* p. 812.
38. Welles, *The Time for Decision,* p. 171.
39. Israel, ed., *War Diary of Breckenridge Long,* p. 183.
40. Ladislas Farago, *The Broken Seal* (New York: Random House, 1967), pp. 196ff.
41. Ruth B. Harris," The 'Magic' Leak of 1941 and Japanese-American Relations," *Pacific Historical Review* (February 1981), pp. 77-96.
42. Hull, *Memoirs,* p. 968.
43. FDRL/PSF/W folder, 1/1941.
44. Israel, ed., *War Diary of Breckenridge Long,* p. 113.
45. Heath to SW, November 22, 1940, SWP.
46. Joseph C. Grew, *Turbulent Era* (Boston: Houghton Mifflin, 1952), pp. 1274-1276.
47. Israel, ed., *War Diary of Breckenridge Long,* p. 107.
48. SW to FDR and FDR to Churchill, November 12, 1940; SW to Matthews, Vichy, November 13, 1940, SWP.

49. SW draft letter prepared for FDR, dated November 13, 1940, SWP.
50. Welles, *Seven Decisions That Shaped History,* pp. 41-43.
51. Ibid.

CHAPTER 23

1. Orville H. Bullitt, ed., *For the President: Personal and Secret* (Boston: Houghton Mifflin, 1972), pp. 504ff.
2. Harold L. Ickes, *The Secret Diaries,* p. 344, Library of Congress.
3. Ibid., p. 329.
4. Interview, Felix Belair, Washington, D.C., 1974.
5. Interview, Marquis Childs, Washington, D.C., 1973.
6. Interview, Frank Waldrop, Washington, D.C., 1977.
7. Interview, Adolf A. Berle, New York, 1970.
8. Interview, Ernest Cuneo, Washington, D.C., 1977.
9. Memorandum from Offie to Orville H. Bullitt, 1970, interviews, Bullitt family members, Philadelphia, 1977.
10. Tamm, later a federal appellate judge, declined to be interviewed, noting that he had previously passed up "material financial advantage" for his FBI reminiscences. Tamm to author, March 1 and April 3, 1974, BWP.
11. Welles's office diary shows that he addressed the Cleveland Foreign Affairs Council on September 27, 1940.
12. Spruille Braden, Columbia Oral History Collection, p. 619.
13. Wallace diaries, December 21, 1944.
14. Elliott Roosevelt, interview, Seattle, Washington, 1978.
15. Elliott Roosevelt, *A Rendezvous with Destiny,* (New York: Putnam, 1975), p. 263.
16. *Greensboro* (N.C.) *News,* September 7, 1940.
17. Robert H. Jackson, his predecessor, had just been elevated to the Supreme Court.
18. Francis Biddle, *In Brief Authority,* (New York: Doubleday, 1962), pp.179-180.
19. Eleanor Roosevelt and Malvina C. Thompson to SW, April 5, 1941, SWP.
20. Fred L. Israel, ed., *The War Diary of Breckinridge Long,* (Lincoln: University of Nebraska Press, 1966), p. 210.
21. Bernard Gladieux, Columbia Oral History Collection, p. 184.
22. Moffat diaries, p. 332.
23. James A. Farley, *Jim Farley's Story: The Roosevelt Years* (New York: Whittlesy House, 1948), p. 341.
24. SW to Pearson, December 22, 1940, SWP.
25. Drew Pearson to SW, December 26, 1940, SWP.
26. SW press conference, December 28, 1940.
27. Harold B. Hinton, *New York Times Sunday magazine,* April 13, 1941.
28. Israel, ed., *The War Diary of Breckinridge Long,* p. 179.
29. R. Henry Norweb, interview, New York, 1976.
30. MTW journal, BWP.
31. Bullit, ed., *For the President,* pp. 512-514.
32. Robert D. Murphy, interview, New York, 1974.
33. Samuel I. Rosenman, *Working with Roosevelt* (New York: Harper & Brothers, 1952), p. 285.

34. H. H. Adams, *Harry Hopkins: A Biography* (New York: Putnam, 1977), p. 223.
35. Samuel I. Rosenman, Working with Roosevelt, (New York: Harper & Brothers, 1952), p. 280.
36. SW to FDR, July 19, 1941, SWP.
37. SW to Hopkins, Burns, Knox, Knudsen and Stimson, July 29, 1941, SWP.
38. SW to FDR, August 26, 1941, SWP.
39. FDR to SW, June 19, 1941; SW to FDR, June 24, 1941, SWP.
40. Sumner Welles, *The World of Four Freedoms* (New York: Columbia University Press, 1943), p.11ff.
41. *New York Times* and *Cincinnati Enquirer,* July 24, 1941.
42. *St. Louis Post Dispatch,* July 24, 1941.
43. Dulles to SW, July 24, 1941, Dulles papers, Princeton University Library, Princeton, New Jersey.
44. *Denver Post,* July 25, 1941, *Troy Record,* July 24, 1941.
45. *New York Daily News,* July 24, 1941.
46. *Washington Times-Herald,* July 24, 1941.
47. James B. Reston, *New York Times Sunday magazine,* August 3, 1941.
48. *Time,* August 11, 1941.

CHAPTER 24

1. Sumner Welles, *Seven Decisions That Shaped History* (New York: Harper and Brothers, 1950), p. 61.
2. Ibid.
3. Before the war, he had been European director of the Chicago Automated Telephone Company.
4. Quai Dorsay Archives, Foreign Affairs, War, 1939-45, London, French National Committee 120-122, 210-213; Algiers, Committee of National Liberation, 460/3/4/5/6, 476-477 (hereafter cited as Quai Dorsay Archives).
5. Years later Leger would win a Nobel Prize for Poetry under the nom-de-plume St. John Perse.
6. Author of the 1947 Monnet Plan for French economic revival; first president of the European Coal and Steel Community (1952-55) and author of the European Common Market.
7. Raoul Aglion, *Roosevelt and De Gaulle,* (New York: Macmillan, 1988), pp. 40ff.
8. *FRUS,* 1941, vol. 2, pp. 204-205, 502ff.
9. Quai Dorsay Archives.
10. Algion, *Roosevelt and De Gaulle,* p. 55.
11. Quai Dorsay Archives.
12. Ibid.
13. *FRUS,* 1942, vol. 2, p. 502.
14. Quai Dorsay Archives.
15. Ibid.
16. Algion, *Roosevelt and De Gaulle,* p. 53.
17. Drafted by Samuel Reber, deputy director of European affairs, but approved by Hull.
18. Welles, *Seven Decisions That Shaped History,* p. 63.
19. Ibid.

20. Don Cook, *Charles de Gaulle: A Biography* (New York: G. P. Putnam's Sons, 1983), p. 143.
21. *FRUS,* 1941, vol. 2, pp. 204ff.
22. Ibid.
23. *New York Times,* April 14, 1942.
24. Cook, *de Gaulle,* pp. 150ff.
25. Ibid.
26. Wallace, Columbia Oral History Collection, p. 2234.
27. Cook, *de Gaulle,* p. 153.
28. Francis Biddle Papers, entry for December 31, 1942.
29. *FRUS,* 1942, vol. 2, pp. 511ff.
30. Ibid.
31. *New York Times,* May 26, 1942, p. 1; Algion, *Roosevelt and de Gaulle,* p. 72.
32. *FRUS,* 1942, vol. 2, pp. 521ff.
33. Cordell Hull, *Memoirs* (New York: Macmillan, 1948), p. 1163-1164.
34. Algion, *Roosevelt and De Gaulle,* p. 157.
35. Earl of Avon, *The Memoirs of Anthony Eden: The Reckoning* (Boston: Houghton Mifflin Co., 1965), p. 394.
36. *FRUS,* 1942, vol. 2, pp. 541ff.
37. Ibid.
38. Henry Wallace referred to him as the "Sumner Welles of France."
39. FDRL, PSF/Welles file/SD.
40. Quai Dorsay Archives.
41. Ibid.
42. Averell Harriman, interview, Washington, D.C., 1971.
43. Algion, *Roosevelt and De Gaulle,* p. 165.
44. Cook, *de Gaulle,* p. 166.
45. Ibid., p. 157.
46. Ibid., p. 170.
47. Ibid, p. 169.
48. Ibid., p. 171.
49. Hull, *Memoirs,* pp. 1212ff.
50. Ibid., p. 959.
51. SW to FDR, March 8, 1943, FDRL, PSF/Welles folder.
52. Fred L. Israel, *The War Diary of Breckenridge Long,* (Lincoln: University of Nebraska Press, 1966), p. 305.
53. Earl of Avon, *Memoirs of Anthony Eden,* p. 438.
54. Harold L. Ickes, *Secret Diaries,* entry for August 15, 1943, Library of Congress.
55. Quai Dorsay Archives.
56. Ibid.
57. SW-Tixier meeting, State Department, August 1943.
58. Robert E. Sherwood, *The White House Papers of Harry L. Hopkins* (London: Eyre and Spottiswoode, 1948), p. 742.
59. Biddle Papers, entry for December 17, 1943; Henry A. Wallace, *The Price of Vision: The Diary of Henry A. Wallace: 1942-46,* ed. John Morten Blum (Boston: Houghton Mifflin, Co., 1973), p. 282.
60. Welles, *Seven Decisions That Shaped History,* pp. 186-187.
61. Sumner Welles, *The Time for Decision* (New York: Harper and Brothers, 1944), p. 158.

CHAPTER 25

1. Sumner Welles, *The Time for Decision* (New York: Harper and Brothers, 1944), p. 173ff.
2. Sumner Welles, *Seven Decisions That Shaped History* (New York: Harper and Brothers, 1950), chapter 1.
3. Lend-Lease, conceived by FDR, was an arrangement to transfer arms and supplies to countries whose defense was deemed vital to the U.S. The program was first administered by Harry Hopkins and later by Edward R. Stettinius, Jr., and Leo T. Crowley. By war's end (1945) when Lend-Lease terminated, it had delivered $50 billion, of which $31 billion went to Great Britain and $11 billion to the then Soviet Union (figures from *Columbia Encyclopedia,* 5th edition [New York: Columbia University Press, 1993]; distributed by Houghton Mifflin).
4. Hull to SW, August 6, 1941, SWP.
5. Theodore A. Wilson, *The First Summit,* (Boston: Houghton Mifflin Co., 1969), pp. 4-7, 63-64.
6. Franklin D. Roosevelt, Jr., interview, Pouqhquag, N.Y., 1981.
7. David Dilks, ed., *Diaries of Sir Alexander Cadogan* (London: Cassell, 1971), p. 379.
8. Ibid.
9. Ibid., p. 250.
10. Sumner Welles, *Where Are We Heading?* (New York: Harper and Brothers, 1946), p. 53.
11. Dilks, ed., *Diaries of . . . Cadogan,* pp. 397-398, FRUS, 1941, vol. 1, pp. 344f.
12. 79th Congress, November-December 1945, Report of the Joint Committee Investigating Pearl Harbor Attack, (Washington, D.C.: U.S. Government Printing Office, 1945) p. 529.
13. Ibid., p. 537.
14. Welles, *Where Are We Heading?,* p. 6.
15. Winston S. Churchill, *The Grand Alliance* (Boston: Houghton Mifflin Co., 1950), p. 433.
16. Robert E. Sherwood, *The White House Papers of Harry L. Hopkins* (London: Eyre & Spottiswoode, 1948), pp. 350-351.
17. Elliott Roosevelt, *As He Saw It* (New York: Duell, Sloane & Pearce, 1946), p. 31.
18. Harriman,'09, Welles,'10, Elliott Roosevelt,'29, FDR, Jr.,'33.
19. *FRUS,* 1941, vol. 1, pp. 355-356.
20. Welles, *Where Are We Heading?,* p. 8.
21. Ibid., p. 8.
22. Dilks, ed., *Diaries of . . . Cadogan,* p. 399.
23. Welles, *Seven Decisions That Shaped History,* pp.177-178; Welles, *Where Are We Heading?,* pp. 4, 19.
24. Churchill, *Grand Alliance,* p. 437.
25. Welles, *Where Are We Heading?,* foreword.
26. Sherwood, *White House Papers,* pp.361-362.
27. Welles, *Where Are We Heading?* p.5.
28. FDR to SW, February 20,1941, SWP.
29. Churchill, *Grand Alliance,* p.440.
30. Sherwood, *White House Papers,* p.364.
31. Dilks, ed., *Diaries of . . . Cadogan,* p.399.
32. Roosevelt, *As He Saw It,* p. 33
33. Ibid., p. 39.

34. Welles, *Where Are We Heading?*, p.18.
35. Ibid., p. 17.
36. British Archives, PRO/FO/371/1941/W 426/9609-10151.
37. British Archives, PRO/PREM 3/485/7 W.
38. Sherwood, *White House Papers*, p. 365.
39. James A. Bishop, *FDR's Last Year: April '44 - April '45* (New York: Wm. Morrow, 1974), pp. 226, 419, 461.
40. Sherwood, *White House Papers*, p. 364.
41. Henry A. Wallace, *The Price of Vision*, p. 128.
42. Moffat diaries, p.354.
43. Fred L. Israel, ed., *The War Diary of Breckinridge Long* (Lincoln: University of Nebraska Press, 1966), p. 212.
44. MTW to Courtney Letts de Espil, September 13, 1941, BWP.
45. Welles, *Seven Decisions*, p.126.
46. Ibid., p.181.
47. Harold L. Ickes, *Secret Diaries*, September 20, 1941, Library of Congress.
48. Sumner Welles, *The World of Four Freedoms* (New York: Columbia University Press, 1943), pp. 16ff.
49. Ibid., pp. 28ff.

CHAPTER 26

1. 79th Congress, November-December 1945, Report of Joint Committee Investigation of the Pearl Harbor Attack, (Washington, D.C.: U.S. Government Printing Office, 1945), pp. 521, 536.
2. Forrest Davis and Ernest K. Lindley, *How War Came* (New York: Simon and Schuster, 1942), foreword.
3. Robert E. Sherwood, *The White House Papers of Harry L. Hopkins* (London: Eyre & Spottiswoode, 1948), p. 438.
4. Edward Murrow, the radio reporter who had just returned from London and who was dining in the White House saw FDR alone later that night; FDR appointment calendar, Edwin M. Watson papers, University of Virginia; Davis & Lindley, *How War Came*.
5. La Razon, (Buenos Aires), January 7, 1942.
6. Sumner Welles, *Seven Decisions That Shaped History* (New York: Harper and Brothers, 1950), p. 100.
7. Sherwood collection, Hopkins papers, container 311, Book 5, Latin American affairs: FDRL.
8. Welles, *The Time for Decision* (New York: Harper and Brothers, 1944), p. 225.
9. Welles, *Seven Decisions*, p. 106.
10. SW to MTW, January 12, 1942, SWP.
11. Eric Sevareid, *Saturday Evening Post*, April 29, 1942, p. 27.
12. Welles, *Seven Decisions*, p. 107.
13. Interview, Emilio Collado, New York, 1976.
14. In his State of the Union message to Congress, January 6, 1942, the day before Welles left for Rio, FDR predicted 60,000 airplanes, 45,000 tanks and 8 million deadweight tons of merchant shipping. Jean Edward Smith, *Lucius D. Clay: An American Life* (New York: Henry Holt & Co., 1990), p. 118.

15. Edward O. Guerrant, *Roosevelt's Good Neighbor Policy* (Albuquerque, NM: University of New Mexico Press, 1950), pp. 173-174, 195-196.
16. Collado, interview, 1976.
17. Adolf A. Berle to SW, January 15, 1942, NA 710, Consultation, 3/330 B.
18. SW to Hull, January 16, 1942, FRUS 1942, vol. V, pp. 27-28.
19. Laurence Duggan, *The Americas: The Search for Hemisphere Security* (New York: Henry Holt Co., 1949), p. 80.
20. Eric Sevareid, *Saturday Evening Post,* March 28, 1942.
21. SW to FDR, January 18, 1942, SWP.
22. Ibid.
23. *FRUS,* vol. V, pp. 28ff.
24. Welles, *Seven Decisions,* p. 109.
25. Duggan, *The Americas,* p. 88.
26. SW to Hull, confidential, #45, 11 P.M. , January 23, 1942, DS records.
27. Welles, *Seven Decisions,* pp. 115-117.
28. Caffery to Hull, January 24, 1942, NA, Consultation, 710.
29. James V. Reeks, interview, Englewood, Florida, 1976.
30. SW to FDR, January 24, 1942; copy of original with SW's handwritten corrections, SWP.
31. *Chicago Daily News,* January 29, 1942.
32. Hull to SW, January 29, 1942; NA 710, Consultation, 3/635A.
33. *New York Journal of Commerce,* January 24, 1942.
34. *Washington Post,* editorial, January 30, 1942.
35. *Philadelphia Inquirer,* January 30, 1942.
36. *St. Louis Post-Dispatch,* February 5, 1942.
37. *Time,* February 9, 1942.
38. Arthur Krock, *New York Times,* February 12, 1942.
39. Berle diaries, January 24, 1942, FDRL, container 213, February-March 42 folder.
40. Berle diaries, February 1, 1942.
41. SW to FDR, November 6, 1942, SWP.
42. Welles, *Seven Decisions,* pp. 118ff.
43. Hull statement, December 14, 1943, DS bulletin #9, December 18, 1943 .

CHAPTER 27

1. Sumner Welles, *Seven Decisions That Shaped History* (New York: Harper and Brothers, 1950), p. 181.
2. Five months after America's entry into the war in April 1917, Wilson directed his aide, Colonel E. M. House, to prepare a peace program before the end of hostilities. House recruited approximately 150 academics and launched "The Inquiry," so-called to avoid publicity. In fifteen months it produced 2, 000 reports but few contained "well-conceived, systematic plans for peace." Lawrence E. Gelfand, *The Inquiry: American Preparations for Peace, 1917-19* (New Haven, CT: Yale University Press, 1963), introduction and p.314.
3. Sumner Welles, *Where Are We Heading?* (New York: Harper and Brothers, 1946), pp.19-20.

4. Robert E. Sherwood, *Harry Hopkins: The White House Papers* (London: Eyre & Spottiswoode, 1949), p.343.

5. Welles, *Seven Decisions,* p.179.

6. Harley A. Notter, *Postwar Foreign Policy Preparation* (Washington, D.C.: U.S. Government Printing Office, 1950), p.51

7. SW to FDR, enclosing Stalin text, December 17, 1941, SWP.

8. Winston Churchill, *The Grand Alliance* (Boston: Houghton Mifflin Co., 1950), p.695.

9. Welles, *Seven Decisions,* p.130

10. Ibid., p.182.

11. Cordell Hull, *The Memoirs of Cordell Hull* (New York: Macmillan, 1948), p.1634.

12. Bowman had been a key member of the Wilson-House Inquiry in World War I and, like Welles, was keenly interested in Latin America.

13. Welles, *Seven Decisions,* pp.125, 132ff.

14. Hull, *Memoirs,* p.1634.

15. The committee was set up with FDR's approval three weeks after Pearl Harbor. Hull was chairman and Welles vice chairman.

16. Minutes of the Advisory Committee, April 4, 1942, pp.1-2, SWP; Harley Notter, Postwar Foreign Policy Preparation, Dept. of State, 1949, pp.34, 89; Hull, *Memoirs,* p.1634ff.

17. Ruth Russell, assisted by Jeannette E. Muther, *A History of the United Nations Charter* (Brookings Institution, 1958), p.98.

18. Welles, *Seven Decisions,,* p.134.

19. Ibid.

20. Ironically, Wilson had followed the same policy in World War I. In May 1917, five weeks after America's entry into the war, British Foreign Secretary Arthur Balfour visited him to discuss postwar settlements but Wilson refused, persuaded by his aide, Colonel House, that discussions might hinder the war effort. Gelfand, *The Inquiry,* p.14.

21. FDR told a press conference in March 1943 that there had been "very little work" done on postwar problems before Armistice Day. Samuel I. Rosenman, *Working with Roosevelt* (New York: Harper and Brothers, 1952), p.401.In May 1945 Stalin told Hopkins, in Moscow, that the Allies were not "properly prepared" at Versailles and should not make that mistake again. Sherwood, *Hopkins,* p.893.

22. Welles, *Seven Decisions,* pp.124-125.

23. American embassy, London, to State Dept., #1095, March 7, 1942, #1116, March 9, 1942, SWP.

24. Earl of Avon, *The Memoirs of Anthony Eden: The Reckoning* (Boston: Houghton Mifflin Co., 1965), p.370.

25. Stalin cables to FDR, February 19 and 21, 1942, SWP.

26. Keith Eubank, *Summit at Teheran* (New York: Wm. Morrow & Son, 1985).

27. FDR to SW, undated, SWP.

28. Earl of Avon, *Memoirs of . . . Eden,* p.376.

29. The only American record of the FDR-Litvinov talks is in the SWP. It bears no indication of authorship but was almost certainly prepared by SW. Cf: *FRUS,* p.533, fn. 64 & 65.

30. Earl of Avon, *Memoirs of . . . Eden,* p.376.

31. *FRUS,* pp.538, 542-543, 560.

32. Hull, *Memoirs,* p.1174

33. *FRUS,* 1942, vol. 3, p.569.

34. *FRUS,* 1942, vol. 3, pp.593-594.

35. Some estimates range as high as 125,000.

36. State Dept. press release, May 29, 1942.
37. Hull, *Memoirs,* p.1229.
38. Moffat diaries, entry for November 13-17, 1942.
39. Fred L. Israel, ed., *The War Diary of Breckinridge Long,* (Lincoln: University of Nebraska Press, 1966), p.273
40. Berle diaries, FDRL, container 214, June 23, 1942.
41. The Subcommittee on International Organization; Cordell Hull, *Memoirs,* p.1638.
42. Welles, *Where Are We Heading?,* p.27.
43. Hull, *Memoirs,* p.1639.
44. Welles, *Seven Decisions,* p.184
45. Hull, *Memoirs,* pp.1640-1643
46. Wallace diaries, entry for February 9, 1943.
47. Thirty senators had just expressed opposition to a postwar international police force.
48. H. G. Nicholas, ed., *Washington Dispatches: 1941-46: Weekly Political Reports from the British Embassy* (Chicago: University of Chicago Press, 1981), entry for March 20, 1943. Dispatches prepared by Sir Isaiah Berlin.
49. Ibid., entry for March 14, 1943.
50. The B2H2 resolution, cosponsored by Senators Harold H. Burton (R-Oh.), Carl A. Hatch (D-N.M.) and Lester Hill (D-Ala).
51. Nicholas, ed., *Washington Dispatches,* entry for March 20, 1943.
52. Robert A. Divine, *Second Chance,* (New York: Athenaeum, 1971), p.115.
53. Nicholas, ed., *Washington Dispatches,* entry for March 20, 1943.
54. Interview, J. William Fulbright, Washington, D.C., 1980.
55. Notes dictated by Harry Hopkins mention Welles's participation. Hull's memoirs say only that FDR "spoke at some length about the structure of the UN organization." Cf. *FRUS,* 1943, vol. 3, p.39.
56. Hopkins.
57. Welles, *Seven Decisions,* p.188.
58. Ibid.
59. Nicholas, ed., *Washington Dispatches,* entry for April 21, 1943.
60. In describing the Tehran conference, Sherwood found no evidence that anyone had considered that one of the Big Four might be an aggressor. Sherwood, *Hopkins,* p.770ff.
61. Sumner Welles, *The Time for Decision* (New York: Harper and Brothers, 1944), p.369; Welles, *Seven Decisions,* p.185.
62. Marshal Pietro Badoglio, conqueror of Ethiopia in 1935-36, succeeded Mussolini as premier in July 1943 and signed an armistice with the Allies in September.
63. Welles, *Where Are We Heading?,* p.28ff.
64. The sketch is reproduced in Sherwood, *Hopkins,* p.789, and in *FRUS,* the Conferences at Cairo and Tehran, p.622.
65. Welles, *Seven Decisions,* p.172.
66. Sherwood, *Hopkins,* p.790.
67. FDR to SW, January 4, 1944, SWP.
68. Welles, *Seven Decisions,* p.139.
69. Dmitri Volkogonov, *Stalin: Triumph & Tragedy* (New York: Grove Weidenfeld, 1988), p.489.
70. Welles, *Where Are We Heading?,* p.379.
71. C. L. Sulzberger, *The Last of the Giants* (New York: Macmillan, 1970), p.304; quoted in Lloyd C. Gardner, *Spheres of Influence* (Chicago: Ivan R. Dee, 1993), p.265.

72. Welles, *Where Are We Heading?,* p.377.
73. Byrnes was Secretary of State from 1945 to 1947.

CHAPTER 28

1. Harold L. Ickes, *Secret Diaries,* Library of Congress, entry for December 7, 1941.
2. H. A. Wallace, Columbia Oral History Collection, March 31, 1942, p.1463.
3. Ibid., March 30, 1942, pp.1145, 1148.
4. Ibid., p.1595.
5. Ickes, *Secret Diaries,* entry for May 24, 1942.
6. H. A. Wallace, Columbia Oral History Collection, p.1676.
7. William R. Castle diaries, Houghton Library, Harvard University, Cambridge, Massachusetts, pp.275-277.
8. Fred L. Israel, *The War Diary of Breckinridge Long* (Lincoln: University of Nebraska Press, 1966) p.281.
9. Hoover memo to Clyde Tolson and Edwin Tamm, October 29, 1942, FBI records, obtained under the FOIA.
10. Ickes, *Secret Diaries,* entry for December 27, 1942.
11. James Rowe, Jr., interview, Washington, D.C., 1976.
12. H. A. Wallace, Columbia Oral History Collection, pp.1677-1678.
13. William C. Bullitt, confidential memoranda of conversations April 23, 1941--June, 21, 1944. Courtesy of the Bullitt family (hereafter cited as Bullitt memoranda).
14. Ickes, *Secret Diaries,* entry for February 14, 1943.
15. Bullitt memoranda.
16. Ibid.
17. Memoirs of Anthony Eden, *Earl of Avon: The Reckoning* (Boston: Houghton Mifflin Co., 1965), p.441.
18. Bullitt memoranda.
19. Ickes, *Secret Diaries,* entry for February 14, 1943; Hoover memo to Tolson and Tamm, May 3, 1943, FBI files, obtained under the FOIA.
20. Bullitt memoranda.
21. Ickes, *Secret Diaries,* entry for May 5, 1943.
22. Bullitt memoranda.
23. Offie confidential memo to Orville H. Bullitt, Philadelphia, 1970, BWP.
24. Adolf A. Berle, interview, January 13, 1970, New York, BWP.
25. MTW to Courtney Letts de Espil, August 1, 1943; Library of Congress, Acc. 10, 078.
26. *The Nation,* August 21, 1943.
27. Interview, Turner Catledge, Madrid, Spain, 1959.
28. Crider to SW, Jan. 29, 1949; BWP. BW interview with Crider, London, 1949; with Belair, Washington, D.C., 1971.
29. SW to MTW, August 12, 1943, BWP.
30. Bullitt memoranda.
31. FDR schedule, August 16, 1943, Edwin M. Watson Papers, University of Virginia, Charlottesville, Virginia.
32. SW to FDR, August 16, 1943, SWP.
33. SW to MTW, August 19, 1943, BWP.
34. Berle memorandum, September 1, 1943, FDRL/Berle.

35. Pearson to SW, August 24, 1943, Pearson Papers, Lyndon B. Johnson library, University of Texas, Austin, Texas.
36. James V. Reeks, interview, Englewood, Florida, 1976.
37. Adolph A. Berle and Travis B. Jacobs, *Navigating the Rapids: 1917-1971* (New York: Harcourt, Brace, Jovanovich, 1971), entry for September 1, 1943.
38. *Washington Times-Herald,* August 30, 1943.
39. Bullitt memoranda.
40. *New York Herald-Tribune,* editorial, August 25, 1943.
41. *St. Louis Post Dispatch,* editorial, August 30, 1943.
42. *Time,* September 6, 1943.
43. *The Nation,* September 4, 1943.
44. *Washington Post,* September 5, 1943.
45. *Washington Times-Herald,* editorial, September 2, 1943.
46. MTW to Courtney Letts de Espil, September 2, 1943, BWP.
47. MTW to Courtney Letts de Espil, September 9, 1943, BWP.
48. Confidential memo on activities of "Mr.A" [Welles] by Daniel H. Clare, Jr., special agent, September 8, 1943, copy in SWP.
49. James B. Reston, interview, Madrid, 1960.
50. Byrnes to FDR, September 3, 1943; James F. Byrnes Papers, Clemson University, Clemson, South Carolina.
51. Pearson to SW, August 30, 1943, SWP.
52. SW to FDR, September 21, 1943, copy in SWP.
53. SW to Hull, September 21, 1943, copy in SWP.
54. Byrnes Papers, 1943, Welles folder, p. 2.
55. W. Averell Harriman, interview, Washington, D.C., 1971.
56. Byrnes Papers, 1943, Welles folder, p.2.
57. Wallace diaries, Columbia Oral History Collection, September 30, 1943, p.2769.
58. FDR to SW, October 15, 1943, FDRL, PSF/Welles/State.
59. E. A. Mowrer, *Philadelphia Inquirer,* November 2, 1943.
60. Pearson notes, November 1943, Drew Pearson Papers, LBJ Library, Austin, Texas.
61. Ickes, *Secret Diaries,* September 13, 1943.
62. Bullitt memoranda.
63. James Rowe, interview, Washington, D.C., June 26, 1971.

CHAPTER 29

1. A new state of Southern Germany, predominantly Catholic; a northern state comprising Upper Hesse, Thuringia, Westphalia, Hanover, Oldenburg and Hamburg, and a northeast state comprising Prussia (although not East Prussia), Saxony and Mecklenburg. The latter two states would be predominantly Protestant. Sumner Welles, *The Time for Decision* (New York: Harpers and Brothers, 1944), p.352 and map facing p.342.
2. Sumner Welles, *The Time for Decision* (New York: Harper and Row, 1944).
3. William Allen Neilson, *New York Herald Tribune,* Sunday, July 23, 1944.
4. Sumner Welles, *Where Are We Heading?* (New York: Harpers and Brothers, 1946), p. 340.
5. Ibid., p. 89.

6. Welles, *Seven Decisions That Shaped History* (New York: Harpers and Brothers, 1950), p.206.

7. Welles, *Where Are We Heading?*, p. 371.

8. Robert E. Sherwood, *Harry Hopkins: The White House Papers* (London: Eyre and Spottiswooode, 1949), p.827.

9. SW to C. P. Curtis, Jr., May 24, 1947, SWP.

10. SW to C. P. Curtis, Jr., March 14, 1946.

11. SW to C. P. Curtis, Jr., July 22, 1946, SWP.

12. SW to BW, September 14, 1946, BWP.

13. SW to C. P. Curtis, Jr., December 1, 1947, SWP.

14. SW to Pearson, January 28, 1948; Pearson Papers, Lyndon B. Johnson library, University of Texas, Austin, Texas.

15. SW to Pearson, February 25, 1948, SWP.

16. SW to MTW, March 11, 1948, BWP.

17. SW to C. P. Curtis, Jr., August 31, 1948, SWP.

18. Laurence Duggan, *1905-48, In Memoriam* (Stanford, CT: The Overbrook Press, 1949), pp.9-11.

19. *New York Times,* editorial, December 23, 1948.

20. Robert Sherwood, *Roosevelt and Hopkins,* (New York: Harper and Brothers, 1948).

21. Published by Harper and Brothers in 1950 under the title *Seven Decisions That Changed History.*

22. A Pittsburgh multimillionaire, Mellon had been U.S. Secretary of the Treasury from 1921-1931.

23. SW to C. P. Curtis, Jr., December 4, 1948, SWP.

24. "Igor Cassini," Cholly Knickerbocker column, "The Smart Set," *New York Journal American,* January 1, 1949, p.8.

25. *Boston Traveller,* January 27, 1949.

26. *New York Times,* editorial, January 28, 1949.

27. SW to C. P. Curtis, Jr., January 15, 1949, copy in BWP.

28. SW to Emily Welles Robbins, February 23, 1949, SWP.

29. SW to Emily Welles Robbins, February 12, 1949, SWP.

30. SW to Eugene Meyer, March 2, 1949, SWP.

31. Pearson Papers, Lyndon Baines Johnson Library, University of Texas, Austin, Texas, July 1, 1949.

32. MTW to Alice van Kaathoven, August 2, 1949, SWP.

33. Later Mrs. Donald McElroy.

34. Pearson Papers, p.76.

35. Private interview, Washington, D.C., April 10, 1975.

36. Interview, Roscoe Hillenkoeter, New York, December 1, 1976.

37. Interview, James J. Angleton, Washington, D.C., 1976. Angleton and the author were colleagues in the Office for Strategic Services and friends during World War II.

38. Interview, R. H. Ives Gammell, Boston, 1976.

39. Pearson Papers, October 28, 1952.

40. SW to BW, June 21, 1952, BWP.

41. To Director from SAC MFO (62-0), May 6, 1953, FBI records obtained through FOIA.

42. Welles attended a Report from the World conference, cosponsored by the Cleveland Council and *Time* magazine, not in September but from January 9 to 11, 1947. Emory

C. Swank, president, Cleveland Council on World Affairs, to author, June 15, 1977, BWP.

43. New York Times, Harrison obituary, February 20, 1978.
44. SW to ANW, April 4, 1956, BWP.
45. Recollections, James V. Reeks.
46. Arnold and Alexander Welles, Arnold's sons by his first marriage; Joan and Cynthia Welles, Arnold's daughters by his second marriage; and Serena and Merida Welles, the author's two daughters.
47. *New York Times,* editorial, September 25, 1961.

EPILOGUE

1. Sumner Welles, *The Time for Decision* (New York: Harper and Brothers, 1944) p. 326.
2. Sumner Welles, *Seven Decisions That Shaped History* (New York: Harper and Brothers, 1950), p. 215.
3. Sumner Welles, *Where Are We Heading?* (New York: Harper and Brothers, 1946), p. 280.
4. Ibid., p. 366.
5. Welles, *Seven Decisions,* p. 13.
6. Welles, *The Time for Decision,* p. 358.
7. Welles, *Where Are We Heading?,* pp. 320-321.
8. Ibid., p. 292.
9. Welles, *The Time for Decision,* p. 335.
10. Ibid., p. 334.
11. Ibid.
12. Ibid., p. 408.
13. Welles, *Where Are We Heading?,* p. 288.
14. Welles, *The Time for Decision,* p. 401ff.
15. Welles, *Where Are We Heading?,* p. 371.
16. Welles, *Seven Decisions,* p. 230.
17. *New York Times,* "Sumner Welles," editorial, January 28, 1948.
18. *Rubaiyat of Omar Khayyam,* trans. Edward Fitz-Gerald, verse 43.

BIBLIOGRAPHY

Adams, Henry H. *Harry Hopkins: A Biography*. New York: Putnam, 1977.

Aguilar, Luis E. *Cuba, 1933: Prologue and Revolution*. Ithaca, N.Y.: Cornell University Press, 1972.

Alsop, Joseph, and Robert Kintner. *American White Paper: The Story of American Diplomacy and the Second World War*. New York: Simon and Schuster, 1940.

Ashburn, Frank D. *Peabody of Groton*. New York: Coward-McCann, 1944.

Bendiner, Robert. *The Riddle of the State Department*. New York: Farrar and Rinehart, 1942.

Berle, Beatrice Bishop, and Travis Beal Jacobs. *Navigating the Rapids*. New York: Harcourt, Brace, Jovanovich, 1973.

Berlin, Sir Isaiah. "Introduction." *Washington Despatches, 1941-1946: Weekly Political Reports from the British Embassy*. Edited by H. G. Nicholas. Chicago: University of Chicago Press, 1981.

Biddle, Francis. *In Brief Authority*. New York: Doubleday, 1962.

Bishop, James A. *FDR's Last Year: April '44 - April '45*. New York: William Morrow, 1974.

Blum, John Morton. *Roosevelt and Morgenthau*. Boston: Houghton Mifflin, 1970.

Bohlen, Charles, and Robert H. Phelps. *Witness to History*. New York: W. W. Norton & Co., 1973.

Borg, Dorothy. *The U.S. and the Far Eastern Crisis of 1933-1938*. Cambridge, Mass.: Harvard University Press, 1964.

Braden, Spruille. Columbia Oral History Collection, Columbia University, New York.

Bullitt, Orville H., ed. *For the President: Personal and Secret*. Boston: Houghton Mifflin, 1972.

Burns, James MacGregor. *Roosevelt: The Lion and the Fox*. New York: Harcourt Brace & Co., 1965.

Byrnes, James F. Papers. Clemson University, Clemson, South Carolina.

Cadogan, Sir Alexander. *Diaries*. Edited by David Dilks. London: Cassell, 1971.

Carillo, Justo. *Cuba 1933: Students, Yankees and Soldiers*. Institute of Inter-American Studies, University of Miami, 1985.

Castle, Wm. R. Diaries. Houghton Library, Harvard University, Cambridge, Mass.

Cave Brown, Anthony. *"C": The Secret Life of Sir Stewart Graham Menzies: Spymaster to Winston Churchill*. New York: Macmillan, 1987.

Churchill, Winston S. *The Gathering Storm*. Boston: Houghton Mifflin, 1948.

———. *The Grand Alliance*. Boston: Houghton Mifflin Co., 1950.

Colville, Sir John. *The Fringes of Power*. New York: Norton, 1985.

Conn, Stetson, and Byron Fairchild. *The U.S. Army in World War II: The Western Hemisphere, The Framework of Hemisphere Defense*. Washington, D.C.: Office of the Chief of Military History, Department of the Army.

Coolidge, Calvin. Papers. Series 1, file 20. Library of Congress.

Council on Foreign Relations. *Survey of Foreign Affairs*. New Haven, Conn.: Yale University Press, 1929.

Cowles, Virginia. *1913: An End and a Beginning*. New York: Harper and Row, 1967.

Crasweller, Robert D. *Trujillo: The Life and Times of a Caribbean Dictator*. New York: Macmillan, 1966.

Cronon, David E. *Josephus Daniels in Mexico*. Madison, Wisc.: University of Wisconsin Press, 1960.

Danelski, David J., and Joseph S. Tulchin, eds. *The Auto-biographical Notes of Charles Evans Hughes*. Cambridge, Mass.: Harvard University Press, 1973.

Davis, Forrest, and Ernest K. Lindley. *How War Came*. New York: Simon and Schuster, 1942.

de Gaulle, Charles. *War Memoirs*. London: Collins, 1955.

Dinesen, Isak. *Out Of Africa*. London: Putnam, 1937.

Divine, Robert A. *Second Chance*. New York: Athenaeum, 1971.

Duggan, Laurence. *The Americas: The Search for Hemisphere Security*. New York: Henry Holt Co., 1949.

Eden, Anthony, Earl of Avon. *Memoirs, The Reckoning*. Boston: Houghton Mifflin, 1956.

Espil, Courtney Letts de, correspondence with Mathilde Townsend Welles, Library of Congress, Washington, D.C.

Eubank, Keith. *Summit at Teheran*. New York: William Morrow & Son, 1985.

Farago, Ladislas. *The Broken Seal*. New York: Random House, 1967.

Farley, James A. *Jim Farley's Story: The Roosevelt Years*. New York: Whittlesy House, 1948.

Freidel, Frank. *Franklin D. Roosevelt, The Ordeal*. Boston: Little, Brown and Co., 1954.

———. *FDR: Launching the New Deal*. Boston: Little, Brown and Co., 1973.

Fuentes, Carlos. *The Buried Mirror: Reflections on Spain and the New World*. New York: Houghton Mifflin, 1992.

Gallup, George H. *The Gallup Poll, 1935-71*. New York: Random House, 1971.

Gardner, Lloyd C. *Spheres of Influence*. Chicago: Ivan R. Dee, 1993.

Gelfand, Lawrence E. *The Inquiry: American Preparations for Peace, 1917-19*. New Haven: Yale University Press, 1963.

Gellman, Irwin F. *Good Neighbor Diplomacy: U.S. Politics in Latin America, 1933-1945*. Baltimore: Johns Hopkins University Press, 1979.

————. Secret Affairs: *Franklin Roosevelt, Cordell Hull and Sumner Welles.* Baltimore: Johns Hopkins University Press, 1995.

German Foreign Policy Documents, Series D, vol. 8. Microfilm. National Archives, Wash. D.C.

Gladieux, Bernard. Papers. New York: Columbia Oral History collection.

Grew, Joseph C. *Turbulent Era.* Boston: Houghton Mifflin, 1952.

Grieb, Kenneth J. *The Latin American Policy of Warren G. Harding.* Ft. Worth, Texas: Christian University Press, 1976.

Guerrant, Edward O. *Roosevelt's Good Neighbor Policy.* Albuquerque: University of New Mexico Press, 1950.

Harris, Ruth B. "The 'Magic' Leak of 1941 and Japanese-American Relations." *Pacific Historical Review* (Berkeley, Calif.: University of California Press; February 1981).

Heinl, Robert, and Nancy G. *Written in Blood: The Story of the Haitian People.* Boston: Houghton Mifflin, 1978.

Hilton, Stanley C. "The Welles Mission to Europe, February - March, 1940: Illusion or Realism?" *The Journal of American History,* vol. 58 (June 1971).

Hull, Cordell. *Memoirs.* New York: Macmillan, 1948.

Ickes, Harold L. *Secret Diaries.* New York: Simon and Schuster, 1953-1954.

Ilchman, Warren Frederick. *Professional Diplomacy in the U.S.: 1779-1939.* Chicago: University of Chicago Press, 1961.

Ingham, Adella. *In the Days of the Monckton Iron Company, 1807-30.* Compiled by Adella Ingham, Vergennes, Vt., 1932. Original copy in Vergennes public library.

Inman, Samuel Guy. *Inter-American Conferences, 1826-1954: History and Problems.* Washington, D.C.: University Press, 1965.

Institute of Public Affairs proceedings, University of Charlottesville, Virginia. 11th session, 1937, vol. 1.

Jackson, Robert H. Papers. New York: Columbia Oral History collection.

Jung, Carl Gustav. *Psychological Types.* Orlando, Fla.: Harcourt, Brace Co., 1925.

Kellogg, Frank B. *Papers, Personal and Confidential.* Minnesota Historical Society, St. Paul, Minn.

Kennedy, Joseph P., and James Landis. "Kennedy memoirs." James M. Landis Papers, Box 51, Library of Congress.

Ketchum, Richard. *The Borrowed Years, 1938-1941: America On The Way To War.* New York: Random House, 1989.

Lester, Langley. "Negotiating New Treaties With Panama: 1936." *The Hispanic American Historic Review* (Washington, D.C.; May 1968).

Lochner, Louis P. *Always the Unexpected.* New York: Macmillan, 1956.

Long, Breckinridge. *The War Diary.* Edited by Fred L. Israel. Lincoln, Neb.: University of Nebraska, 1966.

Marquez Sterling, Manuel. *Proceso Historico de la Enmienda Platt.* Havana, 1941.

Matthews, H. Freeman. *Memories of a Passing Era*. Privately printed, Washington, D.C., 1974. In possession of the Matthews family.

Morison, Samuel Eliot. *"Old Bruin": Commodore Matthew C. Perry, 1794-1858*. Boston: Little, Brown and Co., 1967.

———. *Three Centuries of Harvard*. Cambridge, Mass: Harvard University Press, 1936.

Munro, Dana G. *Intervention and Dollar Diplomacy in the Caribbean: 1900-1921*. Princeton, N.J.: Princeton University Press, 1964.

Murray, Robert K. *The Harding Era*. Minneapolis: University of Minnesota Press, 1969.

Nixon, Edgar. *Franklin D. Roosevelt and Foreign Affairs*. Cambridge, Mass.: Belknap Press, 1969.

Notter, Harley A. *Postwar Foreign Policy Preparation,1939-1945*. Washington, D.C.: Government Printing Office, 1950.

Offner, Arnold A. "Appeasement Revisited: The U.S., Great Britain and Germany, 1933-40." *The Journal of American History,* vol. 64 (September 1977).

Page, Walter H. *Life and Letters*. 2 vols. Garden City, N.Y.: Doubleday, Page & Co., 1922.

Pearson, Drew. Personal Papers. Container G-236. Lyndon. B. Johnson Library, University of Texas, Austin, Texas.

Perkins, Dexter. *Charles Evans Hughes and American Democratic Statesmanship*. Boston: Little, Brown and Co., 1956.

Perkins, Thomas Handasyd. *Memoir: Extracts from His Diaries and Letters*. Edited by Thomas G. Cary. Boston: Little, Brown and Co., 1856.

Phillips, Caroline A. D. Diaries. Schlesinger Library, Radcliffe College, Cambridge, Mass.

Phillips, Ruby Hart. *Cuban Sideshow*. Havana: Cuban Press, 1935.

Pilpel, Robert. *To The Honor Of The Fleet*. Athenaeum, 1979.

Pulliam W. E., diary, in possession of Pulliam family.

Roosevelt, Elliott. *As He Saw It*. New York: Duell, Sloane and Pearce, 1946.

———. *A Rendezvous With Destiny*. New York: Putnam, 1975.

Roosevelt, Franklin Delano, and Elliot Rossevelt. *FDR: His Personal Letters, Early Years*. Vol. 1. New York: Duell, Sloane & Pearce, 1947-50.

Rose, Norman. *Vansittart: Study of a Diplomat*. London: Heinemann, 1978.

Rosenman, Samuel I., ed. *The Public Papers and Addresses of Franklin D. Roosevelt*. 2 vols. New York: Random House, 1938 [c. 1950].

———. *Working With Roosevelt*. New York: Harper Bros., 1952.

Rout, Leslie B. *Politics of the Chaco Peace Conference*. Austin, Texas: University of Texas Press, 1970.

Russell, Ruth, assisted by Jeannette E. Muther. *A History of the United Nations Charter*. Washington, D.C.: Brookings Institution, 1958.

Schermerhorn, Richard. *Schermerhorn Genealogy & Family Chronicles*. New York: Tobias A. Wright, 1914.

Schlesinger, Arthur M., Jr. *The Age of Roosevelt.* Boston: Houghton Mifflin, 1957-60.

————. *History of U.S. Political Parties.* New York: Chelsea House, 1973.

Sherwood, Robert E. *The White House Papers of Harry L. Hopkins.* London: Eyre & Spottiswoode, 1948.

Shirer, William L. *The Rise and Fall of the Third Reich.* New York: Simon and Schuster, 1960.

Skinner, Cornelia Otis. *Elegant Wits and Grand Horizontals.* Boston: Houghton Mifflin, 1962.

Smith, Jean Edward. *Lucius D. Clay: An American Life.* New York: Henry Holt, 1990.

Sulzberger, C. L. *The Last of the Giants.* New York: Macmillan, 1970.

Traina, Richard. *American Diplomacy and the Spanish Civil War.* Bloomington, Ind.: Indiana University Press, 1968.

Volkogonov, Dmitri. *Stalin: Triumph & Tragedy.* New York: Grove Weidenfeld, 1991.

Wallace, Henry A. *The Price of Vision: The Diary of Henry A. Wallace, 1942-1946.* Edited by John Morton Blum. Boston: Houghton Mifflin, 1973.

Watson, Major General Edwin M. "Pa." Papers. University of Virginia, Charlottesville, Va.

Weil, Martin. *A Pretty Good Club: The Founding Fathers of the U.S. Foreign Service.* New York: W. W. Norton, 1978.

Welles, Albert. *History of the Welles Family in England, including an Account of the Welles Family in Massachusetts by Henry Winthrop Sargent.* Boston: Press of John Wilson & Son, 1874.

Welles, Governor Thomas. "The English Ancestry of Governor Thomas Welles." Reprinted from the *New England Historical & Genealogical Register.* (Boston; July and October, 1926).

Welles, Sumner. *Naboth's Vineyard.* London: Payson and Clarke, Ltd., 1928.

————. *The Accomplishments of the Inter-American Conference for the Maintenance of Peace.* Department of State, Confererence Series, #26. Washington, D.C.: Government Printing Office, 1937.

————. *The World of the Four Freedoms.* New York: Columbia University Press, 1943.

————. *The Time for Decision.* New York: Harper and Row, 1944.

————. "Introduction." *The Ciano Diaries: 1939-43.* Edited by Hugh Gibson. Garden City, N.Y.: Doubleday 1946.

————. *Where Are We Heading.* New York: Harper Bros., 1946.

————. *We Need Not Fail.* Boston: Houghton Mifflin, Co., 1948.

————. *Seven Decisions that Shaped History.* New York: Harper and Row, 1950.

Wheeler, Post, and Hallie Erminie Rives Wheeler. *Dome Of Many Colored Glass.* New York: Doubleday, 1955.

White, Francis. Papers. Evergreen House, John Hopkins University, Baltimore, Md.

White, George S. *Memoir of Samuel Slater.* Printed at 46 Carpenter St., Philadelphia, 1836.

Wilson, Hugh R. *Diplomat Between Wars*. London: Longmans, Green and Co., 1961.

Wilson, Theodore A. *The First Summit*. Boston: Houghton Mifflin Co., 1969.

———. *Working With Roosevelt*. New York: Harper and Bros., 1952.

INDEX